W9-BBE-100

BISMARCK: A LIFE

BISMARCK

A LIFE

JONATHAN STEINBERG

OXFORD
UNIVERSITY PRESS

OXFORD
UNIVERSITY PRESS

Oxford University Press, Inc., publishes works that further
Oxford University's objective of excellence
in research, scholarship, and education.

Oxford   New York
Auckland   Cape Town   Dar es Salaam   Hong Kong   Karachi
Kuala Lumpur   Madrid   Melbourne   Mexico City   Nairobi
New Delhi   Shanghai   Taipei   Toronto

With offices in
Argentina   Austria   Brazil   Chile   Czech Republic   France   Greece
Guatemala   Hungary   Italy   Japan   Poland   Portugal   Singapore
South Korea   Switzerland   Thailand   Turkey   Ukraine   Vietnam

Copyright © 2011 by Jonathan Steinberg

Published by Oxford University Press, Inc.
198 Madison Avenue, New York, New York 10016

www.oup.com

Oxford is a registered trademark of Oxford University Press

Library of Congress Cataloging-in-Publication Data
Steinberg, Jonathan.
Bismarck : a life / Jonathan Steinberg.
p.   cm.
Includes bibliographical references and index.
ISBN 978-0-19-978252-9 (alk. paper)
1. Bismarck, Otto, Fürst von, 1815–1898. 2. Statesmen—Germany—Biography.
3. Germany—Politics and government—1871–1888. I. Title.
DD218.S795   2011
943.08′3092—dc22
[B]
2010045387

1 3 5 7 9 8 6 4 2

Printed in the United States of America
on acid-free paper

To my partner, Marion Kant

Contents

Preface

In a preface authors thank those who helped them. In the internet age he or she will certainly not know some of the most important of them: the anonymous librarians, archivists, scholars, researchers, and technicians who put precious resources on line, digitalize catalogues, contribute to online encyclopedia and great reference books such the *Oxford Dictionary of National Biography* or the *Neue deutsche Biographie*. How can I thank personally the archivists at the *New York Times* who provided online the report in its original typeface of the wedding in Vienna on 21 June, 1892 of Herbert Bismarck and Countess Marguerite Hoyos? No Bismarck biographer before me has enjoyed such a wealth of unexpected, unusual and fascinating new material. Whatever the weaknesses of this work, the author had access to more remote and essential material than any predecessor, no matter how diligent, could have exploited.

I know the names of others without whom I could not have written this biography. Tony Morris, publisher and friend, asked me to write a life of Bismarck, and Andrew Wheatcroft, publisher, historian, and friend, saved the project when the first publisher abandoned it. Through Andrew Wheatcroft I gained the help of the perfect literary agent, Andrew Kidd of Aitken Alexander, who guided it safely to Oxford University Press where Timothy Bent steered it through its rough early stage and encouraged me to cut it to a less unwieldy size. His skill and editorial expertise helped me polish and polish again the slimmed down manuscript.

My friend and colleague, Chris Clark, author of *Iron Kingdom: The Rise and Downfall of Prussia, 1600–1947*, read the first draft, all 800 pages, with a care and attention to errors and misinterpretations that only he could have given. Karina Urbach, author of *Bismarck's Favourite Englishman: Lord Odo Russell's Mission to Berlin*, gave me the benefit of her great knowledge of the period and of German society. Rabbi Herb Rosenblum of Philadelphia passed on to me the astonishing fact that in 1866 Bismarck had attended the dedication of the Oranienburg Street Synagogue in Berlin.

An author fortunate enough to be published by Oxford University Press gets two publishers for the price of one. Timothy Bent and his colleagues at 198 Madison Avenue welcomed me with every kind of assistance and support. Luciana O'Flaherty, Publisher, Trade Books, and her colleagues at Oxford University Press, Great Clarendon Street, Phil Henderson, Coleen Hatrick, and Matthew Cotton have been an author's 'dream team'. Deborah Protheroe found illustrations that I had missed and put up with my foibles about the pictures. Edwin Pritchard copy-edited the text with skill and tolerance of the author's irregular habits. Claire Thompson, Senior Production Editor, guided me through the final stages of proof-reading and indexing. Joy Mellor proof-read the text.

Nothing in my long professional career has been as much fun as the composition of this work. I got to 'know' the most remarkable and complex political leader of the nineteenth century and had (and still have) the illusion that I understand him. I met and read the letters and diaries of the greatest figures in Prussian society. That 'imagined society' took me away from, and made me a nuisance to, my family, but all of them supported the enterprise in every way and gave me their love and good cheer, which kept my spirits up. Without my partner, Marion Kant, I could never have written the book and I have dedicated it to her.

Philadelphia, PA
October 2010

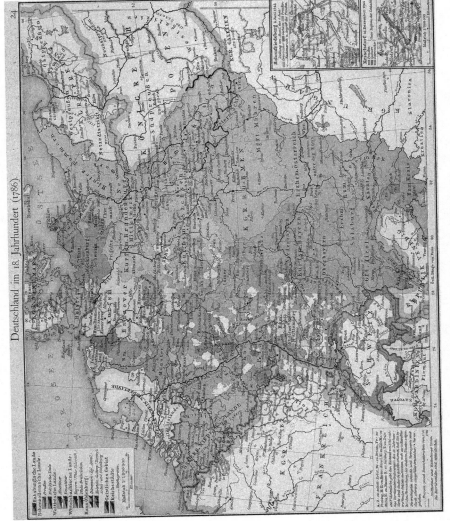

Map 1 Map of Germany showing the political boundaries in 1786.

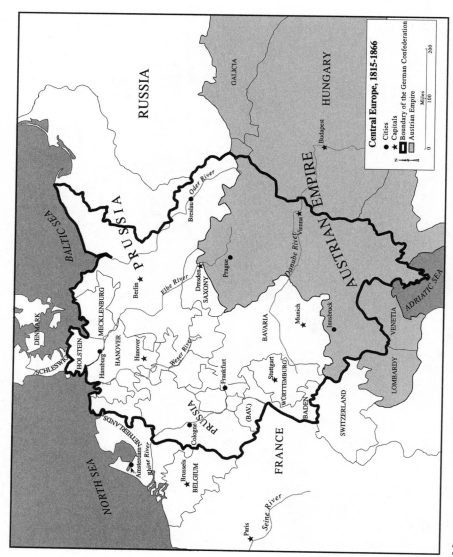

Central Europe, 1815-1866

Cities •
Capitals ★
Boundary of the German Confederation
Austrian Empire

Miles
0   100   200

RUSSIA

GALICIA

HUNGARY

Budapest ★

AUSTRIAN EMPIRE

PRUSSIA

Oder River

Breslau •

Vienna ★

Danube River

Prague •

ADRIATIC SEA

BALTIC SEA

Berlin ★

Elbe River

Dresden ★

SAXONY

Munich ★

VENETIA

Innsbruck •

BAVARIA

LOMBARDY

DENMARK

MECKLENBURG

Hamburg •

HANOVER

Hanover ★

Weser River

Frankfurt •

Stuttgart ★

WÜRTTEMBURG

SWITZERLAND

HOLSTEIN

SCHLESWIG

(BAV.)

BADEN

NORTH SEA

NETHERLANDS

Rhine River

Cologne •

PRUSSIA

FRANCE

Amsterdam •

Brussels •

BELGIUM

Paris ★

Seine River

Map 2

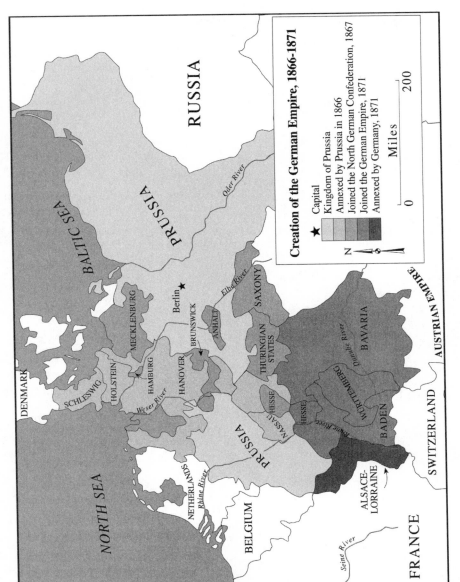

Creation of the German Empire, 1866-1871

★ Capital
Kingdom of Prussia
Annexed by Prussia in 1866
Joined the North German Confederation, 1867
Joined the German Empire, 1871
Annexed by Germany, 1871

Miles

0   200

N

RUSSIA

BALTIC SEA

PRUSSIA

Oder River

MECKLENBURG

Berlin

Elbe River

BRUNSWICK

ANHALT

SAXONY

THURINGIAN STATES

BAVARIA

Danube River

DENMARK

SCHLESWIG

HOLSTEIN

HAMBURG

Weser River

HANOVER

NASSAU

HESSE

HESSE

WÜRTTEMBERG

OLDENBURG

BADEN

Rhine River

PRUSSIA

NORTH SEA

NETHERLANDS

Rhine River

BELGIUM

ALSACE-LORRAINE

Seine River

FRANCE

SWITZERLAND

AUSTRIAN EMPIRE

Map 3

I

Introduction: Bismarck's 'Sovereign Self'

Otto von Bismarck made Germany but never ruled it. He served under three royal masters, any one of whom could have dismissed him at any moment. In March of 1890 one did. His public speeches lacked all the characteristics that we would normally call charismatic. In September of 1878, at the height of his power and fame, the newspaper *Schwäbische Merkur* described one of Bismarck's speeches in the Reichstag:

> How astonished are those who hear him for the first time. Instead of a power-ful, sonorous voice, instead of the expected pathos, instead of a fiery tirade glowing with classical eloquence, the speech flows easily and softly in conver-sational tones across his lips, hesitates for a while and winds its way until he finds the right word or phrase, until precisely the right expression emerges. One almost feels at the beginning that the speaker suffers from embarrass-ment. His upper body moves from side to side, he pulls his handkerchief from his back pocket, wipes his brow, puts it back in the pocket and pulls it out again.[1]

Bismarck never addressed a mass meeting and only attracted crowds after he fell from power, by which time he had become legendary.

From September 1862 to March 1890 Bismarck ruled in Germany but only as a parliamentary minister. He made speeches of the above kind in various parliamentary bodies from 1847 to his dismissal in 1890. He exerted his personal aura over his audiences but never led a political party in the British sense at all. Throughout his career, the German Conservatives, the National Liberals, and the Catholic Centre Party, the largest German parties, distrusted him and kept their distance. The Bismarckian party, the so-called 'Free Conservatives', had influential members but no great following out-side the chambers. Much of Bismarck's time and energy went into the nuts-and-bolts of government administration. He dealt with everything from international treaties to whether stamp duty belonged on postal money orders, an issue—oddly enough—which led to one of his many, many resignations.

He had no military credentials. He had served briefly and very unwillingly in a reserve unit as a young man (in fact, he tried to evade conscription, a scandal which the official edition of his papers omitted) and had only tenuous claims to the uniforms he always wore—to the embarrassment or fury of 'real' soldiers. As one of the so-called 'demi-gods' on General Moltke's staff, Lieutenant Colonel Bronsart von Schellendorf, wrote in 1870, 'The civil servant in the cuirassier jacket becomes more impudent every day.'[2]

He had a 'von' in his name and came from a 'good' old Prussian family but, as the historian Treitschke wrote in 1862, he was apparently no more than a 'shallow country-squire'.[3] He had the pride of his social rank but understood that many occupied higher rungs than he. One of his staff recalled an instance:

> Most of the table-talk was provided by the Chancellor...Hatzfeldt [Paul Count von Hatzfeldt-Wildenburg] would also take part in the conversation, because in the Chancellor's eyes, he enjoyed the highest social standing. The other members of the staff usually remained silent.[4]

He and his brother inherited estates but not rich ones. Bismarck had to keep his expenses down for most of his career. In a society in which court and courtiers occupied the centre of political life and intrigue, Bismarck stayed at home, dined at an unfashionably early hour, and spent much of his later career in the country as far from Berlin as possible.

In a famous passage written in 1918, as Bismarck's empire began to collapse, Max Weber, one of the founders of modern sociology, asked why we obey the authority of the state. He identified three forms of authority or what he called 'legitimations'. The first was

> the authority of the 'eternal yesterday,' i.e. of the mores sanctified through the unimaginably ancient recognition and habitual orientation to conform. This is 'traditional' domination exercised by the patriarch and the patrimonial prince of yore.

The third was:

> domination by virtue of 'legality,' by virtue of the belief in the validity of legal statute and functional 'competence' based on rationally created *rules*.

But it was the second that constitutes Weber's greatest contribution to our understanding of politics, legitimation by what he defined as *charisma*:

> There is the authority of the extraordinary and personal *gift of grace* (charisma), the absolutely personal devotion and personal confidence in revelation, heroism, or other qualities of individual leadership. This is 'charismatic' domination, as exercised by the prophet or—in the field of politics—by the elected war lord, the plebiscitarian ruler, the great demagogue, or the political party leader.[5]

None of these definitions completely describes Bismarck's authority. As a royal servant, he fits Weber's first category: his power rested on tradition, 'the authority of the "eternal yesterday"'. As a prime minister and head of administration, most of the time he behaved exactly as Weber defined his third category: 'domination by virtue of "legality"'... based on rationally created *rules*'. He was not conventionally, as we have seen, 'charismatic'.[6]

In spite of that, Bismarck controlled his contemporaries so utterly that the words 'tyrant' and 'dictator' occur again and again in the letters and memoirs of those who lived under him. Prince Chlodwig von Hohenlohe-Schillingsfürst, four years younger than Bismarck, and after his dismissal one of his successors, described a visit to Berlin a few months after Bismarck left office:

> I have noticed two things during the three days that I have now been here: first, that no one has any time and that everyone is in a greater hurry than they used to be; secondly that individuals seem to have grown larger. Each separate personality is conscious of his own value. Formerly the individual was oppressed and restricted by the dominant influence of Prince Bismarck, but now they have all swelled out like sponges placed in water.[7]

I realized that I needed a new term to explain the Bismarck story. Bismarck commanded those around him by the sheer power of his personality. He never had sovereign power but he had a kind of 'sovereign self'. As the Emperor William remarked, 'it's hard to be Kaiser under Bismarck.'[8] In him we can see the greatness and misery of human individuality stretched to its limits. Take the case of the speech on 17 September 1878, which I cited above. Afterwards Bismarck flew into a rage at the humble stenographers who took down the debates in the Reichstag, and described his dark suspicions a month later on 4 October, 1878, to one his aides, Moritz Busch, who recorded it:

The shorthand stenographers turned against me in connection with my last speech. As long as I was popular that was not the case. They garbled what I said so there was no sense in it. When murmurs were heard from the Left or Centre, they omitted the word 'Left' and when there was applause, they forgot to mention it. The whole bureau acts in the same way. But I have complained to the President. It was that which made me ill. It was like the illness produced by over-smoking, a stuffiness in the head, giddiness, a disposition to vomit etc.[9]

Consider that evidence. Could a sane man seriously believe that a conspiracy of stenographers had developed in the duller corridors of the Reichstag to undermine the greatest statesman of the nineteenth century? And the illness as a result? Hypochondria hardly does justice to the complaints. Lieutenant Colonel Bronsart von Schellendorf had no doubt: on 7 December 1870 he confided to his diary 'Bismarck begins really to be ready for the mad house.'[10] Yet he never got there. He remained sane in his way and healthy in spite of his fears and powerful—though never enough for his desires—from his forties to his seventies. He held office for twenty-eight years and transformed his world more completely than anybody in Europe during the nineteenth century with the exception of Napoleon, who was an Emperor and a General. Bismarck did it while being neither the one nor the other.

This book is, therefore, a life of Otto von Bismarck because the power he exercised came from him as a person, not from institutions, mass society or 'forces and factors'. The power rested on the sovereignty of an extraordinary, gigantic self. What exactly that means has defied precise definition throughout the history of humanity. Here I mean that combination of physical presence, speech patterns and facial expressions, style in thought and action, virtues and vices, will and ambition, and, perhaps, in addition, a certain set of characteristic fears, evasions, and psychological patterns of behaviour that make us recognizable as 'persons', the selves we project and conceal, in short, what makes people *know* us. Bismarck somehow had more of every aspect of self than anybody around him, and all who knew him—without exception—testify to a kind of magnetic pull or attraction which even those who hated him could not deny. His writing has a charm, flexibility, and seductiveness that conveys something of the hypnotic effect his powerful self had on those who knew the living Bismarck.

Only biography can even attempt to catch the nature of that power. This biography tries to describe and explain the life of the statesman who unified

Germany in three wars and came to embody everything brutal and ruthless about Prussian culture. The real Bismarck was a complex character: a hypochondriac with the constitution of an ox, a brutal tyrant who could easily shed tears, a convert to an extreme form of evangelical Protestantism, who secularized schools and introduced civil divorce. He always wore uniform in public after a certain stage in his career but he was one of the few important Prussians who never served in the King's regular army. His fellow Junker aristocrats came to distrust him; he was too clever, too unstable, too unpredictable, not 'a proper chap'. But all agreed that he was brilliant. The British ambassador to Germany from 1871 to 1884, Odo Russell of the great Whig noble family, knew Bismarck well and wrote to his mother in 1871: 'The demonic is stronger in him, than in any man I know.'[11] Theodore Fontane, the Jane Austen of the Bismarck era, wrote to his wife in 1884: 'When Bismarck sneezes or says "prosit" it is more interesting than the spoken wisdom of six progressives.'[12] But in 1891 after Bismarck's fall from power, Fontane wrote to Friedrich Witte: '[it was] not in his political mistakes—which are, as long as things are in flux, very difficult to determine—but in his failings of character. This giant had something petty in his nature, and because it was perceived it caused his fall.'[13]

Bismarck was also that rare creature, 'a political genius', a manipulator of the political realities of his time. His verbal, often improvised, analyses of politics delighted even some of his enemies. General Albrecht von Stosch, whom Bismarck eventually had fired, saw both sides. In 1873, he wrote to the Crown Prince:

It was again an enchantment to see the Imperial Chancellor in full spiritual activity. His flights of thought can become quite striking, when the task of defending the Empire against Prussian particularism falls upon him.'[14]

Several years before Stosch recorded a very different experience:

After a few days Bismarck let me come. He had previously seen in me a man who admired his high intellect and his tireless energy and as long as I possessed a certain importance in his effort to reach agreement with the Princess, I could enjoy the greatest politeness and attention. Now I was just any one of his many aides and I had to feel that. He sat me down and went over my report like a schoolmaster with a dumb and particularly disobedient pupil...Bismarck always loved to give his staff proof of his power. Their achievements were always his; if something went wrong the subordinate got the blame, even if he had acted under orders. When later the Saxon Treaty was attacked openly in public, he said that he had not seen the treaty until it was enacted.[15]

The belief that Bismarck was a political genius, which became universal among patriotic Germans after the unification of Germany in 1870 and is, I think, correct, would have occurred to almost nobody in 1862 when he became Minister-President of Prussia. But one influential person had seen it much earlier and had a position in the King's government. General Albrecht von Roon, Minister of War from 1859 to 1873, who met Bismarck first as a teen-ager, understood from the start that this remarkable person had the stuff of greatness. At Roon's first audience with the Regent and future King of Prussia on 4 December 1858, about his possible appointment as Minister of War,[16] he urged the Regent to name Bismarck head of government. And it was Roon who sent the famous telegram of 18 September 1862: 'periculum in mora. Depêchez-vous!' (Danger in delay. Make haste!), which gave Bismarck the sign that his hour of destiny had come.

When Roon's best friend Clemens Theodor Perthes, professor of law at the University of Bonn and founder of the Protestant 'inner mission', berated Roon in April 1864 for having engineered the appointment of a man 'who calculates so coldly, who prepares so cunningly, who has no scruples about methods'[17] Roon replied:

> B. is an extraordinary man, whom I can certainly help, whom I can support and here and there correct, but never replace. Yes, he would not be in the place he now has without me, that is an historical fact, but even with all that he is himself... To construct the parallelogram of forces correctly and from the diagonal, that is to say, that which has already happened, then assess the nature and weight of the effective forces, which one cannot know precisely, that is the work of the historic genius who confirms that by combining it all.[18]

And Bismarck did just that—'combining it all'.

Yet genius alone could not win power. No sensible monarch—and King William I of Prussia at the age of 65 had good sense and years of experience—would have appointed Bismarck, who had a reputation for utter unreliability, superficial cleverness and extremely reactionary views, unless he had become desperate. The King's brother, Frederick William IV wrote in 1848 'Bismarck—to be used only when the bayonet rules without limit'[19] but in the summer of 1862 a deadlock between the Prussian parliament and the Crown over reform of the army had begun to frighten the royal establishment. Memories of mobs in the streets of Berlin during the revolution of 1848 came back to make the King and court nervous. As the liberal Max Duncker wrote: 'The military are panting after riots "as the hart panteth after the water-brooks" [Psalm 42, verse 1—JS].'[20]

Bismarck gained and held power by the strength and brilliance of his personality but he always depended on the good will of his King. If William I had decided to dismiss Bismarck at the end of September 1862, after the fiasco of 'the blood and iron speech', which all the members of the royal family and most educated people in Germany condemned, Bismarck would have disappeared from history and Germany would almost certainly have been unified by a voluntary federation of sovereign princes. If William I had had the decency to die at the biblical 'three score and ten' in 1867, Bismarck's creation, the North German Federation, might have eventually absorbed the South German kingdoms but not through a devastating war. A 'Liberal Era' under Emperor/King Frederick III and his energetic Liberal wife, the Princess Royal Victoria of Great Britain, might have begun. We know the list of ministers Frederick wanted to appoint in 1888 when he was already a dying man. All were liberal, which to Bismarck meant the British system of parliamentary government, restricted royal power and the end of his dicta-torship. Whether the new Emperor, even if he had been healthy, had the strength of character to resist Bismarck, the Princess Victoria, Queen Victoria's eldest daughter, had enough for both of them. There would have been a clash, and Bismarck would have been dismissed. Germany might then have followed the British model of liberal parliamentary control. We can say these things now because the actors promised them at the time. William did not die at 70, nor at 80, nor at 90 but in 1888 at 91 and that longevity of the old King gave Bismarck 26 years in office.

During those twenty-six years Bismarck forced the King again and again by temper tantrums, hysteria, tears, and threats to do things that every fibre in his spare Royal Prussian frame rejected. For twenty-six years Bismarck ruled by the magic that he exerted over the old man. Bismarck's career rested on personal relations—in particular, those with the King and the Minister of War—but also with other diplomats, sovereigns, and courtiers. William I, King of Prussia and later Emperor of Germany, ruled in part by the rules of written constitutions but in true Prussian tradition also by the Grace of God, a Protestant, Prussian God. Bismarck needed no majorities in parliament; he needed no political parties. He had a public of one. When that public changed, during the ninety-nine days that the dying Frederick III spent on the throne, and when the dynamic and unstable William II succeeded his father, Bismarck's days were numbered. William II dismissed him on 20 March 1890. As a *Punch* cartoon of the time put it, 'the dropping of the pilot'.

But the person and the power existed in a real world. As Bismarck said, a statesman does not create the stream of time, he floats on it and tries to steer. Bismarck operated within the limits of the politically realistic and he frequently defined politics as 'the art of the possible'. The reader needs to know that context, those states and their relations, their government and leaders, the economic and social changes, which turned Europe into the first 'modern' society during Bismarck's lifetime. Bismarck's genius led him to see possibilities in the configuration of domestic and international forces of the 1860s which allowed him to unify—or more accurately divide—Germany by excluding the Austrian lands. He took bold steps, which stupefied his contemporaries, but he lived long enough to fall victim to that maxim of Edmund Burke about unforeseen consequences:

> that which in the first instance is prejudicial may be excellent in its remoter operation; and its excellence may arise even from the ill effects it produces in the beginning. The reverse also happens: and very plausible schemes, with very pleasing commencements, have often shameful and lamentable conclusions.[21]

Bismarck sprang the idea of universal suffrage on a startled German public in 1863 in order to prevent King William from going to a congress of princes called by the Emperor of Austria. It worked. The Austrian move failed. Prussia unified Germany and universal manhood suffrage became the franchise for the new Reichstag, the lower house of parliament in the new German Empire. Between 1870 and his fall from power, Bismarck lived out the truth in Burke's maxim. By 1890 'very pleasing commencements' had become in Bismarck's eyes 'lamentable conclusions'. Germany had industrialized and a new sullen, hostile working class had appeared. The Catholic population had survived persecution and their votes always produced a large parliamentary party. Votes for everybody had by Burkean irony given parliamentary seats to Socialists and Catholics. By 1890 Bismarck's brilliant ploy of 1863 had begun to produce majorities made up of what he called 'enemies of the Reich'. By 1912, Catholics and Socialists, Bismarck's 'enemies', together had an absolute majority of seats in the Reichstag. Universal suffrage, which he had designed to scupper an Austrian initiative in 1863 and to undermine the legitimacy of the lesser German princely states, had yielded the 'lamentable conclusion' of legislative stalemate. As the late Enoch Powell once observed, 'all political careers end in failure'.

The life of Bismarck still matters today, for it expresses a more general problem than just those described above. Bismarck shows us the strengths and weaknesses of the human self when it exercises power. It shows how powerful the large self can be but it also shows how the exercise of supreme political power never leaves its holders unchanged. Since Bismarck was one of the greatest political figures of all times, he has had many biographers of various types. This biography takes its place in a long and distinguished train: Erick Eyck, A. J. P. Taylor, Werner Richter, Edgar Feuchtwanger, Edward Crankshaw, Otto Pflanze, Lothar Gall, Ernst Engelberg, and Katherine Lerman. Then there are huge volumes of J. C. G. Röhl about Kaiser Wilhelm II and Germany after Bismarck, the brilliant study of Bismarck's Catholic adversary, Windthorst, by Margaret Lavinia Anderson, and dozens of other more specialized works. The Van Pelt Library of the University of Pennsylvania lists 201 books with 'Bismarck' in the title. How does this book differ from its predecessors? It does so in two ways: in its aim and in its method. The aim is easy to express and probably impossible to do: to explain to author and reader how Bismarck exercised his personal power. The method is to let those on whom the power was exercised, friend and foe, German and foreign, young and old, anybody who experienced the power of Bismarck's personality close up and recorded the impact, tell the story. I have changed the conventional balance between comment and evidence in favour of the latter. I want to recall the long silenced voices of the many, many distinguished people who met Bismarck and wrote down what they saw. As Bismarck's college friend, the American John Lothrop Motley, explained to Lady William Russell about historical research:

> I go to my archives every day and take a header into the seventeenth century... It is rather diverting... to take the dry bones out of the charnel house and to try to breathe into them a fictitious life. Like Bertram in the third act of Robert the Devil, I like to set the sheeted dead gamboling and pirouetting and making fools of themselves once more.[22]

My 'sheeted dead' do not make fools of themselves. They taught me who Bismarck was and also who they were. Often they confirmed my view of another of Bismarck's contemporaries by expressing an opinion to which I had come on my own.

One example of many will explain the point. General Albrecht von Roon put Bismarck into office and knew it. His reactionary and rigid views could not be further from mine, but he had an odd purity and integrity which moved me. I discovered to my amazement the confirmation of that in an unexpected place. Hildegard von Spitzemberg recorded in her diary on 7 August 1892 that she had been reading Roon's *Denkwürdigkeiten* (his memoirs), just published:

> What a pious, decent, competent man, how loyal and yet how frank. One reads how much annoyance he had to swallow from high and highest persons. And how charming his travel descriptions, how touching his relationship to his wife, and his friends Perthes and Blanckenburg.[23]

That two people from different worlds and times, an obscure academic in the twenty-first century and a grand society lady of the nineteenth century, saw the same character traits, encouraged the hope that my 'feel' for Bismarck's personality and that of his contemporaries had a foundation.

Diaries gave me other unique pleasures. I got a glimpse into the toilet arrangements in the 1870s, when Christoph Tiedemann dined for the first time at the Bismarcks in 1875:

> 25 January. An interesting day! From 5 to 11 pm in the Bismarck house... The Prince complained about poor appetite. Hats off! I would like to see him once with a good appetite. He took second helpings from every course and complained about ill-treatment when the Princess protested energetically against the enjoyment of a boar's head in aspic. He sipped the wine but drank lots of beer from a large silver tankard ...
>
> About 7.30 the Prince invited Sybel and me to follow him to his study. As a precaution he offered us his bedroom, which was next to the study, as a place to relieve ourselves. We went in and found under the bed the two objects we sought which were of colossal dimensions. As we stationed ourselves at the wall, Sybel spoke seriously and from the depth of his heart, 'Everything about the man is great, even his s—!!'[24]

But the main witness is Otto von Bismarck himself. Bismarck wrote uninterruptedly for sixty years. The official collected works run to nineteen volumes, quarto sized, with an average of more than 500 pages each.[25] Volume VIc alone runs to 438 pages just to include the reports sent to the Kaiser, dictation notes, and other official writings from 1871 to 1890. Bismarck wrote thousands of letters to family, friends, and others. He controlled both domestic and foreign policy for twenty-eight years so his correspondence and official writing covered everything from the threat of war with Russia to the state monopoly on tobacco. He seems to have made it his business to know everything about everything. The result was a constant, furious absorption of material and equally stupendous bouts of writing or dictation. Christoph Tiedemann, who served as Bismarck's first personal assistant from 1875 to 1880, recorded in his diary a typical work session with Bismarck at Varzin, one of his country houses:

> Yesterday I spent 2½ hours in his study, today he dictated the whole afternoon a letter to the Emperor—in all 32 folio sides, not interrupted but written right through. He gave not only an exact account of the negotiations with Bennigsen about his joining the cabinet but at the same time a highly political account of the development of our entire party system since the introduction of a constitution. The Prince dictated without stopping for five hours, I repeat five hours. He spoke more quickly than usual and I could hardly keep up with the flow of thought. The room was overheated, and I began to sweat terribly and thought I might get a cramp. I decided quickly and without saying a word to take off my jacket and throw it over a chair. I continued in shirt sleeves. The Prince, pacing up and down, looked at me at first in amazement but then nodded at me with understanding and continued without pause to dictate.[26]

As Bismarck aged and the strains of such a workload weighed more heavily, he became irritable in a way that alarmed his closest collaborators. Robert Lucius von Ballhausen became a member of Bismarck's inner circle in 1870 and after 1879 was a cabinet minister in the Prussian State Ministry. He saw Bismarck frequently and recorded the deterioration. As early as 1875 he wrote increasingly anxious entries in his diary. Here are two:

> 22 February: It is a remarkable feature of Bismarck's character, how intensively he nurses thoughts of revenge and retaliation for real or imagined slights that he has suffered. In his morbid irritability he feels as a wrong what from the other person was never intended to be that . . . It was a highly comfortable evening. He ate, cutting the slices with his own knife, half a turkey, and drank to wash it down a quarter or half a bottle of cognac mixed with two to three bottles of Apollinaris. By day, he said, he cannot enjoy anything, neither beer nor champagne, on the other hand cognac and water agree with him best. He forced me to drink with him so that I did not see how much he consumed.[27]

> 4 March: the domestic situation changes kaleidoscopically quickly . . . Bismarck handles all questions from his own personal point of view, is clearly not about to give up much of his personal influence and changes his mind from day to day. When he himself does not want to do something, he barricades himself behind the Kaiser's will, when everybody knows that he gets his way on anything if he really wants it.[28]

Imagine trying to govern under such a man who tolerates no dissent, who sees disagreement as disloyalty and who never forgets an injury. As Friedrich von Holstein who had worshipped Bismarck as a young diplomat, wrote later in his disillusion:

> It was a psychological necessity for Bismarck to make his power felt by tormenting, harrying and ill-treating people. His pessimistic view of life which had long since blighted every human pleasure, left him with only one source of amusement, and future historians will be forced to recognize that the Bismarck regime was a constant orgy of scorn and abuse of mankind, collectively and individually. This tendency is also the source of Prince Bismarck's greatest blunders. Here his instinct was the slave of his temperament and justified outbursts for which there was no genuine cause.[29]

This 'future historian' can agree only in part. The solitary bachelor and senior civil servant Holstein wrote after 1906, embittered by the way he had been forced from office in the foreign policy establishment. He wrote in deep despair about Germany and its situation. He had known Bismarck intimately from 1861 and had once adored him. But this 'future historian' must also admit how much Bismarck had coarsened and that what Holstein saw others recognized. But in foreign affairs, he never—I think—behaved as he often did in domestic affairs—angrily and irrationally. In foreign affairs he became the prisoner of forces he could not control but took entirely rational action to deal with them as carefully as he could right to the end. The hand never lost its skill. In domestic affairs too, Bismarck showed wisdom and far-sightedness in his introduction of a modern system of accident, invalidity, and old age insurance but allowed his fear and hatred of socialism to blind him on other social questions. Neither author nor reader should judge prematurely the justice of Holstein's indictment but accept, as we begin to follow the story of his life, that we have to do with one of the most interesting, gifted, and contradictory human beings who ever lived.

2

Bismarck: Born Prussian and What That Meant

O tto Eduard Leopold von Bismarck was born on 1 April 1815, the fourth son of the landowner Ferdinand von Bismarck and his wife, Wilhelmine Mencken, on the family estate in Schönhausen in the Mark of Brandenburg to the east of Berlin. Before we consider the personal inheritance of Otto von Bismarck, we have to look at the historical inheritance and note the exact historical moment when he was born, the place of his birth, the meaning of 'landowner' in Prussia, which his father was and he became, the social and political milieu into which the child was born, and finally the ideas and values which those who stood by his cradle had in their heads. Ernst Engelberg called Bismarck an *Urpreusse*, a basic or essential Prussian, and used the word as part of the title of his two-volume biography.[1] But what did it mean to be 'Prussian' and especially at that moment? For Bismarck was born at the end of one period—the French Revolution and Napoleonic Wars—and the beginning of a new one—the 'long nineteenth century', which saw the growth of democracy, the modern state, and the emergence of capitalist industry.

On 20 March 1815, twelve days before the baby Bismarck took his first breath, Napoleon had escaped from exile on the island of Elba and returned to Paris. Everywhere he went, the Napoleonic Empire, which the victorious Allies had abolished the previous year, rose from the dead as if by magic. The Battle of Waterloo on 18 June 1815 put an end to the dream of Imperial resurrection but not to the lasting impact that Napoleon had on Europe and on Bismarck's Prussia. Napoleon had spread and imposed the laws and administration of the French Revolution. That was the first part of Bismarck's historical inheritance.

How did the Markgravate of Brandenburg, in which Schönhausen, the Bismark estate, lay, turn into the Kingdom of Prussia and then the core of the German Empire? It was not because it had rich natural resources. Christopher Clark in his splendid history of Prussia, *Iron Kingdom*, describes the landscape of Bismarck's childhood:

> It possesses no distinctive landmarks. The rivers that cross it are sluggish meandering streams that lack the grandeur of the Rhine or the Danube. Monotonous forests of birch and fir covered much of its surface... 'Sand', flatness, 'bogs' and 'uncultivated areas' were recurring topoi in all early accounts, even the most panegyric. The soil across much of Brandenburg was of poor quality. In some areas the ground was so sandy and light that trees would not grow on it.[2]

That this unpromising small principality became the core of the most powerful European kingdom had everything to do with the rulers who governed it between 1640 and 1918. The most remarkable thing about them was their longevity. In an age when precarious succession and sudden death might destabilize the early modern state, the Hohenzollerns lived on and on. Frederick, 'the Great Elector', ruled from 1640 to 1688, Frederick the Great from 1740 to 1786, Frederick William III from 1797 to 1840, and Bismarck's liege lord, William I, King of Prussia and German Emperor, from 1861 to 1888, dying at age of 91. The average Hohenzollern reigned for thirty-three years. Not only were they long-lived but they threw up two of the ablest rulers in the centuries before the French Revolution: the Great Elector and Frederick the Great, the latter, perhaps, the ablest man ever to govern a modern state.

When the Great Elector died in 1688, he left a prosperous state and a standing army of over 30,000 men. During the reign of Frederick the Great's father, King Frederick William I (1715–40), the so-called 'Soldier king', Prussia had an 80,000-man standing army. Frederick William I was a strict Calvinist who literally would beat those pastors who did not preach properly, but it was Frederick II the Great (1740–86) who transformed his father's realm both in military and civil affairs. Frederick was the genius king—a victorious general, an enlightened despot, a philosopher, and a musician. His legacy loomed over subsequent Prussian history and it is his Prussia which Bismarck inherited.

Frederick was clear that only aristocrats could be proper commanders. Thus the Prussian landowning class, into which Bismarck was born, was a service nobility. It had a monopoly of high office in the army and state. As Frederick the Great put it in his *Political Testament of* 1752:

[The Prussian nobility] has sacrificed its life and goods for the service of the state; its loyalty and merit have earned it the protection of all its rulers, and it is one of the duties [of the ruler] to aid those noble families which have become impoverished in order to keep them in possession of their lands; for they are to be regarded as the pedestals and the pillars of the state. In such a state no factions or rebellions need be feared...it is one goal of the policy of this state to preserve the nobility.[3]

He owed his nobility something, and he knew it. The von Kleist family alone lost thirty members in just one of Frederick's wars, the Seven Years War, 1756 to 1763, and they were not unique in their sacrifice.[4]

The King was famously 'Enlightened'. He was a full-time intellectual, author of theoretical texts and remarkable letters, all written, of course, in French. German was for servants. He corresponded with great luminaries of the Enlightenment. His indifference to religion was an essential tenet of the Enlightenment. Two years before his death Immanuel Kant, the philosopher, wrote a famous essay (1784) 'What is Enlightenment?' and concluded by saying

the obstacles to universal enlightenment, to man's emergence from his self-imposed immaturity, are gradually becoming fewer. In this respect our age is the age of enlightenment, the century of Frederick.

Frederick the Great left a legacy which not even Bismarck could alter. He set an example of the dutiful ruler, the hard-working and all-competent sovereign. One of his servants—and all ministers and officials were just that—Friedrich Anton von Heinitz wrote an entry in his diary for 2 June 1782:

You have as your example the King. Who can match him? He is industrious, places obligation before recreation, sees first to business...There is no other monarch like him, none so abstemious, so consistent, none who is so adept at dividing his time.[5]

Von Heinitz was right. There was no monarch like Frederick and there never has been one since. A genius as king must be an unlikely outcome of the genetic lottery. In practice Frederick the Great left a set of legacies which Bismarck inherited and helped to preserve: first that the king must work as first servant of the state. William I took that injunction seriously. William I may not have been Frederick the Great but he had inherited the conviction that the monarch must do his homework in order to 'govern' properly.

As a second legacy Frederick bequeathed a special identity to the 'Junker class' as the Prussian nobility was called. This sense of service to the Crown among the Prussian aristocracy defined them and their idea of who they were. They served in the army; they served in the diplomatic corps, administered provinces, ran ministries, and had a right to all of that, but the army came first and by a long way. There is a wonderful moment when Botho von Rienäcker, the hero of Theodor Fontane's delightful novel *Irrungen Wirrungen* set in the early 1870s about love between a young Junker lieutenant and the daughter of a Berlin flower seller, has to confront his fierce uncle who has come to Berlin to sort the young lad out. Here is a passage in my translation:

> In front of the Redern Palace he saw Lieutenant von Wedell of the Dragoon Guards coming towards him.
> 'Where to, Wedell?
> 'To the Club. And you?'
> 'To Hiller.'
> 'A little early.'
> 'Yes, but what's the use? I have to lunch with an old uncle of mine . . . Besides he, that is my uncle, served in your regiment, admittedly a long time ago, early 40s. Baron Osten.'
> 'The one from Wietzendorf?'
> 'The very same.'
> 'O, I know him, that is, the name. A bit related. My grandmother was an Osten. Is he the one who has declared war on Bismarck?'
> 'That's the one. You know what, Wedell? You should come too. The Club won't run away and Pitt and Serge will be there too. You will find them whether you show up at 1 or at 3. The old boy still loves the Dragoon blue and gold and is a good enough old Prussian to be delighted with every Wedell.'
> 'Good, Rienäcker, but it's your responsibility.'
> 'My pleasure!'
> In such conversation they had reached Hiller, where the old baron stood at the glass door and looked out, for it was one minute after one. He overlooked the lateness and was visibly delighted, as Botho presented Lieutenant von Wedell,
> 'Sir, your nephew . . .'
> 'No need to apologize. Herr von Wedell, everything that calls itself Wedell is extremely welcome, and if it wears that tunic, double and thrice welcome. Come, gentlemen, we want to retreat from this deployment of tables and chairs and regroup to the rear—not that retreat is a Prussian thing but here advisable.'[6]

This superb vignette tells you what you need to know about this class. First, they all know each other and often turn out to be related. They identify with their regiments the way an Englishman does with his public school or Oxford and Cambridge colleges. The two young Junker lieutenants speak in clipped sentences and have accents which 'cut' or in the German sound *schneidig*. If they have to ask about somebody, the first question would be '*wo hat er gedient?*' Where did he serve? 'Serve' means only one thing: the regiment.

The old Baron detests lateness and would have scolded Botho had the young man not brought a Wedell from the Dragoon Guards as a diversionary tactic. The old man embodies the virtues of the old Prussian nobility: devotion to duty, efficiency, punctuality, self-sacrifice, often based on an authentic Lutheran or Evangelical Protestant piety, and a fierce, implacable pride. Women played no role in this Junker set of values. Bismarck described that in a conversation with Hildegard vom Spitzemberg after his retirement:

> The first Foot Guards Regiment is a military monastery. *Esprit de corps* to the point of madness. One should forbid these gentlemen to marry; I urge anybody who plans to marry someone from this regiment to give the idea up. She will be married to the service, made miserable by the service and driven to death through the service...[7]

One of Bismarck's closest and oldest friends, John Lothrop Motley, the Boston aristocrat who got to know Bismarck when they were both students at Göttingen, wrote to his parents in 1833:

> one can very properly divide the Germans into two classes: the Vons and the non Vons. Those lucky enough to have the three magic letters in front of their names belong to the nobility and as consequences are highly aristocratic. Without these the others can arrange all the letters of the alphabet in every possible combination, they remain plebs.[8]

South and West German 'vons' existed too but few of them had 'served' Frederick the Great. They belonged to the richer, more relaxed, less dour, often Catholic, aristocracy. Many of them held grand Imperial titles such as the title *Freiherr* (free lord), and *Freiherren* only recognized the Holy Roman Emperor as sovereign. They obeyed no territorial princes in whose territories their estates happen to be located. The Austrian nobility and Hungarian magnates, some of whose estates spread over areas the size of Luxembourg or the US state of Delaware, looked at the Junker class with a mixture of admiration and revulsion. The Austrian ambassador to Berlin in the early years of Bismarck's tenure as Prussian Minister President, Count Alajos Károlyi von Nagykároly, belonged to the grand Magyar aristocracy, way above the social standing of a von Rienäcker, a von Kleist, or a von Bismarck-Schönhausen. In January 1864 he wrote to the Austrian Foreign Minister, Johann Bernhard Graf von Rechberg und Rothenlöwen, an equally great nobleman, about the crisis between crown and parliament in Prussia. He argued shrewdly that the conflict was

> the surest sign not only of the political but of the social divisiveness which is inherent in the internal life of the Prussian state, to wit, the passionate hatred of different estates and classes for each other. This antagonism . . . which places in sharp opposition the army and the nobility on one hand and all the other industrious citizens on the other is one of the most significant and darkest characteristics of the Prussian Monarchy.[9]

Bismarck's greatest achievement was to preserve those 'darkest characteristics' of the Junker class through three wars, the unification of Germany, the emergence of democracy, capitalism, industrialization, and the development of the telegraph, the railroad and, by the end of his career, the telephone. Botho's and Wedell's grandsons still commanded regiments under Adolf Hitler. They supported the Nazi's war and led the army until that war was lost and it was they—a von Moltke, a von Yorck, a von Witzleben, and others of their class—who formed the core of the 1944 plot on Hitler's life. It took the Second World War, the deaths of tens of millions of innocent human beings, and the Russian occupation of Brandenburg, Pomerania, Ducal Prussia, and the other 'core' territories to destroy their estates and expel the owners. On 25 February 1947 the Allied occupation authorities signed a law which abolished the state of Prussia itself, the only state in world history to be abolished by decree:

> The Prussian State, which from early days has been a bearer of militarism and reaction in Germany, has ceased to exist.[10]

This act drove the wooden cross through the heart of Frederick the Great.

Bismarck belonged to the Junker class. Nobody doubted that, and the reader will see that his Junker identity located him and many of his values and acts. He boasted of his long Junker lineage, but he never entirely conformed to the type, never quite behaved as a proper Junker. The lunch at Hillers in Fontane's novel that I cited above had begun well. It turned into a disaster when Bismarck became the subject of discussion:

the old Baron, who in any case had high blood pressure, went red across his bald pate and the remaining curly fringe of hair on his temples seemed to want to coil itself tighter.

'I don't understand you, Botho. What does that "certainly, one can say that" mean? It means more or less "one can also not say that". I know where that all will end. It will suggest that a certain cuirassier office in the reserves, who has held nothing in reserve, especially when it comes to revolutionary measures; it will suggest, I tell you, that a certain man from the Halberstadt regiment with the sulfur yellow collar stormed St Privat absolutely on his own and encircled Sedan on his own. Botho, you cannot come to me with that stuff. He was a civil service trainee in the Potsdam government under old Meding who incidentally never had a good word for him, I know that, and all he learned was how to write dispatches. That much I will give him; he knows how to write dispatches, or in other words he is a pen-pusher. But it was not the pen-pushers who made Prussia great. Was the victor of Fehrbellin a pen-pusher? Was the victor at Leuthen a pen-pusher? Was Blücher a pen-pusher? Or Yorck? Here is the Prussian pen. I cannot bear this cult.'[11]

For old Baron Osten, the army had unified Germany not Bismarck. The army had made Prussia and Kurt Anton, Baron von Osten, embodied that army and that state as a Junker landlord and retired officer as did the young lieutenants turning pale before his rage. Prussian Junkers took every occasion to wear uniform and Bismarck insisted on one, even though he had only served briefly and most unwillingly as a reservist. His friend and patron, Minister of War Albrecht von Roon, found Bismarck's insistence on wearing uniform a little awkward. In May of 1862 when Bismarck had arrived in Berlin in the hope that he would soon be made Minister-President, Roon recorded in his diary that at the end of May on Tempelhof field the annual Guards Parade took place, and Bismarck attended:

> His tall figure wore then the well known cuirassier's uniform with the yellow collar but only with the rank of major on it. Everybody knew how much trouble getting that had cost him. Repeatedly he tried to make clear that at least the major's epaulettes were essential at the court in St Petersburg to give the Prussian Ambassador necessary standing and for his personal prestige. The then Chief of the Military Cabinet (General von Manteuffel) could not be moved for a very long time to make the necessary recommendation.[12]

The prestige of the army rested on Frederick the Great's victories. It took a total defeat of Frederick the Great's army in 1806 to allow a team of 'defence intellectuals' loose on the Junkers' prized possession, the Prussian army. They introduced a War Academy with a higher level to train the future elite and to work on the new technology in artillery and engineering. Top graduates of the War Academy would enter a new agency called the General Staff, and there would be for the first time a modern Ministry of War. As Arden Bucholz in his study of Moltke put it, the Prussian Army became 'a learning organization... The Prussian General Staff and Army became pioneers in discipline-based, institutionalized knowledge.'[13] Prussian reform depended on a small group of 'enlightened' army officers, senior civil servants and Berlin intelligentsia. They believed—understandably—that French revolutionary ideas could not be stopped, indeed, should not be. Yet they could not escape the paradox that to reform Prussia meant to make it into something not Prussian. Even distinguished military reformers like Yorck hated what they saw around them. When Napoleon forced Freiherr vom Stein, the most important of the reformers from office in November 1808, Yorck wrote, 'One mad head is already smashed; the remaining nest of vipers will dissolve in its own poison.'[14]

Help for Prussia's embattled Junkers came from an unlikely source, Edmund Burke. Burke became immortal not because of his politics, oratory, or other writings but because, when the French Revolution broke out, he wrote an instantly great book. *Reflections on the Revolution in France And on the Proceedings in Certain Societies in London Relative to That Event in a Letter Intended to Have Been Sent to a Gentleman in Paris*, November 1790. This large unruly masterpiece invented modern conservatism. Burke had a dim view of human nature. Nothing changes. Human vice and folly merely assume new guises. Burke took an equally dim view of human foresight. Plans always go wrong because they ignore the law of unintended consequences.

Burke's legacy was a new Conservatism to match a new radicalism in France.

This new conservatism flourished on the continent of Europe and only very partially and temporarily in the years 1800 to 1820 in England. Burke delivered arguments against any liberalization of reactionary regimes: the people are stupid, men are inherently unequal, planning for improvement is hopeless, stability is better than change. The opponents of France turned Burke's *Reflections* into arguments for rule from above by the aristocracy and, of course, against reforming enlightened despots. They wanted no more of Frederick the Great with his atheism or his rationality than of the French Revolutionaries, since reason itself was bad.

They attacked liberal capitalism, Adam Smith, and the free market and used Burke's arguments in a very different context. Burke had glorified the great English landowners, because land was stable and the 'moneyed interest' was unstable and unrestrained. Money flowed in everywhere. The land became a mere commodity, an object of trade and not the basis of a stable society. Burke explained it in this vivid passage.

> By this means the spirit of money-jobbing and speculation goes into the mass of land itself, and incorporates with it. By this kind of operation, that species of property becomes (as it were) volatilized; it assumes an unnatural and monstrous activity, and thereby throws into the hands of the several managers, principal and subordinate, Parisian and provincial, all the representative of money.[15]

Land ceases to be identity and becomes a commodity. The gainers are the Jews:

> The next generation of the nobility will resemble the artificers and clowns, and money-jobbers, usurers, and Jews, who will be always their fellows, sometimes their masters.[16]

This is eerily accurate. The next generation of nobility in fact included, as Burke foresaw, a Freiherr von Oppenheim, several varieties of Lord and Baron Rothschild, the von Bleichröders, the von Mendelssohns, and so on. For Burke Jews represented everything tawdry and commercial about markets:

> Jew brokers, contending with each other who could best remedy with fraudulent circulation and depreciated paper the wretchedness and ruin brought on their country by their degenerate councils.[17]

Burke's best pupils and most avid readers were reactionary Prussian landlords and enemies of 'progress' in every country. After all, the old ruling classes in Europe 1790 were landowners and feudal lords. Their hatred of free markets, free citizens, free peasants, free movement of capital and labour, free thought, Jews, stock markets, banks, cities, and a free press continued to 1933 and helped to bring about the Nazi dictatorship. It was, after all, a group of Junker conspirators led by Franz von Papen (1879–1969), a Westfalian Catholic nobleman, who persuaded the Junker President of the Weimar Republic, Field Marshall Paul Ludwig Hans Anton von Beneckendorff und von Hindenburg (1847–1934), to appoint Adolf Hitler to Bismarck's old job. The Junkers intended to use the Austrian corporal for their ends, but he used them for his.

Burke, the classical liberal, was now the prophet of reaction, the perfect example of his own law of unintended consequences. There is yet a further

irony. The means by which Burke reached his new Prussian readers involved
one of the most brilliant con-men of the early nineteenth century, a young
intellectual called Friedrich Gentz (1764–1832). Gentz plays a double part in
the life of Bismarck. He translated Burke into German but he gives us an
important insight into the career of Anastasius Ludwig Mencken (1752–
1801), Bismarck's maternal grandfather. Gentz ended up as the most important counsellor to the reactionary Prince Metternich who in Vienna on the
day of Bismarck's birth, was presiding over the Congress of the same name.

When the French Revolution broke out, young Gentz perked up. On 5
March 1790, he wrote:

> The spirit of the age stirs strongly and vigorously in me; it is high time for
> mankind to awaken from its long sleep. I am young, and the universal striving
> after freedom, which breaks forth on all sides, inspires in me sympathy and
> warmth.[18]

Gentz took up and shed principles with the perfect insouciance of a true
trickster. Initially he welcomed the French Revolution, as he wrote on
5 December 1790 to Christian Garve:

> The Revolution constitutes the first practical triumph of philosophy, the first
> example in the history of the world of the construction of government upon
> the principles of an orderly rational constructed system. It constitutes the
> hope of mankind and provides consolation to men elsewhere who continue
> to groan under the weight of age-old evils.[19]

He even read Burke when it first came out in English but disliked it. He was
'opposed to its fundamental principles and conclusions'. Gentz always had
an eye for the main chance. He changed his mind in 1792 after the mob
violence in Paris and especially when he saw that *Reflections on the Revolution
in France* had been a huge publishing success. Within six months, 19,000
copies of the English edition had been sold. By September 1791 it had gone
through eleven printings. Gentz decided to translate the book into German
and it too became a success in the German-speaking lands. Thus Edmund
Burke, the prophet of the new conservatism, had the good fortune to be
translated by 'the greatest German political pamphleteer of his age'. He
wrote to a friend that he translated Burke 'not because it was a revolutionary book in the history of political thought, but because it was a magnifi-
cently eloquent tirade against the course of events in France'.[20]

He wrote the introduction in December 1792 and sent a copy dedicated
to the Emperor in Vienna but got no response. On 23 December 1792

Gentz decided to dedicate his Burke to Frederick William II, who accepted it and promoted him to *Kriegsrat* (military councillor).[21] The book became a best-seller. Two further editions and dozens of offprints poured onto the market.[22] Here is a paragraph from the preface to his translation, which shows how far Gentz had moved from his initial approval of the French Revolution:

> The despotic synod of Paris, internally supported by Inquisition courts, externally by thousands of volunteer missionaries, declares with an intolerance of which since the collapse of the infallibility of the popes no such example has been given, every deviation from its maxims heresy and horror... From now on there shall be one Reich, one People, one Faith and one language. No epoch in history, either ancient or recent, offers a picture of a more dangerous crisis.[23]

This remarkable paragraph deserves a moment of awe. In the winter of 1792–3, a 30-year-old clerk in the Prussian administration under Frederick William II described a potential legacy of the French Revolution that not even Burke could have imagined. One day a distorted and hideous travesty of French revolutionary terror and intimidation would arise in the very city in which he wrote those words, Berlin, and under Adolph Hitler it would proclaim 'one Reich, one People, one Faith and one language' in its Nazi version: 'one Reich, one People, one Führer.' Burke and Gentz together had created modern conservatism.

Some years later Gentz got to know Alexander von der Marwitz (1787–1814), whom Ewald Frie describes as one 'with all the signs of the brilliant romantic'.[24] Alexander was the younger brother of Ludwig von der Marwitz (1777–1837) and with Ludwig von der Marwitz we meet the first Burkean defence of the Junker class and the articulation of the structural anti-Semitism which forms a continuous thread in Prussian and then German hatred of Jews. Jews are enemies of the Prussian state in precisely the sense that Burke described: they 'volatalize' property and represent the dominion of money over real value. Gentz found Alexander von der Marwitz, who happened to be 'in love' with his Jewish hostess, too dour for him and observed 'for [my] gentle nerves too hard as with some people who really give you pain when they shake your hand'.[25] The attractive young Junker belonged to the most enlightened circle in Berlin in the years before and after 1806.

I have no proof that Alexander von der Marwitz actually carried Gentz's translation of Burke to his brother but the identity of view between Burke and the older von der Marwitz cannot be entirely coincidental. We know

from Ewald Frie's moving biography of Ludwig that the brothers corresponded regularly and were close, though utterly different in temperament.
If Gentz found Alexander too hard, Alexander described his older brother
in a letter from 19 December 1811 as a man 'whose good traits and great
abilities have been turned into stone'.[26] Here is the older von der Marwitz
on Stein's reforms:

> These were the traitors and Stein was their chief. He began the revolution-
> izing of our fatherland; the war of the property-less and of industry against
> agriculture, of fluidity against stability, of crass materialism against divinely
> ordained institutions, of so-called utility against law, of the present against the
> past and the future, of the individual against the family, of the speculators and
> money-lenders against the land and the trades, of desk-bred theories against
> customs rooted in the country's history, of book learning and self-styled tal-
> ents against virtue and honourable character.[27]

The argument is pure Burke and written with the same fury that drove the
master's pen in 1790. Friedrich August Ludwig von der Marwitz (1777–
1837) linked the world of Frederick the Great and that of Bismarck's childhood. As a child von der Marwitz stood by the old King's carriage as a court
page. On 9 May 1811 Marwitz organized a revolt. In Frankfurt an der Oder
he gathered the district assemblies of the nobles of Lebus, Beeskow, and
Storkow from the south-east of the Märkisch-Oderland District in
Brandenburg and they addressed a petition to his Majesty the King. It is
worth quoting at some length because it reflects one type of Junker
conservatism:

> In the decree in which the right to own land is granted to the Jews, the phrase
> reads 'those who confess the mosaic religion'. These Jews, if they stay true to
> their faith, are enemies of every existing state and if they are no longer true to
> their faith they are hypocrites and have the mass of liquid capital in their
> hands. As soon, therefore, as the value of landownership has sunk to a point at
> which they can acquire it with profit, it will end in their hands. As landowners
> they will become the chief representatives of the state and so our old, vener-
> able Brandenburg-Prussia will become a new-fangled Jewish state.[28]

Marwitz uses the word *Judenstaat* almost certainly for the first time. A liberal
state is a 'Jew State'. The very phrase Theodor Herzl later used to found the
Zionist movement appears in this attack on Jews as the bearers of capitalism,
free markets, and access to landed property. The Weimar Republic was
denounced as a 'Jew republic'. This is the Junker reply to Adam Smith.
Money and mobile property are Jewish. As von der Marwitz wrote later,

They (Hardenberg's entourage) had all studied Adam Smith but not realized that he speaks of money, because in such a thoroughly lawful county which has a living constitution, as England is, the study of money can be driven to the limits without overthrowing the constitution...[29]

As Ewald Frie writes,

the Jew symbolized the incomprehensibility of post-feudal society, without history-modern, homeless, orientated to capital and profit, revolution-ary... the sharply formulated anti-Judaism [is] at its core anti-modernity.[30]

Carl August Freiherr von Hardenberg (1750–1822), State Chancellor of the King of Prussia, the addressee of Ludwig von der Marwitz's Burkean effusion, was not amused. 'Highly presumptious and shameless', he wrote on the margin of von der Marwitz's petition.[31] In June 1811 he sent von der Marwitz and his elderly fellow rebel, Friedrich Ludwig Karl Count von Finckenstein, to Spandau prison. To von der Marwitz's intense pain, none of his fellow great landlords lifted a finger to help him. They may have shared his views but not to the point of prison. We shall hear Bismarck and other Prussian aristocrats use exactly the same arguments against 'Jewish' liberalism that von der Marwitz used and, as for Scharnhorst's hope that non-nobles would make careers in Prussian regi-ments, von der Marwitz dismissed it. The bourgeoisie cannot produce officers:

Through the children of bankers, of business people, ideologues and 'world citizens' ninety-nine times out of a hundred the speculator or the counter clerk will shine through—the huckster's spirit sticks to them, profit is always before their eyes, i.e. they are and remain common. The son of even the dumbest nobleman, if you will, will shy away from doing anything that could be considered common... And then much learning deadens the spirit.[32]

Von der Marwitz cannot be equated with the entire Junker class though he saw himself as their spokesman, wrongly, as he found out. The Kingdom of Prussia had changed in ways that made his passionate defence of feudal rights obsolete. Market forces had changed minds as well as practices in the east Elbian great estates and new Prussian legislation plus the spread of new agricultural techniques promised many of them better economic condi-tions. Much of East Prussia remained 'liberal' the way the slave owners in the American South before 1860 preached liberalism. Exporters needed free access to foreign markets and hence supported free trade, representative institutions, especially if they controlled them, and freedom from the

meddlesome state. They may have sympathized with the ideas of a von der
Marwitz but they lived in the real world.

In addition, Prussia had acquired a series of unwanted territories in the
Rhine valley. It had very much preferred to absorb the whole of Saxony,
nearer to hand and in 1815 much richer. Metternich who feared the growth
of Prussian power, forced Frederick William III to accept a slice of northern
Saxony and as compensation in the far west of the German lands, sleepy
Catholic communities by quiet rivers like the Ruhr and the Wupper that
ran through farmland. Nobody knew at the Congress of Vienna in 1815 that
beneath the farms and fields lay one of the great European coal seams. By
what Hegel called 'the slyness of reason', the Austrian Chancellor had given
Austria's rival, the Kingdom of Prussia, the fuel for its future industrialization. He had also given them approximately 1,870,908 people in 1816,[33] a
population, which had grown to some 2.5 million by 1838.[34] The region had
some of the highest literacy rates in eighteenth-century Europe and by 1836
only 10.8 per cent of recruits drawn from the new Rhenish territories
could not sign their names.[35] The new territories, organized after 1822 into
the Rhine Province, had a very high proportion of Roman Catholics.
Brophy estimates that about 75 per cent of the population of the Rhine
Province were Roman Catholic and the left bank of the Rhine, especially
the area around Cologne, up to 95 per cent.[36] They had also been occupied
by the French for much longer than the eastern Prussia territories and had
received and accepted the Napoleonic Code with its set of individual and
property rights. The Code became part of the identity of the Rhine Province
known as 'Rhenish Law'. The area with its good communications and
enterprising capitalists became the nursery of German railroads. By 1845
half of all railways in Germany were in the Rhine Province alone.[37]

On 30 April 1815, another new Prussian province came into being. The
territories and principalities between the Rhine and Weser now lost their
independence for good and became the Prussian Province of Westphalia
with a population of about 1 million.[38] The prince-bishoprics of Fulda and
Paderborn and the archdiocese of Münster ensured that in the new province as in the Rhine Province there would be a substantial Catholic population. As Friedrich Keinemann puts it, 'Protestant civil servants in a Catholic
environment' represented the new Prussian royal authority.[39] The inclusion
of the two new provinces changed the political landscape of the Kingdom
of Prussia during Bismarck's lifetime. By 1874 roughly one-third of the
population of the Kingdom were Catholic, according to official statistics.[40]

The western territories of the Kingdom had a more liberal political culture, Catholic sensibilities, commercial and increasingly industrial bourgeois elites, and in due course a different class of representatives in Prussian parliaments. The Junker elites no longer controlled 'their' kingdom as absolutely as they had. This too formed part of the Prussian legacy that Bismarck in a sense inherited.

The Prussian legacy defined but never contained the aspirations of Otto von Bismarck. This legacy—the army inherited from the 'genius-king', Frederick the Great; the fusion of the Junker class with army and the bureaucracy; the pervasive idea of '*Dienst*' or service, the rigid distinction between nobility and bourgeoisie; a military conception of honour; hatred of Jews— all these and more which we shall see in Bismarck's own career, constitute the framework of ideas, behaviour, and values which Bismarck inherited. His genius enabled him to transform his own relationship to this inheritance and ultimately to mobilize the crown and the nobility in wars which he inspired and exploited. He used techniques of the French Revolution to frustrate its ends. In 1890 when he left office exactly a century after the explosion of French liberty, he had blocked the flow of liberalism and staunched the 'providential' doctrines of equality. He transmitted an authoritarian, Prussian, semi-absolute monarchy with its cult of force and reverence for the absolute ruler to the twentieth century. Hitler fished it out of the chaos of the Great Depression of 1929–33. He took Bismarck's office, Chancellor, on 30 January 1933. Once again a 'genius' ruled Germany.

3

Bismarck: The 'Mad Junker'

On 6 July 1806 Karl Wilhelm Ferdinand von Bismarck (1771–1845) married Wilhelmine Louise Mencken (1789–1839) in the Royal Palace and Garrison Church in Potsdam.[1] Ferdinand von Bismarck, the youngest of four brothers, was 'the least educated of them and richly indolent'.[2] 'Uncle Ferdinand' had an amiable and unpretentious character. He was a kindly, decent, mildly eccentric, country squire, rather like Squire Allworthy in Henry Fielding's *Tom Jones*. His son described life with his father in a letter to his sister in December of 1844, and noted how his father liked to organize elaborate hunting excursions in deepest winter in minus 8 degrees Celsius temperature when nothing stirs and when nobody shoots a thing. His father had four thermometers and a barometer, which he would look at one after another, several times each day, tapping each to make sure they were working. Otto von Bismarck urged his sister to write about the small things of life which give their father real pleasure:

> whom you visit, what you have eaten, what the horses are doing, how the servants behave, whether the doors squeak and if the windows let in draughts, in short, real things, *facta*.[3]

His niece Hedwig von Bismarck remembered 'Uncle Ferdinand' fondly: 'he always had a friendly word for us or a cheerful joke especially when Otto and I rode on his knees...and he was often teased when reminded of the entry he wrote in a guest book of a hotel under the heading *character*: 'beastly'. On hearing of the death of a distant relative through whom he gained the inheritance of the Pomeranian estates of Kniephof, Jarz, and Külz he remarked cheerfully, 'a cold uncle served in estate sauce is a very acceptable dish.'[4] Fielding's squires, on the other hand, never controlled serf labour but Ferdinand von Bismarck did. On 15 March 1803 he issued a manorial order addressed 'to my subjects':

I will here once again make known that in future I will hold all strictly accountable to the end that those who do not do their duty or deserve punishment may not excuse themselves by saying they did not know . . .[5]

Like many Junkers he treated his estate as a little kingdom. He exercised a range of feudal powers and had a court on the estate in which he acted as judge and jury. As late as 1837 more than three million Prussian subjects lived under manorial courts of the kind that Ferdinand von Bismarck convened, 13.8 per cent of the total population of the Kingdom.[6] He appointed pastors and schoolmasters on 'his lands' and expected nobody, not state officials nor neighbours, to intervene. Ferdinand von Bismarck and the gentry of Brandenburg constituted what Monica Wienfort describes as the 'stronghold of conservative, feudal politics'.[7] In the years of Bismarck's childhood, the feudal rights of the landlords eroded irregularly but markedly. Many of the gentry defended such rights in the hope that the state would compensate them for their surrender, especially the right to convene manorial courts.

Otto von Bismarck had a difficult relationship with his father. All parents embarrass children but Ferdinand's ineffectual, kindly incompetence did more than embarrass his brilliant son. In February of 1847, a month after his engagement to Johanna von Puttkamer, he wrote her a revealing letter about his parents:

I really loved my father. When not with him I felt remorse concerning my conduct toward him and made resolutions that I was unable to keep for the most part. How often did I repay his truly boundless, unselfish, good-natured tenderness for me with coldness and bad grace? Even more frequently I made a pretence of loving him, not wanting to violate my own code of propriety, when inwardly I felt hard and unloving because of his apparent weakness. I was not in a position to pass judgement on those weaknesses, which annoyed me only when coupled with *gaucherie*. And yet I cannot deny that I really loved him in my heart. I wanted to show you how much it oppresses me when I think about it.[8]

In the same letter, he describes his mother:

My mother was a beautiful woman, who loved external elegance, who possessed a bright, lively intelligence, but little of what the Berliner calls *Gemüth* [untranslatable but 'warm heart' might do.—JS]. She wished that I should learn much and become much, and it often appeared to me that she was hard and cold. As a small child I hated her; later I successfully deceived her with falsehoods. One only learns the value of the mother for the child when it is too late, when she is dead. The most modest maternal love, even when mixed with much selfishness, is still enormous compared with the love of the child.[9]

Wilhelmine Mencken, Bismarck's mother, came from a very different world from that of the eccentric rural squire, Ferdinand von Bismarck. Born in Berlin in 1789 her family had great prospects. Wilhelmine's father, Royal Cabinet Councilor Anastasius Ludwig Mencken (1752–1801), was the son of a cultivated professorial family in Helmstedt in the Duchy of Brunswick. Young Anastasius Ludwig ran away from home to Berlin to escape the family pressure to become a lawyer or professor in the tiny state of his birth. Mencken was so literate, charming, and quick that, though he was without family connections at court or money, he became a diplomat and rose by sheer ability to the rank of cabinet secretary in 1782 under Frederick the Great at the age of 30. He married a wealthy widow, wrote essays, and corresponded with leading figures of the Berlin enlightenment.[10] Under Frederick William II he continued his diplomatic career, and gained a reputation as 'intellectually the most important' of the Cabinet Councillors.[11] An unfortunate publication in 1792 suggested to his enemies that he was a 'Jacobin', that is, a supporter of the French Revolution. The King dismissed him. Since he had his wife's comfortable fortune, he devoted himself to philosophy and political theory as a leading member of a Berlin circle of reform-minded bureaucrats and writers, who hoped for better things under the Crown Prince.

Friedrich Gentz (1764–1832) who later served as Metternich's closest adviser, now turned his ambitious eyes on Mencken. Klaus Epstein describes young Gentz:

> He was determined to 'crash' the narrow circle of the aristocracy by the force of his brilliance and personal charm, and he was unburdened by middle-class scruples in such matters as money or sex. His ability made him the greatest German political pamphleteer of his age; his connections allowed him to become 'the secretary of Europe' at the time of the Congress of Vienna.[12]

Gentz wrote extravagant love letters which are full of tears and imitations of Goethe's young Werther but without the slightest intention to commit suicide. He frequented the salons of Berlin and practised what Sweet calls his 'Parlour Technique'. In 1788 he met the brilliant young philosopher Wilhelm von Humboldt, who said in 1788, 'Gentz is a windbag who pays court to every woman.'[13] Gentz had by now become what Sweet describes as 'an erratic brilliant egoist with a greater capacity for loyalty to ideas than to people'.[14] His judgement on how to climb the greasy pole we can trust and he saw in 1795 that Anastasius Ludwig Mencken had a bright future. Mencken represented the rule of the enlightened bureaucracy, which came to be known as the 'cabinet party'. So Gentz in his ruthless way cultivated Anastasius Ludwig Mencken, the most important figure in the 'cabinet party'. Gentz hoped that Mencken would reward him when the old King died.[15] The calculation came off in 1797. The new King Frederick William III named Mencken on the third day of his reign to the top civil administrative post, which involved, according to Gentz, 'direction of all civil affairs only on terms which reflect everlasting honor upon him and on the King'.[16] In November 1797 Gentz wrote an open letter to the new King on the programme of reform. The King read it out to the court. As Gentz wrote to his friend Böttiger: 'This small and unworthy production has made a sensation among all classes and has brought me actually one of the pleasantest experiences of my life.'[17]

When in 1797 Frederick William III made Mencken his Cabinet Chief, he became responsible for all petitions to the King. Like the White House chief of staff, Mencken filtered requests and his daily notebook listed them, as 'refused' or 'rejected'. As Engelberg writes:

> On the treadmill of bureaucratic work as a royal servant and cabinet chief, a discrepancy opened between the thinker occupied with humanity, enlightenment declarations made in his free hours and the official rigours of daily work with its decisions. A civil service mentality developed very early.[18]

At some point in these years Anastasius Ludwig Mencken wrote out his personal credo as a civil servant, which shows us what a remarkable figure he was:

> I have never crawled, nor thrown myself away. In consideration of my political position I have only seen myself as a passenger on a long sea journey. He will take care to avoid swearing with the sailors, or drinking with the passengers, and pointing out to the conceited helmsman his incompetence, which would only earn him crude insults. He has to learn how to adjust his movement to the rolling of the craft, otherwise he will fall and excite much *Schadenfreude*. I have paid great attention to this and have not fallen. Had I fallen I would not have rejected the hand of him who had tripped me in order to pick me up, but that hand I would never have kissed.[19]

In a few months, however, the brilliant and independent royal adviser fell ill, and though only 46, would not last long. On 1 February 1798 Friedrich Gentz wrote to a friend:

Mencken now directs *all* internal administration. Since he is now extremely sunken and will certainly be torn from us all too soon, you will readily see how much enticement such a career offers to an active, ambitious and self-confident man.

Gentz had to decide whether to stay in post and hope that his fame, charm, and 'parlour skills' would end by earning him Mencken's post or to try something else. He decided not to remain:

> I am not made for banging away at cabals. I have a fear of the military which is not to be subdued, and if the king should put his entire trust in me today, I should certainly go to pieces in less than half a year.[20]

Anastasius Ludwig Mencken died on 5 August 1801, not yet 50 years old. Freiherr vom Stein, who knew him and used many of his position papers and unfulfilled reform schemes for his own programme in 1807, described his predecessor in glowing terms: 'liberal in thought, cultivated, refined in sentiment, a benevolent man of the noblest caste of mind and views.'[21] Mencken, an excellent, gifted and charming senior civil servant, died on the threshold of a great career. He stood at the very apex of power under a young insecure King who preferred to delegate matters rather than to pretend to be Frederick the Great. If Mencken had lived?

Had he lived, Wilhelmine, his younger child and only daughter, would *never* have married so undistinguished a person as Ferdinand von Bismarck. Engelberg argues that

> Ferdinand von Bismarck contracted no misalliance by marrying Louise Wilhelmine Mencken but a social symbiosis. The country gentleman who at Schoenhausen was only a Lieutenant (ret.) won greater social prestige by this marriage.[22]

That cannot be right. In Jane Austen's county society in 1800 or Wilhelmine Mencken's Berlin, a young woman with not enough money had little choice. As Hedwig von Bismarck drily observed, Wilhelmine 'lacked the "von" before her name or money in her purse' and could, of course, not go to court.[23] Thus a very intelligent and beautiful 17-year-old girl married a dull country gentleman eighteen years her senior. It was not a recipe for either a happy marriage nor for a contented life as mother and home-maker. And Wilhelmine Mencken had neither. An acquaintance of Bismarck's mother, who lived to a great age, Frau Charlotte von Quast Radensleben told Philipp zu Eulenburg years later what kind of person Wilhelmine Mencken became:

[she] adopted a curiously serious expression when she spoke about his mother. She shook her fine old head and said, 'Not a pleasant woman, very smart but—very cold'.[24]

A child who loses a parent at an early age—and Wilhelmine was 12 when Anastasius died—never recovers completely. Though no evidence survives, she must have mourned her brilliant, successful father for the rest of her life and for the glamorous life that died with him. We can see that she wanted her sons to fill that void. Here is how she expressed it to Bismarck's older brother Bernhard in 1830, poor decent Bernhard, a chip off his father's block:

> I imagined that my greatest good fortune would be to have a grown son, who, educated under my very eyes, would agree with me, but as a man would be called to penetrate deeper into the world of the intellect than I as a woman could do. I rejoiced in the thought of the intellectual exchange, the mutual encouragement for mental and spiritual engagement, and of that satisfying feeling to have such pleasures with a person who would be through the bonds of nature nearest to my heart, and who, still more, through the kinship of the spirit, would draw ever closer to me. The time for these hopes to be fulfilled has arrived but they have disappeared and unfortunately, I must confess, for ever.[25]

Not a nice letter to get from your mother. We don't know how Bernhard felt but we know that Otto 'hated' her. He blamed her for sending him to the Plamann Anstalt, even though it had a very good reputation and had its inspiration in the gymnastic doctrines of *Turnen*, made famous by *Turnvater* Friedrich Ludwig Jahn (1778–1852). He told the story of his awful six years there again and again to von Keudell, to Lucius von Ballhausen, and repeated it in old age in his memoirs. There are many versions. Here is the one that Otto Pflanze quotes:

> At the age of six I entered a school whose teachers were demagogic *Turner* who hated the nobility and educated with blows and cuffs instead of words and reproofs. In the morning the children were awakened with rapier blows that left bruises, because it was too burdensome for the teachers to do it any other way. Gymnastics were supposed to be recreation, but during this too the teachers struck us with iron rapiers. For my cultivated mother, child rearing was too inconvenient and she freed herself of it very early, at least in her feelings.

And even the food was awful: 'meat of a chewy kind, not exactly hard but impossible for the teeth to soften.'[26]

Bismarck loved his 'weak' father and hated his 'strong' mother. Otto Pflanze speculates that

> Some of Bismarck's habits and attitudes in later years may have stemmed from these early experiences: his contempt for men dominated by wives; his dislike of intellectuals ('professor' was for him an epithet); his hostility towards bureaucratic government and suspicion of Geheimräte (his maternal grandfather's career); his late rising (pupils at the Plamann Anstalt were driven out of bed at 6.00 a.m.); his longing for the country and dislike of cities, especially Berlin; and his preference in agriculture for forestry (he never forgave his mother for ordering a stand of oak trees felled at Kniephof).[27]

The evidence about Bismarck's life that I have seen certainly supports Pflanze's suggestions. Pflanze had become a committed Freudian the longer he worked on Bismarck and used the oedipal mechanism very effectively to explain Bismarck's growing hypochondria, gluttony, rage, and despair. That Bismarck's health, temper, and emotional life deteriorated the more success-ful he became has been one of the most striking findings of my research on his career. His vices grew more vicious; his virtues less effective the longer he exercised the sovereignty of his powerful self. That self had been shaped, possibly deeply damaged in childhood. The death of the father for a girl like his mother or the coldness or absence of a mother for a male child like Bismarck inflicted permanent psychic wounds on both figures. Wilhelmine Mencken suffered from hypochondria like her son, had sensitive 'nerves', and needed to go away for long periods to take cures at fashionable spas. Her son's hyphochondria was as gargantuan as his appetite. What are we to make of the fact that Bismarck confessed that 'as a small child I hated her; later I successfully deceived her with falsehoods' or that he urged Bernhard to do the same: 'Don't write too crudely to the parents. The Kniephof estab-lishment is more susceptible to lies and diplomacy than to soldierly coarseness'?[28] How had she frightened the child so thoroughly that he dared not tell her the truth? We do not know.

By an uncanny set of circumstances, Bismarck ended up in a kind of permanent parental triangle with his sovereigns, not just once but twice. He saw William I of Prussia as a kindly but weak man and his Queen and later Empress Augusta as an all-powerful, devious, and malevolent figure. Nor were these feelings concealed. Here is an example which Lady Emily Russell, the wife of the British Ambassador in Berlin, passed on to Queen Victoria on 15 March 1873. She reported to the Queen the 'exceptional favour conferred upon us' when the Emperor and Empress had dined at the British Embassy, which was a

> high distinction which no other Embassy has ever yet enjoyed in Berlin... Your Majesty is aware of the political jealousy of Prince Bismarck about the Empress Augusta's influence over the Emperor, which he thinks stands in the way of his anti-clerical and National policy, and prevents the formation of responsible ministries as in England. The Empress told my husband he [Bismarck] has only twice spoken to Her Majesty since the war, and she expressed a wish that he should dine with us also. According to etiquette he would have had to sit on the left side of the Empress, and Her Majesty would then have had an hour in which he could not have escaped conversing. Prince Bismarck accepted our invitation but said he would prefer to set aside etiquette, and cede the 'pas' to the Austrian Ambassador. However, on the day of the dinner and a short time before the hour appointed, Prince Bismarck sent an excuse saying he was ill with lumbago. The diplomatists look mysterious and hint at his illness being a diplomatic one. Prince Bismarck often expresses his hatred for the Empress in such strong language that my husband is placed in a very difficult position.[29]

The other royal triangle evoked in Bismarck even more violent feelings of hatred. Bismarck repeated over and over that Victoria Crown Princess of Prussia ruled her husband, the Crown Prince Frederick, and, if I am right about the Crown Prince's state of depression, the rumours may well have been right. On 1 April 1888, a few weeks after the death of Kaiser William I and the succession of the Emperor Frederick and his Empress Victoria, Baroness Spitzemberg

> threw on my finery and went with the children to wish the Princess B good luck... My dear Prince who had greeted me, 'Ah, dear Spitzchen, what are you doing?' took me to the table. To my right sat old Külzer. I 'interviewed' [English in original—JS] the Prince impudently... [Bismarck said] 'My old Master was aware of his dependence. He used to say, 'help me, you know how hen-pecked I am', and so we operated together. For that this one [Frederick—JS] is too proud but he is dependent and submissive to an extent that is not to be believed, like a dog. The painful thing is that one has to remain in spite of it perfectly polite instead of intervening with a 'damn it all!' This battle wears me down and the Emperor. He is a brave soldier but on the other hand he is like those old moustached sergeants whom I have seen creep into their mouse-holes in fear of their wives... The worst was... 'Vicky'. She was 'a wild woman'. When he saw her pictures, she terrified him by the unrestrained sexuality, which speaks through her eyes. She had fallen in love with the Battenberger and wants him near her, like her mother, whom the English call

'the selfish old beast' [English in the original—JS] holds onto her brothers, with who knows what sort of incestuous thoughts.[30]

This disgusting, misogynist, and prurient outburst can hardly be called 'normal'. It and the many other examples, which clutter Bismarck's conversation, would make interesting material for a Freudian case study. Bismarck was physically ill more and more of the time as he aged. Its causes were certainly as much psychic as physical. I believe that when Bismarck said to Hildegard Spitzemberg, 'this constant resistance and the constant punch bag existence wears me down', he meant it and he was right. For twenty-six years, he found himself in the position of the desperate and furious son in a parental triangle, in which the 'parents'—the Emperor and Empress—had in fact literally absolute power over him. The Emperor could dismiss Bismarck at any moment but the old Emperor never did, the younger Emperor Frederick, was too ill to do it, and the youngest, Kaiser William II, with whom Bismarck could only pose as grandfather, very quickly did. Is it not also possible that Bismarck skilfully exploited the royal triangle by playing the 'weak' father off against the 'strong' mother? And that some element of 'personal dictatorship' emerged out of his deep ambivalences about his own parents?

When I began the work on this biography, I saw Bismarck's constant resignation threats, his long stays away from Berlin, his illnesses and hypochondria as in part ingenious tactics to get his way and they were undoubtedly that too. Now I see more clearly that the psychic triangle between a 'weak' emperor and a 'strong' empress must have given Bismarck constant pain as if his political fate required that a wounded psychic muscle be twisted again and again to a point beyond endurance. When Dr Ernst Schweninger arrived in 1884, Bismarck's gluttony, physical symptoms, and chronic sleeplessness were about to kill him. Schweninger treated the Iron Chancellor by wrapping him completely in warm, damp towels and by holding his hand until he fell asleep. Is it fanciful to see that as a surrogate for the warmth of a loving mother?

In 1816 the Bismarck family moved to the Pomeranian estate of Kniephof, which Ferdinand had inherited from the distant relative we mentioned above. It was a bigger estate but had a less developed village and was further from Berlin. During the 1820s Ferdinand transformed the economic basis of his estates from cereal to cattle. Bismarck always preferred the woods of Pomerania to the flood plains of Schönhausen.[31] The child Bismarck loved Kniephof and, as he told von Keudell on a journey to Leipzig in 1864:

up to the age of six I was always in the fresh air or in the stables. An old cow-herd warned me once not to creep around under the cows so trustingly. The cow, he said, can tread on your eye. The cow notices nothing and goes on chewing, but the eye is then gone. I have often thought about that later when people, without noticing it, do harm to others.[32]

At 6 he went to the Plamann Institute and suffered for another six years. From there, on 27 April 1821, we have the first written testimony (I cannot reproduce the quaint spelling) but the quality of the prose attests to the standards of the Institute. Not many 6-year-olds would be able to write this:

Dear Mother, I have happily arrived marks have been given out and I hope you will be pleased. A new springer has come who can do tricks on horseback and on foot. Many, many greetings and so stay as well as you were when we left you. I am your loving son Otto.[33]

The second piece of Bismarckian prose from Easter 1825 shows how much progress the young scholar had made in four years:

Dear Mother,
    I am very healthy. There will now be as every year promotions. I have been put in the second class in sums, in natural history, in geography, in German, in singing, writing and drawing and in gym. Send us quickly a plant drum so that when we go out to collect plants, we can put them in it. The strict teacher has gone away and a new teacher named Kayser has come. Also one student has gone. The new course has begun. Mr and Mrs Plamann are well. Be well and write soon and greet everybody from your true son Otto.[34]

In 1827 Bismarck's life improved. At the age of 12 he went to the Friedrich Wilhelm Gymnasium in Berlin. From 1830 to 1832, he moved to the Grey Cloister Gymnasium also in Berlin; I cannot say why he moved schools but his final school report contained the rubric *diligence*: 'sometimes irregular, school attendance lacked the constant and expected regularity'.[35] He and his brother lived in the family's townhouse at 53 Behrendstrasse in winter with their parents, and in the summer on their own with a housekeeper and a household schoolmaster.

In July 1829 when the two brothers were separated, Otto wrote Bernhard the following letter from Kniephof and, even if I allow for the fact that the writer is only 14, the tone and the vividness of the prose mark the debut of one of the best letter writers of the nineteenth century:

Tuesday we had a big crowd here. His Excellency the Sack (the Provincial President), the bank man Rumschüttel (who did nothing but taste wine), Colonel Einhart and so were here. Little Malwine [Bismarck's young sister—JS] begins to look quite personable and speaks German and French, whichever occurs to her...She still remembers you very well and says over and over 'Do Bennat also come'. She was really pleased when I arrived. They are building a lot in the distillery and they are adding a new house with cellars, the former stable will be a dwelling. The day labourers will move to the sheep pen and where they live now.

Carl will get a house. I have worked a terrible amount. In Zimmerhausen, I shot a duck.[36]

The following summer, Otto wrote Bernhard about a rural comedy in Kniephof:

On Friday three promising young fellows, an arsonist, a highwayman and a thief, escaped from the local jail. The whole neighbourhood swarmed with patrols, gendarmes and militia. People feared for their lives. In the evening the Kniephof Imperial Execution Force, which consisted of 25 militia-men, marched forth against the three monsters, armed as well they could with muskets, flints, pistols, and the rest with forks and scythes. Every crossing point over the Zampel was occupied. Our military men were paralysed with fear. If two units met, they called out, but they were so terrified that the others did not reply. The first unit ran where they could and the other crept behind the bushes.[37]

Needless to say, the 'promising young fellows' were not caught.

On 15 April 1832 Bismarck got his *abitur*, the prized higher school certificate, which entitled the bearer to enroll at a university. On 10 May 1832 Bismarck matriculated at Göttingen 'studiosus of the laws and science of statecraft'.[38] The Georgia Augusta University of Göttingen had been founded in 1734 under George II, Elector of Hanover and King of England, and rapidly became the centre of the 'English Enlightenment' on the continent. Göttingen would not be on first glance the ideal university for a young Junker like Otto von Bismarck, but there were other attractions as Margaret Lavinia Anderson explains: 'What gave Göttingen life its peculiar character was the dominance of the aristocracy.... the promenades of Göttingen were bright with self-styled romantic heroes, conspicuous in velvet frock coats, rings and spurs, flowing locks and long moustaches, and accompanied by the inevitable pair of bulldogs.'[39]

Göttingen may have attracted Bismarck for that reason, but John Lothrop Motley, a gifted upper-class Bostonian, came for the learning associated with it and found it wanting. In 1832 he wrote home to Boston:

> at all events it is not worth one's while to remain long in Göttingen, because most of the professors who were ornaments of the university are dead or decayed, and the town itself is excessively dull.[40]

Motley shared the same birthday as Bismarck but was a year older. Like his friend he came from a social class in which one knew everybody. He corresponded for years with Oliver Wendell Holmes Sr., knew Emerson and Thoreau, and, because of those connections, became US Ambassador in Vienna and later in London without ever having had any serious diplomatic preparation. A gifted linguist, he spoke perfect German, learned Dutch, and wrote a monumental multi-volume history of the Dutch Republic for which he became famous in his lifetime. It had become fashionable in the 1820s and 1830s for upper-class Americans like Motley and well-placed young Englishmen to spend a few years in German universities, which had begun to exercise a powerful attraction on advanced opinion. The great William Whewell, mathematician, philosopher, and long-time Master of Trinity College, Cambridge, learned about *Naturwissenschaft* (natural sciences) and the new type of serious university in Germany and tried to push Cambridge to imitate it. Lytton Strachey in *Eminent Victorians* describes the Tractarian the Revd Edward Pusey, friend of Newman and Keble, as a man of wealth and learning, a professor and a canon of Christ Church, 'who had, it was rumoured, been to Germany'.[41] Strachey plays here on the contrast between staid Oxford clergymen of the proper sort in the late 1820s and 1830 and uppity young men like Pusey 'who had been to Germany' and came back full of the new theology and Bible criticism.

Motley had no such aspirations but he did do something remarkable; he wrote a novel about life in a German university. *The American National Biography Online* dismisses it in a sentence: 'Motley's first novel, *Morton's Hope*, a historical romance, also appeared in 1839. The little critical attention it received was negative: it was condemned for its flawed plot, diction, and characterization.' I agree that *Morton's Hope* has its limits but it has one precious virtue, Otto von Bismarck, thinly disguised as Otto von Rabenmarck, plays the main role. Here we have a remarkable portrait of Bismarck as a student and of the place where he studied.

Motley first met Bismarck as a 17-year-old freshman along with fellow students from Göttingen, who had begun '*eine Bierreise*', a beer-drinking trip, the object of which was to get 'smashed' in as many German cities as possible. Here is the picture Motley/Morton gives us:

> Rabenmark was a 'fox' (the slang term for a student in his first year), who had been just challenging the veteran student to drink. He was very young, even for a fox, for at the time I write of, he was not yet quite seventeen, but in precocity of character, in every respect, he went immeasurably beyond any person I have ever known...His figure was slender, and not yet mature but already of a tolerable height. His dress was in the extreme of the then Göttingen fashion. He wore a chaotic coat without collar or buttons, and as destitute of colour as of shape; enormously wide trousers and boots with iron heels and portentous spurs. His shirt-collar, unconscious of cravat, was doubled over his shoulders and his hair hung down about his ears and neck. A faint attempt at moustachios, of an indefinite colour, completed the equipment of his face, and a huge saber strapped around his waist, that of his habiliment. As he wrote Von before his name, and was descended of a Bohemian family, who had been baronized before Charlemagne's time, he wore an enormous seal-ring on his fore-finger with his armorial bearing. Such was Otto von Rabenmark, a youth who in a more fortunate sphere would have won himself name and fame. He was gifted with talents and acquirements immeasurably beyond his years.[42]

Even then young Bismarck stood out. Several months later, Motley took a walk through the city and reported that

> all along the street, I saw, on looking up, the heads and shoulders of students projecting from every window. They were arrayed in tawdry smoking caps, and heterogeneous-looking dressing gowns with the long pipes and flash tassels depending from their mouths.[43]

Motley/Morton then ran into Rabenmark walking his dog, Ariel. Both man and dog are dressed outlandishly and, when a group of four students laugh, von Rabenmark challenges three of them to duels and the fourth who insulted the dog is forced to jump over Rabenmark's stick like a dog. They go back to Bismarck's rooms. Morton notes the plain furniture and that 'the floor was without carpet and sanded'. The walls were covered with silhouettes:

> a peculiar and invariable characteristic of a German student's room;—they are well executed profiles, in black paper on a white ground, of the occupant's intimate friends, and are usually four or five inches square, and surrounded with a narrow frame of black wood. Rabenmarks's friends seemed to be

numerous, for there were at least a hundred silhouettes, ranged in regular rows gradually decreasing by one from the bottom, till the pyramid was terminated by a single one, which was the profile of the 'senior' of the Pomeranian club...The third side of the room was decorated with a couple of '*schlägers*' or duelling swords, which were fastened cross-wise against the wall.[44]

'There', said Rabenmark, entering the room, unbuckling his belt, and throwing the pistols and *schläger* on the floor. 'I can leave my buffoonery for a while and be reasonable. It's rather tiresome work, this *renommiring* [gaining reputation or *renommée*—JS]...I am a fox. When I came to the university three months ago, I had not a single acquaintance. I wished to introduce myself into the best Landsmannschaft [a duelling society—JS], but I saw little chance of succeeding. I have already, however, become an influential member. What course do you suppose I adopted to gain my admission?'

'I suppose you made friends of the president or senior, as you call him, and other magnates of the club.' Said I.

'No, I insulted them all publicly and in the grossest possible manner...and after I had cut off the senior's nose, sliced off the con-senior's upper lip, moustachios and all, besides bestowing less severe marks of affection on the others, the whole club in admiration of my prowess and desiring to secure the services of so valorous a combatant voted me in by acclamation...I intend to lead my companions here, as I intend to lead them in after-life. You see I am a very rational sort of person now and you would hardly take me for the crazy mountebank you met in the street half-an hour ago. But then I see that this is the way to obtain superiority. I determined at once on arriving at the university, that to obtain mastery over my competitors, who were all, extravagant, savage, eccentric, I had to be ten times as extravagant and savage as any one else...' His age was, at the time of which I am writing, exactly eighteen and a half.[45]

Erich Marcks, who in 1915 published the first full biography of Bismarck which used interviews with the living Bismarck seems to have been one of the few German biographers actually to have read *Morton's Hope*. He concluded that 'out of the features of the Göttingen student Rabenmark, Bismarck stands out with unmistakable accuracy; his experience, his appearance, his way of speaking shimmer through'.[46] Marcks also reports that Bismarck in three semesters engaged in twenty-five duels.[47] Yet the really interesting fact about *Morton's Hope* escapes Marcks. He thinks only of Bismarck, not of Motley. How remarkable both men must have been, the one to inspire, and the other to write, a biography or a biographical novel about the young man. Even at 18 Bismarck had a special aura. Motley makes it absolutely clear that this young man 'in precocity of character, in every respect,...went immeasurably beyond any person I have ever known.'

Motley saw another important attribute in his friend, he saw 'a very rational sort of person... I see that this is the way to obtain superiority and that I intend to lead my companions here, as I intend to lead them in after-life.' Bismarck's urge to rule and dominate others by the force of his personality stood out even at the age of 18. Later in his political career he chose conflict over compromise in most situations, as if conflict had a cleansing or clarifying property by drawing the lines between friends and foes more sharply or defining the possible courses of action.

At Göttingen Bismarck clashed with authority very often. Göttingen, like Cambridge in the nineteenth century, had its own courts and applied *Karzerstrafe* (jail sentences) in the university jail to unruly students who had been caught by the *Pedells* (in Cambridge they were and still are known as the 'Bull Dogs').[48] Bismarck naturally got into trouble and had to serve a sentence. How literally such incarceration was taken I cannot say but we know that he wrote to the Rector of Göttingen in the spring of 1833:

> Your Magnificence had the goodness to postpone the *Karzerstrafe* imposed on me until after my return from the Michaelmas holiday. Now a further recurrence of my illness, the end of which is not foreseeable, requires me to remain in Berlin and continue my studies here since such a long journey would further weaken my already weakened constitution. For this reason I beg Your Magnificence most obediently to allow me to serve my sentence here and not in Gottingen. Your Magnificence's most obedient Otto von Bismarck, stud. jur.[49]

We know quite a lot about Bismarck's state of mind and plans through a series of lively letters he wrote to his 'Corps Brother' (the duelling fraternity 'Pomerania') Gustav Scharlach (1811–81). The first touches a familiar undergraduate problem but does it with Bismarck's literary extravagance:

> There have been uncomfortable scenes with the Old Man, who absolutely refuses to pay my debts. This puts me into a misanthropic mood... The deficit is not so bad because I have huge credit, which allows me to live in a slovenly way. The consequence is that I look sick and pale which the Old Man will, of course, ascribe, when I go home for Christmas, to a lack of means of subsistence; then I will make a scene and say to him I would rather be a Mohammedan than suffer hunger any longer, and that will solve the problem.[50]

The next letter has become justly famous for its wit, style, and brilliant caricature. Bismarck describes to Scharlach what will happen to him if he opts not to go into the bureaucracy but to go home to run one of his father's estates. If Scharlach visits him in ten years he will find a well-fed *Landwehr* [militia—JS] officer with a moustache, who curses and swears a justifiable hatred of Frenchmen and Jews until the earth trembles, and beats his dogs and his servants in the most brutal fashion, even if he is tyrannized by his wife. I will wear leather trousers and allow myself to be ridiculed at the Wool Market in Stettin, and when anyone calls me Herr Baron, I'll stroke my moustache in good humour and sell two dollars cheaper. On the King's birthday I'll get drunk and shout 'Vivat!' and in general get excited a lot and my every word will be 'on my honour!' and 'a superb horse!'. In short I shall be happy in my family's rural circle, *car tel est mon plaisir*.[51]

The vignette of the typical Junker country squire is a perfect miniature, dashed off in a letter to a friend and has justly become famous. The writer at that time had a week earlier celebrated his nineteenth birthday. When Bismarck opted for politics, German literature lost a fine comic novelist.

The third in this set of letters to Scharlach explains his career plans and dates from early May 1834. In it he announces his intention to sit the state examinations and hence

to exchange the honourable estate of candidate in law with that of a royal civil servant, that is, *Referendar* at the Berlin Municipal Court. My plan is to stay here for a year, then go to the Provincial Government in Aachen; after the second year to sit the diplomatic examination and then to leave to the grace of destiny which will render me utterly indifferent whether one sends me to Petersburg or Rio Janeiro...You will, alas, find in this letter my old habit of talking a lot about myself. Do me the pleasure of imitating this and fear not for that reason the slightest shadow of vanity.[52]

At this time, a chance encounter changed his life. In the summer of 1834 he met Lieutenant Albrecht von Roon, a brilliant young officer and graduate of the prestigious Kriegsakademie (the Prussian War College). When the General Staff finally became fully operational in the 1820s, it developed an elaborate project to survey and make maps of the terrain of the Kingdom of Prussia, a tradition, which continued to the Second World War. (The University Library at Cambridge has a complete pristine set of thousands of Wehrmacht maps, so detailed that it is possible to locate landmarks necessary for operations by squads or platoons.) The topography section of the General Staff employed gifted young officers too poor to pay for their own horses and equipment and hence unfitted for immediate assignment to regiments as general staff officers. By an interesting irony, the two generals—Moltke and Roon—who marched in triumph on either side of Bismarck in the parade down Unter den Linden of June 1871 to mark the victory over

France and the unification of Germany, had both spent important years in the topographical unit. Arden Bucholz notes that, like Roon, Moltke took part in the great topographic project under Chief of the Great General Staff Karl Freiherr von Müffling.

Neither Roon nor his wife Anna had any capital and even in the early 1850s lived the life of a simple regimental Commander. As his son wrote, 'they were basically living on his salary.'[53] In the summer of 1834 Lieutenant von Roon was hard at work in the fields and forests of Pomerania, surveying and sketching the landscape for the topography. He invited his nephew Moritz von Blanckenburg to help him and to bring a friend. Moritz brought his best friend, the 19-year-old Otto von Bismarck. The two lads accompanied von Roon on his project in the morning and went hunting in the afternoons.[54] The young Bismarck, who so dazzled his contemporary Motley, must have made an impression on the officer twelve years his senior, who was later to make Bismarck minister-president of Prussia. The link—as so often in Junker Prussia—tied them through the familial net and also through 'service' in the army.

For reasons not entirely clear (Marcks suggests that, since Bismarck fell ill in his last semester at Göttingen, it seemed prudent to study nearer home),[55] Bismarck moved to Berlin where he spent the winter of 1833–4 and at some point changed his matriculation from Göttingen to the University of Berlin. Motley joined him there and a third friend, Alexander von Keyserling, completed the trio. Engelberg calls Motley and Keyserling Bismarck's 'good spirits'.[56] Lothar Gall puts it more strongly—'The American was one of the few real friends that Bismarck had in his life'— and suggests further that Motley introduced Bismarck to Byron, to Goethe, to Shakespeare, and the full flower of German romantic art.[57] Not much of it took. Pflanze points out that Bismarck never showed much interest in the cultural awakening that made Germany between 1770 and 1830 the intellectual capital of the world. He notes that Bismarck was essentially unaffected by his classical education, by German idealism, by the new historicism, by romanticism, by the great era of German musical composition.[58] Hegel left him cold, ditto Schopenhauer. He had nothing to do with either left or right Hegelians, seems not to have cared much for Schelling, Fichte, or most of the romantic poets. But there was one major exception: Friedrich Schiller mattered to Bismarck and even more to the soldiers: to Roon, to Manteuffel, to Wrangel, but interestingly not to the cool Moltke.

Bismarck certainly knew his Schiller well but he preferred the lyric poets with a sense of humour. Baroness Spitzemberg recorded the following conversation in December of 1884, as she sat with Bismarck in his 'corner':

> After dinner he smoked and leafed through a volume of Chamisso's poems, which together with Uhland, Heine, Rückert he treats himself to so that he can have copies in every one of his residences. 'When I am really irritated and exhausted, I prefer to read the German lyricists, they cheer me up'.[59]

In May 1835 Bismarck sat successfully the first stage of the legal examinations to enter the Ministry of Justice. As he wrote to Scharlach in July of that year:

> I have just returned from several weeks of leave in the countryside and have hurled myself back into the duty of bringing to light and punishing the crimes of the Berliners. This high duty to the state, which in my case consists of the mechanical function of taking the minutes, began promisingly but only tolerably while it was new. Now that my beautiful fingers begin to curve under the burden of the constantly moving pen, I wish most ardently to serve the commonweal in some other capacity.[60]

In the spring of 1836 he took time off to prepare for the second examination and this time went to Schönhausen, which he describes in his usual mocking tones:

> For the last four weeks I sit here in this old, cursed manor house with its pointed arches and four metre-thick walls, some 30 rooms in which two have as furnishing splendid damask tapestries, the colour of which can just about be seen on the shreds of cloth that remain, masses of rats, fireplaces in which the wind howls, in the 'old castle of my fathers', where everything which is suitable conspires to maintain a real spleen. Next to it is a splendid old church. My room looks out on the churchyard, and on the other side onto one of those old gardens with trimmed hedges of yew and fine old lindens. The only living soul in these crumbling surroundings is your friend, fed by and cared for by a dried-out old house maid who was a childhood playmate of my 65-year-old father. I prepare my exams, listen to the nightingales, target shoot and read Voltaire and Spinoza's ethics, which I found bound in beautiful pigskin in the library here.[61]

The complexity of this piece of prose needs a word. Bismarck elevates Schönhausen to the 'old castle of my fathers'. In fact, pictures show that the house has an absolutely typical medieval wing with steeply slanting roof and small windows. Next to it a grander late seventeenth- or early eighteenth-century range, three stories high with two plain pilasters running from ground up to the roof, again a modest tiled roof, no pediment and a pleasant curved, baroque arch over the door. Dozens of rural estates would have looked that way and obscure squires, who had enjoyed a good harvest, would add very similar 'noble' wings. The 'castle' has become a ruin in Bismarck's heavy romantic irony, a sentimental and faintly absurd haunt of aristocratic decay, and there alone sits the Byronic young man attended by a hag. The self-dramatization, the pleasure in the word painting, the exaltation of his aristocratic inheritance, and the exuberance of the writing create a powerful impact. It lacks the earlier earthy fun of the 'fat Junker' letter but it suggests that Bismarck has arrived at a new stage in self-dramatization. After all, the place is not a joke but his claim to status in a hierarchical, aristocratic society. He bore the name of the place. He was a Bismarck-Schönhausen, as opposed to the other branches of the Bismarck family with different estate names. Hence its elevation to something from Scott's *Ivanhoe*. This word mastery marks his long career. He became the Bismarck we know because he had a powerful personality and because he could write with such artistry.

In the meantime, he had got fed up with working for the city courts and decided that law would never do, so he applied to be allowed to take the second examination not for the legal profession but for the diplomatic service. Here he needed the permission of the Foreign Minister, who happened to be Jean Pierre Frédéric Ancillon, former tutor to the young Crown Prince Frederick William IV. Through that happy pedagogic employment Ancillon rose to be Foreign Secretary of the Kingdom. Ancillon was a highly cultivated academic and a relative of Friedrich Gentz on his mother's side. What Motley wrote about Vienna in the 1860s applied even more so to the much smaller Prussian society: 'They are all related to each other, ten deep. It is one great family party of 3 or 300.'[62] Ancillon had no very high opinion of the Junker class in general and the young Bismarck in particular and suggested that he should look to something more homespun: the customs service or duty in another domestic capacity. Bismarck got his older brother to pull strings and thus gained the sponsorship of Count Arnim-Boitzenburg, the district president of administration in Aachen in the Prussian Rhineland.[63] But even that connection got him nowhere. In the end Bismarck had to settle for the domestic civil service, which involved facing the second legal examination but this time not in boring Berlin but in Aachen where his patron controlled the local administration.

Aachen, known usually in English as Aix-la-Chapelle, had much to recommend it. The westernmost city in Germany and the ancient capital of

Charlemagne's empire, it had many fine monuments and romantic ruins. It also had a flourishing spa. Aachen advertises itself today as 'the city with the hottest springs north of the Alps', with temperatures between 45°C and 75°C. These springs were the reason Charlemagne chose Aachen as the political centre of his empire. 'Darumb er dann zu Aach sich geren niderge-lassen, und von dess warmen Bad daselbst wegen Wohnung gehabt.' (Thereupon he settled in Aach and from the warmth the same had dwelling.)[64] The spa, the history and the location made it an ideal tourist attraction and certainly attracted the young Bismarck, a handsome 22-year-old, six foot four, slender, a fine linguist who spoke really good English and was utterly, utterly charming. Bismarck took the exams to be admitted to the administrative service, which he passed with distinction, swearing the oath of the civil servant in July 1836.[65]

The year and a bit in Aachen proved emotionally turbulent and very expensive.

Bismarck neglected his work, was frequently absent, and twice (at least) in love. In June of 1836 he wrote to Bernhard and described a trip on the way to Aachen with

> a very strong English party...The trip gave me great pleasure but cost me a lot of money...If one does not weaken at home and let me have a small gratification, I do not see how this can sensibly work out. Then to live here without cash is simply impossible.[66]

Engelberg, who published his two-volume biography in the German Democratic Republic five years later than Gall, makes use of ten Bismarck letters between 30 June 1836 and 19 July 1837 that were omitted from the *Complete Works*. The letters show the hero of German unification in a less than flattering light. There was, first of all, Bismarck's ruthless exploitation of his patron, Adolf Heinrich Count von Arnim-Boitzenburg. Arnim-Boitzenburg was born on 10 April 1803 in Berlin and had enjoyed a mete-oric rise in the Prussian administrative bureaucracy. At the age of 30 he had already reached the high position of *Regierungspräsident* (provincial gover-nor), a post which normally marked the pinnacle of a Prussian administra-tor's career, and was only 33 when he took over at Aachen. He later went on to hold cabinet office and was briefly prime minister during the turbulent years of the Revolution of 1848.[67] As we shall see, by 1864, he had begun to feel 'reservations' about his client's policies. In 1836, Count Arnim-Boitzenburg could not have been more accommodating. He gave Bismarck

special treatment and allowed him to move from section to section 'on
account of my following the diplomatic career path unlike the other
trainees',[68] a 'career path' which Foreign Minister Ancillon had categorically
not permitted.

Bismarck used the time to fall in love. By 10 August he was writing to his
brother that he was utterly overwhelmed: 'to describe how much in love
would leave the wildest oriental hyperbole an inadequate measure'. The
Duke and Duchess of Cleveland and their niece Laura Russell

> and a long tail of authentic Britons who examined me with their lorgnettes
> when His Grace of Cleveland bade me for the first time to have a glass of
> wine with him and with that worthiness and elegance characteristic of me,
> I poured a half gallon of sherry under my waistcoat.[69]

On 30 October Bismarck wrote to Bernhard that the Duke and Duchess
had departed with Laura, with whom I am 'as good as promised' but he let
her go without making it official. He started to gamble to recoup the debts
incurred by living all summer in high society and had considered suicide,
'I put aside for this purpose a cord of yellow silk which I have reserved for
its rarity just in case.'[70] On 2 November he wrote to Bernhard to say that
their father had sent him money but with recriminations.[71] By 3 December
1836 he had discovered that the beautiful Laura was not the niece of the
Duke of Cleveland but a child of a previous indiscretion of her mother's
who had only been the Duchess for two years and was a commoner. He was
now convinced that he had been manipulated and that behind the lor-
gnettes the English were laughing at him. 'They were saying: "look there
that tall monster, that is the silly German baron whom they have caught in
the woods, with his pipe and his seal-ring".'[72]

I see no sign of Bismarck feeling 'dissatisfaction with himself and an inner
emptiness' or that Bismarck was 'in flight and sought distraction', as Lothar
Gall does.[73] Instead, I see every sign of a proud, fatuously self-confident,
provincial gentleman swept away by the wealth and style of the English
aristocracy, so incomparably richer and more confident than the rural squires
who made up the Prussian Junker class. English country houses like Felbrigg
Hall in Norfolk, home of an untitled gentry family, the Wilsons, were bigger, grander, and more impressive than most of the palaces of reigning
German princes, and the Wilsons were much, much richer than any equivalent Prussian family. Robert Walpole's Houghton Hall with its hundreds of
rooms, exceeded any royal palace in Germany except for the Habsburgs of

Vienna and the Walpoles were merely Norfolk squires who through Sir Robert Walpole had made money in the government service.

The *Oxford Dictionary of National Biography* shows how desperately out of his class young Bismarck was. Here is an extract from the entry:

> William Harry Vane, first duke of Cleveland (1766–1842),... left almost £1 million in addition to huge estates, around £1,250,000 in consols, and plate and jewels to the value of a further £1 million.[74]

If we use the exchange rate of 1871 of £1 = 6.72 thaler, then the Duke of Cleveland's realizable fortune, without valuing the lands, amounted to £3,250,000 or 21,840,000 thaler.[75] If the Duke lived frugally on the income of 'gilts' (or consols) only at, say, 3 per cent per annum, he would have had an annual income of £37,500 or 252,000 thaler. When Bismarck became Prussian delegate to the Bundesrat in 1851, he had an income of 21,000 thaler.[76] The Duke of Cleveland must have had an income at least twenty times that of one of the highest-paid Prussian civil servants in the mid-nineteenth century. A 22-year-old country squire, dazzled at the prospects before him, could not entertain the Duke's party in a suitable manner without going into inconceivable amounts of debt. No wonder he considered 'suicide', in October 1836, after the Duke's party with Laura had left Aachen.

He recovered and by July of the next year, he could write to his brother to say that he was 'again on fire', this time a conflagration lit by Isabella Lorraine-Smith, another beautiful English woman 'with blonde hair and incredible beauty'.[77] It was a repeat of the previous summer with Bismarck hosting champagne dinners, incurring debts, and overstaying his leave. Once again he thought he had become engaged. On 30 August 1837 he wrote from Frankfurt to his friend, Karl Friedrich von Savigny, that he had grounds for that belief:

> For the last few days I find myself here with my family (an expression I beg you to consider absolutely confidential). [He asked Savigny to send his dress uniform to Geneva from Aachen.] It would make me very happy if you could be present at my wedding which will probably take place at Scarsdale in Leicestershire. For the moment please tell the Aachen friends that I have gone home to hunt for two months.[78]

The father of the beautiful Isabella could not compete with the Duke of Cleveland. Mr Lorraine-Smith was Rector of Passenham in Leicestershire, and a well-to-do man with lands in three counties but even before the

Frankfurt letter, as he wrote to his brother, Bismarck had begun to get cold feet about the prospect of 'plunging into the hell-fires of a narrow, bourgeois marriage'. His future father-in-law drew an income from the living of Passenham, which would end with his death.

> With my shortage of funds, I do not think I can take a wife who brings less than £1,000 a year, and I am not sure whether L. is willing or even able in the long run to give so much...How do you like these calculations from the pen of somebody who considers himself to be very much in love?[79]

One can see now why the devout editors of the *Gesammelte Werke* left these ten letters out. He had behaved despicably from beginning to end. He had abused the generosity of Count von Arnim-Boitzenburg. He had lived absurdly, had fallen in love with Laura Russell but got out of it as soon as he heard of her illegitimate birth, about which even he had signs of remorse:

> What must poor Laura think of me, when I fell in love with her as the niece of a Duke and turned my back on her as soon as I heard that she had the misfortune to come into the world in a so-so way?[80]

He had then repeated the comedy at a lower level with Isabella but shrunk from his engagement either because of his own monetary considerations or because the Revd Lorraine-Smith had seen through him. He had been absent without leave for months on end and done no work. He had been ruled by his pride and had spent a fortune to save face. Even the long-suffering Arnim-Boitzenburg had finally had enough. He declared that with heavy irony the trainee's conduct was

> no longer appropriate...I can only approve your previously mentioned decision to transfer to one of the royal provincial administrations in the old Prussian provinces where you will be able to return to more intensive engagement which you have desired to find in vain under the social circumstances of life in Aachen.[81]

Bismarck returned to Potsdam and began work again in the civil administration.

In January 1838 Bismarck wrote to his father that he had been trying to evade military service, another letter which the guardians of the flame omitted from the official publication of Bismarck's collected works. He told his Father that he had not yet begun his military service because he made 'one last attempt' to get out of his one-year military service in the reserves 'as a result of muscular weakness which I explained came from a sword-cut under the right arm which I feel when I lift it (!); unfortunately the blow was not deep enough.'[82] Social life could not compare with Aachen but he had been put on the list of *garçons* who were invited to balls by Prince Frederick (1794–1863) and by the Crown Prince.

At the end of September 1838 Bismarck wrote to his father from Greifswald, where he had been stationed as an army reservist, that he had begun to study agriculture at the university and in the agricultural college. He included a copy of a letter he wrote to Cousin Caroline von Bismarck-Bohlen, 'my picture book beautiful cousin with whom—I mention in passing—I am utterly in love', who begged him to continue his career.[83] He copied out the long letter to Caroline for his father and later made a copy for his fiancée Johanna von Puttkammer. Engelberg notes that 'the very fact that he sent it to several addresses, makes it a key document in his development, but above all its content. It is a masterpiece of family diplomacy.'[84] It seems fairly certain that he decided to leave his potentially brilliant career in the civil service because the burden of his huge and still growing debts oppressed him. In July he visited his mother in Berlin who was now terminally ill and poured out his heart. He told her how miserable he was and begged her to help him find some better position, how his life had become unbearable, the work disgusted him, and how the prospect of spending his whole life to end up a *Regierungspräsident* on 2,000 thaler a year filled his great soul with despair. Wilhelmine in turn wrote to Ferdinand who then decided to make over the three Pomeranian estates to the two sons and to withdraw to Schönhausen. By running one of his father's estates he would generate income, live at home, reduce his living costs, and avoid the temptations to gamble and spend conspicuously.[85] Of course he could tell nobody in the family about what actually happened in Aachen so he raised the decision to leave the civil service onto a higher plane. The letter—four pages long—contains one of the most often quoted paragraphs Bismarck ever composed:

> The activity of the individual civil servant among us is very rarely independent, even that of the highest, and for the rest their activity confines itself to pushing the administrative machinery along the tracks already laid down. The Prussian civil servant resembles a player in an orchestra. He may be the first violin or play the triangle; without oversight or influence on the whole he must play his part, as it is set down, whether he think it good or bad. I will make music, which I consider good or none at all.[86]

The reality of his debts continued to plague him. On 21 December 1838, he wrote a grovelling letter to his friend Savigny and apologized for not yet paying him back the

> sum that for years you have had a right to expect. In the next few days I will come to Berlin myself in the hope that I can do in person what I have not achieved in writing, that is, raise some money, which we both doubtless urgently need.[87]

The year 1839 began badly. On New Year's Day Wilhelmine Bismarck died just short of her fiftieth birthday. For the previous three years, his mother had been suffering with an undiagnosed growth, which got progressively worse in 1838. The sources are extraordinarily silent about the woman who so profoundly influenced his life. We can only speculate in a vacuum.

At Easter 1839 Bismarck took up residence in Kniephof and became a full-time farmer. Kniephof was a large estate farmed by *Instleute* with contracts with the lord, a form of rural employment, which resembled the *metayer* in France, the *mezzadro* in Italy, or the 'share cropper' in the American south. In the Prussian case the abolition of bodily servitude, that is, serfdom, had transformed the relations between lord and land worker and in the 1830s and 1840s the 'increasing commercialization of many regions…led to every more frequent demands about unpaid bills for sales or services'.[88] The money economy was turning traditional contracts into relations of the market for labour. *Instleute* were not hired labour nor fully free of traditional ties either.[89] Since 1800 Prussian agriculture had been in a process of increasing professionalization. Agricultural colleges of the kind that Bismarck attended in Greifswald spread, and productivity of agriculture had risen even against the trend of a long depression which followed the end of the Napoleonic wars and did not finish until the early 1850s. Pflanze provides useful figures on agricultural growth and productivity. The population of Prussia grew between 1816 and 1864 from 23,552,000 to 37,819,000 or by 59 per cent. The area under cultivation in the same period rose from 55.5 per cent of the land area to 69.3 per cent, an increase of 24.8 per cent but yield per acre increased by 135 per cent.[90] Bismarck worked hard and began to get results. The trends were moving in his direction.

Although his correspondence with his brother in these years concerns farming, Bismarck now moved into a world dominated by the old Pomeranian noble families, with names which were to play a central part in his career: Dewitz, Bülow, Thadden-Trieglaff, Blanckenburg, von der Osten, von der Marwitz, Wartensleben, Senfft von Pilsach, and others. Hartwin Spenkuch in his book on the Prussian House of Lords put the Pomeranian nobility, according to figures used for the reorganization of the House of Lords in 1854, at the top of the list of knightly estates (*Rittergüter*) with more than 100 years in the same family.[91] Bismarck took up his position as an estate owner with some enthusiasm. As Erich Marcks wrote, 'he had the power to command his lands and his people and the need to obey nobody. He wrote "Lordship" on protocols when bailiffs or pastors or schoolteachers came before him as judge with their complaints. He judged and acted to police his decisions.'[92] He joined his fellow Junker landowners on local and county committees. In spite of all that, the size of the estates meant that the distance between one manor house and another was considerable and he spent a good deal of the time alone, reading and often drinking too much. He hunted with his neighbours and they came to hunt on his lands. Robert von Keudell, who later became one of Bismarck's trusted aides, had taken a post as a junior lawyer in the provincial court at Cöslin. He heard and recorded stories of Bismarck's crazy goings-on from an elderly Herr von der Marwitz-Rützenow who knew Otto well. Von der Marwitz described Bismarck's simple hospitality whenever he had stopped over in Kniephof. He would put out a bottle of strong beer and one of champagne and would say in English 'help yourself'. There would be a simple snack with a lot to drink and much conversation. He was already inventing a more appropriate past. Herr von der Marwitz recalled him saying

> In his youth he had wanted to be a soldier but his mother had wanted to be able to salute him as a well-heeled government councillor. For her sake he spent many years in the Justice and Administrative service but found it not to his taste. After her death, he came to the district and enjoyed the freedom of the country life in big drafts.[93]

One night after a long journey, Herr von der Marwitz and a friend showed up unannounced at Kniephof. Bismarck welcomed them, set out the usual fare, and the visitors and their host sat late and drank a lot.

> He apologized in advance that he would not be able to see them at breakfast because he had to be in Naugard by 7 a.m. The guests needed to go there too and, though Bismarck strongly urged them to sleep as late as they liked, they eventually agreed that Bismarck would wake them at 6.30 in the morning. They drank on and eventually went to bed. The friend said to von der

Marwitz, as they climbed the stairs to the guest room, 'I have had more drink than I am used to and I want to sleep it off tomorrow morning.' 'You can't do that,' Herr von der Marwitz said. 'Wait and see,' replied the friend who pushed a huge chest of drawers against the door. At 6.30 in the morning, Bismarck knocked at the door. 'Are you ready?' No sound from the room. Bismarck turned the doorknob and pushed the door against the heavy chest. A few minutes later he called out from the courtyard. 'Are you ready?' No sound from us. Two pistol shots crashed through the window-glass and knocked plaster onto my friend, who crept to the window and stuck a white handkerchief out on the end of a stick. In a few minutes we were downstairs. Bismarck greeted us with his usual heartiness without a word about his little victory.[94]

His behaviour as a host helped to earn him the title of 'the mad Junker' and stories like the one above, which spread through the county, multiplied as Bismarck behaved with his usual extravagance. He rode like a madman and had many accidents, which also became legendary. His pistol stories, his occasional romances, his extravagant conversation, and unconventional views became the talk of the county society. Keudell visited Moritz von Blanckenburg, who had known Bismarck from childhood and ran into him again at the Grey Cloister gymnasium. Moritz recalled that even in school he was a 'puzzling person. I never saw him work. He went for long walks but still knew everything and always had the homework ready.'[95]

The 'mad Junker' was lonely, restless, and dissatisfied behind the public bravado. He had begun to feel the need for something deeper in his life. He took long trips. One to England in 1842 he described in a letter to his father. He went to York and Hull and took the train to Manchester to see 'the largest machine factory in the world'. England delighted him and, of course, he spoke excellent English after his two years living with or close to Motley. 'The politeness and kindness of the English exceeded my expectations . . . even the common people are well-behaved. They look modest and understanding when you speak.' He was surprised how relatively cheap hotels and meals were.

This is country for heavy eaters . . . They serve huge breakfasts with many cuts of meat and at noon comes fish and an atrocious fruit tart. Soups are so strongly seasoned with white and black pepper that few foreigners can eat them. They never serve by the portion because even at breakfast the most colossal pieces of every sort of meat are available and they put them before you to cut as much or as little as you choose without effect on the bill.[96]

When he was not travelling, as he wrote to his father, 'I am so bored I could hang myself when I am alone at Kniephof.'[97] In August of 1844 he went on holiday at Norderney, and wrote his father a superb description of the boat trip in a thunderstorm. He met for the first time the two people who would most influence his life in the future: Crown Prince Wilhelm of Prussia and his Princess Augusta, who had been born Augusta Marie Luise Katharina von Sachsen-Weimar-Eisenach. He had a pleasant time with them on the beach. He drew vivid word pictures of the long list of gentle-folk present. Bismarck paid particular attention to the young women, one of whom was described as having 'good trotters'.

> Mornings either before or after bathing we play bowls with huge balls. The rest of the time we divide up among playing whist and pharo, mockery and flirting with the women, walking on the beach, eating oysters, shooting rabbits and evenings an hour or two of dancing. A monotonous but healthy way of life.[98]

His private letters from 1843 reveal a kind of desperation: this huge man with his fierce, undirected ambition, his spectacular and extravagant behaviour, his tremendous urge to dominate, and his dread of boredom, resembled a massive engine with a steam boiler at highest pressure and the wheels locked by cast-iron breaks. He was also lonely and at 28 presumably sexually frustrated as well. On the other hand, he recalled only too well the humiliations and folly of his English affairs. On 10 September 1843 he wrote to a friend,

> I love contact with women but marriage is a dubious proposition and my experiences have made me think twice. I feel partly comfortable, partly bored and very chilled in my spirits, and as long as I can hold out, I will... I am toying with the idea of playing the Asian for a few years to bring a change in the stage design of my comedy, to smoke my cigars on the Ganges rather than the Rega.[99]

That his life had become a drearily staged 'comedy' speaks volumes. A month later he wrote to his father to report on developments at Kniephof and explained that he had imported forty day-labourers from the Warthe swamp

> who work much better than our people and help with ploughing but they cost much more. But in the view of the rain I don't know how we would have lifted the potatoes without them... Greet Malwine and come whole and healthy to see me. I am bored to the point of hanging myself.[100]

At the end of the month of October 1843 he confided to his old friend
and future brother-in-law, Oskar von Arnim-Kröchlendorff (1813–1903),
that his financial affairs had

> gradually begun to find a baseline…When I am on my own, I get bored
> which I suppose must happen to every young, reasonably educated man in
> the country who is unmarried and relies on the society of a more numerous
> than interesting clique of Pomeranian squire-bumpkins, Philistines and Ulan
> officers.[101]

Boredom often drove him to the neighbouring estate of his childhood
playmate, Moritz von Blanckenburg, where he met Marie von Thadden-
Trieglaff, Moritz's fiancée. His boredom and emptiness appalled her. On 7
February 1843 she wrote to Moritz:

> I have never seen anybody express his lack of faith or rather pantheism so
> freely and clearly…his bottomless boredom and emptiness…He was very
> upset, was sometimes red in the face but could not get anywhere…a certain
> shyness before the blue haze of his image of God.[102]

This was the beginning of one of the most important relationships of
Bismarck's life. Meeting Marie brought him together with a remarkable
young woman with whom he fell instantly and hopelessly in love. Had she
been free, he might never have unified Germany, no matter how ridiculous
that may sound. She had strength but of a kind that never threatened him.
She saw through his extravagant façade and pitied him. She too fell in love
with him, as this letter to one of her closest friends, Elizabeth von Mittelstädt,
from May 1843, suggests with its disparaging judgement of her fiancé,
Moritz von Blanckenburg:

> Otto B no longer shows his face in Zimmerhausen; very good because dear,
> good Moritz could not survive the comparison. That he stays away out of
> magnanimity I do not believe but because he has something else in mind.[103]

Marie von Thadden and Elizabeth von Mittelstädt belonged to an important group of aristocratic Pietists, Christian believers who in America are
known as 'born-again' Christians. Marie von Thadden's serenity and strength
came from her deep faith in the saving power of Jesus Christ, a power which
worked directly on the souls of men, if they would just believe in him. She
was the daughter of one of the founding members of the Junker version of
Pietism who in 1813 in the 'Christian German Table Club' began meeting
in Mai's Inn in Berlin. The members soon gained the nickname of the

'Maikäfer' (May bugs). The main members were von Alvensleben-Erxleben, Gustav and Heinrich von Below, Leopold and Ludwig von Gerlach, Cajus Count Stolberg, Count Voss, Friedrich Wilhelm Count von Götzen, Adolf von Thadden-Trieglaff, and the Crown Prince Frederick William. Adolf von Thadden-Trieglaff, Marie's father, Ernst von Senfft-Pilsach, and Ludwig von Gerlach married three sisters Henriette, Ida, and Auguste von Oertzen.[104] These men later became Bismarck's 'first political party' and created the platform for everything that followed. They took him up after his 'conversion' and made him—understandably—their polemical sword. Nobody in their ranks could use the profane weapons of wit, commanding presence, brilliance, and literary elegance better than Otto von Bismarck. He became, they thought, the scourge of the ungodly. They were wrong. Bismarck served nobody, neither man nor God but only himself. That discovery in the 1870s tore from him the closest friends and mentors of his youth and left him desolate, and as lonely again as he had been in the 1840s.

The impact of the defeat of Prussia in 1806 and the occupation of the kingdom by the 'Godless' Napoleon had driven many of the great Junker landlords back to Christianity. They rejected Enlightenment rationalism, the horrors of Jacobin fanaticism, the doctrines of equality, the guillotines, but also Frederick the Great's cynical contempt for religion. Though they came out of Lutheran Protestantism, they rejected the official 'walled' churches and like all Evangelicals looked for the stirrings of God's grace not in the Holy Sacraments of the Roman Catholic or Lutheran Churches but in the motions of their own hearts.

In *The Politics of Conversion: Missionary Protestantism and the Jews in Prussia 1728–1941* Christopher Clark traces the peculiarly Lutheran variant of this general Evangelical movement. German Pietism combined evangelical inwardness and preoccupation about salvation through grace alone with organized and very Prussian institutions. The German Neo-Pietists often said mass in homes or in the open air. They communed with simple bread and wine as the early Christians had done. They observed the Sabbath and dedicated themselves to works of charity. Since the Hohenzollern dynasty had been Calvinist since 1603 but the majority of their subjects remained firmly Lutheran, the Pietists with their thrift and discipline became a group from whom the monarchs recruited efficient and pliant civil servants. These Christians brought no baggage of ancient Lutheran claims to feudal rights.

Junker Pietists formed their own missionary society. In January 1822 the Berlin Society for the Promotion of Christianity among the Jews was

founded by General Job von Witzleben. The von Witzleben family produced fourteen Generals between 1755 and 1976, one of whom, Field
Marshall Job-Wilhelm Georg Erwin von Witzleben, was executed for his
part in the plot to assassinate Hitler in 1944.[105] Hitler ordered that he be
hanged from a butcher's hook and filmed in his final agonies so that the
Führer could relish the death of a Junker aristocrat who had tried to kill
him. His ancestor, Job von Witzleben, had been since 1817 chief of the
King's Military Cabinet, an office of the highest importance. The *Allgemeine
deutsche Biographie* describes von Witzleben's position in these words:

> There was no issue of importance—whether it concerned the army, the State,
> the Church or the royal family—which was not discussed by them. Witzleben's
> opinion had great weight in the resolution of such questions... For twenty
> years he was the most powerful subject in the state.[106]

Other founders included Johann Peter Friedrich Ancillon, whom we have
already met as tutor to the Crown Prince and as the Prussian Foreign
Minister in 1832 who prevented Bismarck from entering the diplomatic
service. The reader will recognize the same names as in the Christian
German Table Society and among the Pietists with whom Bismarck now
began to associate, such as Marie's father, Adolf von Thadden-Trieglaff, or
Ernst von Senfft-Pilsach, and the Gerlach brothers.[107]

The milieu in which the members of the Christian nobility moved combined neo-Pietism with millenarian hopes for the conversion of the Jews as
a sign that 'the end of days' had at last arrived. Their high status, personal
connections with the Crown Prince, and the depth and sincerity of their
convictions gave them a cohesiveness that could make them into a political
movement when the right moment came. When Bismarck fell in love with
Marie von Thadden-Trieglaff, he could not, of course, have known it, but
he had taken a step on which his entire career and subsequent life hinged.
The members of the Christian German Table Society, the Society for the
Conversion of the Jews, and his Evangelical Pomeranian neighbours held
office across the spectrum of the army and bureaucracy. Their number contained future court officials and generals. When the Crown Prince Frederick
William came to the throne in 1840, he brought Bismarck's new friends to
power with him and, when the unrest leading to the revolutions of 1848
broke out, his neo-Pietist friends would make Bismarck famous. It was also
through Marie that he met Johanna von Puttkamer, his future wife.

Through the Pietists Bismarck came to know Ernst Ludwig von Gerlach (1795–1877), intellectually one of the most important figures among the group, and a very important person in Bismarck's career. In 1835 Gerlach became Deputy Chief Judge of the Superior Provincial Court in Frankfurt an der Oder. There he gathered round him the smartest and most interesting young lawyers. Privy Councillor Schede recalled:

> In the Collegium of the County Court he was surrounded almost completely by opponents but as a Jurist he had gradually accustomed them to his direction. He had a firm hand on the reins. Nothing gave him more pleasure than to argue a case with well-trained young lawyers, but they could never prevail against his mind and his gifts. It was a joy to listen to him. In his home the impression of the significance of his personality and the unity of his character and life were even more powerful. I have never met anybody who had such a massive personal impact.[108]

The romantic poet, Clemens Brentano, said of him: 'Ludwig was for me from the first moment a frightening figure.' Herman Wagener, one of Bismarck's closest collaborators and first editor of the famous *Kreuzzeitung*, the daily newspaper closest to the Prussian aristocracy, was also a *Referendar* (legal trainee) in Gerlach's court, as was 'little Hans' von Kleist-Retzow, Bismarck's friend. From 1842 both Wagener and Kleist went to the theological evenings which Ludwig organized and which Ludwig's brother, Colonel Leopold von Gerlach, then Chief of Staff of the III Army Corps, also attended.[109] Leopold, later General Adjutant to King Frederick William IV, and his brother Judge Ernst Ludwig von Gerlach became in the late 1840s Bismarck's political patrons and managers. They had direct access to the King. In 1851 they convinced the King to appoint a 37-year-old 'mad Junker' with no diplomatic experience, a reputation for violent and extravagant gestures, too clever by half, and of dubious character, to the second most important diplomatic post in Germany, Prussian Ambassador to the German Bundesrat or Federal Council in Frankurt. The Gerlachs 'made' Bismarck and Leopold in particular saw Bismarck as 'his' creature. That was an error of historic proportions. When Bismarck began to reveal his true objectives and methods, they discovered that they had put an opponent of theirs into power. Ernst Ludwig von Gerlach became a sworn enemy of Bismarck in the late 1860s. In 1874 Bismarck dismissed his old master from his post as a judge on Prussian High Court Judge without a second thought.

This was the milieu that Marie von Thadden and her fiancé Moritz von Blanckenburg moved in. It attracted Bismarck powerfully both as he fell under the spell of the beautiful Marie and came to meet the powerful Junker neighbours who had firm and pleasingly reactionary views. Bismarck would have recognized at once the chance that this group offered him, but it came at a personal price. As a result, Bismarck stayed away from Marie in 1844 but his mood worsened. On 7 February 1844 he complained to his sister: 'Nothing to report from here ... I feel more and more how alone I am in the world.'[110] In desperation he returned to the civil service in Potsdam but could not bear it more than a few weeks. In late May he wrote to Karl Friedrich von Savigny from Naugard to say his sister-in-law had died suddenly and he had to go to his brother's place:

> Would you be good enough to go to my apartment and collect the government stuff for Bülow? ... Forgive me if I rely on your good will in this request but it was you who tempted me to Potsdam and you must now bear the consequences.[111]

In August 1844 he wrote to his university friend Scharlach and summed up his situation:

> For the last five years I have lived alone in the country and have with some success dedicated myself to the improvement in my credit, but I can no longer bear the lonely country Junker life and struggle with myself whether to occupy myself in state service or to go on long journeys. In the meantime I applied for a post in the provincial government, worked for six weeks but found the people and the duties as shallow and unsatisfying as before. Since then I have been on leave, and row without will on the stream of life without any rudder beyond the impulse of the moment and am completely indifferent about where it throws me up on the shore.[112]

On 4 October 1844 Bismarck travelled to Zimmerhausen to attend the wedding of Marie von Thadden-Trieglaff and Moritz von Blanckenburg. It was a memorable day in all sorts of ways. Moritz had long wanted to introduce Otto to 'little Hans' von Kleist-Retzow. On 3 September 1844 Hans Kleist had just passed his third and final law exam with distinction and had gone in high spirits to the Blanckenburg/Thadden wedding. Moritz introduced Otto and Hans having told each that the other was deaf so both shouted at each other for a long time until Moritz had pity on them. Hermann von Petersdorff, 'little Hans's' biographer, observes that 'thus the most important and significant friendship of his life begins with symbolic significance. The day would come when the two really did not understand each and the practical joker of 4 October 1844 could not contribute to their mutual understanding.'[113] The wedding ended disastrously. The family had ordered a fireworks display, which got out of hand and destroyed in a big fire much of the village of Zimmerhausen.[114] A bad omen.

Hans von Kleist-Retzow was undoubtedly the only really close friend that Bismarck made after his friendship with Motley and Keyserling. Hans was born on the family estate in Kieckow on 25 November 1814. The Kleist-Retzow family was 'by far the most powerful in Kreis Belgard' and owned in 1907 about one-fifth of the estates in the district.[115] As a child he had wanted to be a missionary and the persecution of the Old Lutherans by the royal government, which upset him very much, kept that urge alive. Unlike Bismarck's Pomeranian friends, Hans remained a devout but Orthodox Lutheran.[116] At 14 he went to the Landesschule Pforta, the best classical gymnasium in Prussia, which, rather like Dr Thomas Arnold's Rugby School in exactly the same years, was governed by twelve student *Inspektoren*. At Rugby they were called *Praeposters*. There his best friend was Ernst Ranke, younger brother of the great historian, Leopold von Ranke. Hans hated the idea of becoming a soldier. His biographer writes that he had 'a creeping horror of the soulless existence of the parade ground' and refused to serve, 'which caused his father to shed "bitter tears"',[117] understandably when we recall that 116 von Kleists served Frederick the Great in the Seven Years War from 1756 to 1763, of whom 30 died in battle or subsequently from wounds and disease.[118] In May 1835 he matriculated in Berlin University for three semesters and lived with Ernst Ranke,[119] who remembered that he began each morning with a reading of the Greek New Testament. In December 1836 Kleist matriculated in Göttingen, where he rose at four each morning to study the bible, a daily practice which he tried without success to impose on Bismarck. When he met Bismarck, he had already spent three years as a *Referendar* in the Superior Civil Court in Frankfurt an der Oder under Ernst Ludwig von Gerlach but unlike many others he had admired but not worshipped the Master. He was elected *Landrat*, the Prussian chief administrator of a country district, in 1845 for Kreis Belgard, a county of 20 square miles with about 31,000 inhabitants and one substantial village, the town of Belgard, which had 3,327 inhabitants.[120] He, also unmarried, settled down to the life of a rural squire.

In April 1845 Bismarck wrote to his sister Malwine, now married to Oskar von Arnim-Kröchelndorff, that things were getting desperate:

Only with difficulty can I resist the urge to fill an entire letter with agricultural complaints: night frosts, sick cow, bad rapeseed and bad roads, dead lambs, hungry sheep, lack of straw, fodder, money, potatoes, and dung...I must—the Devil take me—marry. That has become absolutely clear to me. Now that father has gone away, I feel lonely and abandoned, and mild, damp weather makes me melancholy, full of yearning, and love-sick.[121]

Bismarck—now that Marie was married—began to visit Zimmerhausen again and not without an impact on Marie. In May 1845, she wrote to her friend Elizabeth von Mittelstädt:

Otto has become much closer to me in these days than for weeks. We have reached out our hands to each other, and I think, that it is not a temporary contact. You have never understood that I see so much behind his often cold elegance so it may appear laughable to you that I have reached out for such a friendship, but it occupies me too much these last days for me to pass over it in silence. Perhaps it is the expression of a personal freedom, which makes so attractive this friendship with a Pomeranian phoenix, who is a prodigy of wildness and arrogance.[122]

In July 1845 Marie von Thadden wrote to Johanna von Puttkamer that the group had read *Romeo and Juliet* with Bismarck present,

Can you believe it? Ademar [code name for Bismarck] read the lover to me [as Juliet]. I don't think it was a trick of our host but just chance...I had so many truths to express, all of which came from the soul that I forgot everything which might have made me embarrassed, even the indecent parts, which we agreed before hand—through Moritz's intervention—to leave out.[123]

Marie von Thadden-Trieglaff was all of 23 when Bismarck, just over 30, played Romeo to her Juliet. She was a beautiful, intelligent, and deeply pious young woman. She had met nobody like Bismarck and that was hardly surprising. There was nobody like him. The two letters suggest pretty clearly that Marie and Otto were in love and also engaged in a struggle for his immortal soul. The latter struggle—the Christian mission—may have made it tolerable for Moritz von Blanckenburg, Bismarck's friend and Marie's husband, to allow the relationship to deepen. But what did Johanna von Puttkamer think then and, more importantly, think later?

A few months after the play reading Ferdinand von Bismarck fell ill and his son Otto rushed to Schönhausen to care for him. As he wrote to his sister at the end of September 1845, to describe their Father's illness, there was a blockage in his throat, which prevented him from taking food and the doctors had to put tubes down his throat.

The way he is being fed that I have described is too artificial and uncertain to allow us to have any hope for him unless he regains in greater measure the ability to swallow naturally.... [Bismarck stayed with him] for it would be miserable for the old man to spend his last few weeks alone and without a member of the family by him.

On 22 November 1845 Ferdinand von Bismarck died.[124] Bismarck had no choice but to move to Schönhausen to run the estate after his father's death and Bernhard took over Kniephof. The relationship with Marie continued to deepen. In April 1846 Bismarck wrote a long letter in rhyming couplets to accompany a pile of poetry books and apples from his orchard. Here are the first three couplets of a very long, elegant, and ironic poem in rhyming verse.

> Am letzten Dienstag sagten Sie,
> Es fehlte mir an Poesie
>
> Damit Sie nun doch klar ersehen
> Wie sehr Sie mich da misverstehen
>
> So schreibe ich Ihnen, Frau Marie,
> In Versen, gleich des Morgens früh.[125]

> Tuesday last you said to me
> That I was lacking poetry
>
> That you may now quite clearly see
> How much you have mistaken me
>
> Madame Marie I write to you
> Verses fresh with morning dew.
>   [trans.—JS]

A few weeks later, he wrote another letter, full of his charm and literary self-awareness:

Dear Frau Marie,
    About to depart, I have just received from Schönhausen a package of green beans, which I cannot completely use up. Regard them, please, not as a sacrifice, which I withdraw from the Moloch which dwells within me, if I lay them at your feet. I include some marjoram and the long promised Schönhausen normal bread, in addition Lenau Part II and some Bech, the pages of which you may cut. Some more I cannot add because for the moment my mind fills itself with field drainage and bog cultivation. Rereading this letter I note three 'somes' in three lines but in an amazing way no 'probably'. Thus one improves. Be well and pass my compliments, if I may ask you, to anybody whom you choose.[126]

Four months later, Marie von Thadden-Blanckenburg died on 10 November 1846, aged 24. Bismarck was shattered in a way that neither the death of his father nor his mother had evoked. He wrote to his sister that he had been startled by the horror of losing somebody from his immediate circle:

> If anything were needed to make the decision to leave Pomerania easier, this was it. This is really the first time that I have lost somebody through death, who was close to me and whose passing leaves an unexpected hole in my circle of life... This feeling of emptiness, the thought never again to see or hear a dear person who had become necessary to me—and of those I have few—was so new that I cannot get used to it and the whole event has not yet become real to me. Enviable is the confidence of the relatives. They think of this death as an early journey, which in the long or short run will be followed by a joyful reunion.[127]

Hans Kleist and Bismarck tried to comfort Moritz after Marie died, as Moritz recalled in a letter to Hans von Kleist forty years later:

> There we sat, the three of us, you, Otto and I as the cold northeast wind blew, on three stools with our legs stretched out onto the kitchen hearth.[128]

The death of Marie triggered a series of decisions in Bismarck's life. On 18 November, scarcely a week later, Bismarck signed a contract giving Herr Klug the tenancy of Kniephof. Klug had formerly been tenant of Pansin. Next he decided to marry Marie's friend, Johanna von Puttkamer. On 16 December 1846, Bismarck wrote the famous *Werbebrief* (suitor letter) to Heinrich von Puttkamer asking for his daughter's hand in marriage. Oceans of ink have been poured by previous biographers in their attempts to make sense of this letter. Had Bismarck really become a Christian, indeed a Pietist, and what relationship had this account of his conversion to his subsequent ruthless use of power? Those are interesting questions but more interesting—and less considered—is why Johanna wanted to marry Bismarck. She must have known and seen with her own eyes Bismarck's passion for her friend. She had neither good looks nor Marie's intellectual interests. Bismarck would not send her books of philosophy.

Johanna von Puttkamer was born on the family estate of Reinfeld in remotest Pomerania, hard by the Polish border, on 11 April 1824, so she was just 21 when she got to know Bismarck through her friend Marie. Her family was—even among the Pietists of Pomerania—well known for their extreme severity. She had an elder brother who died in childhood and thus she grew up as an only child. Pictures of her as a young woman show her with a long face with prominent jaw. She was the daughter of a country squire on a remote estate in a remote region and had never seen much of the great world.

What Johanna may have thought, we do not know, but in any case on 21 December 1846, Otto von Bismarck wrote to Heinrich von Puttkamer the famous *Werbebrief*:

> I begin this letter by stating from the outset its content: it is a request for the highest which you have to grant in this world, the hand of your daughter... What I can do is to tell you with complete openness about myself... and especially my relationship to Christianity... At an early age I was estranged from my parental home and never felt fully at home thereafter. My education was dictated by the intention to develop my understanding and the early acquisition of positive knowledge. After an irregularly attended and imperfectly understood religious instruction, I was baptized by Schleiermacher in my 16th year and had no other faith than naked deism which soon became mixed with pantheistic tendencies... Thus without any control other than the conventional social limitations, I plunged into the world, partly seducer and partly seduced, and into bad company...

He claims that it was the 'loneliness after the death of my mother, which brought me to Kniephof... [where] the inner voice began...'. Through Moritz von Blackenburg, he came into contact with the Trieglaff circle:

> and found there people who made me ashamed... I felt myself soon at home in that circle and with Moritz and his wife who became dear to me as a sister to a brother, and discovered a well-being which I had never experienced before, a family life that included me, a home at last... I felt bitter regret over my previous existence... The news of the death of our dear friend in Cardemin, provoked the first sincere prayer without reflections about the reasonableness of the act that I had ever expressed and tears which I had not shed since my childhood. God did not hear my prayer but He did not reject it either. For I have not lost the ability to pray since that time and became aware of something not exactly peace but a will to live as I had never before known it... What value you place on the change of heart hardly two months old I cannot say...

He asks only to be allowed to come in person to Reinfeld and plead his case.[129]

After years of knowing that such a letter had been written, I approached it in the expectation that I would find the confessions of a 'born-again' Christian. The letter makes no such claim. Indeed it says very little about Bismarck's state of soul or relationship to God. On the face of it, we cannot say why Herr von Puttkamer acceded to Bismarck's request. Shortly after

New Year 1847, Herr von Puttkamer replied affirmatively but asked very properly for some firm commitment to a new Christian life from a possible son-in-law. Bismarck replied on 4 January,

> You ask me, honoured Herr von Puttkamer, whether my feet have taken certain steps. I can only reply in the affirmative to your next question, that I am firmly and in many ways determined to pursue that peace with all and that sanctification without which no one can see the Lord. Whether my steps are as secure as I would want them to be, I am not in a position to say. I see myself rather the lame person who without the help of the Lord will stumble.

He could not come right away because his duty as dyke captain would continue as long as the Elbe threatened to overflow. 'It is the first time in my life, I think, that I yearn for a hard frost.'[130]

On the 12th day of January 1847 Otto Leopold Edward von Bismarck-Schönhausen was officially engaged to Johanna Friederike Charlotte Dorothea Eleonore von Puttkamer. On the same day he dashed off a note to Malwine von Arnim, his sister, which simply said 'All Right'.[131]

The months of the engagement overlap with the beginning of the rumbles of the revolution of 1848 and Bismarck's debut as a politician. Since Bismarck now had important things to do, he had to write Johanna and write he did. He poured out his heart in dozens of rich, long letters, each with a different and more extravagant form of address in English, French, or Italian—'Giovanna mia', 'dearest', 'Jeanne la méchante', because she had not written, long quotes from English poets, Byron, Moore, etc. 'en proie à des émotions violentes'. It is in this period that he wrote the long letter about his mother and father, which I quoted earlier. The letters bubble with wit and extravagant romanticism, as in a letter from March 1847 on

> the long standing rule of conservatism in this house, in which my fathers for centuries have lived in the same rooms, were born and died, as the pictures in the house and the church show, from iron clanging knights to the cavaliers of the Thirty Years War with their long locks and twisted beards, then to the wearers of the huge allonge wigs who strutted round the halls in their red heels and the riders with the neat pony-tails who fought in Frederick the Great's war down to the enfeebled youth who lies at your feet.[132]

A month later he described life at his future in-laws in a letter to his sister:

> As far as my person is concerned, I feel pretty well except for a light headache which my mother-in-law maintains in that she pours a strong Rhine wine for

me at all hours of the day in the sincere conviction that I was nursed and raised on fermented drinks and that I need a quart or two to get through the day. In general I find myself in a state of comfort that I have not had for years and live for the day with the carefree abandon of a student.[133]

On 8 May 1847 Bismarck wrote to his fiancée with important news:

Dearest, only, beloved, Juanita, *my better half* [English in the original] I want to begin my letter with every form of endearment I can imagine because I need your forgiveness very much; I will not leave you to guess why, lest you imagine something worse, but simply say that I have been elected to the Landtag... One of our deputies, Brauchitsch, is so ill that he cannot attend the meetings... Now, since among the six deputies the first position was vacant, the Magdeburg estates ought to have moved the second into the first spot and then elect a new sixth, instead quite unusually they elected me to the first position though I am new in the county and was not even an alternate deputy.[134]

The new Bismarck had emerged—the politician. From that moment to her death in 1894 Johanna would have to suffer his long absences, his tensions, and preoccupations as Bismarck for the first time found his true calling. By violating the rule of the ballot, the electors of Magdeburg had launched the career of the greatest statesman of the nineteenth century and Johanna von Puttkamer lost her husband's full attention even before they had formally been married.

What was Bismarck's Johanna like as a person? Friedrich von Holstein saw her for the first time when he arrived at the St Petersburg embassy in 1861.

Frau Bismarck, like her husband, was a peculiar person. The only attraction she could boast was a pair of arresting dark eyes. She had dark hair too, which revealed the Slav origins of the Puttkamer family. She was entirely devoid of feminine charm, attached no importance to dress, and only lived for her family. She exercised her quite considerable musical talent merely for her own enjoyment, though Bismarck liked to listen when she played classical music such as Beethoven. In society her speech and behaviour were not always appropriate but she moved with a calm assurance, which prevented her from ever appearing ill at ease or unsure of herself. Her husband let her go her own way. I never once saw him take her to task.[135]

A female observer met Johanna von Bismarck for the first time a few years after Holstein had. Hildegard Freifrau Hugo von Spitzemberg (b. 20 January 1843), was 20 and not yet married to Carl von Spitzemberg when she went with her father, the former Prime Minister of the Kingdom of Württemberg, Friedrich Karl Gottlob Freiherr Varnbüler von und zu Hemmingen (1809–89), on his first official call on the new Prussian Minister-President in June 1863:

> On our return we found an invitation to tea, so we threw on our best clothes and drove to 76 Wilhelmstrasse. Frau von Bismarck, a woman in her early forties, tall with dark hair and beautiful brown eyes, received us in a very friendly way and in her entire manner so plain and confiding that we soon felt ourselves very much at home. Later her husband appeared, a very tall handsome man, with an energetic, almost defiant expression on his face. They seem to have an open house...[136]

The next day they called on the Bismarcks again and Hildegard wrote in her diary:

> The whole tone of the house is very plain, natural, and refined and it pleased me very much. After dinner father and Bismarck got involved in political discussions in which they both became very deeply involved...[137]

We must pause now to get to know the first of the important Bismarck diarists. Hildegard Spitzemberg—as a Freifrau she is conventionally titled 'Baroness'—belonged to that rare category of people, the true diarist. Clever, well read, sensitive, and very distinctly not Prussian, she kept a diary every day from her tenth year to her death at 71 in 1914, and it is a wonderful diary, full of human interest and shrewd insights. Her husband, the Württemberg ambassador to Berlin, Carl Freiherr Hugo von Spitzemberg, whom she married on 18 September 1864, took a house on the Wilhelmstrasse next to the Bismarcks. Since Hildegard was beautiful, young, and clever, Bismarck found her a very agreeable conversation partner, and, since she recorded everything she saw and heard, she constitutes one of my most important sources. When in November 1887, the Bismarcks, both Prince and Princess, went to a court function, Hildegard Spitzemberg wrote in her diary: '16 November, B's go to court—a great event. I would like to see the old rag that the dear lady pulls from her clothes closet and happy as can be puts on.'[138]

Baroness Spitzemberg found herself regularly at the Bismarcks, and was often taken in to sit at the host's right. He paid such attention to her that in March 1870 she confided to her diary:

> Count Bismarck is at present more than ever unusually charming to me and seeks me out at every opportunity, is there some object behind it or is it purely personal?[139]

The answer was probably both: there was 'some object behind it' and it was 'purely personal'. Bismarck re-enacted with his 'Hilgachen' the same forbidden and impossible game of love he had carried on with Marie. The beautiful, clever woman—like his mother—could never be achieved and hence in order to survive and put an end to his loneliness he had chosen a plain and limited one. The pattern would repeat itself in the mid-1860s with Katarina Princess Orlov, again with a frankness in his feeling that must have been hard for Johanna to bear. In 1888 Bismarck spoke to Hildegard unusually frankly about his relationship to his wife and daughter:

> When I observed that the Empress had never had a master over her who would have educated her, the Prince replied 'broken but educated is harder than one thinks. With a wife you can do it sometimes but with a daughter that is a great work of art. I have clashed with Marie very hard. She has for all her intelligence a remarkably narrow circle of interests: husband, children, they fulfil her but otherwise almost nobody, let alone humanity, interests her. She is essentially lazy, that's the problem.' I replied, I wondered that she shared so few of his interests given that she so clearly loves him. 'That's the same with my wife. It had its good sides. I live in another atmosphere at home.' On that subject a lot might have been said about real spiritual partnership between married people or between parents and children, but the way it is, what he said laughing in reply to Lehndorff's toast contains the pure truth, 'Yes, she is the best wife that I have had.'[140]

The shrewd Baroness saw with the intuition that made her a great diarist the void at the core of Bismarck's relationship to his wife. There was, as she wrote, the possibility of 'real spiritual partnership between married people or between parents and children' but Bismarck never experienced that. He undoubtedly loved Johanna. His letters show that. But she was, as he admitted to Baroness Spitzemberg, no intellectual, political, nor artistic companion, other than in her music. Nor was she ever prepared to play the role of 'society lady' which Hildegard Freifrau Hugo von Spitzemberg, daughter of a grand seigneur and prime minister of a kingdom, wife of another grand seigneur, played 'as to the manor born'. In June 1885, Baroness Spitzemberg cleared her desk: 'As I looked over the invitation cards of the past winter today for the last time before I tore them up, I calculated that from November to the present I had received 41 invitations to dinner and 53 to an evening.'[141] The arithmetic shows that there were 94 formal invitations for the 197 days or one every other day for six and a half months, and that excludes less formal occasions without written invitations. A lady in the highest society lived that way. Johanna never did. The Bismarcks after a certain point simply stopped going out. As Holstein saw thirty years earlier, Johanna refused to play the game or to conform. Was that her way to repay Bismarck for marrying her on the rebound?

When Johanna finally died on 27 November 1894, Hildegard Spitzemberg discovered that she was no longer welcome 'at Bismarcks' as she had been for thirty years. It suddenly became clear that Johanna had *wanted* her there to play the role that she had filled: to give Bismarck that safe dose of feminine beauty and intelligence that Bismarck needed and Johanna could never supply. On 1 April 1895, Bismarck's 80th birthday, when she was for the first time not invited to the party, Baroness Spitzemberg finally accepted that she had lost her entrée to the Bismarcks with the death of Johanna:

> Since the death of the Princess, I lack the personality through whom I can make my wishes and rights count. Marie is entirely alienated, the sons, even when the Bismarcks were still here, stood apart from me. If I were a man, I could settle somewhere in Friedrichsruh and enjoy everything that happens from A to Z.[142]

The loss of proximity to the great man meant a lot to her on a personal and intellectual level for he had given her that contact with the centre of power that filled the years with interest and the diary pages with content. There was also a social consideration. Bismarck represented the apex of power in Imperial Germany and his favour had raised the prestige of the Spitzembergs in a society still organized entirely by aristocratic rankings. When Johanna died, the contact ceased. The old Bismarck never asked for her, and she never saw him again.

In the spring of 1847, the electors of Magdeburg chose a 32-year-old country squire with a reputation for wild behaviour and irresponsible views. Yet he had something which nobody of his social set and generation could offer—an astonishingly powerful personality and a magnetism which must have attracted them. This self and the gigantic frame in which it rested was his only claim on them. He had no experience, no credentials, and no obvious qualifications, but he was Bismarck. That turned out to be enough.

4

Bismarck Represents Himself, 1847–1851

Bismarck entered politics through his position as a landlord and did so in company with his neighbours. On 19 December 1846 the Prussian Minister of Justice issued an order that reform proposals for the traditional patrimonial justice—the right of Junker landlords to have courts on their own estates in which they served as judge and jury—be submitted to him. As always when Bismarck saw his personal, patrimonial interests threatened, he went into action. He and his influential neighbour, Ernst von Bülow-Cummerow (1775–1851)[1] submitted what came to be known as the Regenwald Reform Programme. The authors submitted the plan because they feared 'that the King could find himself in the end moved to pay attention to the many sorts of attacks on patrimonial justice'. Their plan foresaw a district patrimonial court with a director and at least two lay judges. The judges would sit in the villages on a regular rota.[2] Bismarck called assemblies of his fellow landowners in his own district on 7 January 1847 and spoke at the county diet on 3 March, the convention of the Magdeburg Knights' Assembly on 20 March, and in between, on 8 March, as he reported three days later, he had had 'a conversation of several hours with Ludwig von Gerlach, whose skills he found occasion to admire'.[3] In the meantime the county diet had instructed him to prepare what we would now call a 'position paper' and authorized him to seek a meeting with the minister in Berlin to see how the government proposed to approach the issue. On 26 March 1847 Bismarck wrote to Ludwig von Gerlach and put forward his own plan, without von Bülow-Cummerow, for reform of patrimonial justice, which abolished individual estate courts and replaced them with local judicial districts where the landlords would elect a district judge in exactly

the way local county assemblies elected their *Landrat* or county representative. Gerlach wrote shrewdly on the margin:

> Something which in time becomes feasible through a process of reconcilia-
> tion, can be left for the moment to one side. The majority of estate judges and
> the most influential defenders of patrimonial justice would see this proposal
> as abolition.[4]

Bismarck's new political activity gave him tremendous pleasure. As he
wrote to Johanna, he was 'full of politics to the point of bubbling over'.[5] He
had found his purpose in life. Bismarck had become—and in that respect he
always remained—a brilliant, persuasive and overwhelmingly convincing parliamentary politician. He had rushed around, talked to his constituents, got
them to sign on to his suggestions, drafted resolutions, and eventually convinced them to adopt his radical reform proposals, which, as Gerlach noticed
at once, amounted to 'abolition' of the traditional right to a patrimonial court.
This was the first time Ludwig von Gerlach had to confront the force of
nature he and his brother Leopold had unleashed but could not control.

When Bismarck wrote to Johanna on 8 May 1847 that he had been elected
a deputy to the United Diet, he described it as if it had happened without his
agency. The Magdeburg electors 'quite unusually elected me to the first position though I am new in the county and was not even an alternate deputy'.[6]
The truth was, as we have seen, very different. He had run a campaign to get
his reform proposals for local patrimonial courts accepted which had made
him very well known indeed to the Magdeburg and other electors.

On 3 April 1847 King Frederick William IV invited the entire membership
of the eight provincial parliaments in the Kingdom of Prussia to meet in a
United Diet in Berlin. He took care to make this enterprise as medieval, feudal, romantic, and unlike the French National Assembly as possible, nothing to
do with one man-one vote. Frederick William IV saw the 'state as a work of
art in the highest sense of the word. . . . he wanted to admit and incorporate
into his cathedral those spiritual forces and persons who in any way recognized his kingdom.'[7] Representation would be entirely in *Stände* or estates.
The Lords would form the upper *curia* and knights, towns, and country communities the lower *curia*. He also took care, quite explicitly, not to recognize
the promise made by his predecessor in 1815 that there would be a proper
constitution for the Kingdom of Prussia and a parliamentary assembly, a
promise which Frederick William III had evaded for twenty-five years. The
new assembly would have no function save to approve new taxes.[8] Although

it had the trappings of feudalism, as Christopher Clark points out, the realities had changed from below. The provincial diets had been created in 1823:

> Although they looked like traditional Estate bodies, they were in fact representatives institutions of a new type. Their legitimacy derived from a legislative act by the state, not from the authority of an extra-governmental corporate tradition. The deputies voted by head, not by estate, and deliberations were held in plenary session, not in separate caucuses as in the corporate assemblies of the old regime. Most importantly of all, the 'noble Estate' (*Ritterschaft*) was no longer defined by birth (with the exception of the small contingent of 'immediate' nobles in the Rhineland) but by property. It was the ownership of 'privileged land' that counted, not birth into privilege status.[9]

What Burke and von der Marwitz had most feared had reached the Prussian countryside; the land, in Burke's term, had been 'volatized', turned into a commodity to be bought and sold. Clark writes that 'in 1806 75.6% of noble estates in the rural hinterland of Königsberg were still in noble hands. By 1829 this figure had fallen to 48.3%.'[10]

The King called the new United Diet because a combination of economic distress and intellectual discontent forced him to do so. Between 1815 and 1847 the world had changed dramatically. For reasons which demographers still debate, European population began to grow in the middle of the eighteenth century and continued into the nineteenth as Table 1 shows:[11]

Table 1. The population of Germany (within the borders of **1871**) (millions)

1816	22.4
1820	26.1
1830	29.4
1840	32.6
1850	35.3
1860	37.6
1870	40.8

After 1815 England's industrial revolution produced huge volumes of machine-made goods and British factories flooded European markets with cheap textiles. Domestic craftsmen with their traditional hand looms could not compete; hunger crises—in effect, localized famines—in the Rhineland in 1816–17, in eastern Westphalia in 1831, and in Posen and East Prussia in 1846–7 created unrest and frightened the possessing classes. Bad harvests still meant ruin for local farmworkers, especially if the large estate concentrated on exports. As in the Irish famine of 1845, the impossibility of moving goods before railroads meant that people starved to death when ample supplies lay just beyond their reach. In south-western Germany, partible inheritance, that is, dividing family land equally among the sons, led to sub-divisions of family property and what came to be known as the *Zwergwirtschaft* (dwarf economy). Even though these peasants were free, their smallholdings led to grinding poverty. Finally, the post-war crisis after 1815 had been accompanied by falling prices. Weak harvests and particularly severe winters in 1819 and the mid-1840s made for widespread misery. Though nobody could yet feel it, agricultural productivity had risen and gave promise of a better-fed future. Pflanze shows that in Prussia agricultural productivity in the years 1816 to 1865 went up by 135 per cent whereas the population rose by 59 per cent.[12] As soon as the crops could be transported more easily, and that came with railroads, famine in Germany would disappear. Europe was still far from urbanized, as Table 2 shows. By 1850, only England had really begun to generate serious urban growth.

Table 2. Proportion of population living in cities of over 100,000 inhabitants

	c.1800	c.1850
England and Wales	9.7	22.6
Scotland	—	16.9
Denmark	10.9	9.6
Netherlands	11.5	7.3
Portugal	9.5	7.2
Belgium	—	6.8
Italy	4.4	6.0
France	2.8	4.6
Spain	1.4	4.4
Ireland	3.1	3.9
Prussia	1.8	3.1
Austria	2.6	2.8
Russia	1.4	1.6

Source: A. F. Weber, *The Growth of Cities in the Nineteenth Century* (1899; Ithaca, NY, 1963), 144–5.

The table shows that Prussia in 1850 belonged among the backward continental European states. Though the city of Berlin had grown, Prussia remained overwhelmingly rural and far behind the urban growth in Britain. That too was beginning to change but nobody saw it yet in 1847.

Railroads had just started to transform European life. During the 1830s and 1840s railroad companies sprang up and the first primitive, short lines were built. Within twenty years, European travel and trade had been revolutionized by the railroad boom (see Table 3).[13]

Table 3. Spread of railways in selected countries (Length of line open in kilometers (1km = 5/8 mile))

	1840	1860	1880	1900
Austria-Hungary	144	4,543	18,507	36,330
France	496	9,167	23,089	38,109
Germany	469	11,089	33,838	51,678
Italy	20	2,404	9,290	16,429
Russia	27	1,626	22,865	53,234

German railroad growth outstripped in speed and scale every other continental country. In the 1840s there was a short-lived German railroad 'bubble' as speculative investment piled into the new joint stock companies and raised share prices on insecure foundations. In 1843 a series of bankruptcies set off the first modern depression, though still very small in scale, at the same time that the last European famine crisis had hit East Prussia.

In August 1846 Bismarck wrote to his brother to describe the terrible economic situation in Schönhausen. There had been a prolonged drought and crops were ruined:

> There is absolutely no money in Schönhausen. Daily wages amount to more than 60 thaler a week and with the meadows we are far from finished. In the cash drawer there is nothing and no income to be expected in the near future. In the brick works we have to offer very long credit if we do not want to damage the customers.[14]

In April of 1847 he saw the first riots in Cöslin, a medium-sized town in middle Pomerania, 15 miles south of the Baltic sea coast (Kozalin in Polish today). Bismarck described them in a letter to Johanna:

> In Cöslin there was uproar, even after 12 the streets were so full that we could only get through with difficulty and under the protection of a unit of reserve militia which had been ordered in. Bakers and butchers have been plundered. And three houses of corn merchants ruined. Glass slivers all over... In Stettin a serious bread riot, apparently 2 days of shooting, and artillery was supposed to be deployed. It will very probably be an exaggeration.[15]

On Sunday, 11 April 1847, 543 deputies assembled in Berlin for the largest such assembly ever held on German soil. As David Barclay writes, 'the public mood in Berlin seemed to reflect the weather... The winter had been long and hard. Food shortages and unemployment were becoming increasingly serious problems, and spring had still not arrived. The day was cold and blustery, with a mixture of snow and freezing rain.'[16] The King's mood was solemn and serious. When he delivered his Speech from the Throne he made clear the limited power of the assembly he had convened:

> There is no power on earth that can succeed in making me transform the natural relationship between prince and people... into a conventional constitutional relationship, and I will never allow a written piece of paper to come between the Lord God in heaven and this land.

After this encouraging start, the King pointed out that by calling the United Diet he had merely followed the provisions of the State Indebtedness Act of 1820, which required a meeting of the Estates to authorize new taxes.[17] The members of the diet, regardless of their political views, were stunned. Count Trautmannsdorf declared that the speech had 'hit the assembly like a thunderbolt... With one blow the *Stände* have seen their hopes and desires obliterated; not one happy face left the assembly.'[18]

The odd thing about the diet was how quickly and naturally it turned itself into a normal parliament with all the courtesies and practices of parliamentary life complete with forms of address such as 'the Honourable Gentleman, the previous speaker', and so on. Of the deputies, the overwhelming majority belonged either to the bourgeois liberal groups or the aristocratic Prussian liberal group under the Westphalian Freiherr Georg von Vincke. The group of nay-sayers who rejected any move to transform the gathering into a proper parliament was not large. Erich Marcks estimates that the 'aristocratic ultras' who refused even the slightest alteration in the King's absolute power, cannot have been more than 70, among whom Otto von Bismarck numbered.[19] This was his first public stage and he knew by his innate instinct for showmanship exactly how to use the platform it offered. On 17 May 1847 Bismarck made his maiden speech, as the first speech by a new member in the House of Commons is called. It was a sensational debut. In a manner not unlike the way the young 'fox' Bismarck became the darling of his duelling fraternity, Bismarck outraged the other deputies. He denied that the enthusiasm of 1813, the so-called 'Prussian Rising', had anything to do with liberalism or a demand for a constitution. He portrayed the popular movement against French occupation in a way that mocked the central myth of Prussian liberalism—that the free people had risen to throw out Napoleon and the French in a War of Liberation. It is hard to grasp how offensive Bismarck's remarks were. A whole generation of Prussian liberals had lived through the cold days of reaction by warming their hopes on the glorious memories of the people's war for liberty, which Bismarck belittled. As the stenographic report of the proceedings records, Bismarck asserted that the revolt of 1813 had nothing to do with constitutional liberalism:

> as if the movement of 1813 could have other motives ascribed to it or indeed, as if another motive were necessary, than the disgrace that foreigners in our country brought...
>
> Stenographic report: *murmuring and loud shouting interrupts the speaker; he draws the Spenersche Newspaper from his pocket and reads it until the Marshall has restored order. He then continues*
>
> It does the national honour a poor service (*continued murmurs*) if one assumes that the mistreatment and humiliation which the foreign power holders imposed on Prussia were not enough on its own to bring their blood to boiling point and to let all other feelings be drowned out by hatred of the foreigner.
>
> (*Great noise; Several deputies ask to speak. Deputies Krause and Gier dispute the speaker's right to judge the nature of the movement, which he had not lived through.*)[20]

Otto von Bismarck had arrived on the Prussian political stage, which he was never again to leave until his death in July 1898, and the appearance has all the characteristics of his later speeches in the Landtag and the Reichstag: complete contempt for the members of these bodies, dramatic gestures, violent ideas couched in sparkling prose but delivered in easy conversational tones. He consistently chose conflict over consensus and saw in such clashes what Clark calls a 'clarifying element'. Erich Marcks agrees:

> The lasting peculiarities of his temperament and his way to judge things show up on the very first day and the entirety of his performance contains—I want to say in the ground tones—the whole Bismarck.[21]

However bold he appeared at the speaker's podium, the uproar had slightly unnerved him. The next day he wrote to Johanna:

> I tried my luck at the speaker's platform and aroused yesterday an unheard of storm of displeasure in that body through an observation, not entirely clearly phrased, about the nature of the popular movement in 1813. I wounded the misunderstood vanity of many from our party and naturally caused a great big hello! from the opposition. The bitterness was particularly great because I

only said the truth when I applied the sentence to 1813 that somebody (the Prussian people) who gets beaten by somebody else (the French) to the point where he finally defends himself can hardly claim to have done a great service to a third person (the King).[22]

This was not exactly a stenographic account of what he said; indeed, it was false. Here we meet another permanent and not very agreeable feature of Bismarck's character: he never took full responsibility for his acts. Forty years later he had still not found the courage to take responsibility for his mistakes, even in small personal matters. That Bismarck should have concealed the actual content of the speech from his wife reflects his constant need to be seen to be right, not unusual in politicians, but in Bismarck's case the scale of the correction of his own history has the proportions of his own gigantic ego.

A few days later, Ernst von Bülow-Cummerow met Moritz von Blanckenburg and complained about Bismarck's outrageous behaviour:

'I had always considered Bismarck a sensible chap. I cannot understand how he can disgrace himself in this way.' Blanckenburg replied, 'I think he was entirely right and I am delighted that he has tasted blood. You will soon hear the lion roar in an entirely different way.'[23]

Bülow-Cummerow was not an obscure Junker but by far the most famous and widely read aristocratic pamphleteer, and defender of knightly supremacy, who also advocated the application of modern agricultural technology to Junker agriculture and the development of rural banking facilities in which he himself had engaged, and demanded freedom of the press. Bülow-Cummerow, unlike most of his neighbours, had not been 'born again' and remained untouched by Evangelical Christianity. He had one of the biggest Junker estates in Pomerania, and when in 1848 a 'Junker Parliament' met he was the obvious choice to be its Speaker.[24] Bülow-Cummerow could not understand why Bismarck stirred up unnecessary trouble. He, as a sensible, large landowner, would never have done that.

Within a few days Bismarck had taken a leadership position among the ultra-conservatives, as he explained in a letter to Johanna four days after his maiden speech. He first apologized for not going to Reinfeld, the estate of his in-laws, the Puttkamers, where his fiancée pined for him, over Whitsun because every vote counted and he had to stay in or near Berlin. First things first with Bismarck. He then observed:

I have succeeded in gaining influence over a large number, or in any case several, deputies from the so-called Court Party and the other ultra-Conservatives, which I use as far as I can to keep them from bolting and attempting clumsy jumps to the side which, now that I have spelled out my direction unmistakably, I can do in the least suspect way.[25]

To obtain superiority over the extreme conservatives in the United Diet of 1847, Bismarck turned himself into the most extreme of extremists, the wildest of reactionaries, and the most savage of debaters. All that he could shed as easily as he took off his extravagant costume at Göttingen when he returned with Motley to his rooms. A sensible man like Bülow-Cummerow could not understand the demonic game unfolded before his eyes; very few could.

On 8 June, he wrote to Johanna:

In general I am well and calmer than before, because I have taken a more active part than before...the deliberations have become very serious because the opposition makes everything into a party matter. I have made myself many friends and many enemies, the latter more inside, the former more outside, of the Landtag. People, who before did not want to know me and others whom I do not yet know, overwhelm me with courtesies, and I get many well meaning squeezes from unknown hands... The political assemblies after the Landtag in the evening are a little wearing; by nightfall I come back from my ride, and then go right to the English House or into the Hotel de Rome, and get so deeply involved in politics that I never get to bed before 1.[26]

Bismarck had found a passion for politics, the attendant intrigues, and, I suspect, the growing awareness of his enormous intellectual and personal superiority over the other deputies and their backers. He plunged into politics the way he had hunted in the 'mad Junker' phase, taking risks, drinking too hard, and riding too fast. Above all, he loved the power to manipulate others. The word 'intrigue' pops up again and again in his private correspondence. And then there were other opportunities in his new position of prominence, and the handsome, blonde, 32-year-old giant knew how to value them. On 22 June 1847 he wrote to Johanna, 'The day before yesterday we were with our friend the King and I was very spoiled by their Highnesses.'[27]

His next major speech took place in the debate on the removal of civil disabilities for Prussian Jews. We saw in Chapter 2 that for Junkers like Ludwig von der Marwitz liberalism and equality for Jews meant that 'our old, venerable Brandenburg-Prussia will become a new-fangled Jewish state'.[28] Friedrich Rühs had declared in 1816 unequivocally that 'a Christian state can therefore absolutely not recognize any other members than Christians'.[29] The only good Jew for the Junker Pietists was a converted Jew. When the United Diet debated the Jewish question on 14 June 1847, General Ludwig August von Thile, president of the Berlin Mission to the Jews, argued in these words against full rights for Jews:

> I have also heard today that Christianity and even religion should play no role in the discussions of the state; but one of the honourable delegates put this in words which I could heartily endorse when he said 'Christianity should not be constituted within the state. It should be above the State and should govern it'. With this I heartily agree...He [a Jew] may be the born subject of another nation, he may out of private interest or out of a feeling of general love for humanity make great sacrifices to the circumstances in which he lives, but he will never be a German, never be a Prussian because he *must remain* a Jew.[30]

On 15 June 1847 it was Bismarck's turn to address the United Diet on civil equality for Jews:

> I admit that I am full of prejudices; I have sucked them in, so to speak, with the mother's milk and I cannot succeed in talking them away; if I should imagine having before me, as a representative of the King's Sacred Majesty, a Jew whom I would have to obey, I must confess that I would feel deeply depressed and humiliated, that the feeling of pride and honour would leave me with which I now endeavour to discharge my duties towards the state.[31]

In this case Bismarck merely expressed what almost all of his Junker colleagues thought and here, for a change, he belonged to the majority. On 17 June 1847 the United Diet rejected by 220 to 219 the right of Jews to hold public office or serve in the Christian State.[32] A few days later on 23 July 1847 the *Judengesetz* (the Jew Law) forbade Jews from exercising so-called *ständische* rights, that is rights inherent in class and status. Thus membership in district or provincial diets was closed to them and also the exercise of any rights associated with the knightly estate-ownership, even though a few wealthy Jews had purchased country estates which conferred such rights on them as owners.[33]

The extreme right-wing party of Bismarck and his friends had become—in spite of their protestations—a parliamentary party and, within a little more than a year, Prussia would have a constitution. They needed an ideology and, as Robert Berdahl writes, 'they needed an ideology that developed a theory of strong monarchical power without at the same time, succumbing to bureaucratic absolutism' and in 1847 all they had was the inadequacy of the traditional patrimonial justifications of Adam Müller and Carl Ludwig von Haller which compared the state to an enlarged family.[34]

Help came from a most remarkable and now largely forgotten figure, Friedrich Julius Stahl (1802–61). Born in Würzburg in an orthodox Jewish household, as Julius Jolson, he took the name 'Stahl' and added Friedrich when he converted to Lutheranism on 6 November 1819. Stahl became the philosophical and legal brain of the conservative moment. He wrote a two-volume philosophy of law which attacked not only the Enlightenment philosophers but the entire natural law tradition. Stahl had the intellectual power to take on Hegel and offer an alternative, subjective view of the basis of law. The exclusive reliance on reason was 'as if one considered the eye as the source of light and wanted to discover history not through the observation of events but by examining the inner construction of the eye and its various parts'.[35] He argued for an essentially Burkean conception of history and institutions but based it not on historic liberalism but on a profoundly orthodox Lutheran view of man's sinfulness and failings.

Elected to the Upper House in 1848 he joined the thirteen extreme conservatives among the members and rapidly became their leader. His biographer, Ernst Landsberg, notes what he calls an 'almost world-historical irony' in the fact that the party of neo-Pietist Christian great landowners should have found its intellectual leader in this tiny, delicate little bourgeois, 'simple in his habits, excruciatingly polite to everybody...dressed in his chosen black suits more that of a clergyman than a professor of law, his speaking in a sharp voice but without pathos, in his external appearance the very type of his origins', that is, the little Jewish professor.[36] When Stahl died on 10 August 1861, Hans von Kleist wrote to Ludwig von Gerlach:

> One can truly say that Stahl was the House of Lords. He gave it intellectual significance and thus weight in its decisions in contrast to those of the other House, the Government and in the country at large. He was the soul of his 'Fraction' [the German word for a party grouping—JS], and it determined things again up to the present in the whole house.[37]

Gerlach, who belonged to the 'born again' wing of Lutheran piety, was not so sure. Six years later he wrote to a friend,

> It is painful to write this about a dear friend, who fought so bravely and in whose soul I took such delight and strength and edification, but you have forced me to do so...he fell for the most part into a vulgar constitutionalism

and sought only to temper it in a conservative manner through Christian moral feelings.[38]

The revolutionary years thus gave Prussian conservatism a new ideological direction and that in turn gave Bismarck a platform on which to build his political career. Stahl may have preached 'vulgar constitutionalism' but constitutionalism would happen no matter what he preached. By another 'world historical irony' the arch-conservative Otto von Bismarck needed constitutions and parliaments to show his brilliance. Moritz von Blanckenburg was delighted with Bismarck's speeches on the Jewish question and told Ludwig von Gerlach that since as recently as 4 October 1846 at Trieglaff Bismarck had defended a strict separation of church and state, now his conversion to the ideal of the Christian state was wonderful.[39] Lothar Gall takes this sudden change with a large grain of salt:

> For the spirit of Christian self-righteousness which he met in Pomerania and frequently in his own circle of political friends, he had far too sharp an eye to allow him to fall for such ideas... Bismarck was never entirely comfortable as he entered the thin air of such abstractions...[40]

For Gall and for Marcks the question remained how seriously could either take Bismarck's speech on the Christian State and both devote several pages to casuistical attempts to reconcile the speech with Bismarck's scepticism about the more enthusiastic and doctrinaire aspects of religion and the known peculiarities of his faith. There can be no doubt that Bismarck was religious in his idiosyncratic way, but in this case neither Marcks nor Gall draw the obvious conclusion that the speech on the Jews was pure cynical opportunism. It gave him an opportunity to spread his colourful feathers and enhance his already formidable reputation. Pflanze has, I think, the sharpest view of Bismarck's religion:

> His need to dominate and direct did not spring from a sense of divine mission, but from an earlier, more elemental force in his personality. Conversion did not fundamentally alter his attitude toward his fellowman. His cynical view of minds and motives, his hatred and malevolence to those who opposed him, his willingness to exploit and use others show that the Christian doctrine of love and charity had little influence upon him. His faith provided the reinforcement, not the foundation of his sense of responsibility... Religion gave him a sense of security, a feeling of belonging to a coherent, meaningful and controlled world—the kind of environment that his parents did not provide. The God he worshipped was powerful (in contrast to his father) and loving, supportive and omnipresent (in contrast to his mother).[41]

When King Frederick William IV prorogued the United Diet, Bismarck
had completed the first seven weeks of his long career as a public figure and
from his point of view they had been successful weeks. He had emerged as
the young star of the extreme right and had made a reputation which could
not harm his career among the King's entourage. The royal Princes,
Frederick, Albert, and the Crown Prince himself wrote enthusiastic letters
and Herr von Puttkamer, who had also been a deputy, wrote to Johanna that
Bismarck was 'the spoiled darling of the princes'.[42] As important was his
discovery of the fascination of parliamentary politics, the influence, threats,
and blandishments, the management of men and affairs, the excitement of
the duel in the chamber, and his brilliance as a debater and speaker. The end
of the United Diet left him flat but not unoccupied. He tried to organize a
new conservative newspaper. He busied himself with the next stages of legal
reform and other projects, but the stage lights had gone dark for a while.

And, of course, at some point he had to get married. On 28 July 1847 the
wedding took place in Reinfeld on the Puttkamer estate. The best man was
'little Hans' von Kleist-Retzow, who in his toast 'hoped and prophesied that
the groom would be a new Otto the Saxon', the legendary medieval duke,
Otto the Great.[43] The couple travelled first in Prussia visiting relatives and
then on 11 August 1847 set out for Prague via Dresden (where Johanna, the
quiet country girl, saw her first play), and from Dresden on to the great city
of Vienna, then upriver to Linz and Salzburg. Only a few of Johanna's letters
survive but they testify to an extremely happy life with Otto. On 25 August
she wrote to her parents that 'the world gets ever more beautiful with every
passing day [and] Otto with all his warmth is heartily good and loving.'[44]
On 1 September in Meran they met a Bismarck cousin Count Fritz von
Bismarck-Bohlen, and Albrecht von Roon, who was travelling as tutor to
the young Prussian Prince Friedrich Karl, later a distinguished army commander in 1866 and 1870. On 8 September 1847 von Roon wrote to his
wife Anna that he and Prince Friedrich Karl 'had the pleasure of seeing
Otto Bismarck and his young wife. They promised to visit you in Bonn.'[45]
The Bismarcks decided to join Roon, the Prince, and Cousin Fritz on their
trip to Venice where on 6 September they found King Frederick William IV
and his entourage. On the same night, the Bismarcks went to the theatre in
Venice. Bismarck described what happened in his memoirs:

> The King, who had recognised me in the theatre, commanded me on the fol-
> lowing day to an audience and to dinner; and so unexpected was this to me
> that my light travelling luggage and the incapacity of the local tailor did not

admit of my appearing in correct costume. My reception was so kindly, and the conversation, even on political subjects, of such a nature as to enable me to infer that my attitude in the Diet met with his encouraging approval. The King commanded me to call upon him in the course of the winter, and I did so. Both on this occasion and at smaller dinners at the palace I became persuaded that I stood high in the favour of both the King and the Queen, and that the former, in avoiding speaking to me in public, at the time of the session of the Diet, did not mean to criticize my political conduct, but at the time did not want to let others see his approval of me.[46]

The two essential elements in Bismarck's career had fallen into place: the certainty that he could master political bodies and the favour of the King. From September 1847 to March 1890 he always had both. When he lost the latter, he lost power. He never had any other foundation for his achievements. No crowds followed him and no party acknowledged him as leader. Even his closest Junker allies, the Gerlach brothers, little Hans, and the others were never 'his' party, and owed him nothing for their position in society. Gradually they realized that he shared less of their values than they had thought. The other element to note is the presence of Albrecht von Roon in the story. Bismarck had intended to head for home because the constant rain in Austria had begun to depress him. Did Roon convince him to go to Venice in the hope that he would meet the King? If so, as in 1858 and 1862, he did his friend an incalculable service.

The Bismarcks returned to Schönhausen in late September 1847 and settled in to married life. On 24 October, he wrote letters to his sister and to his brother. To his sister, he wrote that marriage suited him and that he was free 'of the bottomless boredom and depression that plagued me as soon as I found myself within my four walls'.[47] In the letter to Bernhard he complained about his mother-in-law's 'great natural melancholy...She sees a black future.' He then wrote that the honeymoon had cost 750 thaler for 57 days, or 13 thaler per day and he was forced to use Joanna's wedding money, which she had wanted to spend on silver. For his part he was quite happy to go on using his father's old silver plate. As he wrote, tea in Wedgwood 'tastes just as good'.[48] On 11 January 1848, the King kept his promise and invited Bismarck to dine at the palace. He sat next to Ludwig von Gerlach and seems not to have taken Johanna.[49]

As Bismarck made his way home that night, the streets of Palermo in Sicily were buzzing with rumours. The next day a revolt against the King of Naples broke out and the revolutionary year of 1848 had begun. In France on 23 February 1848, full-scale revolution broke out. Within hours, Louis Philippe fled and the Second French Republic had been declared with its fiery Jacobin language and memories of the Terror. As the news from Paris spread across Europe cities from Copenhagen to Naples began to stir. Meetings were held and crowds gathered. On 27 February 1848 in Mannheim a mass meeting demanded press freedom, jury trials, a militia army, and the immediate creation of a German parliament. Revolts and mass meetings took place in all German cities. Peasants rioted and attacked manor houses. In Vienna on 13 March 1848 a rising began and Prince Metternich fled the city. The symbol of repression of the old regime had scurried out of his capital like a fugitive. In Milan on 17 March the news of Metternich's fall arrived and revolt broke out there as well.

The big garrisons in all European cities in March 1848 had no tactics to cope with Parisian style street-fighting: barricades across narrow, winding streets in old urban centres, boiling water and emptied chamber pots poured from upper floors, and the constant danger of fraternization between troops and citizens undermined the army's morale. In northern Italy Marshall Radetzky had overwhelming force, more than 10,000 armed men, and he had garrisons in all the fortresses around Milan but he still lost control of the city. Within a day of the reports that Metternich and the Viennese government had fallen, Milan had become a maze of improvised barricades and fortifications.[50]

In Berlin, the excitement had begun as soon as the news from Paris arrived. Very good weather helped to keep the crowd on the streets. As Christopher Clark writes,

> Alarmed at the growing 'determination and insolence' of the crowds circulating in the streets, the President of Police, Julius von Minutoli, ordered new troops into the city on 13 March. That night several civilians were killed in clashes round the palace precinct. The crowd and the soldiery were now collective antagonists for control of the city's space.[51]

For the next few days King Frederick William IV hesitated, pulled between doves, those advocating concessions, and hawks led by General Karl Ludwig von Prittwitz (1790–1871) the commanding officer of the brigade of Guards Infantry regiments in Berlin, who argued for force. On 17 March the King, shaken by news of the flight of Metternich, finally gave in and agreed to lift press censorship and introduce a constitution for Prussia. Apparently in spite of his bombastic speech from the throne eleven months earlier, he had discovered there was a 'power on earth that [could] transform the natural relationship between prince and people...into a conventional constitutional relationship'—fear. The next morning, as a crowd gathered in the Palace Square to celebrate, a series of clashes occurred between the army and the demonstrators. Barricades went up all over Berlin. The army could not control the city. Just before midnight on 18 March 1848, General von Prittwitz, whom his biographer describes as 'a serious, reserved and closed personality',[52] arrived at the palace to ask the King for permission to order the city to be evacuated and then to bombard the rebels until they surrendered. David Barclay describes the scene:

> The non-committal monarch listened, thanked Prittwitz and returned to his desk. Prittwitz noted 'the comfortable way in which His Majesty sat down at his desk pulling a furry foot-muff over his feet after taking off his boots and stockings, in order, as it seemed, to begin writing another lengthy document'. The document he was drafting was perhaps the most famous of his whole reign: his celebrated address 'To My Dear Berliners' (an Meine lieben Berliner).[53]

By dawn the document had been posted all over Berlin. In it he declared that the army would be withdrawn:

> Return to peace, clear the barricades that still stand...and I give you my Royal Word that all streets and squares will be cleared of troops, and the military occupation reduced to a few necessary buildings.

The order to pull the troops out of the city was given on the next day shortly before noon. The king had placed himself in the hands of the revolution.[54]

For most of the soldiers and indeed for Prince William, the King's brother, and the Crown Prince, Frederick William was a coward who had surrendered to the mob. Roon, stationed in Potsdam, considered emigration. Bismarck instinctively reached for his sword. Two days later, on 20 March, a delegation from Tangermünde arrived in Schönhausen and demanded that the black-red-gold flag of the German Republic be raised on the church tower. Bismarck 'asked the peasants whether they wanted to defend themselves. They answered with a unanimous and vigorous Ja and I recommended to them to drive the city-dwellers out which with the enthusiastic help of the women they rapidly did.'[55] On 21 March Bismarck hurried to Potsdam to see if it made sense to march on Berlin with armed peasants. Bismarck described what happened in his memoirs and the main outlines square with the accounts given by Gall, Engelberg, and Pflanze:

I dismounted at the residence of my friend Roon, who, as governor to Prince Frederick Charles, occupied some rooms in the castle; and visited in the *Deutsches Haus* General von Möllendorf, whom I found still stiff from the treatment he had suffered when negotiating with the insurgents, and General von Prittwitz, who had been in command in Berlin. I described to them the present temper of the country people; they in return gave me some particulars as to what had happened up to the morning of the 19th. What they had to relate, and the later information which came from Berlin, could only strengthen my belief that the King was not free. Prittwitz, who was older than I, and judged more calmly, said: 'Send us none of your peasants, we don't want them. We have quite enough soldiers... What can we do after the King has commanded us to play the part of the vanquished? I cannot attack without orders'.[56]

Gall argues that from this moment on, Bismarck determined to 'take part in all efforts to save the traditional monarchical-aristocratic order even if against the present wearer of the crown'.[57] In one sense, Bismarck had no choice but to do that. Since September when the King invited him to the palace, Bismarck had seen a career through the court as his way to power. With the King in the hands of the revolution, that would not happen. Bismarck could not have imagined that the arrival of constitutional government would offer him the perfect balance between the remains of royal absolutism and the need for parliamentary adroitness. The conflict between King and Chamber would give Bismarck his platform, but not yet.

According to the later Queen Augusta, Bismarck came to her on 23 March of 1848 on behalf of her brother-in-law, Prince Carl Alexander of Prussia, a younger brother of King Frederick William IV and of her husband, Prince William, Prince of Prussia, to ask for her authority 'to use the name of her husband and of her young son for a counter-revolution through which the measures granted by the King would not be recognized and his right to make them and his capacity to act rationally would be contested.'[58] She wrote to the Crown Prince who had fled to England:

I confined myself to talking to Herr von Bismarck-Schönhausen, to whom I said that you had given an example of the truest devotion and obedience and that any measure against decisions of the King would contradict your views. I let him give me his word of honour that neither your name nor that of our son would be compromised by such a reactionary attempt.[59]

Bismarck's version has a very different character:

In this condition of affairs I hit upon the idea of obtaining from another quarter a command to act, which could not be expected from the King, who was not free, and tried to get at the Prince of Prussia. Referred to the Princess, whose consent thereto was necessary, I called upon her in order to discover the whereabouts of her consort, who, as I subsequently discovered, was on the Pfaueninsel. She received me in a servant's room on the *entresol,* sitting on a wooden chair. She refused the information I asked for, and declared, in a state of violent excitement, that it was her duty to guard the rights of her son.[60]

The reader can choose which version to accept but needs to bear in mind that Bismarck always covered up his mistakes, and this headstrong act of folly led to deep hostility between the future Queen and her future Minister-President. In addition, one must reflect that Bismarck wrote the passage after his fall from power and after forty years of his neurotic hatred of her.

The situation then worsened. On 25 March Frederick William arrived in Potsdam and addressed the army commanders and officers:

> I have come to Potsdam in order to bring peace to my dear Potsdamers and to show them that I am in every respect a free King, and to show the Berliners that they need fear no reaction and that all the disquieting rumours to that effect are completely unfounded. I have never been freer and more secure than I am under the protection of my citizens....[61]

Bismarck watched this moment and recorded later in his memoirs his bitterness at what he heard:

> At the words 'I have never been freer or more secure than when under the protection of my citizens,' there arose a murmuring and the clash of sabres in their sheaths, such as no King of Prussia in the midst of his officers had ever heard before, and, I hope, will ever hear again.[62]

Bismarck had no other choice but to return to Schönhausen and confer with his Junker allies. Three days later he wrote in a much calmer frame of mind to his brother Bernhard and commented on the news from Paris:

> As long as the present government in Paris can hold on, I do not believe there will be war, doubt that there's any urge to it. If it is undermined or even overthrown by socialist movements, which is entirely foreseeable, it will have or its successor no money and nobody will lend it any, so that a state bankruptcy or something similar must occur. The motives of 1792, the guillotine and the republican fanaticism, which might take the place of money, are not present.[63]

In this shrewd and absolutely accurate assessment of the French Second Republic, we hear for the first time the cool tones of Bismarck, the diplomat and statesman. From his remote outpost in Brandenburg, he saw what

Tocqueville in the streets of Paris had also noted—that the French Revolution of 1848 was an imitation of 1792 or, in Tocqueville's memorable phrase, 'the whole thing seemed to me to be a bad tragedy played by actors from the provinces.'[64]

On 29 March 1848 the King appointed Ludolf Camphausen (1803–90), a grain and commodity trader, banker, and investor from the Prussian Rhine provinces, as his new Prime Minister and summoned the United Diet to a session on 2 April. Camphausen had the distinction of being the first representative of the new capitalism to hold office under a Prussian king. These changes affected Bismarck, who was a deputy in the United Diet and he therefore left Schönhausen for Berlin. On 2 April he wrote to Johanna from Berlin that 'I am much calmer than I was.'[65]

In the meantime elections for the Prussian National Assembly had been declared. The franchise was indirect. Voters elected a college of electors who in turn voted for the deputies. All adult males were eligible to vote if they were not on relief and had resided in the same place for six months. In a letter to his brother on 19 April, Bismarck reported:

> I have little or no chance to be elected. I don't know whether to rejoice or be annoyed about that. It's a matter of conscience to campaign with all my energy. If it does not succeed, I shall lay myself down in my big easy chair with the satisfaction of having done my bit and spend two to six months sitting around under conditions more agreeable than in the Landtag.[66]

The elections had an electrifying effect on the newly enfranchised peasants and artisans who flocked to the meetings that preceded the elections. Habits of subservience fell off their backs like old clothes and a not insignificant number of middle-class radicals joined them to stir up passions and make careers. The new Prussian cabinet led by David Hansemann and Ludolf Camphausen pursued a combination of liberal economic policies and constitutional proprieties but did little or nothing for grievances of artisans and peasants who wanted guaranteed security, not watered-down Adam Smith. At the same time that voters elected deputies to the new Prussian Landtag, they also chose representatives for the so-called German Pre-Parliament, a kind of constitutional convention for Germany as whole. This led to a second cleavage among supporters of the new order, between those who remained essentially Prussian or Bavarian or Saxon—revolutions had occurred in all thirty-nine German states—and those who wanted to see their state 'go up', in Hegelian language, into the new united Germany.

A coherent account of the revolutions of 1848 requires unusual narrative skills. There was no single revolution but many and often different ones. The events themselves occurred among states and within states. Within a state like Germany thirty-nine revolutions broke out in big kingdoms like Prussia or Bavaria and in tiny German state-lets like the Principalities of Reuss older line and Reuss younger line, one of which was ruled by Heinrich the XX and the other by Heinrich the LXII (this is *not* a misprint).[67] The Habsburg Monarchy had revolutions in almost as many places as there were national identities but in particular in the German, Czech, Hungarian, Italian, and Polish cities and in some rural areas where serfdom, the *robot*, still existed. The attempt to create a German national state foundered quickly on the disagreement about what Germany included. The Habsburg Empire had German and non-German states. Each kingdom, dukedom, principality, or city had its feudal constitution and special relationship to its King, Prince, Duke, Count, Margrave, Landgrave, or Lord. The German nationalists who wanted a 'Greater Germany' laid claim to historic German territories such as Bohemia and Moravia which had non-German majorities. The German national state had to include the 'eternally united' Duchies of Schleswig and Holstein, though only Holstein was a member of the German Confederation both had the King of Denmark as their sovereign. Frictions developed between classes and regions, between entrepreneurs and workers, between anxious artisans who wanted to restrict entry to skilled trades and doctrinaire liberals who applied principles of free markets to all closed corporations. The disintegration of millennial forest and field rights affected Bismarck and his social class who faced the loss of small privileges like the right to a tenth of honey harvests from peasant hives.

Fighting broke out all over Europe as nationalists tried to force the creation of their new states. Charles Albert, King of Piedmont, under the banner *l'Italia farà da se* (Italy will make itself) sent his army into neighbouring Lombardy where radical republicans fought against the Piedmontese and against the Imperial forces of Habsburg rule. To the west and to the east two great powers escaped the turmoil, Great Britain because it already had liberalism, capitalism, a constitution, and a middle class (though it was a close call and radicals in 1848 like the Reverend Frederick Maurice expected the revolution any day) and Russia which had none of those things.

Twenty-five years of censorship came to an end overnight and radicals, conservatives, and liberals of every hue began to make speeches, print flyers, and found newspapers. The sheer kaleidoscopic complexity of places,

persons, issues, heritages, trades, traditions, conflicts, and overlapping juris-
dictions bewildered contemporaries and continues to baffle historians who
have first to understand the events and then describe them.

The kings and princes had suffered a collective loss of nerve but, as the
first shock wave died down, they gradually noticed that they still had their
armies, which, though furious and humiliated at their failure to quell the
mob, were intact and often, as in the case of Prussia, outside the turbulent
capital city. The Austrian armies in northern Italy began to regain control of
Lombardy and Venetia and on 17 June suppressed the Czech revolt in Prague.
From 23 to 26 June General Cavaignac put down the workers' revolt in
Paris in the so-called 'June days'. On 24 and 25 July Marshall Radetzky
decisively defeated the Piedmontese army of Charles Albert and restored
Austrian rule in northern Italy. The old order began to gain confidence.

In Prussia, the conservatives around the Gerlachs had begun their domestic counter-revolution within days of the King's surrender to the crowd by
creating a *ministère occulte,* a secret shadow government, lodged inside the
royal establishment, also known as the 'camarilla'. Since the new constitutional arrangements had not altered the King's powers of command over the
army, the Gerlach brothers became the moving spirits in the creation of the
new secret structure. General Leopold von Gerlach and his brother Senior
Judge Ernst Ludwig von Gerlach were the key figures along with various
royal adjutants-general and the ministers of the royal household. As Hans-
Joachim Schoeps writes of Leopold von Gerlach,

> as a result of the close personal friendship with Frederick William IV—a deep
> spiritual bond linked them—Gerlach had a strong influence over all Prussian
> policy after 1848. He was frequently sent on smaller diplomatic missions. In
> the daily coffee report his counsel and judgement counted for more than the
> minister-presidents in office... Since, on the other hand, the men in the inti-
> mate royal circle had no lust for power—Gerlach was much too scrupulous
> for that—a complete lack of organization distinguishes the Camarilla as its
> most striking feature.[68]

The key feature of the royal government then and in presidential government in those states where it exists today is the social space of power. If you
see the King or President every day, especially if you see him alone, you have
power irrespective of the title of your office or its place in the hierarchy.
Leopold von Gerlach had coffee with the King every day. He had power.

In 1850 or 1851 Leopold von Gerlach became the President of the Berlin
Society for the Promotion of Christianity among the Jews, functioning

exactly as the founder General Job von Witzleben did before him. The date is uncertain because the Annual Reports of the Society for 1850 and 1851 are missing.[69] Like General Job von Witzleben, who combined Christian vocation and office as Adjutant-General, Leopold von Gerlach did exactly the same thing. Anti-Semitism continued to be institutionalized at the top of Prussian society and the prominence of Jews among revolutionary leaders deepened it. Von der Marwitz had said it prophetically in 1811, liberalism meant that 'our old, venerable Brandenburg-Prussia will become a new-fangled Jewish state'.[70]

On 21 June Bismarck told his brother that he was going to Potsdam for a few days of 'political intrigues'. On 3 July he wrote to Alexander von Below-Hohendorff:

> Last week I was in Potsdam and found the high and highest personalities more decisive and much clearer about their position than one would have thought given all that has happened. I also was able to assure myself through sight of a confidential letter from the Tsar that the danger of war with Russia is completely imaginary, as long as civil war does not break out here and our ruler does not call for Russian help. The rest by word of mouth.[71]

On the same day, 21 June 1848, the 'Society for King and Fatherland' was founded, a semi-clandestine association of Junker landlords, not more than ten or twenty in each province, who would, by joining other organizations without acknowledging the existence of the Society itself, influence local people and report to the central committee in Berlin on the atmosphere in the country at large. There was a public committee and a secret one which Ludwig von Gerlach directed.[72]

The camarilla recognized that secret and royal influences would not be enough. They had to do other, more overt, political things. Above all, they needed their own newspaper. Before 1848 there had been talk of one but nothing had come of it. Now in the new more democratic era, the conservatives needed a journalistic voice. Bernhard von Bismarck described the difficulties they faced:

> Although the financial situation and credit of the estate owners stood on wobbly foundations and mine most of all, I succeeded nevertheless through my words, my writing and my example in collecting money to support the conservative press. Through a letter of credit for several thousand thalers which I, my brother and Kleist-Retzow put up to pay the guarantee deposit, we covered the initial expense. Otherwise the paper might well have gone under shortly after it first appeared.[73]

On 1 July 1848 the *Neue Preussische Zeitung* appeared for the first time. Because of the iron cross on its masthead, it became known as the *Kreuzzeitung*. Bismarck took an intense interest in the fledgling paper. He wrote for it and also sent the new editor Hermann Wagener regular comments on it. Here are two from its first days. In July of 1848 he received his first copy and wrote to Wagener to express his delight that a new paper had appeared but complained that

> there are not enough ads. In our rural remoteness ads are a necessity. The women cannot exist without them and in any case the survival of a newspaper rests on the fees from advertising. New papers can help themselves by reprinting the notices in the established papers and so by means of appearance eventually create the reality of an important information paper... Births, deaths, weddings announcements must be taken over from the Spener-Vossische in my view in full, if necessary without phrases. You cannot imagine how many women read papers only for the notices and if they do not find them, forbid their husbands to buy the paper.[74]

In early September Gerlach noted in his diary that Bismarck 'offers himself almost as a minister... a very active and intelligent adjutant for our Camarilla headquarters'.[75] Gerlach's dominance over an entire generation of young conservatives like Wagener, Kleist-Retzow, and Schede rested on his immense personal authority as a legal mind and a judge but also on the extraordinary, almost saintly, qualities of his Christian faith. Bismarck never quite belonged among these disciples. He had not been a *Referendar* in Gerlach's superior provincial court nor could he share Gerlach's comprehensive application of Christian principles to the state.[76]

In the autumn of 1848, Bismarck needed Ernst Ludwig von Gerlach, who helped to set up and direct the camarilla as a political force. Gerlach wrote a column called *Review* every month in the *Kreuzzeitung* and the *Reviewer* became the most widely read and most influential voice on the Right. He never failed to startle readers as in his October 1848 column in which he argued, 'we cannot oppose Revolution only with repressive and security measures, we must always have ideas of justice.'[77] Since his brother Leopold had coffee in private with the King every day, Bismarck reckoned that the brothers Gerlach would be his road to power, and they were.

On 12 July the German Confederation in Frankfurt, which had continued to function alongside the revolutionary German National Assembly, decided to cease meeting but it did so in a way that would affect Bismarck's career. It did not announce 'the end of its existence' but instead 'the end of its previous activity'.[78] When the revolution finally ended, the Austrians could call it back out of its temporary suspension and resume their dominance of the German political structure. That would mean, if Prussia agreed, that there would have to be again a Prussian representative to the Bundestag, the job which Bismarck eventually got.

The Prussian national assembly had debated in July the abolition of all manorial rights and, as a result, in Bismarck's neighbourhood the counter-revolution became still more active. On 24 July an organization for the representation of the great landowners had been founded called the Verein zur Wahrung der Interessen des Grundbesitzes und zur Förderung des Wohlstands aller Klassen (Association for the Protection of the Interests of Landownership and for the Promotion of the Prosperity of all Classes). Although the country aristocracy dominated it, some 26 per cent of the landowners were non-noble. The leading figures were mostly from Brandenburg and their names are already familiar to us: Ernst von Bülow-Cummerow, Hans von Kleist-Retzow, Alexander von Below, and Otto von Bismarck. When the first annual general meeting of members gathered on 18 August, some 200 to 300 men showed up including smallholders and peasants. Since the long name hardly rolled off the tongue, the organizers shortened it to the Verein zum Schutz des Eigentums (the Association to Protect Property) and the journalists immediately called it 'the Junker Parliament'. Although only 34 years old, Hans von Kleist was elected President. Leopold von Gerlach recorded in his diary for 10 December 1855: 'It was the basis and the beginning of the later mighty party which saved the country.'[79] On 22 August 1848 Ludwig von Gerlach addressed the Junker Parliament and gave for the first time his Christian justification for the preservation of manorial rights:

> Property is itself a political concept, an office bestowed by God, in order to preserve his law and the Kingdom of his Law; only in association with the duties which arise from it is property holy. As mere means of enjoyment it is not holy but dirty. Communism correctly rejects property without duties. For that reason we may not surrender the threatened rights—patronage [of church and school], police [estate constables], the legal jurisdiction [estate owners as judges]; for these are more duties than rights.[80]

Bismarck had been tireless in organizing and furthering the Association. He had once again shown his political skills and energy. He wrote to Hermann Wagener on 25 August and put his own, rather different, interpretation on the Gerlach version of *noblesse oblige*:

It is a criterion of nobility that it serves the country for nothing. To be able to do that it must have its own wealth, from which it can live; otherwise the thing simply will not work. As result we have to be as materialistic as necessary to defend our material rights.[81]

Not quite what von Gerlach had in mind. In the midst of the Junker Parliament, on 21 August 1848, the Bismarcks' first child, Marie, was born and Hans von Kleist-Retzow became her godfather.[82]

In the great world beyond Brandenburg, international and national forces had begun to contain, and ultimately crush, the German Revolutions of 1848–9. The day after Bismarck wrote to Hermann Wagener, 26 August 1848, under pressure from Britain and Russia, the Prussian government, whose army had been fighting a quixotic campaign against Denmark for the liberation of the Duchies of Schleswig and Holstein, agreed to sign an armistice with Denmark without consulting the German National Assembly, whose agent in theory Prussia had been. This betrayal of the national cause made clear the evident fact that Frankfurt as capital of the new Germany had no executive force of its own. When on 16 September the National Assembly in Frankfurt ratified the armistice—they could hardly do otherwise—rioting broke out in the street and two deputies, Auerswald and Lichnowsky, were murdered by the mob. The Prussian army entered the city and restored order.[83]

The loss of prestige in the National Assembly affected the Prussian National Assembly in a similar way. On 11 September 1848 the Liberal Prussian Auerswald-Hansemann ministry resigned. The King hesitated. Could he do away with liberals altogether? Bismarck went to Berlin where His Majesty received him and even apparently considered appointing him to office. The King opted for General Adolf von Pfuel, who was 69 when appointed Minister-President of Prussia and had been until 18 March 1848 the military governor of Berlin. Pfuel had been a close childhood friend of the poet and writer Heinrich von Kleist, had been a regular at the Jewish salon of Rahel Varnhagen von Ense, and had an unusual reputation. Though a Prussian Junker of Mark Brandenburg stock, he had genuine liberal sympathies. He tried to keep to the agreements of March 1848 but failed to gain the King's support as the conflict between Crown and Parliament, stirred up and forced by the Gerlachs, sharpened.[84] On 23 September 1848 Bismarck wrote to Johanna:

Either the government shows itself to be weak like its predecessors and gives way, something that I am working against, or it does its duty in which case I do not doubt for a minute that on Monday evening or Tuesday blood will flow. I had not thought the Democrats would be bold enough to accept battle but their whole attitude suggests that they will. Poles, Frankfurter, loafers, freebooters, all sorts of scum, have again appeared. They reckon that the troops will back out, probably through the speeches of a few unsatisfied chatterboxes who thus mislead the troops. I think they are wrong. I have no reason to stay here and tempt God to protect me, for which I have no claim. I shall bring my person to safety tomorrow.[85]

In spite of his letter, Bismarck stayed in Berlin, though in what capacity beyond busybody cannot easily be established. He went here and there, saw this one and that, and generally made sure that he could not be ignored. It seems that he seriously expected to be nominated to high office in the near future and that, in fact, turned out to be quite correct. In Berlin the camarilla had gradually won the King to its views. In early September 1848 Leopold von Gerlach suggested the establishment of a 'military ministry to be headed by a general', which would finally put down the revolution in Prussia. His brother Ludwig told Leopold on 29 September 1848 that the time had come for such a ministry composed of General Count Brandenburg, a member of the royal family, with Otto von Bismarck, Hans Hugo von Kleist-Retzow, and the Prince of Prussia as 'generalissimo'.[86] By 6 October 1848 the camarilla had convinced the King to appoint Brandenburg. Friedrich Wilhelm Count von Brandenburg (1792–1850) was the third and youngest of the three generals who reclaimed Berlin from revolution. Brandenburg, who had grown up in the home of the Minister of the Royal Household, von Massow, must have known Frederick William IV as a child. He had many virtues but no acquaintance with politics whatever when on 2 November 1848 Frederick William IV appointed him to succeed von Pfuel.[87] Bismarck recalled his helplessness:

Count Brandenburg, indifferent to such anxieties, declared himself ready to take the presidency of the Council, and then the difficulty was to find him fit and acceptable colleagues. A list presented to the King contained my name also: as General Gerlach told me, the King had written in the margin 'only to be employed when the bayonet governs unrestricted.' Count Brandenburg himself said to me at Potsdam: 'I have taken the matter in hand, but have scarcely looked into the newspapers; I am unacquainted with political matters, and can only carry my head to market. I want a mahout, a man in whom I trust and who tells me what I can do. I go into the matter like a child into the dark, and except Otto Manteuffel [then at the head of the Ministry of the Interior], know nobody who possesses previous training as well as my personal confidence.[88]

The fate of the revolution in Prussia depended less on von Brandenburg but on another Prussian general, the flamboyant and clever 'Papa Wrangel'. Friedrich Heinrich Ernst von Wrangel was born on 13 April 1784 in Stettin and died on 1 November 1877 in Berlin at the age of 93. In the Napoleonic Wars he had won the highest Prussian order, *Pour le mérite.* During the long peace years he distinguished himself as a dashing and effective cavalry officer. On 19 April 1848 the King gave him command of the Prussian army expeditionary force to go to Schleswig-Holstein and again he won a variety of notable engagements. After the armistice Wrangel returned to Berlin and on 13 September reported to the King who appointed him military governor of 'the Marches', the territory surrounding Berlin. He took up his headquarters in the royal palace in Charlottenburg and deployed 50,000 troops around the city. The scenario had already been established by Cavaignac and Radetzky, but Wrangel was shrewder and more dramatic. On 9 October he organized a military parade to the horror of von Pfuel who advised against it. Wrangel decided that it was high time Berlin saw some soldiers. With drums and flags the army marched from Charlottenburg into the heart of Berlin and drew a huge, cheering crowd.[89] Wrangel spoke fluent Berlin dialect and made himself easily available to the crowd. The parade showed that the revolutionaries had lost support and that the army had regained its prestige especially when commanded by a witty, dialect-speaking, people's general. Eleven days after Wrangel's parade, Bismarck wrote to Johanna:

> Not the slightest sign of revolt here. But instead bitter feelings between workers and civil guard, which can bear good fruit. The workers cheer the King and the army and want the King to rule alone etc.[90]

Meanwhile in Vienna, the Austrian government used force. On 6 October 1848 street fighting broke out and the court fled the city. On 26 October, under the command of General Alfred Prince zu Windisch-Graetz and the Croatian general Count Joseph Jelačić von Bužim, the Austrian army began to bombard the city and on 31 October stormed it with overwhelming numbers. Two thousand people died in the fighting and several prominent leaders, including Robert Blum, a deputy in the Frankfurt National Assembly, were executed by firing squad. Wrangel had done the same job with a parade and no casualties. The German revolution had run its course. On 9 November 1848 Count Brandenburg had decided to remove the Prussian National Assembly from Berlin as a first step to the occupation of the city by Wrangel's troops.

Bismarck had remained in Berlin to make himself as important as possible and seems to have managed that exercise, as he tells us in his memoirs:

> Early in the morning of November 9, General von Strotha, who had been appointed War Minister, came to me, sent by Brandenburg, in order to have the situation made clear to him. I did that as well as I could, and asked: 'Are you ready?' He answered with the rejoinder: 'What dress has been decided upon?' 'Civilian dress,' I replied. 'That I don't possess,' said he. I provided him with a hired servant, and luckily, before the appointed hour, a suit was hunted up at a tailor's. Various measures had been taken for the security of the ministers. First of all, in the theatre itself, besides a strong posse of police, about thirty of the best shots in the light infantry battalions of the guard were so disposed that they could appear in the body of the house and the galleries at a given signal; they were unerring marksmen, and could cover the ministers with their muskets if they were actually threatened. It was assumed that at the first shot all who were present would speedily vacate the body of the house. Corresponding precautions were taken at the windows of the theatre, and at various buildings in the Gendarmenmarkt, in order to protect the ministers from any possible hostile attack as they left the theatre; it was assumed that even large masses, meeting there, would scatter as soon as shots were fired.[91]

None were and on the following day, 10 November 1848, General Wrangel occupied Berlin and put an end to the revolution in Prussia, as it turned out, for good. Now what was there for Bismarck? On the following day he wrote one of those disarmingly honest letters that still have the power to startle the reader:

> I sit here partly as a deputy of our knights' association in Berlin and partly as a court and chamber intriguer. Up to now nothing much has happened except uninterrupted disarming of Berlin, through which as of now, after half of the districts have been searched, eighty to ninety percent of the weapons have been collected. Passive resistance turns out more and more to be cover for weakness. The military in addition to ensuring calm and order turns out to be popular and the number of the angry reduces itself to the fanatics, the rogues and the barricadists.[92]

On the same day King Frederick William IV issued a proclamation, which contained a promise to grant the subjects a new constitution:

> Prussians! I give you once more my unbreakable assurance that you will not be injured in your constitutional rights, that it will be my most immediate effort to be a good constitutional King, and that we together will erect a stately and lasting structure under whose roof to the benefit of our Prussian

and German Fatherland our descendents may enjoy in harmony the blessings of freedom for centuries to come. To that may God grant his blessing![93]

A few days later on 16 November, Bismarck wrote to Johanna:[94]

Yesterday I was invited to dinner by the King. The Queen was English pleasant. I picked a piece of heather from her sewing table and send it to you so you won't be jealous... Afterwards the King summoned me to an audience of about an hour in his cabinet or more accurately his bedroom, which is hardly larger than our little room. The Royals live together in the city palace and are rather cramped. Among other things he said, and instructed me to communicate it to all those well meaning persons, that he will hold to his promises, the right one and the silly ones, without question, without the slightest duplicity, but he intends to secure the rights of the Crown to the last consequence, as long as he has a single soldier and a toe-hold in Prussia.[95]

Years later Bismarck told Lucius von Ballhausen his crushing assessment of the King: Frederick William IV had 'an unsteady character... if one grabbed him, one came away with a handful of slime.'[96]

On 5 December 1848 the Prussian National Assembly was dissolved and the King fulfilled his promise by 'imposing' a constitution on the country. Though it had been *oktroyiert* or 'dictated' from above, the king declared 'as a consequence of the unusual situation which has arisen which made the planned agreement on the Constitution impossible,'[97] the 1848 Constitution was by no means entirely reactionary. It stipulated that all Prussians were equal before the law (Article 4); had personal freedom guaranteed (Article 5); inviolability of their dwellings (Article 6); property was inviolable (Article 8); and religious freedom was guaranteed (Article 11); research and teaching were free (Article 17). Every male Prussian over the age of 24 who had lived in his community for six months and had not been declared ineligible by a court had the right to vote (Article 67). The lower house had 350 members (Article 66) who served for three years (Article 70). Every 250 voters selected one Elector (Article 68) and the Electors elected the Deputies in districts so organized that at least two deputies were elected per district (Article 69). An upper house of 180 members, elected for six years by provincial, county, and districts (Articles 62–5) completed the structure.

On the other hand the core structure of the Prussian state had not been touched. In four articles, the fate of the 'Iron Kingdom' from 1848 to 1918 was sealed. The King exercised supreme command of the army (Article 44). He filled all posts in the same way in the remaining branches of the civil service insofar as the law had not prescribed an alternative (Article 45). The

King had the right to declare war, make peace, and enter into treaties with foreign powers (Article 46). The King had the right to dissolve either of the Chambers (Article 49).[98] Thus, the personnel and command of the army and civil service remained entirely in the hands of the King, who appointed and dismissed ministers and army officers alike, in effect, the spinal cord of the absolute regime. This constitutional structure, as amended by the Constitution of 1850, which eliminated equal suffrage and introduced a suffrage based on the income of the voter, remained in effect to 11 November 1918, when a republic replaced the monarchy.

Among the other prerogatives of the Crown, according to §3 of the Order of 12 October 1854, was the unlimited right to name members of the House of Lords as a sign of 'special All-Highest confidence'.[99] As Hartwin Spenkuch shows in his account of the Prussian House of Lords, successive monarchs named 325 such members between 1854 and 1918. Membership of the House of Lords elevated all sorts of commoners into the service nobility of the new constitutional kingdom but also rewarded nobles who had served in royal office either in civil or military functions. The Prussian House of Lords resembled the modern British version much more than one might expect and in one respect exceeded any equivalent provision of the British House of Lords of today. Between 1854 and 1918, forty university professors received nominations from their institutions to be 'presented' to the King as peers and twenty-one other professors were directly named by the King himself. These academic peerages in Prussia might be compared not implausibly to life peerages for distinguished academics nominated by the British Prime Minister today but with the advantage that the universities themselves selected two-thirds of the candidates. Among the 61 were the theorist of the Christian State, F. J. Stahl (1802–61); the economists of the so-called 'Historical School, Adolf Wagner (1835–1917) and Gustav Schmoller (1838–1917); and the classicist, Ulrich von Wilamowitz-Moellendorf (1848–1931).[100]

From 5 December 1848 the rules of the political game in Prussia were changing in Bismarck's favour. His conservative patrons would need his skills more than they had before and before all else he had to get himself elected to the new lower house, the Landtag. There was not much time. The voters would choose Electors on 22 January 1849 and the Electors would elect Deputies on 5 February. Four days after the imposition of the constitution, Bismarck wrote to his brother,

From September on I have been like a shuttle-cock going back and forth between here and Berlin, Potsdam and Brandenburg...In general I flatter myself that I have poured pepper on the tails of the cowardly dogs and look back at my day's work with satisfaction.[101]

His friends in the Union for King and Fatherland formed an electoral committee and Bismarck joined Julius Stahl, Moritz August von Bethmann Hollweg, Hermann Wagener, and his university friend Karl von Savigny as a member. Their manifesto stated: 'The political way of thinking which moves our Committee, is a unitary one and in many ways has sharper definition than among other fractions of the Conservative side. It consists of an absolute refusal to *negotiate with the revolution*.'[102] Bismarck plunged with his customary energy into the electoral campaign, as he explained to his brother,

> In the electoral assemblies I declared myself for the recognition of the constitution, defence against anarchy, equality before the law (but against abolition of the nobility), equal distribution of tax according to income, so far as possible; election according to interests, and against the abolition of monetary rights without compensation, for strict press and club laws and that is how I intend to behave in the Landtag.[103]

On 5 February 1849 Otto von Bismarck was elected to the Prussian Landtag from Teltow, in Brandenburg. Heinz von Kleist was elected from Belgard. General Leopold von Gerlach noted in his diary: 'Of the reliable people, upon whom we can call, Bismarck, Kleist, and I will assume, Professor Keller, have been elected. It would be important to organize them as a counter-opposition.'[104]

On 28 March 1849 the Frankfurt National Assembly adopted a constitution with universal, manhood suffrage and secret ballot and passed a resolution to offer the Imperial German Crown to Frederick William IV. On 3 April the King received the Frankfurt delegation led by the President of the Frankfurt Parliament, the Prussian Liberal Eduard von Simson. The meeting went badly. Frederick William IV received the '32 Crown Bearers', as Leopold von Gerlach scornfully called them, in the Knights' Hall of the Royal Palace, and told them with great courtesy that, though he was honoured by the offer of the Crown, he would have to see whether the German states accepted the constitution. At the reception that evening, the disappointed von Simson complained that the King had 'nullified' the Frankfurt Assembly, to which Leopold von Gerlach replied with satisfaction 'that is a very correct observation'.[105] The King wrote to his sister Charlotte, as the wife of the Tsar known as the Tsarina Alexandra Feodorovna, later to be a great friend of Bismarck,

> You have read my reply to the man-donkey-dog-pig-and-cat-delegation from Frankfurt. It means in simple German: 'Sirs You have not any right at all to offer me anything whatsoever. Ask, yes, you may ask, but give—No—for in order to give, you would first of all have to be in possession of something that can be given, and this *is not the case!*[106]

Bismarck's view of the Frankfurt crown was not much higher than the King's. On 21 April 1849 Bismarck made an important speech in the Landtag on it:

> The Frankfurt crown may glitter brightly but the gold which lends authenticity to its sparkle must be won by melting down the Prussian crown and I have no confidence that the smelting will succeed with the form of this constitution.[107]

Meanwhile Bismarck had settled into the parliamentary round as he told his brother,

> We are from the mornings at 9 in the expert committees, then plenary sessions, then after lunch in section meetings from 5 to 7 and then party meetings to 10 or 11. In between invitations, tedious visits to pay and to receive, intrigues and working on people and issues. Given my natural tendency to laziness, you will find my silences understandable. The sessions of every kind are the more exhausting because the first word tells you what the whole speech will contain like certain bad novels but you cannot leave because of the possibility of votes.

He had moved to 71 Wilhemstrasse, 'where it is a bit more expensive but then one doesn't get involved in the pubs'.[108]

In August of 1849, he was re-elected to the Prussian Landtag and lived in an inn with Hans von Kleist-Retzow. He wrote Johanna that he had considered taking a *chamber garnie* with him.

> He is for my lifestyle too tyrannical. He wakes me every morning before I want to get up and orders my coffee, so that it is cold when I get to it, suddenly draws Gossner's *Schatzkästchen* [Little Chest of Treasures] out of his pocket and imposes morning prayer on me with hymn that he reads out. That is very nice but often untimely.[109]

Nine days later on 17 August, he conceded defeat:

> I live with Hans here on the corner of the Taubenstrasse, 3 rooms and an alcove, very elegant but narrow, little holes, Hans's bed full of bed-bugs, mine

not, apparently they don't like the way I taste. We pay 25 Reichsthaler a month.[110]

Hans was now dragging him to Lutheran churches, and Bismarck groaned about it to Johanna:

> The singing in Protestant congregations really does not please me. I prefer a church with good church music played by people who know what they are doing and I like to have a church like the Tein church was inside with masses, priests in white vestments, in the fog of candles and incense, that is much worthier, don't you think, Angela?[111]

In September 1849 Bismarck went with his sister Malwine to Friedrichshain to visit the graveyard of the revolutionaries killed in the March days.

> Yesterday I went with Malle to Friedrichshain and not even the dead could I forgive. My heart filled with bitterness at the piety for false gods around the graves of these murders, where every inscription boasts on the crosses of 'Freedom and Justice', a mockery of God and man...My heart swells with poison at what they have made of our Fatherland, these murderers with whose graves the Berliners worship as idols.[112]

This rage at his 'enemies' would become more and more prominent as he got older and more powerful, and would take an increasing toll of his energies and health.

The end of the Frankfurt Parliament brought a new and unexpected complication. Radowitz returned to Berlin on 22 April 1849, from Frankfurt, where he had been a deputy. Joseph Maria von Radowitz (1797–1853) had a story-book career, a young man from a Catholic Hungarian noble family, he arrived on Berlin in 1823 knowing nobody and on the run from his master, the Grand Duke of Hesse. Within a few years he had become an important member of the new Prussian General Staff, a close friend of the Crown Prince who later became Frederick William IV, a founding member along with Count Voss, the Gerlachs, and others of that group of the *Berliner Wochenblatt*, whose aim it was 'to fight the false freedom of the revolution through the true freedom found in right order and never through absolutism, no matter in what guise it shows itself'.[113] In other words, though Catholic, he had taken on the feudal and aristocratic ideology of the Neo-Pietists against revolution but also against Frederick the Great's state absolutism. He rose to high rank in the army, published literary essays, and produced mathematical work as well. He wrote a memorandum on 20 November 1847 entitled 'Germany and Frederick William IV' in which he urged the King to take the lead in a federal, voluntary union of German states under Prussia, an effort which he always believed would have prevented the events of 1848. Only an unofficial, though powerful adviser of the King, he could not convince the ministers to pursue this course and after the March days he retired to an estate of his wife's relatives in Mecklenburg where, rather to his surprise, he was elected a deputy to the Frankfurt Parliament from a Westphalian constituency.

After the collapse of the revolutionary parliament in Frankfurt, Radowitz convinced Frederick William IV to use the new prestige of Prussia—the Frankfurt parliament had offered the German imperial crown to the Prussian king and Prussian force had suppressed tumult in Frankfurt and a peasants' revolt in Baden—to unify Germany in a 'Union' of Princes on a federal basis but without Austria. Radowitz's plan won the King's approval and led to the calling of a meeting of princes.

In Berlin Radowitz's scheme for a Union had little support within Prussia. Radowitz had no office but his close friendship with the King gave him power. The King's ministers mostly disliked the scheme. The camarilla hated it because it introduced an elected German parliament, the equivalent in their eyes of 'revolution'. Radowitz repeatedly offered to withdraw. The King just as repeatedly ordered him to stay. The 'Alliance of Three Kings' concluded between Prussia, Saxony, and Hanover on 26 May 1849 bound the three states to form a union if all other German states, with the exception of Austria, agreed. At a meeting in Gotha on 25 June 1849, 150 former liberal deputies to the German national assembly acceded to the draft of the Union constitution. Under Prussian pressure twenty-eight German states recognized the constitution and joined the union by the end of August 1849 but Bavaria held out and the loyalty of Saxony and Hanover to the idea was never very strong. Radowitz finally took formal office on 26 September 1849 as Prussian Foreign Minister but he had no support around the ministerial table. The King backed him but ever less certainly.

The idea made sense but it ran into two implacable foreign obstacles: the Austrian Empire and the Russian Empire. The Tsar Nicholas I had been furious that Frederick William IV had surrendered to the 'mob' and referred to him as the 'king of the pavements' and the 18-year-old Emperor of Austria, Franz Joseph, had a new adviser, Prince Schwarzenberg. His Serene Highness Felix, the Prince of Schwarzenberg, Duke of Krumlov, Count of Sulz, Princely Landgrave of Kelttgau (1800–52) belonged to the highest European aristocracy and had a powerful personality. He had arranged with the Tsar to help crush the Hungarian revolution, had imposed an entirely centralized government system on the Habsburg dominions, and intended to restore the federal structure of Germany to its pre-1848 position with Austria as sole power as its president.

On 31 January elections for the Union Parliament had taken place. Bismarck was elected and on 20 March 1850 the Union Parliament met in Erfurt for the first time. In spite of his reputation for black reaction Bismarck was elected as secretary of the parliament. He gave his first speech in the Erfurt House of the People on 15 April 1850 in which he objected to the term 'German Empire' because

> it runs the gravest risk a political measure can face, that of becoming ridiculous....Gentlemen, if you make no concession to the Prussian, the old Prussian, the core Prussian spirit more than those made in this constitution and if you try to impose this constitution on the Prussian subject you find in him a bucephalus, which carries the rider whom it knows with courageous joy but the unauthorized Sunday rider complete with his black-red-gold embroidery it will dump into the sand (*Loud applause on the right*).[114]

On 19 April, he wrote to Johanna:

> Things are heading to a crisis here. Radowitz and Manteuffel oppose each other. Brandenburg lets himself be wound round by Radowitz...so that at my urgent pleading Manteuffel set out for Berlin to see the King. For which side he opts will be decided in a day or two, and then either Erfurt is dead or Manteuffel is no longer minister. The little man has behaved very well and decisively; he wanted to break openly with Radowitz yesterday but Brandenburg prevented it...it's awful to live in such a small city with 300 acquaintances. One cannot call a moment one's own. An hour ago the last boring person left and I went to supper in the snug and consumed an entire wurst which tasted delicious, drank a pint of Erfurt Fellsenkeller beer and now as I write I have eaten the second box of marzipan, which may have been meant for Hans, who in any case got none of the wurst. In exchange I'll leave him the ham.[115]

At long last the summer holidays freed Bismarck from his seat on the podium in Erfurt and he had time to write to Hermann Wagener in June of 1850:

> I lead a bottomlessly lazy life here, smoking, reading, taking walks and playing family father. I hear about politics only through the *Kreuzzeitung* so I run absolutely no risk of contamination with heterodox ideas. My neighbours are not inclined to visit and this idyllic solitude suits me perfectly. I lie in the grass, read poetry, listen to music and wait for the cherries to ripen...The bureaucracy is eaten up by cancer in its head and members. Only the stomach remains

healthy and the legal shit that it excretes is the most natural thing in the world. With this bureaucracy including the judges on the bench we can have press laws written by angels and they cannot lift us from the swamp. With bad laws and good civil servants (judges) one can still govern, with bad civil servants the best laws cannot help.[116]

To his old college friend Gustav Scharlach he wrote about Radowitz from Schönhausen on 4 July 1850:

Radowitz is a man who in no respect rises above the average save one, an astonishing memory by means of which he . . . affects in bits and pieces a comprehensive knowledge and memorizes good speeches for the gallery and the centre. In addition he has studied the weaker sides of our All-Highest Lord, knows how to impress him with gestures and grand words and to exploit his nobility and his weaknesses of character. In addition as a private person R. is a decent and unobjectionable human being, an excellent father of his family, but as a politician without an idea of his own, he lives from small expedients and fishes for popularity and applause, driven by immense personal vanity . . . [117]

In July Bismarck too had to face the prospect of being 'an excellent father of his family'. He had to go with his wife and small children to the seaside, a prospect that filled him with gloom and took him away from politics. The letters he wrote to his sister about these holidays show Bismarck as a writer of comic genius. Here is one:

The nearer it comes the more I see this as a ticket to the madhouse or to the Upper Chamber of parliament for life. I see myself with children on the platform at Genthin station, then in the compartment where both satisfy their needs ruthlessly and emit an evil stink, the surrounding society holding its nose. Johanna too embarrassed to give the baby the breast so he screams himself blue, the battle with the crowd, the inn, screaming children on Stettin station and in Angermünde 1 hour waiting for horses, packing up, and how do we get from Kröchlendorf to Külz? If we had to spend the night in Stettin, that would be terrible. I went through that last year with Marie and her screaming . . . I am, I feel, somebody to whom a dreadful injustice has been done. Next year I shall have to travel with three cradles, three nurses, nappies for three, bed clothes; I wake at 6 in the morning in a gentle rage and cannot sleep at night because I am haunted by all sorts of travel pictures, which my fantasy paints in the blackest hues, right to the picnics in the dune of Stolpmünde. And if there were only daily payments for this but instead it causes the ruin of a once flourishing fortune by travelling with infants—I am very unhappy.[118]

September meant parliament, Berlin and, at long last, escape from the stresses of family life. The crisis over the Erfurt Union had not yet been resolved. Austria and Prussia headed for a serious clash. On 27 August 1850 Schwarzenberg declared the Union plans incompatible with the Federal Act and called for an emergency meeting of the German Confederation on 2 September 1850, in Frankfurt. Schwarzenberg shrewdly took advantage of the fact that the old German Confederation, the Bund, still existed, because in July of 1848 it had not announced 'the end of its existence' but instead 'the end of its previous activity'.[119] Then a crisis blew up in the Electoral Duchy of Hesse-Cassel where the reactionary duke had turned the clock back to 1847, annulled the gains of the revolution, and restored absolutism. His subjects who had enjoyed freedoms under their new constitution rebelled by going on a tax strike. On 17 September 1850 the Grand Duke, Frederick William II, appealed to the German Confederation under the terms of its foundation for 'federal execution'—that is, military intervention—to help him restore order. The territories of Hesse-Cassel lay between the western Prussian provinces and the main body of the Prussian Kingdom and the idea that Saxon or Hanoverian troops might block Prussia's east-west axis alarmed and outraged senior officers who otherwise wanted nothing to do with the Erfurt Union, its parliament, or any other such institution.

On 1 November 1850 troops of the German Confederation marched into the Electorate of Hesse. The Prussian action to protect its lines of communication put the King into the absurd position of defending 'revolution' against a legitimate sovereign and Tsar Nicholas made such threats that the King dismissed Radowitz on 2 November. The Prussian government drifted toward a war with Austria and the German Confederation to defend a position which nobody accepted any longer but to admit that would be to suffer a complete humiliation. Things went badly in the military preparations for a war which now had no object. As Arden Bucholz writes:

> from 6 November 1850 to 31 January 1851, the Kingdom of Prussia carried out its first war mobilization for thirty-five years. It was a disaster from start to finish... The War Ministry, and below it, the command and staff headquarters were in chaos.[120]

Members of the royal family argued, the cabinet split, and the atmosphere grew more ominous.

The game of bluff ended when the Prussian government gave in. On 29 November 1850 Manteuffel and Schwarzenberg signed a convention, the Punktation of Olmütz, in which Prussia withdrew her troops from the

Electorate of Hesse and abandoned the Union project. The Prussian surrender to Austria ranks with the Battle of Jena as a moment of national
humiliation. Austria and Prussia agreed to restore the German Confederation
jointly but the Austrians ignored the promise.[121] The shame of Olmütz
crushed even the most bitter opponents of the Erfurt scheme. Otto von
Bismarck was not one of them. On 3 December 1850 he made one of the
most important speeches of his entire career. It had a new tone, one for
which he would become famous:

> Why do great states fight wars today? The only sound basis for a large state is
> egoism and not romanticism; this is what necessarily distinguishes a large state
> from a small one. It is not worthy for a large state to fight a war that is not in
> its own interests. Just show me an objective worth a war, gentlemen, and I will
> agree with you... The honour of Prussia does not in my view consist of play-
> ing Don Quixote to every offended parliamentary bigwig in Germany who
> feels his local constitution is in jeopardy.[122]

The speech made a real impact. His conservative friends had 20,000 copies printed and circulated throughout the country. The tone, realistic, une-
motional, and based on material interest, marks the moment when Bismarck,
the practitioner of *Realpolitik*, made his public debut. The Gerlachs could
not complain because his icy realism had saved them from the humiliation
of an outraged public. Lothar Gall adds another consideration. Bismarck's
parliamentary skills would never bring him power in the new neo-absolutist constitutional structure which post-1850 Prussia would become. Thus
the prospect of leading the conservatives in the Landtag as an unpaid parliamentary performer was 'uninteresting'. Real power would remain in the
King's weak hands and palace figures would control it. Gall writes: 'the goal
of the Olmütz speech was, therefore, to recommend himself for a high state
office.'[123] Without qualifications, without experience, and without a reputation for reliability, Bismarck still hoped to find a post in the diplomatic
service which would move him onto a very different scene, one for which,
as it turned out, he had a natural flair.

1851 began and nothing much seemed to be happening. Bismarck's letters to his wife are full of gossip and small matters. In March he wrote about
a fire in the Prussian House of Lords and how much the Berliners enjoyed
it. He quoted their jokes in dialect 'burning questions'—'who would have
thought that the old place had so much fire in it?' 'At last the light has been
turned on!',[124] and a few days later that Hans had come back from Halle but
had not slept at home for five nights.

I got so worried about him, even though he tyrannizes me, that I had him paged in the visitors lounge [at the Landtag—JS] and he came at once. People talk about his making a very profitable marriage but I doubt it. He is in his personality and his inner nature so buttoned up as if we have only known each other for three days. The young lady in question [Gräfin Charlotte zu Stolberg-Wingerode] is shrewd, pretty, charming and devout, in addition a rich heiress and from a good family. I should like to grant her to him if her parents think as I do.[125]

In early April he wrote home on religion:

Yesterday at your bidding I went to see [Pastor] Knaak again. For my taste he draws the strings too tight. He considers not only all dancing, but also all theatre-going and all music, which is not done for 'the honour of God' but just for pleasure sinful and a denial of God, as St Peter said, 'I know not this man'. That goes too far for me, it's zealotry. But I love him personally and do him no injury in spirit…[126]

On 10 April 1851 the Landtag shut for the Easter holidays and Bismarck went home to Schönhausen for the break with no news about a possible new job. On 23 April he returned to Berlin at Hans's request and, as they lay in the dark in their little flat in the Jägerstrasse, Kleist told Bismarck that he had decided to ask for the hand of Countess Charlotte zu Stolberg-Wernigerode, who was about to be a Deaconess. Then he told Bismarck that he had been to Manteuffel to ask about his future. Manteuffel had told him that he was to become *Regierunspräsident* [Provincial Governor] in Cöslin and Bismarck was to go to Frankfurt as Ambassador. As his biographer writes,

He never forgot that hour, and he came to think of himself as a prophet when he decided to follow the custom of the 'awakened' on solemn occasions, as, for example, in the home of Princess Marianne of Prussia, to give somebody a Bible verse to accompany him or her in life. The 149th Psalm was to serve as Bismarck's guide in his future career, especially verses 5 to 9:

> 5 Let the saints be joyful in glory;
> Let them sing aloud on their beds.
> 6 *Let* the high praises of God *be* in their mouth,
> And a two-edged sword in their hand,
> 7 To execute vengeance on the nations,
> And punishments on the peoples;
> 8 To bind their kings with chains,
> And their nobles with fetters of iron;
> 9 To execute on them the written judgment—
> This honor have all His saints.

Later when his friend solved the German question with the two-edged sword, deposed kings and princes, enthroned an Emperor and humiliated an over-mighty nation, Kleist recalled that hour in the quiet student flat in the Jägerstrasse and saw that the words he had given Bismarck had been fulfilled.[127]

Five days later, Bismarck wrote to Johanna with the news that he had seen 'Fradiavolo' (Bismarck's nickname for Minister-President Manteuffel) and Manteuffel had explained that as a consequence of Olmütz, the vacant post of Prussian envoy to the Bund, the German Confederation, in Frankfurt had to be filled. The plan was to send Theodor Heinrich von Rochow (1784–1854), an experienced diplomat in his late 60s, as the first delegate initially with Bismarck there as successor to take over in two months, when von Rochow would move on to the senior position of Prussian Ambassador to the Imperial Russian court. Bismarck's apprenticeship was over. He was now to make his first appearance on the great stage of European diplomacy which he would eventually dominate in his unique way.[128]

5

Bismarck as Diplomat, 1851–1862

Bismarck had been appointed envoy to a very odd institution: the German Confederation. The German Confederal Treaty of June 1815 (revised by the Final Act of 1820) re-created Napoleon's Confédération du Rhin with Austria in the place of France as guiding power. To do that, Metternich had to accept the way Napoleon had transformed Europe and to make a pact with 'revolution'. He had to abandon the Austrian Habsburgs' justified claims on states which had stolen territory under Napoleon and ignore the claims of disposed princes to get their lands back. He did all that and more to secure the Habsburg Monarchy its rightful place as arbiter of Europe.

The German Confederation or *Deutscher Bund*, which the Congress of Vienna designed, was a loose confederation of thirty-nine states. The Federal Assembly in Frankfurt represented the sovereigns, not the people of those states. The Austrian Emperor and the Prussian King had one vote in the Federal Assembly. Three member states were ruled by foreign monarchs: the Kings of Denmark, the Netherlands, and Great Britain (until 1837 when Queen Victoria could not as a woman succeed to the throne of Hanover). All three foreign kings were members of the German Confederation; each of them had a vote in the Federal Assembly. Six other kings or grand dukes had one vote each in the Federal Assembly: the kings of Bavaria, Saxony, Württemberg, the Prince-Elector of Hesse-Kassel, the Grand Duke of Baden, and the Grand Duke of Hesse. Twenty-three smaller and tiny member states shared five votes in the Federal Assembly. The four free cities Lübeck, Frankfurt, Bremen, and Hamburg shared one vote in the Federal Assembly.

The new German Confederation enshrined in the Final Act of 1820 put the capstone of the Metternichian system into place by 'solving' the German problem.

Article 1 of the Treaty declared that the

deutscher Bund [the German Confederation] is an international association of German sovereign princes and free cities to preserve the independence and inviolability of the member states and to preserve the inner and outer security of Germany.[1]

Article 5 declared that the Bund was permanent and no state was 'free' to leave it—as we shall see, an important provision for Bismarck in 1866. Articles 6 and Article 11 established a general assembly of the Bund as the decision-making body but in addition created a 'narrower' Council where decisions would be taken by absolute majority vote. Article 20 allowed the General Assembly to take action on behalf of member states which had been subject to improper violence or force by another member or members. A large number of the articles concerned the danger of revolution and the means for intervention to suppress it. There was a Federal Court to decide cases of conflict among member states. Article 58 forbade the sovereign prince of each state to allow any existing landständische Verfassung (constitution based on the 'estates of the realm') to overrule his obligations to the Bund.

The structure and arrangement of the Final Act of 1820 have the charm and clarity of the Lisbon Treaty of the European Union of 2007. Nobody but experts ever really cared to understand it, just as today very few outside Brussels can explain how the EU works. In 1858 the Deutsches Staats-Wörtebuch, the leading German legal dictionary, could not define the relationship between the 'narrower Council' and the General Assembly or Plenum: 'The narrower Council is not a senate, there are no chambers or houses... There is only one organ of the Bund, the Bundesversammlung [Federal Assembly]'.[2] The editors could not define precisely what 'the narrower Council' was supposed to do and simply gave up. The Deutscher Bund differed in several fundamental respects from its descendent, the European Union. In the Bund nobody pretended that it represented the 'people'; the EU claims exactly that though with what justice arouses fierce debate. In the second place, the two leading German powers, Austria and Prussia, had retained much greater independence than the European states have today. Not all their territories belonged to the Bund. Their armies remained under the command of their Emperor and King and their domestic tax and spending policies, their internal legislation, and religious establishments had nothing to do with the Bund.

The main difficulty which faced Bismarck on his appointment as Prussian ambassador to the Bund in 1851 lay in the inequality of the two great Powers. The Bund had been revived after the revolutions of 1848 and 1849 because it suited Austria, as it had in 1815, to control Germany in a loose federal scheme. The small states had less to fear from a rambling, decentralized, and multinational empire under the Habsburgs than they had from much more tightly governed and much more single-minded Kingdom of Prussia. The appointment—in spite of the oddity of the institution to which he had been accredited—placed Bismarck in the perfect arena: the place where the two great German powers confronted each other face to face.

In the immediate future the new job made a huge difference to Otto and Johanna von Bismarck. On 3 May he wrote his wife a letter which contains the amazing statement that he had not done a thing to get the promotion:

> Weigh the anchor of your soul and prepare yourself to leave the home port. I know from my own feelings how painful the thought must be to you to leave, how sad your parents are. But I repeat I have not with a syllable wished or sought this appointment. What ever happens, I am God's soldier and where he sends me I must go.[3]

Why did he lie to his wife so blatantly? All the evidence shows that he had been intriguing and scheming to get a proper diplomatic job for months. His efforts had been crowned with more success than he dared to hope, as he admitted in the slightly more honest, excited letter he wrote when he heard the news. He had ended up with the perfect job for him and his talents. Why not rejoice with her on his success? One answer is that he had always lied in personal matters, to his mother and to his father. It had become habitual to avoid the truth in his personal affairs and, as we have seen, he resorted to lies to cover his mistakes. He had to pretend that God had worked in mysterious ways to get her to accept the new life. If God had called, that would be something that Johanna as an evangelical would not be able to contradict or question.

In the second place, the appointment to Frankfurt must have brought home to him with dismay that he had a problem with his wife. She was not beautiful, spoke no languages, had no dress sense, and no experience of the grand world of courts. She would never be a society lady capable of moving gracefully across the grand stage of European high society and Johanna would not make an effort to become one. An old friend from the Pietist circle, Hedwig von Blanckenburg, wrote to Johanna a few days later and warned her about her attitude:

> One thing really pains me, that is that you still see everything the way you did five years ago and *that* I can hardly understand... Everything that belongs to those days lives on in me, but I now have other things to do, more serious things, but do not lack the inner glow. Johanna, dear Johanna! We cannot stay children, who play and fool about, we must become serious people in the service of the Lord.[4]

Bismarck certainly begged her to make that effort. Shortly after he arrived in Frankfurt on 14 May 1851, he wrote:

> It now looks certain that I shall take over Rochow's post here this summer. Then I shall have, if the amount remains constant, 21,000 Reichsthaler salary, but must maintain a considerable staff and household, and you, my poor child, must sit stiffly and nobly in a salon, be called Excellency and be wise and clever with Excellencies... One request I do have but please keep it to yourself and please do not let Mother hear it or she will make a fuss worrying about it, occupy yourself with your French as much as you can in the time but do it as if it occurred to you on your own. Read as much French as you can but not by candle light and not if your eyes hurt... I did not marry you in order to have a society wife for others, but in order to love you in God and according to the requirements of my own heart, to have a place in this alien world that no barren wind can cool, a place warmed by my own fireplace, to which I can draw near while it storms and freezes outside. And I want to tend my own fire and lay on wood, blow the flames, and protect it and shelter it against all that is evil and foreign.[5]

It is a beautiful peace of prose but it conceals the problem. He may not have married Johanna 'in order to have a society wife for others' but he needed her to become one now, and that she absolutely refused to concede. She never did learn French and never provided him with the glamour he needed professionally. As she grew older, she did it less and less. By the time Bismarck had been in the diplomatic service for a decade, she had become what Holstein as a young attaché in St Petersburg described as 'a peculiar person'. Nobody can know the secrets of a marriage but we can see with great clarity that he simply gave up after a certain point. The Bismarcks dined unfashionably at 5.00 in the late afternoon, a custom which everybody in Frankfurt and Berlin thought odd. The Prussian Embassy in Frankfurt and later the official residence at 76 Wilhelmstrasse in Berlin looked as if a rural squire and his 'churchy' wife had settled into the Chancellor's palace. My hunch is that Johanna refused to make an effort to become what Bismarck needed because of resentment. He proposed to her 'on the rebound' from Marie von Thadden and her refusal to make herself attractive was a form of mute protest. For his part, marriage had clearly not satisfied his physical needs, as he wrote in distress to Hans von Kleist from his solitary, bachelor life in Frankfurt during June 1851:

> The chief weapon with which evil assaults me is not desire for external glory, but a brutal sensuality which leads me so close to the greatest sins that I doubt at times that I will gain access to God's mercy. At any rate I am certain that the seed of God's word has not found fertile ground in a heart laid waste as it was from youth. Otherwise I could not be so much the plaything of temptation, which even invades my moments of prayer...Comfort me, Hans, but burn this without speaking of it to anyone.[6]

Four years after his marriage, he confessed to his closest friend a 'brutal sensuality' and his temptation to commit 'the greatest sins'. Whatever Bismarck did in secret, we simply do not know but the letter suggests that his marriage had not removed those urges.

On the other hand, Hans had got engaged to his Protestant nun, Countess Marie von Stolberg-Wenigerode, as Bismarck wrote:

> Hans is unbearably happy, won't go to bed and behaves like a kid. It is still supposed to be confidential but Hans cannot keep it to himself. He wants to carve it in every pavement and tells everybody, friend and foe, in the blissful certainty that all conflict in the world will now cease and everybody will be happy. He has a completely different face, dances and sings the strangest songs when he is alone in his room. In short the old sour puss is no longer recognizable and, if he in his joy would let me sleep at night, that would be nice.[7]

On 8 May the King received Bismarck and promoted him to *Geheimer Legationsrat* (Privy Legation Councillor); as Bismarck remarked it was 'an irony with which God punishes me for my blasphemy against all Privy Councillors'.[8] Ludwig von Gerlach was not enthusiastic about Bismarck's sudden promotion to the top of the diplomatic service and doubted the wisdom of 'violent promotions'. After all, Bismarck's official career amounts up to now to that of a failed *Referendar*.[9] The new post transformed his economic situation: 21,000 Reichstaler amounted to over £3,134 at the 1871 conversion rate. This was a very handsome stipend even by English standards.

In *Barchester Towers*, published in 1857 by Anthony Trollope, Bismarck's exact contemporary, Wilfred Thorne, Esq. the Squire of St Ewold's, had an income of £4,000, which allowed him to be a sportsman with the horses, grooms, and hounds that such pursuits required.[10] And, of course, England was much more expensive than Germany. In comparison to his fellow Prussians, Bismarck had shot up the income table. The Prussian income tax distribution lists taxpayers by tax category and shows the percentage of the population paying each amount. Fortunately there are figures for 1851, which show that Bismarck had now joined the very top of the income pyramid. Prussian incomes as well as income taxes were very low at that time so he had for the first time in his life a handsome annual salary:

Over 1,000 thaler	0.5% of population
400–1,000	3.25%
200–400	7.25%
100–200	16.75%
Under 100	72.25%[11]

On 10 May 1851 Bismarck left Berlin for Frankfurt by train, a trip which he accomplished in the amazingly quick time of twenty-five hours.[12] A week on the job, Bismarck had begun to complain about it and the other envoys:

> Frankfurt is horribly boring... In essence nothing but spying on each other as if we had something worth finding out and worth revealing. Life here is almost entirely pure trivialities with which people torture themselves. I am making astonishing progress in the art of using lots of words to say nothing. I fill pages with nice round script which reads like leading articles in the papers and, if Manteuffel, after he has read them, can say what's in them, then he knows a lot more than I do.[13]

In early June, he wrote to Herman Wagener, editor of the *Kreuzzeitung*, to say that letters were systematically opened by the Austrians and to ask him to send correspondence to Hochstrasse 45, Frankfurt am Main, but addressed to 'Mr Wilhelm Hildebrand', Bismarck's man-servant. Frankfurt diplomacy was ridiculous:

> The Austrians are constantly engaged in intrigue behind a mask of jolly bonhomie... and are always trying with smallish matters of form to cheat us, which so far has been our entire occupation. The envoys from the little states are caricatures of old-fashioned, be-wigged diplomats who immediately put

on their 'report-face' if you ask for a light for your cigar and look as if they are about to make a speech before the old Imperial Aulic Court if you ask for the key to the t——.[14]

The chief Austrian intriguer was a grand aristocrat, Friedrich Franz Count von Thun und Hohenstein (1810–81), a member of one of the oldest dynasties in the Habsburg monarchy. He had heard about the new Prussian envoy and wrote to Vienna about his first impressions:

> In all fundamental issues, which concern the conservative principle, Herr von Bismarck is perfectly correct and will cause damage more by his overly great zeal than by hesitation or indecision. On the other hand, he seems to me, as far as I can judge, to belong exclusively to that party which has its eye only on Prussian interests and places no great confidence in what the Bundestag can accomplish in that cause.[15]

Bismarck sent his impressions of Thun in a private letter to General Leopold von Gerlach:

> He is a mixture of rough-hewn bluntness, which can easily pass for honest openness, aristocratic *nonchalance* and slavic peasant cunning. He always has 'no instructions' and on account of ignorance of the business he seems to be dependent on his staff and entourage...Insincerity is the most striking feature of his character in his relationship to us...There isn't a single man among the diplomats of any intellectual significance. Most of them are self-important pedants filled with little business, who take their letters patent and certificate of plenipotentiary power to bed with them and with whom one cannot have a conversation.[16]

Though he might complain about his colleagues, in fact, Bismarck liked the job and nervously awaited official confirmation of his permanent appointment. It finally came in mid-August 1851. He had received the formal appointment but the ministry had without explanation cut 3,000 Reichsthaler from his salary and had provided no money for setting up his residence. He admitted that 18,000 Reichsthaler would be fine to live 'well and elegantly' but he would need to find a place for the family. He absolutely had to have a garden and a house with large rooms. In early September he found a fine house, 1,200 feet from the city gate, which had a large garden, and cost 4,500 Reichsthaler, which for Frankfurt was cheap. His letter to Johanna on 9 September concluded with the grumble: 'It annoys me that his Excellency the Royal Bavarian Envoy keeps looking over my shoulder as I write.'[17] He would not have had the annoyance, had he not ostentatiously and regularly done his private correspondence during boring speeches in the chamber. And he really did work hard. In a tone of amazement, he told Bernhard in a letter of his present routine:

> From 7 in the morning to dinner about 5 I seldom have an independent minute... Who would have believed it six months ago that I could afford 5000 thaler rent and employ a French chef in order to give dinners on the King's birthday. I can get used to anything but Johanna will find it hard to get accustomed to the pointed and cold contacts in this sort of world.[18]

Bismarck used the time in Frankfurt for other purposes. He continued to travel to Berlin to take his seat in the Prussian Lower House of Parliament. His ruthless and relentless ambition came out in a constant stream of private letters to General Leopold von Gerlach on domestic Prussian matters which he hoped the General would discuss during his daily chat over coffee and cake with the King. The private talk between the King and his General Adjutant made Leopold von Gerlach the most powerful subject in the kingdom. Bismarck's actual superior as Prime Minister and Minister of Foreign Affairs was Otto Theodor Freiherr von Manteuffel (1805–82), a dry, reactionary but highly competent civil servant. Manteuffel had inherited his job when General Count Brandenburg suddenly died on 6 November 1850, in the midst of the crisis with Austria. He had courageously carried the government through the 'shame of Olmütz' and had been shrewd enough to accept the camarilla's pressure to appoint Bismarck as ambassador to the newly reconstituted Bund. During his years in an ambassadorial capacity, Bismarck corresponded regularly around and behind the back of the Minister, his formal chief. Active disloyalty to Manteuffel seems not to have deterred him. By 1853 this double game had become a system as a letter of 25 February 1853 to Leopold von Gerlach makes clear. Manteuffel had requested that Bismarck submit two formal ambassadorial reports monthly on the first and fifteenth of every month. Manteuffel had not made his name as a financial expert for nothing. Bismarck offered to send his dispatches—but *first* to von Gerlach:

> I will send you these as originals with a plea to send them right back via Cologne and commend this indiscretion of mine to your most careful precautions since any discovery of this would have a disturbing effect on my relationship to Manteuffel. That would be not only officially but personally disagreeable since I have a sincere affection for his person and would be ashamed if he were to think that I played him false, even if it were, as here, without foundation.[19]

The sheer effrontery of Bismarck in claiming that he had not played false with Manteuffel when he so obviously had, seems not to have upset the recipient. That the very pious, very Christian, very 'born again' General Leopold von Gerlach accepted the offer shows that camarilla needs trumped Christian morality. Gerlach overlooked a contemptible betrayal by Bismarck of his duty as diplomat toward his chief and an act of gross disloyalty personally to Otto von Manteuffel, who had helped to arrange his appointment. Gerlach's connivance in duping the Minister-President suggests that life in the camarilla had corrupted his ethical sensibilities.

Early in 1852, Bismarck wrote to Leopold von Gerlach and described himself as, 'your diplomatic adopted child'.[20] Johannes Willms compares this and the dozens and dozens of letters which Bismarck addressed to his 'dear Patron and Friend' to 'finger exercises, thought games, which offer fascinating insights into the way his political understanding and knowledge of the European constellations of power grew by leaps and bounds'.[21] Many have the quality of sketches but I see them as much more the pupil showing the master how brilliantly he can describe realities, people, places, conflicts. He also makes certain week by week that his ideas, his energy, and his imagination would flow through the 'dear Patron and Friend' to the King.

Two threats to Bismarck's future emerged early in his Frankfurt years. A group of enemies of Manteuffel and Gerlach had formed in and outside the diplomatic service. In his memoirs, Bismarck describes them and their motives quite accurately:

> The party, or more correctly, coterie, subsequently named after Bethmann-Hollweg, found its original mainstay in Count Robert von der Goltz, a man of unusual competence and energy...[22]

Robert von der Goltz always regarded himself as the natural choice as foreign minister and loathed Bismarck. Holstein records in his *Memoirs* a delightful moment in their rivalry:

> Bismarck was fond of relating how Goltz visited him in Frankfurt one day while he was still a free agent, just to inveigh against everybody and everything. As he left, Goltz had to cross the courtyard, where an extremely fierce watch-dog barked furiously at him. Bismarck, still under the influence of their conversation, called down from a window, 'Goltz, don't bite my dog'...[23]

The second threat arose directly from Bismarck's personality. In March 1852 he got involved in a duel. The story is bizarre. Early on in Bismarck's appointment to the Bund, Count Thun as President had pulled out a cigar and lit it during a session of the narrower Council. Only the President of the Federal Council, the Austrian envoy, had by custom the right to smoke in meetings. Bismarck in order to show the equal status of Prussia immediately lit up a cigar as well. He had told the story to Georg Freiherr von Vincke (1811–75), a deputy from Hagen in Westphalia in the Prussian lower house. Vincke, a fiery character, was widely regarded as the 'greatest Prussian parliamentary orator' of his generation and like Bismarck had been 'a dashing swordsman' as a student.[24] Vincke loved to goad Bismarck. As Hermann von Petersdorff described him, 'on his full, fleshy and sly face, surrounded by a bright red beard, there played a mocking smile. Self-confidence and ease of manner radiated from his body . . . Battle was his life's element.'[25] Bismarck explained the story to his mother-in-law. In a debate in the Prussian Lower House,

> He [Vincke] accused me of lacking diplomatic discretion and said that so far my only achievement had been the 'burning cigar'. He referred to an incident in the Bund Palace which I had recounted to him in private 'under four eyes' as something trivial but rather funny. I replied to him from the podium that his remark exceeded not only the boundaries of diplomatic discretion but even the normal discretion that one had a right to expect from every properly educated man. The next day through his second, Herr von Saucken-Julienfelde he sent me a challenge to a duel of four bullets. I accepted after Oscar's proposal to use sabres had been rejected. Vincke asked for a 48 hour postponement which I agreed to. At 8 on the morning of the 25th [of March] we drove out to Tegel to a lovely spot on the lakeside. The weather was so beautiful and the birds sang so merrily that all sad thoughts disappeared as soon as I got there. I had forcibly to avoid thoughts of Johanna for fear of weakening. With me I had brought Arnim and Eberhard Stolberg and my brother, who looked very depressed, as witnesses . . . Bodelschwingh (a cousin of the minister's and Vincke's) served as neutral witness. He suggested that the challenge had been set too high and proposed that the duel be reduced to a shot each. Saucken speaking in Vincke's name accepted that and further announced that they would be prepared to withdraw the challenge if I apologized for my remarks. Since I could not in good conscience do that, we both took our pistols, shot on the command of Bodelschwingh and both missed . . . Bodelschwingh shed tears . . . the reduction of the challenge annoyed me and I would have preferred to continue the fight. Since I was not the person insulted, I could say nothing. That was it; everybody shook hands.[26]

The life of Otto von Bismarck might have come to an end on 25 March 1852, if Carl von Bodelschwingh had not lowered the stakes or Bismarck might have killed Vincke, which would have almost certainly damaged his career. Nothing happened. Bismarck survived, but it was a close thing.

Bismarck continued to enjoy his position and in letters to his patron, Leopold von Gerlach, he admitted as much. In August 1852 Bismarck began a letter by writing, 'I live here like God in Frankfurt'. Bismarck played with the original aphorism 'to live like God in France', a common German aphorism which means 'I love it here', by substituting *Frank-furt* for *Frank-reich*.[27] (The editors of the *Collected Works of Bismarck*, with perfect German humourlessness, write: '*so in the original—possibly a misprint*'.)

> and this mixture of powdered wigs, railroads, country squire from Bockenheim [Bismarck lived at 40 Bockenheimer Allee—JS], diplomatic Republicanism, cameralist Federal Diet squabbling, suits me so well that in the whole world I would only change it for that post occupied by my All-Highest Lord if the entire Royal Family were to put me under unbearable pressure to accept.[28]

In a letter to his sister, he mocked it by quoting the little verse by Heine: 'O Bund, Du Hund, du bist nicht Gesund' (O Bund! you hound, you are not sound) and predicted that 'the little verse will soon become by unanimous vote the German national anthem.'[29] While he made fun of the Bund, he also observed carefully the behaviour of the small states and concluded that Prussia would always be a greater threat to them than Austria and hence the little states would gather round the Habsburgs for security. A weak protector would be less inclined to gobble them up than a strong one, an assumption entirely justified by Bismarck's later actions.

On 2 December 1851 Louis Napoleon Bonaparte, the elected president of the Second French Republic, carried out a well-planned and bloodless *coup d'état* against the constitution of the Second Republic. The *coup d'état* changed the entire diplomatic situation in Europe. Without it Bismarck could never have unified Germany. Louis Napoleon was as much a prisoner of memory as the conservatives in Prussia. He had to re-create the empire of his uncle in order to fulfil the myth behind his election, in other words, as Article 1 of the new constitution asserted: 'La Constitution reconnaît, confirme et garantit les grands principes proclamés en 1789, et qui sont la base du droit public des Français.' So the great principles of the revolution— 'Liberty, Equality and Fraternity'—had to be asserted but denied at the same time. Above all, he needed the Imperial crown and on 7 November 1852 the Senate re-established the title of Emperor. The dictator became

Napoléon III, and ceased to be called Louis-Napoléon. The next step for the Emperor Napoleon III would follow as surely as night follows day. He had to adopt a Napoleonic posture in foreign affairs and overturn the balance, which Austria had only just restored.

With the emergence of Louis Napoleon Bonaparte, Bismarck's subsequent career became possible. No other conceivable French ruler could have played so perfectly into Bismarck's hands as Napoleon III. No other great state had a reason to destroy Austrian power in Europe, exactly the goal that Bismarck had come to Frankfurt to pursue. Bismarck's reaction shows his unconventional and acute sense of political possibilities: he advocated an accommodation with the new Bonaparte to discomfit Austria and the small German princes. As early as January 1853 Bismarck wrote this to Leopold von Gerlach:

> I am convinced that it would be a great misfortune for Prussia if her government should enter into an alliance with France, but, even if we make no use of it, we ought never to remove from the consideration of our allies the possibility that under certain conditions we might choose this evil as the lesser of the two.[30]

This argument had nothing to do with principle but with realities of power or the appearance of such realities. If Prussia gave the impression to the smaller German states that a deal between Berlin and Paris over their heads might be possible, they would suddenly and in an undignified rush head for Berlin to get assurances that nothing of theirs might have been promised to the French emperor. They would be good little German states and obey Prussia's wishes. In fact, in the period from 1862 to 1870 that is precisely what Bismarck threatened to do and it had the anticipated pleasing effects. A potential alliance with Imperial France would alarm Austria and strengthen Prussia's hand in the game. For Prussia, the enemy could only be Austria, as he wrote to Leopold von Gerlach in late 1853:

> Our politics have no other exercise room than Germany, not least because of the way we have grown and intertwined with it and Austria hopes desperately to use this fact for itself. There is no room for us both as long as Austria makes its claims. In the long run we cannot coexist with each other. We breathe the air out of each others' mouths; one must yield or must be 'yielded' to the other. Until then we must be enemies. I regard that as an 'un-ignorable' fact (if you will pardon the word), however unwelcome it might be.[31]

Courtesy required him to go to Vienna early in his tenure of office. He was presented to the Emperor and he met the new rulers of Austria, who took over after the sudden death of Prince Schwarzenberg on 5 April 1852. In his report to Prime Minister von Manteuffel he commented about the Jews who ran the country and who were, as always for Bismarck and most Junkers, a persistent nuisance:

> People indicated to me that the bearers of the hostile attitude to us, especially in trade matters, was the 'Jew Clique' which the late Prime Minister had elevated to power (Bach, Hock and Jewish newspaper writers, although Bach is not Jewish).[32]

A new Austrian president of the Bundestag had arrived, the formidable scholar-soldier, orientalist, and travel writer, Anton Prokesch Count von Osten (1795–1876). His history of the Greek Revolt of 1821, his travel books, and multi-volume memoirs of his period in the Turkish Empire had made him famous throughout German-speaking Europe.[33] Bismarck loathed him: 'His military appearance, which he affects, is striking. He never appears other than buttoned up in uniform and even in meetings he never removes his sabre.'[34] Metternich who had promoted him wrote of him: 'I adore him, I love Prokesch but if you make him Sultan of Turkey, he would not be satisfied. He is eccentric and vain.'[35] In his reply on 28 January 1853, Leopold von Gerlach expressed a less unfavourable view of Prokesch than Bismarck and insisted in opposition to Bismarck's argument that 'Bonaparte and Bonapartism is our worst enemy.'[36] Nor could he accept that Austria must be the enemy. In a diary entry of 27 July 1853, he wrote:

> I have told Ludwig and others a thousand times the true nature of the Union is that Prussia has a singularly odd relationship to Germany and with it a claim to domination, independent of Austria…Just as important is the union of Prussia with Germany and in this union it must unite first with Austria.[37]

This attitude to Austria did not please Bismarck but he would, in fact, do exactly that in the mid-1860s—ally with Austria against the German princes and then isolate Austria in order to cause a war.

The emergence of a conflict in the Balkans suddenly changed the prospects of the ambitious young diplomat in Frankfurt. In 1853 the conservative alliance of Russia, Prussia, and Austria began to come apart, as Russia and France clashed over the right to act as protectors of the holy sites in Palestine. In May–June 1853 Turkey rejected the Russian claim to be protector of all Christians in the Turkish Empire. On 31 May 1853 a Russian army crossed the Pruth river and occupied the two Danubian principalities of

Moldavia and Wallachia. War broke out between Russia and Turkey in October 1853. This put the Habsburg Monarchy into a difficult dilemma. The presence of Russian troops on the lower Danube threatened the Monarchy, often called the Danubian monarchy, after the river that served it as central artery. Something had to be done to halt Russian advances. On the other hand, conservative politics had united the two courts from 1815 and Russian intervention to help the Habsburgs suppress the Hungarian Revolution of 1848–9 had created a debt that the Russians regarded as self-evident.

On 12 April 1852 Karl-Ferdinand von Buol-Schauenstein became Foreign Minister in place of Prince Schwarzenberg, whose death had removed the one leader of real stature in the post-Metternichian era. Boul was not that. The weakness of Russia tempted Buol to use the occasion to establish Austrian hegemony over the Balkans. The court circles and the Emperor had doubts and so Austrian policy managed to antagonize all parties without any substantial gain.

Bismarck immediately began to urge Manteuffel to use Austrian weakness to expand Prussian power. 'The great crises provide the weather for Prussia's growth,'[38] he wrote, and later in 1854 he urged King Frederick William IV to mobilize 200,000 troops in Upper Silesia where they could be used either against Austria or Russia.

> With 200,000 men your majesty would at this moment become the master of the entire European situation, would be able to dictate the peace and win for Prussia a worthy position in Germany.

The King reacted with surprise: 'A man of Napoleon's sort can commit such acts of violence, I cannot.'[39] Like Buol, the King found himself torn between his close family ties to the Tsar's court (Nicholas I had married Frederick's sister Charlotte), his loyalty to Austria, his emotional commitment to the conservative principles of the old Holy Alliance of 1815, and his own inability to act with decisiveness.

The situation worsened as the Russo-Turkish War dragged on. Britain and France, together with Cavour's Piedmont, formed an alliance of the Western states and Turkey against the Russian empire. Austria now looked to the Bund for support and Prussian-Austrian tension moved beyond clashes over cigars in the conference chamber to issues of war, and peace. On 22 March 1854 Prokesch-Osten, Austrian Ambassador to the Bund, wrote to Buol, the Austrian Foreign Secretary:

I have never expected an honest game from the Prussian side and often ask myself whether we could not put together a coalition, and, when we have it, use it with help of the sea powers to reduce Prussia to a harmless size. We shall never get rid of this rival as long as it has its strength, and still less when it grows. Kaunitz's policies aimed at the insolence of Frederick II, and the Prussia of today is nothing other than Frederick's old state.[40]

Hardly. The Prussia of 1854 had at its head a King who could not make up his mind. As the Tsar wrote contemptuously of him: 'My dear Brother-in-Law goes to bed as a Russian and wakes up as an Englishman.'[41] Bismarck was determined to use the crisis to strengthen Prussia's international standing and that meant refusing to be drawn into an alliance with Austria. He also had to watch the manoeuvres of the smaller German states; as he wrote to Gerlach in April, the smaller German states

want to secure their further existence by joining the stronger powers. In the last few years they went along with Prussia-Austria-Russia as long as they were united, with Austria-Russia as soon as their policies separated from the Prussian.[42]

On 28 March 1854 France and Great Britain declared war on the Russian Empire and joined Turkey in its battle by sending naval units and ground troops to the eastern Mediterranean. On 5 April British troops arrived at Gallipoli. Against this background, on 20 April 1854, Prussia and Austria signed an offensive-defensive alliance, which gave Austria the backing to demand on 3 June 1854 that Russia evacuate the Danubian Principalities. A few days later, on 7 June, the Emperor Franz Josef and King Frederick William IV met in Teschen to coordinate policy. On 24 June 1854 the small and middle-sized German states acceded to the Austro-Prussian alliance. Bismarck opposed all of this, as he wrote to his brother on 10 May 1854:

That at the sound of the first shot against the Russians we shall turn ourselves into the whipping boy for the Western Powers and let them dictate to us the terms of peace while we carry the main burden of war is as clear as a school arithmetic exercise.[43]

A series of defeats shook Russian self-confidence and on 28 July the Russians withdrew behind the line of the Pruth River. The Western Powers had now assembled an amphibious operation and planned to land on the Black Sea coast. Bismarck breathed a sigh of relief, as he observed in a letter of 10 July to his brother:

In grand politics, peace perspectives have begun to pop up. One seems to have calmed down in Vienna, or, rather, one no longer behaves with that impatience they believe they need to impress us.[44]

On 8 August France, Britain, and Austria agreed to present the Russians with four points as the basis for peace negotiations. Russia was asked:

(1) to abandon the protectorate over the Danubian Principalities;

(2) to recognize the freedom of all shipping on the Danube;

(3) to accept a revision of the Treaty of 13 July 1841;

(4) to abandon the protectorate over subjects of the Supreme Porte.[45]

On 2 December a Triple Alliance of France, Britain, and Austria was signed and the three Powers invited Prussia to join them. Bismarck wrote to Gerlach at once:

The text of the Treaty of 2 December arrived the day before yesterday... I would absolutely not join the coalition, because everybody will see that we did it out of fear and conclude that the more they frighten us, the more they get from us. Decorum alone forbids it in my view... The moral is that in all German cabinets from the tiniest to the greatest, fear is the only thing that determines decisions; each is afraid of the other, all are afraid of France...[46]

By the end of the month, Bismarck heard good news from Berlin, as he wrote to Leopold von Gerlach,

Three days ago I got a letter from Manteuffel which made me very happy. He too thinks that we should not join the 2 December... As long as we show relaxed self-confidence, the others will have respect for us. As soon as we betray fear, they will use this ignoble weakness and try to increase and exploit it... In order to fill the Federal states with sufficient fear, as they have of Austria, we have to show ourselves capable, if others make us desperate, to join with France and even Liberalism. As long as we behave well, nobody takes us seriously and then all go where the threat is greater...[47]

Here for the first time Bismarck shows an aspect of his technique: create fear and uncertainty in a crisis, so that opponents cannot be certain how Prussia will act, and be absolutely unscrupulous in the choice of means. Prussia can ally with any force or state if it needs to do so. These techniques, instrumental and unprincipled as they are, marked his diplomatic approach from the Crimean War to the moment he fell from power.

Early in the new year the Austrian Foreign Minister Buol wrote to Count Leo Thun:

> If it comes to a war, I prefer that Prussia does not stay on our side. A war with Prussia against Russia is a great embarrassment for us. If Prussia sides with Russia, so we wage war with France against Prussia. Then we take Silesia. Saxony will be restored and we have peace at last in Germany. For that price France can gladly take the Rhineland.[48]

On 10 January 1855 Bismarck was summoned to Berlin for consultations where he stayed until 18 January. Relations at Frankfurt between Bismarck and Prokesch had entirely broken down. On 20 February 1855 Herr von Buol-Schauenstein wrote to Manteuffel to inform the Prussian government of the forthcoming recall of Prokesch and to announce his replacement, Johann Bernhard Graf von Rechberg und Rothenlöwen. Buol took the occasion to ask whether in view of Herr von Bismarck's 'remarks that have become notorious and especially in conversation with non-German envoys [which] show implacable enmity against Austria' it might not be 'feasible' to substitute Herr von Bismarck, a request which Manteuffel rejected 'decisively'.[49] Bismarck remarked in a letter to his brother that he would like Prokesch to stay, because 'such a clumsy opponent I shall never get again.'[50] In this crisis about an Austrian alliance, Bismarck had his first real diplomatic triumph. The excitement among the small states was growing, he wrote:

> More or less all of them want to mobilize, with Austria against Russia, we are to protect Germany's frontiers. That the French will march through our territory, everybody here takes for granted.[51]

Complex negotiations followed about military mobilization. The intricacies of the rules, the status of votes in the Military Committee as opposed to the Plenum or Narrower Council, seem to have been as incomprehensible to outsiders in 1855 as the proceedings of EU Council of Ministers or the Commission are today. On 30 January 1855 the Bund rejected Prokesch's motion to mobilize and the Austrians withdrew it. Bismarck's countermotion used the word 'neutrality' and, in reply to a further Austrian request of the Bund to mobilize, Bismarck agreed but added the clause that mobilization must be a deployment 'in every direction' (that is, mobilization against France), which removed the anti-Russian thrust and comprehensively outmanoeuvred the Austrians. Bismarck had used the fear of the small

German states that they might find a French invading force marching over their borders, to make neutrality universal, that is, against all possible belligerents, which, of course, included Austria and Britain. Engelberg concludes that 'the Prussian Envoy had delivered his diplomatic master's thesis; his apprenticeship and journeyman period had come to an end.'[52] Prokesch wrote bitterly to Buol:

> Austria today seems to have been put under a ban by the Bund, and there are loud boasts that they have tamed it under Prussia's lead and they must force it to negotiate. 'Armed neutrality' as a rule against France and Austria is now praised as the *ni plus ultra* of diplomatic wisdom, and that we helped to bind us ourselves that way is the stuff of laughter.[53]

Years later, Bismarck told his personal assistant Christoph Tiedemann that he had outsmarted his Austrian counterpart in 1865 by doing exactly the opposite. He challenged Count Blome, the Austrian envoy at Gastein in 1865, to a game of cards and played so wildly and recklessly that Blome assumed that he had the same attitude to his diplomacy.[54] Sir Robert Morier, for many years the British ambassador to several German courts, wrote perceptively of Bismarck's divided self. In a letter to Odo Russell, British ambassador to Prussia, he summed Bismarck up in these words:

> Do not forget that Bismarck is made up of two individuals, a colossal chess player full of the most daring combinations and with the quickest eye for the right combination at the right moment and who will sacrifice everything even his *personal hatred* to the success of his game—and an individual with the strangest and still stronger antipathies who will sacrifice everything *except his combinations*.[55]

And these 'combinations' had worked at Frankfurt. Now Bismarck urged Leopold von Gerlach to stiffen the spines of decision-makers in Berlin:

> For the matter seems to me so obvious and straightforward that the French must know we shall react to troops with troops. That's the only way to avoid complications with France.[56]

The Crimean War ground to its inglorious end and Napoleon III called for a Peace Conference in Paris in 1856, which opened on 24 February. A new young Tsar Alexander II had come to the throne and realized that the Russian defeats represented systemic rather than individual failure. The Tsarist regime needed reform, modernization, and the inclusion of the growing educated middle class. In a way, the defeat in the Crimean War had the same effect on Russia in 1856 that the battle of Jena had on Prussia exactly fifty years before. The Tsar had to infuse the system with patriotism and 'intelligence' without undermining autocracy. The serfs had to be emancipated. Village and county schools had to be introduced, towns had to have municipal governments. The scale and risks of the reform programme confirmed the truth of de Tocqueville's wise remark that 'the most dangerous moment for a bad government is when it decides to reform.'[57] It also meant that Russia, defeated and preoccupied with its internal institutions, would withdraw from great power politics for the foreseeable future. Without Russia's defeat in the Crimea, Bismarck could never have fought his three wars of unification. The rule of central European power had been constant since 1700 (and in a way still is): *when Russia is up Germany is down; when Germany is up, Russia is down.* Equally important, Prussia had stayed neutral and managed to maintain its cordial ties to Moscow. The Austrians had 'betrayed' Russia and could expect nothing from its former ally. When the time came, Bismarck knew exactly how to exploit Russian resentment to destroy Austrian authority in Germany.

Another international event affected Bismarck equally powerfully but less happily. On 29 September 1855 Queen Victoria wrote in her *Leaves from our Journal in the Highlands*, 'Our dear Victoria was this day engaged to Prince Frederick William of Prussia, who had been on a visit to us since the 14th.'[58] In March 1856 the famous radical British politician, Richard Cobden, wrote to a friend that

> Mr Buchanan, the American Minister ... sat next to the Princess Royal. He was in raptures about her and said she was the most charming girl he had ever met: 'All life and spirit, full of frolic and fun, with an excellent head and *a heart as big as a mountain*'.[59]

Bismarck disliked the English marriage from the start. The Prussian sons-in-law of her

> 'Her Gracious Majesty' will find no sort of respect in England ... Among us, on the other hand, British influence will find the most fruitful soil in the stupid admiration of the German 'Michel' for Lords and Guineas, in the anglo-mania of parliament, the newspapers, sportsmen, landlords and presiding judges. Every Berliner even now feels himself elevated if a real English jockey from Hart or Lichtwald talks to him and gives him the chance to grind out the crunched fragments of *the Queen's English*. How much worse will that be when the First Lady of the Land is an English woman.[60]

In 1856 and 1857, another and very important issue began to strain Bismarck's friendship with his patrons, the two brothers Gerlach. Bismarck had begun to think hard and utterly unconventionally about the usefulness of Napoleon III for the achievement of Prussian aims. To think such thoughts, let alone to express them to either of the Gerlach brothers, amounted to an attack on their fundamental principles. Napoleon III embodied 'revolution' and must be quarantined, not accepted. His regime was 'illegitimate'. He was a 'red', 'a usurper', and a 'democrat'. Bismarck disagreed. Possibilities must be matters of rational calculation of forces and counter-forces; the player needs to know the rules of the game, the psychologies of the other players, and the number of moves open to him. As he observed years later,

> My entire life was spent gambling for high stakes with other people's money. I could never foresee exactly whether my plan would succeed... Politics is a thankless job because everything depends on chance and conjecture. One has to reckon with a series of probabilities and improbabilities and base one's plans upon this reckoning.[61]

The metaphors that Bismarck began to use in the 1850s came from his experiences in games of chance, cards, dice, and the like.[62] Politics had, he asserted more and more openly, nothing to do with good and evil, virtue and vice; they had to do with power and self-interest. The exchange of letters between Bismarck and his patrons about Prussia's attitude to Napoleon III marked a turning point in Bismarck's career and the first serious break with the Christian Conservatives to whom he owed his official position. In the summer of 1856 Bismarck visited Paris and received a lecture from Leopold von Gerlach on that account. He replied:

> You scold me that I have been to Babylon but you can hardly expect from a diplomat eager to learn the rules this sort of political chastity... I have to get to know the elements in which I have to move from my own direct observation when the opportunity arises. You need not fear for my political health. I have a nature like a duck and water runs off my feathers and there is a long way between my skin and my heart.[63]

By 1857 Bismarck had stopped joking and wrote two letters to Leopold von Gerlach, which offer us the first sight of the mature Bismarck in full power and clarity. These letters announce the emergence of a new diplomatic style, the birth of what came to be known as *Realpolitik*, for which—interestingly—there is no apt English translation.

Langenscheidt's two-volume German–English dictionary suggests 'practical politics, politics of realism' but neither catches the complete idea. The following exchange of letters between Bismarck and Leopold von Gerlach constitutes a kind of practical definition of the term; do what works and serves your interests. Bismarck quoted these letters in full in his memoirs written nearly forty years later, which suggests that he continued to see them as fundamental even in his retirement and old age. The tone had changed. Bismarck had ceased to be the apprentice, the 'diplomatic child', and had become one of the grand masters of the game of international relations. The first letter is dated 2 May 1857. In it Bismarck wrote his declaration of independence from his patron. The issue was again what stance should Prussian foreign policy take towards Napoleon III. This letter, perhaps the most important he wrote to Gerlach, needs to be quoted at some length:

> You begin with the assumption that I sacrifice my principles to an individual who impresses me. I reject both the first and the second phrase in that sentence. The man does not impress me at all. The ability to admire people is but moderately developed in me, not unlike a defect of vision that gives me a sharper eye for weaknesses than strengths. If my last letter had a rather lively colouring, I ask you to attribute that to a rhetorical mechanism with which I hoped to influence you. What the principle is that I am supposed to have sacrificed, I cannot correctly formulate from what you write... France only interests me as it affects the situation of my Fatherland, and we can only make our policy with the France that exists... Sympathies and antipathies with regard to foreign powers and persons I cannot reconcile with my concept of duty in the foreign service of my country, neither in myself nor in others. There is in them the germ of disloyalty to the lord or the land which one serves... As long as each of us believes that a part of the chess board is closed to us by our own choice or that we have an arm tied where others can use both arms to our disadvantage, they will make use of our kindness without fear and without thanks.[64]

On 6 May 1857 Leopold von Gerlach replied in an unusually defensive and uncertain style:

> If you feel a need to remain in agreement with me on a matter of principle, it is incumbent upon us to seek out this principle, first of all, and not to content ourselves with negations, such as 'ignoring facts' and the 'exclusion of France from the political combinations'... My political principle is, and remains, the struggle against the Revolution. You will not convince Napoleon that he is not on the side of the Revolution. He has no desire either to be

anywhere else, for his position there gives him his decided advantages. There is thus no question either of sympathy or of antipathy here. This position of Bonaparte is a 'fact' which you cannot 'ignore.'. . . You say yourself that people cannot rely upon us, and yet one cannot fail to recognize that he only is to be relied on who acts according to definite principles and not according to shifting notions of interests, and so forth.[65]

Gerlach, in what was for him an unusually long and systematic letter, put the counter-argument very clearly. Politics must rest on principle, because only principle provided the steady foundation for alliances and initiatives. A principled state is a reliable state. Bismarck replied at even greater length in a letter of 30 May 1857.

The principle of struggle against revolution I recognize as mine as well but I consider it mistaken to make Louis Napoleon the only . . . representative of revolution . . . How many existences are there in today's political world that have no roots in revolutionary soil? Take Spain, Portugal, Brazil, all the American Republics, Belgium, Holland, Switzerland, Greece, Sweden and England which bases itself on consciousness of the Glorious Revolution of 1688 . . . And even when the revolutionary appearances of the past have not reached that degree of superannuation that like the witch in Faust with her drink from hell 'here I have a bottle out of which I take a nip from time to time which no longer stinks at all', states did not show the necessary modesty to withdraw from loving contact. Cromwell was called 'dear brother' by very anti-revolutionary potentates and his friendship was sought when they needed it. Very honourable potentates had alliances with the Estates of the Netherlands before their independence had been recognized by Spain. William of Orange and his successors in England were recognized as thoroughly *kosher* by our forefathers, even while the Stuarts still claimed the throne, and we forgave the Unites States of America their revolutionary origins in the Treaty of the Hague in 1785 . . . The present form of government in France is not arbitrary, a thing that Louis Napoleon can correct or alter. It was something that he found as a given and it is probably the only method by which France can be ruled for a long time to come. For everything else the basis is missing either in national character or has been shattered and lost. If Henry V were to come to the throne he would be unable, if at all, to rule differently. Louis Napoleon did not create the revolutionary conditions; he did not rebel against an established order, but instead fished it [power] out of the whirlpool of anarchy as nobody's property. If he were now to lay it down, he would greatly embarrass Europe, which would more or less unanimously beg him to take it up again.[66]

Throughout 1857, Leopold von Gerlach tried to maintain that 'from my side, there's not the slightest reason for bad feeling between us.'[67] In January

1858, he ended a long letter with the pathetic words, 'do come here; it is so necessary that we fix our positions. With old love, yours, L.v.G.'[68] A long break followed until in May 1860 when he wrote,

> You will be surprised to get a political letter from me and even from Sanssouci as in the old days... I write as if things were as they used to be in the old days... It depresses me especially that through your bitterness against Austria you have allowed yourself to be diverted from the simple choice between Right and Revolution. You play with the idea of an alliance with France and Piedmont, a possibility, a thought, that for me lies far away as it should be, dear Bismarck, for you. Forgive me that I have closed this letter 'at random' [English in original—JS]. I do not count on a meeting, but remain always with sincere love your old friend, L.v.G.[69]

Bismarck replied to his old mentor and patron on 2 May 1860, and it cannot have done much to raise the old man's spirits. He put the differences between them very clearly:

> You want to have nothing to do with Bonaparte or Cavour as a matter of principle. I want to avoid France and Sardinia, not because I think it wrong, but because in the interests of our security I consider them very dubious allies. Who rules in France or Sardinia, once the Powers have been recognized, is absolutely unimportant to me, a matter of fact not right or wrong... France would be of all possible allies the most questionable, although I must keep the possibility open, because one cannot play chess if 16 of the 64 squares are forbidden from the beginning.[70]

That was the last letter Bismarck wrote to his 'loving' patron. Leopold von Gerlach died on 10 January 1861 of a cold he picked up at the funeral of Frederick William IV, which Bismarck described in his memoirs.

> Moreover, he was devoted body and soul to the King, even when, in his opinion, the monarch erred. This was plain from the fact that he may be said to have ultimately met his death of his own free will by following behind the dead body of his King bareheaded, helmet in hand, and that in a high wind and very cold weather. This last act of an old servant's devotion to his master's body ruined an already much enfeebled health. He came home ill with erysipelas, and died in a few days. His end reminded me of the way in which the followers of the old Germanic princes used voluntarily to die with them.[71]

This cold farewell to a person to whom Bismarck owed much of his success and almost certainly the appointment to Frankfurt as ambassador in 1851 was typical. Gerlach had been useful but Bismarck in the memoirs made no mention of that. Old Gerlach was a throwback to an earlier age. It may be too crude to note that after October 1857, when King Frederick William IV had a stroke and could no longer govern,[72] Leopold von Gerlach lost his immediate usefulness to Bismarck in any case. Bismarck had used him and his closeness to the King to get ideas and suggestions to the Monarch without censorship by Otto von Manteuffel, the Minister-President and Foreign Minister. The following year, on 7 October 1858, a year after the King's severe stroke, it became clear that Frederick William IV would not recover. His younger brother, William Prince of Prussia, became Regent in his name and formed the government of the so-called 'New Era', which was influenced by the *Wochenblattpartei*, the conservative liberals among whom Bismarck's pet hate, Robert von der Goltz, played a leading role. As Leopold von Gerlach reminded him in his last letter to Bismarck, from 1 May 1860:

> There is another thing that I would like to say to you. You stand entirely alone against the whole Ministry. That is an untenable position... Could you not rely on R von der Goltz? After the 'New Era' he spoke openly to me in a way that gained my confidence. Even Bernstorff might be useful.[73]

Bismarck ignored that advice. The last thing he wanted was an alliance with moderate conservatives. He had another ally in mind which would have shocked Leopold von Gerlach. Bismarck proposed to play the Bonapartist game, as he said in the summer of 1859 to the nationalist liberal Victor Unruh:

> Prussia is completely isolated. There is but one ally for Prussia if she knows how to win and handle them... the German people! I am the same Junker of ten years ago... but I would have no perception and no understanding if I could not recognize clearly the reality of the situation.[74]

Bismarck had seen that the 'masses' in France voted for order not radicalism and had given Louis Napoleon Bonaparte an overwhelming mandate. Would not the German people play the same role in Bismarck's scheme to strength the position of Prussia? He intended to use nationalism as he had used the camarilla, to achieve his goals. He had come to understand that

> politics is less a science than an art. It is not a subject that can be taught. One must have the talent for it. Even the best advice is of no avail if improperly carried out.[75]

Other changes took place against the background of the Crimean War which strengthened Prussia. The first half of the 1850s saw a very rapid expansion of railroad building which transformed the mobilization of the

Prussian army. General Karl Friedrich Wilhelm von Reyher, chief of the General Staff in the 1850s, designated vital operational lines; worked out obligatory building codes for rail cars and railway stations to service cavalry and artillery; drew up a handbook of military regulations for all Prussian railroad companies; and coordinated timetables that acknowledged railroads as the principle mode of transport in wartime. Although Prussia never tested these plans in a full-scale mobilization in the 1850s, an operational timetable was in place by 1856.[76]

In October 1857 the Chief of the Great General Staff Karl von Reyher died and Prince William, whom King Frederick William IV had appointed as Regent for three months on 23 October 1857, appointed Helmuth von Moltke to be his successor, one of the two most important appointments William ever made. The other, on 22 September 1862, was to appoint Bismarck. Moltke was as remarkable as Bismarck but temperamentally and socially his exact opposite. He was born on 26 October 1800 in Parchim in Mecklenburg, the son of an improvident father, who could not manage the family estates and had, as a result, to take a commission in the Royal Danish Army. Modest family circumstances 'decided that Moltke together with his two brothers, Wilhelm and Fritz, without any concern for their own desires, had to become soldiers'.[77] Lack of money led Moltke all his life to a certain obvious frugality. Even as a Field Marshall and the greatest general in Prussian history he travelled second class and usually took a sandwich in a paper bag. In 1822 he transferred from the Royal Danish to the Prussian army and from 1823 to 1826 he studied at the Kriegsakademie (War College). As Arden Bucholz describes it, the Kriegsakademie had developed a new way to train officers, the *Kriegsspiel* or war game:

> War games originated with two Prussian officers, the Reisswitzes between 1810 and 1824. Originally played with plaster terrain and porcelain models at a scale of 26 inches to the mile, it evolved into metal symbols—blue for Prussia and red for the enemy…A set of rules, an umpire—the conductor— who mediated between the opposing sides, and dice standing for the element of chance in war. War gaming was practised at three or four distinct levels. One was indoors around the map or sand table. The other three were all done outdoors.[78]

Moltke graduated top in his class. He was always effortlessly the best at everything but was too poor to take the position he had earned in the Great General Staff because he lacked the private income needed to pay for his horses. As a result, like Albrecht von Roon, Moltke joined the topography section and became a 'land artist'. Moltke took part in the great topographic project under Chief of the General Staff Karl Freiherr von Müffling and spent three years doing this work from 1826 to 1829.

> To do this he [Moltke] lived with local families...He became virtually a member of the family for the old Silesian nobility who took until noon for the *grande toilette* and did not always say what they thought. They lived in beautiful castles set in wonderful parks with French-style gardens and paintings by old masters on the walls. Moltke sketched the counts and countesses, wrote poetry and met all the neighbours...[79]

Moltke painted and drew superbly, spoke six or seven languages (sources disagree on the number), and had immaculate manners. He had every grace and virtue (including discretion) to be the ideal courtier.

In 1833 he finally had enough cash to join the General Staff but in 1835 asked for six months of travel on which he made his way through the Balkans to Constantinople. In 1836 the ambassador of the Sultan asked the Prussian government for a training officer and Moltke, who was already there, got the job. He served as military adviser to the Turkish army for three years, travelled all over the Balkans and middle East, wrote and published his memoirs in 1841, and became instantly famous.[80] The book continues to be reprinted as *Under the Half-Moon* in our own times. In 1842 he married an English woman, Marie Burt, with whom he had no children.

As Arden Bucholz observes,

> Within the age cohort which included hundreds of field grade officers, Molte had now achieved uniqueness. None of his colleagues had any practical military experience. None had served as responsible adviser to an army commander or been decorated with the order Star and Honour Sword by the Ottoman sultan and the *Pour le mérite* by the Prussian king. Such fame for an officer within the general literate public went back two generations—to the wars of liberation. But this was peace-time and more significant for now he had caught the attention of the royal family. And what they found surprised them: a very bright officer, graceful and adept at court, with the additional cachet as an artist. In a society of deference, rife with patron-client relationships, this was gold. His next three appointments put him into close, daily contact with three of them: the king's nephew and most military relative, Prince Frederick Charles, the king's younger brother Prince Henry and the king's other nephew, Prince Frederick Wilhelm. Moltke got along well with the royals. This was certainly one key to his success. Elegantly turned out, perfectly tempered, he fitted in everywhere.[81]

His assignment as adjutant to Prince Heinrich, who lived a solitary life as an art lover in Rome, gave him an opportunity to learn Italian and to draw the great architectural treasures of the Eternal City.[82] Moltke was that rare human being, a universal man. There seemed to be nothing, especially in the arts, that he could not do. Of these appointments by far the most important was that of Adjutant to Prince Frederick William. There he got to know William Prince of Prussia. They had a lot in common. 'Moltke and King Wilhelm were the same kind of people: economical and simplicity loving, moderate and unpretentious. Both used the unwritten parts of letters to make notes and disliked replacing old clothes with new.'[83] Moltke had another qualification, indeed, was the first to have it: he himself had been a product of the General Staff as an educational institution. His predecessors: Grollman, Rühle von Lilienstern, Müffling, Krauseneck and Reyher, belonged to the Napoleonic generation and had had careers before the General Staff formally began to function in 1817. Moltke was an alumnus of the institution he now commanded.[84]

Stories of Moltke's calm detachment circulated throughout his career. In July 1870 Holstein reports that

> Colonel Stiehle [Gustav von Stiehe, chief of staff to Prince Friedrich Karl] also told me that he had found Moltke on the sofa with a novel of Sir Walter Scott in his hand. When the colonel passed some remark about such reading matter at such a moment, the General replied placidly: 'Why not? Everything's ready. We've only got to press the button.'[85]

During the Franco-Prussian War, Lieutenant Colonel Julius Verdy du Vernois was one of the chief staff officers. On 9 January 1871 he wrote his assessment of Moltke as a boss in his private diary. It is remarkable testimony to the great general's character:

> Moltke [...] lives entirely with his staff, and is as kind as ever to everyone of us. No one has ever heard a single harsh word from him during the whole campaign. With us, he is even merry in his simple, cheerful and modest way. We all feel happy in his company, and absolutely love and worship him. But outside of our small circle, there is only one feeling and that is admiration towards him; everyone says he is a truly ideal character.[86]

On the evening of the battle of Sedan, the greatest victory of Prussian arms in the nineteenth century, the King gave dinner for the top commanders. Alfred Count von Waldersee, then a young staff officer, recorded the following passage in his diary:

At dinner were Roon, Moltke and Bismarck. The King raised his glass and drank to the health of 'the man who sharpened the sword for me, the man who used it, and the man who successfully directed my policies.' These words have been frequently quoted differently but I can guarantee that this is what he said.[87]

On the 25 January 1858 the Crown Prince of Prussia Prince Frederick Wilhelm married the Princess Royal Victoria of Great Britain in the Chapel Royal, St James's Palace. Bismarck was not yet grand enough for Windsor but did get invited to the various dinners for the Royal Wedding in Berlin and noted in a letter to a friend that 'in the evening there was a grand gala ball with supper, where the unpractical cut of the civil uniform and the cold corridors gave me a catarrh of the stomach'.[88] As we shall see, Bismarck regarded the palaces as dangerous places, full of germs, draughts, and bossy women. The young Princess was a very young woman of 17 and looked even younger.

As Walburga Countess von Hohenthal, commented in 1858:

> The princess appeared extraordinarily young. All the childish roundness still clung to her and made her look shorter than she really was. She was dressed in a fashion long disused on the continent, in a plum coloured silk dress fastened at the back. Her hair was drawn off her forehead. Her eyes were what struck me most; the iris was green like the sea on a sunny day and the white had a peculiar shimmer which gave them the fascination that, together with a smile that showed her beautiful white teeth, bewitched those who approached her.[89]

During 1858 Frederick William IV had a series of strokes which damaged the speech centres of his brain and made it increasingly impossible for him to conduct the business of the monarchy. On 7 October 1858 he gave his royal powers to his younger brother, Prince William, who took on the role of Regent.[90] The Crown Prince as Regent dismissed the conservative Manteuffel and appointed a new government composed of members of the *Wochenblattpartei,* many of whom Bismarck regarded as 'enemies'. The so-called 'New Era' received the enthusiastic support of Prussian liberals but for Bismarck it spelled disaster. English influence and the so-called 'New Era' under the Regent were in Bismarck's view equally dangerous. Pflanze sums up the change very neatly. 'To shrewd observers, the change did not appear very drastic. Instead of feudal conservatives, aristocratic whigs were now in power.'[91] This assessment is undoubtedly right but at the time Bethmann Hollweg, Rudolf von Auerswald, and the others in the group, including the Hohenzollern prince, Karl Anton of Hohenzollern-Sigmaringen, who became Minister-President, and those members of the new cabinet who had been Liberals in 1848, seemed to promise a new start. The Princess Regent Augusta, a princess of Saxe-Weimar and a hearty liberal, welcomed the 'New Era'. The Prince Regent had doubts. 'What have I done to merit praise from that crowd?' he asked irritably.[92]

The New Era ministry produced one change early in its tenure. On 2 February 1859 it allowed the Jewish owner of a knightly estate, a certain Herr Julius Silberstein of Breslau, the right to vote in the Breslau district diet, that is, to exercise precisely those *ständische* (traditional) rights which Bismarck had successfully helped to close to Jews in 1847. The leading noblemen in the diet protested and refused to accept the decision. A campaign to defend those rights against usurping Jews raged over the next two years.[93] The dreadful prophesy of Burke had been fulfilled: the land had been turned into a commodity. A Jewish plutocracy would replace the true representatives of tradition and honour.

The New Era also meant that Bismarck had lost his direct connection to power and it made him depressed and ill. On 20 February 1859 he wrote to Leopold von Gerlach,

> In foreign affairs I have nothing to write and feel depressed. When, as now in Berlin there are neither pre- nor post-considerations, neither plans nor signs of a stirring of the will, so the awareness of an entirely purposeless and planless employment lowers the spirits. I do nothing more than what I am directly ordered to do and let things simply slide...[94]

To his brother, he complained about his health:

> In the meantime I have been so overworked and so ill that I was happy to find a few minutes for the necessary physical exercise. Because of the lack of that I suffer very much in the form of blood stoppage, congestion and susceptibility to colds.[95]

Hypochondria, illnesses of all sorts, and depression regularly accompanied changes in Bismarck's political situation. With age and—oddly—success they would get worse.

While Bismarck fretted at the loss of influence, Albrecht von Roon had been invited to a ceremony to mark his admission to the Knightly Order of St John. As the Regent gave him the robe and insignia of his knighthood, he said to him, as Roon reported to his wife Anna,

> 'These are the new robes (that is, the cloak) of the gentlemen who are Division Commanders and of those who will become Divisional Commanders. You

(shaking my hand vigorously) are not yet one but will be in the near future.' This 'in the near future', I interpret to mean at least within the year.[96]

Roon came from a very modest background and probably from Dutch bourgeois stock. Certainly 'de Ron' had no claims to nobility, and his paternal grandfather had a wine business in Frankfurt. During the Nazi period, the existence of a significant number of 'Noahs' and 'Isaacs' in his Dutch ancestry gave cause for a certain amount of alarm and they touched up his geneaology.[97] After Roon had served as tutor to the Prince's nephew in 1846 and 1847, General von Unruh informed him on 1 November 1848 that Prince William and Princess Augusta wanted Major von Roon to be military governor of their son, the 17-year-old Frederick William, their eldest child and future Emperor Frederick III.[98] We have seen how rapidly the career of Moltke had been transformed by such royal favour. The General handed the Major a letter from the Princess Augusta in which she explained that with respect to his purity of heart, truthfulness and piety, she could want nothing more of the young Prince. 'Strength of character and intellectual ability, namely sharpness and logic, are not on the same level.' She wanted her son to be brought up to date. 'He belongs to the present and future. He must, as a result, absorb new ideas and learn to digest them, so that he develops a clear and lively awareness of his own time and lives not outside it but within and of it.'[99]

Five days after receipt of this invitation, Roon replied to this remarkable letter with unusual frankness. He declared his

> inability to concede inner truth or outer justification to all the so-called, up-to-date views... I feel myself too old, too rusted into my prejudices, too lame. Will the touch of 'reactionary essence' which is inherent in me, not be harmful to the young gentleman?[100]

Not only did a humble and not very well-heeled Major turn down a golden ladder to a brilliant career but he also had the nerve to suggest to the Princess that the young Prince 'should be removed from Court and all its influences'.[101] Roon had in a sense taken a huge risk with his career prospects by his frankness and he and Anna must have been relieved when a letter of 10 December arrived from the Princess in which she wrote that her choice of him as military governor had

> been perfectly confirmed by your open and honest answer... With respect to separating my son from Court and his parents, our views are far apart and for the moment and for the immediate future we shall not let him go away from us for that reason.[102]

Early in January Prince William courteously informed Roon that Lieutenant Colonel Fischer from the Ministry of War had been appointed military governor to the Prince. The Prince added his own regrets:

> Today I can only say how much I regret that our first choice could not have been permitted to stand and to assure you that our respect for you has not changed in any way.[103]

During 1849, when the Prussian Army suppressed the revolution in Baden, Major von Roon served as chief of staff to I Army Corps of the 'Operation Army of the Rhine', under Lieutenant General von Hirschfeld. The whole operation was under the command of Prince William of Prussia, which allowed Roon to solidify his position with the future King.[104] He became part of the group around the Prince together with Adjutant-General von Kirchfeldt, Lieutenant Colonel Fischer, and one or two others. This group disliked the direction of Prussian politics. It met in the Prince's temporary residence in Koblenz.[105] In December 1850 von Roon was promoted to lieutenant colonel and made commanding officer of the 33rd Reserve Infantry in Thorn; as his wife put it on 31 December 1850, 'this assignment [to command an unfashionable reserve regiment in a remote Polish town—JS] is an expression of the highest disfavour on the part of the Minister of War.'[106] In the following December, he was in spite of the disfavour promoted colonel and the regiment happily transferred from remote Thorn to Cologne, near the royal couple in their residence in Koblenz, where the Prince of Prussia often inspected the 33rd Regiment and saw Roon regularly.[107]

Koblenz was not far from Frankfurt but relations between Roon and Bismarck seem to have been still on a formal basis, as in the letter of 14 July 1852 in which Colonel Roon writes to his 'honoured Friend', as the heading has it, but within the text he addresses Bismarck as 'honoured Excellency', as part of a formal letter in which he asks Bismarck as ambassador to make arrangements for his general to visit the Fortress of Nancy and Louis Napoleon Bonaparte. He passes on greetings from their mutual friends, Kleist-Retzow and Moritz von Blanckenburg, and hopes that the gracious lady will, perhaps, remember him from 1847 and Venice.[108] Roon must have felt his inferiority. After all, he was still a regimental commander of a not very fashionable regiment at nearly 50, while the young Bismarck, still under 40, had shot onto the political firmament with the brilliance of a comet. The Rooms still had to live off his modest salary. Five years later, his career had not advanced much as he wrote to his friend Clemens Theodor Perthes, the Bonn professor, on 9 November 1857: 'I still cannot do more in fact than enlist recruits and send letters without content from above to below and from below to above.' But he reports on a trip to Berlin and 'plans for my future'. A note mentions an exchange of letters with Bismarck about his possible transfer to Frankfurt as Federal Military Plenipotentiary.[109]

On 25 June 1858, the day after Roon was initiated as a Knight of the Order of St John, Prince William summoned him to a private audience and asked for his 'thoughts and plans in writing' for army reform. The Regent wanted Roon to make suggestions for a more efficient management of the recruitment and personnel procedures. In principle, every adult male was subject to military service; in practice a small number actually served as recruits for two years. Recruitment in the 1850s stood at about 40,000 per year. A better army meant more recruits, trained better and serving for longer. It also meant doing something serious about the *Landwehr*, the local militias, who served seven-year terms and could re-enlist for another seven.

Roon submitted his *Bemerkungen und Entwürfe zur vaterländischen Heeresverfassung* (Notes and Drafts for a Structure for an Army for the Fatherland) on 18 July 1858.[110] Roon began his survey by asserting categorically that

1. The Landwehr is *a politically false* institution, because it no longer impresses foreigners and for foreign and domestic politics is of doubtful significance;
2. The Landwehr is at the same time *a militarily false* and *weak* institution because it lacks
   a) a genuine, firm soldierly spirit and
   b) a secure disciplinary control without which no reliable military organization can be conceived.

A reconstruction must, therefore, occur in that:

1. a tight fusion of the Landwehr with the Line units takes place and that
2. the lack of suitable leadership be remedied.[111]

Roon argued that three-year service was essential and that the intake must be greater.

The former Landwehr 'first mobilization' must be completely incorporated into the line units in peacetime . . . If one wishes, the name 'Landwehr' can be preserved. Indeed, the whole army could be called 'Landwehr' if that were preferable.[112]

Ultimately the plan foresaw an annual recruitment of 63,000 men with an eight-year military obligation, three of which were to be active and five in the active reserve. The new Prussian army would have at any time an instant force of over 300,000 fully trained troops, as opposed to the present slack system which could at most generate some 200,000 indifferently prepared soldiers.

The scheme was very radical and not only in its sharp expansion of the army, but also because the Landwehr represented two important principles, which Roon utterly rejected. The right to bear arms had always been the sign of the free man. That faith found expression in the second amendment to the Constitution of the United States, part of the Bill of Rights, ratified on 15 December 1791, which makes it absolutely clear that the free citizen has a right to bear arms:

> A well regulated Militia, being necessary to the security of a free State, the right of the people to keep and bear Arms, shall not be infringed.[113]

Prussia was not a free state. It had no citizens, only subjects. Neither the Regent nor his military adviser intended to alter that. Hence Roon called the *Landwehr* a 'politically false' institution, in that it gave its soldiers ideas beyond their station. It was false in a second sense because it went back to the 'people's rising' of 1813 to 1815, which had for the first time enlisted volunteer units to fight alongside the Royal Prussian Army. The legend of the heroic young men fighting in their stylish black uniforms in a war for freedom comforted a bourgeoisie who could not get commissions in the proper army and who claimed their share of the patriotic War of Liberation. Bismarck had outraged precisely those sentiments by his very first speech in the Prussian United Diet of 1847 when he rejected the idea that there had been a War of Liberation at all. To incorporate the 'free' militia into the traditional Prussian army's *Kadavergehorsam* (obedience of the corpse) attacked the entire self-image of the liberal middle classes. The financial costs would be high and the Prussian Landtag was unlikely to agree to them.

That Prussia could easily afford such costs had not yet entirely penetrated the consciousness of the tax-paying classes. The Customs Union or Zollverein, which Prussia founded in 1819, had become a powerful internal market, from which Austria had been excluded. In the 1860s Prussia accounted for nine-tenths of all the pig iron and coal produced inside the Zollverein, two-thirds of the iron ore, and almost all the steel and zinc.[114]

Less evident but at least as important was the revolution in education that had spread through Prussia from 1815 to the 1860s. In 1833 Victor Cousin, French minister of education, called Prussia 'the land of the barracks and the school room'. In the 1840s, Horace Mann, the famous American educational reformer, toured Prussian schools and noted how free they were:

> Though I saw hundreds of schools and...tens of thousands of pupils I never saw one child undergoing punishment for misconduct. I never saw one child in tears from having been punished or from fear of being punished.[115]

Literacy rates in Prussia in 1850 averaged about 85 per cent, a standard of literacy consisting of both reading and writing skills, whereas in France reading only amounted to 61 per cent and in England reading and writing only reached 52 per cent of the population.[116]

The educated workforce found employment in industries which had begun to exploit science and technology. The Prussian universities turned out scientific pioneers and the system of technical colleges trained generations of engineers who could apply the science to industry. The German university with its doctorates, seminars, research agendas and the technical colleges pushed Germany farther ahead in the struggle for dominance in Europe.

Friedrich Engels, who returned to Prussia for the first time a generation after the Revolution of 1848, was astonished by the change.

> Whoever last saw the Prussian Rhineland, Westphalia, the kingdom of Saxony, upper Silesia, Berlin and the seaports in 1849 found them unrecognizable in 1864. Everywhere machines and steam-power had spread. Steamships gradually replaced sail-ships, first in the coastal trade, then in maritime commerce. The railways multiplied in length many times. In the dockyards, collieries, and iron works there prevailed an activity of the kind the ponderous German had previously thought himself incapable.[117]

As Albrecht von Roon drafted his memorandum for the Regent in July 1858, the Kingdom of Prussia presented a paradox. Frederick the Great still provided the model. The old Frederician absolute monarchy was there in spirit, modified a little by the Constitution of 1850. The Prussian aristocracy still monopolized power in the army and civil service, while society had begun the rapid modernization that accompanies very sudden industrialization. It brought with it the rise of a wealthy middle class and a large industrial working class that demanded more representation and genuine parliamentary politics. Prussia remained Frederick the Great's military state but one with huge factories, big cities, and advanced technology. Yet Roon's army had not changed one iota. In 1862, 85 per cent of cadets entering the Prussian army came from 'old Prussian' territories and 79 per cent came from traditional Prussian families (officers, civil servants, and landowners). In the same period, while 35 per cent of the officer corps was bourgeois, the upper ranks were resolutely aristocratic with 86 per cent of all colonels and generals from the nobility.[118] In other words, Frederick's aristocracy still ruled Prussia but the Prussia they ruled had become utterly different. This paradox framed the careers of Bismarck, Roon, and Moltke. Bismarck's success, if that is the word, lay in his preservation of that paradox to the end of the nineteenth century.

6

Power

Bismarck's position in 1859 depressed him. Though he had not been loyal to Minister-President Otto Freiherr von Manteuffel, Manteuffel had been good to him. Now both the King and Manteuffel had left the stage, the King through illness and Manteuffel through a punctilious sense of duty. In order to give the Regent a free hand, Manteuffel and his ministry tendered their resignations as a group and the Regent accepted them on 6 November 1858. Manteuffel refused the title of count and withdrew to his estate.[1] With the change of Minister President and Foreign Minister, Bismarck heard a rumour that he was to be transferred to St Petersburg, which he regarded—not entirely without grounds—as an attempt to put him, literally, out in the cold. It says something about Bismarck's effrontery or the approachability of Prussian monarchs that Bismarck 'betook himself'—his exact words in A. J. Russell's translation—to the Regent and requested an audience. In it he protested that nobody could replace him. He had done eight years of service in Frankfurt and had got to know everybody who mattered. His successor, von Usedom, was a cretin with an impossible wife and for that matter the entire cabinet of the 'New Era' lacked distinction. As he put it to the Regent,

> After I had expressed myself concerning the post at the Federal Diet, I passed on to the general situation and said: 'Your Royal Highness has not a single statesman-like intellect in the whole ministry, nothing but mediocrities and limited brains.'
>
> *The Regent.* —'Do you consider Bonin's a limited brain?'
>
> *I.* —'By no means; but he cannot keep a drawer in order, much less a ministry. And Schleinitz is a courtier, but no statesman.'
>
> *The Regent* (irritably). —'Do you perchance take me for a sluggard? I will be my own Foreign Minister and Minister of War; that I comprehend.'
>
> I apologized, and said: 'At the present day the most capable provincial president cannot administer his district without an intelligent district secretary,

and will always rely upon such a one; the Prussian monarchy requires the analogue in a much higher degree. Without intelligent ministers your Royal Highness will find no satisfaction in the result.'[2]

Whether Bismarck actually said all that we cannot know. The conversation in question took place thirty-five years before Bismarck wrote his memoirs. Had he taken notes at the time? Yet the text itself still startles me. The idea that a 43-year-old ambassador could slander the entire cabinet and insult the Regent with impunity suggests either that Bismarck could, and did, get away with anything or that the Royal Prussian Court practised a tolerance rather unusual among monarchs. Nobody would have dared to say anything like that to Queen Victoria or Napoleon III.

Bismarck's documents from the time are more modest. He wrote to Johanna in mid-January 1859 that he had been well received at court by the Prince-Regent and had dined with Hans (von Kleist-Retzow), Oscar (von Arnim, brother-in-law), Alexander von Below-Hohendorf, Moritz von Blanckenburg, Wagener, Eberhard Count zu Stolberg, Somnitz, etc. He was likely to remain in Berlin until 24 January and had asked the Regent to be allowed to remain in his present post at Frankfurt.[3] The decision went the other way. On 29 January 1859 Bismarck was named by the Regent the Prussian envoy to the court of Tsar Alexander II.[4] Rather gloomily Bismarck returned to Frankfurt to arrange his affairs and organize the move.

Roon was also in a bad mood. He had run into hostility from the new Minister of War, Eduard von Bonin, who was ten years older than he and incomparably more distinguished as a field commander. Von Bonin had his own ideas about the fusion of the Line and the *Landwehr* and had not been impressed by Roon's memorandum. On 9 January 1859 Roon wrote to Anna that the new minister intended to shove the project to one side as soon as he could.[5] The next day, he dined with the Prince Regent and afterwards the Princess Augusta asked him to stay a while and report to her on the reform project and the meeting of 22 December.

> She discussed my present assignment and sought to cheer me up. I ought not to lose heart. Matters of such importance must be pursued with the greatest eagerness and tenacity...In reply to my remark that the Prince only had to order the changes, she replied evasively. The Prince had been overwhelmed with projects and proposals and his task ought not to be made more difficult if those presenting reports are annoyed or become peevish. In any case it must be obvious that every thing would be better done if the agent carrying it out were convinced of its utility and with that she let me leave.[6]

It cannot have been easy to remain cheerful when the next day Minister von Bonin dismissed him and the project with contempt. Roon wrote angrily to Anna that Bonin had said:

> He really had no time, could not occupy himself with the memorandum, which he had just received and not yet read, had not had time to think it through. He babbled on impatiently like a small boy.[7]

Two days later the Regent called a cabinet meeting at which the military reform project appeared on the agenda. Roon had been invited to join the meeting at the end and heard von Bonin announce in the name of the Cabinet that Roon had been named to chair a commission to study the feasibility of the reform proposal. It all sounded very nice but Roon remained sceptical. He was convinced that von Bonin intended to sabotage the reforms by burying them in the commission and that 'all such commissions threaten to fail on the issue'.[8]

Roon's fate and that of Bismarck were, in fact, being decided in a different part of the world. On 29 January 1859 a Franco-Piedmontese treaty, ratified by both parties, largely codified the terms agreed between Napoleon III and Count Cavour, the Piedmontese Prime Minister, at Plombières in 1858: in the event of an Austro-Piedmontese war in Italy resulting from Austrian aggression, France would join Piedmont in an effort to drive the Austrians from Italy and establish a Kingdom of Upper Italy under the House of Savoy. A few days later, on 4 February 1859, Napoleon published a pamphlet, 'L'Empereur Napoléon III et l'Italie', in which the nephew of the great Napoleon set out his agenda for following in his predecessor's footsteps. He too would liberate Italy and reduce the power of the reactionary Habsburg Empire. This bold attack on the international order of mid-century Europe would set off tremors that would lift both Roon and Bismarck to power and create the conditions in which Germany too could be unified.

Bismarck had reason to be gloomy as he closed the house in Frankfurt and prepared to hand over the post to Guido Usedom. Before he left, he went to dinner at the sumptuous home of Mayer Carl von Rothschild (1820–86), the head of the Rothschild bank in the family's home city of Frankfurt. He wrote enthusiastically about the experience in a letter to Johanna: 'a real, old Jew haggler (*Schacherjude*) tons of silver, golden spoons and forks.'[9] The dinner had long-term consequences since, on Meyer Carl's recommendation, Bismarck appointed Gerson Bleichröder, a banker in

Berlin, who operated as a Rothschild correspondent, to be his private banker and handle his affairs while he was away in St Petersburg.[10] The relationship lasted until Bleichröder's death in 1891 and made a great deal of money for Bismarck. What it did for Bleichröder to be known as 'Bismarck's banker' can easily be imagined and will be described in some detail later in this book.

Bismarck detested moving and even more so when things in remote St Petersburg were so difficult and expensive. On 25 February Bismarck wrote to Karl Freiherr von Werther (1809–82), his predecessor in Russia, about furniture at the St Petersburg residence, which Werther quite naturally wanted to sell. 'What I am supposed to do with a big empty house for the six months until my wife arrives?' Bismarck decided to go to a hotel for the first few months.[11] As he complained to brother Bernhard, the move to Petersburg was going to be very expensive. Yes, he had a grand new salary of 33,000 thaler 'with which under normal circumstances one could live quite comfortably', but Werther had paid 6,400 without furniture for the ambassadorial residence in St Petersburg, a lot more than the 4,500 he was paying in Frankfurt. The Foreign Ministry had promised to give him 3,000 for the move but he reckoned that even with such a subsidy he would in the end be 10,000 thaler out of pocket.[12]

Bismarck left Frankfurt for good on 6 March 1859 and went to Berlin for what he hoped would be a few days. Ten days later, he wrote to Johanna:

> I am still here to my great irritation. I don't know what I should do and what to answer to everybody about my departure. Saturday I had set as a date to leave but now there's a letter from the Prince to the Tsar, which I am supposed to take which will not be ready until next week.[13]

And then without warning, he suddenly had to depart:

> It has turned out exactly as I expected. After keeping me for 16 days without reason, it suddenly turned out yesterday at 5 that I should leave as soon as possible, at the latest tonight. That I am not going to do and will leave tomorrow afternoon.[14]

Bismarck's journey from Berlin to St Petersburg reminds us of the difference between Bismarck's world and ours. Though railroads had begun to spread and he could travel most of the first leg on the train to Königsberg, thereafter he had to travel in carriages of various kinds, which went from one post house or coach stop to the next. Late March brought heavy snow along the Baltic and Bismarck had to get out of the carriage and push at

various points. When he finally reached St Petersburg, he wrote a long letter
to his sister about the exhausting but exciting week it had taken to get from
Königsberg to St Petersburg, a journey that now takes about an hour on a
plane. I quote it at length:

> Day before yesterday early in the morning I arrived here at the Hotel Demidoff
> where I am warm and dry, but it was an effort to get this far. Hardly had we
> left Konigsberg eight days ago, when a lively snow storm began, and since that
> I have not seen the natural colour of the surface of the earth. Already at
> Insterburg, my courier coach took an hour to go one mile. In Wirballen
> I found a miserable coach whose interior was too small for my length, so
> I changed places with Engel [his valet—JS] and passed the whole journey in
> the outer-seat, which is forward and open. There was a small bench with an
> acute-angled back rest, so, that even apart from the cold which at night went
> down to minus 12 degrees, it made sleep impossible. I held out in this position
> from Friday to Monday evening and except for the first and last night on the
> train, I slept 3 hours in Kovno and 2 hours on a sofa in a station house. My
> skin peeled off in layers, when I arrived. The journey took so long because the
> fresh fallen snow covered the sleigh tracks. Several times we had to get out
> and walk because the eight horses of the carriage simply got stuck. The Düna
> was frozen but half a mile upstream, there was an open spot where we crossed.
> The Wilija had wind driven ice floes, the Niemen was open. From time to
> time we were short of horses, because all the post couriers took eight or ten
> and instead of the usual 3 or 4. I never had fewer than six and the carriage was
> not over-weight. Conducteur, Postilion and Fore-rider did their best so that
> I resisted the temptation to ruin the horses. Smooth hills were the worst
> obstacle, especially going down hill the four after-horses piled into each other
> in a tumble. Anyway it is all over and is fun to tell.[15]

In spite of his resistance to his assignment Bismarck actually enjoyed St
Petersburg very much and the letters have a mellow sense of well-being,
which can hardly be found either before or after. His descriptions of the
promenades and boulevards of the 'Venice of the North' have great charm.
He enjoyed watching the oddities of the Russians and wrote at length about
the beauties of the palaces, gardens, and parks, the northern light, the colours. The Petersburg letters describe an idyllic intermission in the life of the
restless and ambitious genius. Since there was no consular service, Bismarck
had a great deal to do as representative of the Prussian King, as he wrote to
his brother in May 1859. His main job was to look after the 40,000 Prussians
in the Russian Empire: 'One is lawyer, policeman, district councillor, and
claims commissioner for all these people. I often have a hundred documents
to sign a day.'[16] He enjoyed matching his skills against those of Prince

Gorchakov, the Russian foreign minister, and used even the least promising occasions to do so. On 28 April, he wrote to Johanna

> Today we funeralled and buried old Prince Hohenlohe with Tsar and Parade. In the black festooned church, after it emptied, I sat with Gortschakov on the black velvet pew with a covering of skulls and we 'politicked', that is, worked, not chatted. The preacher had cited the passing of all things in the psalm (grass, wind, dry) and we planned and plotted as if one would never die.[17]

He reported that the Austrian 'betrayal' of 1854–5 had not been forgiven:

> One cannot imagine how low the Austrians are here. Not even a scabby dog would accept meat from them... the hatred is beyond measure and exceeds all my expectations. Only since I arrived, have I believed in war. The entire Russian foreign policy has no other aim but to find a way to get even with Austria. Even the calm and gentle Emperor spits fire and rage when he talks about it and the Empress, a princess of Darmstadt, and the Dowager Empress are moving when they talk about the broken heart of the Tsar who loved Franz Joseph like a son...[18]

One royal relationship in particular gave him a sense of comfort that he himself noted: he was invited to the Peterhof Palace by the Dowager Tsarina, Empress Alexandra Feodorovna, widow of the late Tsar Nicholas I, born Princess Charlotte of Prussia, the sister of the late King Frederick William IV. Here is Bismarck's account

> For me she has something in her kindness that is maternal, and I can talk to her as if I had known her from my childhood... I could listen to her deep voice and honest laughter and even her scolding for hours, it was homey. I had come in white tie and cut-away for a formal visit of two hours but toward the end she said she had no desire to say farewell to me and that I must have an awful lot to do. I said in reply, 'not in the least' and she said, 'well then stay until I depart tomorrow'. I accepted the invitation with pleasure as a command, for here it is so delightful and the city of Petersburg is so full of stone and pavement. Imagine the height of Oliva and Zoppot, all bound together in a grand park with a dozen palaces with terraces and fountains and ponds in between, with shaded walks and lawns that run down to the water of the lake, blue sky and warm sun, beyond the sea of tree tops the real sea with gulls and sails, I have not felt so well for ages.[19]

Is it reading too much into the text to see this as an intimate meeting between the widowed good Queen Mother and the 44-year-old ambassador son? The language of pleasure and well-being has no parallel in the vast correspondence of Bismarck that I have come to know. He felt at home—loved? Sudden 'elective affinities' across the generations are not unknown and here we have one. In early July, he saw the Dowager Tsarina again and accompanied her to the ship taking her to Stettin for a holiday in Prussia: 'It was so enchanting as we escorted the high lady in Peterhof on board, that I had an urge, in uniform as I was and without luggage, to leap on the ship to travel with her.'[20] In general Bismarck's correspondence gives the impression that the Russian royal family took a shine to the brilliant Prussian ambassador. Bismarck claimed in a letter to a colleague that he was the only diplomat allowed in the Imperial family, 'which gives me the status of an envoy to the family'.[21]

On the wider European scene, the rumble of war between France and Austria grew louder. During April 1859 the Austrians marched blindly into the trap that Napoleon III and Cavour had set for them. On 20 April the Prince Regent ordered the mobilization of three Prussian Army Corps and the entire line cavalry in preparation for a general European war.[22] On 23 April Austria sent an ultimatum to Piedmont-Sardinia to demand that the Piedmontese disarm, which the government of Piedmont rejected on 26 April.[23] The following day at the Austrian Crown Council Franz Joseph decided irrevocably for war, calling it 'a commandment of honor and duty'.[24] How sound the Emperor's judgement may have been can be seen in this letter from Odo Russell to his mother, Lady William, from a few years earlier:

> The little Emperor is full of courage and obstinacy! He delights in reviews— and has them at 4 hours notice once or twice a week—much to the disgust of the soldiers and officers in the winter. His Majesty insisted on having a review during the hard frost—he was advised against it, but uselessly—the review was held. Two cuirassiers fell and broke their necks! The Camarilla concealed this event from fear of giving pain to His Majesty. During a review, an *anständiger Weisswaschwarenhandlungscommis* [a decent employee of a linen and washing powder shop], excited by the sight, passed the Emperor smoking and forgot to take off his hat—he was taken into custody, flogged in prison and condemned to 2 years *schweren Kerker* [a severe prison sentence]. This created bad blood, of course.[25]

Under the rule of such an incompetent, absolute monarch, Austria declared war on Piedmont on 29 April, an act of aggression which triggered the Franco-Piedmontese treaty of alliance. The Austrians had had experience of this sort of war before and had smashed the Piedmontese comprehensively in 1848. But Radetzky and Windischgrätz were no longer in command of the Austrian forces in northern Italy. The new military leadership moved too slowly and got caught in heavy rain in the Po Valley. The French army, though much smaller in numbers, had access to railroads and got their forces into place earlier than the Austrians expected. Giuseppe Garibaldi had also organized his nationalist guerrillas into a force called the 'Hunters of the Alps', a fast unit which harassed the Austrian flanks. Napoleon III had to work quickly because he could not be sure that the Austrians—as the leading German power—would not mobilize Prussia and the Bund on its side. He knew the Russians would not lift a finger to help Franz Joseph and his government which had betrayed them in 1854. On 20 May French infantry and Sardinian cavalry defeated the Austrian army, which retreated, near Montebello and a week later Garibaldi's *Hunters of the Alps* defeated the Austrians at San Fermo and liberated Como. Two big and very bloody battles followed: the Battle of Magenta on 4 June and from 21 to 24 June the Battle of Solferino at which the Franco-Piedmontese Army under Napoleon III defeated an Austrian force under the Emperor Franz Joseph himself. The battle left so many dead and wounded that it moved the Swiss observer Henri Dunant to found the Red Cross.

By this time revolution had broken out in Hungary. The Emperor knew that in this emergency he would not have Russian and Croatian forces to help him suppress the intransigent Magyars and hence had no choice but to sue for peace. On 11 July 1859 he met Napoleon III at Villafranca di Verona in the Veneto. Napoleon III was now in a hurry, because he had lost control of his Italian policy. France had originally planned to take from Austria and give to Piedmont the two northern Italian provinces awarded to Austria in 1815, Lombardy and Venetia. As a result of fighting, the French and Piedmontese had taken Lombardy, but Venetia remained firmly in Austrian hands.[26]

Cavour resigned as Piedmontese Prime Minister in disgust at Napoleon's betrayal and in Italy the nationalist forces of various kinds had no intention of letting the Great Powers dictate to them the nature of their glorious revolution. The treaty of Villafranca assumed that Napoleon III would be in a position graciously to restore the Austrian principalities such as the Grand Duchy of Tuscany and the Duchies of Parma and Modena to their legitimate sovereigns but the Bund and the Prussians might intervene too soon to allow him that luxury. He needed to exit the war and quickly.

Bismarck had from the beginning argued that Prussia must stay neutral in the Austro-French war. 'We are not rich enough to use up our strength in wars that do not earn us anything,' he argued.[27] On 12 May he wrote a long dispatch to the new foreign secretary, Adolph Count von Schleinitz (1807–85) to demonstrate that the Bund must always oppose Prussia, because

> this tendency of middle state policy will emerge with the steadiness of a magnetic needle after any temporary swings, because it is no arbitrary product of individual circumstances or persons but a natural and necessary result of the federal relationships of the small states. We have no means to cope with this in a lasting or satisfactory way within the given federal treaties...I see in our relationship to the Bund an infirmity of Prussia, which we shall sooner or later have to heal with *ferro et igni*.

'Iron and fire' was the precursor of the more famous 'blood and iron' phrase from his first speech as Minister-President in September 1862. It certainly had the same meaning. Prussia would have to carve out its own fate by 'iron and fire', that is, by war. Prussia must use the present Austrian distress to redesign the Bund, send troops to the Austrian border, and threaten to overrun the small states during the war between France and Austria.[28]

On 14 June 1859 Moltke convened a meeting of all corps commanders and their chiefs of staff to consider an unexpected problem. The Prussian mobilization had failed. By the time of the armistice between France and Austria,

> two-thirds of the Prussian army was mobilized and under way, but it was in no position to do anything. What had happened? When the order to mobilize was given, only half the corps were ready to do so. Railroad transportation was ready: war materials—ammunition, food, wagons and supplies—had been collected and stockpiled all over Germany along three railroad lines. But civilian traffic took precedence; troops crawled to the Rhine...Moltke was stunned.[29]

A complete reorganization of the General Staff followed. A railroad department was set up and the second division of the General Staff, the mobilization section, was created.

Roon wrote to his friend Perthes to complain that

> our Prussian pride is headed for another deep humiliation. We have done too much for us now to do nothing...and now we cannot do anything more because without England the risk would be greater than the reward. It is a horrible dilemma. That comes from too much trembling, timidity and hesitation.[30]

And there was much truth in that charge. Neither the Regent nor his Foreign Minister von Schleinitz could decide what to do. Bismarck—with his usual lack of discretion—had argued for an active, anti-Austrian, and explicitly 'German' policy in alliance with the German national movement, now much encouraged by the Italian example. William, the Prince Regent, could not bring himself to break his natural allegiance to the Habsburgs nor to decide to use the occasion to 'make' Germany.

Bismarck's way of influencing policy, as we saw in the previous chapter, had been to write critical letters to the King's General Adjutant Leopold von Gerlach, who would pass them on to the King during their daily chat over coffee and cakes. Bismarck became more and more influential and Minister-President Manteuffel had played with the idea of making him Foreign Minister in 1856. Now the situation internationally suited Bismarck's combative style of politics. The 'national' question had blown up again and the stakes were higher. Bismarck still wrote letters but, as he explained in his memoirs, they were 'absolutely fruitless . . . The only result of my labours was . . . that suspicion was cast on the accuracy of my reports.'[31]

By chance Bismarck had returned to Germany in July, this time really ill, because of the treatment a Russian doctor had given to his injured knee.[32] He needed to be there and the illness gave him the excuse. While he suffered from a poisoning of the body, rage disturbed his mind; as he wrote to his brother from Berlin in August 1859, 'I have worked myself into a rage and for three days have not slept and hardly eaten.'[33] Late in 1859, Bismarck spent a period of recuperation on the estate of his old Junker friend, Alexander von Below-Hohendorf. Below noted with alarm the dangerous and destructive power of Bismarck's terrible rage. In a letter of 7 December 1859 he wrote to Moritz von Blanckenburg that Bismarck had become deranged by his concentration on his enemies and 'extreme thoughts and feelings'. The cure was simple and Christian: 'love thine enemies!' This was the best 'door' through which to release

> the mounting pressures from the darkness of his sick body and the best medicine against the amazing visions and thoughts [*Vorstellungen*] that threaten to draw him to death.[34]

This advice made sense. Bismarck's sick soul needed a release and to his Junker friends that release could be found at any moment through penitence, grace, and the love of God. It was Bismarck's tragedy—and Germany's—that he never learned how to be a proper Christian, had no understanding of the virtue of humility, and still less about the interaction of his sick body and sick soul.

Bismarck had been told by doctors in Berlin that 'my growing *hypochon-dria*' arose from worries about his Berlin existence and the expenses caused by regular dinners with nine people at meals, thirteen domestic servants, and two secretaries. He felt he was 'being plucked at every corner'.[35] This is, I think, the first time that he used the word 'hypochondria' about himself, and in time others used it of him. 'Homelessness', the absence of his stable family life, made him abnormally anxious.

None of this improved Bismarck's temper. In late September he wrote to his sister that

> Now that I have talked myself hoarse to artisans and statesmen, I have almost gone mad from annoyance, hunger and too much business... The left leg is still weak, swells up when I walk on it, the nerves have yet to recover from the iodine poisoning, I sleep badly... flat and embittered and I don't know why.[36]

As we shall see again and again, there is a 'why'. The Prince Regent had rejected him and his advice. Not for the last time Bismarck plunged into a deep despair when his royal master showed displeasure or simply failed to pay sufficient attention to him. A little attention would usually cheer him up and in this case it came from the command to wait upon the Tsar, who had visited Poland to do some serious hunting on the vast Polish royal domains. Bismarck, restored to good spirits, wrote to Johanna from the Lazienki Palace in Warsaw on 19 October:

> The whole day 'en grandeur' with Tsar Alexander II... I can only tell you in plain words that I am very well. Breakfast with the Emperor, then audience, exactly as gracious as in Petersburg. Visits, dinners with his Majesty, evening theatre, really good ballet and the boxes full of pretty women. Now I have just slept splendidly. Tea stands on the table and as soon as I have drunk it, I shall go out. The aforesaid tea consisted of not only tea but coffee, six eggs, 3 sorts of meat, baked goods, and a bottle of Bordeaux... very comfortable.[37]

Recognition from the All-Highest authority and lots of food did wonders for Bismarck's disposition.

On 23 and 24 October a Russo-Prussian summit of the sovereigns took place in Breslau and the Prince Regent had ordered Roon to attend it where he met 'Otto Bismarck', who had 'very serious doubts about the affair',[38] presumably the army reform. The letter does not make clear what the subject of the doubts were, but the next letter, a few days later, makes very clear how unpleasant the whole reform project had become for Roon personally:

How much jealousy and misinterpretation my involvement has aroused even in men who like Steinmetz deserve my respect and recognition. It came to a painful, almost emotional scene. We separated in peace but I had poison in my blood and struggled for a long time to regain my balance.[39]

Roon had objectively a difficult position. He had been asked to chair a commission as deputy to the Minister of War on which he was by far the most junior officer, no insignificant matter in a military organization. Retired General Heinrich von Brandt (1789–1868), one of the most distinguished military theorists of the previous generation of soldiers, that is, those who fought in the Napoleonic War, watched Roon's difficulty from the detachment of one who had seen it all before. He had written the classic study on tactics, which had just been reissued in 1859 and had been translated into several foreign languages.[40] Brandt's most gifted and devoted pupil was the 41-year-old Major Albrecht von Stosch, later like Schleinitz to become one of Bismarck's 'enemies'. He and his former commander, General von Brandt, carried on a private correspondence of remarkable frankness and interest. General von Brandt reported to Stosch on 19 October 1859 what he had heard in Berlin about army reform:

Other than that everything is in the usual confusion. The lack of information about the army organization, plus the nonsense which comes to light begins to be discussed in public. Now they have called on Roon in order to brood further on the project that he came up with in Posen. But he has a difficult problem to solve. He will be expected to patch whereas it really needs a complete break with the old system. Now let God help him. The army is at present in the moulting stage. I believe it would cause unbelievable difficulties if one had to organize it to be able to march.[41]

A series of difficult commission meetings then took place at which field marshals and full generals participated. One, old 'Papa Wrangel', Field Marshall Friedrich Count von Wrangel, though 75, had not retired like his younger colleague von Brandt. He attended the meetings and on 4 November told Roon in a very emotional conversation that he wanted to see von Roon appointed Minister of War:

I must be Minister of War. I was a firm character, he saw that in the debates...I am the only one who can carry out the reorganization and he had recommended my nomination to the All-Highest gentleman in the most urgent possible terms etc. etc.[42]

On 29 November 1859 the Prince Regent appointed Albrecht von Roon Minister of War. The official order was dated 5 December. At 56 years old Roon was the most junior Lieutenant General in the Prussian Army. At the formal audience on 4 December, before the official announcement of the appointment, he asked the Prince Regent urgently to reconsider, 'if he ought not to find a useful man who had his confidence with a more correct constitutional perfume'. Von Bonin had earned the hatred of conservatives because of his 'craving for popularity and his flirtation with liberalism during his earlier tenure (1852–54) as Minister of War'.[43] Roon's first appearance in his new role created an unfavourable impression on the members of the Prussian Landtag and evoked a variety of comments that he was 'austere', 'as if dressed in stiff iron plates', had a face of grim severity' and above all was a 'reactionary'.[44] Nobody accused him of being too soft.

The other side of Roon comes out clearly in his correspondence with his friend Clemens Theodor Perthes, a remarkable professor of civil law at the university of Bonn and a founder of the Christian Union for the Inner Mission in 1855 as well as the founder of the first hostel in Bonn for young workers.[45] Deeply Lutheran, he was also deeply political. He knew almost everybody who counted in Prussian society (the Perthes family owned a distinguished publishing business) and his Christianity never blinded him to the human characteristics of his acquaintances. Roon and Perthes enjoyed an intimate bond that held their friendship stable, even as their stations in life became very different. Perthes, though younger, acted as a kind of confessor to whom Roon confided his thoughts and doubts. Perthes distrusted Bismarck and frequently warned his friend Albrecht von Roon about him. Early in December 1859, Perthes wrote a remarkably prophetic letter to the new Minister of War, warning him not to be too reactionary and advising him to be clear that the *Kreuzzeitung* ultra-conservatives would try to use him and his appointment. He should remember that he had taken on a historic task and not just for the moment:

> The state, on which Germany's fate in the future will depend, should acquire a new basis for its situation in Europe and in its own internal life through you. A piece of history has been entrusted to your hands. You are not merely placed in the present time before the eyes of Prussia, Germany and Europe but have also become a historic man. Who in future will occupy himself with the history of Prussia will not be able to ignore you.[46]

Dierk Walter points out in his recent book on Prussian army reform that there has never been any serious research on the Roon reforms.[47] They have become 'mythical'. Historians see them as 'important' because, without exception, soldiers from the 1860s on and scholars since the 1860s have considered them important. But were they? Even the most modern and standard military histories repeat the old story, as Walter points out,

> without even an attempt to try to establish, why an increase of the recruitment quota by 23,000 men, the creation of 49 new regiments and the exclusion of the Landwehr from the field army should have such wide-ranging, qualitative consequences.[48]

One reason they became important is that William I made them a top priority. On 12 January 1860 the Regent gave an unusual public lecture before the royal Princes and the senior generals in which he discussed the significance of the reforms. Leopold von Gerlach was impressed and found the lecture 'outstanding...I learned many new facts...The military reform is a great measure, whose importance will more and more become evident.'[49] Indeed, the reforms became important because they convinced the King to appoint Albrecht von Roon his Minister of War, and that was really important because Roon had known Bismarck since the latter was a teenager and knew how gifted Bismarck was. Roon constantly urged the King to appoint Bismarck from the first day of his appointment as a minister.

In the second place, the reforms led to a conflict between Crown and Parliament which caused a complete paralysis of the entire government machinery and to generals it seemed to foreshadow Act 2 of the revolutions of 1848. The fear of the Berlin crowd and the memory of the revolutionary unrest—after all, only fourteen years earlier and very well remembered at court and in the army—served as the backdrop to the crisis of 1859–62. In that atmosphere, Roon's constant advocacy of Bismarck became more urgent and irresistible. Bismarck became Minister-President because of the reform programme and the deadlock that financing it created. Roon exercised this power because as a Prussian general and Minister of War he was not bound by the Cabinet Order of September 1852 to consult the Minister-President before requesting an audience with the King. He had, as did other commanding generals, an 'immediate' position. No intermediary could interrupt a Prussian general's access to his commanding officer, the King.

Roon's reforms were, of course, important for military reasons. They increased the size of the active army and active reserves by more than 50 per cent and insured that the larger army would be better trained. They established the doctrine that it took three years of active duty to turn a civilian into a Prussian soldier, a matter which aroused parliamentary opposition from 1859 to the outbreak of the First World War. They reduced the traditional militia reserves, which angered the reserve officers and much of the patriotic bourgeoisie. They raised the annual costs of the army but above all they engaged the Crown and Parliament on an issue which went to the heart of Prussian identity: was the army a royal army or what some called a parliamentary army?

The reforms mattered also because the King cared. Of the Hohenzollern monarchs after Frederick the Great, William was the most committed soldier. He saw himself not only as a commander but as a thinker who had general ideas on the future of the army. In 1832 he wrote several long memoranda on the need for three-year service in order to transform a 'trained peasant into a proper soldier'. The third year made a real difference in creating the *Soldatengeist* or 'military spirit' which in troubled times protected authority. A wave of revolutionary outbreaks had shaken Europe in 1830 and 1831 which made the Prince's reflections more relevant. As he wrote to Karl Georg von Hake, Minister of War under Frederick William III,[50] on 9 April 1832:

> The tendency of revolutionary and liberal parties in Europe is bit by bit to tear down all the supports, which guarantee the Sovereign's power and respect and thus assure him security in time of danger. That the armies are the chief of these supports is natural. The more a true military spirit infuses the army, the more difficult it will be to get around it. Discipline, blind obedience, are things which only through long habit can be created, so that in the moment of danger, the Monarch can rely on his troops.[51]

The lessons of Stein, Scharnhorst, and Gneisenau had been forgotten. The soldier Prince wanted to return to the obedience of the corpse as the only way to preserve his absolute rights as a monarch. If the military has to fire on its fellow citizens, too much thinking can only weaken their ability to do that.

Prince William—rather naively—never reckoned with the hostile reaction which the draft bill received when Roon presented it in February 1860. The liberals in parliament were horrified. Here was a huge increase in the budget to create an army which would be quite explicitly a bulwark against parliament and the growth of representative institutions. After a compromise in 1860 in which moderate liberals agreed to pass the army estimates, the parliament simply refused to approve the Roon expansion and voted against all the measures that might finance it. Crown and parliament locked horns and neither side would yield.

While Roon took his place in the Ministry of War, Bismarck waited for something to happen. He could not return to Petersburg nor get a straight answer about his future. On 21 January 1860 Legationsrat von Zschock, a Prussian diplomat in Stuttgart, wrote to Max Duncker, a leading Liberal and a professor of history,

> Since yesterday the rumour has spread that Herr von Bismarck is to become foreign minister in place of Herr von Schleinitz who will in turn replace Bernstorff in London...The name Bismarck has a repellent sound not only in the ears of all German governments so that the name alone—as Minister Hügel once said to me—is not only enough to effect a split between Prussia and its previous allies, but the name is at the same time—be it right or wrong—a cause of profound hatred in the depth of the soul of every friend of Prussia...[52]

Bismarck, idling in furious impatience, wrote an intemperate and bellicose letter to Moritz von Blanckenburg on 12 February 1860:

> Russia concedes little to us, England nothing, but Austria and the Ultramontanes are worse for us than the French. France will often be our enemy out of insolence and lack of restraint but it can at least live without fighting us. But Austria and her allies,—Reichensperger[53] [a leading Catholic lawyer and politician—JS]—can only flourish on a field where Prussia has been ploughed under as fertilizer. To cling to the Slavic-Romanic mixed state on the Danube and to whore with Pope and Kaiser is just as treasonable against Prussia and the Lutheran faith, indeed against Germany, as the most vile and open Rhenish confederation. The most we can lose to France is provinces and that only temporarily; to Austria the whole of Prussia and for all time.[54]

February turned into March. March passed as did April, and still Bismarck had to wait in Berlin until his royal master made up his mind. On 7 May he wrote to Johanna from Berlin,

> I sit here and the wheel of time has forgotten me like Red Beard in Kyffhäuser. After three days of vain efforts I finally ran into Schleinitz by chance at dinner at Rederns...I explained rather drily that I would rather quit than continue this life of hanging about and worrying in suspended anxiety. He urged me then to be calm 'for a few more days' and made unclear references to undefined alterations.[55]

During Bismarck's enforced idleness at Berlin, he and Moritz von Blanckenburg, his childhood friend, met Roon regularly to discuss the business of the new Minister. As Waldemar von Roon, Albrecht's son and biographer explained, his father sought Bismarck's advice, and since Bismarck was 'intimately tied to Moritz von Blankenburg, chief of the Conservative Party in the Landtag, as was Roon himself', Bismarck 'lost no occasion' when he was in Berlin to consult 'his older friend after Roon had become minister, and in the long conversations that the three had together a growing agreement of political views began to establish itself'.[56] Roon needed all the help he could get in the beginning of his career as Minister, for he came under attack from the liberals in Parliament, for whom he was too reactionary, and from reactionaries in the army, for whom he was too moderate. Of these the most persistent and best connected to the King was General Edwin von Manteuffel.

Edwin von Manteuffel (1809–85) deserves a biography at least as much as Moltke and Roon; indeed Manteuffel created the triumvirate of general officers which shaped Prussian German military affairs until 1918. Unlike Roon or Bismarck, Manteuffel belonged to an immensely distinguished family with many branches and dozens of famous soldiers and statesmen among his ancestors. Yet his own family circumstances were inglorious. His branch had little money, and he suffered from a delicate constitution. He was nearsighted, and in spite of his name had few contacts in higher circles.[57] His cousin, Otto, we have met as the Prussian Minister-President from 1850 to the New Era, who protected and promoted Bismarck. Edwin, unlike his dour and reserved cousin, had a flair for drama and knew thousands of lines of his beloved Schiller by heart. Gordon Craig describes him as an 'incurable romantic'.[58] He served in the extremely posh Dragoon Guards as a young officer, attended the War Academy, held a variety of commands and came to the attention of Frederick William IV and the camarilla. During 1848 and afterwards, the King used this reliable officer on special diplomatic missions. In the 1840s Manteuffel went to the lectures of the famous historian Leopold von Ranke (1795–1886) and became a devoted disciple of the new scientific history which Ranke taught. Ranke reflected years later on Manteuffel and said, 'He had more understanding of my writings and a greater spiritual sympathy than was granted to me elsewhere in the world.'[59]

Manteuffel took his most important post in early 1857 when Frederick William IV named him Chief of the Section for Personnel Affairs in the Ministry of War. Even before Bismarck came to power, Manteuffel had arranged the transfer of the office from control of the Minister of War to the personal headquarters of the King, where the title became Chief of the Military Cabinet. This was done on 18 January 1861, when King William

I issued 'a notable, if momentarily unappreciated, cabinet order that henceforth army orders deciding personnel, service details or matters of command would not require ministerial countersignature ...'[60] The Chief of the
Military Cabinet, in effect, became solely responsible to the King for making suggestions for the assignment of officers of all ranks to their posts.
Thirty years later General von Schweinitz reflected bitterly on this development and the way a successor to Manteuffel, General Emil von Albedyll,
exercised an almost invisible dictatorship:

> The enormous expansion of the army has made it impossible for the Kaiser to
> follow careers and to know the personnel as precisely as he used to do, and to
> regulate it as wisely and justly as formerly. The Chief of the Military Cabinet
> has become in a natural way very powerful and once he had with the help of
> Bismarck [Manteuffel did it before Bismarck—JS] made himself independent
> of the Minister of War who has taken an oath to the constitution, General
> Albedyll has become the second most powerful man in the land. For in our
> people there are very few families of the upper class who are not represented
> by a member serving in the army and hence have either something to hope or
> fear from General Albedyll, the chief of personnel administration.[61]

The most pernicious effect lay in the distortion of decision making. Moltke,
important as he was, had his office in 66 Behrenstrasse; Roon and his successors sat in the Kriegsministerium on the Leipziger Strasse. Manteuffel sat
in an antechamber of the royal palace and as Adjutant-General he saw the
King daily in the normal course of his duties. In a semi-autocratic state like
the Kingdom of Prussia, the fact of proximity trumped all other facts. After
Roon and Moltke had withdrawn to their offices, the head of the Military
Cabinet could listen to the Sovereign's reactions, help him draft his replies,
and gently colour the royal response on broad policy matters. The
Militärkabinet grew steadily in power and authority until finally on 8 March
1883 the Emperor removed the institution from the rank list of the Ministry,
as an official newspaper reported:

> This regulation should come to expression in the rank list of the army in such
> a way that in future under the 'Adjutancy of His Imperial Majesty the Emperor
> and King' the entire Military Cabinet will be listed, whereas under the rank
> lists of the Ministry of War, a listing of such names shall henceforth cease and
> the rubric will simply say: 'See Military Cabinet'.[62]

Manteuffel started the process that led inexorably to a Hobbesian war of all
against all in the German high command, and since under Stosch the new
Imperial Navy adopted the structure of its older model, the Prussian Army,

the chaos soon settled in at the naval headquarters as well. Thus, the centralization and efficiency that Moltke achieved in 1866 and 1870 never occurred again, and that was Manteuffel's legacy. More immediately he made Roon's life difficult by ever more intransigent statements about the conflict between the Ministry of War and parliament. On 10 March 1860, Manteuffel wrote to Roon that 'the unconditional maintenance of the Military Cabinet, particularly at the present moment, is a necessity.'[63] The next day he wrote again to strengthen Roon's resistance:

> When a question of principle arises, all the world counsels concession and compromise and advises against bringing matters to a head, and that when this or that minister has acted upon the rules of prudence and the momentary emergency has passed, then everyone says, 'how could he have given in like that?'[64]

The new regiments promised in Roon's plan should be established right away, whether or not parliament had conceded the necessary funds. On 29 May 1860 Manteuffel wrote to Roon to make it absolutely clear where he—and by implication the Prince Regent—stood on this issue:

> I consider the state of the army morale and its inner energy imperilled and the position of the Prince Regent compromised if these regiments are not established definitively at once.[65]

On the other hand, Roon, Moltke, and later Bismarck all needed Manteuffel's help and support. He shared their ends, disagreeing only on means and on style. Manteuffel played a crucial part in convincing the Prince Regent to appoint Moltke as Chief of the General Staff and to give him wide powers. Nor was Manteuffel as reactionary as some of his utterances in the 1860s suggest. When in 1879 he became Governor-General of Alsace, a post which reported directly to the Emperor, he went out of his way to promote and encourage Alsatian personnel. He went to great pains to reconcile these unwilling German subjects with their fate.[66] The problem that Manteuffel posed for Roon in 1860 arose from his flamboyant temperament, his direct access to the King, his position in the palace, his brilliance and literary flair, and the fact that he had become a general and hence beyond the control of Bismarck, a mere civilian. As early as December 1857 Bismarck complained to Leopold von Gerlach about his treatment by Edwin von Manteuffel, who spoke to him 'as a teacher gives instruction to a child...Edwin's behaviour to me is...always disapproving and suspicious.' Too much 'servility' has spoiled Edwin: '...all the more I need your assurance that this fanatical corporal, this Edwin, did not act on your instructions when recently he treated me as a doubtful political intriguer who had to be got out of Berlin as soon as possible.'[67]

But that was exactly Bismarck's position in late 1857 and afterwards, a 'doubtful political intriguer' always showing up at the palace uninvited, an ambitious, clever, unstable figure, whom Edwin von Manteuffel had every reason to mistrust. Nevertheless, when it became a question of Bismarck's appointment to the Minister-Presidency, Manteuffel backed him loyally. Like Roon he saw that nobody could or would do for the army what Bismarck had in mind.

In 1860 all that lay ahead and Bismarck vegetated in Berlin without orders. Apparently the Prince Regent had specifically issued instructions that Bismarck 'should stay here',[68] and simply wait, not an easy order to obey for somebody of Bismarck's volcanic temperament, but not unusual for the Prince Regent. He combined a genuine concern for his servants with a sovereign disdain for the price his long hesitations would impose on them. The first round of 'Bismarck as Foreign Minister', took four months; the next round of 'Bismarck as Minister-President' to be played out in 1862 would take longer and be even more nerve-wracking. Still, even the lesser prize attracted the restless Bismarck, as he confessed to his brother, if somebody 'put a pistol to [his] breast, it would be cowardice to refuse' the office of Foreign Minister.[69] Nobody did. In early June 1860, he telegraphed Schlözer from Kovno that he would arrive in a day or two.[70] And, apparently this suited him. After his return to St Petersburg, he wrote to Legation Councillor Wentzel, a former subordinate in Frankfurt:

> I have settled in here at considerable cost for many years to come and could not wish for a more agreeable chief than Schleinitz. I have really got close to him and am rather fond of him. I wish sincerely that his desire to change places with me never happens, I would not last six months as minister.[71]

None of this suggests that Bismarck had given up his ambition to be Foreign Minister or Minister-President nor that he had now settled down to enjoy the view over the Neva from his ambassadorial residence. One of his implacable enemies, the Prime Minister of Baden, Franz Freiherr von Roggenbach, wrote on 25 August 1860, to the liberal academic and journalist Max Duncker, that Bismarck was nothing more than 'an unprincipled Junker who wants to make his career in rabble-rousing'.[72] There is something in the charge but there was much more to Bismarck than that. He really yearned for peace and contentment in some imagined countryside but, when he had it, it made him restless. He behaved brutally to friends but cared very much for his brother and sister. The other side of him comes to expression in the following letter which he wrote to his sister, one of the most beautiful I have found:

> I have to be torn from the clockwork mechanism of work here and through an Imperial summons be commanded to have a few free hours to come to my senses and write to you. Daily life controls my every movement from the breakfast cup to about four with every manner of duty, in paper or person, and then I ride until six. After dinner I approach the inkwell on doctor's orders only with great care and in the most extreme emergency. Instead I read documents and newspapers that have arrived and about midnight I go to bed amused and thoughtful about all the strange demands that the Prussian in Russia makes of his ambassador. Before dropping off to sleep I think then of the best of all sisters but to write to that angel becomes possible only when the Tsar orders me to appear for an audience at 1 and I have to take the 10 a.m. train. So I have two hours during which the apartment of the most beautiful of all grandmothers, Princess Wjäsemski, is placed at my disposal, where I write you . . . I look out over the desk and through the window down the hill over birch and maples in whose leaves red and yellow dominate the green, behind them the grass green roofs of the village, to the left of which a church with five onion-shaped domes stands out and that all framed against an endless horizon of bush, meadow and woodland. Behind their brown, grey tints somewhere, visible with a spy-glass could be seen St Isaac's in Petersburg . . . After the long wanderings since the beginning of 1859 the feeling of actually living with my family somewhere is so soothing that I tear myself from the home and hearth very unwillingly.[73]

Both sides of Otto von Bismarck were present at all times: the family man who craved the soothing quiet of his own home, the loving brother who addressed his letter to his kid sister 'my beloved heart', and in the same moment he could behave as the tenacious, devious, and utterly ruthless schemer, determined to get power no matter how.

That Bismarck was unhappy struck the young Friedrich von Holstein, who joined the St Petersburg embassy in January 1861 as an unpaid intern, as we would now call him. Years later he recorded his first impressions of the great man whom he idolized and served for thirty years:

> When I presented myself, he held out his hand and said, 'you are welcome'. As he stood there, tall, erect, unsmiling, I saw him as he was later to appear to his family and the rest of the world: A man who allows no one to know him

intimately...At that time Bismarck was forty-five, slightly bald, with fair hair turning grey, not noticeably corpulent, sallow complexion. Never gay, even when telling amusing anecdotes, a thing he did only occasionally, in particularly congenial company. I have never known anyone so joyless as Bismarck.[74]

The judgement that Bismarck had no 'joy' in life may well reflect Holstein's own 'joyless' last years and his disillusion with the idolized genius he had once adored, but the lack of warmth in the greeting must have made a deep impression on the young diplomat.

On 18 January 1861, thirty-six new infantry regiments, none of which had been authorized by the Landtag, presented their standards at the tomb of Frederick the Great.[75] Minister-President von Auerswald went to ask Manteuffel to intervene with the King and got a dose of Manteuffel's arrogance and provocative attitude:

> I do not understand what Your Excellency desires. His Majesty has ordered me to arrange a military ceremony. Am I to renounce this because there are a number of people sitting in a house on the Dönhoff Platz, who call themselves a *Landtag* and who may be displeased with this ceremony? As a general, I have never yet been ordered to take my instructions from these people.[76]

Manteuffel's outrageous attitude angered a young liberal deputy called Karl Twesten. In April 1861 he published anonymously an 88-page pamphlet entitled 'What can still save us: a blunt word'.[77] He attacked Manteuffel personally as a dangerous political general, long out of contact with the army, which distrusted him. 'Will we have to suffer a Battle of Solferino before we can remove this unwholesome man from an unwholesome position?'[78] Manteuffel demanded to know the name of the author and Twesten acknowledged it, whereupon Manteuffel challenged Twesten to a duel which took place on 27 May 1861. Twesten's shot missed Manteuffel, who offered to withdraw the challenge if Twesten would retract. Twesten refused and Manteuffel, a much better shot, shattered Twesten's right arm. When he offered to shake hands, Twesten apologized for offering his left hand and said, 'he will have to excuse me that it is not the right hand but that he himself has made impossible.'[79] The duel made both participants nationally famous and personalized the issues between the army and the nation in an emotional form, exactly what Manteuffel wanted to do. Twesten's intemperate speeches and vivid language further inflamed the conflict.

The King was beside himself with distress about the duel. He told Roon, 'I have a bucket full of trouble.' It was bad enough that the duel, an act forbidden by law, between Deputy Twesten and Military Cabinet Chief von Manteuffel, forced King William to dismiss von Manteuffel and call for a military court martial; but worst of all, was the personal impact:

> In just this moment to be without Manteuffel's service, a triumph for the democracy which managed to chase him out of my presence; the excitement that the affair must cause in my immediate family circle, these are things that look set to rob me of my sanity, because it puts an unhappy new stamp on my government. Where does heaven want to lead me?[80]

Early in June a group of left liberals, with the wounded Twesten foremost among them, formed a new party, the Deutsche Fortschrittspartei, the German Progressive Party, committed to a national state, a strong government, full parliamentary authority, and communal self-government. It was the first formal party programme in German history.[81] The new party became at a stroke the largest in the Landtag.

In the meantime another row had blown up about the coronation ceremony for William I as King of Prussia. Liberals insisted that he take an oath on the constitution and the King absolutely refused to countenance any such concession. He intended to have a feudal ceremony of homage. Roon now went into action. The time had come to summon Bismarck to take power. On 28 June 1861 he sent Bismarck a telegram with the following wording: 'It is "nothing" [English in the original—JS]. Start your planned holiday without delay. *Periculum in mora* [danger in delay].' The telegram was signed Moritz C. Henning, which Bismarck would at once recognize as his friend, Moritz Karl Henning von Blanckenburg. The phrase *Periculum in mora* would recur in the more famous summons of 1862.[82]

Bismarck took his time in reply, wrote a letter on 1 July, added a paragraph on the 2nd, and sent it with a further addition on the 3rd by the English courier to Berlin. He was in no hurry to take power until his agenda had been accepted. The coronation ceremony was too trivial to topple the Auerswald cabinet and priorities in domestic and foreign policy were exactly the wrong way round—conservative abroad and liberal at home, as Bismarck explained to Roon in a letter in July 1861:

> the good royalist mass of voters will not understand the coronation issue and the Democracy will distort it. It would be better to stick firmly to the military

question, break with the chamber on it and call new elections to show the
nation how the King stands by his people.[83]

The letter shows that by the summer of 1861 Bismarck had the firm outlines of the policy he was to follow in 1863 and 1864. No concessions to
liberalism at home, the battle to be fought over the military question at
whatever cost in bad election results, and an aggressive foreign policy to
catch the popular imagination. 'We are almost as vain as the French. If we
can convince ourselves that we have respect abroad, we will put up with a
lot at home.'[84] Bismarck went to Berlin and then Schleinitz ordered him to
Baden, while Roon travelled in other directions. They simply could not
reach each other and coordinate a place to meet, no matter how urgently
they needed to talk. How the cell phone simplifies arrangements!

In September on holiday in Stolpmünde, Bismarck wrote a summary of
his position on the German question to his close friend, Alexander Ewald
von Below-Hohendorf. It is, I think, the clearest account of Bismarck's
contempt for the world of the petty princes and the most drastic statement
of his own very unconventional conservatism. Remember that this text was
addressed to a dear friend, who had looked after him in 1859 when he was
ill and who prescribed Christian love as the remedy for Bismarck's illness.
Imagine how such a devout rural gentleman would have reacted to the
cynicism dripping from this prose.

> The system of solidarity of the conservative interests of all countries is a dan-
> gerous fiction...We arrive at a point where we make the whole unhistorical,
> godless and lawless sovereignty swindle of the German princes into the dar-
> ling of the Prussian Conservative Party. Our government is in fact liberal
> domestically and legitimist in foreign policy. We protect foreign monarchical
> rights with greater tenacity than our own and wax lyrical about little sover-
> eignties created by Napoleon and sanctioned by Metternich to the point of
> utter blindness to all the dangers to which Prussia's and Germany's independ-
> ence is exposed as long as the madness of the present federal constitution
> survives, which is after all nothing but a green house and storage centre for
> dangerous and revolutionary separatist movements...Beside I cannot see a
> reason why we coyly shrink from the idea of a popular assembly, whether at
> the Federal level or in the Zoll Parliament; an institution, which operates in
> every German state and which we Conservatives in Prussia cannot do with-
> out, can hardly be called a revolutionary innovation.[85]

This kind of *Realpolitik* repelled the pious Christians who were conservatives out of faith and not self-interest. Bismarck no longer hesitated to

broadcast his views to all those who might be persuaded and those who might not.

While Bismarck attacked the 'sovereignty swindle', the King backed down on the feudal ceremony and was crowned without further friction on 18 October 1861, in Königsberg. Bismarck as a royal servant attended the ceremony and wrote a typical letter to his sister about how the ceremony threatened his health:

> Changing clothes three times a day and the draughts in all the halls and corridors still lies in all my extremities. On the 18TH on the palace grounds in the open air I had as a precautionary device put on a thick military uniform and a wig in comparison to which Bernhard's is a mere lock of hair, otherwise the two hours bare-headed would have been very bad for me.[86]

Concessions on the homage question had not improved the atmosphere in the classes that voted in Prussia. On 6 December 1861 Prussian voters returned a lower chamber of 352 deputies, of whom 104 were German Progressives who had remained the largest party, 48 other Liberals, and 91 'constitutionals' (moderate liberals who supported the Auerswald government); in other words, 69 per cent of the new Landtag belonged to the liberal persuasion and of those the most extreme wing had become the largest. Bismarck's conservative friends had shrunk from 47 deputies to a mere 14, a sorry rump for the party of the Junker ruling class.[87]

On 3 April 1862 Edwin von Manteuffel wrote a letter to Roon in which he cheerfully conjured up the threat of revolution:

> I recognize no advances in the battle except with weapons in hand, and we are in the midst of the battle. How can the three-year service be given up during his reign without bringing shame to the personal position of the All-Highest? . . . The army will not understand it; its confidence in the King will slacken and the consequences for the internal condition of the army will be incalculable . . . We shall see bloody heads and *then* good election results will come.[88]

Max Duncker, the liberal journalist, quoted Psalm 42 to sum up the situation: 'As the hart panteth after the water-brooks so the army thirsts for riots.'[89]

In this overheated atmosphere, the kingdom's voters went to the polls on 6 May 1862. By 18 May, the two stages of the elections had been completed and the government of the King had suffered an unmitigated electoral disaster. The left liberals had gained 29 seats compared to 1861 and at 133 members formed the largest *Fraktion*, as the parliamentary parties were called, in the Landtag. The other Liberals had doubled their representation from 48 to 96 and the remaining 'Constitutionals' who had supported the New Era shrank from 91 to 19 seats. The numbers showed an unequivocal shift to the left. The left liberals now controlled 65 per cent of the seats and the King's supporters had shrivelled to a mere 11 deputies.[90]

Was Prussia on the eve of revolution? Was this the great 'turning point where nothing turned'? There are good reasons to think the answer is *no*. Structural factors suggest that there were no grounds to fear revolution. Let us look at the voting figures. The three-class voting system which the constitutional amendment of 1850 had introduced created an odd electoral system. Class I contained the top 5 per cent of taxpayers, Class II the next 13 per cent, and Class III the remaining 81 per cent. It was a universal but very unequal system of suffrage and favoured, as was intended, the well-to-do. If we take the contested election of 6 December 1861, the numbers of those entitled to vote were as follows with figures in percentages showing the share of each class of the total number of those entitled to vote.

Class I	159,200	(4.7%)
Class II	453,737	(13.5%)
Class III	2,750,000	(81.8%)[91]

The share of power granted by this system to the lower orders meant that the vote in Prussian elections mattered most to those with the most. The taxation basis insured that only a tiny number of people could vote in category I in the electoral districts; sometimes no such voters appeared at all, because nobody in the electoral district paid enough tax. At the other end, the complex two-stage voting system (voters voted for electors called *Wahlmänner*, who then voted for candidates), and the rigged system of weighting made it impossible for the masses to get involved. Electoral turnout in Category III was always low, usually well under 20 per cent. Thus the hotly contested elections of the *Konfliktzeit* attracted only the voters in Classes I and II. The German Progressive Party looked threatening to Manteuffel but it represented the well-educated and well-heeled bourgeoisie who were unlikely to erect guillotines on the pavement in front of the royal palace.

We know this now, of course, because the liberals never staged a revolution nor even managed to organize passive resistance such as a tax strike, that is, a refusal to pay taxes until the Landtag's right to control the army's budget had been granted. A tax strike had recently brought the reactionary Prince-Elector of Hesse-Cassel to the negotiating table when he tried to rule without his parliament. Could anybody be certain that constant agitation by the progressive liberals might not in the end have brought the masses into the streets? Manteuffel and a few extremists among the senior officers hoped that a 'bloody heads' scenario would be the pretext to restore the absolute monarchy, abolish the constitution, and quash electoral activity, creating in effect a military dictatorship. Neither the King nor Roon wanted that kind of outcome; indeed Roon had been willing to compromise for a long time, much to the disgust of Manteuffel.

Now as in 1861 the King began to think about Bismarck and in April 1862 he was summoned from St Petersburg to Berlin for consultations. Bismarck wrote to tell Roon that he would soon be in Berlin to discuss a transfer either to Paris or London.[92] A few days later he wrote to one of his former staff in Frankfurt that he was still not certain about his next post and must go to Berlin to find out. 'So I travel without knowing where', and must sell his Russian furniture and possessions at short notice quite unnecessarily, a certain way to lose a great deal of money.[93] When he reached Berlin, he found a characteristic situation: the King could not make up his mind. As he wrote to Johanna on 17 May 1862, 'our future is as uncertain as ever. Berlin has moved to centre stage [a ministerial post—JS]. I do nothing for and nothing against but will drink myself silly when I have my accreditation for Paris in my pocket.'[94] We know by now that Bismarck always told Johanna that he had shunned the post he most wanted and it is clear from other sources that Bismarck had been hard at his palace intrigues to become Minister-President. In May 1862, Roon recorded in his notes that 'Bismarck had been received several times in long audiences by the King. With several ministers he had long discussions and went every day to the Ministry of War. The initiated believed that his appointment to the Ministry must be expected directly.'[95]

In the midst of the ministerial crisis, on 21 May 1862, Roon's friend Clement Theodor Perthes wrote a very significant assessment of Bismarck on the eve of his possible appointment to high or the highest office:

> Bismarck-Schönhausen has great moral courage. A decisive spirit expresses itself in the energetic tone of his voice in all his speeches. He can sweep people along with him. He has no previous political training and lacks a thorough political education...He has a series of contradictions in his character.

His wife, a Puttkamer by birth, is a strict Lutheran, related to Thadden-Trieglaff and very respectful of him. Bismarck inclines to a determined Lutheranism too but is irresponsible. There is an absent-mindedness in him and he can easily be stirred by sympathies and antipathies...He is thoroughly honest and straight but his policies can be immoral. By nature he has an unforgiving, vengeful tendency, which his religious sensibility and nobility of character keep under control.[96]

Perthes catches in this short sketch the deep dualism in Bismarck and the powerful contradictions in his nature. I would doubt that 'thoroughly honest and straight' ever applied to Bismarck. We know from his own accounts that he always lied to his parents and we have seen him lie regularly to Johanna, nor do I see any evidence that his Christianity had the slightest restraining effect on his vengefulness. Von Below showed us how little Christian love the heart of Bismarck contained. But Perthes foreshadowed the internal struggle that marked Bismarck's years in power very accurately. Contemporaries intuit aspects of character which subsequent observers may well overlook.

By 23 May 1862, Bismarck could tell his wife that it would be Paris to which he would be sent,

but the shadow still remains in the background. I was almost caught by the cabinet so I will get away as quickly as I can...perhaps they will find another Minister-President as soon as I am out of sight.[97]

Two days later he wrote to his wife and brother that 'everybody here is sworn to keep me here' and that if he goes to Paris, it will be for a short time only.[98] By 30 May he had arrived in Paris and wrote to Roon on 2 June 1862 to say that 'I have arrived here safely and live like a rat in an empty barn.' He hoped that the King would find another Minister-President and insisted that he would not accept a position of Minister without Portfolio because

the position is impractical: to have nothing to say and to have to bear everything, to stink about in everything without being asked and to be chewed up by everyone where one has something really to say.[99]

Roon replied two days later that 'I took the occasion yesterday in influential quarters to raise the minister-president question and found the same leaning toward you and the same indecision. Who can help here? And how will this end?'[100] Roon described in graphic detail the impossible situation in the new Landtag which had assembled for the first time on 19 May 1862. The only majority for a government would put the Democrats in control and that remained unthinkable. 'Under these conditions, so says my logic, the present government might as well remain in office.'[101] And Bismarck replied a few days later. 'Rest assured that I undertake no counter-moves and manoeuvres...I am not lifting a finger.'[102]

By late June, Roon had become desperate. He expressed it in a passionate outburst to his friend:

> More courage! More energetic activity abroad and at home! More action must be brought into this Ifflandish family drama. For that you are irreplaceable...how is it possible that Prussia will not go under?—And nonetheless, we must fight to the last drop of blood. Can that happen with a knife with a blade and which has no grip? Now you are off to London, Vichy, Trouville, I don't know where and when you will get this letter...[103]

Indeed, as Roon wrote, Bismarck had arrived in London, where he remained until 4 July. It was during this visit that Bismarck met Benjamin Disraeli, at the home of the Russian Ambassador Brunnow. Disraeli, novelist, dandy, brilliant speaker, was the only contemporary of Bismarck's who could match him in wit and political agility. This was the first occasion that these two remarkable men met. In those years, Disraeli, who had already served as leader of the House of Commons and Chancellor of the Exchequer in the 1852 government under Lord Derby, was now going through a long period in opposition. He had in the period out of office established his authority over the Conservative Party which would make him Prime Minister by 1868. Disraeli recorded Bismarck's statement of his political intentions, which he declared in his astonishingly frank way:

> I shall soon be compelled to undertake the conduct of the Prussian government. My first care will be to reorganize the army, with or without, the help of the Landtag...As soon as the army shall have been brought into such a condition as to inspire respect, I shall seize the first best pretext to declare war against Austria, dissolve the German Diet, subdue the minor states and give national unity to Germany under Prussian leadership. I have come here to say this to the Queen's ministers.

On the way home, Disraeli accompanied Friedrich, Count Vitzthum von Eckstädt, the Austrian envoy to his residence. As they parted, Disraeli said to Vitzthum: 'Take care of that man; he means what he says.' And he did.[104]

On 5 July, Bismarck got back to Paris and found Roon's various letters waiting. He reported briefly on his impressions of London. 'Just back from

London where they know more about China and Turkey than about Prussia...If I am going to live here longer, so I must definitely settle down with wife and horses and servants. I don't know any longer what and where to have my lunch...'[105] And to his wife he wrote that the ambassador's house in Paris was 'awful' and made some suggestions on how to make it more habitable.[106] His own plan for his future was typically Bismarckian, as he explained to Roon in a letter of 15 July:'I will not put pressure on the King by lying at anchor in Berlin and will not go home because I fear that on the journey through Berlin I shall be nailed to the guest house for an uncertain length of time...'

Roon too needed a holiday. Just before leaving Berlin, he wrote a long account of his present political position to his friend and confidante, Perthes:

> I am getting determined and poisonous enemies who are a bit frightened of me and warm friends who like to honour my weakness a little. In certain high circles I am *la bête* and in others I am a *pis-aller*, the trusty last nail in the structure. In view of this importance of mine now grown beyond my capacities I feel the need in moments of quiet for my amusement to study the histories of Strafford and Latour, both noble counts, who like me had the passion to enlist themselves for the cause of their sovereigns, although one difference among others is that mine serves a better cause than theirs. As a result the prophecy, which I announced myself years ago 'that I would die by the neck' has acquired also another significance.[107]

In fact, Roon, as he got older, suffered increasingly from asthma and by the end he could have been said to have 'died by the neck'.

Bismarck went off on holiday by himself to southern France. From 27 to 29 July 1862 he was in Bordeaux, then on to San Sebastian by 1 August. On 4 August he arrived at Biarritz where, as he wrote to Johanna, he could see from his hotel, 'the charming view of the blue sea, which drives its white foam between wonderful cliffs towards the light house'.[108] He joined the Prince and Princess Orloff for the next fortnight of sea, sun, and walks. The Orloffs were the grandest of Russian grand nobility. Prince Nikolaus, handsome and charming, had been crippled during the Crimean War, lost an eye, and had his arm shattered. His wife, a Princess Trubetskoy, came from an even grander and much richer family. She was 22 when she met Bismarck, about the age that Marie von Thadden had been when Bismarck first met her. There seems little doubt that Bismarck fell in love with the Princess and in the same way as he had with Marie, a forbidden love of a younger woman who was married to another man. They took walks together, bathed, lay in the sun, exchanged books, and Bismarck recovered his joy in life. As he wrote to Johanna,

> next to me the most charming of all women, whom you would certainly love if you knew her better, a bit of Marie von Thadden, a bit of Nadi, but original for herself, funny, clever and charming... when you two come together, you will forgive me that I go into such raptures... I am ludicrously healthy and so happy, as I can be far from my loved ones.[109]

He wrote to his sister in the same tones and confessed 'you know how these things occasionally hit me, without doing any harm to Johanna.'[110] One wonders what Johanna must have felt when Bismarck compared Katharina to Marie.

What Katharina felt we do not know. Her grandson, who published a collection of letters between his grandmother and Bismarck in the midst of the Second World War, tried to maintain the proprieties and suggested that it was all quite harmless. Bismarck wrote to her as 'Catty' and she to him as 'Uncle', and he was, after all, twenty-five years older than she. My guess is that she was flattered, fascinated by the magnetism and brilliance of the man, but never remotely in love with him in return. Bismarck left the idyllic surroundings in Biarritz but the correspondence continued over the coming years, the most intense and stressful of Bismarck's life. They came to an abrupt and—for Bismarck—painful end three years later, when Bismarck now Minister-President of Prussia, tried to recapture the rapture of 1862 by taking his family to the Hotel L'Europe in Biarritz in late September of 1865. He had written to his 'Catty' to tell her that he intended to be there. When they arrived, it rained the whole time. Catty never appeared and left no notice. She had forgotten her promise and she and her husband had decided to take a holiday in England. On 3 October 1865 she wrote to apologize. 'Dear Uncle, What will you say to me now? I have been a bad niece, for I have broken my word to you. This time, alas, we must renounce our dear Biarritz...'[111] It took Bismarck two weeks to answer and when he did, the bitterness could not be concealed. It begins formally

> Dear Catharine,
>   It is true that you played me a trick which goes well beyond the privileges of a 'méchante enfant', since it was entirely adult and grown up bad manners... You would have done me a great service if you had informed me of the change in your plans... That is the reason I wanted to await the departure of an acquaintance to write to tell you freely the entire *mischief* [English in the

original—JS] which you caused by your silence... Although it was very painful to me to see how quickly the poor uncle has been forgotten even in situations where a small sign of life would have meant a great deal, I have now
gone too far along my road of life and have now too little chance...[112]

The letter breaks off at this point and is allegedly missing. My guess is that
Prince Orloff censored the next few sentences because they were too revealing. There is more than enough in the text to show how deeply hurt
Bismarck must have been. A man of 50 in love with a woman half his age
may look ridiculous but the pain of rejection, if anything, can be more
acute. This yearning for the love of a beautiful woman forms part of the
portrait of the great Bismarck and not an insignificant one.

On the way back to Paris in September 1862, in Toulouse, Bismarck
found a long letter from Roon dated 31 August, in which he set out the
present situation and his hopes for an immediate Bismarck ministry.

My dear B! You will more or less be able to guess why I have not answered
you before. I hoped and always hoped for a decision or even for a situation
which must bring an acute solution... I shall assume your agreement and will
counsel that you be named temporarily Minister-President without portfolio,
something I have so far avoided. There is no other way! If you absolutely
reject this, disavow me or order me to be silent. I have a private audience with
the Gentleman on the 7th... You have time to object... The internal catastrophe will not happen now but in the Spring and by then you have to be
there.[113]

On 12 September Bismarck replied from Toulouse that his present situation had become intolerable. His possessions were scattered all over Europe
and much of them would freeze in St Petersburg if he still had no idea
where to send them before winter set in. He had reached the point where
he would accept anything if it put an end to the uncertainty. 'If you secure
me this certainty or any other certainty, I will paint angels' wings on your
picture.'[114]

On 17 September 1862 Roon made a conciliatory speech in the Landtag.
The government had never in any way speculated on that which had come
to be called a 'conflict' but on the contrary they really wanted to achieve an
agreement over the outstanding questions.[115] In his memoirs Bismarck
wrote:

In Paris I received the following telegram, the signature of which had been
agreed upon:
'Berlin: le 18 Septembre.

Periculum in mora, Dépêchez-vous.
L'oncle de Maurice,
HENNING.'[116]

This formula, as we have seen, had been used in Roon's previous attempt to hoist Bismarck into office and it produced its effect. On 22 September 1862 Roon went to Babelsberg to report that the Landtag by a vote of 308 to 11 had approved the amended budget for 1862 but had rejected by 273 to 68 the entire army reform as part of the budget. Resignation letters had already been submitted by Hohenlohe, Heydt, and Bernstorff. The King asked for Roon's advice. Roon: 'Your Majesty, summon Bismarck.' King: 'He will not want it and now he will not take it on. Besides he is not here and nothing can be discussed with him.' Roon: 'He is here. He will accept your Majesty's command willingly.'[117] Bismarck had arrived in Berlin on 20 September.[118] This is his account of what happened next. He was

> summoned to the Crown Prince. To his question as to my view of the situation, I could only give a very cautious answer, because I had read no German papers during the last few weeks…The impression which the fact of my audience had made was at once discernible from Roon's statement that the King had said to him, referring to me: 'He is no good either; you see he has already been to see my son.' The bearing of this remark was not at once comprehensible to me, because I did not know that the King, having conceived the idea of abdication, assumed that I either knew or suspected it, and had therefore tried to place myself favourably with his successor.[119]

In spite of the King's suspicions, he invited Bismarck to an audience. Here is Bismarck's account of the occasion:

> I was received at Babelsberg on September 22, and the situation only became clear to me when his Majesty defined it in some such words as these: 'I will not reign if I cannot do it in such a fashion as I can be answerable to God, my conscience, and my subjects. But I cannot do that if I am to rule according to the will of the present majority in parliament, and I can no longer find any ministers prepared to conduct my government without subjecting themselves and me to the parliamentary majority. I have therefore resolved to lay down my crown, and have already sketched out the proclamation of my abdication, based on the motives to which I have referred.' The King showed me the document in his own handwriting lying on the table, whether already signed or not I do not know. His Majesty concluded by repeating that he could not govern without suitable ministers.
>
> I replied that his Majesty had been acquainted ever since May with my readiness to enter the ministry; I was certain that Roon would remain with

me on his side, and I did not doubt that we should succeed in completing the cabinet, supposing other members should feel themselves compelled to resign on account of my admission. After a good deal of consideration and discussion, the King asked me whether I was prepared as minister to advocate the reorganization of the army, and when I assented he asked me further whether I would do so in opposition to the majority in parliament and its resolutions. When I asserted my willingness, he finally declared, 'Then it is my duty, with your help, to attempt to continue the battle, and I shall not abdicate.' I do not know whether he destroyed the document, which was lying on the table, or whether he preserved it *in rei memoriam*.[120]

The decision to appoint Bismarck ensured that King William would have trouble at home. The Crown Princess recorded that the Queen would be desperately unhappy. In a diary entry of 23 September 1862, she wrote,[121] 'Poor Mama! How the appointment of her arch-enemy will pain her.' As early as July, Queen Augusta had made her position absolutely clear.

> As the envoy to the Bundestag Herr v. B always filled those *governments friendly to Prussia* with mistrust and affected those houses *hostile to Prussia* with political views which did not correspond to the position of Prussia in Germany but to its status as a threatening great power.[122]

The battle between Queen and Minister-President had begun. In this case, unlike the poor stenographers in the Reichstag, the Queen's hatred was not a figment of Bismarck's disordered imagination. She really was his enemy and did everything possible to get rid of him.

On 24 September 1862 Bleichröder wrote to Baron James de Rothschild:

> We are in the middle of a ministerial crisis. Herr von Bismarck-Schönhausen as Minister-President is occupied with the formation of a new cabinet. Roon, the war minister, remains, and this is proof enough that the conflict between Chamber and Crown will *not* be solved by the change of ministry... it appears as if we were to get an entirely reactionary ministry.[123]

That prospect made even Bismarck's friends uneasy, but for different reasons. The news that Bismarck had been summoned to Berlin spread quickly. On 20 September, even before Bismarck's audience, Ludwig von Gerlach wrote to Kleist-Retzow:

> However great my reservations are about Bismarck, not only in respect to Austria or France but in respect of God's commandments, I would not even dare to work against him—because I know no possible person who would be

better. If he fails too, we fall into God's hands. Will you not summon Moritz
to Berlin as Roon's political soul? Also for Bismarck's sake?[124]

Hans von Kleist replied on 22 September that he had seen his friend:
'Bismarck is fresh and in good humour. I think we do him an injustice if we
mean that he doubts the truth of the Cathecism.'[125]

Bismarck, now in office, had to arrange his affairs. He wrote to Wentzel
in Frankfurt to find out if his former cook in Frankfurt, Riepe, would be
willing to come to Berlin and asked Wentzel to sound him out. First things
first, in Bismarck's mind. Then he told Wentzel that Count Bernstorff would
be leaving for the Prussian Embassy in London sometime between 7 and 10
October, and that he, Bismarck, would then take over the Foreign
Ministry.[126]

On the same day, Major Stosch wrote to his friend, Otto von Holtzendorff,
a liberal judge in Coburg, that the crisis had really now become acute:

> The rumours about the resignation of the King become more and more
> lively, and who knows if that would not be a politically correct step. If the
> King gives in and the Progressives win, we shall be plunged into the whirl-
> pool of theoretical revolution, hair-splitting dogmatism, and impractical
> ambitious democracy. The Crown Prince has done everything to change his
> father's mind. My General [Heinrich von Brandt—JS] says, nothing can hap-
> pen in the army question, because the society of elderly gentlemen whom
> they use as advisers will take care not to say anything that those in highest
> circles will not want to hear. Manteuffel is the man who summons the pup-
> pets and gives them their roles.[127]

Stosch had yet to reckon with the impact of the new Minister-President,
Otto von Bismarck; it was not Manteuffel who 'summoned the puppets',
but Bismarck. In the meantime Bismarck had to confront the Landtag in its
rebellious frame of mind. On the 29th he withdrew the budget altogether,
the first of many provocations. Next he prepared to make his first public
appearance as Minister-President in a speech which he intended to make to
the Budget Committee of the Landtag, the very lion's den of the opposition. It became the most famous speech he ever made, his first parliamentary appearance as Minister-President, and here is the most famous
passage:

> Prussia must build up and preserve her strength for the advantageous moment,
> which has already come and gone many times. Her borders under the treaties
> of Vienna are not favourable for the healthy existence of the state. The great

questions of the day will not be settled by speeches and majority decisions—
that was the great mistake of 1848 and 1849—but by blood and iron.[128]

The attentive reader—and I hope there are a few—will not find that text
surprising. Over many years Bismarck had said more or less the same thing
to all sorts and conditions of listeners. In May 1862 he had advanced exactly
the same argument to Foreign Minister von Schleinitz and had even used
almost the same phrase, *ferro et igni*, iron and fire, rather than 'iron and
blood'. Admittedly, Latin is not German and a private letter not public testimony before a committee of a lower house of parliament. What had changed
was not Bismarck, nor his ideas, but the atmosphere. For once Bismarck
underestimated his own importance.

I have no doubt that he had decided to use that tactic in the relatively
restricted forum of a committee hearing. He had—a rare slip—underestimated his 'old reputation for irresponsible violence'. Liberals in the lower
house and in the country believed that the King had appointed Bismarck to
provoke the Landtag into ever greater folly at which point Bismarck's pup-
pet master, von Manteuffel, would get the King to declare martial law and
suspend the parliament. The army would occupy Berlin and install a royal
military dictatorship. Napoleon III had done exactly that on 2 December
1851, and got away with it, and France had a much greater tradition of revolution and disorder than Prussia. In the overheated imagination of people
like Twesten only that could explain the appointment of so notorious,
implacable, and unreconstructed a reactionary as Otto von Bismarck. The
historically minded could also compare Bismarck's appointment by the
King of Prussia in 1862 to the Bourbon King of France's appointment in
1829 of Prince Jules Polignac, the most intransigent ultra then available.
Charles X used the appointment to signal the end of constitutional monarchy in France and the Revolution of 1830 followed hard on that move.
Why not the same scenario in Prussia?

Bismarck's 'iron and blood' speech, his first as Minister-President, could
easily have been his last and nearly was. Informed opinion in the country
was shocked and outraged. The right-wing liberal, and famous historian,
Heinrich von Treitschke wrote to his brother-in-law:

> You know how passionately I love Prussia, but when I hear so shallow a
> country-squire as this Bismarck bragging about the 'iron and blood' with
> which he intends to subdue Germany, the meanness of it seems to be exceeded
> only by the absurdity.[129]

Much the most important reaction has left no trace but must have happened over the breakfast table or in the royal bedroom, if we assume that the old couple still shared a common bed, at the spa in Baden-Baden, where King William had repaired after his strenuous weeks in Berlin. In any case, no married person will find it hard to understand the impact of Queen Augusta's 'I told you so!' which must have been repeated from every angle. Had she not warned her Lord and Sovereign not to trust Bismarck? Had not the Grand Duke of Baden and the King of Saxony and many other dear relatives not warned the King? etc., etc. And it worked. The King in order to have a little peace and quiet gave in. Yes, he would go to Berlin and have it out with Bismarck and, well, yes, get rid of him.

While we have no record of the conversations in the royal household, we have a fine piece of Bismarck the novelist in his account of what happened next. He was, as always, very careful not to admit fault, let alone that the speech had been a blunder. Bismarck knew he had to see the King urgently so he took the unusual and desperate step of halting the train before it got to Berlin. This account needs to be read with scepticism:

> I had some difficulty in discovering from the curt answers of the officials the carriage in the ordinary train, in which the King was seated by himself in an ordinary first-class compartment. The after-effect of his intercourse with his wife was an obvious depression, and when I begged for permission to narrate the events which had occurred during his absence, he interrupted me with the words: 'I can perfectly well see where all this will end. Over there, in front of the Opera House, under my windows, they will cut off your head, and mine a little while afterwards.' I guessed, and it was afterwards confirmed by witnesses, that during his week's stay at Baden his mind had been worked upon with variations on the theme of Polignac, Strafford, and Lewis XVI. When he was silent, I answered with the short remark, '*Et après, Sire?*' '*Après,* indeed; we shall be dead,' answered the King. 'Yes,' I continued, 'then we shall be dead; but we must all die sooner or later, and can we perish more honourably? I, fighting for my King's cause, and your Majesty sealing with your own blood your rights as King by the grace of God; . . . Your Majesty is bound to fight, you can not capitulate; you must, even at the risk of bodily danger, go forth to meet any attempt at coercion.'
>
> As I continued to speak in this sense, the King grew more and more animated, and began to assume the part of an officer fighting for kingdom and fatherland.[130]

The crisis passed and Bismarck stayed in office—just. Two days later, Kurd von Schlözer, Bismarck's former first secretary in St Petersburg, went to see him. Von Schlözer had clashed with Bismarck in St Petersburg but managed to arrive at a decent understanding with him by the end. Schlözer understood Bismarck's nature from the start, as he wrote to a friend: 'He lives politics. Everything bubbles in him, and strains for recognition and status.'[131] The two went out to dinner and the evening became very convivial, as Schlözer recorded:

> We drank a lot of champagne, which loosened even more his naturally loose tongue. He exulted about pulling the wool over everybody's eyes. Partly by himself and partly by others, he is seeking to get the king to concede the two-year service period. In the House of Lords he paints the reaction he plans in colours so black that, as he puts it, the lords are becoming anxious about the conditions he says he will bring about if need be. Before the gentlemen of the second chamber he appears at one moment very unbending but in the next hints at his desire to mediate. Finally, he intends to make the German cabinets believe that the king is hard put to restrain the Cavourism of his new minister. There is no denying that until now people are impressed by his spirit and brilliance. *C'est un homme!*[132]

The Bismarck who appears in Schlözer's account played the game of a consummate confidence man, acting a part which varied from scene to scene; yet he needed another audience—the Schlözers, the Disraelis, and other witty and cynical people—to whom he could tell the truth, how he fooled this one or that one. Falsehood and honesty, kindness and vengeance, gargantuan energies and hypochondriac frailty, charm and cold remoteness, frankness and deceit, Bismarck was all those contradictions but one attribute never changed. Anybody who said the wrong thing or did the wrong thing in Bismarck's opinion would finish in outer darkness. Witty and charming Kurd von Schlözer made one comment about the 'Pasha' too many and found himself transferred out of Berlin to be legation secretary in Rome (admittedly not Siberia) before he could pack. As Schlözer ruefully put it, 'Tannhäuser, end of Act II. Otto sings: "To Rome, thou sinner." '[133]

7

'I have beaten them all! All!'

In June 1862 Otto von Bismarck explained to Benjamin Disraeli, Baron Brunnow, the Russia ambassador, and the Austrian envoy, Vitztuhm, at the Russian ambassador's residence in London what he intended to do when he took power. Nine years later—almost to the day, Freifrau Hildegard Hugo von Spitzemberg, wife of the Württemberg minister, watched the victory parade pass through Berlin. Otto von Bismarck had accomplished much more than in 1862 he had impudently promised his astonished listeners in the ambassador's parlour in London.

These nine years, and this 'revolution', constitute the greatest diplomatic and political achievement by any leader in the last two centuries, for Bismarck accomplished all this without commanding a single soldier, without dominating a vast parliamentary majority, without the support of a mass movement, without any previous experience of government, and in the face of national revulsion at his name and his reputation. This achievement, the work of a political genius of a very unusual kind, rested on several sets of conflicting characteristics among which brutal, disarming honesty mingled with the wiles and deceits of a confidence man. He played his parts with perfect self-confidence yet mixed them with rage, anxiety, illness, hypochondria, and irrationality.

He created a system of rule that expressed his power over others—his capacity to manipulate King William I, to neutralize the royal family by inserting himself between father and son, between husband and wife, between father-in-law and daughter-in-law with what Russell quite rightly called 'demonic' power. He outmanoeuvred all the generals except Moltke, with whom he eventually arrived at a truce of mutual respect. He undermined and destroyed the power of the sovereign princes of the German states and simply abolished several German states, including a venerable kingdom, when it suited him. He managed to keep all the 'flanking' powers—the Tsarist Empire, Napoleon's France, and Great Britain—out of the German civil war until they had to accept the achievements of his mastery or face destruction as Napoleon III foolishly chose. He used democracy when it suited him, negotiated with revolutionaries and the dangerous Lassalle, the socialist who might have contested his authority. He utterly dominated his cabinet ministers with a sovereign contempt and blackened their reputations as soon as he no longer needed them. He outwitted the parliamentary parties, even the strongest of them, and betrayed all those of the Kreuzzeitungspartei who had put him into power. By 1870 even his closest friends, Roon, Moritz von Blanckenburg, and Hans von Kleist, realized that they had helped a demonic figure seize power.

As early as 1864, Clemens Theodor Perthes wrote to Roon to warn him that Bismarck had no principles. Perthes objected strongly to the way the *Kreuzzeitung* and the *Norddeutsche Allgemeine Zeitung*

> have buried under a mound of mockery, contempt and ridicule the Princes and all those who—truly not without justification—regard them as their legal sovereigns. Where the *Kreuzzeitung* like a revolutionary of the purest kind disregards all justice, because the persons with legitimate entitlement do not please it, the *Norddeutsche Allgemeine Zeitung* in a series of articles with an unmistakable semi-official stamp which began on 16 April, proclaims the essential principle of the Revolution *suffrage universel*.[1]

Roon knew what he had done and took the risk to preserve the Prussian crown from the rise of popular sovereignty. On 27 July, he replied to his friend in a letter which I quoted in the Chapter 1 but deserves to be read here:

> B. is an extraordinary man, whom I can certainly help, whom I can support and here and there correct, but never replace. Yes, he would not be in the place he now has without me, that is an historical fact, but even with all that he is himself... To construct the parallelogram of forces correctly and from the diagonal, that is to say, that which has already happened, then assess the nature and weight of the effective forces, which one cannot know precisely, that is the work of the historic genius who confirms that by combining it all.[2]

Bismarck's first gambit—one he had mentioned to Roon on several occasions and to von Schlözer over champagne—was 'to get the king to concede the two-year service period'.[3] Once the deadlock had been removed by a deal of this kind, he could move swiftly to the rest of his plan. From the purely military side, there had never been a need for the three-year service requirement and a commission of fifteen generals (including Moltke) had conceded in April 1862 that it could accept two-and-a half years or even two years.[4] On 10 October Roon presented a compromise proposal which would have allowed those with means to purchase release from the obligation to serve a third year. The money thus raised would help to attract volunteers. The plan also set the size of the future army at 1 per cent of the population and established a fixed sum per soldier to defray costs.[5] The bill would, in effect, divide liberals on the issue of equity among conscripts but also limit the power of parliament by establishing in future the fixed number of soldiers and the fixed sum for their support.

On 9 November 1862 Adolf Count von Kleist (1793–1866) wrote to Hans von Kleist-Retzow, Bismarck's friend, in some alarm:

> Strange rumours have been circulating for the last four days that mediation and concessions to the Chamber of Deputies are being considered. One wants to promise that three-year service will be allowed to lapse in five years in exchange for approval for the rest of the military reorganization. Heydt is supposed to plan mediation. . . . you are the only one who can work beneficially on Otto. You *must* [in the original] be here to prevent careless measures beforehand, afterwards it will be too late.[6]

Count August had no reason to worry. The plan failed. William I disliked it because it violated the principle of universal service and Manteuffel, who as always had the last military word through his proximity to the King, rejected it because it limited the Crown's command prerogatives. As Mantueffel put it to Roon, 'the game must be played to the end.'[7] Even the Landtag voted against it by 150 to 17. Bismarck, who had no scruples about means, realized that he had to outflank Manteuffel by being more intransigent than the general. He withdrew all compromise proposals and prepared to rule by the iron fist.[8] He began with an attack on the civil service, a category much wider than in the English-speaking world: judges, assessors, referendars, university professors, grammar school teachers, and all the provincial government employees plus employees in state monopolies belonged to the civil service as well as those who worked in central state agencies. Here was a substantial, often liberal, constituency which Bismarck could crush, as he wrote to Prince Henry VII of Reuss on 23 November:

> In domestic affairs we are going to carry out a sharp raid on the civil servants of all types . . . I am for going easy on the Chambers but am intent on bringing the civil service back into discipline at any price.[9]

On 10 December 1862 Count Fritz Eulenburg, Minister of Interior, issued the relevant order to all members of the Prussian civil service to be supporters of the constitutional rights of the Crown. In the administration unity of spirit and will, decisiveness and energy will be evident . . . and the distinction which your position lends you is not to be misused to promote political movements which run counter to the views and the will of the government of the state.[10]

The office which Bismarck assumed on 23 September 1862 was that of Minister-President. It had emerged in March 1849 from the confusions of the revolution of 1848 and the sudden need to have a cabinet able to cope with a legislature.[11] Helma Brunck in her study of the Prussian State Ministry shows that even as late as the year 1862 no very clear constitutional basis for the rights and duties of ministers or, indeed, for the cabinet as a whole had been established. No such office had been foreseen in the Constitution of 1850. The one irrefutable power that Bismarck's predecessor, Otto von Manteuffel, had forced through was the Cabinet Order of 8 September 1852, which gave the Minister-President primacy among the ministers. Ernst Huber, author of a multi-volume constitutional history, argues that the order which forbade ministers to go to the King directly and without notice to the Minister-President made the office something like that of an English prime minister.[12] On the other hand, all the ministers remained servants of the King and the Cabinet Order could not prevent the King from consulting ministers. The Emperor William II in 1890 exercised that right and forced Bismarck to resign, even though Bismarck insisted that the Cabinet Order of 1852 forbade royal interference. On 24 September 1862 Bismarck simply showed up, took the chair, and explained the circumstances of his appointment, as the minutes show:

> In the meeting today of the State Ministry the chair was taken by State Minister von Bismarck-Schönhausen, who gave an account of the negotiations which had led to his nomination as a State Minister and also expressed his regrets at the departure of the two State Ministers von Bernstorff and von der Heydt.[13]

This was not a cabinet which Bismarck had chosen; ministerial nomination remained the prerogative of the King. In time Bismarck's growing dominance of affairs gave him influence but never control over the State Ministry's personnel.

Bismarck wrote to his wife on 7 October that he was having trouble getting used to 'life in the shop window', which he found 'rather uncomfortable and that he ate every day at the good Roons'.[14] Presumably the new

Minister-President walked, unaccompanied by a security detail, from his
temporary office to the Roons' apartment each evening. Pflanze describes
the modest surroundings in which the new Minister-President had his
office:

> In 1862 he moved into the narrow two-story building at Wilhelmstrasse 76
> that housed the foreign ministry. Constructed at the beginning of the eight-
> eenth century as a private home, it was, inside and out, the least pretentious
> building in the Wilhelmstrasse. Bismarck often made fun of its plainness, but
> instigated no changes. On the first floor were the offices and cubicles of the
> counsellors and clerks of the foreign office, and on the second were the min-
> ister's office, reception rooms and private quarters of the Bismarck family. In
> the rear was an extensive private garden shaded by old trees where the chan-
> cellor frequently walked. Visitors were astonished at the simplicity of their
> reception. No porter in dress uniform with 'Cerebus demeanour' guarded the
> portals. 'One must ring just as one does at the homes of ordinary mortals'. In
> the antechambers were no lackeys in gold and silver of the kind favoured by
> diplomats and ministers. Bismarck received his visitors in a plain, sparsely
> furnished office of medium size dominated by a large mahogany desk. 'No
> provincial prefect in France would have been satisfied with such modest
> surroundings'.[15]

This modesty and absence of show continued to mark the Bismarcks
throughout their lives. Visitors could not believe how simple and unpretentious their habits were. Show and possession never mattered to Bismarck.
He worried about money and expenses all his life but spent as little possible
on himself. Johanna shared these puritanical attitudes. As Holstein unkindly
put it, 'Princess Bismarck [Johanna], although she looked like a cook all her
life, had not the slightest idea of how to cook or at any rate how to give
dinner parties.'[16]

Immanuel Hegel, who worked in the Foreign Ministry, recalled his first
impressions of Bismarck as a boss:

> all of us had the impression when he took office that he regarded us with
> mistrustful eyes, speculating whether we had been bought or were otherwise
> under someone else's influence. Once he became convinced that we who
> worked in the cabinet secretariat were all honest people and good Prussians,
> we enjoyed his confidence. Still, we were just instruments for his will. There
> was no room for a pleasant relationship ... Whenever I entered to deliver an
> oral report, I gathered all my wits firmly together, in order to be equal to
> anything unexpected. A relaxed, self-satisfied air was not appropriate with
> him, for one was in that case in danger of being bypassed or run over.[17]

That too would not change over the years. Bismarck worked at a very intense level and expected no less from the staff. Neither clerks nor cabinet officers could expect thanks and almost none got any. In 1884 Lothar Bucher observed bitterly, 'I have worked under him now for twenty years, and yet he has only once (during the constitutional conflict) told me that something I wrote (a newspaper article) was good; and yet I believe I have written many better ones.'[18] And in spite of the way Bismarck treated them, his immediate staff worshipped him, as Albrecht von Stosch wrote to his friend von Normann after his first visit to the Foreign Ministry:

> I arrived between 11 and 12 in the morning. I was told that he was still sleeping. He had worked through the night until morning. The gentlemen of the Foreign Office speak of their chief with a holy awe, as believers do about the Prophet. It sounded really odd. After an hour he received me. He was in his dressing gown but endlessly polite and charming, as he heard from whom I had come.[19]

Nor was he kinder to his cabinet colleagues and in his memoirs he devotes an entire chapter to the members of his first cabinet in which hardly anyone escapes his scorn. Fritz Count zu Eulenburg (1815–81), who served him for more than fourteen years, gets just about the best report which reads like this:

> Eulenburg was indolent and fond of pleasure, but on the other hand he was judicious and ready, and if as Minister of the Interior he should by-and-by be called upon to stand foremost in the breach, the need of defending himself and returning the blows which he received would spur him into activity... when he was in the mood for work, he was an able coadjutor, and he was always a well bred gentleman, though not entirely devoid of jealousy and touchiness in regard to me. When he was called upon for more continuous, more self-denying, more strenuous exertions than ordinary, he would fall a prey to nervous disorders.[20]

Another unfortunate aspect of Eulenburg's character was his tolerance of Jewish liberals, as Bismarck wrote furiously to Roon on 1 March 1863. Eulenburg was

> unwilling to burn all his bridges... Noah, Wolfsheim, Jacobi and the other scoundrels with or without foreskin will betray him and leave him in the lurch. You, I and Bodelschwingh are the most deeply involved in this business, and I would not want to go on living if we suffer a fiasco out of impotence.[21]

The others get poor marks: the Minister of Commerce Itzenplitz (Count Heinrich Friedrich August von Itzenplitz (1799–1883)) was 'unfit... lacked energy'; the Minister of Agriculture von Selchow, who served in the cabinet for a decade (Werner Ludolph Erdmann von Selchow (1806–84)) was 'unequal to the demands of office'; the Minister of Religion Heinrich von Mühler (1813–74) was 'influenced by the energy and amateur participation in affairs of his clever and, when she saw fit, amiable wife'; the Minister of Justice, Leopold Graf zur Lippe-Biesterfeld-Weißenfeld (1815–89) and his 'supercilious air of superiority ... gave offence in parliament and to his colleagues'.[22] Bismarck omits the fact that he sacrificed Count zur Lippe, the most reactionary (and that is saying something!) of all the members of the 'conflict' ministry to the Liberals in the Landtag when in 1866 Bismarck decided to turn 180 degrees and make peace with them. Count zur Lippe did not welcome this form of dismissal and spent the rest of his life as one of Bismarck's most implacable foes. Cabinet officers, no matter how useful, belonged, as did all those who worked for Bismarck, to a group of collaborators who might fairly be labelled as 'use and discard'.

In foreign affairs, Bismarck confronted the Austrian ambassador, Count Karolyi, on 4 December 1862, as he put it in his memoirs:

> I had openly shown my hand to Count Karolyi, with whom I was on confidential terms. I said to him: 'Our relations must become either better or worse than they now are. I am prepared for a joint attempt to improve them. If it fails through your refusal, do not reckon on our allowing ourselves to be bound by the friendly phrases of the Diet. You will have to deal with us as one of the Great Powers of Europe.'[23]

Nobody in the Austrian Foreign Ministry expected anything other than the uncomfortable mix of threats and blandishments from Bismarck, and, of course, nobody trusted him.

On 14 January 1863 the new Landtag session opened and Bismarck continued his policy of dramatic confrontation and provocation. He rejected Liberal claims that he was governing by unconstitutional procedures:

> Whatever the constitution grants you as rights, you shall receive in full; anything that you demand beyond that, we shall refuse ... The Prussia monarchy has not yet fulfilled its mission. It is not yet ready to become a purely ornamental jewel in your constitutional structure, nor yet ripe to be inserted as a dead piece of machinery in the mechanism of a parliamentary regime.[24]

He announced that in a case of conflict between the Crown and parliament—a matter on which the constitution left a 'hole'—residual powers remained with the Crown. Hence the Crown had a perfect right to carry on the business of government, to collect taxes and make expenditures, even if the legislature refused to approve such acts. This theory, which has come to be called the 'theory of the hole in the constitution' or in German *Lückentheorie*, gave Bismarck the confidence to push on with his almost certainly unconstitutional activities.

A week later, he startled the 'narrower council' of the Bund by having Usedom read a statement announcing that the Prussian government favoured a 'German parliament':

> The German nation can find a competent organ through which to influence the course of common affairs only in a representative body chosen directly by the people of each confederate state according to its population.[25]

This, the first occasion when Bismarck reached for the 'people' as a weapon against the Princes, shows how his complete absence of fixed principle allowed him a flexibility denied to his opponents. The small German states feared universal suffrage more than anything else, for it would simply whip away their legitimacy. If the people spoke, they would not cry aloud to preserve the sovereignty of Reuss Elder Line or Schwarzburg-Sonderhausen about which, for the most part, they were indifferent, if not overtly hostile. Even solid states like Catholic Bavaria or the Kingdom of Saxony would not easily be able to resist the German people in their demand for unity. Bismarck had seen, as we noticed in his correspondence with Leopold von Gerlach, that the 'people' could be persuaded to vote for the King against the posturing of the liberal middle classes or the presumptions of the smaller princes.

A different people caused the first international crisis of his tenure of office. On 21 January 1863 a revolt against Russian rule broke out in Russian Poland. Bismarck immediately asked the army to mobilize four army corps in Prussian Poland, though the Poles under the King of Prussia had remained quiet. Bismarck, who knew the Russian scene and the actors intimately, also understood that the 'reform' party at court favoured constitutional rights for the Poles. It was, as he put it, 'simple common sense' to strengthen the reactionaries and to ensure that the Russian Empire did not 'fall into the possession of our enemies, whom we might discern in the Poles, the philo-Polish Russians, and, ultimately, probably in the French'.[26] The Austrians, who like the Prussians ruled a substantial part of historic Poland, had joined with the British and French to propose a new constitutional arrangement for the Poles. Bismarck, who would have done the opposite out of anti-Austrian calculations, wasted no time in supporting the militants at the Tsarist court and sent General von Alvensleben to arrange an agreement on joint action against Polish rebels. On 8 February Alvensleben and the Tsar concluded a military convention which allowed both Powers to cross the borders of the other in hot pursuit of Polish armed units. Whether Alvensleben exceeded his brief cannot be established and for Bismarck it did not matter. As he wrote,

> The Prussian policy embodied in the military convention concluded by General Gustav von Alvensleben in February 1863 had a diplomatic rather than a military significance. It stood for the victory in the Russian cabinet of Prussian over Polish policy, the latter represented by Gortchakoff, Grand Duke Constantine, Wielopolski, and other influential people.[27]

Nor did it matter that the Western Powers put pressure on the Prussian government not to ratify it and that the Convention never came into effect. Pflanze argues that it was 'a rare lapse of judgement' by Bismarck and 'a bad mistake' to have made the agreement,[28] because it got Napoleon III off the horns of a dilemma between his dynasty's historic commitment to Polish independence and his need for a Russian alliance; in my view that was a small price to pay for the certainty that Russia would stay neutral in a Prussian–Austrian final reckoning. Bismarck's immediate support for the reactionary Russian party at court had the further useful aspect that it reinforced his reputation as a latter-day Polignac.

On 27 January 1863 Robert Lucius von Ballhausen (1835–1914), who later became one of Bismarck's closest collaborators and one of the sharpest observers of the great man, attended a debate in the Prussian Landtag and got his first look at the new Minister-President:

> He still wore civilian clothes then, his full moustache was still red-blond as was the thinning hair on his head. His tall broad shouldered figure seemed at the minister's table mighty and impressive, whereas a certain casualness in stance, movement and speech had something provocative about it. He kept his right hand in the pocket of his light-coloured trousers and reminded me of the 'crowing second' at the Heidelberg duelling fraternities. He already had a certain way in which in hesitant sentences he seemed to search for words and always found the most penetrating and showed his knack for sharp crushing responses. He looked to me very 'junkerish', and had the gruffness of the old corps student, especially his manner of good-naturedly pumping malice into his excited opponents. That was the stormy session in which he developed the idea the state would and could live without a budget because it had

to. That aroused the fury of the members, and Count Schwerin-Putzar, then leader of the opposition, a square, rather peasantish figure, who looked like a decent chap, accused Bismarck of developing the principle 'that power takes precedence over justice.'[29]

This posture and attitude had been typical of Bismarck from his first speech in the United Diet of 1847 when he had caused uproar, treated the members with disdain, and pulled a newspaper from his pocket. The 'conflict ministry' had found a perfect 'conflict Minister-President' or, more accurately, Bismarck played that role with his accustomed adroitness. His defence of the Alvensleben Convention—universally condemned by liberals all over Europe—shows him at his impudent best.

> The previous speaker (Henrich von Sybel) observed that I have defended my views today with less than normal certainty. I would regret it most sincerely if the opinion spread that I had in some way seen my opinions as doubtful. I see myself compelled by the statement to make the following declaration, that I have been ill for four days and today against the will of my doctor appear before you because I could not bear to forgo the delights of these deliberations (laughter)...I have often noticed the phenomenon in the press that when the newspapers report a new, hitherto unknown and surprising story they usually add the phrase 'as is well known' such and such is the case. I believe that the previous speaker finds himself in the same position when he says that opinion of Europe on the Convention is absolutely unanimous. The opinion of Europe cannot be unanimous about something of which it knows nothing.[30]

By the end of March, Bismarck had survived six months and opinions about him had now begun to harden. Ludwig von Gerlach welcomed Bismarck's performance with relief, as he wrote to Hans von Kleist:

> Have we ever had such a man at the top? Bismarck has exceeded my expectations. So much calm firmness I had not foreseen. Therefore Bismarck for ever! [English in orginal] Against the whole world and abroad![31]

Bismarck's own reaction to his first half-year in office comes out in a letter to his old Göttingen friend, John Motley. On his 48th birthday, 1 April 1863, he wrote to Motley that

> I never dreamed that in my riper years I would be forced to practise so unworthy a profession as that of parliamentary minister. As an ambassador, although a civil servant, I maintained the feeling that I was a gentleman...As a minister I am a helot. The deputies are not dumb in general; that is not the

right expression. Looked at individually these people are in part very shrewd, mostly educated, regular German university culture... as soon as they assemble *in corpore*, they are dumb in the mass, though individually intelligent. [The letter continues in English—JS] These drops of my own ink will show you at least that my thoughts, when left alone, readily turn to you. I never pass by old Logier's house in the Friedrichstrasse without looking up at the windows that used to be ornamented by a pair of red slippers sustained on the wall by the feet of a gentleman sitting in the Yankee way, his head below and out of sight. I then gratify my memory with remembrance of 'good old colony times, when we were roguish chaps'. Poor Flesh (Graf Hermann Keyserlingk) is travelling with his daughter. I do not know where in this moment. My wife is much obliged for the kind remembrance, and also the children... Deine Hand sieht aus wie Krähenfüsse ist aber sehr leserlich, meine auch? (your handwriting looks like crow's feet but is very readable. Is mine?)[32]

Motley had in the meantime become US Ambassador to Vienna and at the end of May 1863 he wrote to Lady William Russell, the formidable mother of the future British ambassador in Berlin, Odo Russell, about his old college friend:

I am just now much interested in watching the set to between Crown and Parliament in Berlin. By the way, Bismarck Schönhausen is one of my oldest and most intimate friends. We lived together almost in the same rooms for two years—some ages ago when we were both *juvenes imberbes*, and have renewed our friendship since. He is a man of great talent, and most undaunted courage. He is the most abused man by the English newspapers I believe just now going, and I like him the better for that. Don't believe a word of all the rubbish you read. He is a frank *reactionaire* and makes no secret about it. Supports the King in his view that the House of Commons majority is not the Prussian form of government, whatever may be the case in England... I am a great Liberal myself, but I believe that Prussia is by the necessary conditions of its existence a military monarchy, and when it ceases to be that, it is nothing. You as a despot ought to sympathize with Bismarck.[33]

In the Ministry, Bismarck had drafted a press edict which limited the freedom of the Prussian press but had not found a formula which would work. Although Article 27 of the constitution forbade censorship and guaranteed freedom of expression, there was an escape clause: 'every other restriction upon freedom of the press shall be made only by way of legislation' and there was a Press Law of 1851 which gave the government power to license and control all media of printed expression. On 1 June 1863 the King signed a press edict to silence the opposition press by bureaucratic order and to eliminate any recourse to the courts. Henceforth the only appeal would be to the cabinet.[34]

The Crown Prince Frederick William had for some time been aware of the way Bismarck went about perverting the constitutional structures of the kingdom. The press edict was the final straw. He had an engagement in Danzig and had determined to express his disquiet at the violation of the constitution. The host introduced him and said that he regretted that the visit could not be an occasion for complete joy, to which the Prince replied,

> I also lament that I should have come here at a time when a variance has occurred between the government and the people which has occasioned me no small degree of surprise. Of the proceedings which have brought it about I knew nothing. I was absent. I have had no part in the deliberations which have produced this result. But we all, and I especially, I who best know the noble and fatherly intentions and magnanimous sentiments of his Majesty the King, we all, I say, are confident that, under the scepter of his Majesty the King, Prussia will continue to make sure progress towards the future which Providence has marked out for her.[35]

The King flew into a rage, no doubt increased by his own uneasy feeling that by agreeing to Bismarck's press edict, he had indeed violated the constitution. He announced his intention to arrest the Crown Prince on a charge of treason and could only be slowly talked out of that by a nervous Bismarck who saw his whole edifice wobble in the battle between father and son.

The Crown Princess wrote a few days later to her mother, Queen Victoria and expressed her own fury:

> I told you on the 5th that Fritz had written twice to the King, once, warning him of the consequences that would ensue if the constitution was falsely interpreted in order to take away the liberty of the press. The King did it all the same and answered Fritz with a very angry letter. Fritz then sent his protest to Bismarck on the 4th, saying he wished to have an answer immediately. *Bismarck has not answered*... The way in which the government behave, and the way they have treated Fritz, rouse my every feeling of *independence*. Thank God I was born in England where people are not slaves, and too good to allow themselves to be treated as such.[36]

Had Fritz continued his battle, he might have won and the King might have abdicated. That, however, was rather a lot to ask of a Prussian prince who, in spite of his wife's pressure, mainly shared the assumptions of his father about kingship.

The King had already shown signs of agitation about the long-planned meeting with the Austrian Emperor in Bad Gastein. As Bismarck told Roon in a letter from Carlsbad in early July 1863, he wanted to get away on holiday, 'but the King absolutely refused to hear hints that I might go away and I don't want to upset him. He wants me here when the Emperor arrives any day now but he fears that contact with me will upset the western powers and affront the liberals.'[37] On the way Bismarck wrote to his wife to say how 'tedious it was to be stared at like a Japanese . . . [and to be] the object of general ill-will.'[38] Even Bismarck found his national unpopularity uncomfortable. On 24 July he settled into his hotel at Bad Gastein, where on 2 August the Emperor Franz Joseph arrived with an unpleasant surprise. The Austrian 'success' in facing down the Russians over Poland encouraged Anton Schmerling (Anton Ritter von Schmerling (1805–1893)), the ex-revolutionary of 1848 now 'State Minister' of the Habsburgs, to propose a reform of the Bund as a preparatory stage to the voluntary unification of Germany under Austrian auspices. On 3 August 1863, while King William took the waters at Baden-Baden, the Emperor Franz Joseph summoned the German princes to a Congress of Princes to be held in a fortnight in Frankfurt am Main, capital of the German Confederation, the Bund.[39] This posed by far the most serious challenge to Bismarck's plans. The King, a loyal vassal, had received a summons from his liege lord, the Emperor Franz Joseph; all the other German kings had agreed to attend. How could William not do so? This marks the first absolutely unavoidable clash of personalities between the King and Bismarck. Here is his version of the crisis:

> At Gastein, on August 2, 1863, I was sitting under the fir-trees in the Schwarzenberg gardens by the deep gorge of the Ache. Above me was a nest of titmice, and watch in hand I counted the number of times in the minute the bird brought her nestlings a caterpillar or other insect. . . . Queen Elizabeth [widow of Frederick William IV—JS], whom we met at Wildbad on our journey from Gastein to Baden, was urgent with me to go to Frankfort. I replied: 'If the King does not otherwise decide I will go and perform his business there, but I will not return as minister to Berlin.' The prospect seemed to disturb the Queen, and she ceased to contest my view. It was not an easy task to decide the King to stay away from Frankfort. I exerted myself for that purpose during our drive from Wildbad to Baden, when, on account of the servants on the box, we discussed the German question in the small open carriage in French. By the time we reached

Baden I thought I had convinced my master. But there we found the King of Saxony, who was commissioned by all the princes to renew the invitation to Frankfort (August 19). My master did not find it easy to resist that move. He reflected over and over again: 'Thirty reigning princes and a King to take their messages!' Besides, he loved and honoured the King of Saxony, who moreover of all the princes had personally most vocation for such a mission. Not until midnight did I succeed in obtaining the King's signature to a refusal to the King of Saxony. When I left my master, both he and I were ill and exhausted by the nervous tension of the situation; and my subsequent verbal communication with the Saxon minister, von Beust, bore the stamp of this agitation. But the crisis was overcome.[40]

This struggle for the King's soul in August 1863 made Bismarck's subsequent career possible. He 'persuaded' or 'forced' the King of Prussia to refuse an invitation which every fibre in his long, royal frame told him to accept. The intense emotions which both experienced during the confrontation and tears and exhaustion afterwards suggest that a profound struggle, not unlike that between a father and son, took place between the King and Bismarck over the Frankfurt Princes' Congress. Bismarck prevailed because the King must have felt in the depth of his soul that this impossible Bismarck mattered to him. He could not do without him. It has occurred to me that in some way Bismarck might have played the role of the 'good son' which the Crown Prince Frederick William under the influence of the English princess less and less resembled. A kind of love triangle of two sons for the approval of the father may explain this triumph of Bismarck's will over the desires of the King of Prussia in August 1863, the most important achievement of Bismarck's entire career. If he had failed then, as he explained to the Dowager Queen Elizabeth, he could not have remained as minister. In this crucial confrontation, the ultimate fate of Germany rested on the mysterious power of Bismarck's 'sovereign self' and on no other, not office, not command of armies, not prestige. The 'shallow Junker' of Treitschke exerted the force of that self on the King and it worked in August 1863 and continued to work until the day twenty-five years later that William I, by then German Emperor and King of Prussia, died. My explanation of how it worked may not convince the reader; that some mysterious personal power worked on the King cannot be denied. Had Bismarck resigned then because the King felt a duty to attend the Congress of Princes, the history of Germany and the world would have run a different course; that too cannot be denied.

On 29 August 1863 he wrote to Johanna that the King was besieged by 'intrigue' and added that

> I wish that some sort of intrigue or other would install another ministry, so that I could with honour turn my back on this uninterrupted stream of ink and withdraw to the quiet of the country. This restless life is unbearable. For ten weeks I have been doing nothing but secretarial service in a coaching inn.[41]

This too forms part of the emotional pattern. After the spiritual exertions to get the 'old gentleman' to bend to his will, he would feel irritable, exhausted, and depressed. The regularity of the pattern—emotional crisis with the King, terrible struggle, success followed by despair, resignation threats, or dreams of peace in the countryside—suggests that some deep psychic behaviour pattern had become established between the two men, one which was also to last until the King died in March 1888. The odd thing is that on each occasion the King really believed that Bismarck would retire and 'leave' him.

The Princes at Frankfurt had insisted on a reply from Prussia and on 1 September 1863 twenty-four kings and princes wrote to William I to ask him to join them in their project to reform the German Confederation. The King very correctly passed it to the State Ministry, which replied on 15 September 1863 with a list of conditions, of which the most insistent concerned reform of the system of representation. There must be

> a true national assembly which emerges from direct participation of the entire nation. Only such a representative system will grant Prussia the security that it has nothing to sacrifice which will not benefit the whole of Germany. No artificially conceived organism for the Federal departments can exclude the move and counter-move of dynastic and particular interests, which must find a counterweight and corrective in a national assembly.[42]

The threat of universal suffrage for the German people finished the Austrian project. If the nation spoke, it would put an end to the power of the small states in the Bund and, in addition, universal suffrage in the Habsburg lands would empower the subject nationalities in their struggles for representation and autonomy. No Austrian government could accept universal suffrage in the nineteenth century and none did. Here again we see Bismarck's tactical adroitness. By playing off people against princes, nationalities against the Habsburg monarchy, he put Prussia—that is, Bismarck—at the perfect point of leverage. If the princes cooperated, the people would threaten them less, if not, more.

He also used this technique in his sudden interest in the new working-class movement under the leadership of the charismatic and flamboyant Ferdinand Lassalle (1825–64). The liberal bourgeoisie, the owners of capital and disciples of Adam Smith and believers in what the Germans called '*Manchestertum*', caused Bismarck difficulties in the Prussian parliament. If the 'nation' could disarm the German princes, the organized working class could outflank the Liberal middle classes, a classic Bismarckian strategy of alternatives. Lassalle suited Bismarck because he had a flair for publicity and dramatic gestures like nobody else in Prussia. Herman Oncken in his biography of Lassalle sees the logic of the Bismarck–Lassalle alliance in the common enemy—the Progressive Party—with its doctrinaire commitment to free trade and *Manchestertum*. 'What could be for Bismarck more desirable than if the Progressives lost mass support for the party especially in the lower strata of society . . . So the government found the movement [Lassalle's socialists] not unwelcome on tactical grounds and even in principle was by no means opposed to all its points.'[43]

On 11 May 1863 Bismarck wrote to Lassalle, 'In connection with current deliberations on working-class conditions and problems, I wish to obtain considered opinions from independent quarters. I would therefore be glad to have your views on these issues.' The message was brought by an intermediary of Bismarck, Konrad Zitelmann, the writer (1814–89), who had instructions to arrange the meeting. Lassalle accepted and the first meeting took place within forty-eight hours.[44] The next day a flattered Lassalle had been converted to Bismarck, as he wrote to a colleague: 'Workers who allow themselves to be led astray by abuse and slanders of Bismarck, are not worth much. Such workers must be pretty dumb.'[45] The new partnership between the Junker reactionary and the flamboyant Jewish agitator brought two of the most dramatic figures of the nineteenth-century together.

The story of Lassalle defies the imaginative powers of a common-or-garden historian to capture. George Meredith, the now forgotten novelist, as popular in his day as Trollope and Dickens, devoted one of his most successful novels to Lassalle's story, *The Tragic Commedians: A Study in a Well Known Story*,[46] but only concentrated on the mad love affair which ended in a fatal duel. According to Neil Roberts, 'apart from one article on Lassalle, Meredith appears to have done no research on the subject.'[47] Instead he used the memoir of the woman about whom the duel was fought, Helene von Racowitza, entitled *Meine Beziehungen zu Ferdinand Lassalle*. The novel contains, on the other hand, several speeches which appear verbatim in the respectable biographies of Lassalle, so Meredith may have concealed the extent of his use of historical sources.

The real story is much madder than Meredith's Victorian comic temper imagined. Meredith concentrates on Lassalle's infatuation with Helene, called Clotilde von Rüdiger, a 17-year-old coquette, and builds in the true story of Lassalle's liaison with Sophie Countess von Hatzfeldt-Wildenburg (1805–81), mother of Bismarck's ambassador Paul, and a woman twenty years older than Lassalle. The Lassalle character Alvan declares to Clothilde that his relationship with Sophie was not an affair. 'As far as matters of the heart, we are poles apart.'[48] Sophie, a Princess von Hatzfeldt-Trachtenburg by birth, had been forced to marry a descendant of the 'count' line of Hatzfeldts, Edmund Count von Hatzfeldt-Wildenburg, who abused and mistreated her.[49] Out of the depths of his romantic soul the 23-year-old Ferdinand Lassalle absolutely quixotically decided to defend the honour of Countess Hatzfeldt, when he saw how her sadistic husband had imprisoned her. On 11 August 1848 Lassalle was charged at the Assize Court in Cologne with complicity in the theft from Count Hatzfeldt of a cash box. The theft gave Lassalle the pretext he needed to 'try' Count Hatzfeldt before the bar of public opinion. In this case and in thirty-six (!) subsequent trials and in his later career Lassalle used the defendant's bench as an actor uses the stage to present his romantic personality and spread his ideas. He defended the honour of Countess Sophie von Hatzfeldt before the court with romantic flair:

> The family was silent, but we know that when men hold their peace, the stones will cry out. When every human right is outraged, when even the ties of kinship are silent and a helpless being is abandoned by its natural protectors, then the first and last relation of such a being has the right to rise in the person of another member of the human race.[50]

Lassalle then challenged Count Edmund to a duel, who ignored 'this silly Jewish boy'.[51] Lassalle went to jail, of course, which was part of the plot, but he won a moral victory when in 1854 the Count settled a very large sum on the Countess. Since Lassalle had paid the Countess's expenses from his parental allowance, she in turn agreed by written consent to contract to pay him 4,000 thaler a year if he won.[52] The two remained together as an odd couple. Lassalle had endless affairs which he discussed with Sophie and got her approval. Lassalle's liaison with a grand German aristocrat had made him famous when in 1862 he and Lothar Bucher made a pilgrimage to

London to see Marx. Marx wrote to Engels about it and explained that 'to maintain a certain elegance, my wife had to take everything not nailed or welded down to the pawn shop...And so it was established that he [Lassalle—JS] is not only the greatest scholar, the deepest thinker, the most brilliant researcher etc but also Don Juan and a revolutionary Cardinal Richelieu.'[53] Does one catch the whiff of jealousy in Marx's attitude to Lassalle?

Lassalle's family, a modest bourgeois Jewish, commercial family, lost control of him as a teenager. He decided at the age of 14 that he had a great future:

> I believe myself to be one of the best Jews in existence. Like the Jew in Bulwer's *Leila* I could risk my life to rip the Jews out of their present depressing situation. I would not shun the scaffold, could I make them again a respected people. When I cling to my childish dreams, so my favourite idea is to place myself at their head and with weapon in hand to make the Jews independent.[54]

Instead of saving the Jews, he converted to Hegel and went to Berlin to study, where he wrote with characteristic megalomania, 'here is no new phase for me. I have reached the highest level of the contemporary spirit and can develop within this framework only quantitatively.'[55] Hegel had revealed all truth and had given him 'everything: clarity, self-consciousness about content, the absolute powers of the human spirit, the objective substances of human morality'.[56] He must have been an astonishing student if Alexander von Humboldt could call him a *Wunderkind* (wonder child).[57]

After a series of dramatic escapades during Italian unification and a close friendship with Garibaldi, Lassalle returned to Berlin in January 1862. There he met the socialist revolutionary Lothar Bucher (1817–1892) to discuss whether Germany could be transformed in a Garibaldian way. Bucher denied it:

> All the measures you suggest are again only political and legal, one can say they stand on the old basis, and simply create more bourgeois. And these new relations of property, new through a change of persons, not, to use a metaphor, through a change in the chemical properties of property, can only be maintained through a ceaseless war, a terrorism of a tiny minority.[58]

Lassalle and Bucher created a kind of think tank to work through the implications of the industrialization process and the emergence of a new class: the proletariat. Lassalle began a campaign of flamboyant lectures, designed to get himself arrested and to offer him, as in the Hatzfeldt case, a free public platform. Bucher had doubts about the theoretical soundness of his new partner, whose Hegelianism misled him, as he wrote to Bismarck, years later when he had changed sides and become Bismarck's closest collaborator and journalistic assistant:

> This error was not new to me. I had met it in other Hegelians and it can be explained by the essence of Hegelian philosophy which, as is well known, attempts to show a parallelism or an identity, between the development of concepts in pure thought (similar to algebra) and the appearances in nature and the events of history (similar to calculations with known quantities).[59]

Meanwhile, Lassalle attacked liberalism in his speeches as, for example, in one called 'On the special relationship between the present historical period and the idea of the *Arbeiterstand*', delivered at the Manual Workers' Association of Oranienburg:

> If we were all equally, equally shrewd, equally educated, and equally rich, the Idea would be considered as a comprehensive and moral one, but since we are not and cannot be, so the idea is not sufficient and leads in its consequences, therefore, to a deep immorality and to exploitation... You are the rock on which the church of the present will be built... From the high peaks of scientific knowledge, we can see the early morning red of a new day earlier than below in the turmoil of daily life. Have you ever watched the sun rise from the height of a mountain? A purple seam slowly turns colour and bloodies the distant horizon, proclaiming the coming of new light. Mist and clouds stir and move, ball themselves together and throw themselves against the dawning red, casting a shroud momentarily on the rays. But no power on earth can prevent the slow majestic rising of the sun, which an hour later all can see, brightly lighting and warming the firmament. What is an hour in the natural drama of each day, are the one or two decades in which the much more imposing drama of a world historical sunrise will occur?[60]

A few days later Lassalle made a speech to a Berlin District Citizens meeting, 'Concerning the nature of constitutions'. What determined a constitution, he argued, was not the piece of paper but the power relationships that actually exist in a given country. Hence the Constitution of 1850 with its three-class voting and its special Articles 47 and 108 securing the separateness of the army reflected the realities of Prussian society:

> The princes are much better served than you are. The servants of the princes are not fine talkers as the servants of the people often are, but they are practical men who have an instinct for what really matters... Constitutions are not

originally questions of law but questions of power. Written constitutions only have value and last if they express the real power relations in society.[61]

Lassalle's ideas attracted unusual enthusiasts. On 12 September 1862 General Albrecht von Roon quoted Lassalle in the Prussian Landtag: 'According to his analysis of history, the main content of history is not only that between states but also within states there is nothing more than a struggle for power and the extension of power among the various individual factors.'[62] By November 1862 Karl Eichler, a speaker at one of Lassalle's Workers' Meetings in Berlin, told the assembly that Bismarck was on the workers' side. The meeting voted overwhelmingly to hold a workers' congress in Leipzig.[63] On 19 November 1862 Lassalle delivered the 'What Now?' speech in which he urged the Landtag to adopt a resolution that they would no longer meet until Bismarck restored their constitutional powers.[64]

These two themes—the illusions of liberalism and the reality of constitutions as expressions of power—reveal the same realism which we have seen again and again in Bismarck. Lassalle had one advantage which Bismarck lacked. He was a charismatic mass orator, probably the first in Prussian history and, at the same time, a fully paid-up romantic, bursting with romantic metaphors, images, and, unfortunately for Germany, romantic liaisons. In the midst of the campaign of stunning public lectures, clashes with the police and dramatic arrests, he wrote to Sophie Hatzfeldt:

> My sister wants to marry me off. The girl is pretty, of good family, lively and cheerful, can keep her end up in society, but I don't know how deep her education goes...I am very taken with her. She has a lovely body. She is witty and amusing, is quite (not wildly) in love with me...What chiefly keeps me back is the money side. If, as is likely, my money from the Gas Company comes to an end, my income in 1870 will be only about 1,500 thaler or 2,500 or so if my mother dies, I can't keep a wife or children on that without gruesome economies.[65]

In May of 1863 Lassalle founded the Allgemeiner Deutscher Arbeiterverein (the General German Workers' Association) and spent most of 1863 in hectic travel among the branches, where he made exciting speeches to rather sceptical audiences of solid German working men. It was during this period, that Bismarck approached Lassalle and asked him to call. By 1864 Bismarck and Lassalle seem to have met regularly. On 13 January 1864 Lassalle wrote to Bismarck:

Excellency, Above all, I must accuse myself of having forgotten yesterday, to urge you to take to heart that the ability to vote must be conceded to all Germans. An immense means of power. The real 'moral' conquest of Germany! With respect to electoral techniques, since yesterday I have been through the history of the legislation on the French electoral system and there, to be sure, found not much useful material. I have in addition reflected further and am now in a position to be able to give your Excellency a magic recipe for pre-venting vote division and the crumbling of votes. I await the fixing of an evening from your Excellency. I plead strongly for an evening so that we will not be disturbed. I have much to discuss with your Excellency about election techniques and yet more on other matters and an undisturbed and exhaustive discussion is, given the urgency of the situation, an unavoidable need.[66]

On Saturday, 16 January 1864, Lassalle wrote again to Bismarck:

I would not press but external events press powerfully and thus I beg you to excuse my pressing. I wrote to you on Wednesday that I had found the desired 'magic recipe'—a 'magic recipe' with most comprehensive effects. Our next discussion will finally be followed by the most decisive decisions and such decisions, I believe, can no longer be delayed, I shall allow myself to call on your Excellency tomorrow (Sunday at 8 ½). Should your Excellency be pre-vented at that hour, I would ask you to determine another time very soon for my visit.[67]

By 12 March 1864 Lassalle had begun to express these ideas in public. He had been arrested on a charge of high treason. He defended himself by citing Bismarck's wish to impose universal suffrage:

I want not only to overthrow the constitution, but perhaps in a year or less it will be overthrown, and I shall have overthrown it...I therefore declare to you from this sacred place a year will not have passed before Herr von Bismarck will have played the role of Robert Peel and introduced universal and direct suffrage.[68]

At the height of his powers and influence, Lassalle got involved with his maddest romance with a young Roman catholic girl, Helene von Rocawitza, which ended in an utterly futile duel that Lassalle had provoked by his impossible behaviour. On 5 August 1864 Lassalle wrote to a friend, 'Only this I know. I must have Helen—Workers Association, politics, science, jail all pale in my insides at the thought to reconquer Helen again.'[69] The duel took place on 29 August 1864, and Ferdinand Lassalle died of his wounds on 31 August 1864. Marx, who treated Lassalle with a mixture of scorn and envy, as we have seen, and who called him in private correspondence 'Baron

Izzie', wrote an informal obituary to Engels: 'That could only have hap-pened to Lassalle with his strange mixture of frivolity and sentimentality, Jewishness and playing the chevalier, that mixture was utterly his own.'[70]

But there is more to it than that. Serious students of the workers' move-ment in Germany have over the last century and a half devoted much, if heretical, thought to Lassalle as an alternative to Marx. Lassalle had qualities that Marx lacked—the charismatic skills of a mass leader—and his ideas centred on power and the state, two categories which Marx's economic-social model almost entirely ignores. The state and its actors are simply elements of the superstructure. Marx makes that clear in the introduction to the 1867 edition of *Das Kapital*:

> To avoid possible misunderstandings a word. I do not draw the figures of the capitalist or the landlord in a rosy light. But the issue only concerns persons insofar as they personify economic categories as bearers of particular class relations and interests. My standpoint, much less than any other, does not make individuals responsible for conditions of which they are social products, however much they imagine themselves to be above them, since my analysis conceives the formation of the economic structures of society as a natural historical process.[71]

This theoretical position had disastrous consequences for the German labour movement and for the history of humanity. It led the great German Social Democratic Party to view history as determined by economic forces over which neither they nor anybody else had control. They preached rev-olution because Marx's laws showed that capitalism must destroy itself as a result of its 'inner contradictions'. The *Sozialdemokratische partei Deutschlands*, the largest party in Bismarck's empire by 1912, had no strategy for what Lassalle had seen clearly in his 1862 lectures—that political institutions mat-ter, that constitutions rest on power relationships, and that human will can change things.

Lassalle played a unique role in Bismarck's own life. He remained the only figure in Bismarck's career whom he respected to the very end. In 1878, as Bismarck planned legislation to suppress the SPD, Lassalle's ghost came back to haunt him. In July of 1878 the *Berliner Freie Presse* published every day for two weeks letters from Bucher to Lassalle, which very prob-ably Sophie Countess Hatzfeldt had given to Leopold Schapira, the editor of the newspaper, to embarrass Bismarck and block the anti-Socialist Law which Bismarck intended to introduce. In the Reichstag, August Bebel, the leader of the parliamentary fraction of the SPD, challenged Bismarck on his dark past as a crypto-socialist and got an astonishing reply from the Reich Chancellor. Bismarck acknowledged quite openly that he had engaged in secret negotiations with Lassalle, and then added unprompted these words—unique to my knowledge in Bismarck's remarks on his contemporaries:[72]

> What he had was something that attracted me extraordinarily as a private person. He was one of the cleverest and most charming men whom I have known. He was ambitious in grand style...Lassalle was an energetic and witty man with whom it was very instructive to talk. Our conversations lasted for hours and I always regretted when they were over...[73]

This affectionate and unusual tribute to Lassalle calls into question the depth of Bismarck's anti-Semitism. From his respect for Lassalle, his friendship with Ludwig Bamberger, and his admiration for Eduard Simon, we can deduce that, as in every other aspect of Bismarck's hates and loves, no general statement can do justice to his mercurial likes and dislikes. Certainly he had the conventional anti-Semitism of his class and age, but as with Catholics or Socialists, his attitude to Jews reflected how interesting he found them or how useful. He hated Lasker and Windthorst less because one was Jewish and the other Catholic but because they opposed him successfully and became enemies.

There was another legacy of Bismarck's relations with Lassalle that was almost as astonishing as Lassalle's secret meetings. Lothar Bucher, journalist, socialist theoretician, and revolutionary, switched sides. On 15 August 1864, two weeks before Lassalle's fatal duel, Bucher wrote to him with the following news:

> Though I could hope for a favourable outcome, I had decided for reasons that are rather complicated and which should not be set out on paper, to seek another position and in fact, as quickly as possible...In eight days the whole thing was settled.[74]

Lothar Bucher had been employed since 1 January 1863 in the Wolff Telegraph Agency, where he was underpaid and unsatisfied. Christoph Studt offers various versions of how Bucher came to work for Bismarck. One came from Robert von Keudell who claimed the credit. According to Keudell, Bismarck said of the possibility that Bucher might work for him:

> We all cook with water and most of what happens or will happen gets into the press. Take the case that he comes to us as a fanatical democrat, like a worm to bore its way into the state structure and to blow it up, he would soon see that he alone would be destroyed in the attempt. Let that possibility be.

Such perfidy I cannot believe of him. Talk to him without asking for his confession of faith. What interests me is whether he will come or not.[75]

Arthur von Brauer (Carl Ludwig Wilhelm Arthur von Brauer (1845–1926), a Baden diplomat and politician, who also worked under Bismarck)[76] denied that Keudell could have thought of it. The startling idea of the appointment of a former revolutionary in a conservative ministry, Brauer thought, 'looks much more like what Bismarck might do than a Keudell'. The final variant involves a friend of Bucher's approaching Count Eulenburg to ask if there were a chance for a convicted revolutionary to get a lawyer's licence again and Eulenburg asked Bismarck, who replied 'he is completely out of practice in the law, maybe there's some way of using him in the Foreign Ministry'.[77] Bismarck kept the appointment secret for a while and many, including the King, were deeply shocked. Bucher wrote to Bismarck; 'Excellency knows my national standpoint which I would never deny. Bismarck: I know your national standpoint only too well but I need it for the conclusion of my policy and I will only give you work to carry out which moves in the spirit of your national efforts.'[78]

Bucher became a fixture in Bismarck's staff from 1864 to his death. Holstein recalled working in the same office with Bucher during the Franco-Prussian war:

Bismarck regarded Bucher's low status at Court as an advantage, because he knew that Bucher understood that it was Bismarck alone who kept him on. Because of this Prince Bismarck regarded him as his tool, and used him to carry out all kinds of strictly confidential and personal business... He only found fault with Bucher or criticized him to other people when he considered Bucher had not done a job properly. Bismarck never made Bucher's personality and idiosyncrasies the subject of general merriment, as he so often did with Abeken... With his stunted body, his abnormally ugly face and unhealthy complexion, he had that partly timid, partly embittered, reserve of people, who have lost heart because they are social failures. This was combined with a strong interest in the opposite sex, which must have cost him many hours of misery... It so happened that during our last weeks in Versailles, in the big office in the Villa Jessé, I sat between Bucher and Wagener; the man who refused to pay taxes and the founder of the *Kreuzzeitung*, addressed each other in monosyllables. Bucher confided to me that that when he was obliged to flee in the winter of 1848, it was Wagener who signed the order for his arrest to be sent out over the telegraph. Bucher's escape was entirely due to the fact that the telegraph system was not working that day.[79]

Late in August 1863 the King and Bismarck decided to confront the liberals again by calling yet another 'conflict election' and on 2 September 1863, the Landtag was dissolved. The Crown Prince opposed both the elections and the policy of repression. He wrote to Bismarck to say so in early September and the two met for an audience, which Bismarck described in his memoirs:

> I asked him why he held so aloof from the government; in a few years he would be its master; and if his principles were not ours, he should rather endeavour to effect a gradual transition than throw himself into opposition. That suggestion he decisively rejected, apparently suspecting me of a desire to pave the way for my transfer into his service. The refusal was accompanied by a hostile expression of Olympian disdain, which after all these years I have not forgotten; today I still see before me the averted head, the flushed face, and the glance cast over the left shoulder. I suppressed my own rising choler, thought of Carlos and Alva (Act 2, sc. 5), and answered that my words had been prompted by an access of dynastic sentiment, in the hope of restoring him to closer relations with his father...I hoped he would dismiss the idea that I aimed at some day becoming his minister; that I would never be. His wrath fell as suddenly as it had risen, and he concluded the conversation in a friendly tone.[80]

The crackdown on the civil service now extended to the armed forces, to which the King issued a directive that the 'further participation of the army and fleet in elections contradicts the spirit and intentions of the constitution. I consider it therefore as inappropriate.'[81] On 7 October Bismarck issued another order to civil servants to limit their participation. The text of the edict was issued in *The Provincial Correspondence*, an official government paper which had just been founded:

> According to the legal provisions, all military and civil servants, in addition to the general obligations of subjects owed to the King, are bound to special loyalty and obedience, in addition to the special services involved in the office. How can it be compatible with this special loyalty and obedience if they take part in party political activity which is manifestly directed at belittling, limiting or overthrowing the government installed by the King and acting in his name? The simplest intelligence must see that such manifest betrayal of duty is completely incompatible with an ordered tenure of office.[82]

On 20 and 28 October the Landtag elections first and second rounds took place: Wagener and Blanckenburg were elected in Belgard, Pomerania, Kleist's old district. *The Provincial Correspondence* rejoiced:

The little band of eleven Conservatives, who were in the previous house, has been strengthened by four times, and among the new Conservative deputies can be found several of the finest, battle-hardened leaders of those loyal to the King.[83]

The actual results could hardly be called a triumph for the Bismarck Ministry. The shift to the left continued as in the election of 1862. The Progressives won 141 seats as opposed to 135 in the previous legislature. The other liberals went up from 96 to 106 and the 'Constitutionals', the largest fraction in 1858, the New Era liberals, disappeared completely. There were now 35 conservatives instead of 11.[84]

On 6 November Hans von Kleist-Retzow sent his friend an encouraging passage from the Bible. As he wrote:

I read yesterday in Revelations, Ch 2, Verse 27 'And he that overcometh, and keepeth my works unto the end, to him will I give power over the nations: and he shall rule them with a rod of iron; as the vessels of a potter shall they be broken to shivers: even as I received of my Father.'

Bismarck wrote on the margin, 'O Hans, always wrathful with God's thunderbolt'.[85]

On 9 November 1863 William I opened the Landtag with an intransigent Speech from the Throne. The King made clear that he would only give 'My agreement to the necessary household bill which will guarantee and secure the maintenance of the existing structure of the army.'[86] The First Chamber, the House of Lords, welcomed the King's speech. By a vote of 72 to 8 the Lords approved an Address to the King, drafted by Hans von Kleist, which stated explicitly:

Your Majesty's Government has met those undoubted obligations imparted to it and through maintenance of Royal Power as the foundation stone of our Constitution and without any kind of violation of the Constitution or the existing legal system, even without the state budget, it has happily dispelled the danger namely by holding firm to the army reorganization which without committing treason cannot be reversed.[87]

As a sign of the readiness to concede something to the liberals, the government lifted the press edict which both houses welcomed but in lifting the edict the government repeated its 'unaltered conviction that the edict of 1 June to maintain public security and to master an unusual emergency situation was urgently necessary and at the same time absolutely constitutional.'[88] The deadlock continued.

It was to be broken ultimately by events outside Prussia. On 15 November 1863 Frederick VII, King of Denmark, died without an heir, and the crisis of the Danish succession gave Bismarck the chance he needed to outflank domestic opposition by success abroad. On 18 November the new Danish King, King Christian IX, signed the text of a constitution which incorporated Schleswig into the Kingdom of Denmark. Here at last was the foreign crisis that Bismarck wanted. At the end of 1862 he wrote a lengthy letter about the Danish question to an unnamed correspondent:

> It is certain that the Danish business can only be solved in a way which we would wish by a war. One can find a pretext for such a war any time...We cannot get out of the disadvantage of having signed the London Protocol with Austria unless we repudiate it as a result of a break caused by war...[Prussia has] no interest in fighting a war...in Schleswig-Holstein to install a new Grand Duke, who will vote against us at the Bund because he fears our lust for annexation and whose government will become a willing object of Austrian intrigues, forgetful of any gratitude which he owes Prussia for his elevation.[89]

His first move involved securing an agreement with the Austrians to defend the previous agreements about the succession and the status of the Duchies of Schleswig and Holstein. On 28 November 1863 Prussia and Austria sent a joint note to the Danish government which rejected the Danish moves and cited the treaties of 1851 and 1852 as the legal basis for their intervention.[90]

The Schleswig-Holstein question has the reputation of being incomprehensible. Lord Palmerston is supposed to have remarked that 'only three people have ever understood the Schleswig-Holstein question. One is dead, one has gone mad and I have forgotten.' That is a typically Palmerstonian exaggeration. The positions are really quite clear. Denmark had a monarchy which rested on a tradition of royal absolutism and the line of inheritance in that monarchy could pass down the female line. The two historic duchies of Schlweswig and Holstein observed the Salic Law under which only a male heir could inherit. In addition the duchies had historically been joined at the hip in the phrase '*Up ewig ungedeelt*' (forever undivided), though in practice Holstein had been part of the Germanic Confederation, whereas Schleswig had not and hence the King of Denmark in his capacity as Duke of Holstein was a member of the German Bund. When the revolution of 1848 introduced constitutionalism to Denmark, King Frederick VII announced that the duchies would be incorporated into the new kingdom.

The revolutionary German parliament in Frankfurt rushed to defend the German national territory and a war, largely fought by Prussian troops, broke out which Prussia, once it recovered its nerve, unilaterally abandoned. The reappearance of the Danish question suited Bismarck perfectly, because, as Christopher Clark writes,

> modern and pre-modern themes were interwoven. On the one hand, it was an old-fashioned dynastic crisis, triggered, like so many seventeenth and eighteenth-century crises, by the death of a king without male issue. In this sense, we might call the conflict of 1864 'the War of the Danish Succession'. On the other hand, Schleswig-Holstein became the flash-point of a major war only because of the role played by nationalism as a mass movement.[91]

The Schleswig-Holstein crisis had just that combination of complex elements that gave Bismarck room to play with a large number of sets of alternatives: Danish versus German nationalism, dynastic versus popular politics, Prussia versus Austria, Prussia versus the German Bund, royal government versus parliament, and, finally, an international dimension because of the role of the great powers. In 1852 an international congress in London had established that both Austria and Prussia would recognize the 'integrity' of the Danish kingdom and Denmark in turn agreed never to incorporate the duchies or take any steps toward that end.[92] The great powers recognized that, if Frederick VII of Denmark died without issue, the succession to the Kingdom of Denmark *and* to the Duchies would pass to the heir, Christian of Glücksberg, who would thus inherit *both* Schleswig and Holstein. The Duke of Augustenburg, the heir to the Duchies by Salic Law, signed the agreements but never renounced his rights in perpetuity.[93] Hence when Frederick VII in March of 1863 announced a new constitutional arrangement, the crisis threatened to erupt anew but this time the Danes hoped for a better outcome. European diplomats had their attention directed to the Polish Crisis and the Danish cabinet thought it could get enough support to revoke the London Treaties. Frederick's sudden death made the issue acute.

In early December 1863, the King of Prussia called a Crown Council, that is, a cabinet meeting presided over by the King and attended by the Crown Prince. According to his memoirs, Bismarck made clear that the aim of Prussian policy ought to be the acquisition of the Duchies by Prussia. 'While I was speaking, the Crown Prince raised his hands to heaven as if he doubted my sanity. My colleagues remained silent.'[94] The King struggled with the concept, and repeated, 'I have no right to Holstein'. Bismarck observed bitterly that 'the King's way of looking at things was impregnated by a vagabond liberalism through the influence of his consort and the pushing of the Bethmann Hollweg clique.'[95] This was a very wayward description of the King's entirely conservative and legitimist position. He had correctly stated the position. He had no dynastic right nor claim to the Duchies and hence no legitimate way to annex them to his kingdom. Bismarck ran into the King's opposition and immediately blamed the woman who embodied all the malign forces in the royal household, Queen Augusta.

Bismarck, as always, had a second strategy in mind. After the failure of the Frankfurt Congress of the Princes, Baron Rechberg, who had become Austrian Foreign Minister on 17 May 1859, decided in exasperation to work with, not against, Prussia, 'with the remark that an understanding with Prussia was easier for Austria than for the middle states'.[96] Bismarck had clashed bitterly with Rechberg in Frankfurt and the two had been about to go to the woods for a duel at one point. Rechberg had a reputation for temper and was widely known as a *Kratzbürste* (scratch brush), that is, snappish and quick-tempered, but Bismarck got used to him. 'On the whole Rechberg was not bad, at least personally honest, if too violent and quick to explode, one of those overheated red blondes.'[97] Rechberg had a low opinion of his opponent. When it looked like the New Era cabinet would fall, Rechberg said, 'if there is a change of ministry, the horrible Bismarck will be next in line, a man who is capable of taking off his jacket and climbing on the barricades.'[98] Whatever their relationship, Rechberg served Bismarck's purposes perfectly because he had been schooled under Metternich and that meant conventional, conservative diplomacy. Since Rechberg now favoured a dual Austro-Prussian directory for Germany, he naturally agreed to Bismarck's suggestion that the two powers as signatories of the London Treaties must insist that Denmark be held strictly to the letter of the treaties. If King William would not now countenance a policy of naked aggression followed by annexation, Bismarck needed to make sure that no German solution took place by which the small states would ride a wave of national enthusiasm for the young Augustenburg duke. When on 7 December the Bundestag by a one-vote majority voted for the federal 'execution' to force Denmark to abide by the London Treaties of 1852, that suited Bismarck admirably. There were three options in principle: best—annexation of both

Duchies by Prussia; tolerable—the status quo with the Duchies in personal union with Denmark because he knew he could always stir up trouble in that situation; worst—a victory for the Bund and the small states in favour of the Duke of Augustenburg which would add another impossible middle-sized state always ready to vote against Prussia. That by the autumn of 1866 Bismarck had achieved the first and much more than that, he called his 'proudest achievement'. At the close of the war in 1864, he reflected 'this trade teaches that one can be as shrewd as the shrewdest in this world and still at any moment go like a child into the dark.'[99]

Bismarck's tactics in this, his greatest achievement, resemble those we have seen before, constantly shuffling sets of alternatives and playing off one against the other. Rechberg and Karolyi needed a firm guarantee that Bismarck would stay loyally by the London Treaties but Bismarck could genuinely explain that his King under the evil influence of the Queen and the liberals of the court entourage had thrown his emotional support to the young Augustenburg pretender. What could a poor foreign minister do?

The Bund had ordered Saxon and Hanoverian troops to enter Holstein and as a consequence Prussian and Austria troops also crossed the frontier. This period placed a great strain on Bismarck's nerves. He could not control the army nor the vagaries of its commanders. On 12 January Bismarck wrote to Roon to ask about certain military movements, very nervously. He was worried that the Austrians might reach the Eider before the Prussians. 'That would be disagreeable to his Majesty. Or have the orders already been issued? If so, then I have said nothing to you and I can recall the ink already used.'[100]

Bismarck found himself in a double bind. He had a domestic crisis to overcome before he could carry out his Danish policy and he had an international crisis in which he had to prevent British, French, and Russian intervention in his little war, an intervention to which, as signatories of the Treaties of London, they had a perfect right. That Bismarck saw this period as his masterpiece arises from the sheer complexity of the challenges facing him. Let us see if we can sort them by category. In domestic affairs, he had a deadlock with parliament which made it unlikely, if not impossible, that money for the war would be allocated in a legal way. On 15 January Bismarck told the Landtag that he wanted to use legally appropriated funds for the Danish venture, 'but if these were refused, then he would take them wherever he could find them.'[101] In foreign affairs he had to keep Austria under control. On the next day, 16 January 1864, Bismarck and Graf Karolyi signed a protocol that extended the joint military operation of the Austro-Prussian force into Schleswig. Bismarck clearly intended to get involved in a shooting war, if possible, as Roon explained to Perthes on 17 January 1864: 'The first shot from a canon tears up all treaties without our having to break them explicitly. The peace arrangement after a victorious war brings new relationships.'[102]

The King, the court, the royal family and its many relations, and the appeal of the young Duke of Augustenburg, a handsome 34-year-old prince, generated an almost insuperable obstacle to Bismarck's schemes. On 19 November 1863, in response to Christian IX's proclamation about Schleswig, the young Augustenburg proclaimed himself Frederick VIII of Schleswig-Holstein and was widely supported in German public opinion. To make things worse, his wife, Princess Adelheid zu Hohenlohe-Langenburg (1835–1900) was a niece of Queen Victoria and thus a cousin of Crown Princess Victoria. Bismarck had also to cope with generals whom he could not control and who treated him as the civilian interloper he undoubtedly was.

Abroad, Bismarck had to make sure that the Great Powers let him carry out his plan. Napoleon III tried to extort a concession for his support, such as the Prussian territories on the Left Bank of the Rhine, which he had to reject without pushing the Emperor into alliance with Britain. A Liberal government in London, of course, sympathized with little Denmark and deeply distrusted the Prussian reactionary, author of the press edict. The British Foreign Secretary was the grandest of grand Whigs, Lord John Russell, as John Prest describes him in the *New Oxford Dictionary of National Biography* as 'the thinking person's politician'.[103] Lord John served under a very different Prime Minister, Lord Palmerston, a strong and noisy activist. When the Danish crisis blew up, the British cabinet could not agree on a policy. 'Palmerston had encouraged the Danes to believe that they would not stand alone, but the cabinet refused to sanction military intervention.'[104] The French Foreign Secretary would not have been surprised. He told the British ambassador in late 1863 that 'the question of Poland had shown that Great Britain could not be relied upon when war was in the distance.'[105]

On 16 January 1864 the governments of Austria and Prussia presented a joint note to the Danish Foreign Minister, von Quaade, which made clear their determination not to accept the constitution of 18 November 1863. By promulgating the constitution, the Danish government has unequivocally broken the obligations which it undertook in 1852...The above named two Powers owe it to themselves and to the Federal Diet, in consequence of the part they played in those proceedings...not to allow this situation to continue...Should the Danish government not comply with this summons, the two above named Powers will find themselves compelled to make use of the means at their disposal for the restoration of the status quo.[106]

As Michael Embree writes, 'the Danes had thus precipitated a crisis, for which they were unprepared and the consequences of which they completely misjudged.' On 20 January Field Marshall Wrangel assumed command of the Allied Army and entered Holstein on a march to the river Eider. The Danes had played into Bismarck's hands 'blinded by pure nationalism'.[107]

Bismarck still could not be certain that his policy had worked and on 21 January 1864 he wrote to Roon just before a Crown Council to express his anxiety that the King would give in to family pressure and back the young Augustenburg:

The King has ordered me to come to him before the meeting to consider what is to be said. I will not have much to say. In the first place I hardly slept at all last night and feel wretched and then really do not know what one should say...after it has become more or less clear that His Majesty at the risk of breaking with Europe and experiencing a more terrible Olmütz, wants to yield to democracy and the Würzburger in order to establish Augustenburg and create yet another middle state.[108]

On 25 January the King dissolved the Landtag when it refused to pass the 1864 Budget and also rejected a 12 million thaler loan to finance a Schleswig-Holstein action. At least that much Bismarck had achieved.

The next difficulty Bismarck faced involved the generals. Bismarck rested his case against the Western powers on strict adherence to the Treaties of London and a commitment to advance in lockstep with the Austrians. That in turn meant that Prussian generals had to move more slowly than they might have wished. The most intransigent of these was General Field Marshall Count von Wrangel, the Berliner's 'Papa Wrangel'. In January 1864, Wrangel was three months short of his 80th birthday but had command of the Prussian forces in Schleswig. Age had not mellowed the old hothead. Bismarck's needs for restraint passed on through the King's orders infuriated Wrangel and he let loose on Bismarck, as Bismarck describes it in his memoirs:

My old friend Field-Marshal Wrangel sent the King telegrams, not in cipher, containing the coarsest insults against me, in which remarks were made, referring to me, [and] about diplomatists fit for the gallows. I succeeded, however, at that time in inducing the King not to move a hair's breath in advance of Austria, especially not to give the impression that Austria was being dragged along by us against her will.[109]

One tiny incident shows how weak Bismarck's actual position was on the eve of his first triumph. Bismarck needed, quite rightly, a diplomat to represent him at the HQ of Field Marshall Wrangel and had appointed Ambassador Emil von Wagner. Holstein, whom Bismarck sent to serve as secretary to Wagner, recalls in his memoirs that

> when he went to report to the Field Marshall, he came back in very low spirits. This is how he described the scene: the Field Marshall had received him surrounded by royal princes and the whole of his vast military staff. When Wagner presented himself the Field Marshall replied: 'Tomorrow we transfer our headquarters to Hadersleben but you are to stay here—you diplomats are out of place in military headquarters. But you can write to me, my boy.' With that Wagner was dismissed.

Bismarck persuaded the King to overrule Wrangel, who then ordered Wagner to HQ. 'He came back radiant. 'The Field Marshall is a charming man. I didn't see *this* side of him the first time. He came straight up to me and said, "Well, my boy, and where have you been all this time? I shan't let you run away again!" The royal reproof had worked.'[110] It worked but it cost Bismarck extra strain and nervous tension. Here again we can grasp the remarkable way Bismarck succeeded in imposing his will on Prussian conduct without being able to issue an order to the people who had to fight the war.

Luckily for Bismarck the Minister of War, Albrecht von Roon, never wavered in his support of his friend. In turn Bismarck trusted Roon enough to send him military suggestions, though often with the appropriate apology for 'these reflections from a major'.[111] This relationship of mutual trust between Roon and Bismarck must have been the only calculable element in Bismarck's unstable situation of complex and contrasting forces. Bismarck needed Roon, because, as a civilian, he had no power over the course of events once fighting began. Roon could do what Bismarck could not. As a senior officer and Minister of War, Roon was the only member of the State Ministry not bound by the Cabinet Order of 8 September 1852, and could ask for an audience of the King at any time. Roon's *Immediatstellung*, that is, the right to see his Commanding Officer, the King, on request, represented

Bismarck's only means to intervene in matters of command. At this stage, he had not yet become the great Bismarck and was not even 'a major' in more than name. Roon's unswerving loyalty and constant access to the King constituted the invisible basis on which Bismarck had to operate.

Fighting began on 1 February 1864 when Prussian forces crossed the border into Schleswig. Field Marshall Wrangel issued a proclamation to the inhabitants of the Duchy of Schleswig, to say 'We come to protect your rights. These rights are violated by the common Constitution for Denmark and Schleswig.'[112] At this point, the Prussians had a stroke of luck. The morning of 4 February brought very cold weather which froze the waters of the Schlei and the surrounding marshes which meant that the fortified line of the Dannevirke could be assaulted from the frozen flanks. The Prussians and Austrians assaulted the Dannevirke in early February and forced the Danes to evacuate the line over night and in a snowstorm. The Danes retreated across the water to Jutland and to the fortifications and trenches at Düppel in eastern Schleswig. The Danish retreat without a serious fight was a national disgrace but it was not a substantial victory for the Austro-Prussian expeditionary force either which had nearly twice the number of troops. On 18 February Prussian troops—probably by mistake—crossed the border in Schleswig into Denmark proper and took the town of Kolding. Bismarck hoped to use the incursion to raise the military stakes in the war but the Austrians remained on the Schleswig–Danish border. In effect, the Prussian and Austrian armies had occupied most of Schleswig without serious fighting but what now? Both Roon and Moltke told the King how important a victory of arms would be in political terms.

> 'In this campaign your Majesty must win some sort of substantial success, in order not only not to lose the respect gained abroad and at home but also raise it to such an extent that we shall be lifted above many difficulties.' Moltke added: 'In the present state of the war there is no more important objective than the glory of the Prussian army.'[113]

After a week the Austrians and Prussian agreed to push the war into Denmark proper and on 11 March 1864 announced that the Treaties of 1852 no longer bound the two powers. This was a tense period because the invasion of Denmark widened the war and invited the intervention of the Great Powers. The British cabinet discussed an intervention but hesitated to take the step. With France Bismarck took a strong line. If the French intervened, Prussia would halt the Jutland operations completely and make common cause with Austria against France. 'From the moment that you show us *faccia feroce*, we must put ourselves on good terms with Austria.'[114]

The British government had called a conference in London of the signatories of the Treaties of 1851 and 1852 for 20 April 1864. This increased the pressure on Bismarck and ravaged his nerves. Unless the Prussian army could win some sort of military victory, the Prussian delegation at the conference would have no leverage to achieve a favourable decision from the Great Powers. Luckily, all the Prussian Generals agreed that the army needed a victory. On 18 April 46 companies of Prussian infantry stormed the fortified line at Düppel and after six hours of fierce fighting took the main Danish defence in Schleswig.[115] On 24 April 1864, the London Conference began. With the victory at Düppel, the Prussian soldiers had created facts on the ground. Bismarck could now begin to dismantle the restrictions on Prussian freedom in order to move toward annexation. The Austrian and Prussian delegations informed the conference that they no longer considered themselves bound by the London Treaties and suggested a new constitutional arrangement by which the Duchies might be bound to the Danish crown by personal union only. The Danes stubbornly rejected the compromise to the dismay of the Austrians. Meanwhile, on 12 May 1864 a formal armistice began; all troops were to remain in the positions held that day.

The authentic Bismarckian attitude comes out in a private letter to his former boss in Aachen, Adolf Heinrich Graf von Arnim-Boitzenburg, in which he tells Arnim that he intends to use national popular sentiment against the Danes:

> The present situation is so constituted that it seems to suit our purpose at the conference to let loose against the Danes all the dogs that want to howl (forgive this hunting metaphor); the whole howling pack together has the effect of making it impossible for the foreigners to place the Duchies again under Denmark. The Duchies have up to now played the role of the birthday boy in the German family and have got used to the idea, that we are willing to sacrifice ourselves on the altar of their particularist interests...The address will work against that swindle...for me annexation by Prussia is not the highest and most necessary aim but it would be the most agreeable result.[116]

In the midst of the most difficult period of his entire ministry, Bismarck found time to write to Motley in English on 23 May 1864,

Jack, my dear,
    Where the devil are you and what do you do that you never write a line to me?...Do not forget old friends, neither their wives, as mine wishes nearly as

ardently as myself to see you or at least to see as quickly as possible a word in your handwriting. Sei gut und komm oder schreibe! Dein, v. Bismarck.[117]

Motley was startled that his friend had written in the midst of an international crisis and answered four days later:

My dear old Bismarck, It was a very great pleasure to hear from you again. It is from modesty alone that I haven't written. I thought your time was so taken up with Schleswig-Holstein, and such trifles, that you wouldn't be able to find a moment to read a line from me.[118]

Motley's reluctance to disturb his old friend in the middle of war makes perfect sense but why did Bismarck write to him? Why did Bismarck need to have his friend's support and reassurance? There is something mysterious and moving at work here. Bismarck really loved Motley and in this first moment of his world-historical significance, he reached out to him.

Another tiny episode tells us something important about Bismarck's role in Prussian affairs. He was a royal servant and even in the midst of the Schleswig-Holstein crisis he remained subject to the King's whims. On the same day he wrote to Motley he wrote to his cousin Count Theodor von Bismarck-Bohlen to ask for help to carry out a job that the King had dumped on him. The King wanted to mark Field Marshall von Wrangel's retirement from active duty at the age of 80 by buying for him with royal funds the estate Wrangelsburg in the administrative district of Stralsund, County Greifswald. Since the King, always frugal, wanted to pay a reasonable price, Bismarck, in some embarrassment, asked Theodor, who lived in the district, to make discreet enquiries about the market price of the estate and to act as the go-between if a bid were to be made. As Bismarck explained, 'forgive me for bothering you with such matters in All-Highest service, but there is no other way to do it.'[119] Otto von Bismarck, facing his first really great test, caught between conflicting demands of the great powers, intent on dismantling the Bund and establishing Prussian hegemony in Germany, trying to fend off or at least contain nationalist emotions, uncertain about whether the armistice would hold, has to interrupt these serious considerations to shop for a gift for Wrangel. Nor was Bismarck slack in such matters. No matter how irksome he found it, he conducted the King's business, great and small, with exemplary efficiency.

In a letter which Roon wrote to Moritz von Blanckenburg on 24 May 1864, he summed up how the situation looked to the second-best informed man in the Kingdom:

Whether I can do something to settle my old nerves this summer depends upon Lord Pam [Palmerston—JS], Louis Napoleon and a few other highly placed rogues. If we strike again, I can hardly go away ... it all depends whether Vienna prefers to grant us the Duchies rather than the Augustenburger, for separation from Denmark is no longer in doubt.[120]

Rechberg faced exactly that dilemma. The Danes had stubbornly refused the Austro-Prussian proposal for 'personal union' of the two Duchies under the Danish crown. Rechberg thus confronted the choice Roon outlined 'to grant us [the Prussians] the Duchies rather than the Augustenburger'. On 28 May Rechberg suddenly decided to opt for the Augustenburger and the Austrian and Prussian representatives announced at the London Conference their support for 'the complete separation' of the Duchies from Denmark 'and their union in a single state' under the Duke of Augustenburg who 'in the eyes of Germany' had the greatest right to the succession.[121]

This was, as we have seen, Bismarck's least desirable option but he had already considered the Prussian position with the King and the Crown Prince, who—with all due consideration for the claims of young Duke Frederick and ties of family—remained Prussian soldiers and princes. After an exchange of letters between King William and Duke Frederick, the Crown Prince on 26 February 1864 drafted a set of demands which Prussia must put to the Hereditary Duke in a peace settlement:

> Rendsburg to be a federal fortress, Kiel to be a Prussian marine station, accession to the Customs Union, the construction of a canal between the two seas and a military and naval convention with Prussia.[122]

Under such conditions Frederick VIII would have been ruler in name only of what would become a Prussian military district. The Crown Prince believed that he would in the end accept them. To test that hypothesis Bismarck invited the Duke to Berlin for a conference.

While Bismarck prepared to deal with the young Duke, the military clock had begun to tick and on 29 May 1864 Roon with apologies wrote to Bismarck to remind him that 'he had to do with his truest friend, whose task it is, precisely because of this characteristic, to bring disagreements and conflicts into the open.'[123] Roon attached a report in which he complained that the army had become restless about the lengthening armistice and the consequent loss of the gains made by force:

> If a government rests chiefly on the armed portion of the public—and this is our case—so must the opinion of the army about the acts and omissions of

that government certainly not be regarded as inconsequential. Thus if both Duchies are not annexed, the annexation of one is essential. If neither is achieved, it will be an inglorious end of the present government in Prussia.[124]

31 May 1864 Duke Frederick arrived in Berlin for the conference with Bismarck and Roon wrote to von Blanckenburg to express his worries that Bismarck had given too much ground in London:

> unfortunately, I fear that Otto made too many concession in London and has placed himself on another ground. I think that he had no need to do that because I do not believe in the spectre of a general European war.[125]

Bismarck received the Hereditary Duke of Schleswig-Holstein at nine in the evening of 1 June 1864 and the meeting went on for three hours. As he wrote in his memoirs, 'The expectation of his Royal Highness that the Hereditary Prince would be ready to agree, I did not find justified.'[126] Bismarck clearly made the case as strongly as he could and by midnight the Duke realized that whether he accepted or refused the terms would make little difference because Prussia had decided at the very least to turn Schleswig into a Prussian possession in fact, if not in name, and there was little he could do to stop it. In addition to the Crown Prince's conditions, Bismarck added a few of his own (interestingly not included in his memoirs), that Prussia would require 'guarantees of a conservative system of government'.[127] That in turn would turn the Ducal estates against their Prince and lose him the support of the German liberals and nationalists. He thought he had to refuse such terms and did.[128] Bismarck had now eliminated the second option.

As he boasted a year later to Freiherr von Beust, Prime Minister of Saxony, he had 'hitched' the Augustenburg ox to the plough. 'As soon as the plough was in motion, I unhitched the ox.'[129] In fact, he had done nothing of the sort. The Austrians put the Augustenburg solution into the game, and Duke Frederick played into Bismarck's hands. Had he accepted the Prussian terms, he could have declared whatever he liked once he had assumed power and played German nationalism and liberal parliamentarianism against the most hated man in Germany. Instead, the Prince lamely said, as he took leave of Bismarck at midnight, 'We shall see each other again, I suppose...I never saw the Hereditary Prince again until the day after the Battle of Sedan...'[130] Bismarck played his hand perfectly and in a characteristic way. The sudden Austrian decision to choose the Augustenburg option would have rattled a less skilful gamester. Bismarck accepted the move in order to keep the Austrians in step, assuring himself that the King, Crown Prince, and generals wanted the fruits of their victories and even the dreaded Augusta could not block that. Next he needed to box the Duke into a situation in which he would have to refuse the Prussian offer. What options he would have seen if the Duke had been sly enough to accept the conditions with the intention of double-crossing the Prussians we cannot know but Bismarck would have found them. The Duke's territories had a large Prussian army on them. Civil servants had begun to introduce Prussian laws, currency, etc. The Duke's refusal saved Bismarck a lot of bother.

The elimination of the Augustenburg ox from the field left the third and Bismarck's preferred option: annexation of the Duchies. By now he had come close to achieving that, since Rechberg had played his last card. The stubborn Hereditary Prince meant that there would be no Augustenburg solution and when the truce expired on 26 June 1864, fighting began again. The British government, having promised to support Denmark, did nothing. Disraeli, speaking for the opposition, skewered the Liberals with his scorn:

> The most we can do is to tell the noble lord what is not our policy. We will not threaten and then refuse to act. We will not lure our allies with expectations we do not fulfil...to announce to the country that we have no allies and then declare that England can never act alone.[131]

The resumption of fighting caused a new domestic crisis. On 12 June a full Crown Council met to discuss Danish War finances. Karl Freiherr von Bodelschwingh (1800–73) served as Bismarck's finance minister in the 'conflict cabinet' from 1862 to 1870 and in a collection of ministers that he despised, Bismarck absolutely hated Bodelschwingh. As Helma Brunck puts it, Bodelschwingh 'was always restricted in his scrupulous attitude by constitutional, legal reservations'.[132] Roon put it more concretely in a letter to Moritz von Blanckenburg, 'Bismarck's neurotic impatience and Bodelschwingh's bureaucratic niceties and worries have made sure that not all discords have disappeared.'[133] And Bismarck was desperately impatient. The game had reached a moment of the greatest delicacy and at the Crown Council of 12 June 1864, Bodelschwingh reported that to the end May 1864 17 million thaler had been spent, covered by the 1863 surplus of 5,300,000 and the State Treasury reserves of 16 million. More money would be needed but little remained in the treasury. Bismarck demanded that loans be raised without approval of the Chambers but Bodelschwingh and other ministers saw it as a violation of the Constitution of 1850 and the State Debt Law of Frederick William III of 1820. As they declared, 'As long as the ministers of His Majesty must consider themselves bound by their oaths to maintain the Constitution, it cannot be compatible with the oath to accept a state loan without prior authorization of the Diet.'[134] Roon argued fiercely that 'in the case of an urgent need and in order to continue the war, according to articles 63 and 103 of the Constitution a state loan even without the approval of the Landtag can for provisional use be issued constitutionally with the force of law.'[135] Even if that were accepted, it was far from clear whether investors could be found to purchase the obligations of the Prussian Kingdom issued on a doubtful reading of the Constitution. No action could be taken and on 17 July 1864, the King closed the Landtag which had not authorized an additional pfennig of expenditure.

The summer, as usual, saw Europe's royalty depart their capitals for their annual visits to take the waters at the spas. For Bismarck, it meant a wandering existence while he waited on the edge of royal familial holidays for the moments of business. The season opened when on 19 June 1864 the King and Bismarck arrived in Carlsbad for a summit with Franz Josef and Rechberg which ended on 24 June 1864. The next day the London Conference adjourned without a decision on the future of the Duchies. The British had done nothing to help their Danish allies, as the French Ambassador contemptuously remarked, 'they recoiled with vigour'.[136] On 27 June Bismarck wrote to his sister that 'politically things are going so well that it makes me nervous, "pourvu que cela dure". According to the news today, England will stay peaceful.'[137] He had, in fact, pulled off a tremendous coup and knew it.

And the pieces continued to fall into the right holes. On 8 July the new Danish government gave up the struggle and sued for peace. A week later, von Roon warned Bismarck that, if a trade were to be made to return the occupied Danish islands, it had to be compensated by 'a complete cession of the Duchies to the Allies to be acceptable'.[138] The peace negotiations would take place in Vienna and on the day Bismarck left for the conference, 'he [the King], very moved, thanked me as I left and credited me with the whole success that God's support had blessed Prussia. Touch wood!'[139] Bismarck arrived in Vienna early in order to consult Rechberg before the Danish peace delegation arrived.[140] He had time to visit Motley and his family on the second evening after he arrived. Mary Motley wrote at length in a letter to her daughter about the memorable evening:

Your father got a hug from him on the stairs, and then he came into the blue room where we were with the Bowditchs' and gave me three hearty shakes of the hand. I felt in three minutes as I had known him all my life and formed a deep attachment for him on the spot which has not diminished on further acquaintance. He looks like the photograph your father has of him and like some of the caricatures, is very tall and stoutish but not the least heavy, a well made man with very handsome hands. He is possessed of a wonderful physical and mental organization, eats and drinks and works without feeling it, like a young man of five-and-twenty instead of one of fifty or nearly so. He said, of course, he should come to see us whenever he had time to do so and begged your father to let him come to dinner entirely *en famille* so that they might be able to talk over old times together at their ease. Accordingly the following Tuesday, the next day but one, at 5 o'clock was appointed.... It would have done your heart good as it did mine, to witness Bismarck's affectionate demonstration to your father.[141]

I quote the letter at length because it testifies to the extraordinary magnetism Bismarck exercised on his contemporaries. They, in effect, fell in love with him, dazzled by his charm, brilliance, and, yes, warmth. In spite of Holstein's portrait of the cold, joyless Bismarck, the warm, funny, affectionate side existed too and his career cannot be comprehended without getting us close to the mystery of his remarkable personality as this ecstatic letter has done.

At the same time Bismarck was negotiating with Rechberg in Vienna, Disraeli took a long walk with his friend, the Russian ambassador Brunnow, and they talked of Bismarck's successes.

Brunnow thought there was no person whom circumstances had ever so favoured. France, holding back because she was offended with England, English government in a state of impuissance; Russia distracted with conflicting interests; Austria for the first time sincere in wanting to act with Prussia; then, the weak chivalric character of the king, the enthusiasm of Germany.

'Bismarck has a made a good book,' I said. 'He has made a good book but, what is most strange, he backed the worst horse of the lot. For Prussia is a country without any bottom and in my opinion could not maintain a real war for six months.'[142]

The negotiations in Schönbrunn Palace at the end of August 1864 have left conflicting trails of evidence and they remind me a little of those family games of Monopoly when players confront each other with deals. What will you give me to get Trafalgar Square? Rechberg knew perfectly well that Bismarck wanted both Duchies and Bismarck let him think that Milan might be the property to be swapped. On the morning of 24 August Rechberg presented the assembled monarchs and retinues with the draft of just such a swap filled out, as Pflanze puts it, 'with uncomfortable exactness'. Franz Joseph thereupon asked William bluntly if he intended to annex the Duchies and after some hesitation William, embarrassed by the direct question, replied that 'he had no right to the Duchies and hence could lay no claim to them,'[143] exactly the same response he had given to Bismarck's annoyance at the Crown Council earlier in the year.

On 7 September 1864 Gerson Bleichröder wrote to Baron James de Rothschild to report what Bismarck had told him about Austro–Prussian relations. It seems to have been understood between Bismarck and Bleichröder that the Rothschilds would inform the French accordingly:

> The great intimacy with Austria has reached its term and a chill will follow. Schleswig's future is still deeply veiled. My good source still thinks that we must reach an understanding with the French and keep Schleswig-Holstein for Prussia. Russia would not object, and Austria and England would remain silent, however, unhappy they might be. For the time being this ideal is frustrated by the will of the Monarch, who, because of the Crown Princess, is inclined towards the Duke of Augustenburg.[144]

In the summer of 1864 France opened negotiations to create a free trade zone between the Empire and the Prussian-dominated German customs union, the Zollverein. At this point, Rechberg suggested again that a central European customs union would be a natural extension of the existing Prussian-dominated common market. The Prussian Landtag, the Prussian State Ministry, and the smaller German states opted for the French treaty which undermined Rechberg's entire policy of cooperation with Prussia.

Bismarck was furious. He wrote a letter to Roon on 22 September 1864 from Reinfeld, his wife's family estate:

> A privy councillorish rheumatism has afflicted the Ministry of Trade and the Ministry of Finance for which the correct mustard plaster has yet to be found. The gentlemen understand perfectly that they make difficulties for the present government when they worsen our relations with Austria and Bavaria through unnecessary discourtesies, from which we gain not the least advantage.[145]

In spite of Bismarck's anxiety, shortly thereafter the Peace of Vienna was signed, the main clause of which, Article 3, stated that

His Majesty the King of Denmark renounces His rights over the Duchies of
Schleswig, Holstein and Lauenberg to their Majesties the Emperor of Austria
and King of Prussia.[146]

The situation played again into Bismarck's hands. Prussia had in effect
now annexed Schleswig and Austria had an army of occupation in Holstein
hundreds of kilometres from her borders in a territory utterly useless to her.
In the meantime Rechberg had fallen from power in Vienna, and the
Emperor appointed Count Alexander von Mensdorff-Pouilly (1813–71), a
dashing and much decorated cavalry general, to succeed him. Rechberg,
who for all his faults had been apprenticed to Metternich, knew the diplomatic trade. Mensdorff, a very wealthy man, had the highest connections to
the English royal family through his mother, Sophie Duchess of Saxe-
Coburg, but had absolutely no qualifications for the post of Foreign Minister.
In addition, on taking office, he seemed to lose all his dash, and became 'the
picture of a man who wavered with every tendency in court circles'.[147] And
this incompetent, charming but supine figure had to play on centre court
against the greatest gamester in the history of diplomacy. The record of
Austrian incompetence in the nineteenth century hardly has a dimmer
chapter than this appointment.

Bismarck took advantage of Mensdorff's inexperience to stir up trouble
in the Duchies. There were still the Saxon and Hanoverian army units,
which the Bund had sent north to fight Denmark; Bismarck decided to
expel them and demanded that they exit Schleswig at very short notice.
This humiliation of the German Confederation put Austria into difficulty.
They needed to strengthen the Bund, not weaken it. Bismarck managed to
enlist Mensdorff in the enterprise and the two powers issued a joint note on
14 November 1864 which demanded that the allied troops withdraw, which
in due course they did.[148] On 7 December Prussian troops, who had fought
in the Danish War, enjoyed a triumphal march into Berlin, the first public
celebration of success that Bismarck could claim.[149]

The early weeks of 1865 brought tension between Austria and Prussia
closer to the breaking point. Mensdorff kept pressing Bismarck to state
Prussia's intentions and in February Bismarck issued the so-called
'February Conditions': the army and navy of the Duchies were to be
absorbed by Prussia; servicemen were to swear an oath to the King of
Prussia; Prussia was to be granted coastal forts and the right to construct
a canal across the territories; Prussian garrisons were to remain; and the
Duchies were to join the Zollverein, which still excluded the Habsburg

Empire. The Austrians were appalled. The Emperor called them 'quite unacceptable'.[150]

Between February and the summer, the two powers made moves and counter-moves. The Prussian commissioner began to turn Schleswig into a Prussian province, to which the Austrian responded by getting Bavaria to introduce a motion in the Bund that Holstein be turned over to the Duke of Augustenburg which passed by 9 votes to 6.[151] In secret during early March 1865, Bleichröder opened negotiations with the Austrian Jewish banker Moritz Ritter von Goldschmidt (1803–88) on a scheme for Prussia to buy out Austria in Schleswig and Holstein. On 8 March Goldschmidt wrote to Bleichröder: 'it would have to be a fat sum to overcome the immense reluctance against a cash settlement, which would not be very honourable.'[152]

This particular period between the February Conditions and the signing of a new Austro-Prussian convention in August at Bad Gastein has been the subject of more historical debate than any other in Bismarck's long career. How are we to account for the apparent vacillations in Bismarck's policy between the 'Schönbrunn System' (solidarity between Austria and Prussia in joint control of Germany) and the declaration made by Bismarck to Disraeli, Brunnow, and Vitzthum and repeated over and over in many venues that Prussia could only flourish if it destroyed Austrian hegemony by an inevitable Austro-Prussian war. The most famous German historians could not agree. For some the peerless Bismarck always knew—as a genius—what the next step had to be and he only appeared to waver. He changed tactics but not strategy. Others argued that Bismarck really wanted peace but it eluded him. The international conjuncture favoured aggressive moves against Austria. Great Britain had shown itself unwilling or unable under the Liberals to intervene in defence of Denmark. Napoleon III had got involved in an absurd attempt to found an empire in Mexico, and Tsarist Russia had to cope with the social upheaval caused by the emancipation of the serfs in 1861. The engagement of these powers in a German civil war must have been improbable. And yet Bismarck seemed to hesitate.

The King had begun to resent the behaviour of the Austrians. On 25 April he wrote to Roon that Bismarck had shown him the Austrian note about a compromise over Kiel which would involve a reduction of the Prussian garrison. 'I cannot bring myself to do that, since every concession to Austria is met by a new ingratitude and pretensions.'[153] Manteuffel had also been alarmed by the ministerial activities and in early May wrote to the King:

Who rules and decides in Prussia, the King or the ministers?... Your Majesty's ministers are loyal and devoted but they live now only in the atmosphere of the Chamber. If I may express an opinion, it is this, your Majesty should hold no council but should write to Minister Bismarck and say, 'Now that I have read the proposal, I have decided that the government will not agree to it'.[154]

The King rejected this advice and held a Crown Council on 29 May 1865 at which he declared for the first time that annexation of the Duchies was 'almost unanimously' demanded by the 'nation'. 'Only the Democracy which does not want Prussia to become great under the present government stands against this demand.'[155] After the King had declared his determination to annex the territories, Bismarck outlined his expectations about relations with Austria. Sooner or later a war would come; at the moment the international situation was favourable. Nevertheless, the wisest course was to eliminate from the February conditions the two points which had met the greatest objection: the oath of allegiance and the 'amalgamation' of the Prussian and Ducal forces.[156] After the meeting Manteuffel, genuinely alarmed by what he had heard, wrote to Roon:

I beg your Excellency most earnestly to keep your eye on Bismarck and stay in touch with him. I fear this hot-headed approach. That must not be. I beg your Excellency again to follow things closely. This is a game for high stakes and the state is the main thing.[157]

It must have been a stimulating session if the proverbial 'hothead' himself had been alarmed by Bismarck. But what had Bismarck actually said that was rash? He had modified the February Conditions to make them more palatable. He offered various courses of action and seemed not to opt for any.

The trouble was money. The Landtag session had begun in January and, while the obvious and unexpected success in the Danish War had softened the hostility of the liberals towards Bismarck, the lower house still had not yet surrendered its demand to approve state expenditure. On 19 June another Crown Council discussed what strategy to adopt in the deadlock. The minutes reveal that Bismarck said:

for a long time it had been his conviction that with the existing constitution Prussia could not be governed for any length of time...[he referred] to the opportunities which a complication of the foreign situation could yield and noted that it might be advisable by proper financial operations to weaken the present inclination of the money market toward an Austrian loan.[158]

There were several possible sources of funds. The government could issue a public loan without authorization by the Landtag. Bismarck wrote to Fritz Eulenburg, the Minister of the Interior on 5 July 1865 to say that the King had become as convinced of 'the necessity of a money operation as I am. He feels himself free of constitutional reservations. He said to me today his duty to preserve the Monarchy is more binding than his duty to the constitution.'[159] On the same day the State Ministry published its budget in the official state newsletter which contained an item for the fleet approved by the King but not the legislature, which came close to royal rule by decree.[160] A loan by decree could follow that example but might not recommend itself to the bond market. As a result the rate of interest could be punitively high or the sale fall short.

Exasperated by the 'quibbles' and lack of initiative of his Finance Minister von Bodelschwingh, Bismarck turned informally and quite irregularly to August von der Heydt (1801–74) to explore other ways to raise money. Von der Heydt had exactly the qualities that Bodelschwingh lacked: real experience in private banking as a partner in Heydt, Kersten und Söhne, the family firm; long tenure as Trade Minister under Count Brandenburg and then in the Manteuffel cabinet; though a liberal, he had excellent relations with the royal family; and 'as a result of his personal initiative he had insured the development of state-owned railways. By 1860 half of all Prussian railways belonged to the state.'[161] On 22 June von der Heydt wrote to Bismarck to explain his scheme to raise money.

> If it is a question of making liquid considerable sums of money without actual state loans as a floating debt or through their sale, there will be no lack of immediately realizable assets. I draw your attention to the substantial holdings of railroad shares, namely the state participation in the Cologne-Minden, the Bavarian-Märkish, the Upper Silesian, the Stargard-Posen railroads, and then there are the holdings in the Guaranty Fund of the Cologne-Minden line, which in a case of need could be used for sale or for mortgage, then there are the tax credits, perhaps, those of the Saarbrücken Mines or the Upper Silesian pits.[162]

Von der Heydt reckoned that the use of these state assets would finance the government's needs without recourse to unpopular increases in taxation. These were ideas that Bismarck wanted to hear, and it is hardly a surprise that after the victory over Austria in 1866, when he could rid himself of the 'conflict ministry' and the tedious Bodelschwingh, August von der Heydt became Finance Minister. Bismarck called him 'the Gold Uncle', in this case, a term of endearment.

The Protestant banker had come up with a scheme that would work. Bismarck's Jewish bankers, Bleichröder and his Rothschild and Sal. Oppenheim connections had ideas of their own. They too had hit upon a fire sale of Cologne-Minden shares but they had their eyes on the Preussische Seehandlung, which by an irony of history Bismarck, as reporteur of the Finance Committee of the Landtag in 1851, had helped to become 'the bank house of the state'.[163] The Preussische Seehandlung had been founded under Frederick the Great but in 1820 it became an independent institute directly under the Crown.[164] In an era when the joint stock company still required an individual permit from the government, the state bank became a very important agent in financial transactions. The Bleichröder/Rothschild group constructed various schemes to exploit the Seehandlung: floating it on the market; taking out a loan against the reparations to be expected from the Danish government as a result of the Peace of Vienna; selling some of its assets, raising money by selling bank shares or arranging a bond issue.

Bismarck set out the options in a letter to Roon from Carlsbad on 3 July 1865. The money operation had, it seemed, a peaceful side. 'Our task remains by means of our own money operations to block those planned by Austria and thus to assure the maintenance of peace.' He asks why the Seehandlung should not simply accept the demand of the state for credit with an agreement to pay it when and as needed, and if at the same time they raised interest on deposits they would open the gate to a flow of liquid capital to cover the obligation. And there was still the option of the Cologne-Minden railway which Count Itzenplitz had been investigating. 'If neither of the two operations goes forward, there remains only the direct loan available in spite of the constitution.'[165]

Bismarck's intentions cannot easily be deduced from the evidence above but thanks to a piece of luck, we can get a little further towards clarity. In the late 1960s Professor John Röhl, the biographer of Kaiser Wilhelm II, came upon three folders of letters to Fritz Eulenburg in Haus Hertefeld, a home belonging to an Eulenburg descendant. One of them contained 62 hitherto unknown handwritten letters from Bismarck, of which eleven belong to the period between 27 June and 18 August 1865, precisely the period in which Bismarck's intentions have been most contested.[166] The letters show that Bismarck had possibilities to raise the money to finance an Austria war from several sources, and a loan against assets in the Seehandlung had almost been agreed. They make his intentions no clearer but that may be because Bismarck always kept many options open.

When Bismarck arrived in Carlsbad and met the Austrians, he found 'the welcome as cool here as the weather' and on 4 July he wrote to Eulenburg that 'things with Austria stand badly. All the military reports from Holstein tell the King that the situation of troops has become impossible in the face of the press and social chicanery.'[167] While tension mounted between Prussia and Austria, Bleichröder had arranged with the Paris Rothschilds a deal in which the Rothschilds would form a consortium to lend the Seehandlung the money needed to finance the war with security provided by Seehandlung bonds at 1 per cent under the interest payable on Prussian state obligations. As Bismarck wrote to Eulenburg,

> At the moment we could get 4½% at par, the moment war threatens, we would lucky to get 90, therefore we cannot expect a better moment...Bleichröder tells me that Rothschild will take the issue in its entirety and in 10 days the silver would be in the state treasury.[168]

In fact negotiations hit a snag. Carl Meyer von Rothschild offered Otto von Camphausen (1812–1896), President of the Seehandlung,[169] to purchase 9 million thaler of unissued bonds at 98 or 99 but Camphausen insisted on par, that is, 100 per cent of the face value.[170] The margin may seem small but a 1 or 2 per cent 'turn' on a large sum of bonds makes a difference to the profitability of the transaction. Bismarck regretted very much that 'we had not got the money much earlier...Now we lose a lot if the break comes before the money.'[171] Here again we see that Bismarck contemplated the possibility of 'the break...before the money', in other words, he knew that he could make his move if it seemed opportune.

In the end, more than enough money came from an unexpected source. The Cöln-Mindener Eisenbahn-Gesellschaft, founded in 1842, had received money from the Prussian finance ministry in exchange for shares and an agreement that the railway would revert to the government after thirty years. The directors of the line had tried in vain to buy out the government and been refused on several occasion. The summer of 1865 gave them their chance. The directors wanted the state holding back and Bismarck's government needed money urgently. Dagobert Freiherr von Oppenheim (1809–89), a member of the famous Cologne private banking family, had become President of the railway[172] and he approached the government in the summer of 1865. On behalf of the directors, he offered the government

10 million thaler for the shares and suggested that he might be interested in a buy-back of all state claims. The Finance Ministry eventually squeezed the company for 13 million for the shares and another 15 million for the claims. The total sum exchanged amounted to 28,828,500 thaler and the agreement signed on 18 July, notarized on 10 August, was approved by the company on 28 August and the Crown on 13 September. As James M. Brophy explains, 'on three occasions in 1865 officials in the finance ministry demonstrated the illegality of signing a deal that involved the sale of equities in the Guarantee Fund without the legislature's approval, but these legal considerations were overlooked. Bismarck now knew—but not exactly when—that there would be cash in the bank for his war; for the company it meant 'nothing less than salvation'.[173]

On 27 July the Austrian delegation led by Count Blome arrived at Bad Gastein to negotiate a new settlement for the Duchies. Gustav Lehngraf von Blome (1829–1906) had been born Protestant in Hanover but became a Catholic in 1853. He 'seriously underestimated' Bismarck, writes his biographer,[174] and Bismarck thought him an idiot with his 'outmoded Byzantine-Jesuitical method of negotiating, full of tricks and dodges'.[175] Bismarck played cards with him at night, as he told his secretary Tiedemann years later, to scare him by the violence of his play.[176] Bismarck wrote himself to Moritz von Blanckenburg to report that the Austrians were leaning toward peace and the King would probably meet the Kaiser in Salzburg. 'Until then I have to tack and weave. From here on we cannot be crude' but to Eulenburg he wrote more openly:

> As long as the King is here, and as long as we have not carried out our money operations, I have to be glad to let things hang tolerably in mid-air, because the moment we move in Schleswig-Holstein, the ball starts to roll and the stock market sinks.[177]

By this time Bismarck knew that there would be money for a war if he needed it but the arrangements had not been finalized. A letter from Roon to Moritz von Blanckenburg on 1 August confirms that reading of Bismarck's intentions:

> There is money there, enough to give us a free hand in foreign policy, enough if necessary to mobilize the entire army and to pay for an entire campaign.... Where is the money to come from? Without violating the constitution, chiefly through an arrangement with Cologne-Minden railway, which Bodelschwingh and I think is very advantageous.[178]

Blome who had gone to Vienna to get new instructions returned on
1 August with a new proposal which in fact Bismarck had suggested to
him—that the dual powers should divide the Duchies: Prussia to assume
sovereignty over Schleswig and Austria over Holstein. The Austrians disliked the word 'sovereignty' and reduced it to 'administration'. Lauenburg
was to be sold to Prussia outright. Bismarck agreed and Blome returned to
Vienna for final consultations. On 10 August Bismarck wrote to Eulenburg
that he had to stall as long as possible. 'We will need time to make money
and secure France . . . [we have] a stopgap tolerable for us . . . with which for
the time being we can live honourably without the war running away with
us . . .' He asked Eulenburg to tell Bleichröder 'that if any part of my account
with him is still invested in securities, which I don't know here, he should
by no means unload these because of some premature fear of war.'[179] In the
meantime, an Austrian diplomat in Berlin had found out about the money
operations and wrote to Mensdorff in Vienna:

> These financial operations . . . can be justified only by an urgent political
> necessity, not from an economic point of view and [it is doubtful] that the
> Diet will approve them . . . [Prussia had acquired] such an important supply of
> money as one usually keeps in readiness only in anticipation of a war.[180]

On 14 August Bismarck and Blome initialled an agreement which was
signed formally in the Episcopal Palace at Salzburg.[181] A few days before the
formalities Bismarck with his usual casual attitude to matters of secrecy told
Eulenburg the gist of the agreement:

> In Schleswig therefore from 1 September we rule alone and as sovereign.
> Nobody will be able to get us out again and it begins to look as if Austria
> might be willing to sell us Holstein. That we shall get it one way or the other,
> I no longer have any doubt.[182]

In the end the Austrians had no choice but to seek peace. The political
situation in Austria had worsened and on 20 September 1865 Emperor
Franz Joseph revoked the constitution, a move which made it much more
difficult to find a way to cover a budget deficit of 80,000,000 gulden.
During the summer and autumn of 1865 Austrian diplomats in Paris and
London had desperately tried to entice the Rothschilds to float a loan to
cover the yawning budget deficit. They found the Rothschilds very unwilling to form the syndicate and eventually by the intervention of Napoleon
III himself a consortium of big French banks brought a 90,000,000 gulden
loan to the Paris bourse on 27 November 1865. The loan sold out on the

first day, because it carried a 9 per cent rate of interest, a sign of the fragility of Austrian credit. The loan worth 90,000,000 gulden to Vienna would need 157,000,000 to repay and while the investors bought it at 69, the Austrians only received 61¼. The banks made 28,500,000 gulden.[183] The Austrian Empire's bonds might be called 'sub-prime'.

Meanwhile, the Middle States watched these developments with alarm mixed with complacency. In the summer of 1865, the *Budissiner Nachrichten* warned the Saxons that they should beware of getting involved in 'Great Powerdom':

> We have a constitutional life, the like of which neither Prussia nor Austria enjoys. As a result, concord reigns between King and people. We have prosperity, low taxes and healthy finances... Higher political and cultural goals are not neglected here.[184]

The Saxons should mind their own business, the paper urged, and stay out of an Austro-Prussian war. They also had to be careful about the mounting enthusiasm for the creation of a German national state, a possibility which would reduce the Middle States, even those which were kingdoms, to mere provinces in a German Reich.

Schleswig could not enjoy such peaceful complacency. The agreement between Prussia and Austria gave the Prussians sovereignty in their duchy. The acquisition of Schleswig meant that a governor of the territory had to be appointed and Bismarck suggested General Edwin von Manteuffel. The King appointed him on 24 August 1865. It was a happy solution to a perennial problem. The influential general would be in Kiel and not in the King's antechamber and his ego would be gratified by his new vice-regal status. Stosch could not understand the choice as he wrote to a friend, 'I cannot understand how they can send Manteuffel to Schleswig. He will always take orders from the King alone and never from the Ministry...'[185] Bismarck hardly minded that, as long as the King took orders from him and so far he had. On 16 September 1865 the King elevated Bismarck to the rank of count.[186]

While Bismarck negotiated with the Austrians, Moltke had begun to draw lessons from the Danish War, not all of them happy ones. The Prussians had done less well than the official propaganda suggested. The Danes had very effectively used trenches and fortified works and by concentrating their fire had inflicted heavy casualties on the Prussians and Austrians. 'Now that a cannon could hurl a shell seven kilometers and an infantry rifle could bring a man down at 1,000 paces, it would be difficult to redirect a regiment from an enemy's center to his flank in the heat of battle.'[187] Moltke also became convinced that the size of the modern army meant that traditional Napoleonic doctrines of concentrated forces must lead to disaster, a kind of military traffic jam. During the 1850s the General Staff and the railways cooperated more and more closely so that in time of war the army could count on good transport arrangements.[188] The gradual extension of military control of railroads meant that Moltke could work on a very different mobilization timetable and hence a different deployment of troops. The slogan *getrennt marschieren, gemeinsam schlagen* (march separately, strike together) came to be associated with Moltke's bold innovation—to have his armies deploy separately but come together to fight. Great enveloping movements became possible and one of them led to the greatest victory of 1866. The King, who understood military matters, gave Moltke the same ability to experiment that he gave Bismarck, and it is a remarkable fact that the greatest diplomat and the greatest strategist of the nineteenth century served the same monarch and the same state. In addition, the two generals without whom Bismarck could not have unified Germany, Roon and Moltke, came from untypical Prussian backgrounds, Moltke from Denmark and Roon more distantly from Holland. Neither had personal wealth and neither owned estates.

In late September the annual royal manoeuvres took place. Major Stosch wrote to his friend that the King had been very pleased with the efficiency of the army's deployment. He recorded, as closely as he could reconstruct it, a conversation between Bismarck and the Crown Prince about prospects for Schleswig-Holstein:

CROWN PRINCE: 'do you want to annex them?'
BISMARCK: 'If possible, yes, but I do not want to start a European war over them.'
CROWN PRINCE: 'And if one threatens?'
BISMARCK: 'Well, then I confine myself to the February demands.'
CROWN PRINCE: 'And if these are not accepted?'
BISMARCK: 'Prussia needs to fear no war over these; the February demands are our ultimatum.'
CROWN PRINCE: 'And what is happening about Duke Frederick?
BISMARCK: 'That depends on how the cards fall.'
STOSCH CONTINUED: 'At the end the conversation took on a very violent charac-
ter...Bismarck's ruthlessness makes him many enemies in the aristocracy and increases the ranks of the opposition.'[189]

Shortly after the manoeuvres Bismarck left for a holiday in Biarritz with his family. On 4 and 11 October 1865 Bismarck met Napoleon III in Biarritz, though what they actually discussed has never been clearly established. Bismarck would certainly have kept his French options open and would have hinted at the unstable character of the Gastein Convention. Wawro and Eyck argue that Bismarck actually offered Napoleon Luxembourg as compensation for his eventual neutrality in an Austro-Prussian War. Pflanze regards that as unlikely. Whether he promised the Emperor more or less than that we do not know.[190]

Early in the new year, 1866, Bismarck had a visit from Ernst Ludwig von Gerlach, one of his early patrons, which Gerlach recorded in his diary. It was to be a disturbing occasion. This painful meeting showed Gerlach that Bismarck had abandoned any semblance of the rigorous Christian morality which the two brothers Gerlach and many others thought they had discerned in the young Bismarck.[191] Perthes too had concluded that he was cynical and believed in nothing, a cold, calculating rationalist. The next ten years in which Bismarck unleashed two wars, trampled on the sovereignties of the German princes, invoked the 'revolution' in the form of universal suffrage, declared war on the Roman Catholic Church, and introduced secular marriage, divorce, and school inspection into the very heartlands of Junker piety might suggest that he had indeed no religious scruples but—as always—Bismarck defies simple categories. He kept religious and devotional literature by his bedside and strongly denied that he had no faith. His colossal achievements often seemed to him to have been God's work. His abandonment of Gerlach's Protestant Neo-Pietism could not, however, be denied.

On 19 February 1866 the new British Ambassador Lord Loftus presented his credentials to King William I. Lord Augustus William Frederick Spencer Loftus (1817–1904), according to the *Oxford Dictionary of National Biography*, 'was an adequate rather than an able diplomatist, promoted a little beyond his level' but neither 'absurd' nor 'mischievous', as Disraeli described him.[192] He got along well with Bismarck and brought to his new post considerable experience at other German courts. He gained Bismarck's confidence and later in the year witnessed several dramatic moments. There is a passage in his memoirs which is worth quoting at some length because it describes the Prussian court in terms that most commentators have not:

> There is no Court more brilliantly maintained, and no Court where more courtesy and hospitality are shown to strangers than the Prussian. Every member of a royal house in Europe, on arriving at Berlin, is lodged at the

Schloss, and royal carriages and servants are placed at his disposal during his stay. All the expenses of the Court—the appanages of the Royal Family, and the maintenance of the numerous palaces and residences in all parts of the kingdom, always ready for occupation—are kept up by the Sovereign, and are defrayed out of the Crown estates (termed *Kronfideicommis*) which are considerable. These revenues are entirely under the administration of the Sovereign, and are independent of Parliament. All the members of the Royal Family receive the *dotations* appointed to them by the King from the Crown estates without being subjected to any vote or approval of Parliament.[193]

Loftus arrived as the tensions between Austria and Prussia had begun to increase. The King held a Crown Council on 28 February 1866. Everybody who mattered at the apex of the military, political, and diplomatic branches attended and Manteuffel came as Governor of Schleswig.[194] The official *Provincial Correspondence* reported on the event and subsequent meetings between the King and Chief of the General Staff but the paper denied rumours that aggressive intentions lay behind the meeting. It noted that 'the old jealousies on the part of the Austrians had gained ground in Vienna and that the Prussian government would in future be forced to give consideration to its own interests in its deliberations.'[195] At the council Bismarck had made it clear that 'a forceful appearance abroad and a war undertaken for Prussia's honor would have a beneficial effect on the solution of the internal conflict.'[196] Moltke reported Austrian troop movements into Bohemia but he emphasized that Austrian units in Venice 'were not yet in the stage of war readiness... and he emphasized that there had been no signs of horse purchases.' In 1866 120,000 horses were mobilized, so that early mobilization began with large purchases of horses. During the Franco-Prussian War of 1870, 250,000 horses were mobilized by Prussia and more than 300,000 by France. Hence in early 1866 Moltke could safely reckon that the Austrians had not started to mobilize.[197]

On 7 March 1866 Lord Clarendon, British Foreign Secretary, wrote in great distress to Loftus,

In the name of all that is rational, decent and humane, what can be the justification of war on the part of Prussia? She cannot possibly plead her desire for territorial aggrandizement, and she cannot with truth say that the administration of Holstein by the Austrian authorities has been of a kind to constitute a *casus belli*, although Bernstorff has just told me that the license allowed in Holstein by General Gablentz and the hostile articles of newspapers under the inspiration of Austria have produced a state of things intolerable to Prussia...[198]

Even Bismarck at this stage recognized that no ground for war had yet been found. Again it would take stupefying ineptness by Count Mensdorff, Austrian Foreign Minister, to give Prussia even a shred of justification but he had done nothing yet. Mensdorff's well-informed sister-in-law, Countess Gabriele Hatzfeldt, wrote mockingly of Bismarck as a mere subaltern in a Prussian guards regiment and added,

> There is unanimity here that Bismarck is simply mad and has so jammed himself up in domestic and foreign affairs that he has lost his head and wants war *à tout prix*, to get himself out of the affair and maintain his position.[199]

Even Bismarck's friend Roon had begun to worry about his mental and physical health. On 26 March 1866 he wrote a gloomy letter to Moritz von Blanckenburg:

> Things are not good here. Our friend Otto Bismarck in Herculean day and night efforts has worn down his nerves...The day before yesterday he suffered such hefty stomach cramps and was a result yesterday so depressed, so irritable and annoyed—apparently by little things—that I am today not without anxiety, because I know what's at stake....Complete freedom of thought does not combine well with a bad stomach and irritated nerves.[200]

These symptoms, which varied over time, mark the beginning of a pattern that made Bismarck unique in another way: no statesman of the nineteenth or twentieth century fell ill so frequently, so publicly, and so dramatically as Otto von Bismarck. Bismarck trumpeted his suffering and all his symptoms to everybody. He complained loudly and without discretion from the 1860s to his retirement that the vexations of office had ruined his health and disposition, and in a sense they had. His colossal will to power combined with his fury at anybody—friend or foe—who blocked him literally made him sick and he knew it. Yet the very situation in which he operated gave him no choice. The enemies at court, especially the Queen, the Crown Prince, and Crown Princess, worked against him and did everything to undermine and undo his hold on the King. Rage combined with impotence at the 'high persons' whom he could neither convert nor remove ate away at his peace of mind and physical health. He hated them with the intensity of a man in physical and mental pain but he could only escape the agony by surrendering power. That he could never do. Roon saw, as all those close to him confirm, the increasing irrationality, irritability, and intolerance and many like von Below, his old friend, realized that the sickness lay primarily in the mind not in the body.

As the joke has it, 'just because you are paranoid does not mean that you are not being followed'. Bismarck suspected—and he was correct in this—that a conspiracy against him had began to take more formal shape in the mid-1860s. Queen Augusta now received regular foreign and domestic policy reports from Franz Freiherr von Roggenbach (1825–1907), former Prime Minister of Baden. Roggenbach, handsome and distinguished, had enjoyed a brilliant career, becoming Prime Minster of the Grand Duchy of Baden in 1861 at the age of 36. He loathed Bismarck even before he had become a serious threat. In May of 1865 Roggenbach suddenly announced his resignation in protest at Bismarck's policy in Schleswig-Holstein. Major Albrecht von Stosch, who became in time a member of the Queen's private 'shadow administration', wrote to his friend Otto von Holtzendorff to express his regret at the resignation:

> Your news from Baden interested me very much. Roggenbach was like a shooting star among statesmen. It makes me very sad that he gave up his bold project before he had completed it.[201]

From the summer of 1865 on Roggenbach began to supply Queen Augusta with lengthy memoranda prepared with the expertise and authority of an experienced German diplomat and minister. The published collected correspondence of Roggenbach with the Queen and von Stosch which began after his resignation amounts to 453 pages.[202] In Bismarck's memoirs Roggenbach appears always as a source of intrigues and they were that. Other moderate Liberal constitutionalists had close ties to the courts of the Crown Prince and Princess of Prussia, the Grand Duke of Baden, and to the Duke of Saxe-Coburg.[203] General von Stosch belonged to the circle, the rare liberal Prussian general. Bismarck had good ground to be suspicious.

The Prussian King and his ministers had opted for war with Austria and a Crown Council meeting took place on Monday 27 March 1866 at which the King agreed to order a partial mobilization and a call-up of reserves. Roon worried that 'Bismarck's neurotic impatience' would cause a disaster.[204] The next day, like clockwork, Bismarck wrote impatiently to Roon that 'it is very much to be wished that tomorrow the King issues definitive orders. Maundy Thursday he will not be in the mood for such things. You see him tomorrow. Couldn't you arrange that we see him together?' Roon did arrange that and on 29 March, the Wednesday before Easter 1866, the orders were actually signed.[205] Moltke calmly went into action. He knew his mobilization plans had been greatly improved in the last two years and reassured Roon on 5 April:

That the Austrians—if one gives them enough time—will have as many troops in the field as we can summon is nothing new. I have made that clear at all our conferences. It is not a question of the absolute numbers of troop strength but essentially of the time in which both sides can bring them to efficient deployment. Especially for this reason the tables at the end of my report showed clearly and visibly the evident advantage in which we will find ourselves for three whole weeks, if we take the initiative or at least mobilize at the same time as the Austrians.[206]

On 14 April Moltke reported to the king on the next step. His strategy rested on the intelligent use of railroad lines. 'Prussia's three armies were now positioned—on paper—exactly astride the three main and six secondary railway lines. The Elbe army moved on the Berlin-Dresden-Friedland railroad, the First Army on the Frankfurt-Goerlitz-Liegnitz line and the Second Army on the Stettin-Breslau-Lamgaschutz-Rechenbach-Frankenstein and Brieg-Neisse railroads...In short 75 days before it was fought, Moltke envisioned the whole war scenario virtually as it later came out.'[207]

The Crown Prince was horrified and wrote to General von Schweinitz:

The King wants no war but for months now Bismarck has twisted things so that the old Gentleman has become more and more irritable and finally Bismarck will have ridden him so far that he will not be able to do anything but commit us to war, which will stir up Europe. Bismarck's talent to manipulate things for the King is great and worthy of admiration. As an expression of his bottomless frivolity and piratical policies some sort of Reich reform idea will be dumped on the carpet, probably with proposals for a Reich parliament and that in the light of our domestic parliamentary conflict! That is a rich irony and bears its failure on its forehead. With such a man everything is possible.[208]

The Austrians would certainly have agreed with that. They were getting nervous about the German question, as on 7 April Count Blome, Bismarck's counterpart at Bad Gastein, now Austrian ambassador to Bavaria, wrote to State Secretary *Hofrat* Ludwig von Biegeleben in Vienna:

Whoever feels the pulse of public opinion will agree with me that the phrase 'reform of the Bund' has caught fire and pushed the interest for Augustenburg and the independence of Holstein into the background. The fearful and anxious cling to Bund reform; the Bavarian conservatives cling to it since it will make Bavaria a great power. Bund reform attracts the entire 'democracy', which means by it a parliament.[209]

The Crown Prince had guessed right about Bismarck's intentions, and Blome had assessed the aims of the 'democracy' correctly. Neither saw that the two were connected. On 8 April the Prussian–Italian Treaty was signed, which Eyck called a 'breach of the constitution of Germany'.[210] According to its terms the kingdom of Italy was obliged to go to war against the Austrian Empire if war broke out within ninety days, and Bismarck clearly intended that to happen. The next day brought an even bigger shock. On 9 April 1866 the Prussian ambassador submitted a motion to the Bund which changed the entire history of Germany. Of all Bismarck's many dazzling moves in a long career this one must be one of the most important. The official announcement, published on 11 April 1866, read as follows:

> The Prussian government has just taken a step of the greatest importance in the Federal Diet. It has introduced a motion that the Federal Assembly be minded to decide to call an assembly which will be chosen by direct and universal right to vote and at a date to be determined in due course to assemble in order to receive and consider the proposals of the German governments for a reform of the Federal Constitution and in the meantime until the meeting of the said assembly to establish such suggestions by agreement of the governments among themselves.[211]

The Crown Prince had guessed correctly. Bismarck had indeed 'dumped proposals for a Reich parliament on the carpet' but even the Crown Prince had not foreseen the democratically elected parliament. Bismarck had called forth the power of democracy to outflank the Austrians and the German Federal States in the knowledge that the Habsburgs with their eleven national groups and the rising threat of nationalism could never compete on that ground. In 1866 Bismarck brandished democracy at the Habsburgs like a cross in front of a vampire, a not inappropriate image, since Dracula was a Romanian prince, and his castle was in Hungarian-ruled Romania, a territory without universal suffrage.

German opinion was stunned by Bismarck's move. The Liberal *Kölnische Zeitung* commented: 'If Mephistopheles climbed up in the pulpit and read the Gospel, could anyone be inspired by this prayer?'[212] The Austrian Ambassador to Saxony reported on the Saxon Prime Minister Beust's view:

> According to his investigations here *up to now* the reaction in Dresden is that the Prussian motion for a German parliament has caused laughter because they see it as ludicrous to accept such a move from the hand of a Count Bismarck. Whether given the fatuous Germanism of a portion of the Saxon population, this cheerful reaction may not turn to something more reasonable, nobody can offer any guarantee.[213]

The shock was greatest among Bismarck's former patrons and supporters, the faithful Christian conservatives and readers of the *Kreuzzeitung*, his neighbours, friends, and relations. Count Adolf von Kleist was simply incredulous. In a letter to Ludwig von Gerlach he expressed his horror:

> What do you think of the latest twist by Bismarck? Summon up popular sovereignty, forming a constitutional convention!! And more than that the complete embarrassment. Austria is in the right, comes with the old suggestions of 1863 and garners universal applause. For God's sake come to Berlin. You are the only one who still has some influence over him or at least to whom he listens. Our allies are now the revolution in all its nuances. We are absolutely stunned. I am in despair.[214]

A few days later, on 14 April 1866, Prince Albert of Prussia (1809–72), the youngest brother of Frederick William IV, also wrote to Gerlach but more hesitantly.

> What Bismarck's object is with the project, I cannot grasp. In the first place he rejects the entire previous system. A grand slogan of the type of the Congress of Princes does not seem to be the purpose, is it in order to provoke Austria even more?... Not understanding, however, does not make me doubt Bismarck and I wait. But what do you think?[215]

'Little Hans' still stuck by his old friend and wrote to Gerlach on 16 April, from his estate, Kieckow:

> I thank you that you defended Bismarck against Adolf's hasty condemnation. There can be no talk of a constituent assembly. There still remains: universal suffrage, but what else?... In order to judge him, one has to know the entire situation and instead of all us complaining and criticizing, just take it on trust.... May God permit poor Bismarck to get better, illuminate him and preserve us in peace and, if it cannot be preserved, may God purify his conscience by his attempt to have achieved everything through an honourable peace.[216]

The members of the *Kreuzzeitung* party could not accept the resigned piety that Hans von Kleist urged on Gerlach: trust in God and trust in Otto. Many had had enough. On 2 May Privy Councillor J. Bindewald, one of Ludwig Gerlach's former pupils and now a senior civil servant in the Prussian Ministry of Religious, Educational, and Medical Affairs (the *Kultusministerium*), wrote to Ludwig von Gerlach who, as the acknowledged intellectual leader of the extreme Right, had yet to take a public position:

1. Prince Otto von Bismarck, 1896, by Franz von Lenbach

2. Otto von Bismarck aged 11, 1826, by Franz Krüger

3. Johanna von Bismarck, 1857, by Jakob Becker

4. Albrecht von Roon, *c.*1871

5. Helmuth von Moltke, *c.*1870–71, by
Franz von Lenbach

6a. Ernst Ludwig von Gerlach,
1872

6b. Leopold von Gerlach, 1850

7. King Frederick William IV, 1847

8. Field Marshall Friedrich von Wrangel

9. King and Emperor William I of Prussia, 1888

10. Empress Augusta, 1888, by Bernhard Plockhorst

11. Emperor Frederick III

12. Princess Victoria, Princess Royal as Crown Princess of Prussia, by Heinrich von Angeli

13. Otto von Bismarck as Ambassador to the German Confederation, 1855, by Jakob Becker

14. Ferdinand Lassalle, *c.* 1862

15. Hildegard von Spitzemberg, 1869, by
Wilhelm von Kaulbach

16. *Capitulation Negotiations at Donchery*, after a painting, 1885, by Anton Werner

17. Otto von Bismarck in cuirassier uniform, 1875

18. Marie von Schleinitz

19. Supper at a Ball, 1878, by Adolph von Menzel

20. *The Congress of Berlin, 13 June to 13 July 1878, 1881, by Anton von Werner*

21. Eduard Lasker and the National Liberal
Party Leadership

22. Ludwig Windthorst, 1890, by Vilma von
Parlaghy-Brachfeld

23. Otto von Bismarck with German spiked helmet, 1880

24. The Empress Victoria as a widow, 1897

25. Otto von Bismarck, *c.* 1890

26. Otto von Bismarck and his dogs Tyras II and Rebecca, July 1891

27. Ernst Schweninger, 1892, by Christian
Wilhelm Allers

I cannot keep still any longer and after consultation with President von Kleist and Beuttner, I beg you to intervene in the *Kreuzzeitung* so that from our point of view the objections and dangers in the federal reform project are noted and at least the principles are preserved which are more important than a diplomatic move with the purpose of embarrassing the opponent. The proposed parliament and its system of election upsets me less than the modus, the how and the place from which the thing has been staged. Without a parliamentary apparatus these days no statesman can operate and the parliament need not and should not be a constituting body. To treat the chambers at home with a riding crop and because of the complications with them to be standing on the verge of a *coup d'état* and then to hurl the parliament idea into Germany![217]

Two days later, 4 May, Prince Albert wrote to Ludwig von Gerlach again to tell him that as a general officer he had been informed of the partial mobilization. As to politics, he wrote,

I have not been able to see or speak to Count Bismarck. He is still unwell and has only been out once or twice... The leading articles about federal reform have not entirely reconciled my feelings with it. There is much very doubtful about it but I have such boundless confidence in Bismarck that I suspect that it forms part of his long-term, well-thought out plan and is neither a momentary inspiration nor a political chess move.[218]

It is interesting that a royal prince of the older generation should have assessed Bismarck so accurately. Attentive readers may recall the strong language that Bismarck used to the late General Leopold von Gerlach in the famous exchange of letters of 1857 about Napoleon III. Bismarck had seen that democracy and conservatism could be compatible and he intended to use universal suffrage as he used everything and everybody to achieve his end. That was all too much for Ludwig von Gerlach, who on 5 May published an article entitled 'War and Federal Reform' in the *Kreuzzeitung*:

Let us take care not to fall into the dreadful false belief that God's commandments stop at the field of politics. *Justitia fundamentum regnorum* ... The justified calling on Prussia to expand its power in Germany matches the equally justified Austrian claim to maintain its power in Germany. Germany is no longer Germany if Prussia is not there or when Austria is not there... In the midst of the clanging of weapons Prussia introduces at the Bund a demand for universal suffrage. Universal suffrage means political bankruptcy—in place of living relations of law and political thought, instead of concrete personalities, we get numbers and exercises in addition.[219]

Bismarck never forgave Ludwig von Gerlach for daring to criticize him in public. But it bothered him. In later years he would come back to Gerlach in conversation and mock him. Gerlach, a man of principle, continued to criticize Bismarck, the unforgivable sin of sins, so he had to be dismissed as a crank. In 1873 he explained to Lucius von Ballhausen that

> Gerlach has become entirely negative and criticizes everything. Frederick II was not 'great' and his regime was a series of failures and mistakes. He admires 1806 because nobody else does.[220]

An Austrian diplomat commented bitterly on Bismarck's tactics:

> We appeal to the noble sentiments: patriotism, honour, principles of law, energy, courage, decision, sense of independence, etc. He reckons on the lower motivations of human nature: avarice, cowardice, confusion, indolence, indecision and narrow-mindedness.[221]

That list of lower motivations described perfectly the behaviour of the German states. They hesitated. They plotted. They combined and dissolved. In the end on 9 May the Federal Assembly voted by 9 to 5 on a Saxon motion to demand that Prussia explain the grounds for mobilization.

> The High Assembly of the Bund agrees without delay to approach the Royal Prussian Government to request that through an appropriate declaration with due recognition of Art. XI of the Federal Act (according to which members of the Bund may not wage war upon each other but should bring conflicts to the Federal Assembly for resolution) full reassurance will be received.[222]

The Austrians had been outflanked on the Italian front by Bismarck's alliance with Italy and in Germany by his alliance with the people. To the west Napoleon III could not make up his mind nor assure unity among his advisers about what to do: to join Prussia and Italy? To extract German territory on the Rhine from the Prussians as compensation for neutrality? To back Austria to maintain the balance of power? Bismarck played him like a big fish on a line, hauling him in, letting him out. Yes, he would surrender territory, but the King? That was the difficulty, and so on. In the end, on 24 May 1866, Napoleon III—caught between greed and fear—called a conference in the name of France, Britain, and Russia to meet in Paris to mediate between the two German Powers. On 26 May 1866 Albrecht von Stosch, as 2nd Quartermaster General of the II Army under the Crown Prince, attended the Grand War Council with the King, Moltke, Roon, Bismarck,

and all the senior commanders and their chiefs of staff. In a letter to his wife
he described how the King, tearful and upset, remained committed to maintenance of the peace:

> Bismarck gave hints that the war must decisively achieve the rounding off of
> Prussian territory. That caused the Crown Prince to ask the question whether
> there was an intention to annex territory. He had not heard that. The King
> answered angrily, that there is no question of war yet and still less of deposing
> German princes. He wants peace...Bismarck was by far the clearest and
> sharpest. I became convinced that he had brought about the whole situation
> in order to encourage the King to be more warlike...The meeting went on
> for three hours, and as we came out, the Crown Prince said, 'we know no
> more than we did before. The King will not; Bismarck will.'[223]

On 30 May Bismarck wrote to Robert von der Goltz, his ambassador in
Paris:

> I regard the whole uproar and opposition in the country as entirely on the
> surface, stirred up by the upper stratum of the bourgeoisie and nourished in
> the popular masses by unrealistic promises. In the decisive moment the masses
> stand by the Monarchy, without distinction whether it has a liberal or con-
> servative direction at that moment.[224]

The Prussian government had accepted the invitation to Napoleon's
conference in Paris, because Bismarck dared not annoy the Emperor. Stosch
told his wife that Bismarck would soon set off 'to the conference in Paris.
People see that as decisive because by his absence he loses his power over
the King and his opponents, whose number grows each day, gain ground.'[225]
At this point Mensdorff made the first of two serious mistakes. Unlike the
flexible Bismarck, Mensdorff refused to attend the conference in Paris
because the status of Venetia might be discussed and Austrian territories in
Italy were non-negotiable. The conference option fell through.

On 2 June 1866, King William I made one of his most important decisions. He decreed that the General Staff Chief Helmuth von Moltke be
officially put in command of the Prussian army with the right to issue
orders in the name of the King. This broke the tradition of Frederick the
Great that the King had to command his army in the field and gave to
Moltke control of the entire operational leadership in war and its preparation in peace.[226] The years of preparation and attention to small things would
pay off. The General Staff had moved over to the 24-hour clock for its
operations and every commander had orders to keep a war diary from day

1 of mobilization.[227] By 5 and 6 June the Prussian deployment—approximately 330,000 men—on the borders had been completed.[228] But there was still no war nor the crucial pretext for one.

At this point, obligingly, Count Mensdorff made his second serious mistake. The Austrians asked the Federal Assembly to intervene in the conflict and placed the decision in its hands. It also ordered its Governor General in Holstein to call the estates of the Duchy into session. By so doing, it had unilaterally revoked the Bad Gastein Convention and gave Bismarck the chance to declare through the official press that

> by the declarations made to the Bund and through the convocation in the near future of the Holstein estates, Austria has called into question and endangered the sovereign rights of the King of Prussia as co-regent of Schleswig-Holstein . . . Our Government will respond to the treaty violation with its full energy in defence of its rights.[229]

Prussia and Austria now moved toward war. On 9 June Bismarck wrote to the Duke of Saxe-Coburg-Gotha that only 'an act of violence' would solve the German question.[230] On the 10th he presented the text to the German states for a new federal constitution, which would exclude Austria, and had a lower house based on universal suffrage. Bavaria and Prussia would share the military command of the new German state[231] and on the 11th he engaged Heinrich von Treitschke to draft a manifesto for the King to use to address the nation on the eve of war.[232] Heinrich von Treitschke (1834–96) had become a kind of popular idol among German professors. He filled every hall in the university. He addressed crowds on public occasions. He wrote plays, poetry, and literary criticism and lectured on recent German history. His sister compared him to an academic Martin Luther. In 1863 he published a pamphlet called 'Federal State and Unitary State' which took the Bismarckian line. The little states were all fraudulent creations and the justifications of them by the use of the word 'organic' meant nothing. 'We know that the word "organic" appears in politics as soon as thought ends . . . Every German federal reform will be an empty phrase as long as Germany's unnatural ties to Austria continue.'[233] He belonged to the small group of German liberals whom Bismarck had converted. As he put it:

> I find it terrible that the most important foreign minister whom Prussia has had for decades should at the same time be the most hated man in Germany. I find it sadder still that the most promising ideas for reforming the

Confederation that were ever proposed by a Prussian government should have been met by the nation with such humiliating coldness.[234]

Yet when Treitschke actually met Bismarck, he was shocked. After the audience he remarked: 'Of the moral powers in the world he has *not the slightest notion.*'[235]

The Middle States, as they were called, would not surrender their independence easily. A French traveller in the mid-1860s visited Dresden while it still housed the royal reisdence of a ruling dynasty and wondered at the display of monarchical self-confidence:

> Twenty different signs recall at any moment the proximity of the palace ... There are the officers who pass by, with their sabres tucked under their arms, ... Then the troops of men in livery who come and go, invariably wearing ... the royal crown, which image soon ends up encrusted in your retina unless you take good care.[236]

The three dynasties of Hanover, Saxony, and Württemberg had lineages no less impressive than the Hohenzollern and took care to parade them. Bismarck—in one of his very few real miscalculations—overestimated the power of these monarchies and the loyalty of their subjects. Had he known how easily the princes would surrender their sovereignty (Hanover was a stubborn exception), he would never have introduced universal suffrage. The people were not called up because Bismarck had some sort of 'white revolution' in mind or because he had bonapartist urges, as many historians assert, but only to balance the princes in order to preserve the absolute power of the Prussian King. By the end of the 1880s Bismarck planned to repeal universal suffrage because the people turned out to be Catholics and Social Democrats, not obsequious peasants. Bismarck fell victim to Burke's observation that 'very plausible schemes, with very pleasing commencements, have often shameful and lamentable conclusions'.

The first act of war took place on 10 June 1866. Since Austria had unilaterally violated the Convention of Bad Gastein, Prussia now had a right to joint sovereignty of Holstein and Schleswig and Lieutenant General von Manteuffel issued a proclamation to the Holsteiners 'that to protect the threatened rights of His Majesty the King I am obliged to take in hand the supreme authority in the Duchy of Holstein'.[237] Prussian troops heavily outnumbered the Austrians brigades and the Austrian Vice-Regent of Holstein Lieutenant General Ludwig Freiherr von Gablenz (1814–74) issued an order for his troops to withdraw. General Manteuffel allowed them to march out with full honours, drums rolling and flags flying. Bismarck went into one of his notorious rages but he could not issue an order to a Prussian private, let alone a senior and flamboyant character like General Edwin von Manteuffel. He complained to Manteuffel in strong terms and Manteuffel replied equally strongly. Erich Eyck describes what Bismarck then did:

> You say that a violent act would embarrass the mind. I answer you with the words of Deveroux, 'Freund, jetzt ist's Zeit zu lärmen' [now is time to make a din—JS]. Excuse the hasty style of this letter, but your telegram this morning paralysed my nerves, and this is now the reaction. In haste but in old friendship, yours, Bismarck.' While his pen flew over the paper, he thought of some lines from Schiller's 'Wallenstein's Death' which expressed his feelings better still. He ordered a copy to be brought to him. He found the lines at the decisive moment when only open rebellion is left to him, and he wrote under his signature:

> Ich tat's mit Widerstreben,
> Da es in meine Wahl noch war gegeben,
> Notwendigkeit ist da, der Zweifel flieht,
> Jetzt fechte ich für mein Haupt und für mein Leben.
>   (Er geht ab, die anderen folgen) Schiller, Wallenstein, Act III, Scene 10
> [Lingering irresolute, with fitful fears
>   I drew the sword—'twas with an inward strife,
>   While yet the choice was mine. The murderous knife is lifted for my heart!
>   Doubt disappears! I fight now for my head and for my life.][238]
>   (He goes off, the others follow)

> Even the critical reader cannot help feeling overwhelmed by this letter. No other statesman would have been able to write a letter of this scope at so critical a time.[239]

I suspect that Churchill could easily have done something similar, though it is impressive. What Eyck in spite of his stupendous erudition ignores is how weak Bismarck's position was in the situation. He could not order Manteuffel to do a thing, only cajole him, persuade him, seduce him with his favourite playwright. Imagine it: the great Bismarck at the single most desperate moment of his career so powerless that his only ally was Schiller. No doubt, as always with Bismarck, there is self-dramatization at work in the episode, but the fact remains that Manteuffel obeyed the King, not Bismarck.

On 14 June the Prussian delegate in Frankfurt declared that the Constitution of the Bund had been broken and on the next day the Prussian Ministers in Hanover, Dresden, and Hesse-Cassel presented ultimatums to the governments to which they were accredited which demanded a reply by midnight and a complete acceptance of the Prussian proposals.[240] Sentiment in Germany was overwhelmingly anti-Prussian. Baron Kübeck wrote to Mensdorff to report that, as Austrian troops left Frankfurt, the citizenry shouted, "'Three cheers for Austria! Victory for the Austrian army!" Whereas the Prussian contingent left without ceremony in the morning.'[241]

At midnight on the night of 15 June Lord Loftus found himself at a scene of high drama.

> I was with Prince Bismarck on the night of June 15th. We had been walking and sitting in his garden till a later hour, when, to my astonishment, it struck midnight. Bismarck took out his watch and said, 'At this moment our troops are marching into Hanover, Saxony and the Electorate of Hesse-Cassel. The struggle will be severe. Prussia may lose, but she will, at all events, have fought bravely and honourably. If we are beaten' Count Bismarck said, I shall not return here. I shall fall in the last charge. One can only die once and, if beaten, it is better to die.'[242]

That may seem false and theatrical but Bismarck had reason to be nervous. Informed military opinion then expected Austria to win and several distinguished military historians can show convincingly that they ought to have done so. In spite of Moltke's calm certainties, he too had reason to worry. He had to divide his forces with an army in the West which would have to deal with the Hanoverian and Hessian forces, three armies toward the East, one of which would need to subdue the Saxons and the other two had moved into Austrian territory to carry out the encircling movement on which his plans for victory rested. His armies had commanders of varying degrees of quality and equally varying amounts of esteem from the King. Fortunately two of the royal commanders, Prince Frederick Charles, the King's nephew, and the Crown Prince Frederick proved to be outstanding field commanders. The Austrians had similar problems but with unfortunately reversed consequences. The commander-in-chief of the Austrian 'North Army' in Bohemia, Feldzeugmeister Ludwig von Benedek (1804–81), 'the lion of Solferino', had gained a reputation for boldness as one of the few Austrian commanders to come out of the 1859 war with credit. 'The mere name Benedek means that he will come quickly, dealing blows left and right,' Moltke said.[243] Had he done so and caught the Prussian columns one by one, the outcome would have been different, but Benedek, who had done so well as corps commander, proved unable to control an entire army and hesitated at several crucial points. Whereas Moltke had to let the mediocre Eduard Vogel von Fackenstein command the West army because the King liked him, he had good commanders in Bohemia. Franz Joseph chose an obscure, near-sighted Archduke, the Archduke Albrecht, to command the Austrian 'South Army', who proved to be an outstanding and versatile commander. Aided by an accomplished chief of staff, a competent bourgeois officer, Franz John, the Archduke Albrecht achieved victory over the Italians.[244]

Moltke faced another threat which he could not control: the problem of communications. The railroads made it possible to move large numbers of men and the telegraph made control of such movements significantly easier. In effect strategic mobility had greatly improved but once away from the railhead and especially in battle commanders had no way to contact each other. Moltke frequently had no idea where his troops were and no way of finding out. The age of the mobile telephone has so spoiled us that we tend to forget how impossible communications were for most of the nineteenth century.

'Weaponry was the basic evil', claims Frank Zimmer. The Prussian 'needle gun' was much superior to the Austria 'Lorenz' gun.

> That the Austrian Army set its hopes on an obsolete model must rank as one of the most disastrous miscalculations in the history of the armaments industry…The Prussian model was simply the best. Oddly enough its very virtues made it suspect in Austrian eyes and a reason not to adopt it. Kaiser Franz Joseph and many officers thought that its rapid fire power would mislead the ordinary soldier into wasting ammunition.[245]

Gordon Craig adds: 'the *Zündnagelgewehr*…[was] a breech-loading rifle that was capable of firing five rounds a minute with 43 percent accuracy at seven hundred paces' and quotes 'the plaintive cry in the letter of an Austria *Landser*, "Dear Peppi, I guess I won't see you anymore for the Prussians are shooting everyone dead".'[246] In the main engagement the Austrians lost three times as many men on average as the Prussians. The Austrian tactics of bayonet charge simply made certain that, as General von Blumenthal, Chief of Staff of the Prussian I Army, put it, 'we just shoot the poor sods dead.'[247]

Both Bismarck and Moltke had become desperate. Their generals moved in a relaxed manner to their tasks. In exasperation Bismarck asked Roon on 17 June, 'Is Manteuffel in Harburg nailed down by any sort of military order? I hoped, he would fly.'[248] Vogel von Falckenstein was worse. He had settled into the comfortable Hotel Zur Krone in Göttingen and seemed to be taking his time in dispatching the small and ill-organized Hanoverian army. He had a reputation for eccentricity and had once court-martialled a soldier for presenting him a glass of water without the serving tray.[249] Moltke saw that his plan made the Prussian forces terribly vulnerable, deployed in relatively small contingents across hundred of kilometres, as one critic put it, 'like beads on a string'.[250]

After the war Stosch complained that many commanders had been too old and lacked inventiveness but the General Staff was

> fresh, active and, what was best of all, did not stick to formalities but to sub-stance. General von Moltke is one of the most talented and sharp-thinking of generals and has the inclination to grand operations... There is a story that during the difficult hours at Königgrätz somebody asked Moltke what he had decided about retreat to which Moltke answered, 'here it is a question of the entire future of Prussia, here there will be no retreat.'[251]

If Benedek, who enjoyed the advantage of compactness, had launched an attack on the First Army alone before it combined with the two columns of the Elbe and Second Armies, the whole plan would have collapsed. If the Hanoverians or Saxons had fought more tenaciously then the West Army under Vogel and the Elbe Army under Karl Herwarth von Bittenfeld, who, as Wawro writes, 'vied with Falckenstein for the distinction of most medio-cre general in the Prussian army', would not have arrived in time to join the other two columns.[252] On 28 June General Vogel von Falckenstein and the Prussian Army of the Main defeated the Hanoverian army at Langensalza and Hanover capitulated. The first defeat prompted Franz Joseph to change his ministers. On 30 June a new government, the 'Three Counts' govern-ment—Belcredi, Esterhazy, and Mendsdorff—was formed in Vienna, which promised to be more resolute.

On 30 June the King moved the Great Headquarters to Jicin in Bohemia, where Moltke discovered to his dismay that all three Army groups had lost complete contact with Benedek's North Army and had no idea where it was. Time was running out because a French envoy was expected to arrive at headquarters with a demand that the hostilities be halted. The long marches and rain had exhausted the advancing Prussian troops and eroded discipline. The great battle on 3 July 1866 was fought at the village of Sadowa, north-west of the Bohemian town of Königgrätz (now Hradec Králové in the Czech Republic) on the upper Elbe River. It began with an attack by the Prussian Elbe and First Armies.[253] The Crown Prince's Second

Army had not yet arrived to close the encirclement. At 11.30 in the morning Benedek received intelligence that along the Elbe strong Prussian forces had been spotted (the Crown Prince's Second Army). The provisional commander of the Austrian IV Corps, Feldmarschall Lieutnant Anton Freiherr von Mollinary, demanded permission to attack to the Prussian left flank while it lay exposed. 'There I was, standing before the extreme left wing of the Prussian army. A determined attack would have snapped off the enemy's left wing and put us on the road to victory.'[254] Zimmer believes that Benedek intended to attack but only in a conventional frontal assault. The moment passed and by the early afternoon the Crown Prince's II Army 'within a short time broke the Austrian flank, aided by difficult terrain and fog and by exploiting the needle gun and artillery . . . It all went so quickly that Benedek at first would not believe the report and replied to the officer who brought it, "Nonsense, don't babble such stupid stuff". It was 3 pm on the afternoon of 3 July, 1866.'[255]

Later that afternoon Prince Friedrich Karl, Commander of the First Army, suddenly to his surprise met the Austrian Field Marshall Lieutenant von Gablenz, who had come to ask for terms of armistice. 'But why are you asking for an armistice? Does your army need one?' Gablenz: 'My Emperor has no army left; it is as good as destroyed.' Friedrich Karl wrote in his diary: 'Through meeting Gablenz it was clear to me for the first time the scale of the defeat and the breadth of the victory.'[256] Prince Frederick Charles, whose First Army had borne the main burden of the battle, reflected afterwards what had given Prussia the victory and concluded that it was a certain reliable ordinariness:

> It is our well-trained, well-oiled mechanism in which each knows his place, a place which even mediocrity is entirely ready to fulfil its tasks (for it is calculated on mediocrity) which has taught us how to win victories. The reorganization of the army has certainly not alone contributed to this outcome, but it was in its time a necessary perfecting of the mechanism. Geniuses in the proper sense of the word have not shown themselves.[257]

In other words, on balance the Prussians had a more modern, bureaucratic attitude to war than the Austrians. The years of war games, theory, and repeated practice had paid off—but just. Had Benedek let Mollinary attack the Prussian left at 11.30 in the morning and thrown his ample reserves against them from the oblique position his own corps had gained, the Prussians, discipline, bureaucracy and all the rest, would have crumbled as rapidly as the Austrians did in the afternoon and the whole history of Europe would have been other than it became.

Bismarck's own reaction does him credit:

> He felt that he was playing a game of cards with a million-dollar stake that he did not really possess. Now that the wager had been won, he felt depressed rather than elated. And as he rode through fields with dead and wounded, he wondered what his feelings would be if his eldest son were lying there.[258]

Stosch, now a general officer[259] and first Quartermaster General to the Second Army, recorded the arrival of Field Marshall Lieutenant von Gablenz to ask for terms of armistice, to which Bismarck demanded the exclusion of Austria from Germany and the unification of the largely Protestant North German states as a first stage to the full unity. Except for the King of Saxony no sovereign should be deposed. Hessen and Hanover must be reduced to assure the necessary links between the eastern and western provinces of Prussia. The Crown Prince invited Bismarck to dine with the staff of the II Army and Stosch recorded his impressions:

> It was the first time I saw Bismarck personally at a social occasion and I confess gladly that the impression that I got from him nearly overwhelmed me. The clarity and grandeur of his views gave me the highest pleasure; he was secure and fresh in every direction and unfolded in each thought a whole world.[260]

By a fortunate coincidence, the Prussian voters went to the polls on the very day of the battle of Königgrätz-Sadowa and, as the official *Provincial Correspondence* reported with glee: 'The domination of the Progressive Party has been broken. The Party has surrendered a large number of seats in the House of Deputies to more moderate, partly to conservative and partly liberal, deputies but of decisively patriotic temper.' The Progressive fraction fell from 143 members to 83, Conservatives grew from 38 to 123, and centrist Liberals fell from 110 to 65.[261] As Rudolf Bamberger observed to his brother Ludwig, 'It's interesting to observe what effect success has. Ten days ago with the exception of a few thinking people, there were no friends of Prussia; today it's different.'[262] Bismarck had won on both fronts—foreign and domestic—and in exactly the way he outlined to Disraeli. A victory abroad had destroyed the opposition at home. In a matter of twenty-four hours Bismarck had become 'Bismarck', the genius-statesman.

His next step shows that he deserved the title 'genius-statesman'. He made peace with Austria without annexations and without a victory parade

in Vienna. It was his greatest moment in human and diplomatic terms. As
he wrote to his wife, six days after the victory:

> If we do not exaggerate our claims and do not believe that we have con-
> quered the world, we can arrive at a peace worth the effort. But we are as
> quickly intoxicated as we become down-hearted and I have the thankless task
> of pouring cold water into the bubbling cauldron and reminding people that
> we do not live alone in Europe but with three neighbours.[263]

When Stosch went to see him as representative of the Crown Prince, Bismarck
told him exactly the same things, as he reported to Karl von Normann
(1827–88) the influential private secretary to the Crown Prince:

> First of all he explained that it was a question of Austria's exclusion from
> Germany, further damage or surrender of territory and the like should not
> take place, because later we shall want Austria's force for ourselves...he could
> assure me how wonderful he found it that brilliant military victories make the
> best basis for diplomatic arts. Everything went as if oiled.[264]

Moltke agreed absolutely, as wrote to his wife, that he was 'very much in
favour that we do not place the achievements we have made at risk again, if
we can avoid that. That I hope can be done, if we do not seek revenge but fix
our eyes on our own advantage.'[265] General Leonhard Count von Blumenthal,
chief of staff of the Second Army, thought exactly the same thing:

> The peace negotiations are going well and the peace would have been signed
> if the King had not made difficulties. He insists that Austria surrender terri-
> tory to us, which they are only prepared to do as part of reparations for war
> damage. It looks as if this point of honour is the stumbling block.[266]

In 1877 Bismarck gave an account of the events leading to the peace settlement with Austria that gives a very different picture of the attitude of the
generals. He told it to Lucius von Ballhausen, who recorded it in his diary
and he repeated this account in his memoirs in the 1890s:

> I was the only person among the 300 or so who had to rely entirely on his
> own judgement without being able to ask anybody. In the war council, all
> with the king at the head, wanted to continue the war. I stated, fighting a war
> in Hungary in the heat, with the drought and the spreading cholera was
> extremely dangerous, and what was the objective? After all the generals had
> voted against me, I declared, 'as a general I have been outvoted, but as minister
> I must submit my resignation if my judgement were not accepted.' The delib-
> erations took place in my room, because I was ill. After my declaration I left,
> shut and locked the door and went to my sleeping quarters and threw myself,

sobbing and broken, onto the bed. The others deliberated in whispers for a while and then slipped away.

The following day I had a stormy encounter with the King... he called my peace conditions 'shameful'. He demanded Bohemia, Austrian Silesia, Ansbach-Bayreuth, East Friesland, a slice of Saxony etc. I tried to make clear to him that one could hardly fatally wound those with whom later one would want and indeed have to live. He rejected that idea and threw himself weeping onto the sofa. 'My first minister will be a deserter in the face of the enemy and imposes this shameful peace on me.'

I left him, firm in my decision, and had just slammed the door to my room and laid down my sabre when the Crown Prince walked in and volunteered to go to his father. He wanted peace and could understand and approve my motives. I had made the war and must now bring it to a conclusion. After a few hours he brought me a letter from his father which I have kept. The expression 'shameful' appears twice in it. 'Since I leave him in the lurch, and regardless of the brilliant success of the army, so he agrees to submit to the shameful conditions.' These shameful conditions became the Peace of Prague.[267]

Engelberg writes that Bismarck's memoirs are deeply misleading.

Why Bismarck misled generations of readers of 'Reminiscences and Reflections' with a legend about a fronde by the generals against his peace efforts can be explained politically by the period in which they were written. He knew that among the forces which had brought about his fall were leading military men. Thus his false portrayal of the relationship to the generals was an act of political revenge against the Prussian-German General Staff of the 1890s.[268]

That cannot explain the fact that, when Bismarck told Lucius the story in 1877, he had not fallen from power and Lucius had no reason to doubt it. His relationship with the military in 1866 changed during the Franco-Prussian War when he waged an exhausting and bitter struggle against the General Staff officers, whom he called 'the demi-gods', about strategy and politics and it may be that he conflated the two experiences. We have other sources that confirm the King's emotional reaction to the victory and the hysterical behaviour of both King and his chief Minister had by 1866 become part of their relationship. Still it typifies Bismarck's constant tendency, even the stories he repeated at dinner, to rewrite the past. I suppose that more of us do that than we know. Our tales of life never receive the pedantically thorough examination that Bismarck's have had.

On 26 July 1866, Prussia and Austria signed a preliminary peace agreement at Nikolsburg which established the following agreement:

1. Austria is to withdraw entirely from the association of German states;

2. Austria recognizes the formation of a federation of the North German states under Prussian leadership;

3. The relationship between the south German states among themselves and with the North German Federation remains to be decided by freely agreed arrangements.

4. Austria recognizes the alterations of possessions to be carried out in North Germany.

5. Austria to pay a reparation of 40 million thaler for war damage.[269]

The 'alteration of possessions', according to Pflanze, constituted 'Bismarck's most revolutionary act in 1866'.[270] With a stroke of the pen, the historic Kingdom of Hanover lost its independence and King George, a cousin of Queen Victoria, lost his throne. The Duchy of Nassau and the part of Hesse-Kassel north of the Main and the city of Frankfurt were simply swallowed up. If Bismarck's moderation at Nikolsburg shows his best side, his treatment of the Free City of Frankfurt shows his worst. It reveals in miniature the brutal behaviour of the Prussian army in the intoxication of victory. On 16 July 1866 General Vogel von Falckenstein occupied Frankfurt am Main and took command of the city. Three days later the Prussian army seized and transported to Berlin 155 pounds of silver. Manteuffel, who had replaced Vogel von Falckenstein as city commandant then demanded 25 million gulden within 24 hours which was reduced to 19 million when the authorities explained that they had already contributed. The order came directly from Bismarck. Bürgermaster Fellner asked for more time to consult the legislative assembly and, when asked, the assembly refused to pay.[271] The Prussians demanded a list of those who voted against the contribution to punish them; Fellner refused to give them the names. On 23 July Bürgermaster Fellner commited suicide. General Maximilian Count von Roedern (1816–98), who had now replaced Manteuffel as military governor, ordered that Fellner be buried at 5 a.m. but two senators who escaped from the occupied city got the story of Prussian 'atrocities' into the papers. *Appelationsgerichtsrat* Dr Kügler, Senator Fellner's brother-in-law, presented the rope to General von Röder. 'The general told him in the gruffest voice, "that the contribution had to be paid regardless" and continued smoking his cigar.'[272] Irritated by the opposition of the city in which he had spent nine pleasant years, on 25 July 1866, the day before the signature of the preliminary peace at Nikolsburg, Bismarck added Frankfurt to the list of states to be annexed, though it had not been on the 'maximum demands list' before.[273] The citizens of Frankfurt learned what many more were to learn—that Bismarck tolerated no opposition. This little piece of gratuitous brutality reminds us that the victorious Prussian army under the grandsons and great grandsons of the von Röders and von Manteuffels became notorious for atrocities on much grander scale between 1939 and 1945.

The scale of Bismarck's triumph cannot be exaggerated. He alone had brought about a compete transformation of the European international order. He had told those who would listen what he intended to do, how he intended to do it, and he did it. He achieved this incredible feat without commanding an army, and without the ability to give an order to the humblest common soldier, without control of a large party, without public support, indeed, in the face of almost universal hostility, without a majority in parliament, without control of his cabinet and without a loyal following in the bureaucracy. He no longer had the support of the powerful conservative interest groups who had helped him to achieve power. The most senior diplomats in the foreign service like Robert von der Goltz and Albrecht Bernstorff were sworn enemies and he knew it. The Queen and the Royal Family hated him and the King, emotional and unreliable, would soon have his 70th birthday. Beyond Roon and Moritz von Blankenburg, I cannot think of any reliable friends to whom he could tell the truth about his policies. Indeed without Roon's quiet advocacy and complete loyalty he would not have survived politically and physically. With perfect justice, in August 1866, he pounded his fist on his desk and cried, 'I have beaten them all! All!'[274]

8

The Unification of Germany, 1866–1870

Bismarck's great triumph left him in a new situation. He had become a national hero. The Austrian reparation of 40 million thaler had transformed the government's financial situation and he had a completely new structure to construct for Germany. The old Bund had been swept away and Austria expelled from all German affairs to find its new identity as an 'eastern' power. Even before the preliminary peace at Nikolsburg had been signed, the official press announced that elections would be held and that a draft electoral law would be presented to the Prussian parliament. In addition to Prussia and those territories newly included under Prussia (Hanover, Nassau, part of Hesse-Kassel and Frankfurt), invitations to participate would go out to Sachsen-Altenburg, Sachsen-Coburg, Sachsen-Weimar, Schwarzburg-Sondershausen and Schwarzburg-Rudolstadt, Reuß younger Line (Gera), Reuss elder Line, Waldeck, Lippe-Detmold, Schaumburg-Lippe, Mecklenburg-Schwerin, Mecklenburg-Strelitz, Anhalt, Oldenburg, Braunschweig, Hamburg, Bremen, and Lübeck. The Prussian Law of 12 April 1849 would be the basis of the new electoral system according to which every electoral district should have 100,000 voters. The census of the enlarged Prussian state showed that Prussia would now have 19,255,139 inhabitants. Prussia and Posen would, therefore, have 193 deputies.[1] The new federation would as a result be unevenly constructed with Prussia constituting more than four-fifths of the population and land area.

Another outstanding matter had to be settled—the nearly four years in which the Bismarck government had ruled without parliamentary approval of its budget. Bismarck had already convinced the King to make a conciliatory gesture to the liberal opposition over the budget deadlock. Again even before the text of the Nikolsburg agreement had been agreed, Bismarck moved to get the Landtag into session. This time he used his wife to act as agent. He wrote to her on 18 July to tell her that the negotiations in Nikolsburg had begun and asked her, 'why were our chambers not summoned? Ask Eulenburg about it and say to him that it is vital that the parliamentary corps be allowed to intervene before the peace negotiations have been seriously discussed.'[2] Bismarck intended to use the liberal and nationalist forces as a political factor to strengthen his hand in negotiating in the name of the nation but he also let his cabinet colleagues know that the Landtag would be called into session as soon as His Majesty had returned to Berlin to discuss the settlement of the outstanding dispute over the budget. The King had agreed—to the horror of the 'conflict ministers'—to request indemnity for the unconstitutional past.

Even before the King's return to Berlin, the fronts in Prussian politics had begun to shift. On 28 July a new conservative party emerged, dedicated to support Bismarck, which called itself the Free Conservative Union. On the same day Treitschke wrote to his wife, 'the revolution in which we stand comes from above.'[3] Many liberals now admitted the error of their ways. Rudolf Ihering (1818–92), a Göttingen Professor of Law and an expert in property rights,[4] who had called the war an act of 'frightful frivolity', now submitted to the 'genius of Bismarck'.[5] Liberals and nationalists could reconcile their new positions with their former opposition because, as Christopher Clark argues, Bismarck had defeated neo-absolutist and Catholic Austria and hence won a great victory against the forces of reactionary Catholicism. Bismarck's politics and the victory of a Protestant Kingdom, in the eyes of many Liberal Prussian Protestants, must be providential and progressive.[6] For these were the 1860s in which under Pius IX any hint of liberalism had been condemned. Bismarck's wars had put him on the side of the Roman Catholic Church's enemies through his alliance with the 'godless' Kingdom of Italy that had usurped papal territories during its unification struggle and under Prime Minister Count Cavour had dedicated the new Kingdom of Italy to the proposition of 'una libera chiesa nello stato liberale'—a free church in the free state. It was logical too that the Vatican Secretary of State Cardinal Antonelli on hearing the news of the Austrian defeat at Königgrätz-Sadowa cried out in anguish 'Casca il mondo! (the world is falling).[7]

Not everybody welcomed Bismarck's new policy of reconciliation. The text of the Speech from the Throne had been leaked and on 1 August 1866, Hans von Kleist wrote a lengthy memorandum to Bismarck against the indemnity proposal:

How is it remotely conceivable, all old Prussian institutions, all elements of its power, are to be surrendered through this one declaration in the Speech from the Throne and that through it—its finances, its army, its House of Lords, the Monarchy, Prussia itself—is to be given over to the temporary majority of a second chamber which will emerge from its new provisions? It would in the short or long run hopelessly go under in an unfathomable whirlpool. Prussia without the spirit which made it is as good as dead... without an independent Monarchy.[8]

Bismarck, who got word of the leak in Prague where he had gone for the final peace negotiations with the Austrians, dismissed his old friend with contempt. He wrote to his wife on 3 August that there was a

huge feud over the Speech from the Throne. Lippe spreads the great word in conservative sense against me and Hans Kleist has written me an excited letter. These little fellows have not got enough to do, cannot see as far as the ends of their noses and practise their swimming on the stormy waves of phrases. I can deal with my enemies but the friends! They all wear blinkers and only see a patch of the world.[9]

While the *Kreuzzeitung* conservatives drew back with horror from Bismarck, who had been their friend, his former enemies among German liberals drew near to him. As Karl Frenzel wrote in the journal *Deutsches Museum*:

Through its past the government has made an enemy of liberalism, through the war which it fought, the annexations which it prepares, an enemy of feudalism. The success which it achieved in domestic affairs rests in the weakening of both parties and in the creation of a government party which will grow stronger and stronger.[10]

The White Hall of the Palace was crowded with deputies on 5 August 1866 as the King delivered the Speech from the Throne. In it the King admitted that the

government had run the state budget for many years without a legal basis... I cherish the confidence that the recent events will contribute to the necessary understanding to the extent that an indemnity will be willingly granted to my Government in respect to the administration carried on without a budget law and thus the previous conflict will be brought to an end for all time.[11]

During the Speech from the Throne,

Hans von Kleist avoided greeting Bismarck but stood at a place in the White Chamber so Bismarck could not fail to see him. Both waited until the ceremony was over and the White Chamber had emptied. Bismarck approached von Kleist and asked 'Say, old boy, where did you get the Speech from the Throne?' 'I will not tell you.' 'In this matter I don't like jokes. I shall have to get the state prosecutor on to you if you don't.' 'Yes, you can lock me up but you still won't find out.' They parted without a word. As Kleist was changing at home, the Minister President sent a message by his factotum Engel and asked Kleist to come to him. There he found Robert von der Goltz and Karl Friedrich von Savigny. The Minister-President had got his balance back, went to the new arrival in a friendly way and shook his hand. 'It's all forgotten.' An indiscrete minister has confessed at the State Council. 'I suppose, it must have been Wagener.' Then he explained to Goltz and Savigny that he had made peace with the Crown Prince over the word 'indemnity'.[12]

In spite of the apology, the friendship between Bismarck and Kleist never recovered.

Bismarck had now moved into the odd position that he needed Liberals in order to complete his plans for the new German state. The Liberals became his allies from 1866 until he dumped them unceremoniously in the late 1870s. An even odder feature of the new political arena emerges from the paradox that the Bismarck after 1866 rapidly achieved personally a 'cult' status but his Free Conservative Party never had a real following. Three main parties dominated Bismarck's new Germany: Liberals (divided into pro- and anti-Bismarck wings), Conservatives (increasingly anti-Bismarck), and Catholics (anti-Bismarck). At no stage could he rely on any of these three as his party. Thus the new period opens with the paradox that the most powerful figure of the nineteenth century had no real parliamentary support and still depended on the person, the emotions, and the attitudes of a very old monarch. Waves of nationalism swept Germany but Bismarck was no nationalist. Liberals saw unity and liberty but Bismarck was no liberal, and, as Hans von Kleist and Ludwig Gerlach now knew, he was no conservative either. Bismarck changed colour like certain deep pools of water which refract the light in various hues.

On 14 August, August von der Heydt, the new Finance Minister, Bismarck's 'Gold Uncle', presented the indemnity bill to the Budget Committee of the House and stated that the indemnity and the request for new lines of credit had to be considered together, 'because the Government feels itself under no pressure whatever; on the contrary its financial position is entirely positive and hence the Government has no inclination to make concessions.' The Committee voted by 25 to 8 in favour of the double bill, because 'it seems illogical to grant the Government credit and refuse it the indemnity.' The two houses passed the bill and the King signed it on 14 September 1866.[13]

A sign of the changing times took place in another part of Berlin. On 5 September 1866 the new synagogue in the Moorish style on the Oranienburger Strasse was dedicated. With its 3,000 seats it was the largest and most ornate synagogue in Germany. As Emil Breslaur reported the event in the *Allgemeine Zeitung des Judenthums*,

> At 11.30 in the morning the magnificent building was dedicated. Flowers and wreaths, valuable potted plants in artistic arrangements decorated the entrance and the lobby. The sanctuary was filled partly with the Jewish community and partly with the invited guests of honour. Among the latter we noticed Count Bismarck, Minister v.d. Heydt, Field Marshall Wrangel, Police President von Bernuth, in addition to magistrates and members of the City Council, many members of the Prussian House of Deputies among whom were President Forckenbek (sic!), Dr Kosch, Johann Jacoby. A prelude composed for the occasion by Organist Schwantzer opened the ceremony. After that the choir under the direction of the Royal Director of Music Lewandowski, accompanied by organ and brass choir intoned the *boruch habboh* and the *ma tauvu* as the ornamented Torah scrolls entered the sanctuary.

Bismarck and the other guests watched the scrolls proceed down the main aisle where to fanfare and the singing of the *Schema* they were placed in the Ark. Rabbi Aub then preached a sermon on Verse 9, Chapter 2 of the Prophet Haggai: 'The glory of this latter house shall be greater than of the former, saith the LORD of hosts: and in this place will I give peace, saith the LORD of hosts.'[14] No doubt the Rabbi's text applied at least as much to the 'glory' of the new North German Federation as to the great sanctuary of the Jewish community.

The *Konfliktzeit* had ended and Bismarck wanted to rid himself of the 'Conflict' cabinet. Bodelschwingh had gone at the end of May 1866 but the King hated new faces As a result Bismarck only rid himself of Selchow and Itzenplitz in 1873, and Mühler in 1872. The Justice Minister, Count Lippe, he did manage to sack in 1867. As Helma Brunck puts it, 'Bismarck saw himself as the real victor of Düppel and Königgrätz... and the collegial structure of the State Ministry was very soon a thorn in his side.'[15] As always in Bismarck's career the power lay in other hands. These cabinet ministers served the King not the Minister-President and because Bismarck rejected parliamentary government, he deprived himself of that power over a cabinet which the typical Prime Minister of any European country now takes for granted. He could not simply reshuffle his cabinet. Bismarck's dictatorial urges collide with the reality of royal power. He also made the dismissed ministers his permanent enemies but he knew it, as he explained to Gustav von Diest: 'I never underestimated how dangerous Bodelschwingh was. Do you know what he is? He's the fox that you think you have shot, throw over your shoulder to take home and which then bites you in the arse.'[16]

On 21 September 1866 the Prussian army staged its victory parade complete with a solemn *Te Deum* in front of the royal palace. Gustav Mevissen (1815–99), one of the leading Catholic industrialists and bankers of period,[17] stood in the crowd as the troops marched by and recorded his feelings:

> I cannot shake off the impression of this hour. I am no devotee of Mars...but the trophies of war exercise a magic charm on the child of peace. One's eyes are involuntarily riveted on, and one's spirit goes along with, the unending rows of men who acclaim the god of the moment: success.[18]

In February 1867 the *Revue moderne* published Ludwig Bamberger's *Monsieur de Bismarck*. The essay was a great success and it was reprinted in book form in June 1867. Bamberger, a Jewish revolutionary turned successful banker, became one of Bismarck's most intimate advisers. He was certainly among the first to see how radical Bismarck was:

> Now Germany has never made a revolution on its own. It has the glory of having founded Protestantism and developed philosophic liberty but with respect to political enfranchisement it has produced nothing original, spontaneous or durable. It cannot compare itself in that respect with England, nor the United States, nor France, nor Switzerland, nor Holland, nor Belgium. It is the last arrival among the nations and the year 1866 marks the first time it has witnessed a grand organic change without an impulse from abroad...One cannot doubt for a moment that Bismarck is a born revolutionary. Revolutionaries are born—as are legitimists—by some structure in the brain; whereas chance decides whether that same human being will turn into a red or a white one.[19]

By the 1860s the German popular press had begun to develop and it too turned Bismarck into what we would call a media personality. The weekly *Gartenlaube* (the Garden Arbour) founded in 1853 as a new popular middle-class magazine, began in 1867 to publish a column called 'Photographs from the Reichstag'. In its April number it brought a reverent portrait of Bismarck:

> On the raised bench reserved for the Federal Councillors sits the man whom not only Prussia and Germany but the whole of Europe follows with rapt attention and lively interest. Like the biblical King Saul he towers over his

contemporaries by a full head in height, an imposing, aristocratic figure in an elegant cuirassier's uniform, a person who combines the energy of the soldier with the elasticity and flexibility of the statesman.[20]

Pictures and busts of Bismarck were sold by thousands. He had become a symbol.

The King awarded him a 'dotation' from the royal fund on 7 June 1867. With it Bismarck purchased an estate in Pomerania, which contained the village of Varzin. After he had purchased it, in a typical example of Bismarckian parsimony, he offered to sell Kniephof to his brother or to his cousin Philipp, 'but not cheaper than I would get for it on the open market.'[21] The founder of states, the world-historical figure, Otto von Bismarck, retained to the end the tight-fisted pettiness of the impoverished country squire. On the other hand, as we have seen, he also retained the natural and unaffected hospitality that he had learned as a young man. He urged his friend Motley to visit him on his new estate. As he explained to Motley in 1869, though it was far from Berlin, the railroad had changed everything. 'Leaving Berlin at 9 o'clock you are here for dinner.'[22] When Motley finally visited Varzin, he described how the Bismarcks lived there in a letter to his wife Mary:

> The way of life is very simple at Varzin, but the irregularity of hours is great. I usually came down stairs, as well as Lily, [Motley's daughter—JS] between nine and ten. Madame de B, Marie, and the sons came in promiscuously and had breakfast with us. Bismarck came down about eleven. His breakfast is very light—egg and a cup of coffee—and then he has a meerschaum pipe. While he is sitting there and talking to all of us, his secretary hands him the pile of letters with which he is goaded in his retirement, and with a lead pencil about a foot long he makes memoranda as to the answers and other dispositions to be made. Meanwhile the boys are playing billiards in another part of the same room and a big black dog, called 'Sultan' is rampaging generally through the apartment and joining in everybody's conversation... On the courtyard side the house consists of a main building two stories high, with two long wings projecting from the house, in which are servants' rooms and offices, making three sides of an open quadrangle. On the lawn or wood side there is a long veranda running in front of the main house. Inside is a square hall with a wide staircase leading to a large hall above, out of which are four spacious bedrooms. On each side of the hall below is a suite of one or two rooms, which are the family and reception rooms, besides his library and the private rooms of the ladies. The estate is about 30,000 morgens, equal to 20,000 acres.

A great part—certainly two thirds—forest, pine, oak, beech. Of the rest a small farm, some 200 or 300 acres, is in his own hands. The rest is let in large farms of 800 or 900 acres. The river Wipper, which runs through the property, is a valuable water power. He has built two or three mills upon it, one of which is already let and in operation.[23]

Varzin became an essential part of his psychic economy; he needed the woods, the quiet, the long walks and the sense of being on his own land. He returned to that identity as a Junker squire with which he had grown up. It was his retreat.

For much of 1867 he could not get away from Berlin; there was simply too much to do. He had to construct two governments: to rearrange the Prussian State Ministry and to create the new Federal Government of the North German Federation. Bismarck intended to run both but could not at once see how. If the new Prussian-dominated Federation to a large extent recreated the old Bund but without Austria, it might simply carry over the institutions of Frankfurt. It would have a committee of ambassadors as its governing body and a secretary or chancellor of the new federation to execute its collective decisions. The Federal Chancellor might be a civil servant, who would take orders from the Prussian Minister-President, that is, from Bismarck. The votes of Prussia plus those of the swallowed-up German states would give Prussia a blocking veto in any case and the mini-states would never dare oppose Prussia. A statesman who could abolish the venerable Kingdom of Hanover would have Schwarzburg-Sonderhausen for breakfast. On the other hand, as Bismarck's new national Liberal friends desired, the new Federation could be a real state with its own national cabinet, its own laws, weights and measures and national politics. The uneasy and uncertain creation of the hybrid German federal structure would have been difficult in any case but Bismarck's now insatiable ambition made it almost insoluble.

Tidying up had to take place in addition in the formal relations with the South German states which had fought with Austria and now confronted in the North German Federation a victorious, enlarged, and much more threatening Prussia. On 13, 17, and 22 August Prussia concluded peace treaties and identical treaties of alliance with Württemberg, Baden, and Bavaria. On 23 September 1866 Hanover was annexed and became a province of Prussia.

Queen Augusta watched these treaties and transformations with mounting anxiety. She belonged, as a Princess of the Duchy of Weimar, to the

'Ernestine' branch of the royal family of Saxony. She liked to lapse into Saxon dialect and never entirely settled into Prussian ways. She felt sympathy for the middle states and was the mother of the Grand Duchess of Baden. She wrote marginal comments on the long reports from Freiherr von Roggenbach about the political transformation in the four still independent states in southern Germany and she drafted passages of letters to her husband, the King. On 11 October she wrote to King William attaching the Roggenbach memorandum:

> I beg you most earnestly, to do everything possible to seize the hand of friendship which Baden extends to you. I would be neglecting my maternal duty if I did not convey to you the seriousness of the situation described above and not urge you in God's name that you act in good time to protect those dear to us to the advantage of that beautiful country.[24]

The Queen and Roggenbach continued during the autumn of 1866 to exchange lengthy letters which for security they sent by trusted agents. They considered problems of sovereignty and the relationship between Prussia, the new Federation, and the existing states both inside and outside the new federation. The Queen's energy, clarity, and tenacity made her a formidable opponent of Bismarck but an unnecessary one. Had Bismarck offered her the same attentions that Roggenbach did, he might have won her over. Nothing in the letters suggests that in 1866 she rejected the King's or Bismarck's policies as such. She worried, entirely reasonably, about the interactions in what had become a complex, layered, and evolving structure of imperfect sovereignties. In a letter of early January 1867 she wrote with regret that

> Since I have no personal contact with the leading personalities and the director of affairs in the cases when I meet him, is unresponsive, I can say, alas, nothing about his view, whether in the meantime it has been refined...Nor unfortunately can I send you a copy of the Federal Constitution, because I have not been able to obtain one myself.[25]

Had Bismarck been a little less suspicious and misogynist, he would have found this remarkable lady, if not an ally, at least a willing listener, but then that would have involved listening seriously to a woman he could not control or ignore. His policy of grotesque small insults—the Queen had not been sent a copy of the new constitution—reveals that persistent petty vindictiveness with which he treated his enemies.

Bismarck in the meantime had collapsed physically. The strain of the recent months had taken their toll. Thus began a pattern which became more and more common over the years. Bismarcks's frequent illnesses led to longer and longer absences from Berlin. Pflanze calculates that between 14 May 1875 and November 1878, of 1,275 days, Bismarck spent 772 of them, that is 60 per cent, either at his estates or at spas.[26] Bismarck's illness worried senior diplomats. General von Schweinitz tried to find out how he was and recorded the following entry in his diary:

> Count von der Goltz has arrived, he was in Varzin. When I asked whether Bismarck was really ill, he answered with his very peculiar laugh, which people in Paris describe as '*la joie fait peur*'. 'What? That man ill? Bismarck is never ill, I am ill.' Goltz told me a lot but not enough.[27]

In 1866 Bismarck withdrew to convalesce at Putbus on the Baltic. Legend has it that Bismarck and his faithful amanuensis, the former socialist Lothar Bucher, drafted the constitution in two days; in fact, as Pflanze shows, Bismarck had drafted much himself earlier and had received help but it was *his* constitution, designed by him to suit himself and to maintain the peculiar structures of absolutism on which his power rested.

The constitution, like the later constitution of the German Empire, rested on a compact among the Princes who created it. The people played no role and the word only appears once in connection with the Reichstag which represents 'the people'. The sections dealing with the Federal Council and the Federal Presidium are the most characteristic. Article 6 states that the Bundesrat or Federal Council consists of the former members of the old Bundesrat in Frankfurt, 'the voting rights of whom are governed by the regulations for the Plenum of the former German Bund, so that Prussia with the votes formerly held by Hanover, Electoral Hessen, Nassau and Frankfurt, has 17 votes'. According to Article 7 decisions are made by 'simple majority'. Since Prussia had 17 of 43 total votes, any small group of states joined to Prussia could block a measure. The head of the Federation (Article 11) is 'the Presidium which belongs to the King of Prussia'. The Presidium (Article 12) can summon, adjourn, or dissolve the Federal Council and Reichstag and Article 15 states that the chair of the Federal Council and direction of affairs belongs to the *Bundeskanzler* or Federal Chancellor, whom the Presidium names. The office which Bismarck designed for himself depends directly on the King of Prussia as Presidium and on no one else. No cabinet or other officers exist formally. The other important article was Article 20 which states that the Reichstag is elected in general and direct elections with secret ballot.[28] Bismarck had given his word in 1866 and kept it.

The North German Federation had a democratic lower house, comparable with the most democratic in the world at that time. Yet the rights of the democracy had limits. Army strength rested on 1 per cent of the size of the population (Article 60) and the sum of 225 thaler per soldier was settled by Article 62. Thus the Reichstag had no say in fixing expenditure for the army. Bismarck had eliminated from the start any new conflict. The whole draft had the defects that one would expect in a text by Bismarck: no bill of rights, no separate judiciary, no power to collect direct taxes, no immunities and rights for deputies outside the chambers. The edifice—complicated and unwieldy—rested on one fulcrum—the common sovereignty of the King of Prussia and the Presidium of the Bund and the one common officer: the Minister-President of Prussia and the *Bundeskanzler* or Federal Chancellor. In other words Bismarck designed it for Bismarck. The Constitution of the North German Federation became more or less verbatim the Imperial Constitution of 1871 for the new German Empire. It thus transmitted to the united Germany after 1871 *all* the defects of Prussian kingship. Article 63 gives command of all the armed forces to the King of Prussia and his command remains unlimited. Hence court entourages, military and naval cabinets, and camarillas continue to exist under the new arrangements as before. If the Presidium wishes to dismiss the Chancellor, he can. Bismarck built this fragile structure not only to suit himself but also to suit an arrangement in which a strong Chancellor bullies a weak king. As he discovered in 1890 that guarantee could not protect him against a different sort of sovereign.

He made the final corrections after he returned to Berlin on 1 December and presented it on 9 December to the King, Crown Prince, and the Prussian ministers and to a council of ministers representing the states on 15 December 1866. The negotiations with the princes proved to be uncomfortable but Bismarck, as always, had his alternative ready. The new Reichstag would be elected on 12 February 1867. If the King of Saxony or the Grand Duke of Mecklenburg-Schwerin made trouble, Bismarck would have to turn to the democratic forces likely to be elected. He secretly gave orders to the Prussian bureaucracy not to help conservatives as usual but to help radicals here and there in order to exert 'sufficient pressure against recalcitrant governments'.[29]

The results could not have been better. The constituent Reichstag had 297 members, of whom Conservatives gained 63 and the German Reich Party (Bismarckians) 40, National Liberals 80, other Liberals 40, and the

Progressives only 19.[30] The Jewish radical Eduard Lasker defeated Albrecht von Roon for a Berlin electoral district by 4,781 to 1,765 votes.[31] Almost half the members were aristocrats, including one royal prince, 4 non-royal princes, 2 dukes, 27 counts, and 21 barons. From now on Bismarck would play the sovereign German princes off against the people as he wrote to the government of Saxony, 'there are always these alternatives: either to count completely and forever upon the governments now temporarily allied with us or to face the necessity of seeking our centre of gravity in parliament.'[32] A close-fought battle took place for two months until, on 16 April, the Constitution as amended in various small ways was adopted by 230 to 53, and on 31 May 1867 the Prussian Landtag approved it. Bismarck had won again: there was no bill of rights, no independent judiciary, no responsible cabinet, and no remuneration of deputies. This victory, though less celebrated than Königgrätz, meant as much to Bismarck. He had unified millions of Germans in a new state and their elected representatives had sacrificed liberal rights taken for granted elsewhere without a serious fight. The new Germany retained all the worst features of Prussian semi-absolutism and placed them in the hands of Otto von Bismarck.

Bismarck faced another problem in 1867 which complicated his daily life and which still plagues the hapless biographer who has to sketch the course of his activity. Bismarck had become by design the only administrative authority in a new state of 29,572,511 people,[33] who needed thousands of items of legislation, administrative reforms, and changes. The railroads, postal systems, legal structures and codes, roads and canals, banks and currencies, factory inspections, schools, financial systems, universities, and technical colleges had to be made compatible with each other. He had made no provision for a federal cabinet and had no very clear idea how the office of Chancellor would work now that he had decided to combine it with the Presidency of the Prussian State Ministry. From 1867 to his fall from power in 1890 Bismarck's life became an impossible struggle to control and direct everything that happened in his name. Stosch explained to his wife how Bismarck decided everything by himself in negotiating an armistice with the French after the Franco-Prussian war and this typical behaviour can be seen, multiplied dozens of times, in the diaries of all those who served under him:

> I had the opportunity to see Bismarck in action [in the peace negotiations—JS] and must say that I admire the energy of his views and actions. Very odd on the other hand was how he anxiously dismissed everybody from his side for

the decisive negotiations except for those like myself whom he needed for technical questions. He sat alone opposite his opponent and roughed him up. The advantage is that the process goes quickly, the disadvantage that the agreement remains open to different interpretations. Then force must decide between them.[34]

The most rapidly growing modern state in Europe could not be ruled by one genius-statesman but Bismarck refused to let anybody else try.

In addition he had the problem of the identity and function of the Bundesrat or Federal Council. What was it? Was it a Senate, a sort of upper house of his new state? Or was it simply a talking shop for the smaller German states? On 21 July of 1867 he wrote a letter to his deputy in the Foreign Office, Hermann von Thile, which shows how the question of precedence between Prussia and the Bund had to be settled:

> I think it neither necessary nor desirable that the King should formally open the Bundesrat's first session. It would give our colleagues in the Federation the impression that their state representatives were in the same category as a Prussian parliamentary body. In reality only the federal budget and the customs treaty should come before the Bundesrat, both already known realities, which need no All-Highest decisions.[35]

The Bundesrat must not get ideas above its station and interfere with his policies.

But the problem of the burden of office remained and on 10 August 1867 Bismarck proposed to the Reichstag the establishment of a Bundeskanzleramt (Office of the Federal Chancellor), 'an organ in which the different administrative branches come together and find their focal point... [the office was] to prepare with the cooperation of the departments concerned those matters that are to be brought before the Bundesrat and the Reichstag by Prussia as leader and member of the North German Confederation.'[36] At last Bismarck now had a Chancellor's office with its own staff. He chose Rudolf Delbrück (1817–1903) to head the Office of the Federal Chancellor. Delbrück suited Bismarck because he had never been a minister and hence had no following in parliament. He had made a career as senior civil servant in the Ministry of Trade as an expert on customs union affairs. He described his expectations before Bismarck elevated him in these words:

> My relationship to the King and to Count Bismarck was of the sort that I could reckon on the possibility that after a few years I would become the

successor to Count Itzenplitz in the Ministry of Trade. As Prussian Minister of Trade I would end my career. But it all turned out differently.[37]

An office, that of Vice-Chancellor, had been created for him and approved by the new Reichstag on 12 August 1867. The Vice-Chancellor presided over the new Bundeskanzleramt, and represented the Chancellor as presiding officer of the Bundesrat in the Chancellor's absence, which with the passing of time became more and more regular. The new Vice-Chancellor settled in at once and like an administrative dynamo began to regulate all the aspects of the new state. A steady stream of decrees issued from the new office—Bismarck called it 'decree diarrhoea'.[38] Delbrück understood in a way that nobody else ever did how to combine absolute bureaucratic efficiency with complete subservience to Bismarck's will. Bismarck told the Grand Duke of Baden in 1870 that

> Delbrück is the one man of whom I can say that he is completely orientated in every aspect of his office and has an unusual ability to manage affairs and carry them out.[39]

Delbrück soon became known as the 'Vice-Bismarck' but he was in fact completely unlike Bismarck which explains why he remained so long in the service of an autocrat. He worked without the need for personal recognition, refused a title, and served under Bismarck's despotic personality smoothly. Between 1867 and 1870 Delbrück introduced the legislation to create a unified currency, a unified metric system, a unified system of free access to trades and crafts (*Gewerbefreiheit*), freedom of movement and settlement.[40] Bismarck's old friend and rival, Karl Friedrich von Savigny said that 'the strength of Delbrück's position is that he is only interested in the things Bismarck finds boring.'[41]

The relationship between the 'Vice-Bismarck' and other officers was never easy. In February 1873 Stosch, though a General, was now head of the new Imperial Navy. He clashed with Bismarck and Delbück, as he wrote to the Crown Prince:

> I have had the misfortune to countersign an imperial order which was the Imperial Chancellor's business. On the other hand, the Chancellor has interfered in my department through his deputy [Delbrück]. The conflict stemming from that led yesterday to a very stormy scene, when the State Ministry met for a so-called private session at the Imperial Chancellor's. Before the beginning of the session Prince Bismarck invited me to his room, told me that I lacked every ministerial qualification and had to subordinate myself to him

unconditionally no matter whom he employed as his representative. I replied with spirit and we both had flushed faces when we entered the session. Today I asked H.M. to make me the deputy of the Chancellor in naval matters, instead of Delbrück, or dismiss me.[42]

Delbrück irritated Bismarck by consulting members of the State Ministry who happened to be Jews, as Lucius recorded:

> Yesterday noon the Princess had me fetched from a session. The Prince had had a conversation with Delbrück which left him excited and so annoyed that he could not sleep the entire night. I found him in bed but better and more vigorous than on the last occasion. 'He lies here and cannot do anything and feels that neither in the ministry nor in the Bundesrat has he adequate representation. Delbrück always confers with Friedberg, Friedenthal, Lasker, Wolffson, Bamberger, always with Jews which makes the legislative work worse'.[43]

Circumstances forced Bismarck to work with the Liberal parties and that meant dealing with the Friedenthals, Friedbergs, Laskers, Bambergers, and Simons. He attacked them as Jews but they really annoyed him as opponents. Stosch noticed that tendency and on 18 August 1867 he wrote to Gustav Freytag, the novelist, to sum up his view of Bismarck's position:

> The more Bismarck grows in stature the more uncomfortable for him are people who think and act for themselves. And the more nervous he becomes the more he fears abrasive personal contacts ... Common personal weakness and little people irritate the great statesman often beyond the limit of the normal.[44]

A 'little person' who gave Bismarck more trouble than anybody else, Ludwig Windthorst (1812–91), made his debut in national politics in the same month that Stosch wrote to Freytag. On 31 August 1867 the first election to the North German Reichstag took place and Ludwig Windthorst, a Hanoverian lawyer, was elected from the District Meppen-Lingen-Bentheim which he served for the next twenty-four years until his death. Margaret Lavinia Anderson declares that

> Ludwig Windthorst was Imperial Germany's greatest parliamentarian. Considering his terms in the diet of the Kingdom of Hanover, he served thirty-five years in the various legislatures of his country. According to the reckoning of one deputy, he spoke 2,209 times in the Reichstag alone, more than any other member. His skill in debate was equaled by no other deputy; his tactical genius, only by Bismarck.[45]

Central casting could not have found a person more different from Bismarck. Windthorst, a nearly blind, Hanoverian, Roman Catholic dwarf opposed the giant Protestant, Prussian Otto von Bismarck, with nothing but his quick wit. The Catholic politician Peter Reichensperger (1810–92), who served for more than thirty years in the Prussian Landtag and was elected with Windthorst to the North German Reichstag in 1867, served with him in the Reichstag until his death.[46] Reichensperger wrote of him:

> Windthorst must be described as a parliamentary miracle. He alone was equal to Bismarck. With the finest antennae for all things political, he understood how to manoeuvre with a wonderful artistry.[47]
>
> His tiny gnome-like form, his ludicrous mouth, the great bottle-green spectacles shading the sightless eyes would in any case have made him conspicuous... his acerbic wit coupled with idiosyncratic views made him notorious. You never knew whether Windthorst was looking at you from *over*, *under*, or *around* his spectacles.[48]

Windthorst had served in Hanoverian cabinets and in 1867 became the lawyer of the deposed King George V of Hanover (1819–78), for whom he negotiated a settlement with Prussia on Hanoverian royal assets. In the settlement the King received income from his capital of 16 million thaler in exchange for returning state funds he had sent to England during the war.[49] Bismarck seized the royal assets and created the secret 'Guelph Fund', which he used for any purpose he chose. King George, a difficult and rigid man, refused to accept that he had been deposed and posed an awkward problem for his first cousin, Queen Victoria. On 17 August 1866 she wrote in German to Augusta, the Duchess of Cambridge, that she had 'to consider her duty as an English woman, what I am first of all. I can only express my German sentiments by privately asking for possible indulgence and consideration for the Hanoverian royal family and their crown lands.'[50] King George set up a court in exile in Hietzing outside Vienna and did what he could to annoy Bismarck. He created a Hanoverian Legion to fight for restoration and gave his blessing to the formation of a Hanoverian political party which between 1867 and 1914 sent a group of Hanoverian separatists to the Reichstag. Their numbers fluctuated between 4 in the elections of the 1870s and 10 or 11 in the 1880s.[51]

Windthorst, though a Hanoverian, never joined the Guelph Party. Indeed at first he belonged to no party.[52] In 1871 Deputy Braun of Waldenburg described Windthorst's impact in his first years as a member of the Reichstag before he joined the Catholic Centre Party:

> There was once a fraction that consisted of only one member. It was the Meppen Fraction. [Laughter.] And this fraction made itself so felt, so often

took the floor, and exercised such influence—to be sure, because of its high capacities—it was treated with such attention and politeness from all sides of the House, that it gave brilliant proof that minorities are respected here. [Laughter.] Deputy Windthorst then made a bow to the speaker which was returned by the latter. 'I must say, if only because of this living example of our respect for minorities, that I regret most sincerely that this fraction has dissolved itself. [Great laughter.][53]

From the beginning, with his exquisite political sensibility, Windthorst foresaw what he would face. In a letter of 2 November 1867 to Matthias Deyman, he explained that he had decided to enter parliament where 'the situation of the Holy Father might very easily come up for discussion' but he rejected the option of Catholic withdrawal because 'whichever way the locomotive goes, I ride with it in order—with time and opportunity—to halt it or else throw out the engineer and drive it myself.'[54] In December 1867 the Liberal Deputy Falk described this remarkable figure at a royal reception for the newly elected North German Reichstag:

> As I entered the room where the guests were assembling, I noticed a little man in a black frock coat walking to and fro. He wore a star and from his neck hung a ribbon of an order unknown to me. I thought he might be a canon as his decorations seemed to indicate. His head was extremely large, his face quite ugly, while his whole appearance was striking.[55]

Windthorst dominated the Reichstag and the Catholic Centre Party for twenty-four years without ever holding an office or aspiring to one. He held sway by the pure strength of his personality and in that he resembled Bismarck with the difference that he had principles and Bismarck had none. No better example of the 'law of unintended consequences' can be imagined than the way Bismarck's brilliant coup of 1866—the decision to call a German parliament based on universal, direct, secret manhood suffrage—generated a mass, democratic Catholic opposition party by 1871 of 100 deputies with a tiny genius at its head. As a further ironic twist, Bismarck's main opponents in the 1860s and early 1870s were Hanoverians who would never have been there had Bismarck not annexed the Kingdom of Hanover. As Georg von Vincke, Bismarck's old enemy, observed in late 1867 to the Catholic deputy, August Reichensperger (1808–95):[56]

> Do you want to know who are the three cleverest men with us now? They are the three annexed Hanoverians. One is Bennigsen, who is very clever; the second is Miquel who is cleverer still; the third, however, is Windthorst, who is as clever as the other two together.[57]

1868 opened with Bismarck still unable to make progress on the final unification of the North German Federation with the southern states and the institutional questions unsettled. In March 1868 Stosch wrote to the novelist Gustav Freytag about the need for a Reich Cabinet:

> With respect to Bismarck he will run himself into the ground in the growth of his internal power unless he is pulled back. Would you not be willing to float articles in the press in favour of a Reich cabinet? In our official battle for a Reich Minister of War Bismarck accepts that Roon is right, gives him all the powers but not the position. In the Ministry of Trade the situation is the same. A Reich minister of finance will be essential if burdens are to be fairly distributed. The burden of unity would be more easily borne.[58]

Stosch was right but Bismarck never shared power if he could avoid it. His intolerance prevented Imperial Germany from having a proper cabinet and it went to its doom in the First World War with the defects that Bismarck imposed and intelligent contemporaries feared.

In Prussia the proposition to impose schools to which both Protestant and Catholic children might go aroused the opposition of the Catholic Church. On 6 February 1868 Cardinal Count von Ledochowski, Archbishop of Posen and Gnesen, issued an edict to the clergy to warn the faithful to oppose the establishment of the 'simultaneous' public schools (i.e. Protestant and Catholics together). Provincial President von Horn, prefect of Posen, had written to the Minister of Religion von Mühler to suggest that the government discipline the Cardinal. Bismarck intervened in this, as in everything, and forbade the Minister to comply:

> I cannot agree to that... No doubt the edict contains various points in the opinion of the Protestant provincial authorities and of *Oberpräsident* von Horn which ought not to be ignored, but it ought also not to be forgotten that Count Ledowchowski as a Catholic archbishop can hardly speak or write in any other sense. In my most respectful opinion the best thing would be to simply pass over the whole issue in silence and to take those practical actions on the aforesaid ground and views which the authorities think necessary.[59]

Bismarck's sensible answer—in effect, to let sleeping dogs lie—could not stop the inexorable progress towards a clash between church and state. If the war against France lay in Bismarck's hands, the war against the Roman Catholic Church did not. It started with a powerful assault. On 29 June 1868 Pius IX issued invitations for a Vatican Council. The First Vatican Council became notorious to liberals everywhere in Europe because it resulted in the Declaration of Papal Infallibility. It marked the beginning of the *Kulturkampf* which dominated the first years of the politics of the united Germany of 1870. The so-called *Kulturkampf* had begun in Italy well before Bismarck took up the cudgels directly in the 1870s. The Italian Kingdom made clear its intention to have Rome as the capital of its new 'national' state and to impose separation of church and state when it did so. The battle of the church with the state over the 'temporal power' opened the first front in the *Kulturkampf* which led to clashes in Italy, France, Germany, Switzerland, and Austria.

Even greater events happened in 1870. On 8 December 1869 the Vatican Council began its sessions. In Session IV of 18 July 1870, the First Dogmatic Constitution on the Church of Christ was promulgated. Chapter 4 was called 'On the infallible teaching authority of the Roman pontiff' and stated:

> We teach and define as a divinely revealed dogma that when the Roman Pontiff speaks EX CATHEDRA, that is, when,
>
> 1. in the exercise of His office as shepherd and teacher of all Christians,
> 2. in virtue of His supreme Apostolic Authority,
> 3. He defines a doctrine concerning faith or morals to be held by the whole Church, He possesses, by the divine assistance promised to him in blessed Peter, that infallibility which the divine Redeemer willed his church to enjoy in defining doctrine concerning faith or morals.[60]

The reaction to the new doctrine was violent both within and without the Roman Church. Many Catholics were simply unable to accept Infallibility as a binding article of faith. They split from Rome and founded the Old Catholic Movement.

On 8 July 1868 the first Württemberg election with universal manhood suffrage brought the Democratic People's Party and Greater German Club, both of which opposed membership in the North German Federation, an overwhelming victory.[61] As the development toward unity stalled, dissatisfaction mounted about Bismarck's tactics. Roggenbach reported to Queen Augusta from Berlin in the summer of 1869 where he had gone to attend the Zollparlament that 'it is an open secret that Count Bismarck has not only fallen ill physically again under the pressure of all the embarrassments, but in fact no longer knows how to redirect the confusion that emerges from the chaos of the institutions.'[62]

'Chaos of the institutions' described the situation in the Prussian State Ministry very well. For months Bismarck had pressed his colleague Eulenburg to complete the rearrangement of the county structure for the new, expanded

Prussia, and nothing had happened. Bismarck blamed Eulenburg because his frequent illnesses had held up the work—a case of the pot calling the kettle black. In a letter of 19 January 1869 he complained to Eulenburg,

> I am not annoyed with you...I am annoyed with your colleagues in the Ministry...For four weeks nothing whatever has happened, and had I not intervened by today again nothing would have happened...You have at the top an absolute zero, and in my view it is your duty to take care that when you are ill or on leave the state does not suffer under your substitutes.[63]

Exasperation with subordinates coincided with a row with the King over the personnel of the Prussian State Ministry which Bismarck could neither name nor dismiss without the King's agreement. They were, after all, the King's ministers not Bismarck's. There had also been a battle over the reparations to be paid by the city of Frankfurt. Bismarck insisted on 3 million marks, which the Queen thought much too high and William had agreed with her: 2 million would be quite enough. Finally the Usedoms had reappeared in Bismarck's sleepless nights. Usedom had been sent as Prussian ambassador to the Kingdom of Italy and Bismarck wanted him dismissed.[64]

Bismarck sent in his letter of resignation on 22 February 1869 because an ambassador in Italy had been slack, because the county reorganization plan had been moving too slowly, and because the King and Queen had wished to extract a smaller reparation from the city of Frankfurt. The man who had changed the history of Europe submitted his resignation over absurd, trifling, and insignificant issues. How can one explain this or the fact that over the next eleven years this comedy repeated itself, often over matters even more trifling? The King entirely properly replied:

> I repeat there is but one single difference, that concerning Frankfurt-on-the-Main. The Usedomiana I discussed exclusively yesterday in writing, according to your wish; the House affair will adjust itself; we were agreed on the filling of appointments, but the *individuals* are not willing! What reason is there then for going to the extreme?[65]

On the date he submitted his resignation Bismarck told Roon that 'I am at the end of my capacities and cannot hold out spiritually in the battles against the King.'[66] But what battles? The King expressed his respect and affection in effusive terms:

> How can you imagine that I could even think of acceding to your idea! *It is my greatest happiness* (underline twice in the original) to live with you and to thoroughly agree with you! How can you be so hypochondriac as to allow

one single difference to mislead you into taking the extreme step! You wrote me from Varzin at the time of the difference in the matter of making up the deficit, that you were indeed of another opinion than I, but that when you entered your post you regarded it as your duty when you had, as in duty bound, expressed your opinion, always to conform to my decisions. What, then, has so utterly changed the opinions you so nobly expressed 3 months ago? Your name stands higher in Prussian history that that of any other Prussian statesman. And I am to let that man go? Never. Quiet and *prayer* (twice underlined in the original) will adjust everything. Your most faithful *friend* (underlined three times) W. [67]

Roon too wrote to Bismarck to plead with him not to send the resignation letter:

> Since I left you yesterday evening, my honoured friend, I have been continually occupied about you and your resolution. It leaves me no rest; I must once more appeal to you to word your letter in such a manner that a reconciliation may be possible. Perhaps you have not yet sent it and can still alter it. Just reflect that the almost tender note received yesterday lays claim to veracity, even if not fully justified. It is so written and claims not to be regarded as false coin, but as genuine and of full value … in view of the rank of the writer, perhaps even he cannot confess: 'I, I have done very wrong and will amend.'[68]

What did Bismarck want the King to do that he had not done? Is it farfetched or absurd to suggest that he wanted the King to express his love and affection and then, like an unhappy child, the hurt could be 'kissed away'? The King's letter goes well beyond what Roon calls 'the almost tender note'. It says that it is the King's 'greatest happiness to live with you and to thoroughly agree with you! How can you be so hypochondriac as to allow one single difference to mislead you …' It is not quite certain what William I meant by 'hypochondriac' in the next phrase but it would not be incorrect to call Bismarck's difficulties, both personally and politically, utterly imaginary, hence hypochondriac. It made little difference whether the county reorganization bill came out of the ministry a month late or whether Frankfurt paid two million or three or whether Usedom stayed in Italy or not. This is the Bismarck who had transformed the map of Europe and the history of Germany in four years and who in 1870 would engineer the destruction of the Napoleonic Empire. This giant could not sleep because the King refused to sack Guido von Usedom.

General von Stosch picked up the inside information, as he revealed in a letter to Gustav Freytag, about the dismissal of Usedom and the resignation crisis:

Usedom wrote to the King to say that at his last audience the King had been so gracious to him that he could not believe that he had been recalled. The King, furious that Bismarck dismissed an ambassador without consulting him, ordered him to stay and Bismarck got a black eye. Naturally Bismarck turned this adroitly to his advantage and clouted Usedom with it. New outrage and Bismarck submits his resignation. Thereafter Usedom fell anyway but without telling Bismarck the King gave him a decoration and offered him Olfers post.

The Stosch correspondence reveals an important truth about Bismarck. Stosch had himself been badly treated and humiliated by Bismarck. He opposed many of his policies. He became a favourite of the Crown Prince and Crown Princess. Bismarck considered him an 'enemy'. In spite of the damning evidence, which Bismarck assiduously collected on him, Stosch never wavered in his support for Bismarck. The letter just quoted ends with this sentence: 'Without Bismarck, we cannot make progress to a Reich.'[69]

And progress was being made. Delbrück's office churned out bills to unify and liberalize the new state. On 21 June 1869, the Reichstag passed a new law on freedom of trades and crafts, a very contentious issue, because it broke the historic guild restrictions on the practice of a trade, an evil which Adam Smith had condemned in *The Wealth of Nations*. On 3 July 1869 the North German Confederation granted full emancipation to the Jews: 'All existing restrictions on civil and national rights which arise from the diversity of religious confessions are hereby lifted.'[70] On 11 July 1869 a new Public Company's Act removed the requirement to get permission from the government to issue shares; in effect the new law made it possible to found and float new limited liability corporations. That the government of a notorious reactionary had introduced these liberal measures astonished public opinion.

By August 1869 Bismarck had reached such a state of rage and hypochondria that he again threatened to resign, as he wrote to von Roon on 29 August 1869:

> I am sick to death and have gall bladder problems...I have not slept for 36 hours and spent the entire night throwing up. My head feels like a glowing oven in spite of cold compresses. I fear that I am about to lose my mind. Forgive my agitation.... If the cart on which we ride should be smashed up, at least I shall have held myself apart from a share of the guilt. Fortunately it is a Sunday, because I fear otherwise that I would have done myself some bodily harm to let out my fury. We may have both become too angry to be able to row the galley any further.[71]

This insane outburst arose because the Cabinet refused to appoint Bismarck's choice as new North German postal director, a Hanoverian called Helding, a man so obscure that his name appears in neither of the two great German dictionaries of national biography. Ministers objected to the fact that he had not served the necessary three years in Prussian service. By contrast Bismarck wanted to create a Reich civil service open to all without petty restrictions, and was right to be annoyed, but in the disproportion between cause and consequence, there is something seriously deranged. How Bismarck survived these bouts of near madness remains a puzzle; how contemporaries who suffered under them did so is no less remarkable.

His behaviour distressed Albrecht von Roon and Moritz von Blanckenburg. On 16 January 1870 Roon wrote to Moritz von Blanckenburg that

> Bismarck treats business, even the Prussian, more or less as he did years ago. He is in cabinet meetings lively, speaks almost all the time and falls into the old error that through intellectual liveliness and personal charm he can overcome all the difficulties in the way. He will flirt with the National Liberals and ignore old friends and political comrades. He believes that he can win everybody over by diplomatic dialectic and human cleverness and to be able to lead them by spreading bait. He talks conservative to the conservatives and liberal to the liberals and reveals in this either so sovereign a contempt for his entourage or such incredible illusions that it makes me shudder. He wants to remain in office at any cost, for the present and the future, because he feels that the structure he has begun will collapse, making him a laughing stock to the world, as soon as he takes his hand away. That is not entirely incorrect but the means to that end! Are they sanctified for his sake?[72]

Moritz replied five days later:

> What you write about B does not surprise me. That he will not make good the mistakes he has made in his treatment of the conservatives, I know well since [my visit to] Varzin, that he is of the opinion that the progressive unification of Germany requires that we become ever more liberal—that he says right out—admittedly he also maintains that every liberal who by holding office comes nearer to the king, also become eo ipso a more conservative person.[73]

Bismarck had annoyed the only two really close friends he had left in the political world. He had already broken with 'little Hans', Ludwig von Gerlach, Alexander von Below, and most of his close associates in the Junker establishment. From now on, in addition to the recurring bouts of illness, rage, sleeplessness, and indigestion, he would suffer from an almost intolerable loneliness.

While Bismarck made himself sick about the appointment of a post-master general, an important event occurred in Spain that gave him a chance to transform European history again: the crisis over the 'Hohenzollern Candidature', as it is known. In September 1868, a *junta* of generals in Spain overthrew the monarchy of Queen Isabella II, herself the beneficiary of a similar *pronunciamiento* by an equally determined clique of generals in 1843. On 27 March 1869 the Earl of Clarendon, British Foreign Secretary, wrote to Lord Lyons, the British Ambassador in Paris, 'The chaotic state of that Country renders it contemptible at present...there has been evidence already that Bismarck has an eye on Spain as an auxiliary.'[74] Clarendon, who had been British minister during the Carlist War of 1831 to 1837, spoke good Spanish and knew the country well. He was right about Bismarck but could not have known at that stage how right. As early as 3 October 1868 Bismarck issued instructions to the German Foreign Office, 'It is in our interest if the Spanish question remains open...and a solution agreeable to Napoleon is unlikely to be useful for us.'[75] The most important of the Generals was 'the powerful, ambitious and imperturbable President of the Council, Marshall Juan Prim'.[76] In October 1868 Prim convinced his colleagues in the Council that they needed to find a suitable prince to replace the Queen and for the next year agents of the Spanish government approached a variety of French, Portuguese, and Italian royal princes without success. In the spring of 1869 the Generals settled on Leopold von Hohenzollern-Sigmaringen, a member of the Catholic, south German branch of the Prussian royal family and on his mother's side a relative of the Bonaparte dynasty.

In December 1868 Bismarck sent the Prince of Putbus and Colonel von Strantz as envoys to Madrid to assess the political situation and in May 1869 he dispatched the well-known military journalist and commentator, Theodor von Bernhardi, as well.[77] On 8 May Count Vincent Benedetti approached Bismarck to ask if the rumours of such a candidacy were correct and three days later Bismarck confirmed that they were correct but that Prince Karl Anton, head of the Hohenzollern-Sigmaringen branch, had refused the project.[78] Karl Anton, who had been Prime Minister of the New Era Government of 1858, quite rightly worried, as he wrote to Bismarck, that 'a Hohenzoller in Spain would give rise to a wild outcry in anti-Prussian Europe and either precipitate or defer the solution of many pending questions.'[79] That was precisely its attraction for Bismarck. He knew he needed a crisis with France and possibly even a war to overcome the resistance of the southern German states to a final unification under Prussian leadership.

Whether Bismarck wanted war from the beginning of the episode became a matter of high politics from 1870 onward. After 1918 the question of the 'guilt' of Imperial Germany for the First World War became itself the justification for the harsh peace imposed on Germany in 1919–20, and, as a result, the details of Bismarck's machinations in 1870 became a secret of the highest order. On 1 December 1921 Gustav Stresemann, the most important advocate of the politics of cooperation with the Allied Powers in spite of Versailles, cited Bismarck in his address to the right-wing German People's Party at their party conference:

> I ask you to go back in German history, to consider the greatest statesman the world had in the nineteenth century, Bismarck. Were his politics anything other than the politics of compromise?[80]

Bismarck had to be protected from the charge of reckless belligerence and put into the service of post-1919 politics by both Left and Right. After 1945 West German historiography defended the monarchy against all comers, but the complete defeat of Germany in May 1945 had allowed compromising documents to fall into the hands of the Allies. That made conservative historians in Germany even more defensive. In 1973 S. William Halperin, an American, surveyed the literature and the debate over Bismarck's 'war guilt' and concluded that 'complications with France were precisely what he was looking for'[81] but that did not mean that he planned to use the outcry, which Prince Karl Anton rightly predicted, as a pretext to go to war. Bismarck never closed off any option in advance.

In February 1870 Bismarck briefed Lieutenant Colonel Alfred Count von Waldersee (1832–1904) on his appointment as military attaché at the German Embassy in Paris. Waldersee, from a distinguished Anhalt military family, grew up in Prussian service. His father had been a general and Minister of War. Waldersee stood out, along with his contemporary Albrecht von Stosch, as ferociously ambitious and political. He also like Stosch kept a diary and collected his correspondence. By 1866 he had become an adjutant to the King and had excellent connections. In the interview, according to Waldersee's diary, Bismarck warned him to avoid legitimist circles and 'too hasty judgements . . . The political situation is one of an idyllic peace. Nobody can know how long that will last. The French have so much to do domestically that they have no time to think about foreign affairs.'[82] At this stage, 6 February 1870, Bismarck assumed that peace would continue for a while,

as did the British Foreign Secretary, Lord Clarendon, who had written to
the British Ambassador in Madrid in the same vein a few months earlier:

> Happily, there is no longer question, as in former times, of attempts on the
> part of Foreign Powers to turn to their own advantage the variations of
> Spanish politics. There is no desire on the part of any of them to disturb the
> Balance of Power in Europe by seeking to acquire dynastic influence in Spain
> or to aggrandize their dominion at her expense.[83]

The Hohenzollern candidature became a *casus belli* not least because
Marshall Prim refused to take no for an answer and dismissed the likely
response of Paris. On 17 February 1870 Prim wrote to Bismarck to say that
that he 'deemed it more seemly and more expedient at the beginning to make
an entirely confidential approach'.[84] A week later, Eusebio de Salazar arrived
at Karl Anton's residence in Düsseldorf with formal letters for Prince Leopold,
King William, and Bismarck in which an offer of the Crown of Spain was at
last made, subject, of course, to approval by the Cortes. Karl Anton, although
momentarily dazzled by the prospect that his son would found 'a dynasty such
as that has not been known to history since Charles V', recognized that his son
required formal permission from the head of the dynasty, King William I, and
the support of Bismarck before he could give his own consent.[85] The King
opposed the idea but Bismarck had got round such opposition before. On 12
March 1870 the Crown Princess wrote to Queen Victoria, 'General Prim has
sent a Spaniard here with several autograph letters from himself to Leopold
Hohenzollern, urging him most urgently to accept Spain... Neither the King,
nor Prince Hohenzollern, nor Antoinette [Princess Leopold—JS], nor
Leopold, nor Fritz are in favour of the idea...'[86]

Bismarck clearly was. On 9 March 1870 he presented a memorandum to
King William in which he argued that 'it is therefore to Germany's political
interest that the House of Hohenzollern should gain an esteem and an
exalted position in the world analogous to that only of the Habsburgs after
Charles V. The King remained stubbornly against the proposal and wrote
sceptical marginal notes against Bismarck's arguments. After all, the throne
of Spain lacked real stability and might be overthrown by a casual *pronunciamiento* at any time.[87] Bismarck used the occasion of a dinner in Berlin
hosted by Prince Karl Anton on 15 March, which Roon and Moltke also
attended, to hold an informal Crown Council, to try again to persuade the
King, who maintained his 'strong scruples' against it.[88] Bismarck's own
account of his role exceeds in its mendacity the lies we have already recorded
in this book. Here it is:

'Politically I was tolerably indifferent to the entire question. Prince Anthony [Karl Anton—JS] was more inclined than myself to carry it peacefully to the desired goal. The memoirs of his Majesty the King of Roumania are not accurately informed as regards details of the ministerial co-operation in the question. The ministerial council in the palace which he mentions did not take place. Prince Anthony was living as the King's guest in the palace, and had invited him and some of the ministers to dinner. I scarcely think that the Spanish question was discussed at table.[89]

On 20 April Prince Karl Anton and Prince Leopold let Madrid know that they were no longer interested. On 13 May Bismarck wrote to Delbrück to express his rage and frustration:

The Spanish affair has taken a miserable turn. The undoubted reasons of state have been subordinated to princely private interests and ultramontane, feminine interests. My annoyance about all this has heavily burdened my nerves for weeks.[90]

On 21 May Bismarck returned to Berlin and on the 28th told Prince Karl Anton that he had finally changed the King's mind. On 8 June he withdrew again to Varzin to let the royal family negotiate the candidacy without him so that as usual he could shift the blame for whatever went wrong onto princely intrigues. On 19 June Prince Leopold finally sent his acceptance letter to Madrid, which was made public on 2 July. On 5 July the new British Foreign Secretary, Lord Granville, paid his first visit to his new department where the long-serving and experienced Permanent Under-Secretary Edmund Hammond told him that 'he had never during his long experience known so great a lull'.[91] At 12.10 the same day the British Ambassador Layard sent a telegram in which he reported that through an indiscretion he had got news of the acceptance of the Crown of Spain by Prince Leopold.[92] The following day, the new French Foreign Secretary, the Duc de Gramont, announced to the French Chamber of Deputies that the Hohenzollern candidacy for the Spanish throne constituted a serious attempt to change the European Balance of Power to the detriment of the French Empire. The honour and interests of France had been severely injured. He hinted that France would regard it as grounds for war.[93] Later that day, 6 July 1870, the Prussian Ambassador in Paris, Karl Freiherr von Werther (1808–92) arrived at Bad Ems, where the royal family were taking the water of the Lahn, and met Alfred Waldersee, the military attaché in Paris, who as a royal General Adjutant had joined the King there. He told Waldersee in great excitement that 'the devil is loose in Paris. It looks like war.' When yesterday morning he had gone to Gramont to take leave for the holidays, he found him in a very excited mood. A telegram from Madrid said that Prince Leopold Hohenzollern was supposed to be presented to the Cortes as successor to the vacant throne. Gramont was beside himself. He had complained of lack of consideration and deceit on our part and said straight out, the thing was impossible. France could never concede that, the Ministry would be questioned in the chamber. Werther was to an extent in a difficult situation because he had not heard a word about the whole business. He could only take evasive action. Luckily for him that he had previously planned this journey to Ems. I thought he ought not to have gone. The King received him almost at once after his arrival in a long audience. It is really uncomfortable that Bismarck is in Varzin. All decisions are naturally much more complicated.[94]

On the same day, the Crown Princess wrote to Queen Victoria, 'After the Spanish crown had been *decidedly refused* by the Hohenzollerns and the King, the *former* have been applied to again, and, having changed their minds meanwhile, seem likely to accept it—much to the King and Queen's annoyance . . . '[95]

The next day, 7 July 1870, Waldersee complained in his diary about Bismarck's behaviour in the crisis:

Bismarck refused to believe in any approaching danger and was determined to stay in Varzin where he was taking the waters. The sudden prospect of war with France upset the King very much and he wanted earnestly to get the affair settled. As bad luck would have it, Prince Leopold Hohenzollern was not in Sigmaringen but had gone on a trip to the Alps. Nobody knew where he was.[96]

On 8 July Waldersee asked the King for permission to return to his post in view of the threat of war and the King gave him his view of the background of the previous events and then added, as Waldersee recorded:

A few months ago the Spaniards had knocked on the door again and now all of a sudden the father and son Hohenzollern have become passionately in favour of the thing to my great astonishment, whereas before they were pretty uncertain. They allowed themselves to be talked into it by Bismarck, and the Prince who had doubted that he had the guts to be King of Spain, was suddenly filled with idea that he had a mission to make Spain happy. I begged him earnestly to think it over very carefully, but when he insisted I gave him my permission as head of the family . . . I have Bismarck to thank for this because he took the whole matter so casually, as he has so much else. [Waldersee on the margin of the diary entry: 'exact words'] . . . It was the first

time I had ever heard the King talk about serious business. He developed his
ideas with great clarity and without hesitation in his speech.[97]

This testimony—spontaneously given—makes it impossible not to think
that Bismarck engineered the crisis and that the French reacted exactly as
he had imagined they would. His absence in Varzin merely covered his
tracks in the event that things went wrong.

When Waldersee returned to Paris on 9 July, he found the French in high
excitement. At the station he ran into 'Captain Leontiev, an assistant to the
Russian attaché, Prince Wittgenstein. His first words: "you have a war;
believe me, you cannot stop it."' In the evening, Waldersee sent a ciphered
telegram to Bismarck: 'In the War and Navy Ministries elaborate preparations are under way for the conduct of a large war. Reserves have not yet
been called to the colours but it looks as if troop movements will begin
tomorrow. The railroads have been advised. There seems to be an inclination to strike without mobilized troops.'[98]

What happened next could not happen today in the age of instant and
ubiquitous communications. Because Bismarck was still in Varzin, he did not
know that on 9 July 1870 Count Benedetti, the French ambassador to
Prussia, who was in Bad Ems, asked the Prussian King for direct information about the situation. The King replied that the matter concerned him as
Head of the Hohenzollern family not as King of Prussia. He found it hard
to refuse the Catholic Sigmaringen branch in such a matter and could not
intervene. In fact, on 10 July, he wrote to Prince Karl Anton a letter in
which he urged the father to convince the son, Prince Leopold, to withdraw his name. Karl Anton acted at once and on 12 July made public that
the Hereditary Prince Leopold had withdrawn his name. William had also
sent an urgent telegram to Varzin ordering Bismarck to come at once to Bad
Ems as a matter of the greatest urgency.[99]

Bismarck had no idea that these developments had occurred which one
can deduce from the fact that on 10 July 1870 he sent a telegram to his
banker Bleichröder that it would be 'a good idea' to unload the railroad
shares in his portfolio.[100] Today that would be an example of 'insider trading' but it certainly confirms that on 10 July Bismarck expected a war.
When he got to Berlin on the 12th, he learned for the first time that
Leopold had withdrawn. In the late afternoon his carriage halted in the
Wilhelmstrasse and a sheaf of telegraphs was shoved into his hand. Sitting
there in the street he learned for the first time of Karl Anton decision and

the extent of William's involvement in his renunciation. Other messages from Paris told of 'vaunts and taunts' in the Paris press. Descending to the sidewalk, he thought of resigning. Prussia, he judged, had suffered a humiliation worse than Olmütz.[101] Bismarck called a meeting with Moltke, Roon, and Count Eulenburg. Moltke arrived red in the face, 'because he had now made the trip [to Berlin] for nothing, and the war which he had already firmly planned seemed to recede into the distance again ... Old Roon was dejected too.' Bismarck said: 'Until just now I thought I was standing on the eve of the greatest of historical events, and now all I will get from it is the unpleasantness of the sudden interruption of my *Kur*... [to Herbert] I would urge you to work hard because there is not going to be a battlefield promotion.'[102]

Still Bismarck had to do something to save his face and his diplomatic situation. He went to see Gorchakov, who was briefly in Berlin on the way home from taking the waters at Wildbad. 'Apparently he [Bismarck] spoke with Gortchakov about a diplomatic offensive which would be directed at the inflammatory speeches of Gramont. They agreed to criticize the French foreign minister indirectly by emphasizing to the European governments the restraint and moderation of the King and his ministry. In this sense Gortchakov spoke to Lord Loftus and de Launay. Loftus immediately went to see the French *chargé d'affaires*, Le Sourd, and urged on him that the French government should be satisfied with what they had achieved and recognize the conciliatory spirit of the Prussian King.'[103]

Meanwhile in Paris, Waldersee wrote an account of what happened:

On the morning of the 12th, Baron Werther came back from Ems, very tired because of the heat. Immediately after his arrival, a man from the Foreign Office, the Chief of Gramont's cabinet, Count Faverney, appeared and asked if Werther could not visit Gramont as soon as possible. Werther replied, he would come at once. When he came back from the meeting, Solms and I were waiting for him in the Embassy. After we had heard him, we both said that war was now unavoidable. He refused to accept this view. 'A war between France and Prussia is an event of such huge importance, so terrible a disaster for so many people, the cause is besides so trivial that it is the duty of every man of honour to seek to prevent it by every means in his power. That has been my guiding principle and for that reason I have resolved to write to the King.' From a general human point of view he was undeniably right; as Prussian Ambassador he should have behaved to Gramont very differently.... Bismarck's telegram which recalled the ambassador was so crude that I could hardly believe it. As Werther went to take leave of the Duke de Gramont, I accompanied him to the Foreign Ministry. When he came back to the ante-chamber, he said to me, 'this walk marks the end of my career.' He did not deceive himself. Bismarck never spoke to him again.

The editor of the Waldersee diary, Hans Otto Meisner, notes that this is 'wrong. Werther was dismissed in 1871 but recalled in 1874 and sent as Ambassador to Constantinople where he served until 1877.'[104] I pause here to salute Karl Freiherr von Werther for a remarkable act of civil courage, a diplomat who put his honour and his horror of war above his career and his duty to Bismarck as his chief.

If the Duc de Gramont had taken Gorchakov's advice and been satisfied by the public and stunning victory of French diplomacy over Bismarck, again war would have been avoided but he took a further step. He ordered his ambassador who was still in Bad Ems to get a promise from the King that Prussia would take no similar action in the future. On the 13th as Bismarck, Moltke, and Roon sat together over dinner, a telegram from William I arrived from Bad Ems that reported how Ambassador Benedetti had confronted the King and insisted that the King give his solemn word that nothing of the sort would happen again. The King, offended, not only said that he could make no such promise but, when asked by Benedetti if he could have another chance to discuss the matter, refused to see the French ambassador. The King asked Bismarck 'whether the new demand and my refusal should not be communicated to our embassies abroad and to the press'.[105]

Bismarck now had what he needed. He took a pencil and edited what he had received from the King to make it sound more offensive. In the original text the King had written that he had 'let the Ambassador be told through an adjutant that he had now received from the Prince confirmation which Benedetti had already received from Paris and had nothing further to say to the Ambassador.' Bismarck altered the phrase to make it more provocative. In Bismarck's version it read, 'His Majesty the King had thereupon refused to receive the French Ambassador once more and let him know through an adjutant that His Majesty had nothing further to communicate to the ambassador.'[106] Years later Lucius von Ballhausen happened to be present when the three conspirators showed up at an evening in the Wilhelmstrasse and recalled the events of 1870:

> After dinner as we sat around smoking cigars, Field Marshall Roon arrived, coughing and puffing and breathless. He suffered from an asthmatic

condition…Later Count Moltke arrived…He received him very cordially and said, tapping him on the knee, 'the last time we three sat together was on the 13 of July 1870. What a stroke of luck it was that the French went so far! How hard it would have been to find another equally favourable opportunity! We never altered Benedetti's dispatch but condensed it in such way as to show the French pretensions in their full strength. Everything had been surrendered with respect to the Hohenzollern candidacy and had the French not insisted that we promise never to do so again, we might have given up yet more. I asked you both "are we ready?" You said "we are ready".'[107]

On 14 July 1870 the French ministerial council decided to declare mobilization and declared war on 19 July. Bismarck claimed afterwards that his editing of the Ems Dispatch had forced Napoleon III to go to war, though evidence suggests that France had decided to fight earlier. As in the case of the Austrian war, an ill-prepared and badly organized state and army went to war without proper mobilization.

On the Prussian side the Crown Princess was not unrepresentative of the anti-French feeling that had been stirred as a result of French arrogance. On 16 July she wrote to Queen Victoria:

We have been shamelessly forced into this war, and the feeling of indignation against such an act of such crying injustice has risen in two days here to such a pitch that you would hardly believe it; there is a universal cry 'to arms' to resist an enemy who wantonly insults us.[108]

The 16th of July was the first day of mobilization of the Prussian army. Arden Bucholz writes,

By January 1870 railroad mobilization had been reduced to 20 days, 260 per cent better than 1867 with a force nearly three times as large and a mobilization and battle space area seven times larger than 1866. It delivered German forces to the French border like a factory assembly line. And allowed Moltke's timing patterns to begin to dominate war…On the tenth day the first units disembarked on the French border, by the thirteenth day, the troops of the Second Army were assembled there, on the eighteenth the number was 300,000.[109]

On 19 July reserve officers were mobilized. In the Reichstag Lucius von Ballhausen, a reserve officer in the Brandenburg Cuirassier Regiment, went up to the ministers' table and asked Roon and Moltke whether he should remain in parliament or report at once. Roon smiled, 'there's no rush. You can stay here. There is plenty of time before the *Etappen* have to be set up on enemy soil and we have eight to ten days jump on the French.'[110]

The Prussian generals had absolute confidence in their General Staff and in its chief, Helmuth von Moltke. We can catch a little of the atmosphere two days after the French declaration of war on 19 July, from Waldersee's diary:

> Today early in the morning I arrived on the Paris express in good shape but tired by the heat and very dusty. On the platform I ran into Prince Friedrich Karl who greeted me in a very friendly way and told me to go right to Moltke where a meeting was underway. I did that, was admitted and found Moltke with General von Podbielski and the three department chiefs, Bronsart, Verdy and Brandenstein. Moltke conveyed his respects and then pressed me for information. Afterwards I changed as quickly as possible and went to the royal palace. Radziwill was on duty and I was admitted at once. The King was cheerful and friendly as always, gave me his hand and thanked me for the reports. After asking about French conditions, he said, 'you will stay with me.' So my fate was decided for the near future. I was to have the good fortune going to war as the direct companion of this marvellous chief.[111]

The Prussian Army had recently fought a victorious war and in the interim had learned a variety of lessons. In 1866 it had expected a long bloody war but the opposite had occurred. They saw no reason not to repeat the exercise in 1870 and in the first stage of the war, they were right. Moltke in his short summary of the official history of the war gives a desolate picture of French preparations. The French went to war in a collective fit of insanity. 'The regiments had been hurried away from their peace stations before the arrival of their complement of men and without waiting for their equipment. Meanwhile the called-out reservists accumulated in the depots, overflowed the railway stations and choked the traffic.' The planned thrust through the Black Forest which the General Staff had expected never occurred. Careful negotiations on the Prussian side had integrated the southern German armies into the Prussian system and the resulting performance of Bavarian, Württemberg, and Baden units exceeded expectations. Prussian mobilization on the other hand proceeded exactly according to plan. The King declared war on 16 July 1870. Fourteen days later, 300,000 Prussian and allied soldiers had assembled at Mainz all ready to strike into France and, since the French had not used the flank to attack from Strasbourg across the Rhine, Moltke could make his front more compact. The mobilization plan foresaw the same three-part division of forces that had worked so well in enveloping the Austrians in 1866. Three armies under the command respectively of General von Steinmetz (First Army), Prince Frederick Charles of Prussia (Second Army), and Prince Frederick the Crown Prince (Third

Army) which contained the Baden, Württemberg, and Bavarian Corps and the 11th Corps of units from Hesse, Nassau, and Saxe-Weimar, had assumed their initial positions by the beginning of August. The Order of Battle on 1 August 1870 makes instructive reading for the historian of Prussia. Not one corps, divisional, or brigade commander in the line units of the I and II Armies lacked the aristocratic 'von'. The famous names of Prussian history show up in the distribution of commands: several von Kleists (3), von der Goltzes (2), Neidhart von Gneisenau, von Below (2), von der Osten, von Sennft-Pilsach, von Manteuffel, von Bülow (2), von Wedell, von Brandenburg (2), a colonel von Bismarck, von Wartensleben, von Alvensleben, etc. and a sprinkling of royal princes in staff and command posts. In the First and Second Armies, only Major-General Baumgarth, who commanded the 2nd Cavalry Brigade in the First Army, Lieutenant Colonel Lehmann in command of the 37th Brigade in the Hanoverian 10th Corps, and Major General Tauscher of the Saxon 3rd Infantry Brigade, lacked a title. None of the Corps Commanding Engineers, on the other hand, had a title and many of the Commanding Artillery Generals at Corps and divisional levels belonged to the bourgeoisie.[112] Old Prussia went into battle equipped with new technology, transportation, weaponry, and communications.

The spirit that led to bold and dashing acts of heroism had not—to Moltke's intense annoyance—died out. Such bravado led to serious breaches of his careful plans. None was more guilty of disobedience than General von Steinmetz, Commander-in-Chief of the First Army. Karl Friedrich von Steinmetz posed two problems for his fellow commanders and for Moltke. He was 73 when the war broke out and many thought him too old. His biographer writes of him that 'he had few friends in the army during his lifetime. That arose from his gruff nature and the high standards he set in the service. A serious, closed character, he was mostly misunderstood by his contemporaries.'[113] Lieutenant Colonel Waldersee put it more strongly on 25 July:

> That they have given old Steinmetz the I. Army I cannot understand. He was already three-quarters mad in 1866 and is now four years older. He will not lack energy in his moves but that is not enough.[114]

Steinmetz was blamed for attacking at Spichern when Moltke wanted him to wait and in September he was relieved of his command, promoted, and sent off to Posen. Other than that the command structure worked smoothly, and Moltke's reliance on his commanders proved successful. What never worked was the relationship between Bismarck and Moltke. Bismarck showed up on 31 July in the Headquarters of the King at Mainz kitted out in the uniform of a Major General of the reserve, a spiked helmet of the heavy cavalry, and huge leather hip boots, a ridiculous and unmilitary figure.[115] The soldiers may have laughed but the German public began to worship at the altar of the 'German giant' and, as Johnannes Willms shrewdly observes, his distinctive features, instantly recognizable and ideal for pictures, ornamental mugs, and busts looked particularly good in the *Pickelhaube*.[116] The waspish Waldersee kept a sharp eye on Bismarck and recorded in his diary the details. On 2 August he wrote on the quarters taken up in Mainz:

> The King and his entourage have been housed in the grand-ducal palace. Otherwise the rest of the headquarters is scattered across Mainz, about which many are annoyed, in particular, Bismarck, who lives very prettily with a patriotic wine merchant but pretty far out. He complains all the time.[117]

The war began badly for the French. On 4 August there was a fierce skirmish at Wissembourg; on 5 August the battle of Spichern; and on 6 August, the full-scale battle of Wörth, where for the first time 100,000 men on both sides clashed. Here it became clear that the German needle-gun could not compete with the French chassepôt and Moltke soberly records that at Wörth alone the Prussians lost 10,000 men.[118] The victor at Wörth, the Crown Prince Frederick, recorded the event in his war diary:

> I have today completely defeated Marshall MacMahon, putting his troops to utter and disorderly rout. So far as it has been possible to ascertain, his whole corps was engaged, reinforced by Failly and Canrobet as well as by troops brought from Grenoble, approximately a force of 80,000 men against me, who brought 100,000 men into the fighting line. The engagement, which, again!, cost us a very great number of officers and men deserves the title of a veritable battle, in which the greater part of my army fought.... The losses of the French must be extraordinarily heavy; the dead lay in heaps and the red cloth of their uniforms showed up wherever the eye fell. Six thousand unwounded prisoners have been reported to me, including regimental and battalion commanders and 100 other officers. Among them I came upon a Colonel in the Cuirasseurs, who must have recognized me by my star, for he instantly gave me my proper title: 'Ah, monseigneur. Quelle défaite, quel malheur; j'ai la honte d'être prisonnier, nous avons tout perdu! I tried to comfort him by saying: 'Vous avez tort de dire d'avoir perdu tout, car après tout vous avez battu comme des braves soldats, vous n'avez pas perdu l'honneur.' To this

he replied 'Ah, merci vous me faites bien en me traitant de la sorte.' I had him give me the address of those belonging to him so as to send news to the family. Later I came on a great number of other officers in like plight to whom I spoke to the same effect.[119]

There followed several other bloody confrontations and part of the defeated French army regrouped at Metz. When they tried to break out, the greatest battle of the entire war followed, the Battle of Gravelotte-St-Privat, in which the Prussians this time under the direct command of Moltke with two whole armies and over 180,000 men attacked about 112,000 French troops under Marshal François-Achille Bazaine. The attacking forces as in the Battle of Gettysburg in the American Civil War faced withering French fire and the Prussians and southern German allies lost over 20,000, in part, as Moltke admitted through a miscalculation of his. The first fourteen days and six battles had cost the Prussians over 50,000 dead.[120] Bazaine's troops took refuge in Metz and, though, as Moltke wrote, 'the siege of Metz had formed no part of the original plan of campaign', he had no choice but to invest the city.

Meanwhile Marshal McMahon in command of the other French Army very prudently planned to withdraw to Paris to confront the invaders with a strongly fortified city. Napoleon III ordered him to relieve Bazaine in Metz and the newly formed Army of Châlons with Napoleon in command set off northwards along the Belgian frontier to try to go round the Prussians. On 2 September 1870 at Sedan, Moltke caught them in one of his pincer movements and defeated McMahon's army and took Napoleon III prisoner. Within hours of the news reaching Paris, crowds of furious citizens took to the streets and declared the revival of the Republic on 4 September 1870.

Though the war had been much more devastating than Moltke had expected, he had won it by his immaculate planning and the generally orderly operations of the three armies under his command. What happened next had not been imagined. Leon Gambetta, Jules Favre, and General Trochi formed a government of National Defence and rejected Bismarck's relatively moderate demands for an armistice. Jules Favre on behalf of the Government of National Defence declared on 6 September that France would not yield an inch of its territory nor a stone of its fortresses.[121] Gambetta became Minister of War and, as Moltke drily writes, 'Gambetta's rare energy and unrelenting determination availed, indeed, to induce the entire population to take up arms, but not to direct these hasty levies with unity of purpose.'[122] In other words, the Prussian commanders faced a long, wearing and unpopular guerrilla campaign, a 'people's war' which regained much of the popular support that that government of France had lost.

The next few months strained the nerves of all those involved and relations between Bismarck and the General Staff deteriorated. Lieutenant Colonel Waldersee had a choice seat on the edge of the battle for control between Bismarck and the soldiers. As a nosey gossip and intriguer, he had already decided, as his diary entry for 3 August put it, to 'try to maintain my contacts in the General Staff and as a man with the right background I have a basis. Besides, Bronsart, Verdy and Brandenstein are my old friends and acquaintances.'[123] He was the same age and rank as the three lieutenant colonels who ran the three operating divisions under Moltke—Paul Bronsart von Schellendorf, Julius Verdy du Vernois, and Karl von Brandenstein, whom Bismarck bitterly called the 'demi-gods', the agents of God himself, General von Moltke. The three, especially Bronsart, came to hate Bismarck and did everything to prevent him from getting his way. Waldersee recorded that Bismarck also had his 'demi-gods':

> Bismarck, who leads his own team, Abecken, Keudell, Hatzfeld, Karl Bismarck-Bohlen together with several code clerks and councillors, operates with three or four horse-drawn carriages. He himself travels in a very heavy travel carriage with four horses, which cannot keep up with the stallions of the King. For this reason they begin to intrigue against the long marches.[124]

After the declaration of total war by the French Government of National Defence, military and diplomatic considerations became hopelessly entangled. Bismarck needed to get an armistice to keep the Russians, Austrians, and English out of the struggle. Now that Count Beust, the former Saxon Prime Minister, had become the Austrian Minister of Foreign Affairs, there was a real danger that the Habsburgs might fall on the Prussians from the rear to undo the humiliations of 1866. Bismarck needed to get the war over quickly. These anxieties mingled with the wild and uncontrollable rage that seized Bismarck when anyone opposed him, and now Moltke and his 'demi-gods' did so daily.

On 9 September Waldersee recorded the first crisis between the General Staff and Bismarck. The issue was whether a particular police office was to be under Bismarck or the General Staff and Bismarck reacted as he had with the Prussian State Ministry over the Hanoverian nominated to be postal director.

Between Bismarck and the General Staff open war has broken out...One got out the file and showed the Minister President his signature. He said, not stupid, 'I sign so many documents about which I have no idea, that this signature does matter at all. I have no knowledge of any such agreement and consider it to be false.' Negotiations became very lively. Because he had been caught out and proven to be in the wrong, Bismarck took it very badly and this trivial issue led to a quarrel. Moltke stayed out of the business but Podbielski and the department chiefs have ruined their relationship to Bismarck.[125]

On 20 September 1870 the Royal Headquarters moved to the famous villa of Baron James de Rothschild at Ferrières. Before dinner the King walked through the ground floor rooms of the château. In the hall of mirrors, he looked at the many reliefs on the walls and said: 'I am too poor to buy myself such a thing.'[126] Paul Bronsart von Schellendorf also recorded his impressions of Ferrières: 'The ancestors of Baron Rothschild (coats of arms, lions and eagles) are very numerous and often set in marble, bronze, oil and pastel. There wherever possible, the coat of arms has been placed. General Stuckow declared that whole interior decoration was shameless.'[127] The various staff officers joked about coats of arms with JR (James de Rothschild) in them and played with phrases like 'Judaeorum Rex' and 'der Judenkönig'. When Bismarck engaged his private banker Gerson Bleichröder to negotiate off the record about French reparations, Moltke's staff called Bleichröder 'des Kanzlers Privatjude' (the Chancellor's private Jew).[128] During the siege of Paris in January 1871, Bismarck said to his staff:

Bleichröder will come running and prostrate himself on behalf of the whole Rothschild family. Then we will send both to Paris and they can join the dog hunt....Well in the first place Bleichröder should go into battle. He must get into Paris right away so that he and his co-religionists can smell each other and talk with bankers.[129]

Waldersee described the accommodation in Ferrières:

Here in the château, besides the King who has been housed on the ground floor left, there are Bismarck, Moltke, Roon, and the entire entourages of the King and Bismarck. In the beautiful stable buildings, some of which have been converted to guest rooms, the General Staff and Ministry of War have been housed. Everybody else is in the village. In Lagny, Prince Karl, the Grand Duke of Weimar, Prince Luitpold [of Bavaria], the Grand Duke of Mecklenburg-Schwerin, the General Inspector of Artillery and of Engineers.

Naturally great dissatisfaction all round. The second staff want to be in Ferrières and in Ferrières everybody wants to be in the château.[130]

By 19 September, as Moltke writes, the VIth Corps of the III Army had marched on Versailles in two columns and the Bavarian Corps had fought its way to the Paris suburbs. By the evening, he writes, 'the investment of Paris was complete on all sides. Six Army Corps stood in a deployment some fifty miles in circumference immediately in front of the enemy's capital.'[131] What to do next raised a problem. Moltke denied the argument of those who claimed later 'that it would have been possible to capture one of the forts on this day by forcing an entrance with the fugitive enemy.' The forts were formidable and could have been defended even if French troops in retreat were still entering. Moltke believed that 'the escalade of masonry escarpments eighteen feet high can never be successful without much preparation... probable failure would have endangered the important success of the day.'[132] The result was a stalemate which lasted for months during which Paris carried out its own revolution of 1789 against the provinces, known to history as the Commune.

On 24 September Waldersee dined with Bismarck. The Princess Karl had written to let him know that the 'Queen had been vigorously agitating that we should take no land from the dear French. Together with her Princess Radziwill, etc. I should tell Prince Bismarck. As I did so, he said, "I know the clique and their shameful intrigues very well. The King is worked on in every letter from the Queen. I think for a while a bolt has been shoved across it. At my request the King wrote such a rude letter that she will not dare try anything for a while".'[133]

On 1 October 1870 the General Staff entertained Count Bismarck at their table. Lieutenant Colonel Bronsart von Schellendorf recorded a conversation in his diary:

> He had, as it happens, expected that immediately after the arrival of the King Baron von Rothschild would have enquired about the King's orders and arranged for a decent reception of the entourage. That did not happen. Bismarck thereafter decided to treat him as a Jewish merchant. He wished to buy wine from the cellar. The administrator replied that in this house 'où l'argent n'est rien' nothing was ever sold. Bismarck insisted, ordered wine and a bill on which the price of every bottle plus 50 centimes for corkage was added.[134]

What to do with the French popular rising continued to trouble the General Staff and Bismarck. On 4 October Waldersee recorded a conversation

Bismarck had with the American General Philip Sheridan, who had been assigned to the Prussian Army as a military observer. Sheridan (1831–88) had become famous or infamous for his campaign in 1864 in the Shenendoah Valley during the American Civil War, when he ordered his Union troops to set fire to civilian houses and barns in the so-called 'burning', an example of the technique known later as 'scorched earth'. Sheridan said to Bismarck:

> 'You know how to defeat an enemy better than any army in the world, but to destroy him, you have not learned. One must see smoke from burning villages; otherwise you will never finish the French.' And I am convinced that the man is right. Destroy great strips of territory à la Sheridan across the country, that will take the wind out of French sails and put an end to snipers.[135]

Moltke refused to take the guerrilla war seriously. On 7 October he announced with his usual, calm certainty, 'the war is over; there are just twitchings left. There can be no question of more large operations.'[136] But it was not over and went on for months.

On 5 October the entire German headquarters moved to Versailles. Holstein described the conditions in his *Memoirs*:

> Our stay in Versailles was particularly trying to our nerves because of the high room temperature the Chancellor insisted on. One day he complained bitterly of the cold. 'The office staff apparently does not wish me to come downstairs.' We looked at the thermometer; it was between 16 and 17 degrees. When the Chancellor unbuttoned his military greatcoat you could see it was lined with doeskin, but he only undid it when the temperature was 18 degrees Réaumur with a huge fire burning in the grate. [18 Réaumur = 72.5 Fahrenheit or 22 Celsius]

Bismarck's temper worsened as the General Staff debated what to do about the siege of Paris during October and November. They considered uncertainly whether to bombard the city with their powerful siege guns or to try to starve it into submission. Keudell described a characteristic clash between Bismarck and Moltke:

> On 18 October Roon and Moltke went to the Chancellor. Shortly after the conference a pain in his foot began which lasted for several days. I concluded from that, Moltke's refusal to shell Paris could not be overcome, although it was well known that Roon favoured it.[137]

The issue divided the generals and had begun to appear in the press, as Waldersee recorded on 23 October:

In the press great efforts are made to stamp the bombardment of Paris as barbarous. Doubtless female intrigues are behind this and this time in a wonderful way the Queen and the Crown Princess are of the same opinion. I know
with certainty that Stosch, who attaches himself gladly to the Crown Prince,
is involved in this. He turns out to be the most effective ally because he can
say that all the railroad trains and other means of transport are needed for
victualling. Well, we certainly have to live first before we can shoot, so he
alone can hold everything up. There are other conflicts, for example,
Headquarters v Blumenthal; almost all officers against Roon.[138]

While the Prussian victorious progress stalled amidst disagreements and
unfavourable publicity, on 9 November 1870 the Russian government
renounced the Black Sea Treaty of 1856, which had been imposed upon it
after the defeat in the Crimean War. The flagrant gesture of defiance put the
English cabinet in an awkward position. The French Empire under Napoleon
III with whom Britain had fought the war had ceased to exist, and the new
Republic—occupied and humiliated—had no energy to worry about the
eastern Mediterranean. Liberal Prime Minister Gladstone and his Foreign
Secretary, Lord Granville, decided to send Odo Russell to Prussian HQ to
sound out Bismarck on the matter. In London the government believed
that he had secretly urged the Russians to use the favourable diplomatic
situation to wipe out the shame of 1856.[139] Lady Emily Russell wrote to her
mother-in-law, the formidable Lady William Russell: 'It is curious, isn't it?
that he should be going to grapple with Bismarck which is what he said he
wished to do beyond everything and this before he is ambassador to
Berlin.'[140] Odo Russell became an intimate of Bismarck in a way no other
foreign diplomat did and his observations of his extraordinary friend provide one of the best insights into the Bismarck of the 1870s and early
1880s.

Odo William Leopold Russell (1829–84) belonged to the first family of
English Whiggery, the Russells, who were the Dukes of Bedford and who
inhabited at Woburn one of the great lordly houses of England. His father,
who had been the British ambassador at Berlin (1835–41), died when Odo
was 13 and his powerful and eccentric mother, Lady William, decided to
educate her three boys in civilized places, not barbarous English public
schools. Richard Davenport-Hines in his biography in the *Oxford Dictionary
of National Biography* writes that 'as a result he had nothing of the muddied
English oaf about him. He seldom took exercise. He spoke French, Italian,
and German with exceptional purity, though his English accent was always

tinged with continental inflexions.'[141] A flavour of Lady William's character comes from a passage of a letter to Sir Austen Layard on the German victory over France:

> I am GERMANICA to the *pineal gland*. Discipline against disorder, sobriety against drunkenness, education against IGNORANCE. There never was such a triumph of intellect over brutism.[142]

No wonder her three sons, even as grown men, needed to gather their courage to visit Mother.

Odo Russell had spent a good deal of time in Rome and spoke equally impressive Italian. In its obituary *The Times* of 27 August 1884 commented on Odo Russell's remarkable ability as a Protestant to understand Roman Catholicism, an invaluable asset during the crisis of church and state, in which he would soon have to work:

> His intimacy with Cardinal Antonelli enabled him to acquire a thoroughly Italian subtlety seldom to be met with in an Englishman. A close observer by nature, he has learnt by experience how to observe still more closely: he has discovered how to weigh the characters of men, to discern their weaknesses, and to profit by their meannesses and susceptibilities.[143]

On 2 December 1870 Odo Russell wrote to Edmund Hammond, permanent undersecretary in the Foreign Office, about his first impressions of Bismarck and of the political situation at the Versailles Headquarters:

> I am charmed with Count Bismarck, his soldier-like, straightforward frank manner, his genial conversations, are truly fascinating, and his excessive kindness to me have won my heart. His foreign office staff travel with him and form ... his family. At dinner and breakfast he takes the head of the table with his under-secretaries on each side—then come the Chief Clerks—then the junior Clerks and the telegraph clerks situated at the end of the table— everybody in uniform. When I dine there I sit between the Count and the Permanent Under-Secretary [von Keudell—JS] who plays the piano divinely after dinner while we smoke. The conversation is in German and the questions of the day are discussed with perfect freedom, which makes them deeply interesting and instructive.[144]

Again, another sophisticated observer charmed by Bismarck's conversation and personality.

Relations between Bismarck and the General Staff had worsened in the meantime. Paul Bronsart confided to his diary a crushing judgement on the Chancellor:

Bismarck begins really to be ready for the mad house. He complained bitterly to the King that General Moltke had written to General Trochu and claimed that this as a negotiation with a foreign government belonged in his competence. When General Moltke as representative of the Supreme Command of the Army has written to the Governor of Paris, the matter has a purely military character. Since Count Bismarck claims in addition that he had declared to me that he considered the letter extremely questionable, whereas exactly the opposite is the case, I then submitted a written report to General von Moltke in which I demonstrated the falsehood of the assertion and requested in future not to be asked to carry out verbal instructions with the Count.[145]

The pressure from public opinion began to be felt. The Crown Prince recorded in his war diary that his wife had been blamed for the delay of the bombardment and that Johanna von Bismarck and Countess Amelie von Donhöff had spread the lie.[146] Bronsart quoted a popular poem which had made the round in Berlin:

> Guter Moltke, gehst so stumm,
> Immer um das Ding herum
> Bester Moltke sei nicht dumm
> Mach doch endlich Bumm! Bumm! Bumm!
> Herzens-Moltke, denn warum?
> Deutschland will das: Bumm! Bumm! Bumm![147]

> [Good Moltke, why so mum
> As round it all you come?
> Best of Moltkes don't be dumb
> Finally go boom, boom, boom
> Moltke dear, why so glum?
> Germany wants boom, boom, boom—JS]

On 18 December Bronsart put his career on the line to frustrate Bismarck's intervention in military matters. As he recorded in his war diary, he had been ordered by General Podbielski to provide Bismarck with minutes of a Military Council and decided to disobey orders, a court-martial offence. The whole entry records the agony of conscience of one of the most gifted of the 'demi-gods', a lieutenant colonel, a Division Chief in the General Staff, 'for me the hardest day of the entire campaign'. He had received an order from the King approved by the Chief of the General Staff, General Count Moltke, and handed to him by Lieutenant General Podbielski, Quartermaster General of the entire army. As he records the moment of his decision

if a man with the ambitious thirst for power like Count Bismarck were once to be admitted, there would be nothing more to be done...I thought about it for ten minutes; the habit of obedience got me through the address and then it failed me, and the feeling of duty, and the need to be disobedient even to the King, won the upper hand even at the sacrifice of my own person.

He reported to Podbielski that he could not carry out the order in good conscience and submitted his resignation letter at the same time. Podbielski at first flew into a rage and questioned Bronsart's sanity. Then in the face of this act of moral courage by a senior staff officer, he consulted Moltke, who revoked the order and told the King of his decision. Bismarck never got access to the Military Council minutes.[148] Bronsart joins von Werther as two examples of unusual civil courage in the face of Bismarck's increasing dictatorial attitude. As Bronsart concludes the entry:

> Had I done the demanded letters, even if I had weakened it as much as possible and rendered it colourless, it would have been approved and sent. Then Count Bismarck would sit in the saddle. He knows very well how to ride, as he once said about Germany. Where this ride would have taken us is not in doubt.[149]

Albrecht von Stosch, now Lieutenant General himself and Commissary-General in the High Command, took part in the dramas between the army and Bismarck. He reported to his wife the reaction of Bismarck to all the frustrations:

> Bismarck is furious that the military delay disturbs very nastily his political combinations; the King has more than enough of conflicts and would like to take a day off. Both unload their anger or discomfort on the patient Moltke, who is never crude but gets sick from inner fury. The King fears Bismarck's rage, Moltke wraps his anger in aristocratic silence. Roon becomes more ill every day and demands urgently the bombardment.[150]

The next day Bismarck clashed with the General Staff again, as Bronsart recorded, 'the civil servant in the cuirassier jacket becomes more impudent every day and General Roon functions in theses efforts as his true *famulus*. The only question is do we answer very clearly or not answer at all. Probably the latter will happen.'[151] Bismarck summoned Waldersee to see him the day after Christmas. Bismarck unloaded all his grievances to this well-connected adjutant of the King:

> Yesterday Bismarck sent word that he wanted to see me. I found him in his room which serves as living and bed room and was dreadfully overheated. He sat in a long dressing gown, smoked a big cigar, looked as if he were really suffering. He was visibly upset... Then he began to talk in the following way,

'Every thing is made as difficult as possible for me. There, to begin with Grand Duke of Baden and the Duke of Coburg intrigue with the Crown Prince and are on the way to making a mess of the German question... The General Staff refuses to inform me of the most important things; events, which are of the greatest importance for me, on which I have to base my decisions, are concealed from me. I shall have to ask the King to change all that.' He grumbled about this chapter, which I know well, with the greatest violence. His eyes grew bigger. Sweat formed on his brow. He looked seriously disturbed. I fear that he will become dangerously ill because this kind of excitability is not natural. In addition to the heavy cigars that he smokes, I saw from the bottle that he offered me that he drinks very strong wine.[152]

On New Year's Eve an extended Military Council took place in the King's rooms to hammer out a decision: to bombard or not to bombard Paris. The Crown Prince, who opposed 'this wretched bombardment', found himself on the losing side and had to accept the decision. As commanding officer of the III Army he consulted his own staff about the starting date and fixed 4 January 1871 for the beginning of the bombardment. In his war diary, he then entered his despair at what Bismarck had done to Germany's place in the world.

We are deemed capable of every wickedness and the distrust of us grows more and more pronounced. Nor is this the consequence of this War only—so far has the theory, initiated by Bismarck and for years holding the stage, of 'Blood and Iron' brought us! What good to us is all power, all martial glory and renown, if hatred and mistrust meet us at every turn, if every step we advance in our development is a subject for suspicion and grudging? Bismarck has made us great and powerful but he has robbed us of our friends, the sympathies of the world, and—our conscience.[153]

The 4th of January arrived. The Crown Prince wrote:

The eager anticipation with which from daybreak on we watched for the first shot was frustrated by an impenetrable fog, that refused to clear even for one instant, so that there was no real daylight whatever. At the same time an icy wind was blowing that covered the whole landscape with hoar frost.[154]

The next day 'was lit today by bright sunshine, so at quarter after eight this morning the first shell from Battery No. 8 fell on Paris'.[155] The bombardment made no difference to 'the disunity that exists in the highest regions', as Stosch wrote,[156] and on 8 January the Crown Prince found Moltke 'deeply offended at Count Bismarck's arbitrary and despotic attitude... the Federal Chancellor is resolved to decide everything himself, without paying the slightest heed to what experts have to say.'[157] The next day, 9 January 1871, marked the 50th anniversary of Albrecht von Roon's military service but, as the Crown Prince wrote, 'his terrible asthma, which for the last fortnight has been complicated by catarrh... is so indescribably severe that every day he gets choking fits... Count Bismarck is only just recovering from nervous rheumatic pains in the feet that set up a nervous irritation in every part of his body—a doubly unwelcome state of things in such all-important days.'[158] The only one of the Triumvirate who made modern Germany, who continued to function normally was General Count von Moltke.

The Crown Prince took it upon himself to organize a reconciliation between Molte and Bismarck and invited them both to a private dinner in his Headquarters, where the two grand figures really had it out:

> Both talked quite plainly to the other and Moltke, generally so sparing of words, speaking in tones of reproach and quite eloquently, upbraided the Federal Chancellor, brought forward all the grievances he had already confided to me on the 8TH; the other protested in return, and I had repeatedly to interfere to bring back the conversation into smoother water... Then Bismarck attacked the General on his tenderest point, developing the theory that after Sedan we should have stayed on in Champagne to await further developments and ought never to have gone to Paris.[159]

While the war dragged on and eroded the tempers and health of the protagonists, political changes took place with rapidity at home in Berlin and in the new Germany about to be born. All the important actors were not in Berlin and the Reichstag had a period of absentee control to counteract. Two developments took place in December. On 13 December 1870, forty-eight members of the lower house of the Prussian Landtag formed the 'Fraction of the Centre'. The first chairman was Bismarck's old friend Karl Friedrich von Savigny. Among the main leaders were the brothers Peter und August Reichensperger, Hermann von Mallinckrodt, Ludwig Windthorst, Friedrich Wilhelm Weber, and Philipp Ernst Maria Lieber. Though it soon came to be known as the Catholic Centre Party, none of the founders intended it to be just that as the Bavarian Deputy, Edmund Jörg (1819–1901)[160] explained some years later: 'do not forget that the Zentrum has always guarded against being called the "Catholic" Party. Otherwise how would Windthorst have come along with his Hanoverians?'[161]

While the siege of Paris and progress in the war had come to a standstill, the movement to unify Germany got a powerful new impetus from the victories over France in which southern German and Saxon troops had distinguished themselves in the 'national patriotic war'. The North German Federation had to mutate and become something grander to suit the completion of national unity. In mid-October, Captain Count Berchem, adjutant to Prince Luitpold of Bavaria, approached Robert von Keudell at headquarters to ask him confidentially if 'in my view the situation was opportune for a proposal that the presidency of the Bund be decorated by an imperial crown. I replied that to my knowledge the Chancellor had never expressed an opinion on the question but I felt confident that such a suggestion would be highly welcome. The Chief approved the answer.'[162] Ludwig II, the King of Bavaria, would take the initiative if he got certain concessions from Bismarck: money and territory. An equerry of the Bavarian king, Major Max Count von Holnstein, made two trips to headquarters in November to negotiate. Bismarck offered no territory but he paid the King a large sum of money, 300,000 marks from the secret Guelph fund that Bismarck had, in effect, stolen from the Hanoverian king. These payments to the Bavarian King continued until 1886 when the King died. The payments remained entirely secret, and were, in effect, a royal bribe. Then Bismarck gave Count von Holnstein the text of a letter which the Bavarian king would address to William I.[163] The letter duly arrived at headquarters. On 4 December 'Prince Luitpold presented the Federal Field Marshall a letter from King Ludwig of Bavaria in which he gave expression 'to the wish that a German Empire be re-established and also the title of Emperor'. It was known that the King had been consulted and achieved the consent of all the members of the Federation.[164] On the following day in Berlin, 5 December, Karl Rudolf Friedenthal (1827–90), one of the leaders of the Bismarckian Free Conservatives in the North German Reichstag,[165] got hold of a copy of the letter and gave it to Delbrück, who intended to proclaim it and thus astound the Reichstag. Bebel described what happened, as Delbück rose in a portentous way and announced, 'The day before yesterday His Royal Highness Prince Luitpold of Bavaria had presented to His Majesty the King of Prussia a letter from His Majesty the King of Bavaria with the following content... Delbrück stopped. He could not recall in which pocket he had stuck the letter. In highest agitation he searched all his pockets, a spectacle which provoked enormous hilarity in the whole house. Eventually he found it but the effect had fizzled.'[166]

On 7 December the official press published the text as well. The King of Bavaria urged upon King William the need to 'restore the German Empire and the worth of the Imperial title'. The King of Bavaria had consulted all the other German princes to strengthen the appeal.[167] In the following week Bismarck complained to Johanna that the 'princes—and even my most gracious one—plague me with their constant business with all those little difficulties which are linked to the very simple "Kaiser question" by monarchical prejudices and useless finery.'[168] On 14 December the Reichstag of the North German Federation addressed the King in a petition: 'United with the Princes of Germany, the North German Reichstag draws near with the supplication that it may please Your Majesty through the accept-ance of the German Imperial Crown to consecrate the work of unification.'[169] Hans von Kleist wrote to Moritz von Blanckenburg that he was disgusted that the 'Jew Lasker' had been chosen to prepare the draft of the motion. 'Then you will have to take him with you and make him your speaker at Versailles.'[170]

The separatists in the South German kingdoms tried to sabotage the new Reich and the Kings of Saxony and Württemberg dragged their feet. Bismarck engineered the next and very effective step. On the 17th the assembled Princes sent King William a petition to tell him that they had all agreed on the Imperial crown and on the next day, 18 December 1870, Dr Eduard Simson, President of the North German Reichstag led a delegation to petition the King to accept the title of Emperor. The King, much moved, read out a reply which Bismarck had composed and accepted the offer.[171]

The matter now moved to the parliaments of the south German states. In Württemberg and Baden, the measure passed easily but in Bavaria opposition grew. On 11 January the debate began. The Patriot Party denounced Prussia and its militarism. A fierce debate followed and on 21 January the motion passed with the necessary majority but by a margin of only two votes.[172]

The 18th of January 1871 had been chosen as the ceremonial day for the proclamation of the new Reich. The date recalled the day in 1701 when the Hohenzollern dynasty at last became royal. The Elector Frederick III of Brandenburg became Frederick I, King in Prussia (in 1713 the important 'of' replaced 'in'). The coronation of 1701 was the most glorious and expen-sive ceremony ever celebrated in that frugal state up to that point.[173] As 18 January 1871 approached, Bismarck ran into an infuriating new difficulty. The King insisted on the title of Emperor *of* Germany, not German Emperor, which Bismarck had painfully secured from the Reichstag and the German princes. The King stubbornly refused to concede the traditional grandeur of Emperor *of* Germany for the threadbare German Emperor. The Crown Prince on 16 January found his father

excited, disturbed and anxious beyond all belief; he says himself that his inclination to look on the dark side of things has in these truly critical days nota-
bly increased... Von Schleinitz, the Minister of the Household, has arrived;
nevertheless, again today nothing whatever has been settled, and I cannot yet
get any inkling of what exactly is going to be done the 18th January. Nothing
can be quietly thought out and arranged here, for either decisions are indefi-
nitely postponed or else they are slurred over.[174]

The next day matters came to a head, as the Crown Prince wrote in
his diary:

In the afternoon a meeting was held at the King's quarters, which Count
Bismarck, Minister of the Household von Schleinitz and I attended. When
Count Bismarck met von Schleinitz in the ante-room, he told him pretty
sharply he really did not understand what the Federal Chancellor in conjunc-
tion with the Minister of the Household would have to discuss with the King.
In an over-heated room the discussion dragged on for three hours over the
title the Emperor was to bear, the appellation of the heir to the throne, the
relation of the Royal family, the Court and Army to the Emperor, etc. With
regard to the Imperial title, Count Bismarck admitted that in the discussions
as to conditions, the Bavarian Deputies and Plenipotentiaries had already
refused to agree to the designation 'Emperor of Germany', and that finally to
please them, but all the same *without consulting his Majesty*, he had substituted
that of 'German Emperor'. This designation, with which no special idea is
connected, was as little to the King's liking as it was to mine, and we did all
we possibly could to secure the 'of Germany' in lieu of it; however, Count
Bismarck stuck to his point, that, as this title would be adopted simply to
secure a combination with the Bavarians... in the greatest agitation he [the
King—JS] went on to say he could not describe to us the despairing mood
he was in, as tomorrow he must bid farewell to the old Prussia to which he
alone clung and always would cling. At this point sobs and tears interrupted
his words.[175]

The 18th of January 1871 dawned grey and lowering but as the honour
guards marched beneath the King's window a ray of sunlight came through
which lifted the King's black mood. The ceremony took place in the Palace
of Versailles in the Hall of Mirrors and an overflow into the *Salon de la Paix*.
A simple field altar had been erected on a platform in the well of the hall at
which the King stood covered in all his orders and decorations. Paul Bronsart
von Schellendorf observed with amusement, that 'the improvised altar stood
right next to a naked Venus, a relationship which in the Palace of Versailles
cannot easily be avoided.'[176]

Many of the officers, including the Crown Prince, could not get into gala and appeared in service boots and field dress. No rehearsal had been possible and the order to the men 'off helmets for prayer' had been forgotten, which the Crown Prince remembered at the last moment and gave out loud. Chaplain Rogge, pastor in Potsdam and Roon's brother-in-law, gave 'a rather tactless and tedious historical religious disquisition'. After the 'Te Deum' and a simple address by the King, William I, followed by the assembled princes, moved back to a special platform, where they stood on either side of the King:

> Count Bismarck came forward, looking in the grimmest of humours, and read out in an expressionless business-like way and without any trace of warmth or feeling for the occasion, the address 'to the German People'. At the words, 'Enlarger of the Empire', I noticed a quiver stir the whole assemblage, which otherwise stood there without a word. Then the Grand Duke of Baden came forward with unaffected, quiet dignity that is so peculiarly his and with uplifted hand cried in a loud voice: 'Long live His Imperial Majesty the Emperor William!' A thundering hurrah at least six times repeated shook the room, while the flags and standards waved over the head of the new Emperor of Germany [*sic!*—JS] and 'Heil Dir im Siegerkranz' rang out.[177]

Thus Bismarck lived the moment of his greatest triumph, the proclamation of the German Empire, in a foul temper, clear to everybody in the Hall of Mirrors. As Lucius von Ballhausen heard from Bismarck later, 'His Majesty took the opposition to the latter title so badly [German Emperor] that on the day of the proclamation of the Empire, he cut him completely.'[178] Nor were the princes assembled full of joy. Prince Otto of Bavaria, heir to the throne, said: 'I cannot even describe to you how infinitely sad and hurt I felt during the ceremony ... Everything was so cold, so proud, so glittering, so showy and swaggering and heartless and empty.'[179] That evening, Bismarck returned from the ceremonial dinner, as Holstein recalled years later,

> I can still hear Prince Bismarck's angry outburst on the evening of 18 July, when he spoke of the tactless sermon preached by pastor Rogge (Countess Roon's brother). He had chosen a text which ran: 'Come hither, ye Princes, and be chastised.' Certainly not a happy choice. Bismarck said: 'I've said to myself more than once, why can't I get at this parson? Every speech from the throne has first to be considered word by word, yet this parson can say just what comes into his head.' In lighter vein, by contrast, was Bismarck's tale of how vain young Schwarzburg (nicknamed 'Prince of Arcadia')

addressed the assembled royal personages with the words: 'Greetings to you, fellow vassals'.[180]

Nor was joy universal in the rest of the royal family. The row between the King and Bismarck had led to the peculiar situation that Queen Augusta had not been informed that she had been elevated to the rank of Empress, as Crown Princess Vicky wrote to Queen Victoria on 20 January:

> I was going to tell you by the Empress' (Queen's) own desire that she knew nothing whatever of the adoption of the Imperial title on the 18th nor of the Proclamation. The Emperor is so averse to the whole thing that he did not like it spoken of beforehand and no one else took the initiative of informing us here what was going to be done. Of course this was an embarrassing and awkward position for my mother-in-law—who resented the proceedings very much. I had a deal of difficulty in calming her down. She calls me to witness her having known nothing until the day came . . . You say you are glad that my Mama-in-law and I get on well now together. The wretchedness of my life when we do not, you do not know. I am only too glad when she will let me be on a comfortable footing with her. . . . I feel a deep pity for her as nature has given her a character and temper which must tend to unhappiness and *Unbefriedigung* wherever she be, and she had many a sore and bitter hour to go through during her life.[181]

On 23 January Jules Favre arrived at Versailles to negotiate the final capitulation of the French Republic, which Bismarck conducted absolutely on his own, with only a few technical advisers. The capitulation was signed on 28 January and the Prussian army now had to provision the starving city. Bismarck made that more difficult by his incalculable outbursts of rage, which nobody could escape. The peacemaker, Commissary-General Albrecht von Stosch, found himself accused of using state money to provision Paris. Bismarck had demanded that he be prosecuted for criminal negligence. Two days later Bismarck asked him to carry out the provisioning of Paris, as if nothing had happened.[182] The Crown Prince despaired over the situation:

> Count Bismarck has won for himself the reputation of being the instigator of all the cruel reprisals we have, alas, been forced to carry out; they even say of him that he means to establish a reign of terror in Paris of quite another sort from what Gambetta's was. Occasion is certainly given for such suppositions by the monstrous maxims and savage expressions one hears openly given utterance to here, and which his wife repeats in Berlin . . . so impossible is it to count on Count Bismarck and so fitful his policy that nobody can form a clear conception of his views, still less feel any confidence in his secret plans.[183]

Paul Bronsart von Schellendorf had no doubt about Bismarck's 'secret plans', as he wrote in his diary on 25 January 1871:

> General Moltke, whom posterity will recognize as one of the greatest field commanders of all time, falls victim to the ambition of a talented but inwardly base personality who knows no rest until he, as a modern *major domus*, has insured that all respectable existence in his environment has been crushed.[184]

Now that the capitulation had been signed, the vexed issue of the French reparation payment began. On 8 February the Prussian State Ministry set the French reparations at 1 billion thaler (3 billion francs), 95 per cent of which was earmarked for the army. Otto Camphausen (1812–96), former President of the Seehandlung, who had become Bismarck's Finance Minister in 1869, after he discarded 'the Gold Uncle' von der Heydt,[185] made the claim very forcefully:

> The German nation had after all suffered so many additional losses in blood and material goods which are beyond all accounting that it is entirely justifiable to assess the price of the war generously and in addition to the estimated sum to demand an appropriate surcharge for the incalculable damages. The State Ministry concurred.[186]

Bismarck, as usual, chose his own methods to accomplish the end and sent his private banker, Gerson Bleichröder, to act as intermediary with French financial circles and the new Republic. Bronsart found the presence of this Jew absolutely repellent and recorded two entries in his War Diary to give vent to his feeling:

> Now he [Bismarck] confers eagerly with the Jew Bleichröder, his banker, whom he lets come here for *official* discussions concerning the war indemnity to be demanded from Paris. One wonders for what purpose we have an institution like the Prussian State Bank if the Chancellor's *Privatjude* and not one of its officials operates as adviser in state business . . . Bleichröder was at the General Staff this morning. In his buttonhole he wore an artistically arranged rosette of many colours which attested the *Ritterschaft* of many Christian orders. Like a true Jew he bragged about the private audiences he has had with the King, about his other exclusive connections, about the credit people like him and Rothschild can command etc. About the political situation and the inclinations of Count Bismarck he was sufficiently informed; now he wanted to enlist the help of the General Staff and gain access even to Count Moltke.

On 26 February 1871 a preliminary peace between France and Germany was signed at Versailles. French reparations were set at 5 billion francs. Bleichröder wrote to the Crown Prince: 'Count Bismarck would seem to have conducted himself during the negotiations with monstrous brusquerie and intentional rudeness, and by such behaviour to have shocked the Paris Rothschild who in the first instance addressed him in French.[187] On 4 March 1871 *The Economist* commented on the reparations:

> to extract huge sums of money as the consequence of victory suggests a belief that money may be the object as well as the accidental reward of battle. A flavour of huckstering is introduced into the relations between States which degrades the character of statesmen, and is sure sooner or later to infect the character of the people.[188]

On the last day of the Prussian stay in Versailles, the Crown Prince tried to convince Bismarck to nominate the Baden aristocrat, Freiherr von Roggenbach, Governor of Alsace. Bismarck, who undoubtedly knew through his many spies that Roggenbach had a close relationship to the Queen, naturally rejected the name. The Crown Prince, not inaccurately, concluded that Bismarck intended to appoint 'only persons of a sort to carry out his orders directly and implicitly. I gathered the impression today more than ever that he means to play the "All-Powerful", "the Richelieu" in these countries.'[189]

The Emperor and the Crown Prince arrived in Potsdam on 17 March 1871 after a rapturous reception at every stop in Germany. The victory and the unification of Germany had dazzled the German people across the political spectrum. On 21 March the State Opening of the new Reichstag elected in early March took place. The occasion was unusually grand as befitting the first assembly of a united German parliament. Baroness Hildegard von Spitzemberg, as wife of the Württemberg envoy, had a good seat in the diplomatic balcony,

> where in very nice company we could watch the whole scene. In contrast to usual practice, Princes, Princesses and the Empress were arranged around the throne on the left and on the right…Just before the king came Moltke with the sword, Roon with the sceptre, Peuker with the Reich orb, Redern with the crown, Wrangel flanked by Kameke and Podbielski with the flag. The Kaiser was very moved as he began the speech from the throne, which was interrupted with lively bravos by the evidently excited assembly. It also struck me that the Kaiser removed his helmet before reading the speech, whereas he normally keeps his head covered. The entire ceremony was beautiful and gripping.[190]

On the following day, the Emperor raised Bismarck to the status of prince (*Fürst*) and the next evening the Bismarck family entertained a grand gathering to mark the occasion and the Spitzembergs from next door attended the party.

> Carl and I in a large gathering of gentlemen at Bismarcks. On the day of the opening, the Kaiser '*princed*' the count, which is all fine and good, but in order that it is not a gift borne by the Greeks there will have to be a corresponding endowment of which as yet not a sign. In house they consider the things quite calmly enough, the 'Serene Highness' seems to him as odd as it does to us.[191]

Among the odder honours that Bismarck received in 1871 as national hero was the dedication to him of a fish. In Stralsund, the trader and brewer Johann Wiechmann had established a prosperous fish cannery. In 1853 he opened a store and in the backyard his wife Karoline pickled fresh, filleted Baltic herring and sold them in wooden boxes. Herr Wiechmann wrote to Bismarck on his birthday in 1871, presented him with a barrel of his best pickled herring, and humbly asked if he could call them 'Bismarck Herrings'. The Prince generously agreed and this unusual and lasting monument to the great man joined the paperweights, statues, and portraits.[192]

On 16 April 1871 the Reichstag approved the new Constitution, and the first phase of Bismarck's great career had been concluded. The Genius-Statesman had transformed European politics and had unified Germany in eight and a half years more. And he had done by sheer force of personality, by his brilliance, ruthlessness, and flexibility of principle. He had again, as in 1866 'beaten them All!'

9

The Decline Begins: Liberals and Catholics

The victory over France and the foundation of the new Reich marked the high point of Bismarck's career. He had achieved the impossible and his genius and the cult of that genius had no limits. When he returned to Berlin in March 1871, he had become immortal, but he now faced a completely different challenge: to preserve his creation and to make it work. As a result, the second stage of Bismarck's career has a completely different substance. His days filled up with the detail of government: tax rates, local government reorganization, unification of the legal system, factory inspection, educational regulations, the charges for postal transfers and packages, railroad finances, budgets and estimates. For the next nineteen years, more than twice as long as the unification period, the daily business of government occupied his time and energy. In it the same Bismarck operated with the same ruthlessness and lack of principle that had marked the heroic days but in different areas. Since he could never delegate authority, hated opposition, and considered—rightly—that he was smarter than everybody else, he ran into obstacles, both personal and material, at every stage. Nobody understood him, nobody carried out his wishes properly, and nobody could be trusted. He fell into a more or less continuous rage against everybody and everything.

Preservation of his great achievement meant constant watchfulness for threats from abroad as well as enemies at home. The great powers had reason to fear the new Germany. Disraeli summed up their feelings in a prophetic speech from the opposition Front Bench on 2 February of 1871:

> The war represents the German revolution, a greater political event than the French revolution. I don't say a greater, or as great a social event. What its social consequences may be are in the future. Not a single principle in the

management of our foreign affairs, accepted by all statesmen for guidance up to six months ago, any longer exists. There is not a diplomatic tradition that has not been swept away. You have a new world, new influences at work, new and unknown dangers and objects with which to cope... The balance of power has been utterly destroyed, and the country that suffers most, and feels the effect of this great change most, is England.[1]

The French and Austrians might well have contested the idea that England, which had not been defeated by Prussia, 'suffers most, and feels the effect of this great change most', but in a deeper sense, Disraeli was right. He saw a fundamental reality which the world would slowly and painfully understand. The *Pax Britannica* rested on the European Balance of Power. Metternich had known that and worked with Lord Castlereagh in 1814–15 to make sure that no one state gained too much from the defeat of Napoleon. Bismarck had destroyed that balance. Between 1871 and 1914 the German Empire would become an economic superpower. Its coal, steel, and iron production grew larger than the entire production of its continental rivals put together. Whereas in 1871 Germany and France had roughly the same population, by 1914 Germany had half again as many people, better educated, better disciplined, and more productive than any people in the world. In science, technology, industrial chemistry, electrical engineering, optical instruments, metallurgy, and many other areas, Germany had become the most advanced manufacturer anywhere. 'Made in Germany' meant the very highest quality. By 1914 the Reich had the most powerful army and had constructed the second largest navy. Germany had achieved a supremacy in Europe which only the French Empire of Napoleon had reached at a few moments but Germany had a much more powerful industrial and technological foundation.

Bismarck had explained to Leopold von Gerlach that one could not play chess if 16 out of the 64 squares were blocked in advance. Politics as the art of the possible required flexibility. Yet Bismarck's own achievements made that flexibility harder to attain. Bismarck saw that clearly in the Peace of Prague in 1866. By rejecting the King's wish for a victory parade in Vienna and by refusing to take Habsburg territory, Bismarck quite explicitly left the door open for an eventual reconciliation with the Habsburg Monarchy. In 1879 that reconciliation became an alliance. He equally explicitly, as we have seen, rejected a soft peace with France. He insisted as part of the peace on the annexation of the two provinces of Alsace and Lorraine. Here even the Crown Princess, his enemy on most matters, backed the decision, as she wrote to Queen Victoria in December 1870:

About Alsace and Lorraine there is but one voice all over Germany, that if we do not keep them (or part of them), we shall be doing a wrong thing, as we shall be exposing ourselves to the same calamity as threatened us in July— being attacked and overrun by the French whenever it suits them, as our frontiers are too weak to keep them out.[2]

Whatever the motives that made Bismarck agree to the annexation of the two French territories, he could no longer play chess with all the squares open. Sixteen of the sixty-four had been blocked permanently: France would never ally with Germany as long the territories remained in German hands. France had one foreign policy—revenge—and one goal—the 'lost' territories. If Germany—so new, so fragile in Bismarck's eyes—were to be protected from its enemies, it would need allies but which? England? Unlikely. The traditional English distrust of continental Europe, still present today in Euro-sceptic attitudes to the European Union, would make it at best a temporary collaborator but never a reliable ally. It followed that the only defence against French revenge must lie in the recreation of the Metternich coalition of conservative powers, a league of the Three Emperors—the Tsar, the Habsburg Emperor, and the new Hohenzollern Emperor—against democracy and revolution. In the 1870s he used his matchless skills to do that.

The second stage of Bismarck's career differs from the first eight and a half years. Peace replaces war in international affairs. Liberalism takes the place of conservatism in domestic matters. Both in diplomacy and in domestic policies the plot thickens as the details of treaties and bureaucratic administration multiply and blur the clear narrative lines of the story. The traditional sources for study of Bismarck's career reflect this division. The editors of the 'New Friedrichsruh Edition' of the collected works, which began publication in 2004, point out that in the nineteen volumes of the original *Collected Works*, published between 1924 and 1934, five volumes (2,860 pages) cover the eight years of the foundation of the Reich, while only one volume (449 pages) covers domestic policy during the two decades of his career after 1870. The editors of the original *Collected Works* declared in 1924 that they wished to build 'a monument that Germany erects to the Founder of the Reich in the moment of its deepest humiliation'.[3] Hence the omission of documents which showed Bismarck in unfavourable postures or acts.

The years 1871 to 1890 mark the decline of Bismarck's political position. Not even he could run a modern state by himself and he would allow nobody to share it with him. Even his 'combinations' in international affairs

could not hold back tides of nationalism and popular pressure on governments. The gigantic figure at war with all the forces of his age makes an
arresting image but the actual stages remain complicated and not all developments move in the same way or direction. The narrative that this biography follows tries to highlight the contours of the years 1871 to 1890 by
looking at the nineteen years in stages. The first period, the Liberal era leads
to the struggle against the Roman Catholic Church and the final break
between Bismarck and his Protestant conservative friends. In those years the
'Great Depression' begins in 1873 and worsens toward the end of the decade. That leads to a 'great turn' in 1878–9 when Bismarck drops his liberal
allies, makes peace with Roman Catholic Church, attacks Socialism, and
introduces welfare and social security. This chapter takes the story to the
historic break in the late 1870s.

One of the forces he could not control was the voter. The very first elections to the Reichstag took place on 3 March 1871, when 51 per cent of the
adult males eligible to vote went to the polls. 18.6 per cent of them voted
for the Centre Party which with its 63 seats became at a stroke the second
strongest party in the chamber. By 1874 it would grow to ninety plus representatives, a solid, anti-Bismarckian block. Of the 382 deputies, 202 could
be called Liberal, though there were several Liberal parties. The National
Liberal Party with 100 seats and 30.2 per cent of the vote became the largest
party. The Conservatives divided 23 per cent of the vote between the old
Kreuzzeitung Party with 14.1 per cent and the smaller pro-Bismarckian
German Reich Party with 8.9 per cent.[4] Among the 37 Reich Party members were Robert Lucius von Ballhausen, elected as a Reich Party
Conservative for Erfurt, and Bismarck's staff member Robert von Keudell
elected for Königsberg-Neumark, who on election also joined the Reich
Party. On hearing the news of his election Bismarck told Keudell: 'I do not
care which fraction you go into; I know that when you can you will vote
for me.'[5] At the height of his power and fame, Bismarck's endorsement only
garnered 8.9 per cent of the vote. In all the elections between 1871 and 1890
the Bismarckian party only once managed to achieve double figures and
that in the panic election of 1878 when the it won 13.6 per cent of the vote
and gained 56 seats. Thereafter it declined steadily and in the election of
February 1890, a month before Bismarck fell from power, it only won
20 seats or 6.6 per cent of the vote. Not exactly a monument to the Reich's
founder from the German voter.

The other crisis in this phase of Bismarck's career had begun even before the Franco-Prussian war finished. The Prussian victory at Sedan not only destroyed the Empire of Napoleon III but allowed the Kingdom of Italy to seize Rome on 22 September 1870. The new French Republic had withdrawn the French garrison stationed there since 1849 and maintained by Napoleon III as a gesture to his own Catholic supporters. Bismarck's third war indirectly ended the sovereignty of the Roman pontiff over the eternal city, a sovereignty which had lasted from the fall of Rome. The loss of temporal power coincided with the greatest ever public extension of papal spiritual power in the declaration of Infallibility promulgated in July 1870 at the first Vatican Council. The Crown Prince had noted the connection in his war diary on 22 September 1870:

> The most important news I heard today was that the troops of the King of Italy have occupied Rome. So at last the Roman Question is done with . . . The miserable regime of priestly domination is at an end and once more the triumph of German arms has done the Italians a good service . . . The occupation of Rome within a few weeks of the publication of the dogma of Infallibility is a strange irony of Fate.[6]

The connection made it certain that the Vatican and the new Prussian, Protestant Reich would collide. Even before the election of the first Reichstag, on 18 February 1871, the Centre Party in the Prussian lower house sent a message to the Emperor asking for his support in the restoration of the 'temporal power', as Papal sovereignty in Rome was called. The Emperor replied indirectly in the Speech from the Throne when he declared that the German state would not intervene in the affairs of others, a sentiment reinforced by the Address in Reply adopted by the Landtag. Only the Centre voted against it.[7] During a vigorous debate in the new Reichstag in early April 1871, the majority rejected by 223 to 59 a Centre motion to enshrine in the new Reich constitution six articles from the Prussian constitution on freedom of speech, freedom of the press, of assembly, of religious belief, of science, and the autonomy of religious institutions.[8] The majority Liberals allowed anti-Catholicism to trump their liberal principles, though there was something odd about the party of the Church militant in its most assertive phase asking for freedoms in Germany not accorded by the Vatican to faithful Catholics and actually condemned in the Syllabus of Errors.

Bismarck reacted very strongly. In a confidential dispatch to Georg Freiherr von Werthern (1816–95), Prussian minister in Munich, he wrote that the debate showed 'a hostile tendency to the Reich government . . . which will be forced for its part to act with aggression against the Party'.[9] Margaret Lavinia Anderson comments on Bismarck's violent reaction that 'for Bismarck with his nervous sense of the fragility of his new creation, the Zentrum was by definition subversive . . . too powerful to be left autonomous . . . Bismarck struck at what for him was the root of its power, the Catholic Church, launching what Heinrich Bornkamm has aptly called "a domestic preventive war for ensuring the empire".'[10] Thus began what came to be called the 'War over Culture' or *Kulturkampf*.

Bismarck's aggression against the Centre had the effect of strengthening it. Margaret Lavinia Anderson has analysed the voting patterns in those districts from which Centre deputies came and found that of the 397 seats in the Reichstag 104 were *Stammsitze* (trunk or solid seats, i.e. safe) and seldom changed hands. The Centre voters concentrated in certain areas of the 104 such districts and thus 73 of the Centre's deputies represented safe seats. Hence the core of the party never changed over the rest of Bismarck's period in office. Between 1874 and 1890 76 per cent of the party's seats were solidly safe. This made sure that the aristocratic founders continued to hold sway and there was no influx of new elements. The grand gentlemen of the party tended to be less obedient to the parish priests and bishops than the lesser flock. If Bismarck had been more subtle, he might have gradually pried the party apart from the hierarchy. His aggression solidified those bands. Unless he abolished universal suffrage or revoked the constitution, he could not win the battle against the Catholic Centre Party and the Roman Catholic population in the new, much more Catholic, unified Germany.

The new Italian Kingdom had expropriated cloisters and church property and seized papal palaces on the Quirinale. The Pope was once again a prisoner as in 1809 Pius VII had been. The temporal power was abolished and Pope Pius IX went into inner exile. The great gates of the Vatican closed in mourning. The new Italian parliament in 1871 passed the Law of Guarantees as a gesture of good will and offered a large monetary compensation for the loss of the Vatican's property. Pius IX's reaction was an encyclical UBI NOS (On Pontifical States) promulgated on 15 May 1871. In it, the Pope rejected all relations with the godless Italian state and the struggle intensified in the 1870s. Crown Prince Frederick was wrong. The Roman Question was not over; it had just become much, much worse. The *dissidio* (dispute) on the Roman question poisoned church–state relations in Italy for fifty years. In 1874 the Pope declared it *non-expedit* (not desirable) for devout Catholics to take any part in the government of the Kingdom of Italy. In 1877 the decree was strengthened to *non-licet*; it was now not allowed for a Catholic to serve the blasphemous kingdom in any capacity, even to vote in its elections.

The Liberal State rejected everything that Pius IX represented. It proclaimed its commitment to free speech, freedom of religion, freedom of the press, separation of church and state, tolerance of all religious beliefs and none, freedom of scientific inquiry, Darwinian evolutionary theory (*Origin of Species* appeared in 1859 and was an instant best-seller), secular education, civil marriage, and civil divorce. During the 1870s, in Germany, Italy, Switzerland, France, and Austria, the state defended these values against the Roman Catholic Church and its priests. It was the holy war of liberalism against the Black International of Catholicism. Bishops and priests were arrested or expelled from countries, even in democratic Switzerland.

Bismarck, as usual, followed two policies, one an aggressive and punishing reaction to the Catholic Centre Party, and the other caution and moderation in dealing with the Vatican. On 1 May 1871 he wrote to Joseph Count von Brassier de Saint Simon, the German ambassador in Florence (where the interim Royal Italian capital still was before the final move to Rome), to ask him to warn the Italian government that its acts would affect

> not only its own parties and its own parliament in its own land but it must reckon with the Catholic Church outside its own borders and for those Powers who are friendly to it. Clever and tactful behaviour especially with respect to a magnanimous consideration of the person of the Pope, will make it possible to preserve the existing friendly relations without offending the feeling of their Catholic subjects.[11]

Bismarck showed here that subtle and tactful side of his diplomacy, as he tried to insert a wedge between the German Catholic political party and the faithful by being harsh to the former and considerate to the latter, the Holy See. The *Kulturkampf* arose everywhere as a problem of international relations, national solidarity, and domestic policy. In any country with a substantial Catholic population, what sort of schools, what sort of hospitals (nurses or nuns?), what sort of poor relief, what marriage ceremony and divorce provisions, what charitable status for churches and convents, in short, the whole apparatus of daily life for the Catholic faithful became the subject of intense debate. The Roman Church and all its traditional pastoral and ecclesiastical activities challenged the growing power, competence, and intrusiveness of the modern state. The *Kulturkampf* represented the most serious challenge to Bismarck's authority during the rest of his career, and it is a rich irony that the reconciliation between Bismarck and Windthorst in March 1890 led to his dismissal.

During June of 1871 Bismarck's irritation with the Centre Party hardened and he became particularly annoyed at Adalbert von Krätzig (1819–87), head of the Catholic section of the Prussian Kultusministerium (its full title was the Ministry of Religious, Educational and Medical Affairs). He told Hohenlohe on 19 June that he intended 'to expel the Krätzig clique' from the government because they protected too strongly Polish interests.[12] A few days later in Upper Silesian Königshütte, a Polish riot occurred which gave Bismarck what he needed to blame Krätzig. On 8 July 1871 the Catholic Section was dissolved and Krätzig assigned to minor duties.

In the meantime the press campaign—undoubtedly orchestrated by Bismarck—began in earnest when on 22 June 1871 a *Kreuzzeitung* article called 'Centre Party' attacked it as unpatriotic and declared that a new chapter in the struggle of 'Germanism' against 'Romanism' had begun.[13] Father Karl Jentsch (1833–1917), a priest and social activist,[14] wrote about life under the *Kulturkampf*:

> Every day the Catholic had to read in *Käseblattchen* [low level newspapers] as well as in the great newspapers that he was an enemy of the Fatherland, a little papist, a block-head and that his clergy were the scum of humanity. So he founded his own newspapers which at least did not insult him every day.[15]

Bismarck bombarded his envoy in Rome, Karl Count von Tauffkirchen-Guttenberg, (1826–95) the Bavarian minister to the Holy See, who acted for the Prussians, with letters in which the Pope and Cardinal Antonelli were reminded that the collaboration of the 'black' and 'red' parties stirred up the population in many districts. Such agitation called into question the Pope's opposition to radicalism or his professions of good will to the German Reich. On 30 June 1871 he warned Tauffkirchen that

> We see in the behaviour of this party a danger for the Church and the Pope...The aggressive tendencies of the party which controls the Church forces us to resist, in which case we shall seek our defence...If the Vatican decides to break with this party so hostile to the government and to prevent

its attacks on us, that would be welcome. If it cannot or will not do that, we reject all responsibility for the consequences.[16]

Bismarck now had to deal with one of the survivors of the 'Conflict Ministry', his *Kultusminister*, Heinrich von Mühler, a strict, orthodox, Lutheran, conservative. Bismarck, who normally avoided face-to-face confrontation with his subordinates, finally went to see von Mühler in the summer of 1871 and we have von Mühler's notes on what he said:

> He revealed to me without ambiguity his entire game and his system, which he could no longer conceal from me. His goals were: battle with the ultramontane party, in particular in the Polish territories West Prussia, Posen and Upper Silesia—Separation of church and state, separation of church and school completely. Transfer of school inspection to lay inspectors. Removal of religious instruction from the schools, not only from gymnasia but also from the primary school.... 'I know how the Kaiser stands on these matters but if you don't stir him up, I shall lead him nevertheless where I want'. Bismarck described the clash between us—outwardly once more in a calmer tone—quite rightly with the words. 'You deal with things from the religious perspective, I on the other hand from the political'.[17]

Apparently Frau von Mühler, who had been eavesdropping, dropped to her knees to pray when she heard Bismarck's intentions.[18] Von Mühler held out until January 1872 when he finally submitted his resignation. He explained his decision in a letter to Maximilian Count von Schwerin (1804–72), one of his predecessors in the Kultusministerium, who had accused Bismarck on 27 January 1863, in the Prussian Landtag that his motto was '*Macht geht vor Recht*' (power trumps justice/law—JS]).[19] Schwerin might be expected to understand von Mühler's reaction.

> Bismarck's approach in the Kulturkampf is to be explained by the entirely realistic—dare I say?—materialistic understanding which lies at the root of his entire political life. Bismarck despises all spiritual and moral levers in politics. Blood and iron—materialistic means of power—these are the factors with which he reckons. He would prefer to ban the church and religious ideas from public life and turn them into private matters. Separation of church and state, removal of the church from the school system and the school from religious instruction, these are very familiar views of his, as are the many steps he has taken and many public and private utterances in this direction, for which I have proof, make clear. He shows clearly a characteristic feature that, if not decisively anti-Christian, is at least anti-clerical and separationist and which borders on a middle ground between delusion and

enmity. And on top of that comes his overly large ambition which tolerates no opposition and no longer even respects the personal convictions of the Kaiser.[20]

The pious, very Christian von Mühler was replaced with a formidable liberal lawyer Adalbert Falk, whose name came to symbolize the *Kulturkampf*. Falk came from a Protestant pastor's family in Silesia. A child prodigy, he entered Breslau University at 16 to become a lawyer, served in various of the elected bodies in the 1860s, and made a steady but not spectacular career in the Ministry of Justice, when to his surprise on 22 January 1872 he received a summons to the Chancellor who offered him the job as *Kultusminister*. When Falk asked Bismarck what he expected of him, Bismarck replied in one of his lapidary phrases 'to restore the rights of the State against the Church and to do it with as little noise as possible'.[21] Falk served Bismarck during the entire *Kulturkampf*, drafted most of the legislation and defended it in the Landtag. Falk believed in the state as an abstract entity, what Bornkamm called 'practical Hegelianism';[22] Bismarck wanted to smash the Catholic Centre Party. The two went at the issues in completely different ways and the mixture of Bismarck's brutality and Falk's conceptual purity undoubtedly made the actual attack on German Catholicism more damaging and politically more disastrous. Falk really believed in the ideal of separation of church and state; Bismarck wanted to assert his power. By appointing Falk Bismarck indirectly made certain that his old Prussian Conservative friends would join the Catholics in defence of their Protestant patriarchal control of schools and society.

From 1872 on Falk introduced a series of stringent pieces of legislation in both Prussia and Reich. Even before his appointment an amendment to the Reich penal code made it an offence, punishable by up to two years of prison, for clergymen to make political statements from the pulpit that might endanger the peace. This anti-clerical gag law continued to be part of the German criminal code until 1953, when the Catholic Centre, now in its new guise as the Christian Democratic Party, under the old Centre politician Konrad Adenauer, finally abolished it.[23]

The next battle was fought out in February 1872 in the Prussian Landtag over the *Schulaufsichtsgesetz* (the School Supervisory Law), which required the replacement of clerical by state supervision in 'all public and private institutes of instruction'. Here was an issue that pitted Liberals against Catholics and also increasingly conservative Protestants. Eduard Lasker, the indomitable little liberal purist, challenged the house by saying that the law abolishes 'the school supervisor with rights of his own, who has the audacity to say to the State: "You have no right to prescribe for me in what way I supervise and direct the school." '[24]

The theatrical quality of the occasion was heightened by the contrast among the speakers and the intensity of the debate. All the leading speakers of the parties went to the rostrum but the main bout was that between the 250-pound giant Bismarck, sweating and swaying, and the tiny, blind Windthorst with his green, glass spectacles and his minute shape. He unnerved and annoyed Bismarck. On 24 January the Catholic deputy, August Reichensperger noted with satisfaction in his diary:

> Bismarck's irritation seems to me to be based on the fact that his project of a German national church has shipwrecked, and that the believing Protestants, for whom Windthorst in Hanover forms the bridge, are more and more joining ranks with us.[25]

On 30 January Bismarck launched a direct attack on the Catholic Centre Party in the Landtag and ended in a duel with Windthorst, which Bismarck openly lost. Windthorst caught him in one of his inconsistencies:

BISMARCK: When I returned from France, I could not consider the formation of this fraction in any other light than as a mobilization of a party against the state.

WINDTHORST: I do not know what the Minister-President regards as struggle against the state . . . But, gentlemen, I make so free as to suppose that it is not yet correct that the Minister President is the state . . . When, however, the government jerks from Right to Left at such a suspiciously hasty tempo as is happening now (for today the Minister President has proclaimed unconditionally the rule of the majority) . . . I must take my ministers from the majority [he said] . . . therefore I can take no Catholics, because Catholics are not in the majority, . . . the Zentrum's support is not possible.[26]

On 8 February Windthorst in turn attacked Bismarck for abandoning conservative and monarchical principles with the School Inspection Bill.

> These words affected Bismarck visibly. His hands shook and he needed both of them to hold a glass of water. He replied: The deputy from Meppen with an adroitness that is too perfect . . . arranges the words I have spoken to suit his momentary ends . . . I have passed my years-long examination in the service of the monarchical principle in Prussia. For the Herr Deputy, that is still—or so I hope—to come.[27]

The next day, Bismarck returned with a new attack on the Guelphs (a term to describe the Hanoverian royal family and its followers such as Windthorst) and accused the 'Guelph leadership' of stirring up trouble. He attacked Windthorst personally:

> Before the Centre Party had been founded, there existed a Fraction which people called the Meppen Fraction. It consisted, as far as I can recall of one deputy, a great general without an army, but in the meanwhile he has succeeded like Wallenstein to stamp an army out of the ground and ring it round him.[28]

and concluded that: 'for Guelph hope can only succeed when strife and subversion reign.' The President of the House, Max von Forcenbeck, gave Windthorst unlimited time for a point of personal privilege. Windthorst replied:

> such an excess of personal attacks has been directed against me, and indeed with such violence, that I am beginning to believe that I possess a significance of which, until now, I had never dreamed. [Laughter.] . . . For my part, you may be assured: I will NOT submit to this pressure. Nevertheless, it is something as yet unheard of in parliamentary history that a man of this rank spent nearly an hour in order to attack me personally.[29]

In the debate next day, 10 February 1872, the Catholic deputy, Hermann von Mallinckrodt, replied to Bismarck:

> We are proud to have in our midst so distinguished a member as the Deputy from Meppen. [Bravo!] They have annexed a pearl, Gentlemen, and we have brought that pearl into its proper setting [Very good!—in the Zentrum; and great, continuing laughter elsewhere.][30]

To which Bismarck, always quick-witted, replied mockingly:

> The honourable gentleman has called the Deputy from Meppen a pearl. I share that view in his sense completely. For me, however, the value of a pearl depends very much on its colour. In that respect I am rather choosey.[31]

On 13 February 1872 the School Supervisory Law passed the Landtag by 207 to 155.[32] The relatively narrow majority in the lower House where the Centre only had 63 deputies indicates how much opposition the bill evoked among Conservatives. It had been a victory of sorts for Windthorst. On the day of the vote, Eberhard Freiherr von Brandis, a former Hanoverian general, said with evident delight to Sir Robert Morier

What do you say about Bismarck's and Windthorst's duel? We rather think that Windthorst has had the best of it. He has become a giant, having been a liliputian and Bismarck is diminished in size and power.[33]

On 5 March 1872, the day before the School Supervisory Law went before the House of Lords, Hans von Kleist went to dinner at the Bismarcks and after the other guests had gone, they discussed the School Supervisory Law. 'In the course of the conversation the excited Prince grabbed a letter opener and made a gesture as if to divide the table cloth and cried, "if that's the way things are, it's all over between us." The die had been cast. Nothing remained to Kleist but to take his hat and go.'[34]

The next day, 6 March, Bismarck opened the debate on the School Supervisory Law in the House of Lords. He dismissed the objections of believing Christians, his old friends, about the assault by the secular state on Protestant religious education. He rejected Kleist's assertion that 'through this law the government of the state opens the gates through which the turbulent waters of unbelief in time will flood from the de-christianized State over the schools. I disdain even to go into such ideas.' The Law passed 126 for 76 against. Among the yes voters were Bismarck, Moltke, Roon, and Eberhard Stolberg, Kleist's brother-in-law.[35]

The reaction among Bismarck's former allies was bitter and angry. One of them, Andrae-Roman, expressed that bitterness in a remarkable letter of 15 February 1872 to Ludwig von Gerlach. Ferdinand Ludwig Alexander Andrae (1821–1903) came from a solid bourgeois family in Hanover. He went to Berlin and to Bonn as a student to learn agricultural theory and with a command of scientific agronomy he bought an estate in the Pomeranian district of Kolberg called Roman and from then on called himself Andrae-Roman. He met and became a close friend of Bismarck through the Pietist circle around Moritz von Blanckenburg. Andrae-Roman cut a unique figure as a bourgeois landowner and a Hanoverian among the Prussians but he served for years in the Conservative Party in the Prussian Landtag.[36] As he wrote to Gerlach,

> It is hard to see a man like Bismarck go down hill in big slides, he who openly confesses himself true to principles that he so victoriously fought with your help. History cannot offer another example, somebody for whom twenty years ago even Stahl was not conservative enough. I recall going to see him in Frankfurt—it must have been 1850 or 1851 one morning rather late and I found him in bed. Frau von Bismarck explained he had slept badly and for hours had tossed and turned with hefty groans and finally cried out: 'He is

after all only a Jew!' namely, Stahl as he then declared and said to me later. 'What do you think would have become of Stahl if he had not had Gerlach at his side? Never a Prussian Conservative.'[37]

The *Kulturkampf* poisoned Bismarck's relationships with his old friends and embittered the Catholic minority in the new Reich; Bismarck and Falk pushed on nonetheless. On 1 August 1872 Kleist wrote to Schede,

> It's not easy in such a struggle to stand up against the government, which has engaged itself so deeply. Apparently the next Landtag will have legislation before it against the Bishops. It horrifies me. Krements' sentence is right: 'Obey God more than the government.' On the other hand those measures of the Catholic Church, or a Bishop, to defend the doctrine of infallibility cannot be identified by us with God's commandments. The state law must have precedence.[38]

In the midst of these grand battles a small political event needs to be recorded. On 18 April 1871 Robert Lucius von Ballhausen (1835–1914) introduced a bill to speed packages to troops and officers in occupied France. Delbrück gave an evasive ministerial reply. Bismarck appeared late and invited Lucius to come to the Ministers' room behind the Speaker's podium.

> He spoke at such length and with such an absence of reserve, to me a total stranger, that I was surprised. It was the first time that I had talked to Bismarck alone and in his lively and confidential way he treated me as if I were an old acquaintance. It made a remarkable and captivating impression on me.[39]

This first conversation between the Chancellor and the 35-year-old medical doctor and landlord turned into a lifelong relationship which Lucius recorded in copious notes, published in 1920, unedited, six years after his death. Lucius had gone into politics after 1866, as an agricultural protectionist and lapsed Catholic; he joined the German Reich Party and served in the Landtag and Reichstag for many years.[40] Lucius moved quickly into the charmed circle of those who enjoyed the privilege to know the Prince at home. On 9 May he received an invitation this time to a political soirée and described how these occasions worked:

> he [Bismarck] gathers a large group of people around him and simply dominates the conversation, while those sitting next to him kept the threads by as it were spinning him more occasions to carry on. This sort of conversation clearly gives him pleasure and he never tires of it. The groups around him were often very interesting people. He treated every single guest with the same friendly warmth and concern. People formed groups casually and at will. There reigned an absolute social equality in the way guests were treated

and a splendid hospitality without pretence or affectation. In the many years afterwards, as I became an intimate of the house, I never noticed the slightest difference in his behaviour. He showed every guest the same courtesy and consideration. At most he might make a distinction by age.[41]

At other occasions and in private, Bismarck might do nothing but complain about how wretchedly he felt physically. This happened to Waldersee, who called on Bismarck on 27 April 1871, and found his host in bad shape.

> I went yesterday evening to Bismarck. He looks really miserable and complains also about his health. The hours in which he gets to sleep are between 7 and 12 a.m. He only really feels well for the first time each day late in the evening and then he gets to work.[42]

On 10 May 1871 Germany and France signed the peace treaty in Frankfurt. Bismarck and Count Harry Arnim, German Ambassador in Paris, signed for Germany.[43] Two days later, Bismarck received a hero's welcome in the Reichstag. Gustav von Diest (1826–1911) a strict Evangelical, noted with distaste how his 'whole nature changed... He no longer tolerated contradiction; he was accessible to flattery; but even the smallest, alleged disregard for his ego and his position exasperated him.'[44] Everything exasperated him. He lost his temper with the Reichstag about Alsace and Lorraine. He lost his temper with Moltke and the generals about the victory parade scheduled for 3 June, and blamed the Queen for not wanting to interrupt her holiday as the cause.[45]

Prussia and the Reich had to be reorganized in all sorts of ways and the Emperor-King had to approve hundreds of appointments—down to the level of heads of teacher-training institutes. All that hugely increased Bismarck's workload. Everyone of those appointments came to Bismarck either from the Household Minister down or from Delbrück in the Reich Chancellery up. Hence even in Varzin, the daily burden of work never let up. He complained to von Mühler that a certain Lizenziat August Langer in Glogau, 'an extremely worked up Infallibilist', had been appointed by the Kultusministerium to be principal of the teacher training school in Habelschwerdt, a small Silesian town. Bismarck was furious. The whole idea of the abolition of the Catholic Section in the ministry had been to prevent the attitudes of the people in that department from 'disturbing the peace in the country'. His Excellency must take care in future to put all such nominations before the State Ministry for 'a very searching' examination before they went for All-Highest approval.[46] The great Bismarck blocked the appointment of the head of a teacher-training college in a tiny community.

Summers brought no break from work, because monarchs went to the grand spas to take the waters and make treaties. August 1871 was no exception. Bismarck attended the Emperor in Bad Gastein and learned on 22 August that the King intended to meet Emperor Franz Joseph in Salzburg on 5 or 6 September, 'at which I cannot be absent'.[47] For some months Bismarck had been writing press releases and dispatches in favour of the Habsburgs and ordered the official organs to make clear that the constitutional crises in the 'Austrian half' of the now divided Austro-Hungarian Monarchy should not be understood as a crisis about nationality (which it undoubtedly was—especially Czech national rights) but about 'political currents' and, as in Germany, 'both elements, the ultramontane and the socialist, are born enemies of Germany'.[48] The Emperors William and Franz Joseph met informally in Bad Gastein on 24 August. Bismarck issued a notice to all German missions abroad to say that 'the meeting of the two Monarchs can only further contribute to show the world that the disturbance in the friendly relations, to which both lands, in contrast to the feelings of the two rulers, had been pushed by their historic developments, must now be seen as a completed and finished episode.'[49] 'Pushed' (gedrängt is the word Bismarck used) 'by their historical developments' very neatly evades the fact that 'the historical developments' stood for a war that was caused by the Chancellor who drafted the circular letter. In any event, Bismarck had the first link in place for the new conservative alliance. Between 1871 and 1879 the Austro-German friendship, carefully and patiently cultivated by Bismarck, turned into a formal alliance.

The next step involved the Tsarist Empire and Alexander II. Here a stroke of luck helped Bismarck arrange things. The Emperor Franz Joseph decided that he would cement the new friendship with Germany by a state visit and the Emperor William could hardly say no. Bismarck had reassured the Russians again and again that Germany would not sacrifice its ties to Russia but the visit of the Austrians made the Russians uneasy. Bismarck had tried to bring those European states together 'which had substantial numbers of Catholic subjects... for an exchange of ideas' in May of 1872[50] and later had proposed a conference on combating socialism and terrorism, but it was the visit of the Kaiser Franz Joseph that made the Russians move. The Tsar decided that he would join the visit of the Emperor of Austria and so the two Emperors would visit Berlin in September of 1872.

The visit of the Three Emperors went extremely well and established a foreign policy construction which remained a set and fixed element of Bismarck's foreign policy to the moment of his resignation. How much he planned that outcome can never be established. He was a brilliant diplomatic chess player who always saw moves well in advance, but whether he foresaw the future Three Emperors' League cannot be shown. On the other hand, as we saw in Chapter 5, Bismarck had always supported a Russian connection, had established intimate relations with the Russian royal family, and had enjoyed his embassy in St Petersburg more than any other post. He never forgot how much Prussia and his success depended on Russian support.

On 12 September the British Ambassador to Berlin, Odo Russell, wrote to the Foreign Office on the origins of the meeting of the Three Emperors in Berlin and what Bismarck had told him about it:

> In an after dinner conversation I had with Prince Bismarck at the Imperial Palace, the Chancellor, who was unusually cheerful, pointed to the three Emperors and made the following remarks in English, which, quaint as they were, I must endeavour to give verbatim: 'We have witnessed a novel sight today; it is the first time in history that three Emperors have sat down to dinner together for the promotion of peace. My object is fully attained, and I think your Government will approve of my work...I wanted the Three Emperors to form a loving group, like Canova's three graces, that Europe might see a living symbol of peace and have faith in it. I wanted them to stand in a silent group and allow themselves to be admired, difficult as it was, because they all three think themselves greater statesmen than they are.'[51]

This was the foundation of the Three Emperors' League, which was formally signed on 22 October 1873. In the long run the attempt to hold the two great Eastern powers together proved to be impossible. The slow but steady decline of the Ottoman Empire sucked Austria-Hungary into Balkan affairs in a competition with Russia, a rivalry which contributed to the outbreak of the First World War. The Balkans and the Orthodox kingdoms of Serbia and Bulgaria were an area of Russian 'interests'. The Russian Tsar saw himself 'protector of the Balkan Slavs'. The dilemma for Bismarck, given Austrian-Russian rivalry in the Balkans, was how to stay 'one of three' in Eastern Europe. The Three Emperors' League provided an answer, although temporary. It allowed Germany to achieve two objectives: first to avoid the choice between Austria and Russia and, second, to maintain France in isolation. In the end France was bound to be the natural ally of Russia against a growing and ever more powerful Germany, even though France was a Republic and Russia an autocracy. As long as Bismarck ran German foreign policy, he prevented that alliance but by the time he fell he could only do so by subterfuge and deceit so alarming that his successors could no longer continue it. The drag in foreign affairs meant that Bismarck's combinations worked steadily less well. Of the sixty-four squares on the chessboard, half— the enmity of France and the alliance with Austria—were covered. German foreign policy see-sawed from 1873 on between Russia and Great Britain. Bismarck spun his web with great skill and subtlety but he had no permanent solution. The forces against his combinations proved too strong.

Just before the conclusion of the Three Emperors' League, an epoch-changing event occurred, now unfortunately so familiar that the story tells itself; there was an economic 'crash'. Between 1866 and 1873, in the euphoria of the victories of 1866 and 1871, Germany had moved from the long wave of growth since 1849 until the final stage of a bubble economy. The post-war boom in the years 1870 to 1873 gained the nickname the *Gründerzeit* (the time of the founders), because of the sheer numbers of new companies which had been founded, many as solid as the 'collateralized debt obligations' of 2008. For example, the now famous Deutsche Bank was founded in 1870 in the euphoria of unification. There was a stock market boom because the French paid off in four years the huge reparations payments which the victorious Germans had imposed on them: it amounted to the stupendous sum of 5 billion gold marks. If the sum is converted using the retail price index, it amounts to 342 billion, using GDP deflator to 479 billon and much more with other indicators such as GDP per head but all these conversions understate the actual value at the time, for these were gold francs.[52] Imperial Germany, a semi-developed economy with chronic capital shortage, suddenly floated up on this vast flood of liquidity, the perfect conditions for an asset bubble. The resulting property boom, the unjustifiable mortgage deals, the enterprises lifted by artificially low borrowing rates, the fraud in banking and brokerage business, the sudden enthusiasm to get rich quick, all that occurred in more or less exactly the same way in the first years of the unified Reich as it did between 2001 and 2008. Arthur von Brauer (1845–1926), a young lawyer from Baden, joined the Prussian Foreign Ministry and moved to Berlin in 1872. He had, as a *Korpsbruder* (a member of the same duelling fraternity as Bismarck), good connections to the Chancellor and rose to be an important official relatively quickly.[53] Here are his impressions of his new home:

The hunger for profits and wealth possessed the new capital of the Reich, and even a large part of the once so solid Prussian officialdom and officer corps had joined the dance around the Golden Calf with no pangs of conscience. Swindlers gained large fortunes in a few days. Everyone, from princes to workers, gambled on the bourse. An obtrusive, undignified opulence predominated everywhere.[54]

That could have been written in July 2008 in London or New York without changing a word except 'princes', who had disappeared from the scene.

One of those who profited from the property boom was Field Marshall Albrecht von Roon. On 8 June 1875 he sold his estate Gütergotz, bought with money granted him by a grateful Emperor and for which he paid 135,000 thaler (roughly equal to 402,000 marks) to the Jewish banker Gerson Bleichröder, for a price of 1,290,000 marks, a tidy profit for the old soldier who had lived for so long on his salary. Waldemar von Roon, his son, when he published the papers of his father in 1892, omitted from the memoirs the name of the buyer and thus the uncomfortable fact that his father, hero of the Reich, had sold his estate to a Jew.[55]

On 9 May 1873 the Vienna Stock Market crashed, ushering in the first modern globalized financial crisis. Within a week Bismarck reported to William I that the Austrian Emperor had enabled the Austrian State Bank to issue a larger volume of bank notes than had been previously authorized. His experts argued that the crisis arose because 'the Vienna Stock Exchange had been the arena in which speculation had called forth a lot of companies, mainly joint stock limited companies, for which the existing capital proved insufficient.' As in 2008 the lenders had simply withdrawn capital from good as well as speculative investments which in turn worsened the crisis.[56] The next day Bismarck wrote to the Emperor to reassure him that a similar crisis would not occur in Berlin because 'the stock of metal is greater here and fraudulent business has not reached in our case the same dimensions as in Vienna'.[57] That reassurance proved to be as false as similar reassurances by governments in 2008 who were certain that it could not happen to them. It did. London and Paris followed and on 18 September, the leading Philadelphia banking firm, Jay Cooke and Company, went bankrupt. The worldwide crisis ushered in a period of slow growth and falling prices which continued from 1873 to 1896/7 and has been called the 'Great Depression'.

The depression fell into two distinct parts, an agricultural depression and the first modern industrial depression in which the heavy industrial sector suffered badly and revealed certain vulnerabilities that recurred from 1929 to 1938. The agricultural depression arose because from 1869 with the completion of the first trans-continental railway in the United States, the supply of very good American and then also Canadian grain began to flood the European markets. Henckel von Donnersmarck complained bitterly to Thiedemann about the sixfold increase in American exports of grain, flour, and meat 'in truly unbelievable numbers, for German agriculture, there must be a grain, flour and meat tariff as an unconditional necessity if we are not to expose it to the same fluctuations as industry'.[58] Michael Turner provides a useful set of indices of agricultural prices for the period 1867 to 1914 for the UK which can be used as a surrogate for the German price level as well.

(1867–7=100)	
1873	108.3
1891	75.7
1896	68.6
1901	76.7
1914	94.8[59]

The list makes clear that it took two generations for the agricultural price level even to come near to the level it had reached by 1873. The fact that the European upper classes including the Russells of Woburn Abbey and the Bismarcks of Schönhausen depended on agriculture made these price falls a matter of survival. Hence Bismarck's class faced a crisis of survival by 1878 and remained in it until their estates disappeared under Russian tanks in 1945. The Junkers could not—even with heavy application of fertilizer—compete with the vast riches of the American and Canadian Great Plains, the Argentinian Pampas, or the Russian Black Earth regions.

On 9 June 1873 the Reichstag passed the *Reichmünzgesetz* (the Reich coinage law) which established the legal exchange rate of the new German mark to the old Prussian thaler at 1 thaler = 3 marks and proclaimed that the new German currency would have 'in principle' a gold basis.[60] The adoption of gold as the basis of the new Germany currency in 1873 added a deflationary element to the other changes in the economic conditions. The amount of gold depended on its production. When economic growth exceeded the growth of money supply which it did until the late 1890s, then something had to give. When too many goods chase too little money, prices fall. By the 1890s in Junker Prussia and American Kansas, gold and its advocates had become the villains. As William Jennings Bryan cried out at the Democratic Party Convention in 1896, 'thou shalt not crucify the American people on a cross of gold.' Hans Count von Kanitz (1841–1913) read Jennings Bryan's speech into the records of the Prussian House of Lords.

Falling prices in industries with heavy fixed investment raised the cost of the interest they paid to investors and banks at the very moment when revenues fell below marginal costs and approached fixed costs. Competition among heavy industrial enterprise ended in a zero sum game and bankruptcy for some of the players. It made sense to limit production, cut wages or fire workers, and to combine in Kartells or Trusts, so by the 1880s, big industry had tightened its cost bases, employed accountancy to manage its outgoings, and worked out anti-competitive policies of all sorts.[61] A moment's reflection will suggest that all the developments in the depression of 1873 undermined liberal economic attitudes. By 31 October 1874 Baron Abraham von Oppenheim wrote to Bleichröder to say that he shared Bleichröder's 'pessimistic attitude entirely, and I do not see whence an early recovery could come. We did not—alas!—reduce our security holdings and must await better times. I have been in business now for almost fifty-six years and cannot recall such a protracted crisis ever before. According to my view the national wealth of Germany has shrunk by one-third, and therein lies the chief calamity.'[62] The crash of 1873 thus ushered in a new era, one which nobody had experienced before in human history: an international crisis of capitalism. The full impact took several years to work its way through society and into the priorities of Otto von Bismarck, a landowner, a timber merchant, and a tight-fisted country squire.

In 1873 and 1874 Bismarck and his Liberal colleagues continued their battle against the Catholic Church. A year before the Vienna Stock market crashed, on 14 May 1872, the Reichstag had passed a motion asking the Reich government to introduce a draft bill governing the legal status of Catholic religious orders and their subversive activities, particularly the Jesuit order. On the same day Bismarck sent a circular to German missions abroad in which he accused the Prussian Catholic bishops of being agents of the Pope:

> The bishops are only his tools, his subordinates, with no responsibility of their own; toward the government they have become officials of a foreign sovereign, of a sovereign who, because of his infallibility, has become an absolute one—more absolute than any absolute monarch in the world.[63]

On 3 June 1872 Bismarck wrote to Delbrück from Varzin that the Jesuit law must make clear that government will take action against those undermining state authority. 'It is a case of emergency defence and we cannot defend ourselves with Liberal phrases about civil rights.'[64] A week later he urged Falk to make sure that the state helped the lower Catholic clergy by arranging better salaries.[65] Here again we see the Bismarckian technique of alternating strategies—carrots and sticks. In July, the Jesuits were legally banned from Reich territory. However shocking this may appear now, it may be easier to imagine if instead of Jesuit you insert communist and think back to the Cold War. To European liberals in the nineteenth century, Jesuits stood for a pernicious, secret conspiratorial order of 'Soldiers of God', capable of anything.

Even democratic Switzerland banned Jesuits from all Swiss territory in the new Federal Constitution of 29 May 1874. According to Article 51 of the new Constitution

> the Order of the Jesuits and organizations affiliated to it may not seek a place in any part of Switzerland and every activity in church and school is forbidden to its members. This prohibition can be extended by Federal decision to other religious orders whose activity endangers the state or disturbs religious peace.[66]

It took ninety-nine years for Swiss voters to approve the repeal of this article, which they duly did on 20 May 1973. Bismarck's Jesuit Law was not more severe than the Swiss expulsion by constitutional amendment.

Bismarck welcomed the Swiss as allies in the war against the Black International and on 23 February 1873 the Swiss Minister to Germany, Johann Bernhard Hammer, who was Swiss Envoy in Berlin from 1868 to 1875, wrote to the President of the Swiss Confederation and head of the Political Department, Paul Jacob Cérésole. Hammer had received a telegram that the Swiss Federal Council had refused to allow Monsignor Gaspar Mermillod to remain in Switzerland as 'Apostolic Vicar'. Hammer informed Bismarck who invited him to a private talk, the kind of invitation that a diplomat from a small state could only dream about.

> You well know how difficult access to Prince Bismarck is for personal exchanges with diplomats ... He said 'We fight on the same ground in the same cause'. . . He takes pleasure in his awareness of the attitude which Switzerland takes in response to clerical presumptions and emphasized how the character of our situation makes freedom of action much more favourable, whereas he has been

lamed by a variety of obstacles to his freedom of action and hemmed in. In detail he named the opposition of 'high placed ladies' as especially obstructive...The Prince closed the conversation with these words: 'I hope at least Switzerland will stand by the principle in its present struggle with the church that on its territory it will tolerate no other sovereignty than its own.'[67]

This attitude led to the infamous May Laws of 1873, a set of laws passed in the Prussian Chamber that stipulated (1) future clergymen of both confessions had to be 'German' and fully educated in German gymnasia and universities; (2) only German ecclesiastical authorities could exercise disciplinary powers over clergy and such discipline was subject to review by the provincial governor and by a state court, 'the royal court for church affairs'; (3) ecclesiastical appointments were to be subject to the provincial governors; (4) clergy guilty of disobeying these laws would be fined and jailed; (5) *Kirchenaustritt*, leaving the church, was made easier for an ordinary person.[68]

The May Laws were an outrage in two senses. They violated the rights of subjects under the Prussian constitution and every principle of liberal society. They attacked the very idea of the Roman Catholic Church as 'the mystical body of Christ Incarnate'. The Roman Catholic Church cannot be treated like a civilian organization and it had no intention to accept such treatment. On 9 May 1873 Windthorst announced 'passive resistance against the May Laws: Against this passive resistance everything that is intended in these laws will sooner or later be dashed to pieces. God grant that the Fatherland not suffer harm thereby.' When on 15 May the Prussian May Laws passed anyway, the Prussian bishops declared themselves 'not in the position to cooperate in the execution of the laws published on the fifteenth of this month.'[69] The failure of Bismarck's policies became clear in the Reichstag elections of 1874. The Centre doubled its vote from 718,000 in 1871 to 1,493,000 in 1874, in percentage of votes from 18.4 to 27.7 per cent with 95 seats.[70] The Catholic population had rallied to the cause.

Odo Russell, who saw Bismarck regularly and enjoyed his confidence, believed that Bismarck had made a big mistake in starting the *Kulturkampf*. On 18 October 1872 he wrote to Lord Granville:

I fancy that Bismarck utterly misunderstands and underrates the power of the Church. Thinking himself more infallible than the Pope he cannot tolerate two infallibles in Europe and fancies he can select the next Pope as he would a Prussian general...Hitherto the anti-clerical measures have produced the very state of things the Vatican was working for through the Oecumenical

Council, namely, unity and discipline in the clergy under an infallible head, or the Prussian military system applied to the Church.[71]

These measures bred hatred and violence on both sides. In September Georg Count von Hertling (1843–1919), later to be Reich Chancellor during the First World War,[72] wrote from Belgium to Anna von Hertling on the hatred of Catholics by their fellow Germans:

> Again and again I have the same experience: scarcely has one exchanged two words with a countryman, than in some place or other, crude or refined, hatred of Catholics comes out.[73]

By June of 1875 the *Frankfurter Zeitung* reported that in the first four months of the year, 241 clergy, 136 editors, and 210 other Catholics had been fined or imprisoned; 20 newspapers had been confiscated, 74 houses searched, 103 people expelled or interned, and 55 public meetings broken up; 1,000 rectories, nearly a quarter of all parishes in Prussia, were vacant. By 1876 all Prussian bishops were either in custody or in exile.[74] Odo Russell, who had predicted that Bismarck would lose the *Kulturkampf*, reported to his brother Hastings on the Catholic hierarchy's reaction to these severe measures:

> In Germany his [the Pope's] success has been complete for all the bishops who voted against the new dogma in the Vatican Council now go cheerfully to prison and pay enormous fines and suffer martyrdom for that very infallibility they voted against 3 years ago and think they will go to heaven like skyrockets when they die for their trouble.[75]

History has no record of German Catholic bishops seen flying up to 'heaven like skyrockets' but it records the monstrous tally of damage to the structure and practice of the Roman Catholic Church and systematic violations of the Prussian Constitution. The anti-Catholic hysteria in many European countries belongs in its European setting. Bismarck's campaign was not unique in itself but his violent temper, intolerance of opposition, and paranoia that secret forces had conspired to undermine his life's work, made it more relentless. His rage drove him to exaggerate the threat from Catholic activities and to respond with very extreme measures. Prussia was never threatened by its Catholic population. Pius IX had no reason to overthrow the Hohenzollern Monarchy nor the means to do so. Bismarck made miserable the daily life of millions of Catholics. As Odo Russell wrote to his mother, 'The demonic is stronger in him, than in any man I know.'[76]

Bismarck told Lady Emily Russell how he reacted to Windthorst and the Catholic Centre in the Reichstag:

> When the Catholic Party cried 'shame' and shook their fists at him, his first instinct was to take the ink stand in front of him and fling it at them—his second instinct was to measure the distance, spring upon them and knock them down—his third impulse overcame the two first and he merely told them that 'he felt contempt for them but was too civil to say so'.[77]

The bully, the dictator, and the 'demonic' combined in him with the self-pity and hypochondria to create a constant crisis of authority which he exploited for his own ends. Nobody believed him when he threatened to resign. Prince Hohenlohe-Schillingfürst recorded a conversation with the Liberal MP Eduard Lasker in November 1874 on Bismarck's position in government:

> Lasker...talked of Bismarck's projects of retiring. He regards them as mere pretence and says that Bismarck is too much of a demon to let the reins out of his hands. To my remark that the situation was ominous on account of the feeling at Court, Lasker replied there was nothing to fear there. At the decisive moment no one would be willing to let Bismarck go, because they had no one to substitute for him. There were plenty of straw-men who imagined they could replace Bismarck, but the Kaiser would think twice before he put one of them in Bismarck's office.[78]

Opponents, friends, and subordinates all remarked on Bismarck as 'demonic', a kind of uncanny, diabolic personal power over men and affairs. In these years of his greatest power, he believed that he could do anything. Roggenbach wrote to Stosch on 30 August 1874 that

> nobody can hold out with the Reich Chancellor any more... As long as it's just an outburst of raw, brutal moodiness and a result of the juice of the grape, it might be ignored...but it's another matter when the method in madness and a specialization in dishonourable humiliation take place. Nobody knows better how to use *avilir, puis détruire* [humiliate then destroy] and to shatter his victim in the eye of the public through poisonous publications arranged at long distance and finally to expose him to the future fatal blow.[79]

His enemies, of which Roggenbach was certainly one, concentrated their criticism on his brutality and demonic qualities but they tended to ignore the sheer pressure that he had to face—admittedly, a stress he had helped to create. He ran by himself two governments, the German and the Prussian, faced two very different parliaments, and had to operate with two conflicting political agendas. Some issues that looked harmless at first developed into serious political crises. It was clear that local government in the enlarged Prussian kingdom needed reform. This subject had been on the agenda of successive Prussian governments since 1859 and had led to what Patrick Wagner in his study of the growth of state power and Junker resistance calls 'the twelve year reform debate'.[80] The conquests and annexations of 1866 and afterwards, the foundation of the Reich itself in 1870, had left a patchwork quilt of types of local government. It needed cleaning up, and for that Bismarck had to turn again to his Prussian cabinet, which still contained four holdovers from the 'Conflict Ministry': arch-conservatives Eulenburg, Selchow, Itzenplitz, and Roon. They became disorientated because Bismarck was never there. As early as September 1869 Itzenplitz wrote to him:

> If you don't come, we have to see how we get on by ourselves or go. How you intend to be Federal Chancellor and say goodbye to the Prussian State Ministry my simple head cannot grasp. That must be Roon's view too and that must be why he has not answered. In true affection—even if I cannot grasp the above—as always your devoted Itzenplitz.[81]

Itzenplitz may have been a reactionary but he was a count, a gentleman, and Bismarck's social equal.

On 23 March 1872 a new Prussian local government statute was submitted to the Landtag. It abolished the police and administrative powers of *Rittergutsbesitzer*, the owners of knightly estates, that is, estates like Bismarck-Schönhausen and the estates of literally *everybody* from Bismarck's social class. The local government statute, which included an elected element on a three-class voting basis, passed the Chamber of Deputies 256 to 61. Estate owners and *Landräte* from eastern provinces including Bismarck's own brother Bernhard, had voted against it.[82] It would almost certainly fail in the Lords.

Eulenburg, the minster responsible for the legislation, wrote to Bismarck to ask for guidance. Bismarck had been in Varzin for months while this crisis festered. Indeed he told Moritz Blanckenburg that he intended to stay as long as possible, 'until the filthy mess is so big, that I can push through everything'.[83] In addition he saw the Local Government Reform, which was bound to create a constitutional crisis because of resistance in the House of Lords, as an opportunity to get rid of Eulenburg as Minister of the Interior. Moritz von Blanckenburg warned Hans von Kleist on 15 August 1872 that 'Bismarck and Roon want to use the Local Government bill to topple Eulenburg. You know that. They will not identify themselves with draft of

the Lower House.'[84] On 22 October 1872 in the House of Lords two leading conservatives, Wilhelm Freiherr von Zedlitz und Neukrich (1811–80),
whom a Catholic member of the Landtag, Ludwig Hammers (1822–1902)
called 'a very conservative landowner',[85] and Friedrich Stephan Count von
Brühl confronted the government directly on the principle of inherited
rights. Brühl put it bluntly: 'If there is no longer any hereditary authority in
the kingdom except the Crown, God preserve us from the threat that somebody lays hands on that too, the one last hereditary authority, and shakes
it.'[86] As Ludwig von Yorck had warned Prince William, sixty years earlier, 'if
your Royal Highness deprives me and my children of my rights, what is the
basis of yours?'[87] In desperation Eulenburg wrote to Bismarck on 25 October
1872, the frankest possible letter from a decent man, also a count and a
gentleman, to his chief. I quote it at some length because here as in the case
of Itzenplitz one sees the discomfort of the ministers under Bismarck:

Dear Friend,
    Only the importance of the matter could bring me to you give you discom-
fort by a letter. The debate in the House of Lords has unfolded in such a way
that the success of the bill must be highly improbable. So yesterday the House
of Lords voted by name with a two-thirds majority against the government bill
and against the decision of the House of Deputies, the Lords accepted a provision that in the raising of the local tax base in the country districts the ground-
and building-tax shall never be higher than the half of that percentage which
is set as the basis for income and classified taxable income for suffrage. This
decision will never pass the lower house. In all probability there will be decisions approved with regard to the composition of the district assemblies, whose
acceptance by the House of Deputies is also inconceivable. Count Lippe, Kleist
and Senfft are the spokesmen. With them more than half the members will
vote: Putbus, Oscar, Arnim and so on. What is to be done? A local district ordinance must be passed and as soon as possible. I shall fall with this one but what
then? A conservative district organization has no chance in the House of
Deputies, a liberal one none in the House of Lords, but something has to
happen. Without an organization of district government, all the legislative
programme stalls: school organization, roads, administrative organization, provincial funding; everything just stops. I beg you, dear friend, to let me know
urgently how you stand on these things. The uncertainty is driving many people into the enemy camp. Do you want me to submit my resignation at once
and would you like to try it with somebody else? Or do you want openly to
speak out and strongly in support of my efforts? Or should there be ready for
the time when the draft law returns a second time to the House of Lords,
provision for a *Pairschub* [creation of new lords to form a majority—JS]. There
is no time to lose. From my heart your Eulenburg.

PS The Catholics will vote against the district organization because they fear that the office holders will be an appropriate organ for conducting civil marriages.[88]

Bismarck refused to give an answer or to leave Varzin. His reply, written on 27 October 1872, is beneath contempt. He had not

> yet formed an opinion about every detail...Even if our draft in its virginal purity had gone to the House of Lords, I would have not expected it to be accepted as a whole...I think your considerateness has led to a growing degeneration of the social order and I have to live here under a *Landrat*, who to save his own honour has made it his object to portray me before the dwellers here as an incompetent and un-Christian minister. There lies the evidence of how far my power extends in other ministries.

Bismarck refused to make the required *pronunciamiento* or indeed to say anything and reminds Eulenburg about

> his beloved Wolff who during your illness made any legislation impossible...I hope to come in December but if I have to write many more letters like this, I shall not come before the Reichstag and will lay my presidency of the State Ministry to rest in the files. Responsibility without corresponding influence on what has to be responded leads directly to medical institutions. In old friendship, yours[89]

The sheer effrontery of this farrago of evasion of responsibility and irrelevance really shocked me the first time I read it. Bismarck sinks in this to a level of cowardice, irresponsibility, petty vindictiveness, and absurdity. How could Eulenburg's gentleness as police minister have been responsible for the opinions of the *Landrat* in Bismarck's district? The *Landrat* simply said of him what every respectable conservative landlord in the eastern areas said ten times a day and many said it in the House of Lords. How could the most powerful statesman of the nineteenth century claim that he had 'responsibility without corresponding influence on what has to be responded'? It puzzles me that Fritz Eulenburg did not resign on the spot but stayed on for another six years.

One has to sympathize with the Junkers in the House of Lords, who like Ernst von Sennft-Pillsach (1795–1882) had written to Bismarck:

> The war with France should have deepened the German people in the fear of God, but instead it drove it to arrogance. And your Excellency has not resisted that turn from God and His Word with that steadiness in faith, that holiness the Lord had commanded you in so wonderful a way. Turn in faith to our

Lord Jesus Christ, who under Pontius Pilate 'hath well acquitted' himself. Now in Luther's spirit acquit yourself in a German way. Then the Lord will turn to you and bring back to you many noble and pious men who now stay far from you.

Bismarck wrote on the margin with contempt: 'Gerlach? Windthorst! Bodelschwingh? Or Ewald?'[90] He found out when on 31 October 1872 the local district organization bill was defeated by 145 votes to 18 in House of Lords. As Pflanze puts it, the 'Stahl Caucus' rejected the transformation of the *Ständestaat* involved in abolition of manorial rule.[91]

Bismarck's reaction was another bout of illness, as on 16 November 1872, Bucher explained to Bleichröder:

> You know how spiritual and somatic conditions are reciprocally related with the Prince. Excited or annoyed by affairs, he becomes vulnerable to colds and lapses in his diet, and, when he has physical complaints, any kind of work makes him impatient.[92]

Bismarck responded in his usual violent way with a *Promemoria* dated 2 November and written still in Varzin clearly in a rage.

> In the light of the attitude of the core of the House of Lords in the School Supervisory Law, the district organization and other questions, a reform of this body seems to me more important than the passage of any sort of district order…The factious attitude of the House damages and discredits the system of two chambers and endangers the monarchical system…

The solution was to abolish the House of Lords and replace it with 'a first chamber, a Senate [which] should be essentially an organ of government and of monarchical interests in Prussia.'[93]

On 3 November the State Ministry met, still without Bismarck, and Eulenburg took the occasion to go over the district reorganization draft with his colleagues, to make what changes might give it a better passage and to consider the possibilities of a *Pairschub*. The minister conveniently omitted any discussion of the Promemoria on the abolition of the House of Lords. The cabinet calculated that at least twenty-four new peers would have to be named to ensure a majority and to intimidate the others. Helma Brunck, to whose fine analysis I owe my insight into this bizarre affair, gives the real credit for the outcome to the King. Eulenburg had made mistakes, which he admitted, but he had no reason to blame himself on moral grounds. Brunck writes:

the King saw it that way too. He saw through the game of intrigue and the unjust treatment of Eulenburg, which through his permanent absences he [Bismarck] had driven to a crisis point, in order to leave the Minister of Interior standing alone in the rain and to impose on him alone the battle for the district reorganization.[94]

On 30 November 1872 the *Pairschub* took place. King William, offended by the attitude of 'his Junkers', named twenty-five new peers to the House of Lords with whose votes the disputed district ordinance passed by a major-ity of twenty-five on 9 December 1872.[95] The law abolished the patrimonial police and Junker-controlled village administration. Baroness Spitzemberg observed in her diary that the Kaiser spared the Junker right-wing the humiliation of 'sitting next to Jew barons and speculators... It would have annoyed me if the *nouveau riche* had got into the House of Lords, because I am becoming more and more high Tory and conservative. Father says autocratic and violent.'[96] On 13 December King William signed and sealed the new local district law.

The crisis did not end with the passage of the local district law but gen-erated further discontent in the cabinet. Several ministers had complained to the King about Bismarck's continuous absences.Von Selchow, the Minister of Agriculture, felt insulted that he had not been involved in the local gov-ernment business. Roon also thought of resigning, and Itzenplitz had been thinking of it for years. Bismarck could not afford to lose the Conflict Ministers because it would look as if he had opted for a new liberal course, the last thing he had in mind. In mid-November he wrote gloomily to Roon about his health

> In the last days I have been in bad shape again, am back in bed since the day before yesterday and have lost much heart as a result of this relapse, since I had been markedly getting better. God be with you; things cannot get worse very soon in human affairs, above all no dissolution.[97]

A day later he wrote to William I to express his apologies that, as a result of his weakened health, he had not been there at the Kaiser's side during the continuing crisis. His attempt at Eulenburg's request to intervene from a great distance had led to misunderstandings and to a further weakening of his health. 'I have therefore asked Roon to summon me only if Your Majesty specially commands it and have notified him that I shall not correspond individually with the colleagues any more.'[98] This account falsifies reality. His refusal to intervene at Eulenburg's request had *caused* the crisis as had his prolonged absences. This once again shows Bismarck in his Pontius Pilate guise, washing his hands of responsibility when things went wrong.

In mid-December he got news that Roon too had submitted his resignation and this triggered his own desire to do likewise. In a formal reply addressed to 'Your Excellency' of 13 December, he wrote that he decided to ask His Majesty to allow him 'to divide functions entrusted to my person, which presupposes that His Majesty wishes to retain my services, . . . so that I restrict myself to the direction of the Reich's affairs, with inclusion of foreign policy.'[99] In the private 'dear Roon' letter written the same day, he writes that the situation now requires him to return to Berlin 'not while I feel healthy but because I have a duty to discuss the situation with his Majesty and you in person.' There follows a remarkable passage in which he describes an 'unheard of anomaly that the foreign minister of a great empire also bears the responsibility for domestic policy'. What must old Roon have thought who had watched Bismarck intentionally accumulate office and power at every level? He continues his letter to Roon with a moving account of his state of mind:

> In my trade one accumulates many enemies but no new friends, instead loses the old ones if one carries it out honestly and fearlessly for ten years. I am in disgrace with all[sic!] the members of the Royal family and the King's confidence in me has ebbed. Every intriguer has his ear. As a result foreign service becomes more difficult for me.... In domestic matters I have lost the basis that is acceptable to me because of the treacherous desertion of the Conservatives in the Catholic question. At my age, and in the conviction that I have not long to live, the loss of all the old friends and ties has something disheartening about it for this [sic!] world; it produces paralysis. The illness of my wife which in the last months has afflicted her more severely, compounds that. My springs have been crippled through overuse. The King in the saddle has no idea how he has ridden a sturdy horse into the ground. The lazy last longer.[100]

This *confession* of the great Bismarck, the most famous statesman of his or perhaps any age, raises profound questions about his personality. If you threaten to put the police on your closest friend and wave a knife at him over dinner, you might just offend him. If you mock the principles which you used to espouse, those who hold them might despise you. If you pursue vendettas against subordinates until you destroy them, they might in self-defence resort to intrigue against you. Bismarck literally destroyed the career of Count Harry Arnim, because he threatened to become a rival. Vain, irresponsible, a stock exchange speculator, Arnim certainly was, but Bismarck used the courts to accuse him of treason, drove him out of the country, and to an early death.[101] His policy on local government reorganization removed the ancient patrimonial jurisdiction of the Junker class and moved the countryside a small step toward modernity and justice for the peasants employed on Junker estates. Their opposition to the measure never amounted to treason to the state. It was political opposition and defence of their interests. None of this he recognized or admitted. Here we have the cleverest political actor of the nineteenth century, a person for whom the word 'genius' exactly fits the political insight and imagination Bismarck often displays, who cannot see the simplest political reality: that acts have consequences. He resorts to self-deception and self-pity in a manner so crass that even Roon and Moritz von Blanckenburg who still stuck to him, must have doubted his sanity. Yet neither they nor anybody else seems to have had the courage to tell him the truth at any stage. The demonic power of the sovereign self and the combination of awe and delight which all the intimates record, seems to have lamed them. The dour Christians, Ludwig von Gerlach, Ernst von Sennft-Pilsach, 'little Hans' could face him and tell him the truth, as they saw it, but he had banished them. His enemies in the Reichstag and Prussian Landtag regularly attacked him but hardly any saw the underside of the giant figure, though many such as Roggenbach had a good idea what Bismarck was really like.

On 21 December 1872 the King accepted Bismarck's resignation as Minister-President of Prussia and by cabinet order relieved him of the post. Roon became his successor and suffered eleven painful months in the post. Already weakened by his chronic asthma, the old soldier took the job until he collapsed completely and resigned on 5 October 1873. On 23 October 1873, on the way back from the World's Fair in Vienna, the Kaiser and Bismarck had a leisurely discussion of the ministerial question and Bismarck accepted William's request to resume the Presidency of the State Ministry. On 4 November Bismarck formally accepted and asked his Majesty to appoint the liberal Otto Camphausen (1812–96), who had been von der Heydt's successor as Finance Minister, Vice-President of the Ministry and to make his friend Moritz von Blanckenburg the Minister of Agriculture. General of the Infantry Georg von Kameke (1816–93) became Minister of War on 9 November 1873 and was to hold the post for a decade. The rest of the cabinet remained the same, slightly more liberal with the disappearance of von Selchow and Roon. The last conflict minister, Count Eulenburg, the great survivor, continued in office until 1878.[102]

Throughout 1873 and 1874 relations between Bismarck and the Conservatives deteriorated. The final break came when Bismarck lost his temper in a speech in the Reichstag and attacked the *Kreuzzeitung*: 'Everyone who receives and pays for [the *Kreuzzeitung*] shares indirectly in the lies and slander that are published in it, in slanders such as the *Kreuzzeitung* contained last summer against the highest officials of the Reich, without the slightest proof.'[103] On 26 February 1876, the so-called *Deklaranten*, 400 of the most prominent Conservatives, signed a declaration defending the *Kreuzzeitung* and renewed their subscriptions. Hans Joachim Schoeps writes, 'This was the core of the Prussian old conservatives, many from the Old Mark and Pomerania, many personal and ideological friends of the Chancellor, at the top Adolf von Thadden who put the postscript after his name "with pain".'[104] Hans von Kleist—interestingly—refused to sign.[105]

This break with his old allies remained. Four years later Hildegard Spitzemberg recorded a remarkable discovery on a visit to the Bismarcks:

> The Princess has an alphabetically ordered list of the 'Deklaranten', that is, those who signed the declaration in favour of the Kreuzzeitung which the Prince had attacked. All these are seen as personal enemies who will never be forgiven and to whom visiting cards will not be returned.[106]

On 18 January 1875 the Prussian Landtag began a new session and an usher from the Foreign Office handed the National Liberal member, Christoph Tiedemann, a note from Prince Bismarck requesting the recipient to call at the Prince's residence in the Foreign Office at 9 p.m. that evening. Tiedemann recorded in his diary: 'How very odd. I wrack my brains without success during the course of the day for an explanation of this surprising invitation.'[107] Nothing in his past record explained it. He was born on 24 September 1836 in Schleswig and had studied law as preparation for a career in the Danish civil service. When Schleswig became Prussian, Tiedemann transferred seamlessly to the Prussian civil service and rose to be Landrat (district administrator) for the Mettmann district which became part of Prussia in 1816 after the Congress of Vienna. He had won a seat in the Prussian lower house and had risen to a place of influence within the leadership but his position could by no means be said to be among the most prestigious figures in the party. He was not yet 40 years old.

At 8.45 p.m. Herr Tiedemann presented himself at the Foreign Office. He described the episode in his diary.

In a large room, dimly lit by one lamp, which seemed to be used as a dining room, I had to wait a quarter of an hour. Punctuality seems to be the rule in this house. The servant explained that he dare not announce me until 9, for I had been invited for 9 and not before. I passed the time looking at the interesting Chinese tapestries on the wall.

As the clock struck nine, I was ushered into the Prince's work room. He rose from his desk, offered me his hand in greeting and gestured me to a seat opposite him. During all this, the 'Reich Dog', Sultan, emerged from the darkness, sniffed me suspiciously but soon satisfied, lay down again by the hearth. The Prince asked me if I smoked to which I naturally assented cheerfully. He gave me a cigar and lit his pipe. I shall try to reconstruct the conversation literally:

HE: There are several draft bills in the Ministry of the Interior on which I must report to His Majesty in the next few days. They concern the organization of the civil administration in the western provinces: the structure of the provinces, of the districts and the communes. Look at this pile and the accompanying memoranda. It is no trifle to read that stuff. I have been rather ill, have not slept for three nights and have eaten more or less nothing.[108]

In effect, Bismarck had invited Tiedemann to do his homework on the complexities of the new local authority structure in the western districts of the Prussian Kingdom. Tiedemann knew the problems both from his own experience as district officer of Mettmann and from service in the parliamentary committee dealing with the legislation. Tiedemann set out his views and Bismarck took notes. The Prince observed wryly that, unlike his cabinet colleagues, he as a landowner knew what it felt like to be ruled by the Prussian bureaucracy with its rage for perfection. Tiedemann, who from the evidence of the diary had a quick wit and a sense of humour, also knew his brief and gave Bismarck the answers he wanted. Above all, not too much democracy in the new provincial and local authorities.

Tiedemann, who over the next five years spent weeks in the great man's company, could never get over the scale of Bismarck's way of life. The huge chamber pots corresponded to the incredible quantities of food served and consumed at the Prince's table. A diary entry for 22 January 1878 reads in its entirety as follows:

22 January 1878,   Menu:
                        Oysters, caviar
                        Venison soup
                        Trout
                        Morel mushrooms Smoked breast of goose

> Wild boar in Cumberland sauce
> Saddle of venison
> Apple fritters
> Cheese and bread
> Marzipan, chocolate, apples[109]

Bismarck could not control his emotions. When Sultan, 'the Reich Dog', died of a heart attack at Varzin in October 1877, Bismarck would not be consoled.

> He cannot stop talking about the death of his dog and especially that he hit him shortly before he died. He tortures himself with the thought that he caused the dog's death because of that. He accuses himself of violent temper, brutality with which he hurts everybody who comes into contact with him, and on and on berates himself for mourning so long and so deeply for an animal.[110]

He clearly needed help in all sorts of ways, and for reasons not entirely obvious he decided to choose this youngish, middle-ranking National Liberal deputy to provide it. At first young Tiedemann served as a recipient of Bismarck's complaints. On 7 May Bismarck gave a dinner party to which Tiedemann was again invited:

> As I had taken my coat to leave, a servant whispered to me, that the Prince wished to see me . . . The Prince unburdened himself in observations about the difficulties of his position, which neither the outside world nor posterity can justly assess. Historians only see through their own glasses. He praised Carlyle highly because he understood how to put himself in the soul of another person. He then continued more or less as follows. 'I find it as a particular burden that my personal enemies grow more numerous from year to year. My profession demands that I step on the corns of lots of people and nobody ever forgets that. I am too old to find new friends, and in addition have no time for that, and then the old ones disappear from the scene, as soon as they realize that I will no longer be a useful vehicle for their careers. So I end up surrounded by enemies. Hopefully you do not belong among them.'[111]

Bismarck's physical and psychological condition deteriorated during 1875. He slept so badly that he often received cabinet ministers and officials in bed. His temper worsened and the smallest irritation—a servant not placing a chair somewhere quickly enough—would cause an outburst of uncontrolled rage.

In mid-January 1876 Lothar Bucher informed Christoph Tiedemann that Bismarck had decided to appoint him as a kind of personal adjutant who would be a member of the Staatsministerium—roughly the equivalent of White House Staff in the USA or the Cabinet Office in the UK—but who would be assigned to no department and have no other duties than those Bismarck requested. Tiedemann saw the Prince at eight in the evening of 25 January 1876 and recorded the event in his dairy:

> He received me lying on a cot wrapped in blankets. He looked very pale and terribly serious and complained vigorously about his physical condition, especially his extreme irritability which was tied to his insomnia . . . He begged me to excuse him that he received me lying down but I might see from that how great his interest in my appointment was . . . In any case at the beginning I was not to be too dutiful and overwork. There would be plenty of times in which I should have my hands full.[112]

For the next five years, from his fortieth to his forty-fifth year, Tiedemann served Bismarck as his administrative assistant and adjutant and provided posterity with an intimate account of Bismarck both as a person but also uniquely as chief executive officer of the new German Empire and the old Kingdom of Prussia. It was, as he wrote to Herbert Bismarck in September 1881, 'the pride of his life . . . to have worked as apprentice to the greatest Master on the loom of world history'.[113] For us he offers an independent, amused, and curiously approachable view of the great man, his family, his environment, and his estates but also the details of policy and administration. Tiedemann had that indefinable something which makes a great diarist, an ego no doubt robust but leavened by a natural curiosity, a good ear for conversation, an eye for oddities, and an irrepressible sense for the absurdity of life, something that Bismarck had himself demonstrated in his early life but lost as he grew greater and more miserable. Tiedemann's account of the two huge chamber-pots in Bismarck's bedroom and von Sybel's earnest admiration of them as signs of Bismarck's grandeur ought to have a place in any collection of nineteenth-century comic memorabilia (see p. 10).[114]

On 5 February 1875 Pius IX issued an encyclical *Quod Numquam* (On the Church in Prussia) in which he declared:

> We must vindicate the freedom of the Church which is depressed by unjust power. We intend to fulfil these aspects of Our duty through this letter announcing to everyone to whom the matter pertains and to the whole Catholic world that those laws are invalid insofar as they totally oppose the divine order of the Church. The Lord did not set the powerful of this world over the bishops in matters which pertain to the sacred ministry.[115]

Bismarck responded with more pressure on Catholic civil servants and on 22 April 1875 the Prussian Landtag passed a law 'concerning the cancellation of payments with state funds for Roman Catholic Bishoprics and Clergy, the so-called "Breadbasket Law".' Bismarck told the house that he expected little success from the withdrawal of the money, 'but we simply do our duty when we defend the independence of our state and nation against foreign influences, and when we defend spiritual freedom against its suppression by the Jesuit Order and by a Jesuitical Pope.[116]

Hildegard Spitzemberg recorded a comic aspect of the 'Breadbasket' debate. She reported the Princess's story that Bismarck had decided not to go to the Landtag to hear the debate on the suspension of state payment for the Catholic Church. As he dressed that morning, he discovered that he had put on his winter rather than his light trousers.

> Superstitious as he is in such things, he saw it as a sign to go to the Landtag and arrived just at the moment that Sybel had been reading a passage about Diocletian and his 'bald-headed Minister Mark' from the writings of Konrad von Boland as a satire on the Ultramontanes. At the end the 'evil Mark' sinks in swamp. As Sybel came to that point Bismarck suddenly appeared as if on cue and the house erupted in enthusiastic applause.[117]

On 15 April 1875 thirty ultra-conservatives followed Kleist-Retzow and voted in the Lords to reject the *Sperr- und Brotkorbgesetz* (the Breadbasket Law), which suspended 889,718 marks of 1,011,745 of Prussian subsidy to the Catholic Church.[118] After the passage of the Breadbasket Law, the active and aggressive phase of the *Kulturkampf* came to an end in spite of Bismarckian rhetoric on the Reformation and the threat to Protestantism. A stalemate ensued in which the bishops and clergy practised passive resistance and the state gradually lost the will to enforce new legislation or even police the old. Everybody waited for the death of Pius IX, who at 83 and ill could not last much longer. He died on 7 February 1878, and an important phase in the history of the Roman Catholic Church and European history closed with him. His legacy continues to the present in the absolute claims of papal supremacy and in resistance to so-called modern trends.

In the summer of 1876 Bismarck went to take the waters at Bad Kissingen and forbade Tiedemann to send him any business whatsoever. Anything urgent had to be sent via Bismarck's son Herbert who would pass the matter on and transmit his father's reply. He told Tiedemann on the day of his departure that he hoped 'to bring back a skin colour as fresh as your own'.[119] After a few days at the end of July, the Prince went to his estate Varzin in Pomerania where he stayed until 21 November 1876. The huge estate had a classical park with terraces leading up a Greek temple in the distance and the scale of the rooms and arrangement suited Bismarck's new princely status.[120]

On 3 December 1876 William chaired a meeting of the Privy Council, attended by the Crown Prince Frederick William, Bismarck, all the members of the State Ministry (the cabinet), and Tiedemann as minute-taker. After the Privy Council, Tiedemann took a stroll with Friedrich Count zu Eulenburg, the Minister of the Interior, who confirmed that the Emperor regularly insisted that the full documentary and legal dossiers about new legislation be sent to him before meetings. Eulenburg offered as example a recent meeting of the Privy Council on the revocation of the customs duty on iron at which

> the Emperor gave us a short lecture on the history of Prussian tariff policy which was so illuminating and sharp that it amazed us all and when in the course of the debate he argued for the maintenance of the existing tariffs, he showed how carefully he had read the reports of the provincial governors from the Rhenish-Westphalian industrial areas and how accurately he assessed the often conflicting views of the industrialists themselves.[121]

While Bismarck supported the National Liberal insistence on free trade, William I had remained a convinced protectionist. As he stated at the December Privy Council,

> I have always considered reduction of tariffs very questionable and in the last meeting of the Council fought the decision to revoke the iron tariffs. The consequences of our incorrect measures show themselves already and will show themselves even more in the future. I shall not live to see it but my successor will surely witness our return to a system of moderate protective tariffs.[122]

Within three years that prophecy had become reality. The new German Reich and its powerful Chancellor Bismarck had indeed abandoned free trade, adopted tariffs, and ended the relationship between the Crown and the liberal parties. The Emperor made one mistake. He, not his successor, presided over the great 'shift' to conservatism which Bismarck engineered.

The sessions of the Privy Council teach us some interesting things about the constitutional formalities and the actual politics of Bismarck's new Germany. The King/Emperor retained the final say. In spite of convivial relations between the Royal Family and leading parliamentarians, he remained an all-powerful sovereign executive who intervened, often with handwritten notes directly to cabinet ministers, which absorbed a great deal of their time, effort, and correspondence. Nothing seemed too small for the All-Highest attention. In June of 1877 Bismarck, Falk, and other cabinet officers had to soothe the Emperor about the handling of a row over progressive clergymen in the Evangelical Synod of Berlin which Tiedemann claimed showed 'tactless and unworthy behaviour...and power-seeking and restless elements within the Evangelical Church'.[123] The All-Highest, as head of the Evangelical Lutheran Church, could and did express opinions on such matters and wrote one of the participants a four-page handwritten letter on matters of faith and doctrine. But he might intervene on the question of sugar beet production in Prussia, the Berlin-Dresdner Railroad, the reorganization of the system of courts, local government reorganization, building sites in the Voss Strasse, patent law, legislation to care for abandoned children, the organization of the Ministry of Trade, the regulation of auditing and the government audit office, etc., many of which required an All-Highest decision or signature.

Ministers understood the Emperor's strong prejudices and acted to calm or allay his anxieties but they could never ignore them. As we have seen, William I chose not to dismiss his cabinets over tariffs or other questions. He conducted such meetings in what Tiedemann called 'a free and easy form'.[124] Ministers could speak their minds openly. Yet William could dismiss them at will as he could dismiss Bismarck. Why he chose to be overruled on matters by his Chancellor remains one of the most mysterious and yet important themes of Bismarck's career and hence of this book. The constant tension between a Chancellor who could not bear opposition and a conscientious and careful Sovereign who opposed him at every step must have contributed to that sense of futility, exhaustion, and despair which Bismarck expressed again and again. Thus, on 4 January 1877 Tiedemann wrote in his diary: 'The Prince unwell, and has cancelled all appointments.'[125] Four weeks later Bismarck told Tiedemann that he was suffering from a headache on one side of his head and would have to postpone the dinner for members of the House of Deputies he had wanted to host for some time. For that he needed to be well enough to do some serious drinking. 'If I have to eat with members of parliament, I must drink myself the courage.'[126]

Foreign affairs, on the other hand, never provoked the rage, psychosomatic ailments, and physical exhaustion that domestic matters increasingly did. Not even a revived France disturbed his digestion. On 12 March 1875 the French National Assembly approved the addition of a fourth battalion to each regiment and a fourth company to each battalion. Moltke calculated that the law would add 144,000 men to the French army.[127]

Bismarck turned his attention to an effort to reduce France to second-class status. Articles on a possible coalition of France and Austria began to appear and on 8 April the *Berliner Post*, a paper often used by Bismarck to plant stories, published a front-page article, 'ist Krieg in Sicht?'(Is war in sight?), written by Constantin Rössler, a journalist known to be close to the Chancellor. The paper answered its own question, 'yes, war is in sight but the threatening clouds may yet blow over.'[128] The publication, Tiedemann noted, 'aroused great excitement'.[129] Odo Russell took it all calmly and assured Lord Derby that

> Bismarck is at his old tricks again alarming the Germans through the officious press and intimating that the French are going to attack them and that Austria and Italy are conspiring in favour of the Pope... This crisis will blow over like so many others but Bismarck's sensational policy is very wearisome at times. Half the diplomatic body have been here since yesterday to tell me that war was imminent, and when I seek to calm their nerves... they think that I am bamboozled by Bismarck. I do not, as you know, believe in another war with France.[130]

The crisis developed as both Bismarck and the French Foreign Minister tried to blame the other. On 21 April the French Ambassador to Germany was told by a high official in the German Foreign Office that a preventive war would be entirely justified, if France continued to rearm, indeed it would be 'politically, philosophically and even in Christian terms' entirely justified.[131] The Prussian military also began to consider preventive war and leaked their comments. The French used the bad reputation that the Prussians now had to alarm the other powers and the Kaiser as well. On 6 May Henry Blowitz published an article in *The Times*, 'A French Scare', in which he took the French side. Lord Derby observed that 'Bismarck either is really bent on making war, or he just wants us to *believe* he is bent on it.'[132] The Russian ambassador to Great Britain, Peter Shuvalov, whom Bismarck preferred to Gorchakov, saw Bismarck in Berlin and on arrival at his post in London told Lord Derby on 10 May that Bismarck was suffering from sleeplessness and talked of resignation. 'He appeared to think that all Europe was inclined to coalesce against Germany and was also much haunted by the idea of assassination... fatigue, anxiety and other causes had produced in

[Bismarck] a state of nervous excitement that may explain many of his sayings and doings.' In fact Bismarck had submitted his resignation on 4 May for the umpteenth time and with the usual phrases, 'I am incapable of performing further the work and duties inseparable from my office, and that after 24 years of active participation in the field of higher politics...my powers are no longer adequate.'[133] As usual Bismarck did not resign. The new British Prime Minister Disraeli, a Tory committed to more international activity than Gladstone, convinced the Russians to intervene jointly in Berlin to preserve the peace. Gorchakov leapt at the chance to teach Bismarck a lesson. He and Tsar Alexander travelled to Berlin to persuade the Kaiser not to go ahead with a preventive war against France, something he had no intention of doing. The visit from 10 to 13 May allowed Tsar Alexander to calm Bismarck and persuade him not resign. Gorchakov and Odo Russell confronted Bismarck on 13 May in the Foreign Ministry and tried to get him to declare publicly that he had no intention to attack France. He refused but he had lost face. He had to give in to the pressure from the Tsar and his own Emperor, the first serious reverse he had suffered. The Tsar observed that 'one should not believe the half of what he said, for he says things that he does not really mean and are only an expression of his passions and his momentary nervous excitement. One must never take him "au pied de la lettre".'[134] On 31 December Bismarck wrote gloomily, 'a bad year';[135] it was certainly the first in which he had been outplayed in the game of diplomacy.[136]

In mid-July of 1875, a revolt broke out in Herzogovina against Turkish rule, which the Turkish authorities repressed with great brutality. The emergence again of the Eastern Question confronted the three Emperors with a dilemma. On 1 August Schweinitz reported from Vienna on proposals for collective mediation that eventually resulted in the so-called Andrassy Note written in the name of the three powers to demand reforms. With the approval of the United Kingdom and France, the Note was submitted to the Sultan, whose agreement was secured on 31 January 1876. The Herzegovinian leaders, however, rejected the proposal. They pointed out that the Sultan had already made promises to institute reforms but had failed to fulfil them.[137] Within a few months, the Sultan had been overthrown but unrest continued until Abd-ul-Hamid II came to power. Revolt spread across the Balkans and in May Sir Edward Pears, the senior member of the bar in Constantinople, sent reports of atrocities in Bulgaria.

The reports contained passages which, alas, are now only too familiar after Pol Pot and Ruanda but then marked the beginning of a development of nationalist violence that has yet to die down. The British public were horrified to read descriptions such as these:

> They had seen dogs feeding on human remains, heaps of human skulls, skeletons nearly entire, rotting clothing, human hair, and flesh putrid and lying in one foul heap. They saw the town with not a roof left, with women here and there wailing their dead amid the ruins. They examined the heap and found that the skulls and skeletons were all small and that the clothing was that of women and girls. MacGahan counted a hundred skulls immediately around him. The skeletons were headless, showing that these victims had been beheaded. Further on they saw the skeletons of two little children lying side by side with frightful sabre cuts on their little skulls. MacGahan remarked that the number of children killed in these massacres was something enormous.[138]

The crisis became suddenly acute when, on 5 May 1876, the German and French consuls in Saloniki were murdered. Bismarck wanted a big naval demonstration to intimidate the Turks. France and Britain sent squadrons but Stosch refused to send any capital ships. Bismarck was furious: 'We have a fleet that can't go anywhere so we must have no trouble spots in the wide world.'[139] From 11 to 14 May the Foreign Ministers of the Three Emperors met in Berlin to coordinate policy about Turkey. The rise of an extreme Pan-Slav party at the court of the Tsar had begun to threaten that the Russians, as 'protector of the Balkan Christians', would invade Bulgaria and assist the orthodox Serbs in their revolt against Turkish rule. The three Powers could not get the other Great Powers to join them so on 8 July 1876 the Tsar and Emperor Franz Joseph met at Reichstadt and agreed to divide the Balkans in the event of a collapse of the Ottoman Empire. The Emperors had been too hasty. The Turkish army attacked the rebellious Serbian forces in July and August 1876 and routed them. Both Disraeli and Bismarck now faced difficult decisions. The Liberals, and especially the leader of the opposition, William Ewart Gladstone, had rallied behind the angry public in their horror at the Bulgarian Atrocities. Gladstone had written a powerful pamphlet with that title. Disraeli and the Tories, on the other hand, stood for the maintenance of Ottoman Turkey since it prevented the Russian fleet from entering the Eastern Mediterranean and threatening British lines of communication with its Indian Empire. That support and its apparently immoral premiss became harder to maintain.

Bismarck faced the equally delicate question of support for the Russians, who had not forgotten their aid to Prussia in the unification of Germany. The Tsar and Gorchakov wanted their reward in the form of overt German support for Russian intervention or at least German sponsorship of a conference at which the Russians could achieve their protectorate without war. Bismarck's trusty ambassador in St Petersburg, General von Schweinitz, had gone on a generous leave to hunt in the Austrian Alps and could not be reached. On 1 October the Tsar used the German military attaché, Bernhard von Werder (1823–1907) to carry an urgent message to Bismarck, 'would Germany act as Russia did in 1870, if Russia went to war with Austria?'[140] Bismarck was furious that a military attaché should let himself get into such a situation. He wrote to Bernhard Ernst von Bülow (1815–79), who had replaced Hermann von Thile as State Secretary in the Foreign Ministry, in effect, Bismarck's deputy, a private letter written from Varzin on the same day:

> Von Werder is worse than clumsy in letting himself be used as a Russian tool to extort from us an uncomfortable and untimely declaration. For the first time in his telegram the Tsar talks of 'war against <u>Austria</u>' [so in the original— JS], whereas up to now one has spoken of saving the Three Emperors' Alliance . . . and now to pose the insidious question of Austria with a yes or no is a trap set by Gorchakov. If we say no, he stirs up Alexander; if we say yes. he will use it in Vienna.[141]

Bismarck tried various dodges but the Russians continued to press him and, worse, they put pressure on Emperor William I, who had a close and affectionate relationship with his nephew, the Tsar. In November, the Tsar wrote to his uncle and urged him to support Russian military action in the 'interest of Europe'. Bismarck dictated an answer a week later in which he cynically remarked that he usually heard 'the word "Europe" in the mouth of those politicians who demanded from other powers what they in their own name dare not request'.[142]

The Turkish Sultan's forces were advancing rapidly on Belgrade. On 31 October 1876 the Russian Emperor sent the Sultan an ultimatum to halt the advance within forty-eight hours and accept an armistice of six weeks. The Porte yielded, and Britain proposed a conference in Constantinople, which the Turks accepted. Lord Salisbury, the British Foreign Secretary, travelled to Turkey for the opening session. On the same day, the Grand Vizier 'proclaimed with thundering cannon' a new constitution that, the Turks announced, made the conference of the powers unnecessary, and on

18 January 1877, an assembly of notables rejected the Russo-English proposal for a settlement.[143] Bismarck's efforts to avoid a choice between his two allies succeeded when on 15 January 1877 the Austrian and Russian Empires agreed in the Convention of Budapest to reconcile their measures and decisions in the event of war, and on 24 April 1877 Russia declared war on Turkey.[144]

The Russo-Turkish War, the sixth since the eighteenth century, turned out to be a bitter and protracted set of campaigns. The Russians invaded across the Danube in Romania and also sent a large army to the Caucasus to seize the Turkish provinces along the Black Sea coast. At first the Russian forces in the Balkans advanced so rapidly that Disraeli's cabinet on 21 July 1877 resolved to declare war on Russia if the Russians should defy British warnings and seize Constantinople. Luckily for the British, Turkish resistance stiffened and the Russian advance stalled from 10 July to 10 December 1877. After very heavy fighting in which a reorganized Serbian army had distinguished itself, the Turks asked the neutral powers for mediation.

During the summer of 1877, in July, when Bismarck took the waters at Bad Kissingen, he wrote the famous *Kissinger Diktat* (Kissingen Dictation) in which he stated his foreign policy maxims for the new German Reich:

> A French newspaper said recently about me that I suffered from 'le cauchemar des coalitions'. This sort of nightmare will last for a long time, and maybe forever, an entirely justified worry for a German minister. Coalitions against us can be formed on the western basis if Austria joins one, more dangerous, perhaps, the Russian-Austria-French combination; a greater intimacy among two of the above would give the third means to exercise a not inconsiderable pressure on us. In my anxiety about such eventualities, not at once, but in the course of years, I would regard a desirable outcome of the Oriental Crisis if the following occurred.
>
> 1. gravitating of Russian and Austrian interests and mutual rivalry towards the East;
> 2. an occasion for Russia to need the alliance with us in order to achieve a strong defensive position in the Orient and on its coasts;
> 3. for England and Russia a satisfactory status quo, which would give both the same interest in maintaining the existing situation as we have:
> 4. Separation of England because of Egypt and the Mediterranean from France which remains hostile to us.
> 5. Relations between Russia and Austria, which make it hard for both to create anti-German coalitions which centralizing or clerical forces at the Austrian court are somewhat inclined to pursue.

> If I were capable of work, I would perfect and refine this picture, which
> I have in mind, not that of the acquisition of territory but of an overall politi-
> cal situation in which all the powers except France need us and are held apart
> from coalitions against us by their relations to each other.[145]

This dictation offers the most succinct representation of Bismarckian
foreign policy aims after unification and can be said to explain the increasing complexity of the formal alliances that Bismarck contracted in the 1880s.
His admirers wax eloquent about the ingeniousness of the scheme. Yet it
failed within a year of its composition the first time he attempted to apply
it. In February 1878 he announced that he intended to act as 'an honest'
broker in the Oriental question by summoning a conference to Berlin to
settle all the outstanding issues left from the Russo-Turkish War and associated changes in the Balkans. The conference took away many of the Russian
Empire's gains from what had turned out to be a very nasty and costly little
war, and the Russians blamed Bismarck. True, he managed to renew the
Three Emperors' League in 1881 and 1884 but in 1887 he had to do it in
secret and by violating equally solemn, binding, and secret agreements with
other powers. By 1890 the Kissinger Diktat had failed and the first thing
Bismarck's successors had to do was to repudiate the 1887 Reinsurance
Treaty which Bismarck had negotiated with the Russians.

A second reason for its failure lay in Bismarck's misunderstanding of
Germany's new position in Europe. Even in his time the German Empire
had become an economic and military superpower. It had no need of these
subtle and secret agreements which rested on his elaborate combinations
and duplicity. Indeed as we shall see, Bismarck's nightmares rested on the
sort of pessimism and paranoia which marked his wider view of life. Its
legacy led to the pessimism of his successors in 1914 who unleashed an
unnecessary preventive war because they were surrounded and would be
overrun. In fact, had they waited on their borders with machine guns,
barbed wire, and artillery, both the French and Russian attackers would
have been massacred and Germany would have won the war. Bismarck's
pessimism had deep roots in his psyche and possibly also in his social identity as well, the feeling that his class had no future.

A third reason was Bismarck's own personality and record as a ruthless, unprincipled warmonger. As he desperately tried to preserve the
procrustean stretch between Austria and Russia and peace in the Balkans,
the British ambassador in Constantinople wrote to Morier and expressed

the general view that Bismarck was somebody who stirred up war everywhere.

> Bismarck is aiming at upsetting every pacific solution and involving Russia in an expensive and dangerous war; he will continue to use Andrassy as his tool and he will thus prepare two great results: the weakening of Russia and the partitioning of Turkey.[146]

In the midst of this great international crisis, Bismarck staged another resignation drama. On 27 March 1877 he told the State Ministry that 'he had decided to submit a request to the Emperor for retirement. If it is rejected and only leave is granted, he proposes to ask that a fully empowered deputy be created so that he Bismarck would be relieved of responsibility.'[147] Hildegard von Spitzemberg recorded her dismay at the prospect, not least because the loss of the connection to the Bismarcks meant a huge loss of prestige for the Spitzembergs:

> I cannot really believe it—the new *Reich* without Bismarck, 76 Wilhelmstrasse without him, one cannot imagine it but the talk was all of packing up and sending family pictures to Schönhausen. That sounds very like reality... I spoke earnestly to the Prince to ask him to give me his reasons, 'Arrange the murder of Augusta, Camphausen and Lasker with the hangers-on and I will continue to stay in office. But this constant resistance and the constant punch bag existence wears me down'...Then he took my hand and said 'you will still come to see us in Varzin?'...How loving and good and touching the great man was, as he spoke to me with tears in his eyes and stroked my hand lightly... The possibility goes round in my head, we shall lose infinitely if Bismarck goes—socially, humanly and in our position in society, for our trusting friendship with them has served us very well and made things easier. I have never concealed that from myself. The way since 1863 in exemplary loyalty I have been loved, honoured, cuddled there will never be given me anywhere again. I know only too well their great weaknesses, our views are often heavens apart, but how I love them all, how thankful, how devoted to them I am, I recognize in the deep melancholy which their departure has caused in me.[148]

A few days later, on 4 April, newspapers reported on Bismarck's resignation, whereupon the Emperor granted him leave of absence for a year.[149] The left Liberal leader, Eugen Richter wrote to his brother on hearing the news of the furlough for a year.

> Naturally Bismarck's retirement is our chief interest. That will produce changes in party relationships so colossal that they cannot be predicted. The tariff protectionists, who have become especially dangerous, have the greatest

cause to mourn. If he actually remains away from all business for a full year, that will be the equivalent of a complete retirement.[150]

The well-informed Odo Russell wrote to Lord Derby and gave him his own reading of the crisis:

I have told you in a dispatch all about the crisis, which is simply that Bismarck is *really nervous* and in want of rest—and the Emperor reluctant to part with him altogether. Besides physical ill-health, Bismarck is morally upset by the decreasing support his policy suffers from, on the part of the Emperor and of Parliament, which he attributes to the Empress's hostile influence on his Majesty, and to the Pope's influence on the Catholic Party in Parliament, instead of attributing it to his very disagreeable manner of dealing with his Sovereign and his supporters, and to the violence of his dealing with his opponents. What he wants is the power to turn out his colleagues from the new cabinet at his pleasure—a power this Emperor will never concede to his Chancellor. At Court on Thursday last the Emperor told me he would give him as much leave as he pleased but would not let him resign. The Empress told me that Bismarck must be taught to obey his Sovereign.[151]

The next day the Kaiser rejected his resignation and the appointment of a deputy on the grounds that 'any serious substitution would make it difficult for you to return'. Bismarck told the State Ministry in private that the Kaiser regarded his request as an 'insult and declared he would lay down his crown if Bismarck went'.[152]

On 14 April Hildegard von Spitzemberg learned from Princess Bismarck that the Chancellor Crisis had been resolved and that Bismarck told her the Kaiser had

wept like a baby and spoken of his abdication and hence his insistence on his resignation became impossible. But nobody believes—and rightly—that Bismarck could not have had his way had he really in full seriousness insisted on his resignation. Either he ought to have gone, cost what it costs, or ought not to have created the whole spectacle, which now all seems like a pure comedy—'scaring people does not count'...in short his authority has suffered by the result of this crisis and that depresses me very much, although I rejoice personally that everything will stay the same.[153]

On 16 April 1877 Prince Bismarck and the family departed for Friedrichsruh, the estate which the Emperor had given Bismarck in 1871. Bismarck had converted an old coaching inn in Aumühle outside Hamburg into a family house. In 1877 Lucius von Ballhausen visited him for the first time:

I took the 3.20 train to Hamburg, slept there and travelled early Sunday morning to Friedrichsruh—roughly 26 kilometres from Hamburg—where the Prince and Count Herbert waited for me at the station. Very warm reception. They live only five minutes from the station in a friendly, little cottage, which would be comfortable for a family of three or four people but not for a family with seven or eight servants. The area is beautiful but opener than Varzin. We soon mounted our horses and rode for about four hours through the wood. The Prince after fourteen days of country life and quiet days seems refreshed, sleeps better and generally seems quieter in spirit. He was full of the intrigues of Her Majesty and complained repeatedly...[154]

Bismarck worked in Friedrichsruh with the same ferocious energy he repeatedly claimed he no longer had. He went to Bad Kissingen. He travelled to Berlin. He wrote dispatches, conducted foreign policy with the same finesse as ever. On 6 October he moved to Varzin, where he noticed very painfully how the depression of agricultural prices had affected the profitability of the estate. He spelled it out in a conversation with Moritz Busch:

'Varzin brings me nothing. It is hardly possible to sell grain because railway rates for foreign grain are too low. The same is true of timber, which realizes very little owing to the competition. Even the proximity of Hamburg to the Sachsenwald is of little use to me at present.' Busch says there's a rumour that Bismarck is buying an estate in Bavaria 'Bavarian estate! I have not the least idea of buying. I have lost enough on the one I bought in Lauenburg, where the purchase money eats up the whole income of the property. How can an estate yield anything when a bushel of grain is sold at the present low price?'[155]

The summer and fall of 1877 marked an important stage in Bismarck's political career. For a while, how seriously meant we cannot say, he entertained the possibility that he might introduce Rudolf von Bennigsen, leader of the National Liberals, into his Prussian cabinet, no doubt as part of a reshuffle in which he could rid himself of ministers who had begun to irk him. Negotiations with the National Liberal party in the House of Deputies began when Bismarck asked Tiedemann to invite Rudolph von Bennigsen, its leader, to the Chancellery privately and without fuss; if that could not be accomplished right away, then to arrange a visit in Varzin. On 1 July 1877 Tiedemann wrote to von Bennigsen to explain that the Prince wished to see him without the press and public notice and hence hoped that Bennigsen could come to Berlin; if not, Tiedemann asked whether it would give rise to 'certain misinterpretations' and inconveniences if Bennigsen visited Bismarck in Varzin.[156] Bennigsen replied two days later:

> I should hope that political ignorance has not gone so far in Germany that a visit, in my capacity of President of the House of Deputies and a party leader, to the Imperial Chancellor and Minister President at his country house in Varzin could cause misunderstanding. I am entirely prepared to pay the price of any silly misunderstandings which may arise.[157]

On 30 November 1877 Tiedemann recorded another resignation crisis in a letter to his wife, one so bad 'as we have not had for ten years and it is to be feared that it will end with the definitive resignation of the Prince'. On 7 December he wrote again that

> the Prince makes his return to the job depend on conditions which in part involved a change of personnel in the higher civil service and in part on a reorganization of the offices of the Reich. If his conditions are not accepted, he is determined to submit his resignation. He is tired of having every step obstructed either from left or right. The family and his doctor had urged him to resign.[158]

At the same time as the resignation crisis Bismarck invited the leader of the National Liberals to talk about the National Liberals as a government party and Bennigsen as a minister.[159] Lucius, always well informed, analysed the resignation threat and the invitation to Bennigsen with his usual clarity:

> Bismarck [...] wavering in his attitude to an attempt to set up a partial parliamentary ministry... The general idea was the unification of the most influential Reich and Prussian ministries: the Chancellor and the Minister-President, the Vice-Chancellor in the Reich and also the same in Prussia, the Reich Justice Minister at the same time Prussian Justice Minister, the same in finance etc. The plan was to represent Prussian chief ministers in the Reich through directors or under-secretaries... As I heard from a reliable source, there was before the Kaiser a resignation request, which contained a kind of ultimatum and demanded the dismissal of certain palace officials. On the other hand, the long absences of Bismarck, the existing confusion in the coalition, have favoured anti-Bismarck forces... Besides there was a danger that Bismarck had screwed his demands too high for the Kaiser, especially in the delicate situation of the court and almost all family relations and thus the decision might go against him. The impertinence of the demand that he act against his own wife was very painful for somebody of the old monarch's courtly character. All the ultramontane, high feudal elements were active in the plan to destroy Bismarck's work.[160]

If the Emperor had ever wanted to dismiss Bismarck, this would have been the moment. He had put up with constant moral blackmail: three resignation threats in a year, two within a month; constant political activity behind his back; and the Chancellor's long absences on the pretext that he was too ill to work, etc. Yet planted articles, manoeuvres, meetings, trips to Varzin and Friedrichsruh by important people continued and the Emperor received no solid information about it all. On 29 December 1877 the *Norddeutsche Allgemeine Zeitung*, which acted as Bismarck's house organ reported rumours of impending major changes in the Prussian cabinet. That was the last straw. The next day the Emperor—entirely understandably—wrote Bismarck a furious letter in which he complained 'you have not communicated a single syllable on this subject'. He told Bismarck that he could not accept Bennigsen who was 'not quiet and conservative'.[161] Bismarck reacted to the rebuke with a complete psychological collapse. He put himself to a bed, like a child who had been scolded by an angry father. The letter of rebuke and the Kaiser's 'lack of consideration' made him ill, sleepless, and bilious, and, as Pflanze concludes, 'pathologically sick with anger', at the thought that the Kaiser could write him a critical letter.[162]

Here I have to stop to express some sympathy with Bismarck. His power rested on the old King, who had a wife who hated Bismarck and who gathered round her a camarilla of his enemies. In his weak position as a subject of a semi-absolute monarch he could never reach and crush that camarilla as he normally crushed and humiliated lesser opponents. He needed the King's approval not only psychologically but practically. Bennigsen would have been the King's minister not Bismarck's. Thus he had put himself into a position of the utmost stress in which real forces constrained him to re-enact these humiliations on a daily basis. He had only himself to blame since he had used his great powers to preserve for the King the absolute rule with which he could indirectly torture Bismarck with his own powerlessness.

The psychic tensions made worse the real and insoluble problems. The real forces in government and society ground relentlessly on and he had less certainty that he could master them. Take parliamentary government. Had he moved after 1870 towards a parliamentary system, he could have done so. The King always gave in to his genius–minister and in that case Augusta and the Crown Princess would have been on Bismarck's side, but that would have reduced the derivative absolute power so necessary to his 'sovereign self'. These double and interlocked dilemmas destroyed his peace of mind and physical well-being but like an addict he had to repeat the drama again and again.

Karl von Neumann, the Crown Prince's private secretary, summed up the situation in a gloomy letter to Roggenbach sent from Wiesbaden on 22 November 1877:

> These are hopeless conditions in which we live, and we can hardly be surprised if independent and free natures quit the public service one after another. Resignation is still better than ruining themselves by degrading themselves to mere tools of the All-Powerful One... The Chancellor has one advantage that almost the whole world agrees with him that things cannot continue for long as they are.[163]

Two days after Christmas 1877 Stosch wrote to Roggenbach to report that von Friedberg had spent three days at Varzin and heard the new plans to merge the Reich and Prussian ministries, to clear out most of the cabinet and introduce new policies.

> Friedberg asked 'and what about Stosch?' Answer: 'he enters the cabinet as an independent minister'. Isn't that gracious? The man thinks he can trample all over me and then still dispose of me freely... Another person, less adoring, who was also in Varzin and arrived just after the dog died, came home convinced that the Chancellor was already crazy or soon would be.[164]

Thus ended the year 1877, Bismarck's fifteenth in power, at the lowest point in his career. Neither the Chancellor nor his enemies knew what to do next. Harold Macmillan, British Prime Minister in the 1950s and early 1960s, was once asked by a journalist what might blow a government off its course and replied 'events, dear boy, events'. In Bismarck's case the events of 1878 had the opposite effect. A lucky combination of events gave him and his policies a sudden new direction and new life.

10

'The Guest House of the
Dead Jew'

At 12 I found him at lunch, as fresh and cheerful as possible, after he had
once again spoken in the Reichstag, (which they now call the 'Gasthof
zum toten Juden').

Baroness Spitzemberg, 15 March 1884, Spitzemberg, Tagebuch, 205

O n 11 January 1878 Bill, Bismarck's son, told Tiedemann that the Kaiser
was 'very angry' because Count Eulenburg 'as a joke' had shown him
the new cabinet list composed of the most prominent National Liberals and
Progressives—'Bennigsen, Forckenbeck, Stauffenberg, Rickert etc.'[1] On
18 January 1878 Tiedemann on orders from Bismarck had a meeting with
Bennigsen, who regarded his appointment to the ministry as 'beyond doubt'
but insisted on 'one or two colleagues from the National Liberal party' joining the cabinet with him.[2] On 19 January 1878 Tiedemann travelled to
Varzin to report on the meeting. A week later in Berlin, Rudolf von
Bennigsen told Lucius at a parliamentary dinner that the Liberals held two
trump cards:

1) the rising need for new money which cannot be satisfied without our help;
2) the approaching end in two years of the Septennat [the seven-year Army
bill which fixed the financial contribution and the size of the army—JS]. . . . If
an understanding is now reached between parliament and government, a
steady development will be guaranteed for the next twenty years; if not, incalculable complications could ensue.[3]

On 18 February the National Liberal caucus met. Julius Hölder, a deputy
from Württemberg, was there and recorded the event in his diary. Hölder
belonged to the pro-Bismarckian wing of the National Liberals in the

Reichstag but in Württemberg's parliament often curbed the enthusiasm of the Bismarckians on state level.[4] Now Hölder accepted that a showdown with Bismarck had to be faced because

> a truly responsible government is necessary, one in close touch with the Reichstag's majority...the grant of new taxes must be kept in hand as a means of pressure not only against the Bundesrat but also (as it appeared to me, at least according to the sense of their remarks) against Bismarck and the Kaiser in order (briefly said) to force a parliamentary administration of the Reich. In particular, the finances of the Reich and Prussia must come into one person's (Bennigsen) hands.[5]

This moment falls into the category devised by the late A. J. P. Taylor to describe German history: 'a series of turning points where nothing turns'. Had Bismarck raised an eyebrow or lifted a finger of approbation, three National Liberals would have joined the cabinet and Germany might have moved slowly towards a more parliamentary regime. Bismarck would have shared power, made compromises, and accepted opposition as a necessary element in all political life. He would have surrendered his dedication to a semi-absolutist monarchy and settled for less than complete control. Can Bismarck ever have considered such a possibility? There is no evidence that he did and much that he could not have. The negotiations with Bennigsen fell into the category that Morier called 'his combinations', a move on the chessboard, never more.

Before Bismarck's motives could be tested, events came to his aid. On 7 February Pius IX died. Suddenly Bismarck had room to manoeuvre. Peace with the Vatican in exchange for pressure on the Centre to get rid of Windthorst? A possible Blue-Black (Conservative-Catholic) majority in the Reichstag to move toward protectionism and conservative schemes of government? Above all, he could get rid of the Liberals, too bourgeois, too pedantic about rights and representation. He suddenly felt much better, and on 14 January he returned to Berlin. He reappeared in the Reichstag for the first time for months. On 19 February Bismarck made his 'honest broker' speech in which he invited the Great Powers to a conference on the Russo-Turkish War to be held in Berlin. Three days later, on 22 February 1878, Bismarck announced to a startled Reichstag that 'My aim is a national tobacco monopoly...as a provisional measure and a stepping-stone...'[6]

The National Liberals were appalled and placed in a dilemma. A few weeks earlier Bismarck had been chatting with Bennigsen about the terms for three National Liberal ministers in the Prussian cabinet and now he came out for state intervention and a repudiation of the free market, then and now an essential liberal demand. Bennigsen wrote to Max von Forckenbeck, the president of the Chamber, to ask: 'Do you not agree that we cannot partici-pate in setting up this monopoly? If so, I shall go to the Chancellor and tell him that our negotiations are at an end.'[7] In the Prussian State Ministry his Finance Minister and Vice-President Otto Camphausen (1812–96) resigned because he could not accept interventions in free trade.[8]

In these tense days, Ludwig Bamberger, the Liberal finance expert and long-serving Reichstag deputy, sat opposite Bismarck at a dinner and recorded from across the table certain features of his face and conversation:

> Behind the curtain of his heavy moustache one can always only partly observe him. With his usual chattiness there appears something soft and always lightly smiling across his broad lips, but directly behind lies something powerfully tearing, definitely like a predatory beast. This charming, lightly smiling mouth can open suddenly and swallow the interlocutor. He has a bulging chin, an upside-down teacup of flesh, with the convex side turned outward. The eyes are mistrustful/friendly, lurking/bright, cold/flashing, determined not to reveal what goes on behind them unless he intends it. Though he had given two long speeches in the Landtag, he chatted from 5.30 to 8.30 without a pause, listened only to himself and will not be distracted from the thread of thoughts that he spins.[9]

Nothing in Bismarck's personality suggested to Bamberger that he would enjoy a parliamentary regime.

On 20 February Cardinal Gioacchino Vincenzo Raffaele Luigi Pecci was elected Pope and took the name of Leo XIII. He was 68, and his reign was expected to be short. In fact, he lived until 20 July 1903, when he died at the age of 93. Although an aristocrat as Pius IX had been before him, Leo XIII took a very different attitude to the modern world. His famous encyclical *Rerum Novarum* of 15 May 1891, in which he wel-comed the discoveries of science and the productivity of industry but asserted that human labour could not be considered as just a factor of production, set the stage for a new Catholic relation to the industrial world and its social problems. Bismarck now had a possible partner at the highest level of the church. That was the first change in the political constellation.

The second happened a month later when on 31 March Wilhelm von Kardorff (1828–1907) had an audience with Bismarck. Kardorff, a wealthy industrialist and landlord, had been one of the founders of the Bismarckian

Reich Party and had become its most eloquent orator and effective leader. He made a fabulous fortune during the *Gründerzeit* but swung to protectionism earlier than his party. He founded the Free Economic Union in 1874 to advocate protective tariffs and in 1876 the most important industrial pressure group, the Central Association of German Industrialists.[10] When he arrived, Bismarck startled him by telling him that he now wanted 'moderate protective and finance tariffs' and continued:

> Earlier I was myself a free trader, being an estate owner, but now I am a complete convert and want to make good my earlier errors...I want tariffs on tobacco, spirits, possibly sugar, certainly petroleum, perhaps coffee, and I am not afraid of grain tariffs which could be very useful to us against Russia and also Austria.[11]

In April Bismarck began to work on new legislation for the era in which he could dispense with the Liberals. High on his agenda was a plan to crush the Social Democratic Party which had gained votes and benefited from the long depression. He drafted a law which would have given the Bundesrat exceptional powers to suppress publications and organizations which advocated Social Democratic aims. On 24 May 1878 the Reichstag rejected the exceptional legislation to limit socialist activity, 251 to 57, led largely by Liberal opposition to the bill's violation of civil rights.[12] Bismarck's indifference to the defeat surprised Tiedemann:

> When the Reichstag majority disturbs his plans, he usually does not lack caustic remarks in airing his displeasure. But this time he limited himself to a few joking remarks about the unfortunate ministers whose duty it had been to defend the ill-fated bill.[13]

For once the shrewd Tiedemann missed the point. The Liberals had voted against internal security. Bismarck knew that they had handed him the best weapon he could find. Again Macmillan's 'events, dear boy' would soon give him the moment to use it. On 11 May 1878 a worker named Max Hödel fired three shots at the Kaiser as he rode with his daughter, the Grand Duchess of Baden, in an open carriage along *Unter den Linden*. Nobody was hurt and Hödel was arrested. On 2 June Dr Karl Nobiling, a failed academic, tried again from a second-story window overlooking the same avenue and this time the Kaiser was hit by pellets in three places. The wounds would not have been serious but the Kaiser was by now 81 years old.[14] Tiedemann's account of how Bismarck reacted to the news must be one of the most remarkable eye-witness pictures of Bismarck's quickness of mind and political adroitness ever written. Here it is in full. The scene took place in Friedrichsruh that afternoon.

> As I was underway to the Aumühle and Friedrichsruh Park, I caught sight of the Prince, who, accompanied by his dogs, was walking slowly in the bright sunshine across the field. I walked towards him and joined him after a brief greeting. He was in excellent humour and chatted about his walk and on the beneficial effect which a long walk in the forest air had on his nerves. After a short pause, I said, 'some very important telegrams have arrived'. He answered in a joking tone, 'and they are so urgent that we have to attend to them here in the open field?' I replied, 'unfortunately! They contain shocking news. Another attempt has been made on the Kaiser's life and this time the shots have hit him. The Kaiser is seriously hurt.' With a jolt, the Prince stopped. He drove his oaken walking stick into the ground and said taking a deep breath as if a mental lightning bolt had struck him, 'then we dissolve the Reichstag'. Quickly he walked back to the house and while walking inquired about the details of the assassination attempt.[15]

The instant 'combination', as Morier put it, made him the most gifted political tactician of the nineteenth century. He saw in a flash that he could run a scare campaign and get rid of the Liberal Party who would be accused of lack of patriotism. He returned at once to Berlin and went to see the Kaiser in hospital. Hildegard von Spitzemberg was there when he returned:

> The Prince had just come from a conversation with the Kaiser. The strong man was so deeply moved that he had to take a drink before he could speak. 'The old man lies there, propped up in a bed, in the middle of the room, the hands wrapped entirely in gauze and stretched out far from his body, on his head an ice-pack—a pitiful sight! Behind him there was a lamp. I found him thinner in the face but businesslike as always and as clear; it is obvious that he suffers a lot, then, although he had a lot to say on matters that really interest him, after a while he nodded to me to go away.' From there the Prince went to the Crown Prince for several hours, who was at first annoyed that he had not been present at the hospital conversation. The Prince told Carl that the Crown Prince had demanded security for his person, because everything indicated that the Internationale was behind the two assassination attempts. They 'want to sweep Kaiser and Crown Prince away so that a child comes to the throne and they will have a free hand'. Today there was a grand Council of Ministers. The trouble is that the case of the temporary incapacity of the Kaiser has not been considered in the Reich Constitution, and the Crown Prince cannot step in without the declaration of a full regency. There are so many decisive decisions to take: state of emergency, dissolution of the Reichstag etc. The Prince has let a snow-white full beard grow so that he

looks ridiculously like his brother Bernhard. In the evening he came back to the Kaiser several times: 'I cannot get the old man out of my mind'. So heavy and bleak was our mood, the old firm German loyalty is broken, a stain on our honour that nothing will wash away.[16]

A Crown Council under Crown Prince approved the dissolution of the Reichstag in spite of National Liberal protests.[17] On 30 July 1878 German voters went to the polls with a turnout of 63.4 per cent, the highest since 1871. The National Liberals lost 4.1 per cent of their vote and 29 seats, and the Progressives 1 per cent and 9 seats, while the German Reich Party, Bismarck's party, won 57 seats, a gain of 19 seats, and secured 13.6 per cent of the vote, more than the *Kreuzzeitung* Conservatives, who only secured 13.0 per cent of the vote with 59 seats. The Centre, solid as always, returned the same delegation plus one new member.[18] Conservatives and Catholics together now had 210 seats, eleven more than an absolute majority of the 397 seats in the Reichstag. On the other hand the two Liberal parties with 125 seats together with the 94 Centre deputies made up a majority as well. Bismarck could play off each of the main blocks against the other. The Liberal threat had been banished and, as it happens, forever. Liberal votes declined until, on 30 July 1932, in Hitler's triumphant summer election before the seizure of power, the two great parties of 1871 had dwindled to 1 per cent each of the votes cast.

The elections took place not only against the background of a security panic but in the immediate aftermath of the Congress of Berlin, the most glittering summit since Metternich's Congress of Vienna. On 11 June 1878, a Tuesday evening, Benjamin Disraeli (1804–81), Earl of Beaconsfield, British Prime Minister, arrived in Berlin. Disraeli may have been the only statesman at the Congress who matched Bismarck in cleverness and flair. They found, as we shall see, that they liked each other. The official language of the Congress was, of course, French, which Disraeli spoke with a bad accent and the vulgar vocabulary he had acquired in his extravagant youth. Odo Russell, the British ambassador, who had been alerted by the staff that the 'Chief' had decided to speak French, welcomed him and used Disraeli's favourite device to manipulate people, flattery:

> A dreadful rumour had reached him that Beaconsfield would address the Congress in French. That would be, said Lord Odo, a very great disappointment to the Plenipotentiaries. 'They knew that they have the greatest living master of English oratory and are looking forward to your speech as the intellectual treat of their lives.' Lord Odo tells us that...[he] never knew whether he took the hint or accepted the compliment.[19]

Disraeli arrived rather unwell and at 74 somewhat fragile. He also bore the not inconsiderable burden of war or peace. The Queen and cabinet had come to the conclusion that Russian expansion had to be stopped at all costs and a fleet had been sent to the sea of Marmora. Odo Russell wrote the next day to his brother, Hastings, the Duke of Bedford,[20] 'Lord Beaconsfield seems excited, Lord Salisbury anxious and all the other Plenipos are in a nervous state which is scarcely pleasant.'[21]

Disraeli had developed a close relationship to Queen Victoria and wrote to her in extravagant terms throughout the Congress. The elegant, literary, Conservative leader pleased her much more than the stern, moralizing, Liberal leader William Ewart Gladstone (1809–98). 'You have heard me called a flatterer,' Disraeli said to Matthew Arnold, 'and it is true. Everyone likes flattery, and when you come to royalty you should lay it on with a trowel.'[22] This note to the Queen is not untypical:

> Distant from your Majesty in a foreign land and with so awful a responsibility, he feels more keenly how entirely his happiness depends on his doing duty to your Majesty and your Majesty's kind appreciation of his efforts.[23]

On 12 June Disraeli wrote to Queen Victoria to tell her that, to his surprise, Bismarck had insisted on seeing him on his arrival.

> Accordingly at a quarter to ten o'clock, Lord Beaconsfield waited on the Chancellor. They had not met for sixteen years but that space of time did not seem adequate to produce the startling change which Lord B. observed in the Chancellor's appearance. A tall pallid man with a wasp-like waist was now represented by an extremely stout person with a ruddy countenance on which now he is growing a silvery beard. In his manner there was no change except he was not perhaps quite so energetic, but frank and unaffected as before... He talked a great deal but well and calmly, no attempt at those gro-tesque expressions for which he is, or has been, celebrated,...B let us deal with the great things that concern England for England is quite ready to go to war with Russia.[24]

On 13 June 1878 the Congress of Berlin opened and Disraeli described the proceedings in a long letter to Queen Victoria:

> At two o'clock, the congress met in the Radzivill Palace—a noble hall just restored and becoming all the golden coats and glittering stars that filled it. Lord B. believes that every day is not to be so ceremonious and costumish. Prince Bismarck, a giant of a man, 6 feet 2 at least and proportionately huge, was chosen President. In the course of the morning, Prince Gortchakoff, a shriveled old man, was leaning on the arm of his gigantic rival and Prince

Bismarck, being seized with a sudden fit of rheumatism, both fell to the ground and unhappily Prince Bismarck's dog, seeing his master apparently struggling with an opponent, sprang to the rescue. It was said that Prince Gortchakoff was not maimed or bitten thro' the energetic efforts of his companion...At seven o'clock was a gala banquet at the Old Palace, a scene of extraordinary splendour. It is a real palace, but, strange to say, all the magnificent rooms and galleries of reception are where in the days of Queen Anne poor poets used to reside: the garrets. It must have been much more than 100 steps before Lord B. reached the gorgeous scene, and he thinks he would have sunk under it, had not, fortunately, the master of ceremonies been shorter-breathed than himself, so there were many halts of the caravan.[25]

Before the conference, the Russian had conceded that the entire Treaty of San Stefano would be negotiable and the British had conceded that the decisions of the Congress would be unanimous, in effect, to give the Russian a veto. Odo Russell turned out to be at least as good in the flattery game as his chief, as he wrote to Hastings:

I overwhelm Lord Beaconsfield with honours and respect and give him my place at the table as if he were the Queen or the Prince of Wales, at which he seems well pleased, for he calls me 'his dear and distinguished colleague' and assures me that one of his chief objects in coming to Berlin was to see my 'dear wife who is the most agreeable woman he ever knew...'[26]

Bismarck puzzled and discomfited Disraeli and Lord Salisbury, the Foreign Secretary, by his odd behaviour. On 16 June Disraeli and Salisbury had been invited by the Emperor and Empress to wait on them at Potsdam, but, as he wrote in his diary, Bismarck insisted on seeing him before he left:

Before I went down to Potsdam, I had by his invitation an interview with Prince Bismarck, which lasted upwards of an hour. What his object was, or is, I have not yet discovered. There was no business done; it was a monologue, a rambling amusing, egotistical autobiography. As His Highness had requested this interview, I would not open on any point. Lord Salisbury, equally invited, had an audience almost immediately after me and of the same surprising character...not a word of business from Prince Bismarck, either to Lord Salisbury or to myself.[27]

The next day, 17 June, he had another long exposure to the oddities of Bismarck. There was a formal dinner—a very rare occasion—at the residence of the Bismarcks, as Disraeli wrote to Queen Victoria:

In the afternoon at 6 o'clock great dinner at P. Bismarck's. All these banquets are very well done. There must have been sixty guests. The Princess was present. She is not fair to see tho' her domestic influence is said to be irresistible. I sate on the right hand of P. Bismarck and, never caring much to eat in public, I could listen to his Rabelaisian monologues: endless revelations of things he ought not to mention. He impressed on me never to trust princes or courtiers; that his illness was not, as people supposed, brought on by the French war but by the horrible conduct of his Sovereign etc etc. In the archives of his family remain the documents, the royal letters which accuse him after all his services of being a traitor. He went on in such a vein that I was at last obliged to tell him that, instead of encountering 'duplicity' which he said was universal among Sovereigns, I served one who was the soul of candor and justice and whom all her Ministers loved. The contrast between his voice which is sweet and gentle with his ogre-like form, is striking. He is apparently well-read, familiar with modern literature. His characters of personages extremely piquant. Recklessly frank. He is bound hand and foot to Austria whether he thinks them right or wrong: but always adds: 'I offered myself to England and Lord Derby would not notice my application for six weeks and then rejected it'.[28]

The German Ambassador to Russia, von Schweinitz, had become seriously worried about the Congress and wrote to his wife that 'the conference is going very badly. Everybody against Russia except us. Andrassy makes a play for old Beaconsfield, flatters him, everything he says is wonderful and will vote in everything with him against Russia.'[29] Bismarck suddenly got serious, and as Disraeli recorded in his diary, took an unusual step on 21 June:

I was engaged to dine today at a grand party at the English embassy, but about 5 o'clock Prince Bismarck called on me, and asked how we were getting on and expressed his anxiety and threw out some plans for a compromise, such as limiting the troops of the Sultan etc etc. I told him that in London we had compromised this question, and in deference to the feelings of the Emperor of Russia, and it was impossible to recede. 'Am I to understand it is an ultimatum?' 'You are.' 'I am obliged to go to the Crown Prince now. We should talk over this matter. Where do you dine today?' 'At the English Embassy.' 'I wish you could dine with me. I am alone at 6 o'clock.' I accepted his invitation, sent my apology to Lady Odo, dined with Bismarck, the Princess, his daughter, his married niece, and two sons. He was very agreeable indeed at dinner, made no allusion to politics, and, tho' he ate and drank a great deal, talked more.

After dinner, we retired to another room, where he smoked and I followed his example. I believe I gave the last blow to my shattered constitution, but I felt it was absolutely necessary. I had an hour and a half of the most interesting conversation, entirely political. He was convinced that the ultimatum was not a sham, and, before I went to bed, I had the satisfaction of knowing that St Petersburg had surrendered.[30]

The following morning, 22 June, at 10.30 a.m. Disraeli telegraphed the Queen and Chancellor of the Exchequer: 'Russia surrenders and accepts the English scheme for the European frontier of the Empire, and its military and political rule by the Sultan. Bismarck says, "There is again a Turkey-in-Europe". "It is all due to your energy and firmness" was the Queen's reply.'[31]

A few days later, on 26 June, Disraeli sketched another vivid portrait of Bismarck for Lady Bradford, his special confidante.

> Bismarck soars above all: he is six foot four I shd think, proportionately stout; with a sweet and gentle voice, and with a peculiarly refined enunciation, wh. singularly contrasts with the awful things he says: appalling from their frankness and their audacity. He is a complete despot here, and from the highest to the lowest of the Prussians and all the permanent foreign diplomacy, tremble at his frown and court most sedulously his smile. He loads me with kindness, and tho' often preoccupied with an immediate dissolution of parliament on his hands; an internecine war with the Socialists, 100s of whom he puts daily into prison in defiance of all law, he yesterday extracted from me a promise that, before I depart, I will once more dine with him quite alone. His palace has large and beautiful gardens. He has never been out since I came here, except the memorable day when he called on me to ascertain wh[ether] my policy was an ultimatum. I convinced him that it was, and the Russians surrendered a few hours afterwards.[32]

Disraeli was delighted to find 'all the ladies are reading my novels from the Empress downwards. The ladies are generally reading *Henrietta Temple*, which being a "love story" and written forty years ago, is hardly becoming an Envoy Extraordinary.'[33] Odo Russell found, as he wrote in a letter to the Foreign Office, that even the Chancellor 'is deeply interested in Lord Beaconsfield's novels which he is reading once again. Prince Bismarck informed Monsier de St. Vallier that, while he read novels, his mind enjoyed perfect rest, because it ceased to govern Germany for the time being—but that if he did not write novels, it was because the government of Germany required the whole of his undivided creative powers.'[34]

No doubt Bismarck and Disraeli dominated the Congress of Berlin, and equally there is no doubt that Disraeli found Bismarck a fascinating and bizarre figure. Bismarck behaved in an unusual way to Disraeli as well. He called upon him, something he *never* did after he achieved his great status, and he invited him to a family dinner, a confidence accorded to literally no other foreign statesman. I am not even certain that Odo Russell ever enjoyed the intimacy of the Bismarck family. Here is Disraeli's account of that memorable evening on 5 July 1878:

I dined with Bismarck alone i.e. with his family who disappear after the repast, and then we talked and smoked, If you do not smoke under such circumstances, you look like a spy, taking down his conversation in your mind. Smoking in common puts him at ease. He asked me whether racing was much encouraged in England. I replied never more so... 'Then,' cried the Prince eagerly, 'there never will be socialism in England. You are a happy country. You are safe as long as the people are devoted to racing. Here a gentleman cannot ride down the street without twenty persons saying to themselves or each other, "Why has that fellow a horse, and I have not one?" In England the more horses a nobleman has, the more popular he is, So long as the English are devoted to racing, Socialism has no chance with you.' This gives you as slight idea of the style of his conversation. His views on all subjects are original, but there is no strain, no effort at paradox. He talks as Montaigne writes. When he heard about Cyprus, he said 'you have done a wise thing. This is progress. It will be popular; a nation likes progress'. His idea of progress was evidently seizing something. He said he looked upon our relinquishment of the Ionian Isles as the first sign of our decadence. Cyprus put us all right again.[35]

Bismarck ran the Congress of Berlin entirely by himself. He used three languages interchangeably—English, French, and German—and composed the necessary documents in French either by hand or in dictation. He managed to get the business done in twenty sessions and negotiated a package of compromises. Britain gained Cyprus, a reduction of the size of Bulgaria, preservation of Turkish sovereignty over Macedonia and the Mediterranean coast. In other words, Russia could not affect the supply route to India. The straits remained under Turkish control. Russia received Bessarabia, Kars, Ardahan, and Batum but none of that satisfied the Pan-Slav groups and the Russian imperialists. As a compensation, the Austrians gained control of Bosnia and Herzegovina and the Sandjak of Novi-Bazar. Bismarck had rearranged south-eastern Europe, avoided war, and increased his own and the prestige of the German Empire. In diplomatic matters he negotiated, cajoled, discussed, and compromised, all the forms of behaviour that he showed so rarely in domestic affairs. But in the end he had opted not to support Russia in order to maintain his impartiality and the Tsar and the court were offended.

After the glamour of the Congress he had to return to domestic affairs. During the summer at Bad Kissingen, he met Cardinal Aloisi Masella on a regular basis from 30 July to 16 August, but the negotiations with the Catholic church got nowhere. As he wrote to Falk on 8 August, 'The Pope does not have the least influence on the Centre Party' but he wanted nobody to know that. As he continued, 'In my opinion the uncertainty must be maintained as long as possible. The belief in an approaching reconciliation between state and curia will unquestionably be beneficial for the conduct of the curia, the Centre and the liberal parties.'[36]

On 9 September 1878 the new Reichstag met for the first time. A chastened and smaller National Liberal Party had already agreed to the adoption of a law against subversion. The question was only how severe to make it. A week later Bismarck returned to Berlin for the first reading of the Anti-Socialist Law.[37] One of the first speakers was none other than Hans von Kleist-Retzow, who made a fierce attack on Social Democracy and accused them of high treason:

> I stick to the view that the whole of Social Democracy is the way to high treason, that they carry out the work of moles, they undermine the foundations of the state. Are then the things you do, the battle songs you sing on the streets—the Marseillaise of the future, just childrens' games, are they lesser preparations as if somebody bought powder or shot? ...

As Kleist finished, the Reich Chancellor came down from the ministers' platform and went over to the old friend. Much moved, Bismarck reached out his hand and carried out before the whole country an act of reconciliation. Kleist too was deeply moved. Two days later he directed a thank you note to his old and now re-found friend:

> Let me just before I go off thank you with all my heart that you recently gave me your hand after so long and so painful a separation. With great joy I see in the gesture an expression of your wish to restore the old friendship and familial band and the previous traffic between our houses.[38]

The friendship never returned to the old basis and Kleist rarely saw Bismarck except in and around the House of Lords. It mattered very much to von Kleist; did it matter to Bismarck? He had lost his dear 'Mot', John Lothrop Motley, who died in London on 29 May 1877. He rarely saw 'Flesch', Alexander von Keyserlingk, the other college friend, whose scientific interests Bismarck did not share and whose estate lay in distant Latvia, then part of the Russian Empire. He began more and more to feel lonely and isolated.

On 23 September Bismarck left Berlin for Varzin but had to return because the committee on the socialist law had been unable to agree on the appeals procedures.[39] From 9 to 15 October a fierce debate raged on the question of civil rights. Eduard Lasker fought a last ditch battle to preserve the constitutional rights of the Socialists. On 11 October he found an unexpected ally. Ludwig Windthorst rose to make one of his great speeches:

> 'Conservative' means to conserve the given, legitimate institutions in State and Church. It does not mean to arm a government with omnipotence, with which it can modify those institutions at will. So long as you confuse conservatism with *Polizeiwirtschaft* [a police state] an alliance with you is certainly unthinkable.[40]

Windthorst's courageous stand at the head of a conservative Catholic Party reflected a position he had always held—that the defence of Catholic rights in the *Kulturkampf* covered all rights, the rights of everybody, Jews, Catholics, Socialists, or Atheists. The consistency, integrity, and sheer courage with which Windthorst fought Bismarck's authoritarianism and violations of the law, often against the reactionary instincts of his own parliamentary party, deserve to be better known and honoured in the Federal Republic of Germany than they are. Even Lasker gave in under the pressure of what he saw as public opinion and confessed that 'contempt for the laws should no longer be tolerated and the Deputies were almost challenged to vote for an exceptional law.'[41] On 19 October 1878 the Reichstag passed the Anti-Socialist Law with 221 to 149 votes. The German Conservatives, Free Conservatives, and National Liberals created a pact to see the law through. The government had to accept a Lasker amendment in second reading that the law would in the first instance only last until September 1881 (2½ years).[42] The law contained severe restrictions: 'Paragraph 1. Associations which through Social Democratic, Socialist or Communist activities intend to overthrow the existing state and social order are to be forbidden.' Paragraph 9 outlawed public meetings which urged the overthrow of state and society and paragraph 11 outlawed publications which did the same. A variety of other measures added to the burdens on the Socialist organizations.[43] Bismarck blamed his new Minister of the Interior, yet another Eulenburg, cousin Botho Count zu Eulenburg (1831–1912), for the fact that the law continued to allow citizens to vote for socialists and did not take away rights of railways workers and other state employees to do so. Bismarck told Lucius, 'I do not believe it possible to let citizens, legally proven to be socialists, retain the right to vote, the right to stand for election and the pleasure and privilege of sitting in the Reichstag.'[44]

Before the vote on the Anti-Socialist Law on 17 October 1878, a group of deputies from three parties—87 from the Centre, 36 conservatives, and

27 liberals, amounting to 204 in total or a majority of the 397 Reichstag members—had formed 'The Economic Association of the Reichstag'. It was chaired by Friedrich von Varnbüler from Württemberg, a long-time advocate of tariff protection. The Association showed that there was now a clear majority in favour of the abolition of free trade. This was the second great alteration in German politics. No bill had been introduced and details had to be worked out but the sense of the House was now clear.[45]

On 23 October Bismarck left Berlin and returned to Friedrichsruh. On the way, Tiedemann noted that Bismarck hid the beer bottles from which he had been drinking under the table in the train every time it halted at a station. He explained to Tiedemann that the public should not be disillusioned about their Chancellor.[46] On 9 November Bismarck wrote to Emperor William I to apologize for his absence at the Landtag:

> My health leaves much to be desired. I need for some time absolute rest, which I have not been able to enjoy for years past; I hope to find it at Friedrichsruh while the Landtag is sitting, and will not let my own weakness interfere with the gladness with which I hear through Lehndorff of your Majesty's returning strength.[47]

As mentioned earlier, Pflanze did the sums and found that between 14 May 1875 and the end of November 1878, of 1,275 total days, Bismarck spent 772 either at his estates or at spas, or more than two years away from Berlin.[48] The remarkable thing is how little rest Bismarck actually took when not in Berlin. He wrote memoranda, he saw ministers, he drafted legislation, and planted articles in the official press. For example, on 6 November official newspapers attacked the Centre for its failure to welcome peace moves between Leo XIII and Bismarck. The *Provincial Correspondence* wrote:

> This striking behaviour is only understandable through the character, composition and leadership of the Centre Party, which for years has posed as the representative of the clerical interests of German Catholics but which in reality pursues purely political ends which have nothing to do with the real interests of the Roman Catholic Church.[49]

For the next few years Bismarck tried to drive wedges into the crack between the Curia in Rome and the Centre Party in Germany and in the Reichstag. The crack existed. The Centre refused to act as the agent of the Vatican and demanded an autonomy which the Curia found difficult to accept. Bismarck sensed that tension and had the cunning to try to exploit it. Windthorst had the cunning to cut off the move before the crack widened.

In response to the new campaign by Bismarck Windthorst introduced a bill on 11 December 1878 to allow those religious orders still on German soil to stay and for the reinstatement of Articles 15, 16, and 18 of the Reich Constitution, which protected civil rights of Catholics. Windthorst knew that Lasker and the Left Liberals would support the move and the Bishops and the Centre would form a solid phalanx behind such an unexceptionable bill. After all, how could a few convents and monasteries undermine Bismarck's mighty Reich? And if Bismarck blocked such a modest and reasonable bill, the Roman Curia would drop its private negotiations and fall in behind the Centre Party. Windthorst played Bismarck's game as quickly and flexibly as the Chancellor could. He had a marvellous facility for exploiting the weakness of the Church in the *Kulturkampf* to embarrass Bismarck and encourage the Catholic faithful.

The approaching end of the *Kulturkampf* and the election of 1878 had ended Bismarck's need for Liberal votes. Now he could introduce protection. On 12 November 1878 he proposed that the Bundesrat create a Tariff Commission to prepare new legislation. In December Bleichröder, who visited Friedrichsruh regularly, told Bismarck and Tiedemann that his English correspondents informed him that American competition had begun to have a serious effect on English monetary policy and that it was likely that the UK would also soon adopt tariffs. On 15 December the official press published the news that Bismarck had sent the text of a set of requirements for tariffs to the Bundesrat. Bismarck declared in the Reichstag that the Reich income should in future come from indirect taxes rather than direct ones. Tariffs would allow financial reform, since indirect taxes 'were less burdensome than direct ones' and since 'other states surround themselves with customs barriers it seems to me justified...that German products have a small advantage over foreign ones.'[50] These two standard arguments for protection had become Bismarck's policy even though as opposition papers quickly pointed out, Bismarck had in 1875 wanted most of the state's income to come from 'income tax from the really rich people'.[51] The opposition stressed the fact that indirect taxes have a regressive effect, a penny on a loaf of bread costs the poor man a larger share of his income than the same penny on a loaf purchased by a rich man.

Bismarck was in fighting mood, as he told Tiedemann on 11 January 1879,

if his ideas on tax and tariff policy meet serious resistance among the Prussian ministers, he will travel to Berlin, call a meeting of the State Ministry and put to them the future of the cabinet. If the gentlemen will not go along with him, so he will ask them to look for other employment and will form a ministry with new cabinet officers from lower ranks if necessary. The Emperor agrees with him.[52]

He also sent a draft bill to the Bundesrat to make sure that punishment of excesses in speeches in the Reichstag be introduced, the so-called *Maulkorbgesetz* (the muzzle law). The Prussian Landtag took up the issue and Lasker spoke for the majority when he said 'freedom of speech is untouchable and must remain so and expressed the confidence that the Reichstag will know how to preserve it'.[53] Even Bismarck could not introduce restrictions on free speech in the Reichstag and the motion failed.

On 19 January Max von Forckenbeck (1821–92), president of the Reichstag, wrote to Franz Freiherr Schenk von Stauffenberg (1834–1901), the leader of the Bavarian Liberals about his anxieties. Forckenbeck and Stauffenberg were the two ministers whom Bennigsen had wanted to bring with him into Bismarck's cabinet. Both were far too liberal for the Chancellor. Forckenbeck he called 'dark red'.[54] Forckenbeck's letter sums up the change that had been going on:

> The Bismarck system is developing with fearsome speed just as I always feared. Universal military conscription, unlimited and excessive indirect taxes, a disciplined and degraded Reichstag, and a public opinion ruined and made powerless by the struggle between all material interests—that is certainly the politics of popular impotence, the end of any possible development towards constitutional freedom, and at the same time a terrible danger for the entire Reich and the new imperial monarchy. Is the National Liberal party a suitable instrument to combat such dangers with its present politics, its present programme and its present composition? Will we not be led deeper and deeper into the quagmire? Has pure opposition not become a duty?[55]

Ludwig Bamberger took a cynical view of Bismarck's motives in introducing tariffs and in a diary entry just dated 1879 he speculated that self-interest played a big role:

> The progress of Bismarck's thinking arrived at protective tariffs from the protection of agriculture. The industrial tariffs served as a mere pretext. Among agrarian tariffs the tariff on lumber came at the head of the list. He is, after all, proprietor of woods. Senator Plessing from Hamburg who substituted for Krüger in the Federal Council was astonished by the exuberance of Bismarck when it came to this subject. He took part personally in all the negotiations, was inexhaustible in his speeches, knew his way through the most minute

details of the lumber trade like an office clerk. According to the Senator's account, the axe rages in the woods of Lauenburg and huge piles of timber have piled up in the warehouse. . . . Bismarck asked his own advisers, those whom he trusts, to send the final draft of the tariff bill to Bad Kissingen where he made corrections in his own hand in the rates on the various categories of timber products.[56]

Later in February he lost another of his old friends. On 27 February 1879 Albrecht von Roon died, age 76. Robert Lucius von Ballhausen assessed the man whom he had known well:

> Roon was the perfect type of the severe, dutiful, conscientious, Prussian. He was endowed with very high intellectual abilities, great talent for organization, an unshakeable determination, strength of will. In manner, occasionally rash, off-putting but genuine through and through.[57]

Roon had an inner integrity and decency which high office, fame, and success never spoiled or corrupted. Bismarck owed him a greater debt than to any other figure in his career. Roon's persistence with the King from 1859 to 1862 secured Bismarck the chance to become Minister-President in the 'Conflict Time' and his loyalty through their relationship allowed Bismarck to become what he did. In bad health and very tired, Roon answered Bismarck's call to become Minister-President of Prussia in 1872—to allow Bismarck to indulge himself in hysterical hypochondria. Here is Bismarck's verdict.

> Roon was the most competent of my colleagues. He could not get along with others. He treated them as a regiment which he marched too long. The colleagues in due course complained about this and I had to take over the Ministry of State again.[58]

So much for the adieu to the most loyal and far-sighted of Bismarck's companions.

On 7 February 1879 Bismarck announced that the government intended 'to make it a goal to complete the system of state railways, which was outlined in the draft of 1876, as far as the main trunk lines are concerned'.[59] The retreat from private enterprise had become a rout. On 24 February 1879 the Congress of German Landowners, the pressure group of the 250 largest landowners, adopted protectionism.

There remained a problem about what to do with the customs receipts which would flow to the central authorities from the new tariffs. The German Reich was a federal state. When ministers addressed the Reichstag, they spoke in the name of 'The Allied Governments' not 'the Reich' let alone 'Germany'. If the income from tariffs went exclusively to the federal government, the federal balance would tilt against the Allied Governments. The Roman Catholic Centre Party had its power base in Bavaria, the Catholic districts of Württemberg and Baden, and the Catholic Rhineland, areas very unwilling to see the Prussian-dominated Reich grow. When the Reichstag opened on 12 February it became increasingly clear that the Centre with its 94 votes could give Bismarck his majority or withhold it.

The immediate result was that Bismarck had to learn to be nice to Windthorst. On 31 March he had a conversation with Windthorst and granted a pension to the Dowager Queen of Hanover, a convenient gesture since Windthorst, as a lawyer, represented the exiled Hanoverian royal family.[60] Bismarck then told him that he had proposed diplomatic recognition of the Curia in exchange for maintenance of the *Anzeigepflicht*, the obligation of the Vatican to get the approval from the state for the appointment of bishops. Windthorst replied that he and his friends had 'received no communication at all from the curia over the content of the negotiations, and were therefore not in a position to express a view of them'. Bismarck and Windthorst agreed on the need for tariffs.[61]

In the midst of these complicated negotiations, on 8 April 1879, the French ambassador, Saint-Vallier, wrote to the French Foreign Secretary Waddington about the reality of the power of parliament in Bismarck's Reich:

> it is a common enough error among newcomers and superficial observers here in Berlin to take for real the parliamentary system as it exists here: with more experience and reflection, one quickly realizes that Germany is endowed with a fine and beautiful façade, finely embellished on the surface, faithfully representing a picture of a parliamentary and constitutional system; the rules are correctly applied; the play of parties, turmoil in the corridors, lively debates, stormy sessions, defeats inflicted on the government and even on the powerful Chancellor (only in matters of course that he considers of secondary importance), in short everything is done that can give the illusion and make one believe in the gravity of the debates and importance of the votes; but behind this scenery, at the back of the stage, intervening always at the decisive hour and always having their way, appear Emperor and Chancellor, supported by the vital forces of the nation—the army dedicated to the point of fanaticism, the bureaucracy disciplined by the master's hand, the bench no less obedient, and the population, skeptical occasionally of their judgements, quick to criticize but quicker still to bow to the supreme will.[62]

This view of Germany, the authoritarian state, finds easy assent but is too simple. Parliamentary government twisted and turned to free itself from Bismarck's control. There was nothing inevitable about the longevity of King/Emperor William I. His death almost any time before 1887 would have ushered in the era of parliamentary sovereignty in Germany. The combination of the reactionary Emperor and the brilliance of Bismarck managed to prevent it but only just.

In April Windthorst travelled to Vienna to see his Hanoverian clients and while there had a meeting on 20 April 1879 with the *nuncio* Archbishop Ludovico Jacobini, who had been acting as the intermediary between Bismarck and the Vatican. Windthorst told the nuncio 'Bismarck is more powerful than King William and the dynasty. No one is able to do anything against him. "A second Wallenstein," the historian Klopp inserted eagerly. "More than that", was Windthorst's laconic reply.'[63]

When Windthorst returned to Berlin at the end of April 1879 he had a surprise awaiting him. For the first time Bismarck invited him on 3 May to a parliamentary *soirée* at 76 Wilhelmstrasse. Centre deputies had been rigorously excluded from such convivial occasions and the press gathered outside the palace to hear what happened. Bismarck received Windthorst with extra cordiality but spilled punch over his white waistcoat and tried—to the amusement of Windthorst and the bystanders—to dry him off with a table-cloth. It might, in view of Bismarck's deep loathing for Windthorst, be considered a 'Freudian slip'. When the tiny little man emerged on the steps, the journalists asked him how he had been received and he replied with his usual quick wit 'extra Centrum nulla salus' which for those less familiar with Catholic dogma may need a gloss.[64] In traditional Catholic doctrine, the church taught 'extra ecclesiam nulla salus'—outside the church, no salvation. Windthorst's pun played on the fact that Bismarck could accomplish nothing in the Reichstag without the Centre; there would be no 'salvation without the Centre'. Canon Franz Christoph Ignaz Moufang (1817–90), an intransigent ultramontane and rigorous theological conservative,[65] was horrified at the spectacle of Windthorst and the Antichrist Bismarck in polite conversation:

> the exiled and harassed bishops and the punished and harried priests, and the zealous Catholics who listen and read in the newspapers that Herr Bismarck and Herr Windthorst have met together very amiably, do not understand how one is able to be a persecutor of the Church and a friend of Herr Windthorst at one and the same time.[66]

Apparently the pious Canon had not heard that to eat with the devil one needs a long spoon.

On 9 May 1879 Eduard Lasker accused Bismarck in the Reichstag of pursuing 'the finance policy of the propertied'. Bismarck replied in a rage,

> I can say with just as much justice that the Herr Deputy Lasker pursues the finance policy of the property-less. He belongs among those gentlemen, who at all stages in the promulgation of our legislation form the majority of whom scripture says 'they sew not, the harvest not, they spin not, they weave not, and still are clothed.'[67]

The real quote reads very differently. It is from the Gospel of St Matthew, Chapter 6, verse 26: 'Behold the fowls of the air: for they sow not, neither do they reap, nor gather into barns; yet your heavenly Father feedeth them. Are ye not much better than they?' Bismarck continued by personal attacks on Lasker so sharp that the president of the Reichstag rang the bell to warn the Chancellor to use parliamentary language. Bismarck in a rage (*wütend*) created an 'embarrassing scene':

> what's the meaning of that bell? It's perfectly quiet in the house...I am the highest official in the Reich, and am here as President of the Bundesrat. I am not subject to the discipline of the president. He may not interrupt me nor warn me with the bell, as he did today. At the end he may criticize my speech or those of the members of the Bundesrat. He may even complain to their superiors, but if he tries to exercise discipline in this way, it will be one step closer to a dissolution.[68]

The heated debates continued. Over 155 speakers took part in the debates in the Reichstag alone, let alone in the committees. The special interests swarmed round the chamber pressing for protection for this or that product, haggling over rates and conditions. One condition became essential and the Centre took it to the floor, proposed by its parliamentary leader, Georg Freiherr von und zu Franckenstein (1825–90). Franckenstein chaired the committee which drafted the legislation for protective tariffs, and included a clause, which came to be called the 'Franckenstein clause', which limited the amount of customs revenue and tobacco duty payable to the Reich to 130 million marks. Everything beyond that would go to the federal states. On 9 July 1879 the Franckenstein clause was adopted by 211 (Conservatives, Free Conservatives, Centre) and 122 against (National Liberals, Progressives, Poles, Guelphs, and SPD).[69] It had long-term and important effects. By limiting the Reich to a fixed amount of customs revenue, the Centre and the

Franckenstein clause prevented the central government from profiting from the great economic boom and the staggering growth in imports after the end of the great depression in 1896. Niall Ferguson argues that the squeeze on the budget in the years before 1914 made the General Staff and the War Ministry so nervous about Russian and French growth in military strength that they resolved to act in July 1914 before Germany with its constant budget crises was overrun by them.[70] Another example of Burke's principle of unintended consequences.

On 26 May 1879 the Reichstag completed the committee stage of its debates on the tariff and on 25 June 1879 Bismarck accepted the Franckenstein Clause as the precondition of passage of the tariff bill. On 9 July Bismarck gave his last speech to the Reichstag on tariffs: 'Since becoming a minister, I have belonged to no party; nor could I have belonged to any. I have been successively hated by all parties and loved by few. The roles have continually changed.'[71] Windthorst replied for the Centre: 'What we are doing, we do on grounds inherent in the matter itself, and for no other reason.' To the charge that Bismarck had duped him into support for the bill, 'In any case, I want to say to you that whoever wants to dupe me must get up a little bit early.' (Universal, stormy laughter.)[72] On 12 July 1879 the protective tariff bill passed with a majority of 100.

The next stage was to get rid of superfluous ministers. On 29 July 1879 Adalbert Falk resigned and was replaced by the arch-conservative Robert Freiherr von Puttkamer, a member of one of the largest and most influential Pomeranian Junker families and a relative of Bismarck's wife. By 1880 fifteen Puttkamers had the rank of general in the Prussian Army, and another 250 officers of various ranks, even more than the Kleists.[73] Robert Puttkamer had a very large and handsome full beard. Bismarck later said, 'Had I known that he spent half an hour every day combing his beard, I would never have made him a minister.'[74] Puttkamer loved to hear the sound of his own voice, to which Bismarck remarked, 'He is an excellent swimmer; too bad, he swims in every puddle.'[75]

The dismissal of Karl Rudolf Friedenthal was much nastier. Friedenthal was one of the founders of the Bismarckian Reich Party in 1867 and became Minister of Agriculture on 19 April 1874.[76] In 1874 and for some years afterwards Bismarck had been delighted with Friedenthal because as an estate owner he lived as Bismarck did in the real world. By the summer of 1879 he wanted to be rid of all the remaining Liberal members of his cabinet. On 3 June 1879 he wrote to the Kaiser, who had a high opinion of Friedenthal in his usual dismissive way about the ministers in the Prussian State Ministry:

> He (Friedenthal) is ambitious and his wife perhaps even more so, but his ambition rests on the future. He keeps in touch with a tiny group of 'future ministers', who reckon with their expectation that when God calls His Royal Highness to the throne, he will name a liberal ministry. Among the five or six minister candidates who make this calculation, Friedenthal is by far the cleverest.[77]

At a parliamentary soirée toward the end of June, Bismarck called Friedenthal, who was a Lutheran convert married to a Catholic, a 'jüdischen Hosenscheisser' (a Jew who shits his trousers, i.e. a coward) and this got to Friedenthal. On 4 July Lucius went to see Friedenthal and recorded what Friedenthal said to him. He was:

> Not willing to be trodden under foot. Under no circumstances would he allow himself to be talked into staying. He was now packing and prepared to be expelled from the country etc. The grounds of his anger are remarks of Bismarck at the last soirée at which he called Friedenthal 'a semitic pants-shitter [Hosensch——] which with certain circumlocutions got into all the newspapers.[78]

Bismarck appointed the loyal Lucius to be Friedenthal's successor and on 14 July Lucius received important post, the large blue envelope from the palace with his appointment to the ministry of agriculture and forestry.

> I went to Friedenthal at once and found him in great distress. He had heard nothing and apparently feared that he would receive his dismissal in an ungracious form. While I was there, two blue envelopes were delivered, in one he found confirmation of his resignation but with the rank and title of Minister of State; the other contained a patent of nobility. He gave me the impression that the latter was unwelcome to him. Later he refused the ennoblement.[79]

Friedenthal's treatment at Bismarck's hands shows again his inability to recognize service given him by others. Hans-Joachim Schoeps, who spent his career as a Jewish apologist for the Prussians,[80] claims that Bismarck called him a 'jüdischen Hosenscheisser' because Friendenthal refused to become Minister of the Interior, for which nobody else offers any evidence. But even if the story had been true, what gentleman insults a valued colleague in that vulgar and disgusting way? Friedenthal's real crime lay in the fact that he had the nerve to resign at a time of his choosing, not Bismarck's.

Liberals had been expelled from the cabinet. Draconian laws against the Social Democratic Party now violated the civil and political rights of tens of thousands of citizens. Tariffs and customs duties had replaced free trade. Schemes for state ownership had multiplied but it never occurred to Bismarck to resign or explain the great changes. He had no need to do so. He was Bismarck. Quite the contrary. He wanted to revenge himself on the Liberals as is clear from the letter he wrote to King Ludwig of Bavaria on 4 August 1879:

> The fiery speeches addressed to the property-less classes by Lasker and Richter have displayed the revolutionary tendencies of these deputies so clearly and nakedly that for a supporter of the monarchical form of government no political cooperation with them can be possible anymore... These are learned gentlemen without property, without industry, without a trade. These gentlemen are the ones who deliver the revolutionary ferment and who lead the Progressive National Liberal parliamentary parties. Splitting these fractions is in my most humble opinion an essential task of conservative politics.[81]

The Liberals merely wanted the standard protections of the rule of law, freedom of speech, protection against arbitrary arrest, freedom of religious worship, freedom of the press, and freedom of learning and research, all freedoms enshrined in the Prussian Constitution of 1850 and ruthlessly ignored by Bismarck, who had not included them in the Reich Constitution of 1870. Such persons had in his eyes become guilty of revolutionary tendencies, not against the 'monarchical principle' but against the tyranny of Otto von Bismarck.

In August 1879 Tsar Alexander II complained about German policy to Ambassador von Schweinitz and on 15 August wrote to the Kaiser to complain in even stronger terms. Bismarck reacted by moving toward Austria and arranged to meet the Austrian Foreign Minister, Gyula Count von Andrassy (1823–90) at Bad Gastein on 27 and 28 August. The official press noted that 'confidential discussions' had taken place but made no further comment.[82] Andrassy represented the Westerners at the Habsburg court, a grand Hungarian magnate who had fought with Kossuth for a liberal, independent Hungary, had fled to England, which he admired, and had been an architect of the Dual Monarchy in 1867, the system under which the Hungarian Kingdom had equal status with the Austrian lands. As his biographer writes, Andrassy sought *Rückendeckung* (cover for his back) in Berlin[83] and a glance at the structure of European politics shows why. The Magyars ruled over some 17 million people (Magyars, Germans, Slovaks, Serbs, Romanians) but never constituted a majority of the total population in the 'Kingdom of Hungary', as it was resurrected in 1867. They had to defend their rights both against the Austrians, especially those Austrians who favoured greater rights for the Slavic peoples of the Monarchy, and against the Slavic peoples themselves inside and outside the frontiers. Hence the Magyars of Andrassy's persuasion looked to Berlin to counter those forces. Dualism had made Hungary a Great Power and Andrassy intended to keep it that way. An Austro-German alliance would secure that support.

Bismarck had come to recognize that an Austrian alliance would serve German security, as he wrote after the Austro-German Alliance was signed on 7 October 1879:

> I have succeeded in carrying out what I would like to call the first stage of my security policy by erecting a barrier between Austria and the western powers. In spite of the summer clouds, which in my view will blow away, I do not doubt that I can reach the second stage, that is, the restoration of the Three Emperors' League, the only system which in my view secures the greatest prospect of European peace.[84]

Trouble arose when William I refused categorically to see things that way. He loved his nephew, Tsar Alexander II, the son of his favourite sister, Charlotte. He had grown up in the Napoleonic Era when the Russian Empire had destroyed Napoleon, liberated Prussia, and guaranteed the domination of genuine conservative values. On 31 August Bismarck saw the Emperor, who flatly refused to allow him to go to Vienna, and, as Bismarck wrote to von Bülow, 'My nerves were most affected by William's prohibition against my going to Vienna.'[85] The usual psycho-drama unfolded. Bismarck always collapsed when the Kaiser disapproved or scolded him. These collapses had very real somatic consequences and he suffered sleeplessness, rage, severe indigestion, neuralgia, and facial pains. He wrote to Radowitz that 'I have not recovered from the consequences for my health of similar frictions that occurred at Nikolsburg and Versailles; today my health is so diminished that I cannot think of attempting to do business under such circumstances.[86]

But, as always, he did. On 3 September, the Kaiser visited the Tsar at his hunting lodge at Alexandrovo in Russian Poland to resolve differences, while Bismarck continued to negotiate the terms of an alliance with Austria. Again, very typically, he played another option to keep his combinations flexible. On 16 September 1879 he authorized Count Münster, the German ambassador to Britain, to ask Disraeli about the possibility of an Anglo-German alliance. The sources suggest that Münster never reported sufficiently clearly Disraeli's positive response and as a result Bismarck noted on the margins 'sonst nichts?' (is that all?). He gave up on the British option, which he may not have taken seriously in any case.[87]

In spite of the Emperor's reservations, Bismarck went to Vienna, where he received the treatment reserved for modern superstars. He was mobbed at railway stations, huge and cheering crowds gathered along his carriage routes in Vienna. Over the two days, 23 and 24 September 1879, Bismarck and Andrassy negotiated a treaty with very limited terms: if either treaty partner were attacked by Russia, that would trigger the casus foederis, which meant that it would have to intervene. If either power were attacked by another power, the other would maintain benevolent neutrality unless Russia joined the attacker. If that case arose, then the other partner would have to fight. The provisions so designed ensured that Austria would not get involved in a second Franco-German war for the defence of Alsace-Lorraine. Bismarck wanted more and Andrassy refused to yield it. At one point, Bismarck lost his temper and he leaned his great bulk over the Austrian and said with menace 'either accept my proposal or...'. Andrassy remained silent, and Bismarck laughed as he finished the sentence, 'otherwise I will have to accept yours.'[88] The official Provincial Correspondence recorded the highly laudatory articles in the Vienna papers and the warm welcome the press had given to the new Austro-German entente.[89]

On 25 September Bismarck returned to Berlin and had an extremely difficult audience with the Emperor. After a long emotional conversation, the Emperor gave in and remarked afterwards that 'Bismarck is more necessary than I am.'[90] On 29 September Bismarck addressed the Prussian cabinet for two and a half hours on the Austrian treaty and Robert Lucius von Ballhausen, now Minister of Agriculture, heard Bismarck in full flow, the experience that Stosch in 1873 had described as an 'enchantment'. Lucius wrote that Bismarck had held the cabinet 'absolutely enthralled...All the ministers support the Austro-German dual alliance as a recreation of the old German Confederation in a new more modern form.'[91] On 5 October Bismarck held another cabinet meeting before which Lucius heard Bismarck read out his resignation request which he had prepared if the Emperor had not given in on the treaty with Austria. 'His Majesty had in the meantime written him all sorts of soothing remarks...they had never had any serious differences in the seventeen years of joint work and joint achievement.

Bismarck laughed out loud about this comfortable memory. Now once again peace has been restored.'[92] On Tuesday 9 October he left for an extended stay in Varzin.[93] The Austro-German Treaty, signed on 7 October, remained secret.

While Bismarck walked the woods at Varzin, another crisis broke out, this time a wave of public anti-Semitism, which completed the end of the liberal era and began another stage in Germany history that ended in the Holocaust. Bismarck played a vital role in the process and he welcomed it. He shared, as we have seen, the visceral hatred of Jews among the Prussian Junkers, though he made exceptions for a few Jews such as Lassalle or, for a while, Friedenthal, Friedberg, and Bamberger. In 1811 Ludwig von der Marwitz attacked the Prussian reform movement and its liberal aims because they would end in a *Judenstaat*. No Junker dissented from that view and Bismarck shared it. His Pietist friends shared it because Jews could have no place in a Christian state but, as Bismarck abandoned the Christian state in the name of the secular state, he retained the unspoken belief, still widely and equally unconsciously held in today's Germany, that *ein Jude* cannot be a German. In 1850, in an essay called 'Das Judentum in der Musik' (untranslatable but roughly 'Jewishness in Music') Richard Wagner gave that view a new sharpness by arguing—even before Darwin— that Jews by race could not express true German art; they could not be more than parasites on authentic German creativity. Wagner also saw 'the Jew', as von der Marwitz and Bismarck did, as the embodiment of commercial life. Wagner declared:

> According to the present constitution of this world, the Jew in truth is already more than emancipated: he rules, and will rule, so long as Money remains the power before which all our doings and our dealings lose their force.[94]

According to Wagner, 'the Jew' (always in the abstract) corrupts art by turning it into a market for 'art commodities' (*Kunstwarenwechsel*). This theme, repeated ad nauseam, reflects the romantic distaste for the fact that even a genius has to sell tickets. Wagner's radical anti-capitalism was directed at Jews and the key figure, of course, was Nathan Meyer Rothschild and his brothers:

> in this respect we have rather had to regret that Herr v. Rothschild was too keen-witted to make himself King of the Jews, preferring, as is well known, to remain 'the Jew of the Kings.'[95]

In Wagner's view, 'The Jew' corrupted morals and culture by money. The message would be transformed into racial terms in the arguments used by the Nazis. The connection is there, however often Wagnerians try to deny it. 'The Jew' corrupted pure speech. Jews were unable to speak German properly. The word *mauscheln* is a German verb which is defined as 'mumble' in modern, politically correct, German dictionaries, but the real definition is 'to speak like a Jew, sound like Yiddish'. Wagner here too was a pioneer:

> But far more weighty, nay, of quite decisive weight for our inquiry, is the effect the Jew produces on us through his speech; and this is the essential point at which to sound the Jewish influence upon Music. The Jew speaks the language of the nation in whose midst he dwells from generation to generation, but he speaks it always as an alien... The first thing that strikes our ear as quite outlandish and unpleasant, in the Jew's production of the voice-sounds, is a creaking, squeaking, buzzing snuffle: add thereto an employment of words in a sense quite foreign to our nation's tongue, and an arbitrary twisting of the structure of our phrases—and this mode of speaking acquires at once the character of an intolerably jumbled blabber (eines unerträglich verwirrten Geplappers); so that when we hear this Jewish talk, our attention dwells involuntarily on its repulsive how, rather than on any meaning of its intrinsic what.

When Wagner invented modern anti-Semitism in 1850, he had to conceal his identity by writing anonymously. When he republished the essay in 1869, he could use his own name, because the attitudes he pioneered had become widely held.

Wagner was the first prophet of modern anti-Semitism, because his gigantic artistic achievement, like Nietzsche's philosophy, rejected reason, free markets, private property, capitalism, commerce, and social mobility, just those very attributes of the modern world that Bismarck and the Junker class loathed. They were joined by the very large artisan class, which had never accepted free markets and free entry into the trades called *Gewerbefreiheit*. This restrictive attitude to trades and crafts and who may practise such enterprises continues to the present in the defensive attitudes of the German *Handwerkerstand*. The origins of this powerful craft-guild mentality come from the fact that Germany—uniquely in Europe—had disintegrated into thousands of little political authorities, whose princes and senators lacked the power to suppress guilds and corporations. When the French Revolution cleared away the mini-states of the old Reich, and abolished all closed corporations, it left a legacy of dissatisfaction and rage among the artisans at their lost privileges which never died away. Anti-Semitism was thus endemic in large sectors of the German Protestant population and in Catholic regions it belonged to Catholic doctrine until the Second Vatican Council and the papacy of John Paul II.

The most important novel of society of the nineteenth century spread the picture of the repulsive Jew beyond the circles of those who read music journals. In 1855 Gustav Freytag's *Soll und Haben* (Debit and Credit) appeared and became one of the best-selling novels of the period. The book sang the virtues of the new German mercantile class. Its hero Anton Wohlfahrt (the name means 'welfare'), the honest and worthy young man from humble beginnings, rises to wealth and prestige in the new commercial world because of his bourgeois virtues. The anti-hero is the Polish Jew from Ostrau, Veitel Itzig, who begins his career at the same time. Itzig has every vice in contrast to Anton's virtues; he is vulgar, servile, and sly, where Anton is upright, correct, and honest.

> He [Itzig] understood what always counted as the highest in this society, how to give his obsequious humility a touch of farce, and was a master of the absolutely most tasteless bows and scrapes. He had the science to turn old brass into silver gilt and old silver to high polish. He was always ready to buy worn-out jackets—which passed among the initiate for the highest cunning.[96]

The book, a huge six-volume work, paints Jews and the Jewish community in such loathsome and lurid vignettes that it could pass for Nazi propaganda. There is, however, hope, the son of Itzig's boss, Herr Ehrental (again a sly joke—valley of honour), Bernhard Ehrental has become assimilated and German. Freytag sketches him as a positive and sympathetic character, the 'reform Jew'.

For some observers, the Germanized Jews were worse than the Veitel Itzigs, because at least the Polish Jews stood out. In 1865, one of the main newspapers of the Protestant church could write this about reform Jews:

> The true reform Jew is a thoroughly specific and peculiar being of a particular smell and taste. Even among the rodents which gobble and slobber everything and leave traces of their gluttony, there is a variation in the degrees of their repulsiveness. The mouse with its gnawing tooth is not as odious as the caterpillar with its soft, cold body and countless legs, or the snail which leaves behind its thick slime and always arouses disgust. Both are sometimes at large and eat up everything which is green, so that nothing remains but the bare stalks. Similarly, the reform Jews gnaw away at everything which is still green in human life, at everything which warms the soul, which is beautiful, which

is lofty and lovely, and, if it were up to them, nothing would be left over but bones and brushwood.[97]

The Nazis could not better this piece of Protestant hate literature.

Jews had become prominent in the industrial and commercial boom economy of the *Gründerzeit*. Fritz Stern gives some numbers for the concentration of Jews in certain professions and activities. In 1881 the Jews of Berlin represented 4.8 per cent of the population but 8.6 per cent of writers and journalists, 25.8 per cent of those engaged in the money market and 46 per cent of its wholesalers, retailers, and shippers. In 1871 43 per cent of the residents of Hamburg earned less than 804 marks but only 3.4 per cent of the Jewish population belonged to this group. Ten per cent of all students enrolled in Prussian universities and even higher in the gymnasia were Jewish.[98] Peter Pulzer points to other areas where Jews were very strongly over-represented. In 1887 in Prussia Jewish lawyers made up 20.4 per cent of the profession, Catholics with thirty times the population had only 26.3 per cent.[99] Jews stood for liberalism. Pulzer has assembled the party affiliations of all Jewish members of the Reichstag between 1867 and 1878. The total amounted to twenty-two, of whom six were baptized Jews like Karl Rudolf Friedenthal, Bismarck's Minister of Agriculture. Of these, only one was a conservative, two were members of Bismarck's Reich Party, the rest were liberals of one kind or other.

Jews in politics, the law, the universities, and journalism gave offence to those who cared but Jews in banking and finance greatly worsened the situation. W. E. Mosse in his pioneering study *Jews in the German Economy* shows how influential Jews were in this area. Jews dominated private banking in the 1850s and 1860. 'With the doubtful exception of Gebr. Schickler, there are no Gentile houses to compare with [them].'

Mosse supplies a list of the major German cities and the bankers in them:

Berlin: Mendelssohn & Co., S. Bleichröder, F. Mart. Magnus, Robert Warschauer, and H. C. Plaut;
Frankfurt: M. A. von Rothschild, Erlangers, Speyers, Wertheimers, Goldschmidts;
Mannheim: W. H. Ladenburg & Söhne and Hohenemser;
Cologne: Sal. Oppenheim;
Hamburg: Heines, Behrens, Warburgs;
Breslau: Heimanns;

Dresden: Kaskels;

Mainz: Bambergers;

Munich: Hirsches, Seligmanns, Kaullases, and Wassermans.[100]

The super-rich had a disproportionate share of Jewish millionaires. Prussia has to serve as surrogate for Germany as a whole because it had income tax whereas the Reich as such had none. The tax returns for 1908 show that 'of the 29 families with aggregate fortunes of 50 or more million marks, 9 (31 percent) were Jewish or of Jewish origins.'[101] Of the six names at the top of the table two were Jews.

Benjamin Disraeli, who cannot be accused of anti-Semitism, gives us a vivid description of a visit to one of the super-rich in 1878, Bismarck's banker, Gerson Bleichröder, whose mansion he visited during the Congress of Berlin:

> The great banker of Berlin is Mr Bleichröder. He was originally Rothschild's agent, but the Prussian wars offered him so great opportunities that he now almost seems to rival his former master. He has built himself a real palace, and his magnificent banqueting hall permitted him to invite the whole of the Plenipotentiaries and Secretaries of Embassy and the chief ministers of the Empire. All these last were present except P. Bismarck, who never appears, except occasionally at a Royal table. Mr Bleichröder, however, is Prince B's intimate, attends him every morning and, according to his own account, is the only individual who dares to speak the truth to his Highness. The banqueting hall, very vast and very lofty, and indeed the whole of the mansion, is built of every species of rare marble, and, where it is not marble, it is gold. There was a gallery for the musicians, who played Wagner and Wagner only, which I was very glad of, as I have rarely had an opportunity of hearing that master. After dinner we were promenaded thro' the splendid saloons and picture galleries, and a ballroom fit for a fairy tale, and sitting alone on a sofa was a very mean-looking little woman, covered with pearls and diamonds, who was Madame Bleichröder and whom he had married very early in life, when he was penniless. She was unlike her husband, and by no means equal to her wondrous fortune.[102]

This kind of extravagance gives rise to ill feeling in any society but the public rarely worry about it until things begin to go wrong. After the crash on the Vienna stock exchange things went very wrong indeed. August Sartorius von Watershausen, whose massive study of the German economy in the nineteenth century still commands respect, gives us startling figures of the ferocity of the collapse and the length of the first phase of the crash. In 1872 the 444 largest listed companies had a nominal worth of 1,209 billion marks. By 1879, they had fallen to 400 billion. Industrial prices plummeted between 1873 and 1877. In marks per ton Westphalian iron fell from 120 to 42, steel rails and Bessemer steel from 366 to 128, and iron bars from 270 to 122.[103] Sartorius calls 1879 the 'deepest point' in the depression era. This necessarily led to a struggle for survival in heavy industry where the massive scale of capital investment needed for an iron foundry or Bessemer steel plant meant that heavy fixed costs had to be assumed before a bar or ton was sold. These fixed costs weighed even more heavily when prices fell and competition pushed them lower. Heavy fixed costs forced really big enterprises to try to combine to cut ruinous competition, and cut the one marginal cost which can be shed: labour. The second half of the Great Depression shows this clearly. Between 1882 and 1895, the number of large companies (those employing 51 or more persons) rose from 9,974 to 19,953 and in employment terms 1.61 million to 3.04 million and of those companies with more than 1,000 workers, the number doubled from 127 to 255, and employment rose from 213,160 to 448,731.[104]

Hans Rosenberg's classic work *Grosse Depression und Bismarckzeit* of 1967 explored the interaction of economic change and what we would now call *mentalité*. He noticed a fundamental change in the nature of anti-Semitism:

> In the course of the trend period 1873 to 1896 a revolutionary change took place in the character, intensity and function of anti-Semitism... in numerical growth, in qualitative restructuring and social location of economic anti-Semitism, in the rise of racial anti-Semitism and in the emergence of political anti-Semitism... Thus the trend period of the Great Depression was the great foundation stage and the first epochal peak of modern anti-Semitism. There followed a decline during the very satisfying high industrialization era between 1896 and 1914.[105]

This can be seen in the emergence of a new kind of journalistic exposé—the financial scandal articles and books in which Jews are the villains. In 1874 the *Gartenlaube*, a popular middle-class weekly, published the first of this new genre of literature, the anti-Semitic article. It was called *Der Börsen-und Gründungsschwindel in Berlin* (The Stock Exchange and Foundation Swindle in Berlin) and was written by Otto Glagau (1834–92). It began with the familiar complaint, 'Speculation and swindle are the two powers which today sit on the throne of the world, under which civilized humanity sighs and groans, weakens and fails.' Economists, Glagau writes, call boom and bust 'a necessary evil' but much of it is the work of crooks and fraudsters.

The shining comet of these is 'Dr Bethel Henry Strousberg, a son of the Chosen People from Polish East Prussia, where fox and wolf say "good night" to each other.'[106] Glagau, who wrote vivid prose, outlined the collapse of the Strousberg Romanian railway company which had been launched in 1868 by a 65 million thaler loan with a 7½ per cent rate of interest by a consortium headed by Strousberg, the Duke of Ratibor, the Duke of Ujest, and Count Lehndorff and when the railroad collapsed could be bought for under 40. Glagau compared Strousberg to an anti-Hercules, 'Strousberg, the semite, filled the Augean stable with rubbish and depravity'.[107] Glagau continued the story with other articles and eventually published a book of his journalism two years later. Wilhelm Marr (1819–1904) invented the word 'Anti-Semitism' in his pamphlet *Der Sieg des Judentums über das Deutschtum* written in 1878 and published in 1879.[108]

On 17 March 1879 Heinrich von Treitschke wrote to Franz Overbeck, an Evangelical Theologian and academic colleague, to let out his exasperation with the Jews:

> Sometimes it presses deeply on my soul to see how the character of our Folk has been ruined by the Jewish press. Is there a single name—with the exception of Moltke—which Semitic impudence has not spat upon and soiled?[109]

On 15 November Heinrich von Treitschke, a Bismarck admirer and editor of the influential *Preussische Jahrbücher*, published an article under the title 'Unsere Ansichten' (Our Opinions) in which he attacked the Jews for their role in German public life and for the part they played in the economic collapse after 1873.[110] As the historian Theodor Mommsen said of the article, 'what *he* said was thereby made respectable.'[111] And *he* was the incomparable Treitschke, the most famous, the most successful, the most popular historian of his age, a respected member of the Reichstag, a popular poet and critic and the editor of the most important intellectual and political monthly journal in the German language. Treitschke represented the Liberal intellectual establishment and his attack on the Jews transformed the debate.

'Unsere Ansichten' is a long editorial. It begins with Treitschke's views of foreign affairs, the Austrian alliance, relations with Russia, the instability in the Balkans, and the liberal defeats in the recent Prussian elections. Finally after ten pages, Treitschke claims to have discovered 'a wonderful, mighty excitement in the depths of our people's life' of which 'one of the symptoms of the deep change of mood is the passionate movement against the *Judenthum* [Jewry—JS]'. Treitschke is, after all, no Glagau nor Marr, no

Grub Street gutter scribbler but a grand figure, a civilized man, a historian, so he has to be even-handed. He admits that Spanish Portuguese Jews have in England and France caused no trouble but Germany has to do with the Polish Jews, whose behaviour, he admits, has historic causes. The Jews should become Germans but, inconsistently he attacks not just the new immigrants but the cultivated German-speakers. For Treitschke 'the most dangerous aspect is the unfair preponderance of Jews in the Press . . . For ten long years public opinion was "made" in many cities by Jewish pens. It was a disaster for the Liberal Party that its press gave the *Judenthum* too great a freedom to act.' Of course, the Germans owe the clever Jews a great deal but they introduced a cynical, witty style which lacked 'respect' and contributed to the degradation of morals in society. Their jokes and slanders about religion were 'simply shameless'. As a result, what has happened may be 'brutal and ugly but is a natural reaction of the Germanic folk feeling against an alien element which has taken up too much space in our public life'.[112]

Anti-Semitism had now reached the heights of the establishment and soon would reach the court and highest aristocracy as the Court Preacher Adolf Stoecker began to preach sermons against Jews and Jewish influence. One of his disciples was the young Prince William, later Kaiser William II, another was Alfred Count von Waldersee, who had by the 1870s intrigued his way into the succession to Moltke. The Court Preacher sowed dissension in the royal household and ultimately contributed to the fall of Bismarck.

In the German-Jewish community the effect of all this was devastating. Berthold Auerbach (1812–82) may have been even better known than Treitschke and certainly outside Germany much more so. He came from an orthodox Jewish family and would have been a rabbi, had he not been arrested for revolutionary activities. He became a journalist and unsuccessful novelist. Between 1843 and 1858 he published four volumes of 'Schwarzwälder Dorfgeschichten' (Village stories from the Black Forest) which became an 'incomparable world success, which made Auerbach together with Gustav Freytag the most popular German story-teller of the nineteenth century'. The stories went into many editions and into translation in every European language.[113] This patriotic, national writer happened to be Jewish; suddenly in his late sixties he found that it mattered. In November, a week before Treitschke's article, Auerbach wrote to his brother Jacob:

Lasker has not even been nominated as a candidate in Breslau. The inflammatory campaign against Jews has been at work here too. Yesterday in the local

'Observer', there was a piece from a Breslau newspaper, that Jews live in houses they have not built, etc. That is incitement to murder and theft, and we must now experience that.[114]

Bismarck said nothing throughout the whole crisis. It suited him that anti-Semitism undermined his enemies like Lasker. Windthorst said again and again that one must condemn anti-Semitism. In a speech in the Reichstag on 16 April Windthorst declared that he demanded equal rights and equal protection for all. 'I will on every occasion represent the rights I claim for the Catholic Church and her servants for Protestants also and not least for Jews. I want this right for all.'[115]

The Jews under this mounting attack tried two strategies. On 18 June 1880 Bleichröder wrote to William I personally:

> I dare call for Your Majesty's high patriarchal protection for myself, but not only for myself, rather for a whole class of loyal subjects of Your Majesty who surely are not useless citizens of the state. The bitter struggle against Jews [is] a social struggle against property as such…My name is now on the tip of every Christian Social agitator's tongue; it is invoked not only as a target for persecution but is branded as a prototype of all capital, of the stock market, of all prosperity, and of all evil…[this is] the beginning of the misfortune of a terrible social revolution.[116]

There was some truth in Bleichröder's argument that anti-Semitism represented the revolt of the property-less against property but in a much larger sense it represented a revulsion of a deeply conservative society against liberalism. In the Catholic community, Carl Constantin Freiherr von Fechenbach saw in the anti-Semitic agitations a way to end the *Kulturkampf* by creating a union of conservative Catholic and Protestant groups in a Social Conservative Association dedicated to anti-capitalism, anti-Semitism, and state socialism which would include nationalization of basic industries.[117] On 18 July 1880 he wrote to Adolf Franz, the editor of the main Catholic newspaper *Germania*, that he wanted to unify 'all truly Christian elements on the basis of a common social programme'.[118] Windthorst understood at once that Fechenbach represented a double threat to his leadership and programme. It diverted attention from the struggle to dismantle the May Laws and other Catholic disabilities and it moved the political attention from the Prussian and Reich parliaments where Windthorst's mastery allowed him to run the Centre Party without formal office to outside organizations. Hence, when on 10 November Fechenbach invited Franckenstein and Windthorst to meet to discuss an anti-Semitic union of

Catholics and Protestants; both declined.[119] The Catholic lawyer August Reichensperger, like his brother Peter, a Centre deputy, relates in his memoirs that most Catholic parliamentarians were eager at that time to participate in the anti-Semitic campaign. So the threat was real.

On 20 November 1880 the Prussian House of Deputies debated the anti-Semitic agitation. In the name of the Progressive Party, Albert Haniel had asked the Minister of the Interior what position the Prussian government was preparing to take on the Anti-Semites' Petition. August Reichensperger described it:

> The most notable parliamentary event was the great debate on the Jewish question (die grosse Judendebatte) of November 20 and 22 [1880]. It was brought about by Haniel's interpellation. Within the Catholic Centre group the discussion of the Jewish question had led to very agitated discussions between Windthorst, who was rather friendly toward the Jews, and the great majority of the group which was raring to join the attack. Windthorst stood almost completely alone in his opinion that the Catholic Centre should be as neutral as possible. . . . The debate before the House was a defeat for Jewry and the Progressive Party whose phrases turned always against them as *Kulturkämpfer*. The anti-semitic agitation has greatly increased since.[120]

Berthold Auerbach who heard the debate despaired: 'I have lived and worked in vain... the awareness of what lies concealed in German breasts and could explode at any time, cannot be eradicated.'[121] Eça de Quieroz, a Portugese novelist in Berlin at the time, was appalled by the government's response:

> It leaves the Jewish colony unprotected to face the anger of the large German population—and washes its ministerial hands, as Pontius Pilate did. It does not even state that it will see the laws protecting the Jews, citizens of the Empire, are enforced; it merely has the vague intention, as vague as a morning cloud, of not altering them *for the moment*.[122]

On 29 November 1880 Bamberger wrote to his sister-in law Henriette Belmont:

> I shall write nothing about anti-Semitism. The newspapers are too full. The characteristic feature is that the ordinary people have nothing to do with it. It is the hatred and envy of the educated, professors, jurists, pastors and lieutenants, stimulated by the spirit of reaction and brutality from above.[123]

In December Windthorst destroyed Fechenbach's project by a brilliant parliamentary manoeuvre. He introduced a bill to exempt the administration of the sacraments from criminal prosecution. 'This motion... forced the Conservative Party to choose between antagonizing Bismarck or exposing the vacuity of its own calls for confessional peace.'[124] The Conservatives voted against the bill and thus helped Windthorst destroy Fechenbach and the others who wanted to unite conservative Catholics and Protestant on social questions by showing that Protestants would never give Catholics an inch. He renewed it year after year and thus by restoring the Centre's freedom of movement allowed it to make electoral alliances with the Progressives in the 1881 elections between the first and second ballot. It removed the possibility that Bismarck might imagine he would *not* have to pay in concessions on religious matters for the 100 Centre votes he used to pass his conservative tariff legislation.

On New Year's Eve 1881 a group of men who had attended an anti-Semitic rally rioted, smashed Jewish shops, and shouted 'Juden raus!' (Jews out!).[125] On 12 January, when the Landtag reopened, Eugen Richter, a brilliant parliamentary Liberal debater, whom Bismarck hated as much as he hated 'that dumb Jew Boy Lasker and his following, those theoretical speech-makers',[126] connected Bismarck to the anti-Semitic agitation: 'The movements begin to cling to the coat-tails of Prince Bismarck and, however much he rejects them and lets his press scold them for their excesses, they go right on cuddling up to him and call to him as noisy children surround their father.'[127] That is deeply true. The 'Jew debate' reflects a malevolent prejudice in Bismarck against the intelligentsia, against people like Lasker, who insisted on rights and protections against the state and against dictators like Bismarck. In November 1880 he wrote to his reactionary Minister of the Interior, Robert von Puttkamer, that 'moneyed Jewry' has 'interests on balance inter-connected with the maintenance of the institutions of our state and whom we cannot do without' but property-less Jewry 'which...attaches itself to all political opposition' must be crushed.[128]

Bismarck destroyed German liberalism, his real enemy. If Jews got hurt, so be it. It was not his habitual but characteristic anti-Semitism that caused the damage but his intolerance of opposition. The legacy was so pervasive at the time and afterwards that one has not got to look hard to find its traces. One sees it in a letter from April 1881 from Theodor Fontane, the German novelist, to Philipp zu Eulenburg on Bismarck's role:

> Bismarck is a despot, but he has a right to be one, and he *must* be one. If he were not, if he were an ideal parliamentarian, who allowed his course to be determined by the most stupid thing there is, by parliamentary majorities, then we wouldn't have a chancellor at all and least of all a German Reich. It

is true on the other hand, of course, that under such a despot only dependent natures and powers of the second and third rank can serve, and that any free man will do well at times to resign. In doing that, the free man does right for him, but the chancellor *also* does what is right for him, when he doesn't allow that to cause confusion in his action or inaction.[129]

Consider what that means. Society in Germany could not achieve anything on its own because parliaments are 'the most stupid things', that is, we the people are unable through exercising their rights, to achieve anything. Germany needed to be governed by a genius-statesman who followed his own course. Fontane made a fundamental mistake in that analysis, the free man cannot do what is right for him, because his attitude—the surrender to the genius—shows that he has chosen slavery not freedom. The freedom to resign is not real freedom; that the subtlest social observer of the age fails to see that is Bismarck's real gift to Hitler.

On Christmas Eve 1881 a truly free man, Eduard Lasker, wrote his political testament in a long letter to the novelist Berthold Auerbach, whose spirits had been deeply depressed by the events of the previous two years. Lasker, a bachelor, a Jew from an orthodox family in Jaroczyn, had risen to be spokesman of rights and liberty in Prussia and Reich by sheer ability. A trained lawyer, he devoted his entire life to a comprehensive and untiring preoccupation with the legislative process. In 1868 against Bismarck's ponderous opposition, he pushed through legislation to protect free speech in the chambers of the Reichstag and in 1873 he exposed a case of 'insider trading' in railway shares carried out by Hermann Wagener, Bismarck's friend and first editor of the *Kreuzzeitung*, inside the Ministry of Trade. The ring included the Princes Putbus and Biron and enjoyed the tolerance of the Minister Count Itzenplitz. Lasker exposed them fearlessly, caused the resignations of all involved, and ensured the passage of a law making it illegal for civil servants to engage in commercial transactions connected with their office. He wrote the petition of December 1870 in which the North German Reichstag asked King William I to become Emperor and the first Reply to the Address from the Throne of the new German Reichstag in March 1871.[130] Only Windthorst surpassed him as a parliamentary speaker and legislator. On 25 December 1881 Lasker wrote to Berthold Auerbach and set out his understanding of the crisis in Germany about the Jews:

My dear, old friend, I have granted myself a festive pleasure in that I can settle down alone and composed on the first day of Christmas to write to you. . . . In the moment of danger many in the German Fatherland, among the best of them, have come to understand what you mean to us and expressions of sympathy and compassion from all sides, even from the enemy camp in public life, have been sent. Were these testimonies or even a part of them to come to you, you would no longer cling to the melancholy doubt that your impact on the nation has been ignored or in substance destroyed. After all, it is like a blue streak in the dark clouds that ugly anti-Semitism in a moral sense can be seen to be done for, by which I do not mean the end of the tension. For each revolutionary epoch takes on a confessional colouring and we stand in the middle of a violent revolution, perhaps the most violent I have experienced. But with regard to the particular anti-Semitic agitation the mud has settled and now lies on the ground... In the elections the people have definitely rejected anti-Semitism in its ghastly form and in its dirty content, as completely as could be wished. Not so easily will we be able to deal with the other element of the reactionary power. Bismarck is no enemy to underestimate even when he makes mistakes and acts in passion. In the present stage of society many too many problems exist, and when a powerful government looks around for popular programmes, then they can find effective levers, which after a lot of tapping about and getting lost, will not fail them. In fact it requires great vigilance, careful thought and the most selfless sacrifice to pull the good cause undamaged from the struggle. By good cause I mean the liberation of individuals and the reduction of situations when people see as dictated by fate what is really a situation the powerful seek to control.[131]

If Fontane missed the deeper meaning of his acceptance of the dictatorship of the genius-statesman in the name of the greater cause, Lasker greatly overestimated the power and civil courage of decent people. The Germans followed Fontane into slavery and not Lasker into freedom.

On 5 January 1884 Lasker died suddenly in New York after a long and successful speaking tour in the USA. Lucius summed up his view of Lasker in his diary on 6 January:

With him ends the one of the most significant and popular parliamentarians of the new Reich. Next to Bismarck and Bennigsen, he was the best known figure in the Reichstag. Thoroughly patriotic, unselfish, full of idealistic aspirations, he had a more destructive than constructive impact.[132]

The US House of Representatives resolved that 'this loss is not alone to be mourned by the people of his native land, where his firm and constant exposition of and devotion to free and liberal ideas have materially advanced the social, political and economic conditions of those peoples but also by lovers of liberty throughout the world.'[133] When the text of the resolution arrived in Berlin, Bismarck refused to accept the message and returned it to the senders because the description was erroneous. Five Prussian cabinet ministers desired to attend Lasker's funeral and asked Bismarck for permission. He replied 'most certainly not'.[134]

On 28 January 1884 Lasker's funeral took place in the famous Oranienburg Synagogue in Berlin, the very synagogue at whose dedication Bismarck had been present. Lasker's parliamentary colleague, Ludwig Bamberger, recorded the event in his diary:

> Today the funeral. No minister, no member of the Bundesrat, not one high civil servant, neither Friedberg nor Achenbach, not even the Swiss Minister Roth—apparently the '*Ordre de Mouft*'. Kapp gave a mediocre speech. Tonight I talk in the Singakademie.[135]

A month later, on 28 February, Bamberger reflected in telegraph style in his diary on the death of Lasker and the political implications: 'the aftermath of Bismarck's opposition to Washington confirms my view. Whether he will be proved right? The people is not born to be free.'[136] On 7 March the Reichstag had to be adjourned because of the angry debate when they protested at Bismarck's discourtesy to their dead colleague and the US House of Representatives. On 13 March Bismarck appeared in the Reichstag at 1 p.m. and made a statement before the opening of formal business with regard to the message of condolence which the American House of Representatives had directed to the government. Bismarck attacked sharply revolutionaries and republicans. In response to an interjection by Hänel he responded wittily: 'He had no obligation to exchange sentimentalities and in the political duel to let himself be shot down.' He added his best wishes for the liberal party which Lasker had always led down the wrong path. 'Solemn assertions of personal regard and friendship only make political opponents more dangerous.'[137] He described Lasker as somebody with 'superior but destructive eloquence'.[138] He clearly enjoyed kicking a dead Jew and, when Hilga Spitzemberg called on him two days later, she found him in highest good spirits: 'At 12 I found him at lunch, as fresh and cheerful as possible, after he had once again spoken the Reichstag, which they now call the "*Gasthof zum toten Juden*"—"The Guest House of the Dead Jew".' It might also be called *Gasthof zum toten Liberalismus* (the Guest House of Dead Liberalism) because Lasker's death marked the end of the hope of a liberal regime in Germany.

In November 1881 Bismarck commented on the 'Jew Debate' at a cabinet meeting of the Prussian State Ministry:

With respect to the anti-Semitic movement he criticized it as inopportune. It had shifted its aims. He was only against the progressive not the conservative Jews and their press. He would always prefer the Socialists and Catholics to the progressives, the former aim at the impossible, which in the end must be smashed by the use of the sword; the progressives aim at a possible form of state: the republic.[139]

On 26 November 1881 Bismarck told Lucius that 'the "Jew Hunt" was not opportune. He had declared himself against it but had done nothing to stop it because of its courageous attack on the progressives.'[140] He had not declared himself against it: as usual, he lied about his acts.

During February and March 1880 Bismarck's health deteriorated suddenly and dangerously. On 31 March 1880 Tiedemann found the Prince in really alarming condition:

At report, I found the Prince wretched, his tongue seemed to be lamed and his appearance horribly altered. He thinks he had a stroke last night, got no sleep, and threw up continually. Struck declared that it was nothing but a cold in the stomach with effects on the tongue. The Princess told me that her husband had eaten yesterday evening an endless mass of white wine punch ice cream and then six hard-boiled eggs. Evening council of war with the Princess, the Rantzau couple and me in the Princess's boudoir about rules to be set for the morning. The Prince is more difficult than ever and shouted at Struck so furiously that the poor man fled, completely crushed. He had chicken soup, meat and vegetables for lunch, although Struck had quite specifically forbidden such food and equally categorically forbidden a walk in the rain in the garden. Now he sits alone in an irritable mood before the fireplace in the garden room and only wants his dogs for company.[141]

Bad health stirred Bismarck's increasing irrationality and impossible rages. On 3 April 1880 the Bundesrat (the Federal Council) which Bismarck had designed to serve as his faithful legislative agency, met to consider the Reich Stamp Duty Law, not exactly the most exciting item on the parliamentary calendar. The Council began to consider its provisions, which the small states disliked, and small here includes tiny principalities like Reuss, elder Line (population 72,769 in 1910) and Reuss, younger Line (population 139,210), political units so little that they could not afford permanent ambassadors in Berlin and had to give proxies to larger neighbours. The small states particularly disliked the provision that placed stamp duty on postal transfers and on receipts given for advance payments into postal accounts. The vote on the issue produced a small sensation. The Federal Council rejected the provision by 30 votes to 28.[142]

Bismarck flew into one of his increasingly intemperate rages. Tiedemann went to Friedrichsruh to discuss current business and arrived late on 4 April 1880. He was awakened early the next morning by a servant who told him that the Prince wished to see him at the unexpectedly early hour of 10 a.m. He found the Chancellor in a foul mood. He had again not slept and in his rage had risen to go to work at 9 a.m. By the time Tiedemann reported for duty, Bismarck was sitting at his desk, making notes from the *Almanach de Gotha*. He declared that the thirty states which had voted against the provision represented 7½ million to the 38 million behind the losers. Voting down Prussia by such a majority went directly against the spirit of the constitution, he declared, and such things must never happen again:

> He ordered me to draw up a direct submission to the Kaiser in which he asked to be relieved of his office. Basic idea: he could neither represent the majority decision against Prussia, Bavaria and Saxony nor could he make use of his right to address the Reichstag which Article 9 of the Reich Constitution granted representatives of the Bundestag minority... Nor was that enough; in his furious impatience, the resignation request had to be sent to the Kaiser with the greatest possible haste, and by the evening edition of the official newspaper, the *Norddeutsche Allgemeine Zeitung*, formal notice of his resignation had to be published.[143]

The combination of his terrible temper, gluttony, and hypochondria made him the 'patient from Hell'. In this frame of mind he could do anything, including the absurd resignation over the stamp duty on postal transfers. He invited his neighbour and regular member of the inner circle at 76 Wilhelmstrasse, Carl Freiherr Hugo vom Spitzemberg, the Württemberg envoy to the Bundesrat, to 'straighten the matter out' and the conversation degenerated into a row as Hildegard recorded in her diary on 6 April 1880:

> It would be laughable were it not so sad. The Prince is sick and nobody in his immediate circle calms him. On the contrary they stir him up, sometimes without realizing it, sometimes to ingratiate themselves, or out of fear. Of course he will not resign but the fact that everybody knows that makes it all into an unworthy threat—and on account of such a trivial matter. Carl was very angry and stood his ground against the Prince.[144]

Nothing could dissuade him and a crisis, which Tiedemann accurately described as a 'storm in a water glass', blew up. The little states had an attack of nerves. Ambassadors scurried about. The Kaiser rejected Bismarck's request and the non-official press assumed that it had been just another of Bismarck's cunning ploys. It worked. On 12 April 1880 the Bundesrat reversed its decision and restored stamp duty on postal transfers and on receipts for pre-payment of bills at postal counters. The Reich had survived the crisis. But Bismarck had again given evidence of his growing emotional instability. Everything annoyed him. 'The Prince visits the King of Saxony, very bitter that the King had not come to him.'[145] After all, what was a King of a smallish Kingdom to him? His servants and his ministers could not reason with him, and his unique power and prestige made him immune to any control other than that of the Emperor. He said no to everything that displeased him. The Prince had stopped riding and the press of business had grown. Friedrichsruh, unlike Varzin, could be quickly reached from Berlin and official visits filled the days. Nor had overeating ceased. As Tiedemann wrote in October 1880 to his wife,

> I took a quick walk with Countess Marie [Rantzau, Bismarck's daughter—JS] and prepared myself for the dinner, which in addition to dessert consists of six heavy courses. Nothing has changed. Here we eat until the walls burst.[146]

And breakfast was no better:

> we rise at 9 and breakfast at 10: roast beef or beef steak, cold venison, wild birds, roasted pudding, etc.[147]

By early 1881 Bismarck's erratic behaviour had begun to damage his projects in both the Reichstag and the Prussian Landtag. Count Udo zu Stolberg-Wernigerode (1840–1910), the bluest of blue bloods, married to an Arnim-Boitzenburg and descended from Dönhoffs and related to the von der Schulenburgs, wrote to Tiedemann to complain about the 'impossible situation' which the German Conservative Party and his own Reich Party faced when 'a man of the stature of the Reich Chancellor stands at the apex of business and his own party which is most willing to support him, is left completely in the dark about such questions'.[148]

Tiedemann had begun to face his own 'impossible situation' and realized it could not continue. Bismarck literally worked him to the edge of exhaustion. In an age before the telephone, the typewriter, carbon paper, the xerox, and the fax, Tiedemann spent hours, indeed whole days, copying out dictation from the Chancellor, drafting letters and piece of legislation, transcribing notes of sessions and conversations. Luckily for the historian, Tiedemann had the sort of obsessive personality which led him, 'as a conscientious statistician', to count the number of pages he produced on busy days or the number of times he lunched with the Chancellor (133 in 1879).[149] Then there were the long residences in either Varzin and Friedrichsruh, weeks on end away from his wife and family, and the need to carry urgent documents or messages all over Berlin when on rare occasions Bismarck deigned to honour the capital with his presence. Bismarck's hypochondria, sleeplessness, irregular hours, huge meals, terrible temper, rapid and alarming mood swings, had finally after six years taken their toll of the cheerful, flexible, and always available Tiedemann. He too had lost his capacity to sleep and never saw his children. His wife actually sent a formal invitation to the Bismarck house inviting the 'Herr *Oberregierungsrat* Tiedemann to tea at the family residence (dress morning coat) at 8 pm'. The gesture amused the Bismarcks but it sent Tiedemann a serious message. Finally, he knew that on a deeper level he could no longer survive closeness to Bismarck.

> There is something great to live one's life in and through a great man, to enter into and be absorbed by his thoughts, plans, decisions, in a certain sense to disappear in his personality. One's own individuality runs the risk of being ground down. I yearned for freedom of movement, for independent activity, and for my own activity and creativity... When I asked him in Spring 1881 to recall his promise to arrange a suitable post, he flew into a rage and accused me in bitter, angry words, that all I thought about and worked for was designed to abandon him. It was the first and only time that he ever spoke to me in such a way. This scene too strengthened my resolve to leave the Reich Chancellery.[150]

Bismarck could not imagine a better or more important job than one close to his person. What could be better than to serve Bismarck? Grudgingly Bismarck found Tiedemann a suitable post and bid him farewell.

He respected nobody and paid no attention even to his royal visitors. On 20 April 1880 King Albert of Saxony had an uncomfortable hour with him:

> When the king uttered a differing opinion, Bismarck changed his expression, and the king immediately yielded. It is Bismarck's misfortune, the king declared, that he cannot listen to a contrary opinion and immediately conjectures ulterior motives. This is what happened in the vote on the stamp tax bill, when no one knew that the matter was important to him. Everyone does his will, the Kaiser first of all.[151]

In the end, Bismarck's erratic behaviour led to a serious reverse. On 4 July 1880 Lucius wrote in real exasperation that the final vote on the church policy bill had been a disaster and most of the bill had been rejected.

> The Prince is entirely to blame, who systematically rejected with irritation any moderate attempt at criticism. Thus the only result of this episode general

annoyance on all sides and against the government...In the Bundesrat also excited negotiations took place...The Prince let loose on Minister Hoffmann and Postmaster General Stephan in such a way as if he wanted to be rid of both. The draft of the stamp duty bill had been the cause of his irritation.[152]

The use-and-discard employment system remained an abiding feature of Bismarck's treatment of his subordinates. Bismarck used the occasion to abolish the Reich Chancellor's Office and create instead a series of 'State Secretaries' of various departments, which at first looked like an Imperial Cabinet but appearances deceive. These state secretaries reported to Bismarck only, not to the Emperor, had no collective cabinet identity, and had no responsibility to the Reichstag. He now had a system in which he had a set of advisers and department chiefs whom he could dismiss at will, ignore when it suited him, or pretend that they had real authority when he wished to shirk responsibility for something that had gone wrong. As Friedrich Wilhelm Count von Limburg-Styrum (1835–1912) observed cynically, 'Bismarck is to his ministers the way Don Juan was to his lovers. First he cajoles them, and when he catches them, he lets them go without caring about what happens to them.'[153] Discarded ministers had the modest consolation that Prussia had a uniform for retired ministers: tailcoat with embroidery and epaulettes[154] and the King often rewarded them with titles and orders, as if he felt guilty that his Minister-President had treated them so badly.

In April 1881 a family crisis broke out which fused the destructive elements in the characters of Otto and Johanna von Bismarck to seething point and broke the heart and spirit of their eldest son. Herbert von Bismarck was born on 12 December 1849, and had become his father's most faithful amanuensis and disciple. After the obligatory Prussian military career in which he served in the very aristocratic First Dragoon Guards, he entered the 'family business' by joining the Foreign Service in 1874 and, as the boss's son, rose rapidly, though nobody questioned his competence as a young diplomat. Eberhard von Vietsch in his biographical entry in the *National German Biography* writes of him that 'he always stuck strictly to his father's instructions, to whose will he subordinated himself'.[155] He lived for long periods with his parents in Varzin and Friedrichsruh and served together with Christoph Tiedemann as a confidential correspondent during the late 1870s. At some point, he met and fell madly in love with the Princess Elisabeth von Corolath-Beuthen (1839–1914), one of the wittiest, most beautiful, and most popular figures in Berlin high society. Prince Philipp zu

Eulenburg-Hertefeld (1847–1921) knew Herbert and Elisabeth well and indeed the Princess had been an early flame of his. He wrote of her:

> The Princess Elisabeth loved Herbert from the depths of her soul. She was a rich, gifted nature. Beautiful, vain in the way that most beautiful women are, but much too brilliant a person to succumb to vanity. She glowed with interest for the arts and was unusually musical. Proud, elegant in her character, she had gone through a hard school of life in her father's house where the most unedifying circumstances reigned.[156]

Herbert and Elisabeth began a passionate affair in 1879 and Herbert convinced her to get a divorce from her husband, Carl Ludwig Prince zu Carolath-Beuthen, a Silesian prince and grand seigneur, with whom Elisabeth had been unhappily married for some time. In 1881 the divorce was granted and Herbert could now imagine a life with his beloved, who was ten years older, divorced, and a Catholic, not the ideal set of attributes to bring home to Varzin. The story had been circulating in society and finally the *Vossische Zeitung*, a Liberal up-market, anti-Bismarckian daily paper, got hold of it. Georg Brandes (1842–1927), the famous Danish critic and writer, had been living in Berlin for several years and wrote columns for his Danish readers. On 15 March 1881 he wrote a long piece about how Bismarck 'had never been so unpopular with the cultivated middles classes' as he was at that moment and how his 'bilious outbursts and nervous symptoms' had alienated many. He thought the cause might be deduced from the following 'mischievous notice', which he copied out from the 'Voss':

> Member of the Reichstag, Prince Coralath-Beuthen, has requested a lengthy leave to withdraw to his estates—Princess Carolath has arrived in Messina in Sicily—Count Herbert Bismarck recently left Berlin. The news that he has been travelling on a special mission had not been confirmed.[157]

Public scandal had, indeed, made the Bismarcks angry, but there was something worse, indeed, a fatal flaw in the Princess Carolath's character that damned her from the start. Both her sisters had married 'enemies' of Bismarck: one, the famous hostess Marie, known as Mimi, had married Alexander von Schleinitz, briefly Bismarck's chief as Foreign Minister in 1861; and the other had married Walter Freiherr von Loë (1828–1908), a General Adjutant to the Kaiser and the only Catholic to rise to the rank of Field Marshall in Imperial Germany.[158] In Bismarck's eyes the connection ruled the Princess out of consideration. Her family belonged to the 'counter-government' around the Empress Augusta and he spoke of them as the

'Hatzfeldt-Loë-Schleinitz clique'. No son of his could entertain relations with these hated foes, a hatred which the implacable Johanna with her card file of enemies further stirred up to white heat. Johanna declared that 'I will fight tooth and nail to see that the society of Loë, Schleinitz and Hatzfeldt do not come to our table.'[159]

After her divorce, Elisabeth Carolath went to Venice, where Herbert had promised to meet and marry her. During April 1881 Herbert, caught between his love and his parents' intransigence, hesitated. He postponed his departure for Venice and Elisabeth had a breakdown. She wrote to Philipp Eulenburg on 14 April, 'I was so sick that it was believed that I wouldn't live and even now I am so weak that I can scarcely take a few steps.'[160] Bismarck tried to buy her off. On 23 April Bleichröder's Italian agent called on the Princess with an offer. She rejected it with contempt, as the agent advised his chief in a telegram, 'Princess Carolath wants no interference from third parties and Prince Bismarck could write to her directly.'[161] On 28 April Herbert went to see his father to make one last attempt and an epic confrontation followed. Herbert told his father that he intended to go to Venice to marry his Elisabeth. He received in recompense the full dose of the great Bismarck's threats—he would commit suicide, he would die of a broken heart. There were tears, pleas, rage, attacks of his many illnesses. He also used his legal powers over his son to make the plan impossible on practical grounds, as Herbert wrote to Philipp Eulenburg on 31 April 1881:

> In the meantime I am forbidden to leave the service. Therefore I cannot marry without permission (there is no legal possibility until after the lapse of ten months). I must remember that I have nothing to offer the princess, since according to the law of primogeniture, as recently changed with the Emperor's approval, any son who marries a divorced woman is automatically disinherited. Since my father has nothing but the two great entailed estates, I should have no inheritance whatever. This would be all the same to me, since the split with my parents and their ruin would be the death of me.[162]

Herbert never went to Venice and something certainly died in him as a result. Eberhardt von Vietsch concludes his biographical entry in the *NDB* by writing that it is possible 'that his own will, especially in the struggle with his father over the marriage, had been broken.' He became known for his 'coarseness and contempt for people'.[163] On New Years' Day 1888 Hildegard Spitzemberg reflected on Bismarck's family and especially on Herbert and Bill, his sons:

The sons get their light and glitter from the parents, but it is hard to take their ruthless pleasure-seeking, their gruff, materialistic tendencies, the brutal use of the right of the stronger, their complete lack of sensitivity for anything fine, educated, cultivated and disciplined. Their love of animals is attractive but the Princess often talks to me about Herbert, whose cynicism deeply troubles her and whom she would really love to see married.[164]

Herbert was ruined in 'society'. He had behaved like a cad. He had let down a beautiful and valued member of high society and had not treated a woman with honour. He had breached a solemn promise of marriage, a legal offence. He was a coward, selfish, insensitive, and so on. General von Loë put it very clearly in his military brevity. 'If Herbert were not the son of the Almighty Chancellor, he would be brought before a court of honour and it would be a farewell appearance.'[165] Thus Bismarck's infinite capacity to hate his enemies, indeed anybody who contradicted him, destroyed his eldest son and added to the long list of victims of the distorted and disturbed personality that his genius had allowed to go unchecked. Philipp Eulenburg, who knew everybody in the tragedy, concluded that Bismarck had made a terrible mistake:

> Somebody who knew the Princess Elisabeth as well as I did inclines to the view that it was a mistake. For with the destruction of his deepest hope of happiness the son was driven not only into inescapable self-condemnation but also it must bring the pessimism and contempt for people in the once so happy and sunny nature, a development which damaged his future. The Prince had influenced his own future much more deeply by the transformation of his son's character for which he bore the blame than he could have imagined as the waves of pain, of anxiety and his passion crashed over him.[166]

Herbert's brutality, arrogance, and insensitivity undermined his father's position and helped to bring about the end of his father's chancellorship and his own career. Here from Waldersee's diary is an example of Herbert's impossible behaviour in public, after he became his father's deputy as State Secretary in the Foreign Office. This event took place in December 1886:

> On the Thursday, Count Lerchenfeld, the Bavarian Ambassador, gave a dinner for Prince Luitpold. At table Herbert Bismarck took the top place, ranked therefore above the Field Marshall, Stolberg, Puttkamer, Boetticher etc. He excused himself by saying that the Chancellor demands that at diplomatic functions the State Secretary of Foreign Affairs must have the first place. There will be a scandal. Moltke announced that he will no longer attend diplomatic dinners. The strange thing about the whole business is that Herbert accepted

the place. Were he a sensible person, he would never have done it, now he has the whole reasonable world against him.[167]

Herbert, who had become a heavy drinker, died in 1904 just 55 years old, a victim of his father.

Bismarck too paid a price because he loved his cherished eldest son and knew what he had done. Wilhelm von Kardorff wrote to Bleichröder that 'It seems to me that in political matters we are ailing because of Herbert and Venice; at least the renewed illness of the Chancellor must essentially be blamed on this.'[168] Throughout May 1881 Bismarck had been unwell and, when Lucius visited him on 12 June, Bismarck's condition shocked him. Bismarck had an infection in the veins of one of his leg and could not walk.

> He lies on the sofa with the infected leg and with his stubble on unshaven beard looks old and doddery. Complained with a broken voice: 'he must throw in the towel. He cannot go on. Nothing that he takes up can he get rid of...' Bismarck has suffered terrible stomach cramps and passed blood. He blames the constant friction of his job but it must be caused by stomach ulcers...[169]

His chief attending physician had finally given up treating his august but incorrigible patient. On 17 July Lucius noted in his diary that Dr Struck had asked to be relieved of the post of house doctor,

> because his health is too fragile to bear the stress that the practice in the Bismarckian house involves. Dr Struck has learned to profit from Bismarck's style. Tiedemann has repeatedly asked for a government presidency in either Trier or Bromberg, which Bismarck evidently holds against him. Why is he in such a hurry to get away from him?[170]

We know only too well why Tiedemann wanted to get away by this point in Bismarck's career and the odd thing is that the perceptive Lucius could not see it.

On 27 October 1881 Reichstag elections took place. The results infuriated Bismarck because the main gainers had been his enemies. The two conservative parties lost heavily. The Reich Party lost half its seats and its share of the vote fell from 13.6 to 7.5 per cent. The Centre, solid as ever, gained seats to hit 100, but the big winners had been the left liberals, still split into three parties, but they were the clear victors. They increased their share of the vote by a fraction more than 15 per cent and together now had 109 seats, a gain of 86 seats, largely at the expense of the National Liberals, who had cooperated with Bismarck.[171]

Bismarck's contempt for the public reached new heights of bitterness laced with dollops of self-pity. They had failed him again, as he told Moritz Busch:

> The elections have shown that the German philistine still lives and allows himself to be frightened and led astray by fine speeches and lies...Folly and ingratitude on all sides. I am made the target for every party and group, and they do everything they can to harass me and would like me to serve as whipping boy for them. But when I disappear, they will not know which way to turn, as none of them has a majority or any positive views and aims. They can only criticize and find fault—always say, 'No.'[172]

He also developed new symptoms, this time a facial neuralgia (*trigeminal neuralgia*) 'like a sword being shoved through my cheek'.[173]

On 14 January 1882 the Landtag opened and Robert von Puttkamer represented the Minister-President, who was still away. One important item needed no emphasis and Puttkamer declared it with satisfaction: 'the friendly relations to the present supreme head of the Catholic Church put us in the position to take account of practical needs by re-establishing diplomatic connections to the Roman Curia. The means to pay for this will be requested of you in due course.' He also announced what came to be known as the Second Discretionary Bill, which would allow exiled bishops to be pardoned, eliminate the German culture examination for priests and pastors, and lift the *Anzeigepflicht* (compulsory notification to the Prussian state of clerical appointments) for assistant pastors.[174]

On 8 February Eugen Richter (1838–1906), leader of the Left Liberals and along with Windthorst and Lasker one of the critics who most provoked and enraged Bismarck, explained the compromise with the Catholics as part of a deep plan:

> Prince Bismarck wants a docile majority...one that is also perhaps amenable to altering universal, direct, equal suffrage, for this, it seems to me, is now coming into question. That is the goal, and this bill is only one piece of the total policy that is meant to lead to it. Now, gentlemen, it must have been clear to Prince Bismarck that he cannot attain such a docile majority from Protestant districts alone. [Cheers from the Zentrum.] After the last election it may have become clearer still. He needs, therefore...tractable deputies from Catholic districts. Consequently it was obvious to him that he must seek a way to get those regions and their deputies into his special power, and such a means is this bill. That is the actual point to this matter. The Catholic clergy, gentlemen, are to be made hostages to the good behaviour of the Zentrum party. Other than this, this entire policy of discretionary authority has no purpose.[175]

Bismarck returned to Berlin for the Landtag and Reichstag sessions and on 18 February Holstein saw him.

> I asked him (B) if he was going to attend the debate on the *Kulturkampf* in the Landtag. 'Why should I? The more undecided things are the better. The question is by its very nature an open one, and the conflict will never be resolved because ever since Colchas there has been a group of people in every nation who hold as an axiom, "We know God's will better than the rest of you." If I had been able to conduct the *Kulturkampf* entirely in accordance with my own ideas, I should have been satisfied with inspection of schools and the suspension of the Catholic Section of the Ministry of Ecclesiastical Affairs. But the attitude of the Conservatives obliged me to reckon with a majority which liked to beat the *Kulturkampf* drum as loudly as possible.'[176]

Once again we see all the characteristic features of Bismarck's approach to politics: to leave affairs open-ended, or in the words used to Holstein, 'the more undecided things are the better', and that linked with denial of his responsibility for what had gone wrong. It was ludicrous to say, and by this time a disillusioned Holstein knew it, that 'if I had been able to conduct the *Kulturkampf* entirely in accordance with my own ideas'. Whose ideas and whose absolute authority had been behind it, if not Bismarck's? The frustration at his defeat came out in his furious attacks on Windthorst, who on 17 March 1882 wrote to Professor Heinrich Geffken: 'I cannot speak with the Prince at all; the full bucket of his fury is pouring over me ... Bismarck will not cease persecuting me until I lie in my grave.'[177] These three attributes— wonderful flexibility of strategy and tactics, shirking responsibility for what went wrong, rage and brutality to his enemies—almost always ended in hypochondria and withdrawal to bed. Like clockwork that followed, as Lucius recorded on 5 March 1882, 'For three weeks Bismarck has been unwell, sees no one, lets matters go, and gives no directives, neither on church nor on tax policy.'[178]

He got up from his bed on 27 March 1882 and admitted defeat in the Landtag. He surrendered two days before Windthorst was set to reintroduce the sacrament motion, and asked him if he would accept the bill if he (Bismarck) dropped the *Anzeigepflicht* completely. Windthorst accepted and the Conservatives did likewise. On 31 March 1882 the Second Discretionary Relief Bill, as amended, passed the Landtag.[179] Bit by bit the apparatus of persecution of the Catholic Church had begun to come down. Bismarck had been comprehensively outmanoeuvred by Ludwig Windthorst and the Catholic Centre Party in the Reich and Prussia. On 24 April diplomatic relations between Germany and the Vatican were restored and on 25 April the Conservatives and Centre introduced a resolution to abolish completely the Falk system of interference with the disciplinary and pastoral life of the Catholic Church.[180] The wounds would never entirely heal, as Catholics well into the twentieth century felt themselves to be second-class citizens. On 15 October 1882 many prominent Catholics, the leadership of the Centre, August Reichensperger, Windthorst, and others boycotted the national festival, in the presence of the Imperial Family, to celebrate the completion of Cologne Cathedral. On 31 October Windthorst wrote to Bishop Kopp, 'We cannot be sure that Bismarck won't make a *coup de main* [i.e. call a snap election] . . . Il est le diable.'[181]

On 14 November Lucius confided to his diary his distress at Bismarck's handling of the end of the *Kulturkampf*:

> Bismarck has underestimated the curia, the Conservatives say, and made great mistakes in dealing with it. All the concession made so far have not been matched by any concession on its part. He acts too hastily under angry impulses and listens to no advice.[182]

In October Bill Bismarck brought his doctor to see his father. Bill suffered from obesity and the doctor, a remarkable South German, Ernst Schweninger, seems to have helped him to lose weight. Schweninger, who was born in Freystadt in the Upper Pfalz, went to Munich, where he qualified as MD and had a brilliant career ahead of him. In 1879 he was arrested and sentenced to four months in prison for what a contemporary American newspaper called 'an atrocious act in a public place'. His offence was against the widow of his best friend and it was committed at his grave, to which she had gone with flowers.[183] Quite how Schweninger got to Bill Bismarck with that past is a mystery, but he did. Schweninger played an important part in Bismarck's life and his treatment reveals certain traits in Bismarck's psyche. Schweninger practised a type of medicine utterly at variance with the scientific, white-coated model dominant in the nineteenth century and not unknown in the twenty-first either. The handsome 32-year-old with his great black beard and sparkling eyes made an impression on Johanna von Bismarck, who had by this stage become desperate about 'Ottochen's' health. On 10 October 1882 she wrote to Herbert: 'We liked him very much, and now he has sent all kinds of little bottles for Papa.'[184] But Schweninger brought something more fundamental to the bedside than little bottles; he brought a different way to treat patients.

In the academic year 1904–5 a young medical student Richard Koch (1882–1949) attended a seminar by Schweninger, now, of course, famous as Bismarck's doctor. The seminar took place in the old Charité hospital building in Berlin:

> Only a few students were present, all of them strange characters, young and old, types one usually meets in vegetarian restaurants. Dr Schweninger himself was a striking figure. At that time he was 55 years of age. He was of medium height, rather skinny, had pitch black hair as well as a big beard, very lively eyes, a typical Bavarian. He wore a top hat, morning dress, a white waistcoat and an elegant tie. This elegance was unusual for an academic and did not fit his rustic features.[185]

No other faculty member showed up in such garb; it caused a scandal—a doctor with no white coat! He said outrageous, unscientific things and enjoyed provoking his white-coated medical students. Koch only returned because he wanted to argue:

> So I returned, got even angrier, but came again. Schweninger's theory was roughly as follows: 'school medicine treats illness as abstract things that seldom happen in reality, only in textbooks. One should not treat illnesses but ill people.'[186] ... Schweninger's examination of patients had the students in an uproar. They argued with him but he had a way to deal with patients that nobody else taught. 'There is a rule—answer as if you were the patient.'[187]

In May 1883 Schweninger arrived from Munich and began his treatment of his difficult patient. Here is his account of his first evening with Bismarck as told to K. A. von Müller:

> Bismarck was on the verge of physical collapse. He believed that he had already had a stroke and suffered from severe headaches and complete sleeplessness. No treatment had done him any good. He mistrusted all doctors. A relative, [he said] had taken his life because of a similar disorder; 'That will also be my fate'. 'Tonight, your Highness,' said the doctor, 'you will sleep.' 'We shall wait and see,' Bismarck replied sceptically. Schweninger wrapped him in a damp body roll [Leibwickeln] and gave him some drops of valerian, telling him, however, that it was not a sleeping potion. Then the doctor sat in the easy chair next to his bed and took one of Bismarck's hands in his own, 'like a mother with a restless child' until the chancellor fell asleep. When he awakened in the morning, the doctor was still at his side and Bismarck could not believe that it was day and that he had actually slept the entire night. 'From that moment, he trusted me.'[188]

Schweninger set out his therapeutic technique in these words:

I determined as far as possible the working time and the tasks to be under-taken during it; regulated the time and amount of recreation, exercise and rest; supervised eating and drinking, according to time, quantity and quality; regu-lated getting up and going to bed, intervened whenever necessary either to moderate or stimulate; and finally had the satisfaction of noting real progress in body and spirit.[189]

The pains, the facial neuralgia, and the headaches vanished; Bismarck was able to ride again. His weight began to go down as the list below shows (in pounds):

1874	227
1878	267
1879	272
1881	255
1883	222
1885	225

From 1886 on he never went above 227 pounds, a perfectly reasonable weight for a man of six feet four. Schweninger had, in effect, saved Bismarck's life.[190]

How did he do it? Richard Koch explained it this way:

The real secret of Schweninger's power over Bismarck was in his absolute honesty. He did not hide behind scientific jargon but talked to him about his illness, treatment and cure in his own language...He felt the vocation to spread his conviction to destroy conservative 'pseudo-scientific' medicine and replace it by own new 'natural way of healing'.[191]

Schweninger practised holistic medicine in the age of Pasteur and the white coat. It looked unscientific to his students in 1905 but it had one peculiar technical advantage that Bismarck's previous physicians seemed unable to understand: Schweninger treated Bismarck, the person, who needed care and attention. One could say that he had come near to death by being Bismarck. His destructive urges and rages, his need for revenge, his paranoia and sleeplessness had psychological causes. They lay in the dark recesses of his colossal and complex nature. Bismarck made himself ill by his turbulent psychic reactions. He needed tender loving care and support, and, for rea-sons that we have seen, Johanna, angular, full of vindictiveness herself, stirred his hatreds rather than calmed them. She could not give that maternal care that he desperately needed. If we look at Schweninger's own account of his first treatment, we see what he did. He put the child to bed, 'wrapped in a damp body roll [*Leibwickeln*]' (warmth of the womb?) and gave him 'some drops of valerian, telling him, however, that it was not a sleeping potion'. Valerian is a herb that grows wild all over western Europe and probably worked because it came from the loving comforter. Then the doctor sat in the easy chair next to his bed and took one of Bismarck's hands in his own, 'like a mother with a restless child'. This is exactly what a parent does when a little child has a nightmare—holds his or her hand for comfort until the child falls asleep. Wilhelmine Mencken Bismarck failed to give the child Otto that elementary maternal care. He knew it and hated her for it. Schweninger saved Bismarck's life by giving him a surrogate for that missing care and by controlling the eating habits of the entire family.

On 8 June 1883 Johanna wrote to Herbert that Schweninger had prescribed a new diet for the entire family—tea or milk with eggs for breakfast, a 'little' fish and roast meat (no vegetables) at noon, a small jug of milk at 4.00 and yet another in the evening. To eat 'less and more frequently'. Johanna had developed 'a mighty trust' and prayed that this 'pleasant, modest, cheerful and unspeakably demanding' personality would remain by her husband's side for the rest of the summer.[192] He stayed for the rest of Bismarck's life and in gratitude Bismarck imposed his 'House Doctor' on the Berlin medical faculty, which regarded him as a charlatan and refused to speak to him. As Koch writes, 'only in 1900 did Schweninger get a position befitting his qualifications. He became head of the medical department in the county hospital in Gross-Lichterfelde.'[193]

The other great change in the 1880s lay in social policy. On 9 January 1882 Bismarck answered a parliamentary question from Georg Freiherr von Herling, a rising younger leader of the Centre, who during the First World War briefly served as one of Bismarck's successors as Chancellor.

> Have the Allied Government plans, as part of their concern for the working classes, to expand the existing factory legislation, in particular to the end that Sunday working be abolished as soon as feasible, that female labour be further restricted and that...the legal regulation of artisans be augmented by special protective rules and the factory inspectorate's officials charged with that task be also equipped with comprehensive powers?

Bismarck's reply indicated that the answer would be a qualified yes and that such provisions would be included in the large forthcoming package of legislation that the Allied governments would submit in the Spring. He then let slip in passing during a long and unusually flaccid speech one of the prime motives that had moved him:

the perception that the mass of workers regard even the attempts of the government to improve their conditions with such deep mistrust that they prefer to vote for those parties which in the area of economic activity advocate the right of the stronger and abandon the weak in the battle against the might of Capital...[194]

In other words, workers trusted left liberals like Lasker, in spite of his free market ideas, and not Bismarck. Bismarck believed that the anti-Socialist legislation had not gone far enough. Voters could vote for, and candidates could stand as, Social Democratic representatives in the Reichstag. The SPD had not been crushed in the October elections but had, in fact, gained three seats. Bismarck knew that he had to do something and he had for some time been working on a plan. In the Ministry of Trade, he found a willing, if not always biddable, civil servant in Theodor Lohmann, a Hanoverian Christian with social reformist urges. Bismarck in this case had a clearer concept of the next step than the expert, though both agreed that accident and illness insurance had to be provided. Lohmann wanted to foster Christian self-discipline; Bismarck wanted a state insurance system with compulsory contributions by employer and worker. Bismarck was right.[195] In spring 1883 Bismarck launched the first part of the new social welfare legislation, an accident insurance bill and a sickness insurance bill to cover the period of thirteen weeks after accidents. On 15 June 1883 the official government gazette, *Neueste Mittheilungen*, saluted the passage by the Reichstag of the sickness insurance legislation:

> By the acceptance of the principle of compulsory state insurance, an end has been put to all those attempts to make health insurance a private matter for those affected and formally and publicly asserts the role of the state in the provision of care for workers who have become ill in the course of employment.[196]

Bismarck as a non-liberal could do what the liberal democracies found and still find hard: to see the state as the guarantor of justice for the poor.

During the 1880s Bismarck completed the social security network by getting an accident insurance system into place which the Reichstag accepted on 27 June 1884 and an old age and disability insurance bill passed in 1889. The state system of social security gave Germany the first modern social welfare safety net in the world and still forms part of the modern German social security system, a significant achievement and entirely Bismarck's doing.

His restlessness continued in spite of better health. During 1884 and 1885 he again began to tinker with the institutions of the Reich. He set up a State Council. It caused much ill-will and confusion and did not work. He tinkered with the acquisition of colonies for a while in 1884 and 1885. The pressure from a new type of merchant adventurer, the illusion that colonies might supply a protected market for German goods and yield cheap raw materials, the importance of some sort of foreign policy success to maintain his reputation and the chance to exercise his wizardry, all contributed to his sudden conversion to colonialism. On 24 April 1884 the German Reich extended 'its protection' over Walfisch Bay and other adjacent territories which then became German Southwest Africa (today's Republic of Namibia), Togoland, German East Africa (Tanzania today), and some islands in the Pacific. The colonies never played a significant economic or social role. By 1903, the total German population of the colonies amounted to 5,125, of whom 1,567 were soldiers and administrators.[197]

On 1 April 1885 Bismarck celebrated his 70th birthday. The event became a national celebration. All over Germany there were huge festivals. A fund to purchase the Schönhausen estate as a national birthday gift met its target. The Emperor and the entire group of royal princes called on Bismarck. Lucius attended the occasion.[198] The aged father, well pleased with his son, shed tears. But the son had now become old himself during the twenty-three years he had served the father.[199]

Bismarck had grown old in other ways. As Phili Eulenburg noticed on a visit to the Bismarcks, the two well-known rooms had not changed save for the addition of 'a red silk couch cover with a yellow pattern'. The rooms showed the taste of the typical Pomeranian Junker family of an earlier generation, that is, 'its absence of taste...but then we old Prussians have always been tasteless'. On the walls Johanna had hung a selection of conventional landscapes. One by Morgenstern had been sent back to the artist because the Prince on seeing it had said 'too many clouds'.[200] He began to wear a long black tunic buttoned up to the neck around which he tied a handkerchief, which made him look uncannily like a Cathedral canon in the Catholic Church.

He seems to have read no contemporary German literature, no Freytag, no Heyse, and apparently no Theodor Fontane either, even though Fontane confessed to the journalist Maximilian Harden in March 1894 that 'in nearly everything I have written since 1870, the Sulphur-Yellow (*der Schwefelgelbe*) [Bismarck's sulfur-yellow, cuirassier uniform—JS] goes around and, although the conversation touches him only fleetingly, the talk is always of him as of Charles or Otto the Great.'[201] He never went to a Wagner opera nor listened to music much after Beethoven. He had become the national grandfather, though he alone failed to see that.

If he was old, the Emperor and court circle were extremely old, as Phili Eulenburg wrote in his diary on the occasion of the visit of the Emperor to Bavaria in 1885. General Hartmann called them 'walking corpses'. Eulenburg watched with particular interest 'the old General Physician Lauer who for years has been completely mummified. He had attached to himself a fat staff doctor with vulgar legs, and the two of them stare uninterruptedly at the Kaiser with great Argus eyes. God spare us a treatment by these two for their only case is the one old man.'[202] The 88-year-old Emperor continued to be the foundation of Bismarck's power, though most of the time he refused to admit it.

When the Reichstag opened on 5 November 1886, the speech from the Throne announced that the Allied governments would demand a renewal of the Septennat, for another seven years to begin on 1 April. Both the increase in army size under it and the cost fell within the 1 per cent of the population (now much larger than in 1871) and the 225 marks per head but the bill advanced the renewal of the previous Septennat by a year, a move evidently designed to provoke the Reichstag. Bismarck began to stir the press with threats of war and many found it convincing.

On 20 August 1886 the handsome, young Prince Alexander of Battenberg had been kidnapped by a group of rebellious officers and taken from Bulgaria. On 4 September Prince Alexander announced his intention to abdicate and was allowed to take his leave of his subjects in Sofia which he did with great dignity. He returned to Germany and rumours began again that he would get engaged to the Princess Victoria of Prussia, the sister of the future Kaiser William II. On 23 October 1886 the Crown Princess wrote to her mother Queen Victoria:

> The attacks of the Berlin press on Sandro continue—it is mean, and shameful, besides utterly ridiculous. It is, of course, to flatter the Tsar, and the great man...[203]

Bismarck went into a super-rage at the Crown Princess and women who intended to undermine his diplomacy by arranging a marriage with Sandro Battenberg. The Russians would threaten the Reich and war might ensue because the Crown Princess Victoria really had lurid urges of her own to have Alexander close to her.

The crisis in the Imperial family coincided with an outbreak of trouble internationally. The appointment of the bellicose General Georges Boulanger (1837–91) as French Minister of War in 1886 caused alarm in the German General Staff. Boulanger had pledged to strengthen the army and made aggressive public speeches which earned him the nickname *Général Revanche*. Bismarck decided to respond in kind. On 11 January 1887 Bismarck made one of the most famous speeches of his career. The speech began with the assertion that 'we have no warlike needs, we are so to speak a saturated state', one of Bismarck's most famous phrases. He continued that Imperial policy in the last sixteen years had been 'to preserve the peace. The task was not light.' He then reviewed the excellent results of his policies, especially the relations between Austria and Russia, both united by the Three Emperors' League, renewed in 1884, and the Dual Alliance. France was, alas, another matter. French military improvements and the threat posed by Boulanger made it essential to increase the army and to do it now. Of course, that was hardly the real reason, since the new Septennat called for a very modest expansion in troops and funds. He then threw down a challenge to the Reichstag which nobody could miss:

> The Allied Governments stand by the full Septennat and will not deviate by a hair from it. You will never make the army dependent on shifting majorities. Annual appropriations, eliminating battalions already approved is a fantasy, and an absolute impossibility. We want an Imperial Army not a parliamentary one, which is to be commanded by Messrs Windthorst and Richter... The Allied Governments will not enter into long negotiations. The Reichstag shall accept the bill as soon as possible and in all its provisions.[204]

The news that Bismarck intended to open the debate on the Septennat had spread through Berlin and the crowd wanting to hear Bismarck was so great that even Baroness Spitzemberg, well connected as she was, could not get a ticket. She dined with Count Wartensleben and

> many distinguished people, especially ministers, who told me all the details of the session so that I was almost there. The speech of the Prince, which I read in the evening, was splendid. Whatever else there will be a dissolution, if the Septennat is not approved. Woellwarth even told me today of a possible Staatsstreich [*coup d'état*—JS], that is, an alteration of the franchise, since better election result are not to be expected.[205]

The gamble had high stakes. Bismarck hoped to ram the army bill down the throats of parliament. If they refused the peremptory demand, there would be an immediate dissolution and Bismarck would go to the country with his usual scare tactics, as he had done successfully in October 1878. That time he had broken the Liberals' strong position and given himself room to pass the tariff and other anti-free market legislation. This time he wanted to reduce the leverage of the Centre by a 'war in sight' election and with strengthened conservative and National Liberal fractions he could abolish universal suffrage, formerly his best weapon but now increasingly impossible to control. On 14 January Bismarck dissolved the Reichstag and the campaign began.

The Centre immediately recognized that it was in danger and the fraction leader von Franckenstein wrote to Monsignor Angelo di Pietro (1828–1914), nuncio in Bavaria, two days after the dissolution. Vatican circles had let it be known that it would please the Curia and speed the final demolition of Catholic disabilities if the fraction would support the Septennat:

> I do not know whether the Holy See finds it a matter of indifference whether or not the Zentrum returns in the same strength or whether the Holy See harbours the wish that the Zentrum might disappear from the Reichstag. I do not need to say that the Zentrum was always happy to act on the orders of the Holy See when it was a question of ecclesiastical legislation. I allowed myself, however, as early as 1880 to call attention to the fact that it is absolutely impossible for the Zentrum to obey directives on non-ecclesiastical legislation.[206]

On 21 January 1887 Archbishop Ludovic Jacobini, the nuncio in Vienna since 1879 and the main channel between the German government and the Vatican, sent round a note to the German episcopate:

> Considered as a political party, the Zentrum is allowed freedom of action always . . . If the Holy Father believed that he should notify the Zentrum of his wishes in the controversy over the Septennat, then that is to be ascribed to the circumstance that connections with the religious and moral order were tied in with that affair. Above all, there were cogent grounds for believing that the final revision of the May Laws would receive a strong impulse from the government if the latter were satisfied with the Zentrum's vote on the Septennat.[207]

Windthorst had a big speech to make in Cologne and on the night of 4 February 1887 he was boarding the train when he heard the station newsboys yelling, 'Pope against Windthorst! Pope against the Zentrum! Pope for the Septennat!' He bought the paper and, as the train pulled out of Hanover and his travelling companion Deputy Dr Adam Bock began to read the article aloud, he discovered that it contained the text of the Second Jacobini Note. He knew that one of the German bishops, almost certainly the Bismarck fellow-traveller, Bishop Kopp, had leaked it to the Bismarck press to 'break his back', but as Windthorst had once warned Bismarck, he would have to rise very early indeed to outwit Ludwig Windthorst. On 5 February Windthorst rose to speak in the Gürzenich Hall, Cologne, and was received with 'deafening applause and foot stamping'. He deftly turned the Papal letter on its head:

> If anyone has the right to rejoice it is we...Of course, it cannot be over-looked that the Holy Father *wished* that the law might be adopted. In this proclamation, however, he based his wish not on the material content of the bill, but rather on grounds of expediency, from the standpoint of diplomatic considerations and relations...had it been possible, we should have granted it of our own accord, without compulsion...the impossible no one can do [opposition had been in the party's programme]...And above all, away with that wicked Guelph, with Windthorst!...But, gentlemen, *old Windthorst is still alive.* He will not do these people the favour of dying...And, however difficult the situations are, if we are true to ourselves and to the cause we represent, then God will also be with us. For what we preeminently strive for is God's cause.

Windthorst said to a friend as he climbed down from the rostrum, 'Well, I lied my way through that one.'[208] But he had survived—just! On 9 February the German bishop's conference supported Windthorst and the Zentrum against Leo XIII. When on 21 February 1887 Reichstag elections took place, the Centre survived intact. It lost 2.5 per cent of its vote but only one seat. Ninety-eight members were returned and voted as a bloc against the Septennat. On the other hand, the two conservative parties and the National Liberals had formed an electoral 'Cartel' that stated whichever party had the highest vote on the first ballot would get the support of the other two in the second round. It worked. The two conservative parties gained 15 seats but the National Liberals gained 48 at the expense of the left parties, which lost 42. The Socialists held their share of the vote but because of coalitions against them between first and second ballot they only got 2.8 per cent of the seats and lost 13 deputies.[209]

Windthorst had survived with his party behind him but the collapse of the left Liberals meant that Bismarck no longer needed to negotiate for his support. He came close to despair. On 22 February August Stein recorded Windthorst's reaction:

He sat—or lay, actually—next to me on the sofa and for the first time spoke bitterly of the 'inspired calumnies' he had heard. 'They do not hit me, but after this election I am beginning to doubt the future of a people who allows its best friends to be so vilified... After my death it will surely conquer. Because I believe in the divine governance of the world. Perhaps you are laughing now, dear friend. I cannot see you. No matter. What I say sounds old-fashioned but I have fared very well by this belief. It alone has allowed me to hold out.'[210]

In the camp of the defeated Liberals, bitterness was also great. On 25 February Ludwig Bamberger wrote to Franz Schenk Count von Stauffenberg, the Bavarian left liberal, and expressed his dismay:

Although it was accomplished by crude cunning and coercion, I say to myself: the new representation is a true expression of the German popular will. Junkerdom and the Catholic church both know very clearly what they want, while the *Bürgertum* are childishly innocent, politically naïve, and in need of neither justice nor freedom. Junkerdom and Catholic church will join hands, and the burghers will get what they deserve, with the National Liberals contributing the political music. *Il faut que les destines s'accomplissent.* The crown prince is now relieved of all embarrassment. He will do what Bismarck wants.[211]

The shrewd political general, Alfred Graf von Waldersee, saw what Bismarck had accomplished, as he recorded in his diary on 11 March:

Things goes excellently in the Reichstag. The Septennat went through smartly and there are distinct signs that the Zentrum has begun to fall apart. Without doubt Bismarck has against all the doubters once more done one of his master strokes.[212]

In foreign affairs, Bismarck had apparently achieved another 'one of his master strokes', as Holstein reported to his cousin Ida von Stülpnagel on 14 March:

Two days ago ratifications of various treaties between Austria, Italy and Germany were exchanged. Above all we now have a defensive alliance with Italy against France. There is in addition an agreement between England and Italy, loosely knit it is true, concerning 'attempts to preserve the status quo in the Black Sea'. Hatzfeldt telegraphed yesterday evening that Austria had adhered to this agreement. Thus my exertions of the past six months have been crowned with success... After a long gap I have been seeing the Chancellor in recent weeks. He has become an *old man*. The days when he could claim to think of everything are past: now one has to try to help and support him whenever possible...[213]

The Chancellor had secured this complex set of agreement only by conceding to Austria and Britain a set of assurances about Russian expansion into the Mediterranean, the issue which had nearly caused Britain to go to war with Russia in 1878. The so-called Mediterranean Agreement had been concluded two months before the Three Emperors League was about to expire. The gap between Russia and Austria had now widened to such an extent that the Tsar would no longer renew the Treaty. During May and June 1887 Bismarck and the Russian Ambassador in Berlin drew up a separate agreement that has come to be known as the Reinsurance Treaty, a secret agreement signed on 18 June 1887. In it Bismarck promised 'to give moral and diplomatic support' for any measures that the Tsar might deem necessary to defend the entrance to the Black Sea.[214] The complexity of these diplomatic ties, according to Herbert von Bismarck, had an ulterior motive, as he explained to Holstein:

> The secret treaty, nowadays called the Reinsurance Treaty, had existed since 1887. Prince Bismarck eagerly indulged in his treaty spinning in every direction. The more tangled the mesh, the more difficult it was to find one's way about in it without Prince Bismarck. 'My father is the only person who can handle this business,' as Count Herbert Bismarck used to say.[215]

The treaty—whatever its merit or demerits—shows that Bismarck no longer had room to manoeuvre. All the squares on the board had now been blocked and no Bismarckian combinations could conceal that. His victories in domestic and foreign affairs rested on unsteady conditions which must change and soon. The next Reichstag election returned the Reichstag to its balance which the temporary war scare election had upset. The cartel parties lost a catastrophic 84 seats. Windthorst's Centre returned 106 deputies and became the strongest party in terms of seats in the Reichstag. The hated Social Democratic Party raised its share to 19.7 per cent and won 1.4 million votes. It became the largest party in the parliament measured by numbers of votes. Bismarck's 'enemies of the Reich' now controlled its parliament. Thus in both foreign and domestic politics the Bismarckian system of government had ceased to function.

11

Three Kaisers and Bismarck's Fall from Power

The year 1888, 'the year of Three Kaisers', changed Bismarck's position in Germany and the history of Europe. Within the space of a hundred days, William I died, his son Frederick III died also, and a 29-year-old became Kaiser William the Second (1859–1941). This accident of heredity undid Bismarck because he had always depended on royal favour, and that favour no longer sustained him. The way he fell showed up the destructive features of his grip on power in the most lurid of lights. He fell victim to exactly the kind of palace intrigue which had made him great: the secret operations of an unofficial camarilla composed of young Prince William, Philipp Count zu Eulenburg, Friedrich von Holstein, the 'grey eminence' of the German Foreign Office, who owed his career to Bismarck, and the 'political general', Alfred Count von Waldersee, Moltke's successor as Chief of the Great General Staff. Bismarck, who had always disdained those in his entourage, now became their victim.

The first link in the conspiracy came about by accident at a chance meeting at the hunting lodge of Eberhard Graf von Dohna-Schlobitten in Prökelwitz in East Prussia. On 4 May 1886 Herbert Bismarck's friend, Philipp Count zu Eulenburg (1847–1921), scion of one of the most important Prussian dynasties (his uncle Fritz had been Bismarck's long-serving and long-suffering Minister of Interior; his first cousin Botho had succeeded his uncle in the same office; another cousin August would become Household Minister to Kaiser Wilhelm II) went to join the hunting party. There he met the young Prince William of Prussia and in effect 'fell in love' with the Prince. From 1886 to 1900 when the relationship cooled, Phili and William had a relationship so intense, on Phili's side 'boundless love', that nasty tongues began to wag.[1] They had something to wag about when on 8 May 1908, 'Philine', as Axel von Varnbüler called him in a letter, was arrested on his grand estate Liebenberg and accused of 'abnormal' sexual relations with two fishermen on the Starnberger See near Munich. Phili and his close friends in the high aristocracy had an intense set of interlocking relationships and, though many were married with children (Phili had eight), the surviving correspondence shows unmistakable signs that the group belonged to a clique of what would now be called gay men. They called the young Kaiser 'Liebchen' (little Darling) in their correspondence. Kuno Count von Moltke (1847–1921), one of their group, which came to be known in the press as the 'Liebenberg Round Table', had risen to the rank of Lieutenant General, and had become a General Adjutant of the Kaiser. He was 'outed' in 1907 by the journalist Maximilian Harden and at a series of trials lurid details of his activities—and, with his wife of nine years, non-activities—titillated the taste of the new mass public. There were several suicides in the group of friends around Moltke and Eulenburg and six officers in exclusive guards regiments also committed suicide during the early years of the twentieth century, as homosexuality became a public theme in European societies.[2]

On 4 June 1898 Axel Freiherr von Varnbüler, son of the former Württemberg Prime Minister and brother of Hildegard von Spitzemberg, wrote to Kuno Moltke that he had met Kaiser William II recently. '*Liebchen* stopped me in the Tiergarten and, after he had suitably admired my yellow boots and the matching colour tones of my riding habit, he asked me: "what do you know about Kuno? I cannot get anything out of him nor Phili".' In the course of the conversation the Kaiser emitted 'a few strong expressions not to be repeated here', which showed Varnbüler 'that he is completely informed and has no illusions any longer'.[3] Isabel Hull provides a remarkable portrait of the Kaiser recorded by Walter Rathenau (1867–1922), the businessman, intellectual, and foreign secretary who was murdered as a liberal and a Jew on 24 June 1922 by the right-wing secret military 'Organization Consul':[4]

> There sat a youthful man in a colorful uniform, with odd medals, the white hands full of colored rings, bracelets on his wrists; tender skin, soft hair, small white teeth. A true Prince, intent on the impression [he made], continuously fighting with himself... neediness, softness, a longing for people, a childlike nature ravished... This man must be protected, guarded with a strong arm, against that which he feels but does not know, that which pulls him into the abyss.[5]

None of this would have mattered, had Phili Eulenburg not made himself into Bismarck's most insidious foe by becoming an unofficial adviser of the young Prince. Phili poured gushing streams of extravagant, romantic, and exaggerated flattery over the young man and eased his friends and allies into positions of future power. Eulenburg had many real gifts. He preferred the arts to the barracks and after brief military service in the Prussian foot guards, chose a diplomatic career. He rose fairly rapidly, though Bismarck neither trusted him nor set much store by his abilities. Bismarck wrote to Herbert that 'I like him personally. He is charming but in political matters he has no judgement for what matters and what does not; he lets himself be influenced by carping gossip, which he passes on and causes annoyance without reason.'[6]

Phili indulged in all the fashionable irrationalisms of the late nineteenth century—spiritualism and séances, nordic mythology, and racism. He wrote song cycles and poetry set in the imaginary swirling mists of Nordic antiquity, and played and sang them to the Kaiser; he had a close and possibly intimate relationship with Count Arthur Gobineau, one of the founders of modern racism, and admired late, overripe romanticism in the visual arts. His politics expressed an equally romantic conservatism, contempt for the masses, mixed with great sensitivity and shrewdness about people, and a light and charming prose style and manner.

At this time, Eulenburg made his first contact with Friedrich von Holstein, the most senior, non-ministerial civil servant in the Foreign Office, and the third member of the camarilla. Holstein, a secretive bachelor, had once been a devoted admirer of Bismarck but had become alienated from his former master. He believed—not without reason—that Bismarck's foreign policy had become too complicated and had no other purpose than to buttress Bismarck's power by making it impossible for anybody to replace him. Holstein had no other life than the Foreign Ministry. He worked long hours, read everything, knew everything, and now began to spin intrigues against Bismarck and even more against his immediate superior, Herbert Count von Bismarck, Phili's close friend. If Phili in Bismarck's eyes lacked judgement and listened too much to 'carping gossip', Holstein had judgement enough for both of them and provided Eulenburg with informed opinions on policy and personnel as well. Holstein wanted neither promotion nor honours, so, in the simple sense, he served without fear or favour. On a deeper level, he knew that he was right, that the Bismarcks had become power-mad and utterly self-involved, and hence a danger to the state. He was thus a principled traitor, powerful and invisible, a kind of spider in a web of intrigue. Holstein flattered and patronized Eulenburg in equal measure, because he saw that the triumvirate—William–Eulenburg–Holstein—could give him the power that he needed to rectify the errors of the late Bismarck Era.

Holstein and Eulenburg wanted to enlist the full-time intriguer and future Chief of the General Staff, Alfred Count von Waldersee, to work with them. They first had to overcome Waldersee's suspicion, as this frank extract from his diary makes clear.

> In the great game of intrigue, more clarity emerges. It concerns, as I correctly supposed, power in the future royal house. Bismarck father and son intend to rule alone. They imagine they can control the Crown Prince. They make the mistake of alienating everybody with whom they might have worked together and show that they do not understand the Crown Princess. I am certain that she will soon tire of her new friends. In order to rule alone everybody in the way, who has influence or might have it, must be eliminated. In that they use contemptible methods. One of the worst agents is Legation Councillor von Holstein. He is so clever as never to show himself in the world so that lots of people are scarcely aware he exists. I too am on the list of the condemned! This is particularly strange since up to now I have belonged to the group who stuck immovably to the Chancellor and intervened on his behalf.[7]

It took Holstein a year to recruit Waldersee for the camarilla but on 31 May 1887

Waldersee joined the plotters, as he recorded with satisfaction:

> Today I was at the Foreign Office and restored the old friendly relationship with Herr von Holstein. Third parties seem to have had an interest in this reconciliation and assert that there were misunderstandings in the way. That may be so. I took the hand offered gladly and had the impression that a weight fell from Holstein's heart.[8]

He who rises by camarilla will fall by camarilla seems to be the conclusion here. Bismarck comprehensively and systematically betrayed his chief Otto von Manteuffel in the 1850s. He sent secret dispatches written for Manteuffel first to Leopold von Gerlach and only then to the Minister-President. He wrote frequently to von Gerlach, a key figure in the camarilla around Frederick William IV, behind Manteuffel's back, and tried to influence policy and to advance his career. With his one-sided morality he could not see the irony in his situation in 1888–9. Holstein justified his treachery with more claim to our consideration; his intrigues had nothing to do with personal advantage. The letters flowed regularly and confidentially between Holstein and Eulenburg. They discussed personnel and policy with equal frankness but had to be careful. On 16 June 1886 Holstein wrote to Eulenburg that 'Herbert writes me that he has asked you for letters and if they are sufficiently factual and objective, as is to be expected, he will send them unchanged to His Highness. So be warned. With best wishes, your devoted Holstein.'[9]

The time for the camarilla to grab the levers of power had not yet arrived but it moved closer when, on 6 March 1887, Dr Gerhardt, Professor of Medicine at the University of Berlin, diagnosed a small growth on the left vocal cord of the Crown Prince. He failed to remove it surgically so he tried to burn it out but also without success.[10] The Crown Prince Frederick, the most successful field commander during the Austro-Prussian and Franco-Prussian wars, had been gradually losing heart and equanimity. He had written to Stosch:

> In the present regime ... every capable person is subordinated. They can only obey; they no longer think independently. There is the further consideration that I feel little inclination to do business through a major-domo [Bismarck] ... I am resigned. I lack a joyful or assured spirit. I am inspired by no other wish than to spend the couple of years that yet remain to me as quietly and as retired as possible in my household and be swiftly placed in the background by the new sun [William].[11]

On 4 May 1886, Stosch wrote to von Normann:

> he [the Crown Prince] began to unburden his heart. Bismarck, father and son, treat him simply with scorn. He feels so isolated; only Albedyll has taken up with him, because he is in bad with Prince William—What could I reply? I have sympathy for the Prince in the depths of my soul. You must have attended the Good Friday Lamentations in a Catholic Cathedral. They have always deeply moved me. I had exactly the same feelings at the unending laments of this poor weak soul. I do not know any help for it.[12]

What had happened to the confident and successful soldier of 1870? That Frederick had energy and curiosity. On his free days he went off to look at French cathedrals and châteaux with his guidebook. He intervened vigorously in debates and confronted Bismarck. By 1887, the Crown Prince had become a 'poor weak soul' and may have been what today we could call clinically depressed. In March of 1887 it became clear that he had cancer of the throat.

There began a desperate struggle between the Crown Princess and the German medical establishment over his treatment. On 29 April 1887 the Crown Princess wrote to her mother, Queen Victoria, from Bad Ems:

His spirits are far better here than at Berlin, and his throat seems daily improving. All the irritation, swelling and redness is fast subsiding, he never coughs, and has not the feeling of soreness, but part of the little 'granula' which Professor Gerhardt could not take off with the hot wire, because the throat was too much irritated, is still on the surface of one of the *Stimmbänder* [vocal cords] and will have to be removed when we go home.[13]

The royal couple then moved from Bad Ems to San Remo on the Italian Riviera for the winter. Everything she did was wrong and earned her criticism, as she wrote to her mother on 27 October 1887: 'I am driven quite wild with the newspapers of Berlin and dear Ct Radolinsky keeps writing that people are so angry with me for choosing San Remo and for not calling in another German doctor. Really it is excessively impertinent of these people.'[14] On 6 November Sir Morell Mackenzie, the most famous English oncologist, arrived in San Remo to examine the Crown Prince, who asked if it was cancer. Morell replied: 'I am sorry to say, sir, it looks very much like it, but it is impossible to be certain.'[15] The struggle became embittered because Bismarck and his captive press had waged a campaign of vilification against the Crown Princess for years, which she recognized and described in another letter to her mother:

> To return to Prince Bismarck, he has so much that is brutal and cynical in his nature, so little that is noble and upright, he is so completely a man of another century than ours, that as an example or ideal he becomes very dangerous. He is a patriot and is a genius, but as a school there could not be a worse one. Opinions such as William holds are very much the fashion nowadays in Germany—they have half created the immense power Bismarck possesses and he has half created them.[16]

Bismarck planted spies in the royal household at the Neues Palais to watch the Crown Princess. Hugo Prince von Radolin (1841–1917) was appointed Marshall of the Palace in the entourage of the Crown Prince. Radolin, a Germanized Polish prince, belonged to the Bismarck connection and rose through Bismarck to ambassadorial duties in due course. Lady Ponsonby (1832–1916), the wife of Sir Henry Ponsonby, private secretary to the Queen, watched the situation of the royal couple at close hand:

> I don't think the Queen realizes what an extraordinary state of things exists in Germany in the way of espionage and intrigue. They, the foreign office, which means Bismarck, wanted to put a man of their own about the Crown Princess so as to more effectually control the Crown Prince when he became Emperor. Seckendorff refused to play the spy . . . then they appointed Radolinsky (Court

Marshall to the Crown Prince) with orders to get rid of Seckendorff...
Radolinsky's manner of defending the Crown Princess simply consists in
spreading these reports and trying to detach her family from her.[17]

Early in January 1888 the well-informed General Waldersee wrote in his
diary that the Bismarcks had begun to suspect that there were those who
wanted to influence Prince William against him:

> We, including Albedyll, are agreed that the Chancellor is jealous of those
> people who want to alienate Prince William from his son Herbert. Here as so
> often he sees ghosts and goes ruthlessly after them... Given the tendency to
> revenge in the Bismarck family war will be waged on them all, if at first in a
> careful way.[18]

On 3 February 1888 Bismarck published the text of the secret Austro-
German treaty concluded on 7 October 1879. Waldersee noted it in his
diary: 'Today's publication of the German-Austrian Alliance has caused an
immense sensation. I hardly believe that overall situation will change
much.'[19] In fact, it made a significant difference. The Hungarian elite recognized to their relief that the treaty had an entirely defensive character, and
the Russians saw to their dismay that the Treaty had them as its object. On
6 February Bismarck delivered one of his grand speeches on foreign policy
in the Reichstag. The final paragraph whipped up the members of the
Reichstag and led to such demonstrations in the street that Bismarck had
trouble getting through the cheering crowds:

> We Germans fear God but otherwise nothing in the world and that fear of God
> is what has let us love peace and cultivate it. Whoever breaks the peace will soon
> convince himself that the pugnacious love of the Fatherland of the then weak,
> small and exhausted Prussia which called the entire population to the colours,
> has today become the common possession of the entire German nation and that
> whoever attacks the German nation in any way will find it uniformly armed and
> every soldier with the firm belief in his heart: God will be with us.[20]

On 9 March 1888 William I, German Emperor and King of Prussia, died
a few weeks short of his 91st birthday. The old King had for more than
twenty-five years supported Bismarck in both senses of the word, approving
his work and policy as well as tolerating his increasingly impossible and
irrational behaviour. He had been well rewarded for that support. In 1859,
he became Regent of a small, not very powerful German kingdom and by
the time of his death it had become the greatest and most powerful state in
Europe. He had become an Emperor and seen his beloved Prussian army

win three brilliant military campaigns. The King's contribution may not be obvious but it was essential to that success. He let Moltke command his armies and Bismarck run his state. He recognized early that fate had given him the greatest military strategist and the most developed political genius of modern times and to them he entrusted his fate, that of his dynasty and his people. He worked hard, read government papers and always had well-founded opinions on subjects but he never let his own views, even when he knew they were correct, as they often were, overrule Bismarck's policies. He had a strong sense of loyalty, a virtue his Chancellor completely lacked, and rewarded many of those whom Bismarck had savaged. He refused to let his favourite ministers go just because Bismarck had suddenly turned against them. He was a kind, decent, honourable, and unpretentious man, in effect the only kind of King who would and could have tolerated life with Otto von Bismarck. William I made Bismarck's career possible and his longevity made it into an institution.

His death confronted Bismarck with the drastic possibility that the new Emperor would simply dismiss him. As in September 1862, after the 'Blood and Iron' speech, on 11 March 1888 he boarded the new Emperor's train at Leipzig, who 'repeatedly embraced and kissed him'.[21] The next day, the Emperor Frederick wrote a two-page memorandum on constitutional issues, which began with the following introduction:

> My dear Prince,
> On assuming power, I feel the necessity of addressing you, the long-tried, first servant of my father, who now rests in God. You have been the faithful and brave adviser who gave shape to the aims of his policy, and secured their successful realization. I and my House are and remain most grateful to you.[22]

Bismarck realized that he now had nothing to fear. On 13 March, the next day, he told the Prussian Cabinet,

> I feel relieved of the great concern I had that I would have to fight with a dying man against inappropriate intentions to the point of demanding my release from office. Everything is going easily and pleasantly with his majesty, like a *jeu de roulette*.... The Kaiser wishes to make no changes at all in the cabinet, neither do I. This is no time to change course. In view of his earlier utterances in younger years, there was reason to fear he would pursue all kinds of deviant aims—but I do not fear that any more.[23]

Others were less pleased. The new Emperor rewarded some of his faithful friends and Waldersee disliked what he saw. He deplored the names on the new honours list:

Among the first acts of government in the new reign was the granting of the Order of the Black Eagle to the Empress and to the Minister Friedberg... Friedberg has been for a long time a friend and in many affairs an adviser of the Crown Prince and Princess. He has the reputation among Liberals as being one of them and is of Jewish origin. I believe in fact was a Jew himself. The decoration stakes out a programme. It reveals the effort to make them popular with Liberals and Jews. The Ministers Puttkamer, Maybach and Lucius were passed over by the decoration of Friedberg...[24]

The great chronicler of Prussian life, the novelist Theodor Fontane, exploded at the Liberal newspapers which dared to suggest that the new Emperor might graciously allow Bismarck to continue in office. On 14 March 1888 Fontane wrote to his wife Martha to express his rage:

After the greatest *political* achievement in a millennium (for Frederick's was smaller and Napoleon's more fleeting) to have to be told by a Jewish rascal, behind whom unfortunately many, many stand: he was only a 'servant' and can, if he is nice and polite, remain in his *servant's* position. Unheard of! Frightful!... Now they will all creep out of their swamps and holes and make their monkey business with him and tell him that it serves him right.[25]

Two days later the old Emperor was laid to rest. The Empress Frederick, as she was now styled, described the day vividly in a letter to her mother, Queen Victoria:

All went off well, there was no hitch in spite of the bitter cold weather—sharp frost and deep snow. The public was respectful and silent; there were no great crowds. The service I thought rather conventional, stiff and cold; the singing was very good... The hearse was very simple indeed... It is an inestimable blessing to be relieved of the thraldom and tyranny which was exercised over us in the poor Emperor's name, as now the right thing can be done for Fritz's health. But oh—if it is not too late, too late.[26]

Waldersee had become genuinely alarmed for his position. Bismarck had begun a press campaign to get him out of Berlin and to break his links to others, as yet unknown to him, who had been intriguing against him. Waldersee went to see the new Crown Prince William and opened his heart.

The conversation turned to the Chancellor, and I took the occasion to turn it to the attacks on me in the press and to the Chancellor's intention to remove me from Berlin. The Prince said to me very confidently that I can be reassured on that point. He would stick to the rule that nobody should be moved from his post and not allow the Chancellor to interfere in military matters. I referred explicitly to this danger, which is, in fact, very real. Thank God, the Prince understands the situation very well.[27]

On 21 March Bismarck had a rude shock. Frederick III refused to sign a two-year extension to the anti-socialist act, and a bill to make Reichstag elections every five years instead of three. Bismarck, of course, threatened to resign, because 'the existence of the cabinet is most seriously in question'. Bismarck summoned his carriage and drove to Charlottenburg in person, where he was received by the Empress. He explained that a bill passed by the Reichstag could not be subject to an Imperial veto. The Kaiser had no such power. The Empress Frederick went into the Emperor's bedroom and came out with the signature on the two bills. With his paranoid misogyny, he blamed the Empress and her three ladies-in-waiting, Anna von Helmholtz, Baroness von Stockmar, and Henriette Schrader, who, he believed, had conspired to intervene between the Emperor and his cabinet.[28] The only incident in Bismarck's long career of rage and revenge crazier than this was his accusation that the Reichstag stenographers had ganged up to undermine him.

While Bismarck blamed nefarious 'feminine intrigues'. Waldersee saw the Jews as the real culprits. He knew, as always, exactly what had happened and blamed Frederick III, not the women of the household, for the crisis. The real culprits were the Liberals, that is, the Jews, who had voted against both reactionary bills in the Reichstag:

> The opponents of the two laws were the 'enemies of the Reich'. One can easily see in what direction the Emperor would have taken us, had he been healthy... Jewish circles have been unusually active, in order to gain some advantage for themselves out of it all. Even liberal people take the view that the Progressive Party to which the Jewish circles belong has operated in an unbelievably stupid way. The Crown Prince will have an easy time finishing those people off.[29]

Waldersee believed that 'World Jewry' had initiated a conspiracy to defame and undermine the Crown Prince William. The fact that the Crown Prince and Princess had become enthusiastic congregants of Court Preacher Stoecker and showed that in public had inflamed the press:

> In the whole hostile press the word has gone out to make the Crown Prince unpopular... Foreign newspapers achieve amazing things. The Jew papers, above all *Die Neue Freie Presse* and *Pester Lloyd*, make the running. Every time they drag Stoecker in, often naturally Puttkamer, and from time to time I get mentioned. In general attacks against me seem to have rather slowed down lately.[30]

On 4 April 1888 Moltke rejected the Kaiser's request to give Waldersee command of an Army Corps, in effect, to reduce his malign influence on his son by sending Waldersee to a remote posting. Moltke told Waldersee:

> I see that my powers are declining. I can in any case not continue my position for much longer. It would, therefore, be nonsense to take you away, when it will not be a year before you are back here and this time as Chief of the General Staff.[31]

On 15 June 1888 Frederick III, German Emperor and King of Prussia, died in Berlin. Philipp Eulenburg's father described the scenes from the palace after the Emperor's death in a letter to his son written on 17 June 1888:

> The Empress is beside herself. Kessel heard her not only weeping but scream-ing. She said to him on one occasion, 'what will become of me at my age without a home?'...He says that with all the grief that he feels, he also feels relief to be freed from an unnatural, artificial English intrigue, and that he can now think and be honestly himself. Tomorrow at 10 is the funeral and by 12 it will all be over. Many wreaths have arrived from regiments but more from the Jews. There is a whole room full of Bleichröder, Schwabach, Heimann etc.[32]

Within three months, three generations had passed across the stage of German history. William I, born in 1797, Frederick III born in 1831, and now William II born in 1859, all Emperors one after another. Frederick's illness and death have always been a great 'might have been' in German his-tory. Had he arrived healthy and strong, would the course of events have been different? Obviously the question has no answer but one thing can be said definitely—the mid-century generation, Frederick's contemporaries, never came to power with him. Instead an uncivil, illiberal, unsteady, and insecure 29-year-old came to the throne and the 'lost generation' of the German mid-century never came to power.

The struggle of the generations had, however, another long-term effect, as Christopher Clark argues in his biography of Emperor William II. The great age of the old Emperor, his reactionary views, and the absolute power he exercised over the royal family weakened the power of the young Prince's parents over him in ways that made an alliance between the old and young a reality, the great hope that the Bismarck family cherished. In October 1886, the Prince, then 27 years old, explained the situation to Herbert von Bismarck, who then passed on the substance to his father:

> The prince...said that the unprecedented circumstance of there being three adult generations in the ruling family made things difficult for his father: in

every other case, in ruling and other families, the father had the authority and the son was financially dependent upon him. But he [Prince Wilhelm] was not under his father's authority, he received not a penny from his father, since everything derived from the head of the family, he was independent of his father... that was, of course, unpleasant for his Imperial Highness [the Crown Prince].[33]

Clark argues that this alliance of old and young had foreign and domestic significance. The Prussian Kingdom, as a 'state in the middle', had always been torn between the Western powers, France and Great Britain, and the Russian option. William I had been a 'Russian' in sympathy, tied to the Romanovs by bonds of family and by his natural reactionary instincts; Frederick III and Victoria represented England, liberalism, and the hated Jews, who embodied all those aspects of a commercial and open society that the old Kaiser and most of his entourage disliked. Bismarck who belonged to neither camp, made it possible for the old Emperor to gratify his instincts just enough to keep him happy but never tied his foreign policy or the German Reich to a pro-Russian line, quite the opposite. He considered the English option at various stages but got too little encouragement from Disraeli and the Tories and none whatever from the Liberals whose leader William Ewart Gladstone embodied everything he detested about Liberalism save that he happened to be a devout Anglican rather than a Jew. Now Bismarck had to cope with a headstrong young man who from the beginning intended to rule in his own name and not as an agent of the great Bismarck. He shared most of Bismarck's values but he had too much of the irrationalism, showiness, and ambivalence about the new industrial society which the younger members of the Prussian ruling class, his contemporaries, also shared, to be a comfortable master for the old man of Friedrichsruh.

William II became the most controversial figure of modern German history and gave his name—Wilhelm—to a period in that history, the Wilhelmine era, 1888 to 1918, in the way that his grandmother Queen Victoria gave her name to the era 1837 to 1901. And rightly so. His flamboyance, his aggressive speeches, his public image and dress, his quick wit and capacity to create slogans, the exaggeration of his uniforms and his bellicosity, all those aspects came to embody the period of explosive economic and military growth that the German Empire unfolded from the 1890s to the First World War. He led Germany when it went to war in 1914 and his abdication on 10 November 1918 cleared the way for the armistice.

Many in Germany and almost everybody abroad blamed him for the First World War and 'hang the Kaiser' was a popular slogan in the British 'khaki' election of 1918.

William II was born on 27 January 1859. During a traumatic birth, his left arm was damaged and he could never use it properly in later life. In May 1870 the Crown Princess wrote to Queen Victoria: 'Wilhelm begins to feel being behind much smaller boys in every exercise of the body—he cannot run fast because he has no balance, nor ride nor climb nor cut his food.'[34] He had a very strict tutor who used brutal methods to get him to overcome his disability and to excel intellectually. His mother wanted him to 'be something of what our beloved Papa was, a real grandson of his, in soul and intellect, a grandson of yours'.[35] What effect this combination of physical handicap and high maternal expectations had on the young Prince has attracted the attention of psychologists and psychiatrists, including Freud. William's impulsiveness, outbursts of brutality, and changes of mood made many fear that he would not be able to rule steadily. His mother wanted him to understand the lives of ordinary people, so his tutor took him to see the poor and later he became the first Hohenzollern to attend an ordinary school, a *gymnasium* in Kassel, and to spend a few years at university. Like Bismarck he never had a proper Prussian upbringing, no *Kadettenanstalt*, as a small boy and Christopher Clark speculates that as a result he never 'internalized the habits of self-subordination and discipline that a fully Prussian military education was designed to instill'.[36] He rebelled against his parents' values (perfectly normal) and sought solace in his grandfather (not unusual either) but, since his grandfather happened to be Emperor of Germany, a soldier by avocation, a reactionary in politics and the uncle of the Tsar Alexander II, young William had an alternative political model. He did his military service and became a caricature of the young Junker officer in a posh regiment complete with the language, demeanour, and prejudices.

On the other hand, he fell for the romanticism and myth-making of Phili Eulenburg and his song-cycles, not the sort of material that Botho von Rienäcker and the other guards officers described by Fontane knew anything about. He was intelligent, charming, and interested in modern technology but had a quick temper and a cruel sense of humour. The Bismarcks had done everything to win him over and cultivate him as a tame and flexible Emperor but by June 1887, they had begun to doubt whether it would work. Holstein recorded a conversation with Herbert on the subject:

I was very struck by a talk I had two days ago with Herbert about Prince Wilhelm...The Prince had no staying power—he simply wanted to be amused. And all that really interested him in army life was wearing a handsome uniform and marching through the streets to music. He fancied himself as Frederick the Great, but had neither his gifts nor his knowledge. And Frederick the Great, as a young man, had ceaselessly worked and exercised his intellect, whereas Prince Wilhelm allowed his talents to deteriorate by constantly consorting with Potsdam lieutenants. And as cold as a block of ice. Convinced from the start that people only exist to be used—either for work or amusement—and that even then they only do duty for a given period, after which they may be cast aside...I found Herbert's changed attitude towards Prince Wilhelm particularly interesting psychologically in that it revealed that *he* does not enjoy the status with the Prince which he desired and imagined he had.[37]

During his father's illness, William's relationship with his mother deteriorated and he had nasty spats with her, one of which the Crown Princess described in a letter to Queen Victoria:

You ask how Willy was when he was here! He was as rude, as disagreeable and as impertinent to me as possible when he arrived, but I pitched into him with, I am afraid, considerable violence, and he became quite nice and gentle and amiable (for him)—at least quite natural, and we got on very well. He began with saying he would not go out walking with me 'because he was too busy—he had to speak to the doctors.' I said the doctors had to report to me and not to him, upon which he said he had 'Emperor's orders' to insist upon the right thing, to see that the doctors were not interfered with, and to report to the Emperor about his Papa! I said it was not necessary, as we always reported to the Emperor ourselves. He spoke before others and half turning his back to me, so I said I would go and tell his father how he behaved and ask that he should be forbidden the house—and walked away. Upon which he sent Ct Radolinsky flying after me to say he had not meant to be rude and begged me not to say anything to Fritz.[38]

William's reaction to his mother became increasingly bitter and on 12 April 1888 he wrote to Eulenburg to express 'the shame for the sunken prestige of our once so high and untouchable House...That our family's shield should be spattered and the Reich brought to the edge of ruin by an English princess who happens to be my mother is the worst of all.'[39]

On 15 June 1888 Frederick III died and William now assumed his new role. At once the new camarilla came under fire from the well-informed press. Waldersee hastened to cover his flank by visiting Bismarck in July 1888 and had an interesting afternoon with the Chancellor. He was his old self. We drank two bottles of Grünhäuser and had a very agreeable conversation.... With regard to France he asked whether it would not be useful for us to violate Belgian neutrality in order to march through Belgium. I explained to him that I would advise against that but did think it would be extremely helpful if the French marched through Belgium.[40]

This remarkable conversation on the violation of Belgian neutrality took place three years before the first sketch of the Schlieffen Plan was drawn up in the German General Staff, a plan for a two-front war against Russia and France that involved in the first version a violation of both Belgian and Dutch neutrality. The plan foresaw a gigantic encircling movement by the German army to come into France from the north and cut the French army off from Paris. It is extraordinary that the idea came from Bismarck not the soldiers. Had the Chancellor considered the diplomatic consequences of such an attack? That Great Britain, a guarantor of Belgian neutrality, would be forced to join France, as, indeed, happened in 1914? That Germany would reap a whirlwind of hatred and contempt for its violation of the rights of peaceful, small states?

William II began his reign with a variety of visits abroad, where he made a very bad impression. In November 1888 he visited Rome for an audience with the Pope and a state visit to the Italian Kingdom. On 17 November Ludwig Bamberger summed it up as 'in short, a total fiasco'. He had received a letter from his old friend, the novelist Heinrich Homberger (1832–1890), which told the story:

> Now, all voices agree, that He did not please. 'Unripe, impolite, ruthless, bad manners'. When he came back from the Vatican, he described what happened during the visit at the court table with all sorts of bad jokes and made fun of the Pope. Further, with the young Crown Prince of Italy, an eighteen-year-old who had in the Roman way been largely educated in a cloister, he used 'des discours lestes', asked questions which made the poor lad red with shame. That he took no interest in art or antiquities was held against him.[41]

In addition to his gaucheries abroad, he showed hostility to Catholics and Jews at home. In September 1888 the ever watchful Waldersee recorded in his diary that the Kaiser 'could not bear Jews' and 'often stated' this.[42] Nor was this a superficial attitude. John Röhl, the author of the great multi-volume life of Kaiser William II, writes that the Kaiser's 'animosity towards Jews, recorded in such marginalia and also in Waldersee's diary, was anything but peripheral; it formed a key element of his thinking.'[43]

The inevitable clash between the young Kaiser and the old Chancellor gradually emerged in early 1889. On 14 January the Kaiser opened the Landtag in the White Hall of the Palace. He announced that a draft bill for reform of the income tax in Prussia would be forthcoming to 'lighten the burden on the less well off'.[44] Since Bismarck had not entirely approved the proposal and certainly not the direction it took, tensions emerged within the cabinet and between Bismarck and the Kaiser, who had begun to think of himself as 'the King of the Poor'. This self-image would be put to the test when on 3 May 1889 the Ruhr miners began a strike which spread to the Saar, Saxony, and Silesia. The strikers demanded eight-hour shifts underground including transport down and up from the shaft, a 15 per cent wage increase, an end to prolonged shifts, and better working conditions. From 14 to 20 May there were 7,000 on strike in Upper Silesia, 13,000 in Lower Silesia, 10,000 in Saxony, in the Saar and Aachen 20,000, and in the Ruhr district 90,000 of the 120,000 employed. The government sent in so many troops to the Ruhr basin that the *Nationalzeitung* joked it looked the spring manoeuvres.[45] The panic and arrogance of the coal barons annoyed the army chiefs. On 11 May General Emil Albedyll (1824–97), formerly head of the Military Cabinet and now commander of the VII Corps stationed in Münster,[46] sent a message to Chief of the General Staff Waldersee:

> Every ten minutes I get a telegram announcing the overthrow of everything if immediate military help does not come, and absolutely nothing has happened which might look even remotely like damage to property.[47]

The Kaiser on 6 May 1889 ordered local authorities in strike areas to report directly to him. He also tried to force owners to raise wages immediately without consultation with Bismarck. On 7 May three miners were killed by police fire and on 12 May at a meeting of the Prussian cabinet William II suddenly appeared unexpectedly and unannounced his intention to preside over the strike discussion. After the Kaiser left, Bismarck said to his colleagues: 'The young master has Frederick William I's conception of his authority and power, and it is necessary to protect him from excessive zeal in this regard.'[48] Bismarck's reaction reflected his tactical approach more generally. He said on 25 May that in his view it would 'be useful if the settlement of the strikes and its unfortunate after-effects were not too smoothly and quickly resolved, the latter in particular to make the liberal bourgeoisie feel it.' He wanted to use the strikes to remind the liberals how useful the anti-socialist law would be after all. So, above all, no rush to conciliate the strikers.[49] He was not at all fussed by the strikes but the Kaiser's tendency to govern by himself without consultation made him uneasy.

The mounting tensions between the Kaiser and the government led Bismarck—unusually for him in high summer—to return on 10 August to Berlin. On 17 August Bismarck presided at a cabinet meeting and discussed the issue of strikes:

> If the mine administration should no longer have the freedom to dismiss a worker without the consequence of a general strike, that would mean the establishment of mass rule, which would present a great danger for public life.[50]

On 20 August Bismarck left Berlin but went to Friedrichsruh, which was, of course, nearer Berlin. On 9 October Bismarck returned to Berlin to welcome Tsar Alexander III on an official visit and three days later, on 12 October, the following conversation between them took place:

ALEXANDER III: Are you sure of your position with the young Kaiser?
BISMARCK: I am certain of the confidence of Kaiser William II and I do not believe that he would ever dismiss me against my will.
ALEXANDER III: It would give me great pleasure if your optimism were to be fully confirmed.[51]

The last act of the great drama began on 1 December when 3,000 miners in Essen gathered to protest against employers' blacklists which had locked them out of employment. Unluckily for Bismarck, Hans Hermann Berlepsch (1843–1926), a rare Liberal at the top of the provincial government system, was Superior President of the administration of the Rhine Province. Berlepsch had been involved in the strike movement from the beginning and had seen and got to know workers well. He had become convinced that the workers were part 'of a great historical movement which cannot be suppressed with force'.[52] He convinced the employers to lift the blacklist and reinstate the sacked workers. Bismarck was distinctly unhappy with that decision but, as usual, he was away in Friedrichsruh and unable to reverse it. In fact, even Bismarck's personal assistant, Franz Johannes Rottenburg, who had replaced Christoph Tiedemann in 1881, believed that a 'new course' in social policy would be needed and later he caused a scandal as Curator of the University of Bonn in his inaugural lecture by advocating official recognition of the Social Democratic Party, for which he was investigated by the police.[53] Bismarck's deputy, Karl Heinrich von Boetticher, as his biographer describes him, was 'the model civil servant, shrewd, adroit and agreeable in manner. It was his good fortune to be persona grata with Bismarck and William II.'[54] But not for long, because Bismarck refused to accept their advice. On 19 December Rottenburg informed Boetticher that the 'Chief' had rejected conciliation and Berlepsch's policy. Bismarck had ordered that Boetticher draft an *Immediatbericht* (a direct report for William II) in which he wanted it said that:

> We are cultivating in the workers a great danger that will ultimately be felt not only at the polls but also in the army. The efforts of the workers to obtain ever more pay for ever less work has no limits ... If we let the mistake they [Berlepsch and the local authorities—JS] began (i.e. mediation in favour of workers) exert an influence, its consequences can only be corrected later by hard and perhaps bloody disciplinary measures (*harte und vielleicht blutige Massnahmen*).[55]

On the same day, Albert Maybach, the Minister of Trade, and Herrfurth, the Minister of the Interior, ordered the provincial authorities to cease conferring with labour representatives. This was more or less the opposite of the Kaiser's intentions, as events would soon show.

On 24 January 1890 Bismarck returned to Berlin for a Crown Council in something of a hurry because the Kaiser, without informing him, had called one for that evening at 6 p.m. Neither Bismarck nor his son had any idea why the Council had been called. When on 23 January 1890 Herbert asked for an audience, the Kaiser granted it and explained that the Council had been called because he wished to put his ideas on 'the handling of the labour question to the ministers; if your father wishes to take part, I shall be very pleased.'[56] Herbert sent a telegram to urge his father to come to Berlin as soon as possible. Bismarck had to rise early, something he hated and made him irritable. He took an early train, which arrived at 1.50 p.m. At 3.00 he met the cabinet, at 5.30 the Kaiser alone, and at 6 p.m. the Kaiser chaired the Crown Council. Holstein, who had been in bed on Tuesday, 23 January, with influenza, had received a visit from Herbert Bismarck, who was in a great state of agitation. Holstein told him his opinion and then with a pencil sent him the same views in writing, dated 24 January, the day of the fateful Crown Council. He warned Herbert not to push the Kaiser too hard. The letter did no good, for that very afternoon the session of the Imperial Council took place at which sparks really flew for the first time.[57]

A few days later, he wrote a full account of the fateful Council to Phili Eulenburg. The Kaiser opened the Council by saying that the anti-socialist law would certainly pass without the expulsion paragraphs and then added that 'it would be lamentable if I were to colour the beginning of my reign with blood . . . I cannot and will not be forced into such a situation.' Bismarck then announced that

> under the circumstances he had no choice but to submit his resignation since he could not accept the views of His Majesty. The declaration was brief and without any attention to the Kaiser's arguments. The Kaiser then asked each minister individually for his view; *all declared that they shared the Chancellor's view.* The Kaiser then gave in . . . He behaved with admirable self-control and was right not let the Chancellor go. He must take a personal stance which is not identical with that of the ruler. In addition, Kaiser, Chancellor, Ministers, Bundesrat, Cartel, Parties are all in a dreadful mood.[58]

Lucius wrote in his diary that 'we parted with our differences unresolved, with the feeling that an irreparable breach had occurred between sovereign and chancellor. His Majesty exerted himself to be friendly toward the prince, but he was boiling. At any rate he possesses great self-control.'[59] The next day, as expected, the anti-socialist law was rejected in the Reichstag by 169 to 99 and thus would expire on 30 September 1890, unless a new bill were introduced in the next Reichstag after the February elections.

Bismarck had become seriously worried now about his position and suddenly called on his 'enemies' for help. On 18 February 1890 Bismarck visited Waldersee, who was not at home so he left his card. Waldersee was astonished, as he wrote in his diary: 'The chancellor wanted to visit me! I didn't trust my ears when I heard that. For years he has made no visits whatever, and now he drives to me and the Field Marshall [Moltke—JS] in order to call. He is indeed becoming weak.'[60] At the same time Bismarck requested an audience with the Empress Frederick, which she refused. If he wanted to call, it ought to be a social call and hence with the Princess. Bismarck had no choice but to agree. Victoria was even more startled than Waldersee, as she wrote to her mother, the day after the visit on 19 February:

> Prince Bismarck and his wife came to see me yesterday. He spoke a long while on the subject of William's newest coup! He also spoke of retiring soon, as he could not keep pace with innovations so suddenly resolved on and carried out in such a hurry and on the advice of people he thought in no way competent to give it. I dare say he quite means what he says in this instance but I do not suppose his resignation would be accepted . . . I thought Prince Bismarck looked remarkably strong and well and inclined to take things philosophically.[61]

Baroness Stockmar, who had lady-in-waiting duty that day, passed on to 'neighbour' (their agreed code-names) Ludwig Bamberger some more of the conversation. Apparently the Empress Frederick had asked Bismarck whether he had composed the February Decrees which he claimed (implausibly) to have edited to make them less 'impossible'. Frau von Stockmar continued:

> Bismarck had made it clear that he intended to go. William took counsel from any and everybody, without listening to him. It was all vanity; he wanted to be a great world historical monarch... Bismarck saw the time coming when he will be ignored and denied. As Victoria asked, 'what is then to be done?' He answered, 'Majesty if you meet me later in a salon, be gracious enough to greet me...'[62]

While the Empress and Bismarck gossiped like old friends, Germany went to the polls, and the results were fully as bad as National Liberals had feared. It is just possible that Bismarck hoped for such an outcome, because it would make him irreplaceable, and that might be why he refused to remove the expulsion clause from the anti-socialist bill. Voter participation fell to 71 per cent and was thus lower than the crisis election of 1887. The election was a disaster for the Cartel Parties, which lost 85 seats. The Socialists raised their vote to 19.7 per cent (about 1.4 million votes) and became for the first time the strongest party in terms of votes.[63] The 'enemies of the Reich' now controlled its parliament; 106 Centre deputies plus 35 Socialists and 66 Progressives gave a majority of 207 of the 397 seats in total, easily enough to put an end to the anti-Socialist Law and frustrate reactionary military bills.

On 2 March 1890 Bismarck startled the Prussian State Ministry with a new and daring plan. He intended to introduce into the Reichstag an anti-Socialist law far more stringent than the one the old Kartell-dominated Reichstag had rejected five weeks earlier. Social Democratic 'agitators' would be banned from voting and from standing in elections and could be summarily exiled. The inevitable rejection would lead to a dissolution and a conflict election, very like the scenario in Prussia in 1862, which gave him power in the first place. There would be elections in which radicals and Socialists would gain until Bismarck announced a new electoral law with an end to universal suffrage. Since the German Empire rested on an alliance of princes and not of states, Bismarck declared, according to the minutes of the meeting 'the princes... could decide, if need be, to withdraw from the joint treaty. In this way it would be possible to free oneself from the Reichstag if the results of the elections continued to be bad.'[64] The authentic Bismarck stands revealed here. Domination mattered and nothing else. He would destroy the Reichstag rather than surrender power.

On 5 March William II went to the annual dinner of the Brandenburg provincial estates and gave the toast: 'Those who want to help me are heartily welcome, whoever they are, but those who oppose me in this work I shall crush.'[65] Both the Kaiser and Bismarck had now begun to use violent language and plan for extreme situations. Holstein wrote that 'the present preference of His Highness for extreme situations is a sign of the irritability of old age. Earlier in spite of his decisiveness he was the most superior statesman there has ever been.'[66] Waldersee had another and much more profound explanation for Bismarck's behaviour. In an entry for 5 March 1890, which the editor of the Waldersee diary omitted, he wrote that Bismarck

cannot leave because he is afraid of his successor and of the anger which will be unleashed in many whom he has oppressed, lied to and deceived...he has a very bad character; he has not hesitated to disclaim his friends and those who have helped him most; lying has become a habit with him; he has made use of his official position to enrich himself on a colossal scale and has had his sons promoted with unbelievable ruthlessness although no one thinks them competent![67]

Waldersee made two mistakes in that assessment. He had always lied from his earliest childhood, and he had not the least fear of any successor. He wanted absolute dominance and would do anything to retain it. In fact Bismarck had begun to play his combinations as he always had. As Paul Kayser (1845–98), head of the Colonial Department in the Foreign Office and one of the camarilla, said of Bismarck's plan to cause a crisis in the Reichstag, it was 'the most masterful move in the whole game of chess: it means checkmate for the king.'[68] After all, Bismarck would be able to claim that the trouble lay not with him but the new master who refused to accept realities. Bismarck had engineered the defeat of the Cartel by refusing to compromise on the expulsion clause to please the National Liberals. They, not he, had paid the price in a huge electoral defeat and he still had his room to manoeuvre. Now he had to steer a big Army bill through and renew the anti-socialist law. His Minister of War, Julius Verdy du Vernois, who had been one of the three 'demi-gods' of 1870, contemplated offering the hostile Reichstag two-year compulsory service in exchange for the passage of the bill, an irony of history, for it was precisely that compromise which Bismarck wanted to offer the Landtag in October 1862, that the King had vetoed.

Bismarck had another option—to entice the Centre to give him both bills in exchange for the final abolition of the remaining restrictions on the Catholic Church. On 10 March Windthorst called on Bleichröder, who urged him to meet Bismarck privately—whether he acted on his own or on Bismarck's request is not known. On 12 March 1890 Ludwig Windthorst presented his card at the Bismarcks and was immediately received. Margaret Lavinia Anderson provides a vivid account of that meeting:

> Bismarck welcomed his old opponent warmly, seating him on the sofa and plumping up cushions to support his back. Then he sat down beside him, leaned his head back on the sofa rail, and outlined the general political situation. He needed support and he asked Windthorst his price. It was Windthorst's great moment. 'The repeal of the Expatriation Law', he began. 'Done!' Bismarck interjected. Revision of the *Anzeigepflicht* in accordance with the formula of the Prussian Bishops' Conference, Windthorst continued; free activity of missions, the establishment of the *status quo ante* in Catholic matters, including the readmission of the Jesuits. To the last demand, Bismarck replied equivocally, but concluded, 'It should be feasible. Not of course at once, but step by step...' In this un-dramatic manner Bismarck agreed to concessions for which Windthorst had been fighting for eighteen years...In their unexpected need for each other, the barriers of rank, manners and long enmity dissolved and the old men treated each other as the intimates that they in some ways were. Windthorst cautioned Bismarck, 'If anyone says to you, turn in your resignation, that in a fortnight they will be calling you back—don't believe him. I went through that sort of thing twice in Hanover. Don't believe a word; if you go, you won't come back. Stay in office.' Bismarck was not offended at this familiarity. 'That's true,' he mused, 'you have experience on your side. I must say you have spoken frankly with me.' As he left, Windthorst was poignantly aware of how slim the chance that the concessions he had obtained would ever see the light of day. When he met Porsch that evening he look surprised and dazed. 'I am coming from the political deathbed of a great man,' he confided.[69]

The next day, 13 March 1890, Count Otto von Helldorf-Bedra (1833–1908), the leader of the Conservatives in the Reichstag, called an extraordinary meeting of the Fraction and bound them to accept no concessions on the Septennat and none on religious and educational questions. This decision meant that no deal with the Centre in spite of its 106 seats would have a majority in the Reichstag. Bismarck's approach to Windthorst would compromise him without assuring his survival.

On the 14th Bismarck sent word to the Kaiser to beg an audience, which the Kaiser ignored. Bismarck gives a vivid account of the scene which followed in his memoirs. At 9 a.m. on the morning of the 15th the Kaiser sent word that he would arrive in thirty minutes. Bismarck had to be awakened, dressed hurriedly, and awaited the Kaiser without having time to breakfast.

Bismarck began the report by announcing that he had seen Ludwig Windthorst, to which the Kaiser replied, 'and you did not show him the door'. Bismarck declared that all parliamentary colleagues, provided they were well mannered, had always been received. The Kaiser then confronted Bismarck with the accusation, 'you negotiate with Catholics and Jews behind my back.' Bismarck reacted furiously that soon he would have to submit his menus.[70] The Kaiser described the scene to Phili Eulenburg very vividly:

> I sat at the table, my sabre between my knees, smoking a cigar. The Chancellor stood before me and his growing anger made me calmer. Suddenly he picked up a huge folder and hurled it down on the table in front of me with a big bang. I was afraid he was going to throw an inkwell at my head. Well, I took hold of my sabre! I could not believe it.[71]

The discussion had gone badly wrong from the beginning. Next the Kaiser demanded that the cabinet order of 1852 be rescinded to allow him to contact ministers directly since the Chancellor was always in Friedrichsruh. This further infuriated Bismarck. The Kaiser then said that he would amend the military bill to make sure that it found a majority in the Reichstag. The Kaiser thus removed the only conflict which might have assured Bismarck's survival.

That afternoon the Chief of the Military Cabinet General Wilhelm von Hahnke (1833–1912), the Adjutant-General Adolf von Wittich, and the Chief of the General Staff Waldersee had an audience with the Kaiser, who told them what had happened. The Kaiser believed that 'there is collusion between the Jesuits and rich Jews'. Waldersee argued, according to his diary, that Bismarck could not resign for fear of what his successors would find and 'unfortunately also because he was too closely allied with the Jews and could not escape from them'. He then gave the Kaiser 'a frank account of my views on the Chancellor without sparing him anything. Hahnke and Wittich were astonished, but the Kaiser not at all.' The only disagreement between the Kaiser and Waldersee was over what to do next. Waldersee urged the Kaiser to dismiss Bismarck; Wilhelm II wanted to provoke Bismarck to resign.[72]

The next day von Hahnke arrived at the Reich Chancellery with the Kaiser's demand that the 1852 order be rescinded and Bismarck refused. On 17 March August Eulenburg reported to Phili that no reply had been received to the Kaiser's demand so that Hahnke would go again in the morning with a summons to the Chancellor to order him to come to the palace that afternoon with his resignation in his hand.[73]

Meanwhile at the palace, the Kaiser waited for Bismarck's reply. His friend Phili Eulenburg spent the tense hours with him in his study and by the evening, when 'Uncle Ernst', the Duke of Coburg, arrived for dinner, nothing from Bismarck had been received. The Kaiser said, 'now we have had enough; lets make music'. After dinner, Phili sat at the piano and played and sang his various ballads while the Kaiser sat next to him on the piano bench and turned the pages. The adjutant on duty slipped into the salon and the Kaiser went out for a second. When he returned and settled down next to Eulenburg, he whispered 'the farewell is here'.[74] Eulenburg may have got the date wrong or the Kaiser may have read more into the adjutant's message then was actually there, for, according to other sources, nothing seemed to have arrived at the palace on 17 March.

That evening the entire cabinet assembled at Boetticher's house and voted to appoint him as their spokesman. He was to beg an audience of his Majesty, as Lucius wrote in his diary,

> in order to express our regret at the resignation of the Prince and to submit collectively our resignations in order to offer his Majesty in this respect complete freedom. The meeting became known that very evening through the Kölner Zeitung. All the papers according to their position published a political death notice and approved without exception the resignation of the Prince as right. With respect to the succession nothing positive has emerged. All the commanding generals have assembled.[75]

This unanimity from left to right in the press that Bismarck should go gives an indication of how much his political status had eroded and how little he understood that.

On 18 March Hermann von Lucanus (1831–1908), the Kaiser's Civil Cabinet Chief, arrived at the Wilhelmstrasse to ask why the Prince had not replied to the Emperor's demand. Lucanus, a senior civil servant, whom Bismarck had placed in the delicate office of Civil Cabinet Chief, must have found the assignment uncomfortable.[76] Bismarck answered that the Kaiser had power to dismiss him at any time and needed no letter of resignation, nor could Bismarck see any need to submit one. He intended to write an explanation of his position which could be published and sat down to do so. While he composed this statement, General Leo von Caprivi had arrived to take over the Chancellorship and began work in the next room. Bismarck described his reaction in the Chapter 'My Dismissal' in Book Three of his memoirs: 'My indifferent feelings gave way to a sense of injury... That was an expulsion without warning which at my age and after the length of my service I had every right to regard as rudeness and I am still today not free from the sense of injury at the mode of my expulsion.'[77] He then wrote a long memorandum on the importance of the Cabinet Order of 8 September 1852, an order 'which since then has been decisive for the position of the Minister-President and alone gave him the authority which made it possible to exercise that level of responsibility for the collective policies of the cabinet.' He then stated that he could not in good conscience carry out the Emperor's demand that he rescind the Cabinet Order and still serve as His Majesty's Minister-President and Reich Chancellor. He concluded the memorandum by writing:

> With the devotion to the service of the royal house and to Your Majesty and the long years of habitual activity in a relationship, which I had considered lasting, it is very painful to withdraw from the accustomed connection to the All-Highest person and from my responsibility for overall policy in the Reich and Prussia. After conscientious consideration of All-Highest intentions, to the execution of which I must be ready, if I am to remain in service, I can only humbly beseech Your Majesty to relieve me of the office of Reich Chancellor, of that of Minister-President of Prussia and that of Prussian Minister of External Affairs with Your grace and with the obligatory pension.[78]

Thus ended the extraordinary public career of Otto von Bismarck, who from 22 September 1862 to 18 March 1890 had presided over the affairs of a state he had made great and glorious. In the convoluted language of the promemoria, the experienced courtier used the language of subordination and royal power which he had mastered and used for forty years but which had never impeded his ability to act as he saw fit. Now the humble posture that he had always necessarily adopted in his written communications with his royal master had become his real posture. The old servant, no matter how great and how brilliant, had become in reality what he had always played as on a stage: a servant who could be dismissed at will by his Sovereign. He had defended that royal prerogative because it allowed him to carry out his immense will; now the absolute prerogative of the Emperor became what it had always been, the prerogative of the sovereign. Having crushed his parliamentary opponents, flattened and abused his ministers, and refused to allow himself to be bound by any loyalty, Bismarck had no ally left when he needed it. It was not his cabinet nor his parliamentary majority. He had made sure that it remained the sovereign's, and so it was that he fell because of a system that he preserved and bequeathed to the instable young Emperor. On 20 March the Kaiser replied in gracious tones and the resignation became official and public. The Kaiser wrote a twenty-page private letter to explain what had happened and why he had been forced to dismiss Bismarck. His conclusion uses a term which comes up again and again in contemporary assessments of Bismarck, 'lust for power had taken a demonic hold on this noble, great man.'[79] The Kaiser was not alone in that view.

Hildegard von Spitzemberg took time to reflect at some length in her diary how far and in what ways Bismarck had been the author of his own downfall. On 20 March, the day of Bismarck's official resignation, she recognized that he had been to blame in the catastrophe for his long absences and his tendency to confuse public and personal business:

> a series of necessary laws fell under the table because they did not suit his private interests as a landlord or simply because he had no time for them—As far as the family is concerned, nemesis breaks over them not unjustly for the brutality and heartlessness with which they trampled so many people, great and small into the dust, but the prospect will not be pleasant. My God, the vulgarity which will now show itself after the servility of earlier days.[80]

On 23 March 1890 the new Chancellor, Leo von Caprivi, the new Foreign Minister Adolf Marschall von Bieberstein (1842–1912), and Holstein met to decide whether or not to renew the Reinsurance Treaty with Russia. Neither Caprivi nor Marschall had any experience of foreign affairs or diplomacy. Marschall had served in the Reichstag and from 1883 had been Baden's ambassador to the Federal Council. He knew so little that he was jokingly described as the 'minister étranger aux affaires'.[81] Herbert Bismarck's resignation had still not been accepted by the Kaiser and he continued to occupy the office of State Secretary of Foreign Affairs, Marschall's new job. When he heard that Caprivi had been shown the secret Reinsurance Treaty, he became very angry with Holstein:

> Thereupon the Count sent for me and said, maintaining his self-control with difficulty: 'you have been guilty of something which in past circumstances I should have been obliged to punish most seriously. Under present conditions all I can say is that you have been in too big a hurry to regard me as a past number.' I had no difficulty in justifying the professional propriety of my behaviour, and we parted, shaking hands for the last time.[82]

Holstein had not, of course, been honest with Herbert for some time but in this case he had behaved correctly by giving the text of the treaty to the new Reich Chancellor and Foreign Minister. Herbert behaved the way Hildegard Spitzemberg noted and confused personal and public.

On the night of 23 March 1890 the Prince and Princess Bismarck gave a farewell dinner for the entire State Ministry and the new Chancellor, General von Caprivi. Lucius, who attended, described it on the last page of his long record of life under Bismarck:

> Caprivi gave his arm to the Princess, on whose left sat Boetticher. Maybach and I sat on either side of the Prince. The initial, stiff and depressed mood lifted gradually. The Prince and Princess had already during the afternoon taken leave of the Empress Frederick. The Princess expressed loudly and without reserve her view of the events of the recent days. Bismarck treated Caprivi with great warmth, wished him as he left everything good and offered his advice, if should need it.[83]

On 24 March the annual dinner of the Black Eagle Order, the highest Prussian decoration, took place. Everybody who counted and who had made a reputation in the Hohenzollern Kingdom regularly attended. Prince Chlodwig zu Hohenlohe-Schillingsfürst, who kept a splendid diary, recorded the event:

> At half past one—dinner at which I sat between Stosch and Kameke. The former told me about his quarrel with Bismarck and was as chirpy as a wren that he could now speak openly and that the great man was now no longer to be feared. This comfortable feeling is universal here. Here again it is true that the meek inherit the earth.[84]

Hildegard Spitzemberg went back to see them a week after her previous visit and found the atmosphere already very unpleasant, as

> a consequence of the sad and subjective view of people which for a long time determined the tone in this house and how much is now personal hatred and bitterness?... It is highly distressing to hear how dreadfully the violence and petty urge to rule had gained the upper hand in the Prince's behaviour.[85]

On 29 March 1890 Hildegard Spitzemberg called at 77 Wilhelmstrasse as the Bismarck family were about to leave. She found movers and packers dismantling the house, and

> empty, smoke-stained walls...Only when the Princess told us how yesterday the Prince had gone alone to the old Kaiser's mausoleum to take leave of his old master, did we all burst into tears. 'I took roses with me,' the Prince explained, 'and laid them on the coffin of the old Emperor. I stood there for a long time and called down to him a variety of things.'[86]

News of their departure had spread in Berlin and large crowds lined the route to the Lehrter Bahnhof. The public had expected that William II would appear to see Bismarck off but he did not. 'A squadron of guards cuirassiers with band and standards had assembled on the platform. All the ministers, ambassadors, generals were present... There was a deafening "hurrah" and "auf Wiedersehen". As the train began to move, the public joined in singing the "Wacht am Rhein". Thus the last act has been played out and an event of incalculable scope has taken place.'[87] With these words, Robert Lucius von Ballhausen ended his long diary. Ludwig Bamberger noted the event on the same day: 'departure today. The Bismarck legend begins. If the National Liberals were not slaves, they could use it to become great again. He is gone as the Great Devil who towers over his nation.'[88]

Nobody who knew Bismarck or Johanna could imagine a serene retirement and a quiet old age. Within days he had set up a 'shadow government', the shrine to his genius and the headquarters of the anti-Kaiser William II fronde. Two weeks was all that Bismarck needed to mobilize his own press corps. He no longer had the 'Reptile Fund' at his disposal to pay for planted articles, but he had no need to pay in cash. He paid in secrets revealed, in interviews, and in his incomparable authority, the authority of 'the Great Devil who towers over his nation', as Bamberger called him. War between Friedrichsruh and the new government would soon break out. To the surprise of the family, he no longer interested himself in the management of his now considerable landed property. It worried Herbert that his father looked 'uninterested or bored or actually never listened' when farm management needed decisions. He interested himself only in reading newspapers and in what Herbert called 'playing pseudo-politics'.[89] Herbert moved to Schönhausen, where he actually enjoyed the life of the country squire, and never returned to Berlin politics.

On 15 April 1890 the Prince received Dr Emil Hartmeyer (1820–1902), the proprietor of the National Liberal daily, the *Hamburger Nachrichten*. Hartmeyer, who inherited this substantial regional newspaper from his father in 1855 and ran it as owner-editor for almost fifty years, invited Bismarck to use the services of the paper and its chief political correspondent Hermann Hofmann (1850–1915) as his own personal newspaper, and Bismarck accepted.[90] The paper launched on that very day a sharp attack on the new Chancellor's first Reichstag speech. Bismarck had no intention of going quietly into retirement. He lusted for revenge.

Hatred and revenge had always moved him strongly and, now in impotent retirement, no positive activity nor satisfaction could distract him from the absolutely ruthless settlement of grievances—against the Kaiser, his successors as Chancellor, and against all those ministers who had not followed him into exile. Those on the list of enemies who had already died, like Guido von Usedom, would have their reputations blackened in every way possible when he came to write his memoirs. Those still alive and in office could be compromised and destroyed by leaks to the press. Heinrich von Boetticher, his subordinate and deputy, had stayed in office after Bismarck left, an offence for which the minister could not be forgiven. In March 1891 Bismarck leaked the story through his tame press that he had arranged a loan of 100,000 marks from the Guelph fund so that Boetticher could pay off the debt of his father-in-law. A few days later Philipp Eulenburg wrote to Boetticher a kind of condolence letter in which he expressed his horror and amazement:

> I had not remotely considered it possible that somebody would be capable of playing such a trick. If I take the personal grudge out of the picture, the entire affair must be seen as an *unpatriotic act*, which makes the line between personal wickedness and high treason very hard to draw.[91]

Bismarck had no hesitation in crossing that line and wickedness is not a bad word for his act. He devoted six pages in his memoirs, an entire chapter, to the ingratitude and treachery of Karl Heinrich von Boetticher,[92] and not a word about his leak of the compromising loan.

The new Chancellor, Leo von Caprivi (1831–99), found himself in a delicate situation. He had no political background but, as a soldier and as Imperial State Secretary of the Navy, after Bismarck had fired his enemy Stosch, Caprivi enjoyed a reputation as an upright, competent man, a conservative Christian but with a social conscience. *The Times* of 21 March 1890 gave its readers a picture of the man. He was unmarried, did not smoke, and had no independent income. His physical presence commanded attention:

> A typical Teuton of the hugest, most impressive type. He might very well pass for a brother or even a double of Prince Bismarck himself... In point of stature and breadth of shoulders, General von Caprivi even has the advantage of the man he is going to succeed... He is a good enough speaker but a brief one, and when at the head of the admiralty, he never failed from his place on the Federal Council bench in the Reichstag to put his case clearly and well.[93]

Caprivi determined to adopt, as Heinrich Otto Meissner writes, 'a *Versöhnungspolitik* [a politics of reconciliation] which would take the good from where it came... even hoped to win Social Democracy for the state.'[94]

The Reichstag which Bismarck had bequeathed to him had a negative majority. Caprivi had to govern with shifting majorities assembled for each bill, 'which was no peculiarity of Caprivi's system but of non-parliamentary constitutionalism in general'. The difficulty lay in appearances. 'Without the characteristics of a demonic genius . . . it looked like wavering.'[95] Windthorst had decided to support Caprivi's army bill and did so. On 27 June 1890 'the military bill passed with 211 against 128. The majority contained the votes of the entire Cartel Parties, the overwhelming majority of the Centre and the Polish Party. To the minority belong the Progressives, the People's Party, the Social Democrats, a few Guelphs and 21 South German Centre deputies.'[96] Windthorst explained why he had opted to support Caprivi to one of his aides on 23 June 1890, who took down the remarkable argument verbatim:

> If the bill had been rejected, then a serious constitutional conflict stood in prospect and universal suffrage would have been extremely endangered. One may think what one wants of universal suffrage—I would never have introduced it—but to do away with it now would mean to make way for revolution and to weaken essentially the power of the Catholics. The latter lies in the masses. Catholics are positively the poorer [of the two confessions]; the ruling classes in the state, in municipal government, and, on account of their greater wealth, in social life as well are Protestant. The position of the new Chancellor Caprivi would have been violently shaken, if not destroyed, through the rejection of the military bill. These political considerations alone forced its adoption.[97]

Windthorst, who always understood Bismarck's tactics, showed again his acuteness. Bismarck had intended to create a crisis to abolish universal suffrage. If a crisis occurred now after his fall, he might be recalled. Windthorst and the Centre Party had to support Caprivi for fear of somebody worse and, above all, to keep Bismarck safely in retirement.

In Friedrichsruh, the former Chancellor received visitors and played politics through his tame press. He also let it be known that he had begun working on his memoirs with the aid of his old amanuensis, Lothar Bucher. In March 1891, Baroness Spitzemberg visited and asked Bismarck if there were a chance of a reconciliation with the Kaiser and Bismarck made clear that there was not:

> No, that's all over and done with. Imagine what it would be like if I lived in Berlin. How could I present myself to all those who have shamelessly dropped me as soon as they saw I no longer counted? Given the miserable way people

behave would I not harm my friends? Everyone to whom I spoke, anybody who came to my house would be accused of 'plotting with Bismarck!' The Kaiser sent me packing like a lackey. I have all my life felt myself to be a nobleman, whom one cannot unpunished simply insult. From the Kaiser I can demand no satisfaction, so I just stay away.[98]

When she asked him the next day why the Kaiser dismissed him, she got an unexpected answer from the Chancellor:

I certainly can. A word from Versen, the chief flatterer,[99] expresses it. He told him that if Frederick the Great had had or inherited such a chancellor, he would never have been 'the Great', and he wants to be 'the Great'. May God give him the talent for it. I am the thick shadow there that stands between him and the sunshine of fame. He cannot allow as his grandfather did that some glamour of rule fall onto his ministers. It is inconceivable that he and I should work together. Even seeing each other is painful. I am a standing rebuke.

Gradually Bismarck's contemporaries began to die. On 15 March 1891 Windthorst died, on 24 April Moltke. In June 1891 Hans von Kleist visited Bismarck in Friedrichsruh. He had been moved to do so by 'the public accusation that his old friends did not come to visit him. He was very friendly and dear. I caught not a trace of bitterness. That he gave up saying grace at table years ago, made me sad.'[100]

During 1891 Herbert went to Fiume to stay with the family of his old friend from the diplomatic corps, Count Ludwig von Plessen, who had married the eldest daughter of Count Georg Hoyos and Alice Whitehead, daughter of the English inventor of the Whitehead torpedo. Count Georg had gone into his father-in-law's business and ran the *Silurifico Whitehead* in Fiume. There he met another daughter, Marguerite Hoyos, a beautiful 22-year-old, and they got engaged. The marriage was planned for Wednesday, 21 June in the Protestant church in the Dorothea Gasse in Vienna's fashionable First District. A marriage between the Bismarcks and one of the great Magyar noble houses would have been a social event in any case but in view of the status of the groom's father, it became a political crisis for the Kaiser and Chancellor Caprivi. They assumed—wrongly—that Bismarck had arranged the occasion to make his re-entry onto the diplomatic stage in Vienna and the Kaiser reacted with his usual intemperance. Bismarck had, of course, notified the officials at the Hofburg that he would be in Vienna during the week of 15 to 22 June and would wish to pay his respects to the Emperor Franz Joseph, whom he had known for four decades. On 9 June the Kaiser ordered Caprivi to notify the German embassies everywhere to take no notice of the former Chancellor's presence and to Franz Joseph he wrote on 14 June to ask the Emperor his 'true friend' not to receive 'this *disobedient* subject until he comes to me to say *peccavi*'.[101]

The Austrian Emperor had no choice but to close his door to Bismarck and to order the official establishment in Vienna to ignore the most glamorous social event of the summer to which some 600 guests had been invited. As the *New York Times* wrote, 'the Austrian officials were conspicuous by their absence. The Austro-Hungarian aristocracy were represented by Hungarian magnates attired in their gorgeous national costumes... The ex-Chancellor was attired in the uniform of the German Garde du Corps and wore a helmet surmounted with a silver eagle.'[102] The event in spite of the Kaiser's petty vindictiveness became a huge triumph for Bismarck. He was received by cheering crowds at every point on the journey to Vienna and in the city itself. He spent a week as a fantastic celebrity, loudly welcomed everywhere in Vienna and in cities in Germany which had officially been forbidden to receive him.

Every kind of German patriotic body made a pilgrimage to the shrine at Friedrichsruh. The real Bismarck, the real history, no longer mattered. Bismarck became a public idol even in places like Munich where he had been hated. He had come to symbolize German greatness and pictures of the Iron Chancellor in his uniform and helmet hung in school rooms and parlours. His image had become and remained especially after the First World War a potent symbol of German greatness and articles and books appeared, as Robert Gerwarth shows in *The Bismarck Myth*[103] with titles like 'the Bismarck Legend', 'Bismarck's Shadows'. His uniform and his aggressive facial expression in these souvenirs conveyed the image of blood and iron and contributed to the cult of German militarism and its deep-seated roots in German culture.

Reality, as always, looked very different. On 18 March 1893 Baroness Spitzemberg visited Friedrichsruh:

> I found them entirely alone, the old couple, both now entirely white, she pathetically asthmatic. First they kept us company after lunch, and then we chatted and asked about each others' friends and family. The death of Countess von Arnim before her decrepit husband, led Bismarck to remark, 'I often think that our Creator and Lord does not do everything himself but lets the direction of certain areas pass to his ministers and civil servants, who then do dumb things. You see how imperfect we are and the Saviour is supposed to come to us. I cannot believe that. A police chief arrests a woman instead of a man. Those things happen.'[104]

Relations between the Kaiser and Bismarck began to thaw in 1894. On 21 January Herbert von Bismarck was invited for the first time for years to the annual *Ordensfest* (the Festival of the Royal Orders), to which he was entitled as former Reichstag deputy and the holder of the Hohenzollern *Hausorden* (Family Order) with star and chain but Baroness Spitzemberg noted in her diary that the Kaiser 'cut him' even after Eulenburg had placed Herbert in the front of him. 'Count Cramer told me that the fat deputy Alexander Meyer said that the Kaiser had placed him ostentatiously in such a way that he could intentionally cut Herbert.'[105] Prince Hohenlohe, who had almost every order imaginable was also there and reflected on it: 'Hence great indignation among the Bismarckians. They declared that the Emperor had notified Herbert Bismarck that he would speak with him. This, however, cannot be true. For when the Emperor sends anyone a message like that, he does not cut him in so marked a manner.'[106]

A visit by the Chancellor to Berlin to see the Kaiser happened very shortly after the insult to Herbert. On 26 January 1894 Bismarck in his general's uniform took the train to Berlin. Huge crowds waited at every station between Friedrichsruh and along the Hamburg line to Berlin and at the Lehrter Bahnof when the train arrived in Berlin. Prince Heinrich, the Kaiser's younger brother, received him and escorted him to the palace where the Kaiser received him in a short private audience of which no record of any kind seems to have survived.[107] Baroness Spitzemberg reported that the lunch party was very intimate and friendly: those present were the Kaiser and Kaiserin, Count Klinckstroem, twin brother of the commanding officer of the Halberstadt Cuirassiers of which Bismarck had been named Honorary Colonel, Prince Heinrich, the King of Saxony, Herbert, and Bill. 'Everything went very cheerfully.'[108] Hohenlohe noted that 'the very numerous crowd that had gathered round greeted the carriage but there was no sign of any great enthusiasm... It is certain that this reconciliation has earned the Emperor great popularity through the whole of Germany. In the afternoon I left my card at the Bismarck house.'[109] On 19 February 1894 William II returned the visit. Official relations had been restored between William II and Bismarck but there was never to be cordiality between them.

During 1894 another structure designed by Bismarck for his own purposes came unstuck and led to the dismissal of Caprivi. After Caprivi's failure to get a school bill through both the Reichstag and the Landtag in 1892, the Kaiser decided with Caprivi's agreement to divide the Reich Chancellor's post from that of the Prussian Minister-Presidency, and appointed Botho

Eulenburg (1831–1912), nephew of the former Interior Minister under Bismarck and a hard-line Bismarck protégé.[110] This was exactly what Bismarck had tried in 1872. It had not worked twenty years before and could not work in the 1890s either, indeed, could work even less well. Caprivi and Eulenburg had diametrically opposite views. Worse still, the Prussian Constitution of 1850 with its House of Lords and three-class voting system assured the owners of the Junker estates a permanent veto on change in the federal state which contained three-fifths of the population and most of the heavy industry. Its electoral districts, in addition, took no account of the growth of cities, working-class districts, and population trends. Even in the late 1890s, rural districts still voted for their lords as they had done fifty years earlier. During 1894 the Kaiser demanded that his two chief executives pass legislation against subversive and revolutionary activities, the so-called *Umsturz-Vorlage*, the overthrow bill. Caprivi faced a Reichstag elected in 1893 which had shifted rightwards but not far enough. The Cartel Parties had gained 18 seats but still only had 153 seats, short of 199, the minimum for a majority, but the opposition of Centre Left Liberals and SPD only had 188, also short of a majority. The logic of the system demanded that Caprivi introduce a mild bill against subversion while Botho Eulenburg demanded a harsh one in the hope that the Reichstag could be forced either to accept it or to face the *Staatsstreich*, or *coup d'état*, that Bismarck had also wanted: abolition of universal suffrage. On 26 October 1894 both Eulenburg and Caprivi submitted their resignations.

In December 1894 Caprivi summed up the problem that the successor of Bismarck faced. Bismarck had done great damage and reduced the civil service 'to servility... In my opinion, the successor—even if his capabilities had been greater—had to strive to give the Nation back its self-esteem; one must get along, indeed, with average—or, if you will, normal people.'[111] This deep truth shows how much Germany lost when the unsteady Kaiser got bored with the sober, competent, and honourable soldier and dismissed him. Bismarck had left a system which only he—a very abnormal person— could govern and then *only if* he had as superior a *normal* Kaiser. Neither condition obtained, and the system slithered into the sycophancy, intrigue, and bluster that made the Kaiser's Germany a danger to its neighbours.

The Kaiser decided to appoint Chlodwig Prince zu Hohenlohe-Schillingsfürst, Prince of Ratibor and Corvey (1819–1901) as the new Reich Chancellor and summoned him to Potsdam by a telegram. He arrived on 27 October and after a day of long negotiations accepted the Emperor's request to become Imperial Chancellor and, once again, Prussian Minister-President. Chlodwig Prince zu Hohenlohe-Schillingsfürst belonged to one of the grandest and richest of German dynasties. He was born on 31 March 1819 and was thus only four years younger than Bismarck, a Catholic but not an ultramontane, a Prince but an experienced politician, a Bavarian but one who had supported unification as Bavarian Prime Minister in the late 1860s, and a friend of the Hohenzollern family. Bismarck knew him well, got on with him, and had appointed him Viceroy in Alsace-Lorraine. The Kaiser called him 'Uncle Chlodwig'.[112] Except for his age and his emollient temperament he had the perfect pedigree to fill the job. In January, 1895, Freiherr von Roggenbach wrote to Stosch that he was following Hohenlohe's moves

> with melancholy fellow feeling... He is cunning and smooth but he has the Privy Councillor [Holstein—JS] against him... How shall he, Bavarian and Catholic, make people fear him? He would have to have a monarch stand behind him, who knows what he wants and supports him vigorously. As it is his chancellor post is a slow death.[113]

On 27 November 1894 Johanna, Princess Bismarck died at Varzin. Baroness Spitzemberg reported that Bismarck's first reaction to Johanna's death was 'were I still in office, I would work without rest, that would be the best way to help me get over this, but now...'[114] Another, unexpected change occurred with the death of Johanna von Bismarck. Hildegard Spitzemberg lost her entrée to the Bismarck household.

> Since the death of the Princess, I lack the personality through whom I can make my wishes and rights count. Marie is entirely alienated, the sons, even when the Bismarcks were still here, stood apart from me. If I were a man, I could settle somewhere in Friedrichsruh and enjoy everything that happens from A to Z.[115]

This change casts an interesting light on the relationship which Baroness Spitzemberg had cultivated for nearly forty years. Bismarck could have summoned her at any time, which in view of his emotional moments with her might have been expected, but he did not. Was it really Johanna who used Hildegard Spitzemberg to provide attractive and intelligent female company which she knew she could not provide? 'Higachen' served as a safe flirt and an intelligent listener, a Marie Thadden or Katarina Orlov with whom Bismarck never fell in love and with whom Johanna actually felt comfortable.

Bismarck carried on life on his own. He hosted an official visit by the new Reich Chancellor and Prussian Minister-President who travelled to Friedrichsruh to pay a condolence call on 13 January 1895. Prince Hohenlohe took his son Prince Alexander (1862–1924) with him, who proved to be as gifted a diarist as his father. It is his account which I cite:

> Bismarck, large, massive, broad shouldered with a small head for his size but finely shaped, under bushy eyebrows his eyes—something that one often sees among heavy drinkers—teary but remarkably beautiful from which sudden bolts of lightning would flash. He covered his massive body with a one-piece black, long and remarkably old-fashioned tunic, more appropriate for a priest than a statesman. He wrapped a white neck cloth around his neck of the kind people used to wear in the 1830s or 1840s... While Bismarck spoke, his soft gentle voice struck me and those unforgettable eyes... On the way home I asked my father about that remarkable, gentle voice. He said to me with a laugh, 'In those gentle tones he read the death sentence for many careers and twisted the neck of many a diplomat who had provoked his hate.'[116]

On 26 March 1895 the Kaiser himself visited Friedrichsruh to pay respects to Bismarck on his 80th birthday. The Kaiser arrived 'on horseback with spiked helmet and glistening breastplate and led a small army of infantry, artillery, hussar cavalry and naturally the Halberstadt cuirassiers'.[117]

After the festivities Bismarck settled into old age and loneliness. As he wrote to Bill on 30 July 1895:

> I continue to vegetate in peace here, put my clothes on and take them off and would have pleasure in driving through the good harvest in Schönhausen, if I did not come back in the evening punished with more acute *Gesichtsreissen* in spite of the good weather. According to medical opinion my pains come from too little, according to my opinion, from too much outdoor exposure. A similar dilemma confronted Merk with his palace dog (Hofhund); he wanted to beat him because he barked too much. I offered him the thought that the dog might take the view that he had been punished for not barking enough. My incapacity to judge the cause of my facial pains is as great as the dog's about the reason for the beating.[118]

The old Chancellor had one more sensation to spring on his successors. On 24 October 1896 the *Hamburger Nachrichten* published the terms of the Reinsurance Treaty and reported that it was

> Count Caprivi who rejected the continuation of this mutual assurance, where Russia was prepared to continue it.... So came Kronstadt with the Marseillaise

and the first drawing together of the absolutist Tsardom and the French Republic, brought about, in our opinion, exclusively by the mistakes of the Caprivi policy.[119]

A curt official note a few days later denounced this revelation as a 'violation of the most confidential secrets of state which constituted a blow to the serious interests of the Empire'.[120]

The revelation of the treaty naturally caused a huge sensation. On 27 October Eulenburg wrote a secret memorandum for Bernhard Bülow in which he argued that the revelation 'certainly qualifies as betrayal of a state secret for which not less than two years in prison is the penalty. It has crashed like a bomb in the Foreign Ministry.' Nobody, including the Chancellor, could imagine the motive that might have prompted it. Eulenburg believed that it had no purpose other than 'to stir up dissatisfaction—in general increase the disquiet'.[121]

A few days later, Eulenburg wrote a long letter to Kaiser William II and made another attempt to explain the revelation. He rejected Holstein's theory that Bismarck wanted to destroy the Austro-German-Italian Triple Alliance of 1882 and the Chancellor's explanation that Bismarck simply wanted to stir up trouble: 'I believe that the evil old man found the articles very irritating that appear from time to time that say (and rightly!) he had caused our bad relations with Russia. With him everything is explained *personally*.' He went on to describe how Alfred Marschall von Bieberstein, the Foreign Minister, had arranged a lunch to discuss the government's response and

> sat there with a long, pear-shaped face. First as the fruit was served, he cheered up. His own home-grown pears awakened him from his state prosecutorial reflections about the two year jail sentence that awaited the wicked old man in Sachsenhausen according to § so and so. And still, if the old Prince had gone to jail, he would have offered him a slice of his 'Beurée Marschall' or the 'Marschall long-lasting pear'. C'est plus fort que lui. These pears are his joy, his sunshine. Everybody has his 'pear', so why should not he?[122]

The debate in the Reichstag and in the public concentrated on the treaty's terms, but which treaty? All the Three Emperor's League treaties were secret and the Reinsurance Treaty of 1887 most secret of all so commentators thought that Bismarck had revealed the terms of the 1884 agreement which—they reasonably assumed—had been set for six years and thus needed renewal when Caprivi came into office. Herbert complained to

Kuno Rantzau, who was living with his father-in-law in Friedrichsruh on 16 November about the confusion. On 17 November Rantzau replied that apparently even Bismarck had begun to get the treaties muddled, perhaps, the first sign of failing powers:

> He continues to think in spite of everything that the treaty of 1884 which was revealed had a six-year term. I have up to now been unable to convince him. Maybe you can get him to understand when you come.[123]

The shock abroad was no less great. Kaiser Franz Joseph in Vienna was 'beside himself about the evil old man in Friedrichsruh', and even Lord Rosebery, the former British Prime Minister, wrote a personal letter to Herbert on 25 November 1896 to ask for an explanation:

> I wish, if it seems good to you, you would throw some light on the recent 'revelations' and their cause. But if you prefer to say nothing. I will understand. I don't think I have ever asked you a question of this kind on paper in my life before.[124]

Manfred Hank in his remarkable study of these last years could not find an answer and has no reliable explanation.[125] I suspect that a combination of Bismarck's habitual 'frankness', his irresistible urge to show the world that he did everything better than his successors, and sheer malice combined to create the conditions for the revelation. He had always been beyond and above the laws that bound mortals. The only sign of a difference is that he muddled the 1884 and 1887 treaties; Bismarck in full command of his powers would never have done that.

In other respects, during 1896, Bismarck's health began to decline and the disintegration of his household without the firm grip of Johanna did not help. Schweninger diagnosed gangrene of the foot, which he treated but Bismarck refused to accept the treatment. He was supposed to stand up and walk but no longer did so. During 1897 he was often reduced to a wheelchair and by 1898 he rarely went out to his woods and fields. In July 1898 he could only get about in a wheelchair and was in such pain and often feverish he had difficulty breathing. On 28 July Schweninger got him onto his feet and he sat at the table, talking and drinking champagne. Afterwards he smoked three pipefuls and read the newspapers, the old Bismarck once more but for the last time.

The Kaiser and the entourage were aboard the SMS *Hohenzollern* on the annual North Sea cruise on 29 July 1898 and were heading for Bergen in Norway, when, as Eulenburg recorded in his diary,

Today news arrived that Schweninger had left Friedrichsruh...That Schweninger would make every effort to arouse the impression in Germany that the Kaiser was indifferent to this deeply moving event is certainly to be expected and his departure from Friedrichsruh is an adroit chess move which he placed through the *Tägliche Rundschau*. It is probably safe to assume that he only left because the Prince is now beyond hope.[126]

The fact that Bismarck had improved on 28 July would not have been known to the Kaiser or the court on board but they immediately assumed that Schweninger's move had a nefarious purpose—to undermine the Kaiser. Even the last forty-eight hours of Bismarck's life were darkened by suspicion and recrimination.

Over the next two days his condition deteriorated and he had trouble breathing. Just short of midnight on 30 July, he died. Herbert was with him to the end. On 31 July Herbert wrote to his brother-in-law Ludwig von Plessen:

yesterday morning his breathing grew worse and at about 10.30 he spoke to me and stretched out his hand to me, which I held until he went to sleep...Toward 11 it was all over for us. I have lost the best and truest father and most splendid and noblest spirit in the world.[127]

Even after death the Bismarck's family needed to revenge itself on its enemies and Moritz Busch had found a way to get at the Kaiser. On 31 July the *Berliner Lokal-Anzeiger* published an article by Moritz Busch which contained the complete text of Bismarck's resignation letter. Eulenburg asked,

Who had fired this unhappy reminiscence into the public, a provocation in view of the fact that the dead Prince still lay on his death bed? Without having asked Herbert, Rantzau and the family, Busch would never have reopened this feud.[128]

The Kaiser had ordered the 'Hohenzollern' to return to Kiel as quickly as possible. On the journey home, William II planned a magnificent funeral in the Cathedral of Berlin and burial of 'Germany's greatest son...by the side of my ancestors'.[129] But when the royal party reached Friedrichsruh, they learned that Bismarck's final wishes had been set out: no postmortem, no death mask, no drawings, no photographs, and a burial place on the grounds. There were to be no flamboyant gestures from Kaiser William II and no ceremony in Berlin. He had chosen as his epitaph 'A loyal German servant of William I.'[130] A brief memorial ceremony on 2 August then took place. Hildegard Spitzemberg read about the simple ceremony at the house in the Sachsenwald and saw at once what it meant: 'I can well understand it. Blood is blood and the Bismarcks are defiant, violent men, unrestrained by education and culture and not noble in temperament.'[131] Phili Eulenburg recorded how painful the occasion was:

> Next to me stood Herbert, to whom I was the truest of friends, when he had to choose between Elizabeth Hatzfeldt and his father. There he stood, cold and still at war for his father ... Never has the poison of politics been brought so crudely to my sight, as now in this house ...[132]

Conclusion
Bismarck's Legacy: Blood and Irony

Blood and Iron
'The great questions of the day will not be settled by speeches and majority decisions—that was the great mistake of 1848 and 1849—but by blood
and iron.'

Otto von Bismarck, 30 September 1862

Irony n.
2. fig. A condition of affairs or events of a character opposite to what was,
or might naturally be, expected; a contradictory outcome of events as if in
mockery of the promise and fitness of things. (In F. ironie du sort.)

Oxford English Dictionary

Many contemporaries believed that Bismarck's power—and his ability
to hold on to it—had something inhuman to it. But what? Not even
the devout Roman Catholic Windthorst could have believed that Bismarck
was literally *le diable*, which he once called him but, as the greatest German
parliamentarian of the nineteenth century and, perhaps, the shrewdest,
Windthorst sensed, as others did, that there was an unearthly dimension to
him, perhaps what Ernst Rentch and later Freud would call *das Unheimliche*
(uncanny). When Odo Russell and Robert Morier called Bismarck the
Zornesbock, the raging billy goat,[1] did they choose the *Bock*, knowing that
the devil used the goat as one of his many disguises?

Yet Bismarck's personality had such contradictions in it that it could be
experienced as positive or negative—angelic or demonic—sometimes both
at the same time. Hildegard von Spitzemberg, who saw him regularly over
thirty years, could never get over the contrasts in her great friend. She

admitted in her diary on 4 January 1888 that 'the apparent contradictions in the powerful personality are of such an intense magic, that I am bewitched anew every time'.[2] Both Stosch and Baroness Spitzemberg used words like 'bewitched' or 'enchantment' to describe the impact of his presence. Bismarck in conversation or in a formal speech seems to have had a special charm, not, as we have seen, charisma in the Weberian sense, but, nonetheless something irresistibly compelling. Disraeli wrote a diary entry about Bismarck's conversation: 'His views on all subjects are original, but there is no strain, no effort at paradox. He talks as Montaigne writes.'[3] Ludwig Bamberger, who knew him well, described the terrifying and yet charming way he looked:

> Behind the curtain of his heavy moustache one can always only partly observe him. With his usual chattiness there appears something soft and always lightly smiling across his broad lips, but directly behind lies something powerfully tearing, definitely like a predatory beast. This charming, lightly smiling mouth can open suddenly and swallow the interlocutor. He has a bulging chin, an upside-down teacup of flesh, with the convex side turned outward. The eyes are mistrustful/friendly, lurking/bright, cold/flashing, determined not to reveal what goes on behind them unless he intends it.[4]

There were times when Bismarck revealed what went on behind those eyes: once in October 1862 when he bragged to Kurt Schlözer how he had successfully deceived all the political actors in the conflict over the army,[5] and the other when he explained his tactics in gaining dominance in student life: 'I intend to lead my companions here, as I intend to lead them in after-life.'[6] Both Schlözer and Motley believed that they had heard the authentic Bismarck. Motley built it into a novel when he returned to Boston in the 1830s, long before his friend had become *the great Bismarck of history*. That cynical cunning startled even the sceptical Schlözer in October 1862. He began to see Bismarck as a kind of malign genius who, behind the various postures, concealed an ice-cold contempt for his fellow human beings and a methodical determination to control and rule them. His easy chat combined blunt truths, partial revelations, and outright deceptions. His extraordinary double ability to see how groups would react and the willingness to use violence to make them obey, the capacity to read group behaviour and the force to make them move to his will, gave him the chance to exercise what I have called his 'sovereign self'.

Another, very perceptive contemporary saw what lay behind the charm and fluency—an absence of principle. Clement Theodor Perthes warned Roon against Bismarck in early 1864, 'the man in Prussia, who calculates so coldly, who prepares so cunningly, who is so careless of the means that he chooses...'[7] 'Cold', 'cunning', and 'careless about means' add up to a kind of evil or what Queen Victoria quite openly called 'wicked'.[8]

Even old and close friends received rough treatment if they refused to bend to Bismarck's will. When his childhood friend Moritz von Blanckenburg refused to accept his offer of a ministry, 'he threatened me with a transfer to Stettin in the most ruthless way.'[9] He drew a knife on Hans von Kleist on one occasion and warned him on another that he would have him arrested for not revealing the source of a leaked memorandum. He dismissed his old mentor, Ludwig von Gerlach, from the high court in 1874 without an apparent twinge of remorse. No sentiment withstood his unbridled urge to dominate. General Alfred Count von Waldersee summed up what many thought in a diary entry from March 1890. Bismarck, he wrote, 'has a very bad character; he has not hesitated to disclaim his friends and those who have helped him most.'[10]

His contemporaries used a variety of terms to describe Bismarck's unusual role in transforming Prussia and Germany. With what historical figure might he be compared? He was the over-mighty courtier, or a Richelieu, or a *major domus*. However, none adequately caught the breadth and depth of his huge personality. Often his friends and enemies called him a dictator, an odd usage in a state with an absolute monarch. Disraeli wrote in 1878: 'He is a complete despot here, and from the highest to the lowest of the Prussians and all the permanent foreign diplomacy, tremble at his frown and court most sedulously his smile.'[11] As one of his friends, General von Schweinitz observed in 1886: 'The dictatorship of Bismarck, which has had on the whole an educational and positive influence on the mass of the people, has degraded the higher levels of the official world. It leaves room in a strange way for a very impressive secondary tyranny.'[12]

Schweinitz was wrong. Dictatorship always degrades those who exercise it and those subject to it. When Bismarck left office, the servility of the German people had been cemented, an obedience from which they never recovered. The upper reaches of society had been debased as the general rightly noticed, and they too never recovered. Government by intrigue had brought Bismarck to power and intrigue around Kaiser William II brought him down. Like the traditional palace favourite, he rose by camarilla and fell by it. He was a dictator but one dependent on the will of the King.

Among the seven deadly sins, Bismarck committed repeatedly and without limit the sin of wrath. He bubbled with rage. Nobody ever indulged himself so utterly in vehement or violent anger as Otto von Bismarck. He raged and

hated until he nearly killed himself. He lost his temper at the slightest provocation. He wrote to his brother that he had got into such 'a rage over those who
keep knocking at my door and annoy me with questions and bills that I could
bite the table'.[13] The rest of his life he stewed and fumed and suffered the
aftermath of these fits in sleeplessness and psychosomatic illnesses. The pretexts
were often trivial. The Federal Council rejected the appointment of an obscure
Hanoverian to head the postal service. The stenographers at the Reichstag
took down a speech incorrectly and he saw in a harmless mistake a conspiracy
against him. The absurd conflict over stamp duty on postal transfers caused
one of his most famous rages. He flew into a rage when the President of the
Reichstag rang the bell to call him to order. Alexander von Below-Hohendorf
got it right when he called Bismarck 'sick unto death'. In a letter of 7 December
1859 he wrote to Moritz von Blanckenburg that Bismarck had become
deranged by his concentration on his enemies and 'extreme thoughts and feelings'. The cure was simple and Christian: 'love thine enemies!' This was the best
'door' through which to release 'the mounting pressures from the darkness of
his sick body and the best medicine against the amazing visions and thoughts
[*Vorstellungen*] that threaten to draw him to death'.[14]

That advice made sense. Bismarck's sick soul needed a release and to his
Junker friends that release could be found at any moment through penitence, grace, and the love of God. Prayer, as von Below urged on him, has as
its object change; the need to accept responsibility for one's sins, to acknowl-
edge one's weaknesses, as the Book of Common Prayer's general confession
of 1662 puts it: 'We have followed too much the devices and desires of our
own hearts. We have offended against Thy holy laws. We have left undone
those things which we ought to have done; And we have done those things
which we ought not to have done; And there is no health in us.'

This surrender to divine will must have been hard for Bismarck. The
liturgy repeatedly urges penitents not only to come humbly to God but to
seek forgiveness from those we have hurt or offended. I cannot recall a letter
in which Bismarck apologized for anything more serious than not writing
or forgetting a family birthday. He certainly made no apology to his enemies and, when five cabinet ministers asked permission to go to Lasker's
funeral, he said 'certainly not'—and this tells us a great deal—none of them
went. It occurred to none of these high-placed gentlemen that Bismarck's
refusal to curb his vindictiveness even before the open coffin was an outrage. Why indeed did they need his permission? Why did they not simply
go to pay their respects?

His wrath destroyed his eldest son, Herbert, who could not marry the woman he loved because Bismarck hated her family. They belonged to the clique of his 'enemies'. The objects of his rage and hatred mattered more to him than his child. Rancour destroyed this precious bond—the love of father for his son—as it destroyed almost all his old friendships. It poisoned his mind and soul and it led him to seek revenge, never repentance.

His unbridled misogyny needs a further word. Bismarck turned his life into a physical and psychic hell because he so implacably despised the Queen/Empress Augusta and the Crown Princess Victoria. Again and again the 'strong woman' played the role of evil enchantress in his psyche. These all-powerful women dominated their weak husbands and threatened Bismarck from all sides. He sensed conspiracies everywhere. The women caused all his difficulties. He imagined their influence as malign and pervasive to a degree that can fairly be called paranoid. One need not be a Freudian to see how the hatred that Bismarck felt for his cold, intelligent, and unloving mother became an obsession as he exercised his genius and will in politics. Here Bismarck got caught in a convolution from which he could not extricate himself. He relied on William I's weakness to be able govern. Yet that weakness arose in part from the strength of the Queen. Had William I not been pliant in dealing with Augusta, he would not have been pliant in dealing with Bismarck. This desperate struggle to control an emotional old man who actually held power that neither Bismarck nor Augusta could entirely control wore Bismarck's nerves to shreds. He had to re-enact day after day, year after year, the agony of his childhood, the little boy at the point of an upside-down triangle and at the mercy of the struggle between the threatening woman and weak man. His rage, his sweats, his sleeplessness arose frequently from this impotence. The most powerful man in Europe, swollen with pride and bilious, had to bow to the old lady who happened to be the Queen. The humiliation must have been unbearable.

His confession to Hans von Kleist in 1851 that he could not control his sexual urges adds a further twist to the pain. The stubborn refusal of Johanna von Bismarck to make herself into a society lady for him meant that nowhere could he find consolation or a way to escape the Oedipal triangle which Prussian kingship forced him to re-enact every day. Indeed Johanna von Bismarck expressed her love for her husband by learning to hate as fiercely as he did. Hildegard Spitzemberg, Holstein, and many others noticed how bitter and vindictive Johanna was. Nobody in the Bismarck household saw that they did him harm by stirring his poisonous feelings.

The king would not always give in to Bismarck's demands. He was a conscientious Mason and protected Lodge brothers. He cared about many of his ministers. He felt, as a decent man, real loyalty to his 'servants' and could not allow them to be brutally discarded by his all-powerful subject. The king's kindness and consideration for others further enraged Bismarck. If the king wrote or spoke sharply to him, Bismarck collapsed into bed and was sometimes ill for weeks on end. Whatever William I meant by writing 'How can you be so hypochondriac as to allow one single difference to mislead you into taking the extreme step!' he had reason to complain. William could not have shown Bismarck more love and attention. Yet in conversation with Disraeli, in June of 1878, Bismarck had the nerve to complain of the horrible conduct of his Sovereign.[15] This monologue astonished Disraeli because Bismarck said these things in public at a state dinner. They were almost certainly imaginary. I have not seen one word to substantiate the charge. Augusta certainly hated Bismarck and with reason, but she was sane. She knew that she had to live with the demonic Chancellor and his hypnotic power over husband. She sought moments when reconciliation without loss of face on his side might be possible. When in March 1873 Odo and Lady Emily Russell enjoyed the 'unique favour' of a visit from the Emperor and Empress to the British embassy for a private dinner, protocol required Bismarck to sit on the left of Her Imperial Majesty for an hour or so and to make polite conversation. He could not do it and refused the invitation. The greatest political genius of the nineteenth century lacked the courage and self-control to behave like the 'nobleman' he claimed to be in the presence of his sovereign and his sovereign lady. All he had to do was chat for an hour. The Iron Chancellor, who caused three great wars, feared a little old lady with a Saxon accent.

Furious and commanding he could be but Bismarck always managed to evade responsibility when things went wrong. He had lied to his mother from early childhood and continued to lie all his life. He lied to Johanna in 1851 that he had done nothing to gain the appointment to Frankfurt, when the evidence shows that he had intrigued for more than a year to get it. He always lied when he might be blamed for something. As Waldersee observed, 'lying has become a habit with him.' His memoirs twist and suppress the truth. He lied to the King about his relationship with Eulenburg during the crisis about local government 1872. His reply to Eulenburg's letter contains falsehoods that anyone could spot. His preoccupation with military uniforms could be called another kind of lie. He had been a draft dodger in

1839–40 and lied about that, aided by the editors of the *Collected Works*, who removed the compromising correspondence from the record.

Finally he was guilty of yet another of the deadly sins: gluttony. The *Oxford English Dictionary* defines it as 'the vice of excessive eating. (One of the seven deadly sins.) Also *rarely* an instance of this.' Gluttony may not be the most obvious of the deadly sins but it nearly killed Bismarck. Had Schweninger not given him the maternal care he needed in 1883 and reduced his intake, he would certainly have died of the combination of wrath and gluttony. If pride kills the soul, rage and gluttony ravage the body. Eating as a substitute for whatever Bismarck lacked represents yet again his utter unwillingness to exercise self-control over his appetites or to submit to the charge of another, even his personal physician. He was the great Bismarck from the age of 17 to the day he died, subject to none of the limitations which ordinary mortals must accept.

And then there were the virtues. The contradictions in his character that Hildegard Spitzemberg described earlier in this chapter apply to other aspects of Bismarck's personality. He had many virtues. He was courteous to visitors, irrespective of status. He had both charm and warmth which over-whelmed Mary Motley and Lucius von Ballhausen when they first met him. The modest way the Bismarcks lived struck everybody as remarkable, and his irresistible sense of humour could win over enemies. Bismarck enjoyed the love and affection of his family and friends. The King, General Leopold von Gerlach, Roon, Motley, Moritz von Blankenburg, and count-less others loved him and continued to do so in spite of his neglect and brutality to them. Marie von Thadden certainly loved him and so did his devoted wife, his sister, and brother. Nobody can read Bismarck's letters to his sister without seeing how much love he could show. His successes in his career rested as much on the faithfulness, love, and loyalty of friends and patrons as well as subordinates such as Tiedemann and Keudell.

He could not, on the other hand, forgive and forget. Bismarck's hostility to Queen Augusta concerned her politics. She was a Saxon princess, liberal in a sort of Coburgian way, friendly with Catholics, sympathetic to the middle states, and very intelligent. She threatened Bismarck because, as he constantly complained, she had the breakfast table at her disposal. There is little evidence that Augusta's coterie of liberal advisers accomplished a thing or had much if any influence over the Emperor. He had his own firm views on most issues and seems not to have had a close enough relation to his wife to take her views too seriously. The real threat came from the Crown Prince and Crown

Princess. They represented another Germany. Had William I done the decent thing and died at a reasonable age, at least young enough to allow Frederick and Victoria to rule for a few years, the conflict between the Crown and Chancellor would have ended Bismarck's career smartly and finally.

Bismarck saw politics as struggle. When he talked about 'politics as the art of the possible', he meant that in a limited sense. He never considered compromise a satisfactory outcome. He had to win and destroy the opponents or lose and be destroyed himself. Very early in his career, he had a clash in the Prussian Landtag in which he showed his preference for conflict. On 27 January 1863, in one of his first speeches, he told the deputies his view of constitutionalism. 'Constitutional life is a series of compromises. If these are frustrated, conflicts arise. Conflicts are questions of power, and whoever has power to hand, can go his own way.' Maximilian Count von Schwerin cried out in amazement, 'power comes before morality'.[16] The Count missed the point; the issue was not morality but compromise. Whoever has power in a normal political system may win a round but must then continue the struggle to reach consensus. That was not Bismarck's way. He set out to 'beat them all' and did. In a political system where principle stood at the centre of political activity, he had none but the naked exercise of his own power and the preservation of royal absolutism on which that power rested. If politics according to Bismarck were the 'art of the possible', but without compromise, what sort of art or craft was it? And to what end?

In international relations, it meant absolutely no emotional commitment to any of the actors. Diplomacy should, he believed, deal with realities, calculations of probabilities, assessing the inevitable missteps and sudden lurches by the other actors, states, and their statesmen. The chessboard could be overseen and it suited Bismarck's peculiar genius for politics to maintain in his head multiple possible moves by adversaries. Since the international system of the nineteenth century rested on five (or six, if one counts Italy) great powers, Bismarck could deploy his 'combinations, as Morier called them, with some assurance. He had his goals in mind and achieved them. He was and remained to the end master of the finely tuned game of diplomacy. He enjoyed it. In foreign affairs he never lost his temper, rarely felt ill or sleepless. He could outsmart and outplay the smartest people in other states and, even better, no Queen could get in his way. On occasion when he was ill or wallowing in self-pity, he considered the surrender of certain burdens of office. He never once suggested that anybody else should be Foreign Minister. Indeed, his miscalculation in 1890 arose in part because he believed that young Kaiser William II would never sacrifice his Chancellor's thirty years of success and expertise.

Domestic politics posed a very different challenge. There were endless details, messy and insoluble problems, lots of different actors with conflicting interests, issues that had unforeseeable consequences, and the constant buzz of irritating criticism from tedious people in parliaments—two, the Reichstag and the Landtag, within a mile of each other. He had to know everything and decide everything but he was always ill, away for months and constantly impatient. Even more taxing was the fact that he had no very strong principles on practical matters and shifted his position all the time on issues of local government, trade, commercial regulations, legal codes, and the machinery of the modern state. He chose to complicate his life by stirring up the *Kulturkampf* and in due course provoking conservatives, liberals, progressives as well as the Guelphs, Poles, and Alsatians who sat in the Reichstag.

The Gerlachs were not wrong that principles matter in politics. Neither reality nor power has unequivocal or objective meanings. Human beings have values, faiths of various kinds, and preferences. The Bismarckian assumption that a master player can 'game' the system worked only to a point at which irrational emotions, violence, confusion, incompetence, began to mix themselves up with his plans. What is the purpose of the art of politics if not to serve some cause, to improve the conditions under which people have to live, to make societies, freer, more just and more humane or, with the Gerlachs more Christian? Bismarck practised his wizardry to preserve a semi-absolute monarchy and, when it suited him, he would preserve the rights of a narrow, frugal, fiercely reactionary Junker class, who hated all progress, liberalism, Jews, socialists, Catholics, democrats, and bankers. He differed from them only in his ruthlessness.

Bismarck used the German people, the King, the Gerlachs, in order to gain power but, as the German philosopher Kant warned, 'Act so that you use humanity, as much as in your own person as in the person of every other, always at the same time as end and never merely as means.'[17] Bismarck ignored this both in his grand schemes and in his treatment of colleagues and subordinates. Count Albert von Pourtalès, a very distinguished diplomat in the Prussian Foreign Service, wrote to Moritz August von Bethmann Hollweg: 'Bismarck uses and misuses his party comrades. To him they are...just post horses with whom he travels to the next stop...From him I am saddled and ready to meet the blackest ingratitude.'[18]

Bismarck bequeathed to his successors an unstable structure of rule. The constitution of Prussia had been thrown together in the muddle of the revolution of 1848–9. Bismarck preserved it with its grossly unbalanced representation system. It continued to give the small class of Junker land-lords a permanent veto on progress. Since Prussia amounted to three-quar-ters of the population, territory, and industrial power, it served as a surrogate for Germany as whole. Prussia's House of Lords, gerrymandered and patched with difficulty, gave Hans von Kleist and his friends a place to dig in. The lower house with its three-class voting system did the rest. The fact that Germany never had its own army or Foreign Ministry (Prussia retained both) meant that the country went into the war of 1914 run by exactly the same families whose names make up the order of battle in 1870 and with the same impossible structure of rule.

Neither he nor his successors found a way to protect the semi-absolute power of the monarch in the unstable double legislative structure which Bismarck had cobbled together. The entire period from 1866 to 1890 is one long institutional tinkering—separate the Minister-President's office from that of Reich Chancellor (1872–3 and 1892–4) and then reunite them because separation had not worked. Fuse the Reich and Prussian ministries and then decide against it; Bismarck fell over one of these jerry-built struc-tures, the act of 1852 which, he believed, prevented the King/Emperor from consulting ministers directly without the Minister-President's permission. In the Reich, there were no ministers, only so-called 'State Secretaries' who assisted the Chancellor but in theory had no independent power. Under Bismarck's much weaker successors, the greater figures among the State Secretaries gained freedom to enjoy direct access to the Kaiser. Admiral Tirpitz, the powerful Reich Minister of the Naval Administration from 1897 to 1916, as an officer had an 'immediate' position, that is, direct access to the Emperor, and he used it. Without Bismarck, only Kaiser William II could coordinate policy and he could not or would not try.

In one of his most brilliant and fateful ploys, Bismarck announced in 1863 that the new Germany would have universal manhood suffrage. He used the people to undermine and tame the German princes, whose power and intransigence he grossly overestimated. On the other hand he underes-timated the power of the people because he failed to see how the people had changed by the middle of the nineteenth century. He saw that the peo-ple had put Napoleon III into power and assumed that the masses were monarchical. But France was overwhelmingly agricultural throughout the nineteenth century, and Prussia/Germany was not. By the 1880s he could no longer prevent the growing forces of Social Democracy, the Catholic Centre, and bourgeois liberalism from representing their constituents. He had not used universal suffrage as anything other than a temporary tactic and it backfired. By the end of his career, no pro-government majority could be constructed without concessions, which Bismarck rejected.

In March of 1890 he explained to the State Ministry how he intended to provoke the Reichstag with reactionary legislation, to create a split between all the 'enemies' and the established order. He would then get the princes who made the Constitution of 1870 to unmake it and with that decision end the Reichstag with its irksome universal suffrage. To stay in power he would destroy the Reich of 1870, his greatest creation.

In 1863 when Bismarck used universal suffrage as a means to a political end, neither he nor anybody else could imagine that in three decades Germany would dominate central Europe with its heavy industries, its excellent technological institutes, its skilled, literate, and increasingly urban workforces, its mines and mills, its railroads, steamships, telephones and tel-egraphs, its thriving ports and harbours, a vigorous shipbuilding industry, its great trading companies and giant factories, its advanced medical facilities, its physics and chemistry and excellent engineering. It had the best army, the second largest navy, a huge trade surplus, and an archaic government of country squires. Max Weber and Thorstein Veblen warned that such a mix was not stable.

Mass society meant capitalism and capitalism brought its liberal ideology and the demand for free trade, free movement of people and goods, free access to crafts and professions, banks, stock exchanges, insurance compa-nies, and traders. Into this thriving new capitalist state, Jews emerged as its most adept practitioners and its most ambivalent symbols. Anti-Semitism in the nineteenth century became a surrogate for everything that the Junkers, churches, peasants, and artisans most feared and distrusted. From 1811, with von der Marwitz's 'Jew State', to July 1918, and Colonel Bauer's condemna-tion of Jews as draft-dodging, black marketeers,[19] the Prussian Junker class regarded Jews as enemies. They represented the corrupt and dangerous flu-idity of money, capitalism, and markets. They controlled a significant share of newspapers and pioneered the department stores.

By the late 1850s anti-Semitism was flourishing among the bourgeoisie as well as among the Junkers. Wagner published *Jewishness in Music* in 1850, and Gustav Freytag his anti-Semitic best-seller in 1855. By 1865 the main

Protestant church newspaper could compare reformed Jews to vermin. The crash of 1873 and the resultant depression made these views respectable and Heinrich Treitschke, Germany's most prominent historian, adopted and made' them acceptable to the upper orders of society. The Reverend Adolf Stoecker, the court preacher, took them into court circles and converted the young Prince and Princess William of Prussia and General Alfred and Marie, Count and Countess von Waldersee. From top to bottom anti-Semitism flourished in Bismarck's Germany.

In March 1890 the Kaiser had to replace Herbert Bismarck with a new Foreign Secretary. It said a lot about the wasteland Bismarck left behind that not one of the seven senior ambassadors had the necessary qualities. Friedrich Wilhelm Count zu Limburg-Stirum (1835–1912) clearly did but Phili Eulenburg rejected him, because, as he wrote to the Kaiser, Limburg Stirum 'was of Jewish extraction on his mother's side, which permeates his being'.[20] Wilhelm II furiously upbraided Bismarck for 'collusion' with 'Jesuits and Jews'.

Bismarck shared all of these prejudices and expressed them regularly. On the other hand, he clearly thought highly of Lassalle, got on well with Disraeli, Eduard Simon, and Ludwig Bamberger. He shared and often expressed loathing and disdain for Jews but he himself took no part in the extreme anti-Semitism of the Treitschke kind. On the other hand, he did great damage to Jews in Germany indirectly, because he took no steps to enforce the laws or protect Jewish citizens during the crisis of 1880. He used anti-Semitism to attack the Progressive party in order to destroy its 'Jewish' leadership.

Bismarck always destroyed 'enemies' and hence he let the anti-Semitic agitation of the 1870s and 1880s run because it would undermine Eduard Lasker and the left Liberals, whom Bismarck considered Jews, whether or not they actually were. A party which believed in free speech, free press, parliamentary immunity, separation of church and state, free markets, abolition of the death penalty, constitutional monarchy, representative cabinets, that is, the *Deutsche Fortschrittspartei*, must be crushed as an 'enemy of the Reich' and as 'Jewish'. As von der Marwitz claimed, such reforms were advocated by persons who wanted '*den neuen Judenstaat*'. For Bismarck the way to split the liberal 'revolutionary' movement, a typical example of Bismarckian paranoia, lay in anti-Semitism. If he could drive a wedge of anti-Semitism between the Jews and respectable German progressives, the Progressive Party would lack the leadership and cutting edge provided by the Jews. He used the same wedge technique by trying to slide the Vatican between the Catholic masses and the Centre Party. Hatred fired the energy with which he drove his wedge in both cases. Thus, when Lasker, the courageous, incorruptible leader of the Progressives, died in New York in 1884, Bismarck took his revenge on the 'dumb Jewboy',[21] as he called Lasker, by sending back the message of condolence passed by the US House of Representatives.

Bismarck certainly did not create the anti-Semitism, which was universal at all levels of German society, but he used it to crush his enemies irrespective of the consequences. Anti-Semitism and its anti-liberal poison passed into the bloodstream of Germany to become virulent in the overheated atmosphere of the First World War and to become lethal in its aftermath. That too was a Bismarckian legacy, and it is richly ironic that Kaiser William dismissed Bismarck in March 1890 because he had been consorting 'with Jesuits and Jews'.

By the 1890s, rather to his surprise, Bismarck had become genuinely popular. He drew huge crowds to hail him on his trip to Vienna in 1892 and enjoyed the homage of the German people. His image became an icon, a symbol of the German nation. When Bismarck died, as the poet Auden wrote in 'In Memory of W. B. Yeats',

> The currents of his feeling failed; he became his admirers.
> Now he is scattered among a hundred cities
> And wholly given over to unfamiliar affections.[22]

What did these admirers see in him? We all know the picture of the stern figure with his heavy eyebrows and moustache, in uniform, often with a glittering *Pickelhaube* on his head. He became the Iron Chancellor, the all-powerful, all-wise, genius-statesman, the man who unified Germany. His image hung in every schoolroom and over many a hearth. He embodied and manifested the greatness of Germany. The image became itself a burden to his successors. He made it impossible, as Caprivi wished, that Germany should get along with 'normal people'. Germany had to have a genius-statesman as its ruler. Kaiser Wilhelm II outdid the Iron Chancellor in military display but failed the test. He could not control himself, still less the complicated ramshackle structure that Bismarck had left him. The First World War destroyed much of Bismarck's Germany and defeat ended the monarchies in all the many German states. In 1925 the citizens of the unloved Weimar Republic elected Paul von Beneckendorff und Hindenburg (1847–1934), a Prussian field marshal, to be their President. Hindenburg, born in Posen on 2 October 1847, had gone to the typical *Kadettenanstalt*, to which Junker nobility sent their sons, and become an officer in the 3rd Regiment of the Foot Guards. He led his troops at the Battle of Königgrätz, 'which became for him all his life the greatest event in his own personal development and for the glory of Prussian arms'.[23] He belonged to, and had grown up in, Bismarck's world and looked it. He had the same frown, the same military severity and bulk. Historians of Germany often speak of him as an '*ersatz Kaiser*' or a Kaiser substitute, but I think rather that he represented an '*ersatz Bismarck*', a surrogate for the Iron Chancellor. It was Hindenburg, the last ruling Junker, who handed Adolf Hitler the office that Bismarck had created—that of Reich Chancellor. His only reservation typically had to do not so much with Hitler's policy but his rank. Hitler had been only a corporal and Hindenburg found that fact deeply distasteful. Every wrinkle in the fossilized Prussian Field Marshall stirred at the degrading need to elevate that 'Bohemian Corporal' to Bismarck's chair. Bismarck's legacy passed through Hindenburg to the last genius-statesman that Germany produced, Adolf Hitler, and the legacy was thus linear and direct between Bismarck and Hitler.

Bismarck, the living human being; Bismarck, the genius-statesman; Bismarck the Iron Chancellor as icon, make up a complex legacy. Patriotic biographers left out the uncomfortable aspects of his actual life and the editors of documents omitted or censored them. A generation of conservative German historians exalted the wisdom, moderation, and vision of the statesman; the public and propagandists exalted the strong man, the essential German. The real Bismarck, violent, intemperate, hypochondriac, and misogynist, only appeared in biographies late in the twentieth century. What the three Bismarck images have in common as phenomena is the absence of the redeeming human virtues: kindness, generosity, compassion, humility, abstinence, patience, liberality, and tolerance. Bismarck the man, Bismarck the statesman, Bismarck the icon embodied none of those virtues.

There are deep ironies in the career of Otto von Bismarck: the civilian always in uniform, the hysterical hypochondriac as the symbol of iron consistency, the successes which become failures, the achievement of supreme power in a state too modern and too complex for him to run, the achievement of greater success than anybody in modern history which turned out to be a Faustian bargain. For twenty-eight years he crushed opposition, cowed cabinets, poured hatred, scorn, and anger on political opponents in public and private. It required courage of a high order to resist the Chancellor.

Almost nobody dared. He smashed the possibility of responsible parliaments in 1878 when he used the two attempts to assassinate the Kaiser to destroy moderate bourgeois liberalism. He persecuted Catholics and Socialists. He respected no law and tolerated no opposition. His legacy in culture was literally nothing. He had no interest in the arts, never went to a museum, only read lyric poetry from his youth or escapist literature. He paid no attention to scientists or historians unless he could enlist them like Treitschke. He was the most supple political practitioner of the nineteenth century but his skill had no purpose other than to prop up an antiquated royal semi-absolutism—and to satisfy himself. The means were Olympian, the ends tawdry and pathetic. All that fuss to give Kaiser William II the ability to dislocate rational government and cause international unrest. Sir Edward Grey compared Germany to a huge battleship without a rudder. Bismarck arranged it that way; only he could steer it. He gave the German workers social security but refused them the protection of the state. He preferred to shoot workers rather than to listen to their complaints. He made his Junker friends into enemies and then ridiculed them. He mocked their Christian beliefs and offended their faith and values.

This biography began with Max Weber's analysis of legitimacy which he set out in a lecture in 1918. In the same year, he wrote his 'Parliament and Government in the new order in Germany'. Section 1 asks 'what was the legacy of Bismarck?' Max Weber, born under Bismarck in 1864, grew up in the home of committed National Liberals and knew the main figures in politics. He was both participant and observer. Weber began the section with Bismarck's destruction of National Liberalism in 1878 and the resulting dilemma which he had created. Bismarck refused to govern with the Catholic Centre but could not govern without it. He then turned to the actual legacy of Bismarck's long tenure of office:

He left a nation *totally without political education . . . totally bereft of political will* [italics in the original—JS] accustomed to expect that the great man at the top would provide their politics for them. And further as a result of his improper exploitation of monarchical sentiment to conceal his own power politics in party battles, it had grown accustomed *to submit patiently* and fatalistically to whatever was decided for it in the name of 'monarchical government'.[24]

This crushing verdict by Germany's greatest social scientist brings us full circle to the lecture room in Munich in October 1918 when Weber first explained the idea of charismatic leadership. Bismarck lacked the attributes that we normally associate with the charismatic leader. He moved no crowds at mass meetings and in parliament he roused his listeners more by insults and scorn than by overwhelming oratory, but he had that 'demonic' power that made him an irresistible political figure and a disastrous one.

The deepest and most impenetrable irony lies in Bismarck's own personality.

He ruled Germany by making himself indispensable to a decent, kindly old man, who happened to be a king. He drew the King from his family and inserted himself between man and wife and between father and son. He worked his personal magic in that tiny space and his rule depended absolutely on the bond between William I and his chief minister and on nothing else. He stirred the hatred of the Queen and of the Crown Princess by his control of their husband and father-in-law. Both king and minister had terrible rows, burst into tears, and collapsed afterwards. In the end Bismarck got his way but paid a price in physical symptoms, sleeplessness, attacks of neuralgia, stomach problems, and anxiety symptoms. He could not live without the power that he extracted from the royal person but could not live with it either. For twenty-six years Bismarck and the King lived in this constant love/hate relationship. The King retained his good temper and serenity through all that time. Bismarck could not. The ultimate and terrible irony of Bismarck's career lay in his powerlessness. Contemporaries called him a 'dictator' or a 'despot' but he knew better. Perhaps that is why he insisted that the only epitaph on his simple grave should tell the truth about his career: 'A faithful German servant of Kaiser Wilhelm I.'

Notes

CHAPTER I

1. Schoeps, 15–16.
2. Bronsart, 249.
3. Gall, *Bismarck: The White Revolutionary*, i. 206.
4. Holstein, *Memoirs*, 52.
5. 'Politik als Beruf', *Gesammelte Politische Schriften* (Munich, 1921), 396–450. Originally a speech at Munich University, 1918, published in 1919 by Duncker & Humblot, Munich. <http://tiunet.tiu.edu/acadinfo/cas/socsci/psych/SOC410/Readings/Weber/Works/politics.htm>.
6. Ibid.
7. Chlodwig Hohenlohe-Schillingsfürst, *Memoirs*, 429, Berlin, 18 June 1890.
8. Börner, *William I*, 221.
9. Busch, 4 Oct. 1878, ii. 197.
10. Bronsart, 212.
11. Urbach, 69.
12. Craig, *Fontane*, 115.
13. Ibid. 116.
14. Stosch to Crown Prince, 24 Jan. 1873, Hollyday, 126.
15. Stosch, 120.
16. Roon, i. 355–6.
17. Ibid. ii. 239.
18. Ibid. ii. 260–1.
19. Engelberg, i. 315–16.
20. Craig, *The Politics*, 137.
21. Edmund Burke, *Reflections on the Revolution in France* (1790), para. 97, p. 61.
22. Motley, *Family*, 297.
23. Spitzemberg, 304.
24. Tiedemann, 13, 15.
25. *Bismarck Die Gesammelten Werke*, ed. Wolfgang Windelband and Werner Frauendienst, 1st edn. (Berlin: Deutscheveralgsanstalt, 1933). Abbreviated below as *GW*.
26. Tiedemann, 221.
27. Lucius, 129–30.

28. Ibid. 131.
29. Holstein, *Memoirs*, 118.

CHAPTER 2

1. Engelberg, *Bismarck: Urpreusse und Reichsgründer*.
2. Clark, *Iron Kingdom*, 1.
3. 'Primary Source'. <http://www.thenagain.info/Classes/Sources/Frederick%20 the%20Great.html>.
4. Sigurd von Kleist, *Geschichte des Geschlects v. Kleist*, 5. <http://www.v-kleist. com/FG/Genealogie/AllgemeineGeschichte.pdf>.
5. Clark, *Iron Kingdom*, 241.
6. Theodor Fontane, *Irrungen Wirrungen* (1888) in Theodor Fontane, *Gesammelte Werke: Jubiläumsausgabe. Erste Reihe in fünf Bänden* (Berlin: S. Fischer Verlag, 1919), 152ff.
7. Spitzemberg, 291.
8. Engelberg, i. 126.
9. Stern, 40.
10. Clark, *Iron Kingdom*, p. xix.
11. Fontane, *Irrungen Wirrungen*, 154.
12. Roon, ii. 86.
13. Bucholz, 30–1.
14. Paret, 4.
15. Burke, para. 322, p. 192.
16. Ibid. para. 322, p. 192.
17. Ibid. para. 77, p. 48.
18. Gentz, 19.
19. Epstein, 436.
20. Sweet, 21.
21. Ibid. 28.
22. Guglia, 147–8.
23. Mann, 40-1.
24. Frie, 57.
25. Guglia, 33.
26. Alexander von der Marwitz to Rahel Varnhagen in Frie, 58.
27. Marwitz, *Preussens Verfall und Aufstieg*, 184.
28. 9 May 1811, *Last Representation of the Estates of the Lebus Circle, joined by the Beeskow and Storkow Circles meeting in Frankfurt an der Oder to His Majesty the King*, Marwitz, *Preussens Verfall*, 241ff.
29. Marwitz, *Preussens Verfall*, 224.
30. Frie, 280.
31. Ibid. 281.
32. Marwitz, *Preussens Verfall*, 204.

33. <http://www.deutsche-schutzgebiete.de/provinz_rheinland.htm>.
34. Brophy, *Popular Culture*, 14.
35. Ibid. 22–4.
36. Ibid. 257.
37. Brophy, *Capitalism, Politics, and Railroads in Prussia*, 25.
38. Keinemann, 20.
39. Ibid. 20.
40. *Provinzial-Correspondenz* (*PC*), 12/33, 19 Aug. 1874, p. 1. <http://amtspresse.staats-bibliothek-berlin.de/vollanzeige.php?file=9838247/1874/1874-08-19.xml&s=1>.

CHAPTER 3

1. Engelberg, i. 61.
2. Ibid. 48.
3. Bismarck to Malwine, *GW* xiv. 29.
4. Engelberg, i. 102.
5. Ibid. 51.
6. Wienfort, 15.
7. Ibid.
8. Bismarck to Johanna, 23 Feb. 1847, *GW* xiv. 67.
9. Ibid.
10. Engelberg, i. 37 ff.
11. *Neue deutsche Biographie*, xvii. 36. <http://mdz10.bib-bvb.de/~db/0001/bsb00016335/images/index.html?id=00016335&fip=70.20.182.111&no=5&seite=52>.
12. Epstein, 593.
13. Sweet, 18.
14. Ibid. 8.
15. Ibid. 33.
16. Ibid. 34.
17. Ibid. 35.
18. Engelberg, i. 46.
19. Ibid.
20. Gentz, i. 243–4, 1 Feb. 1798.
21. *Neue deutsche Biographie*, xvii. 36. <http://mdz10.bib-bvb.de/~db/0001/bsb00016335/images/index.html?id=00016335&fip=70.20.182.111&no=5&seite=52>.
22. Engelberg, i. 64.
23. Ibid. 107.
24. Pflanze, i. 34, n. 3.
25. Engelberg, i. 100.
26. Pflanze, i. 33–4, Bismarck, *Gedanken und Erinnerungen*, 49–50, Lucius von Ballhausen, 9 Apr. 1878, von Keudell, June 1864, pp. 160–1.

27. Pflanze, i. 38.

28. Engelberg, i. 97, quoting Marcks.

29. Lady Emily Russell to HM Queen Victoria, 15 Mar. 1873, *Empress Frederick Letters*, 131–2.

30. Spitzemberg, 248–50.

31. Engelberg, i. 93.

32. Keudell, 160.

33. Bismarck to Mother, 27 Apr. 1821, *GW* xiv. 1.

34. Bismarck to Mother, Easter 1825, *GW* xiv. 1.

35. Engelberg, i. 104.

36. Bismarck to Bernhard, Kniephof, 25 July 1829, *GW* xiv. 1.

37. Bismarck to Brother, 12 July 1830, *GW* xiv. 2.

38. Engelberg, i. 116.

39. Anderson, 18.

40. Ibid.

41. Lytton Strachey, *Eminent Victorians* (London: Penguin Books, 1986), 26.

42. Motley, *Morton's Hope*, i. 125–7.

43. Ibid. 151–2.

44. Ibid. ii. 160–1.

45. Ibid. 163–5.

46. Marcks, *Bismarck*, 95.

47. Ibid. 89.

48. For a fascinating account of the last woman to be arrested by the Proctors and Bull Dogs in 1891 and tried by the Vice-Chancellor's Court, see Deborah Kant, 'Daisy Hopkins and the Proctors', M.Phil Dissertation in Criminology, University of Cambridge Institute of Criminology, 2008.

49. Bismarck to the Rector of Göttingen, *GW* xiv. 3.

50. Bismarck to Scharlach, 14 Nov. 1833, *GW* xiv. 2–3.

51. Bismarck to Scharlach, 7 Apr. 1834, *GW* xiv. 4.

52. Bismarck to Scharlach, 5 May 1834, *GW* xiv. 5.

53. Roon, i. 280.

54. Ibid. i. 68.

55. Marcks, *Bismarck*, i. 104–5.

56. Engelberg, i. 125.

57. Gall, *The White Revolutionary*, i. 35–6.

58. Pflanze, i. 38–41.

59. 27 Dec. 1884, Spitzemberg, 212.

60. Bismarck to Scharlach, 18 July 1835, *GW* xiv. 5.

61. Bismarck to Scharlach, 4 May 1836, *GW* xiv. 7.

62. Motley to Lady William Russell, 31 May 1863, *Motley Family*, 174.

63. Gall, *The White Revolutionary*, i. 38.

64. Aachen city website:
    <http://www.aachen.de/DE/tourismus_stadtinfo/100_kuren_baden>.

65. Engelberg, i. 131–2.

66. Ibid. 132.

67. Biographical details from German Wikipedia. <http://de.wikipedia.org/wiki/Adolf_Heinrich_von_Arnim-Boitzenburg>.

68. Engelberg, i. 133.

69. Ibid. 134.

70. Ibid. 136.

71. Ibid. 139.

72. Ibid.

73. Gall, *The White Revolutionary*, i. 39.

74. Entry by William Carr, rev. K. D. Reynolds; *Oxford Dictionary of National Biography Online* (Oxford: Oxford University Press, 2004–8).

75. C. P. Kindleberger, *A Financial History of Western Europe*, 2nd edn. (New York: Oxford University Press, 1993), 237.

76. Bismarck to Johanna, 14 May 1851, *GW* x. 211.

77. Engelberg, i. 144.

78. Bismarck to Karl Friedrich von Savigny, Frankfurt, 30 Aug. 1837, *GW* xiv. 9.

79. Bismarck to Bernhard, 10 July 1837, Engelberg, i. 143–4.

80. Ibid. 142.

81. Ibid. 146.

82. Ibid. 146.

83. Bismarck to Father, 29 Sept. 1838, *GW* xiv. 13–17 and Caroline von Bismarck-Bohlen, 18 June 1835, *GW* xiv. 6.

84. Engelberg, i. 149.

85. Gall, *The White Revolutionary*, i. 41.

86. Letter to Father, 29 Sept. 1838, *GW* xiv. 13–17.

87. Bismarck to Savigny, Kniephof, 21 Dec. 1838, *GW* xiv. 17. See also Engelberg, i. 150.

88. Wienfort, 213.

89. Theodor von der Goltz, Die ländliche Arbeiterklasse und der preußische Staat (Jena, 1893), 144–7.

90. Pflanze, i. 103.

91. Spenkuch, table 3, p. 160.

92. Marcks, *Bismarck*, i. 184.

93. Keudell, 13.

94. Ibid. 14.

95. Ibid. 16–17.

96. Bismarck to Father, London, 28 July 1842, *Bismarck Briefe*, No. 4, p. 6.

97. Bismarck to Father, Kniephof, 1 Oct. 1843, *Bismarck Briefe*, No. 7, pp. 9–10.

98. Bismarck to Father, Norderney, 8 Aug. 1844, *Bismarck Briefe*, No. 11, pp. 14–15.

99. Bismarck to Louis von Klitzing, 10 Sept. 1843, *GW* xiv. 21.

100. Bismarck to Father, 1 Oct. 1843, *GW* xiv. 22.

101. Bismarck to Oskar von Arnim, ibid.

102. Engelberg, i. 192.
103. Ibid. 198.
104. Clark, *Conversion*, 125 n. 3; Engelberg, i. 186.
105. Witzleben (Adelsgeschlecht) German Wikipedia. <http://de.wikipedia.org/wiki/Von_Witzleben#Namen>.
106. Cited in Clark, *Conversion*, 126.
107. Ibid. 130–1; Fischer, 60–1.
108. Petersdorff, 60 ff.
109. Ibid. 62.
110. Bismarck to Sister, Berlin, *GW* xiv. 24.
111. Bismarck to Karl Friedrich von Savigny, 24 May 1844, *GW* xiv. 25.
112. Bismarck to Scharlach, 4 Aug. 1844, *GW* xiv. 25.
113. Petersdorff, 69.
114. Engelberg, i. 205.
115. Petersdorff, 73.
116. Ibid. 20.
117. Ibid. 39.
118. Sigurd von Kleist, *Geschichte des Geschlects v. Kleist*, 5. <http://www.v-kleist.com/FG/Genealogie/AllgemeineGeschichte.pdf>.
119. Ibid. 43 and 81.
120. Petersdorff, 81.
121. Bismarck to Sister, Kniephof, 9 Apr. 1845, *GW* xiv. 33.
122. Engelberg, i. 299.
123. Ibid. 201–2.
124. Bismarck to Sister, Schönhausen, 30 Sept. 1845, *GW* xiv.35.
125. Bismarck to Marie von Thadden, 11 Apr. 1846, *GW* xiv. 41.
126. Bismarck to Marie von Thadden-Blanckenburg, Kniephof, Saturday, July 1846, *GW* xiv. 42–3.
127. Bismarck to Sister, 18 Nov. 1846, *GW* xiv. 45.
128. Blanckenburg to Kleist, 15 May 1885, Petersdorff, 93.
129. Bismarck to Heinrich von Puttkammer, 21 Dec. 1846, *GW* xiv. 46–8.
130. Bismarck to Puttkammer, 4 Jan. 1847, *GW* xiv. 48–9.
131. Bismarck to Sister, 12 Jan. 1847, *GW* xiv. 49.
132. Bismarck to Johanna, 4 Mar. 1847, *GW* xiv. 74.
133. Bismarck to Sister, 14 Apr. 1847, *GW* xiv. 83.
134. Bismarck to Johanna, 8 May 1847, *GW* xiv. 86.
135. Holstein, *Memoirs*, 9.
136. Spitzemberg, 49–50.
137. 4 June 1863, ibid. 50.
138. Ibid. 235.
139. 19 March 1870, ibid. 90.
140. 11 Apr. 1888, ibid. 248–50.
141. 12 June 1885, ibid. 220.
142. 1 Apr. 1895, ibid. 335–6.

CHAPTER 4

1. Ernst von Bülow-Cummerow had a very large estate in Pomerania but belonged to the Liberal side of the debates in Prussia after 1815. He approved of the reforms of Hardenberg, opposed the protectionist theories of Friedrich List, disliked the feudal pretentions of his fellow great estate owners, and made himself rather unpopular among Bismarck's backers. On the other hand his pamphlets on political matters and economic theories and the huge size of his holdings made him too big to antagonize. *Allgemeine deutsche Biographie & Neue deutsche Biographie (Digitale Register)*, vol. iii (Leipzig, 1876), 518 ff.
2. Wienfort, 113f.
3. Marcks, *Bismarck*, i. 387–8.
4. Bismarck to Ludwig von Gerlach, 26 Mar. 1847, *GW* xiv. 82.
5. Marcks, *Bismarck*, i. 388.
6. Bismarck to Johanna, 9 May 1847, *GW* xiv. 86.
7. Friedrich Meinecke quoted in Barclay, 36.
8. Marcks, *Bismarck*, i. 395.
9. Clark, *Iron Kingdom*, 408.
10. Ibid. 408.
11. *Historical Atlas.* <http://www.tacitus.nu/historical-atlas/population/germany.htm>.
12. Pflanze, i. 103.
13. Modern History Sourcebook: Spread of Railways in 19th Century. <http://www.fordham.edu/halsall/mod/indrev6.html>.
14. Bismarck to Brother, 26 Aug. 1846, *Bismarck Briefe*, No. 29, p. 40.
15. Bismarck to Johanna, 28 Apr. 1847, *GW* xiv. 84.
16. Barclay, 127.
17. Clark, *Iron Kingdom,* 460.
18. Barclay, 128.
19. Marcks, *Bismarck*, i. 397.
20. Text in *GW* x. 3.
21. Marcks, *Bismarck*, i. 426.
22. Bismarck to Johanna, 18 May 1847, *GW* xiv. 89.
23. Keudell, 9.
24. 'Ernst Gottfried Georg von Bülow-Cummerow', *Neue deutsche Biolgraphie*, ii. 737–8. Online Digitale Bibliothek: <http://mdz10.bib-bvb.de/~db/0001/bsb00016318/images/index.html?id=00016318&fip=71.242.201.13&no=22&seite=757>.
25. 21 Jan. 1848, Holstein, *Diaries*, 333–4.
26. Bismarck to Johanna, 8 June 1847, *GW* xiv. 94.
27. Bismarck to Johanna, 22 June 1847, ibid. 6.
28. Cf. Ch. 2.
29. Rühs, 128.
30. Clark, *Conversion*, 166.

31. Bismarck, *Die politischen Reden*, i. 25–6.

32. Ibid. 28.

33. Wagner, 292.

34. Berdahl, 349.

35. Ibid. 356.

36. 'Friedrich Julius Stahl', *Allgemeine deutsche Biographie*, vol. xxxv (Leipzig, 1893), 400.

37. Kleist to Ludwig von Gerlach, 25 Aug. 1861, ibid. 377–8.

38. Berdahl, 354.

39. Marcks, *Bismarck*, i. 421.

40. Gall, *Der weisse Revolutionär*, 56 and 59.

41. Pflanze, i. 53.

42. Marcks, *Bismarck*, i. 429.

43. Petersdorff, 94.

44. Marcks, *Bismarck*, i. 446.

45. Roon, i. 503.

46. *Bismarck, Man & Statesman*, i. 20.

47. Bismarck to Sister, Schönhausen, 24 Oct. 1847, *GW* xiv. 99–100.

48. Bismarck to Brother, Schönhausen, 24 Oct. 1847, ibid.

49. Marcks, *Bismarck*, i. 453.

50. Jonathan Steinberg, 'Carlo Cattaneo and the Swiss Idea of Liberty', in *Giuseppe Mazzini and the Globalisation of Democratic Nationalism*, ed. C. A. Bayly and Eugenio Biagini (Proceedings of the British Academy, 152) (London and New York: Oxford University Press, 2008), 220–1.

51. Clark, *Iron Kingdom*, 469.

52. Bernhard von Poten, 'Prittwitz', *Allgemeine deutsche Biographie*, vol. xxvi (Leipzig, 1888), 608.

53. Barclay, 141.

54. Clark, *Iron Kingdom*, 474–5. Clark's account of the Berlin revolution is the best short account of the dilemma of authority in a rebellious city during 1848 that I have read anywhere. He catches the difficulty of communicating with crowds and troops, of misunderstandings and confusions, in only seven pages.

55. Engelberg, i. 270.

56. *Bismarck, Man & Statesman*, i. 24.

57. Gall, *Der weisse Revolutionär*, 70.

58. Ibid. 70.

59. Engelberg, i. 273–4. Augusta gave this letter to William in September 1862 to warn him against appointing Bismarck as minister-president.

60. *Bismarck, Man & Statesman*, i. 24–5.

61. Engelberg, i. 275.

62. *Bismarck, Man & Statesman*, i. 29.

63. Bismarck to Brother, 28 Mar. 1848, *GW* xiv. 102.

64. *Souvenirs d'Alexis de Tocqueville*, introd. Luc Monnier (Paris: Gallimard, 1942), 63–4.

65. Engelberg, i. 280.

66. Bismarck to Brother, 19 Apr. 1848, *GW* xiv. 105.

67. Familienartikel Heinrich (Reuß); *Neue deutsche Biographie*, vol. viii (Berlin, 1969), 386.

68. *Neue deutsche Biographie*, vol. vi (Berlin, 1964), 294–5 (Digitale Bibliothek).

69. Clark, *Conversion*, 167 and n. 83.

70. Cf. Ch. 2, p. 24.

71. Engelberg, i. 298.

72. Ibid. 298–300.

73. Ibid. 296.

74. Bismarck to Hermann Wagener, 5 July 1848, *GW* xiv. 109.

75. 9 Sept., Gerlach, *Aufzeichnungen*, ii. 2, cited in Engelberg, i. 307.

76. Engelberg, i. 297.

77. Ibid. 298.

78. Zeittafel zur deutschen Revolution 1848/49. <http://www.zum.de/ Faecher/G/BW/Landeskunde/rhein/geschichte/1848/zeittafel.htm>.

79. Holborn, i. 75–6 and Petersdorff, 129–33.

80. Engelberg, i. 304.

81. Ibid. 305.

82. Petersdorff, 133.

83. *Zeittafel zur deutschen Revolution* 1848/49. <http://www.zum.de/Faecher/G/ BW/Landeskunde/rhein/geschichte/1848/zeittafel.htm>.

84. Bärbel Holtz, 'Ernst Heinrich Adolf von Pfuel (3.11.1779–3.12.1866)', *Neue deutsche Biographie*, vol. xx (Berlin, 2001), 362–3.

85. Bismarck to Johanna, Berlin, Saturday evening, 23 Sept. 1848, *GW* xiv. 113.

86. Barclay, 178.

87. Anton Ritthaller, 'Friedrich Wilhelm Graf von Brandenburg', *Neue deutsche Biographie*, vol. ii (Berlin, 1955), 517.

88. *Bismarck, Man & Statesman*, i. 55–6.

89. B. Poten, 'Friedrich Heinrich Ernst von Wrangel', *Allgemeine deutsche Biographie*, vol. xliv (Leipzig, 1898), 229–32.

90. Bismarck to Johanna, Berlin, 18 Oct. 1848, *GW* xiv. 114.

91. Ibid. 56–7.

92. Bismarck to Brother, Potsdam, Sunday evening, 11 Nov. 1848, *GW* xiv. 117-18.

93. Rbbonline: <http://www.preussen-chronik.de/_/episode_jsp/key=chronologie_ 006490.html>.

94. Bismarck to Johanna Potsdam, 16 Nov. 1848, *GW* xiv. 119.

95. Ibid.

96. 14 Apr. 1872, Lucius, 20.

97. *Verfassungsurkunde für den Preußischen Staat* 5 Dec. 1848 (Preußische Gesetz-Sammlung 1848, p. 375) Source:. Homepage des Lehrstuhls für Rechtsphilosophie, Staats- und Verwaltungsrecht Prof. Dr. Horst Dreier, Universität Würzburg. <http://www.jura.uni-wuerzburg.de/lehrstuehle/dreier/startseite/>.

98. *Verfassungsurkunde für den Preußischen Staat*, 5 Dec. 1848.

99. Spenkuch, 385.

100. Ibid. 366–7.

101. Bismarck to Brother, 9 Dec. 1848, *GW* xiv. 120.

102. Engelberg, i. 325.

103. Bismarck to Brother, Schönhausen, 10 Feb. 1849, *GW* xiv. 123.

104. Engelberg, i. 329; Petersdorff, 151–2.

105. Engelberg, i. 354.

106. Clark, *Iron Kingdom*, 494.

107. Bismarck speech in the Landtag, 21 Apr. 1849, *GW* x. 29–32.

108. Bismarck to Brother, 18 Apr. 1849, *GW* xiv. 127.

109. Bismarck to Johanna, 8 Aug. 1849, *GW* xiv. 131. Johannes Evangelista Gossner (1773–1858) was a missionary, preacher, and writer active in the religious awakening in Germany. The 'little treasures' to which Bismarck refers was a book of devotions, *Das Schatzkästchen* of 1825, written for his congregation in St Petersburg. Cf. Friedrich Wilhelm Bautz, *Biographisch- bibliographisches Kirchenlexikon*, vol. ii (Spalten, 1990), 268–71. <http://www.bbkl.de/g/gossner_j_e.shtml>.

110. Bismarck to Johanna, 17 Aug. 1849, *GW* xiv. 133.

111. Bismarck to Johanna, 9 Sept. 1849, *GW* xiv. 140.

112. Bismarck to Johanna, 16 Sept. 1849, *GW* xiv. 143, also in Engelberg, i. 337.

113. R. von Liliencron, 'Radowitz', *Allgemeine deutsche Biographie*, vol. xxvii (Leipzig, 1888), 143.

114. Speech 15 Apr. 1850, *GW* x. 95–6.

115. Bismarck to Johanna, Erfurt, 19 Apr. 1850, *GW* xiv. 155.

116. Bismarck to Hermann Wagener, editor of the *Kreuzzeitung*, Schönhausen, 30 June 1850, *GW* xiv. 159.

117. Bismarck to Sharlach, Schönhausen bei Jerichow an der Elbe, 4 July 1850, *GW* xiv. 161–2.

118. Bismarck to Sister, Schönhausen, 8 July 1850, *GW* xiv. 162.

119. Zeittafel zur deutschen Revolution 1848/49. <http://www.zum.de/Faecher/G/BW/Landeskunde/rhein/geschichte/1848/zeittafel.htm>.

120. Bucholz, 44–5.

121. Clark, *Iron Kingdom*, 494–9; *Encyclopedia of 1848 Revolutions*. <http://www.ohiou.edu/~Chastain/dh/erfurtun.htm>.

122. Bismarck's speech on Olmuetz, 3 Dec. 1850, *GW* x. 103ff.

123. Gall, *Der weisse Revolutionär*, 119.

124. Bismarck to Johanna, Berlin, 12 Mar. 1851, *GW* xiv. 199.

125. Bismarck to Johanna, Berlin, 29 Mar. 1851, *GW* xiv. 202.

126. Bismarck to Johanna, Berlin, 7 Apr. 1851, *GW* xiv. 204.

127. Petersdorff, 190–1.

128. Bismarck to Johanna, 28 Apr. 1851, Pflanze, i. 76.

CHAPTER 5

1. Dreier website: <http://www.jura.uni-Wuerzburg.de/lehrstuehle/dreier/dokumente_und_entscheidungen/dokumente_am_lehrstuhl/schlussakte_der_wiener_ministerkonferenz_15_mai_1820/>.

2. *Deutsches Staats-wörterbuch*, ed. Johann Caspar Bluntschli and Karl Ludwig Theodor Brater. Published by Expedition des Staats-Wörterbuchs, 1858 Original from the University of Michigan, Digitized 8 May 2006, p. 61.

3. Bismarck to Johanna, Berlin, 3 May 1851, *GW* xiv. 208.

4. Hedwig von Blanckenburg to Johanna von Bismarck, 7 May 1851, Engelberg, i. 369.

5. Bismarck to Johanna, 14 May 1851, *GW* x. 211.

6. Bismarck to Kleist-Retzow, 4 July 1851, Pflanze, i. 51.

7. Bismarck to Johanna, Berlin, 5 May 1851, *GW* xiv. 208.

8. Bismarck to Johanna, 8 May 1851, *GW* xiv. 209.

9. Engelberg, i. 367.

10. Anthony Trollope, *Barchester Towers* (1857) (London: Penguin Classic, 1994), 188.

11. Ferdinand Lassalle's 'Open Answer of 1 March, 1863' in Oncken, 281.

12. *GW* xiv. 209.

13. Bismarck to Johanna, 18 May 1851 *GW* xiv. 213.

14. Bismarck to Wagener, 5 June 1851, *GW* xiv. 217.

15. Engelberg, i. 386.

16. Bismarck to General Leopold von Gerlach, 22 June 1851, *GW* xiv. 219–20.

17. Bismarck to Johanna, Frankfurt, 16 Aug. 1851, *GW* xiv. 237 and 6 Sept. 1851, ibid. 240.

18. Bismarck to Brother, Frankfurt, 22 Sept. 1851, *GW* xiv. 241.

19. Bismarck to Leopold von Gerlach, 23 Feb. 1853, *GW* xiv. 292.

20. Bismarck to Leopold von Gerlach, 6 Feb. 1852, *GW* xiv. 249–50.

21. Willms, 97.

22. Ibid.

23. Holstein, *Memoirs*, 22–3.

24. Herman von Petersdorff, 'Georg Freiherr von Vincke', *Allgemeine deutsche Biographie*, vol. xxxix (Leipzig, 1895), 748.

25. Ibid. 750.

26. 25 Mar. 1852, Bismarck and Vincke have a duel: Bismarck to Mother-in-law, 4 Apr. 1852, *GW* xiv. 258.

27. This saying according to Georg Buchman's *Geflügelte Worte: Der Citatenschatz des deutschen Volkes*, 510–11, goes back to the sixteenth century and originated with Emperor Maximilian I.

28. Bismarck to General Leopold von Gerlach, Frankfurt, 2 Aug. 1852, *GW* xiv. 275.

29. Bismarck to Sister, Frankfurt, 22 Dec. 1853, *GW* xiv. 336.

30. Pflanze, i. 86–7.

31. Bismarck to Leopold von Gerlach, 19 Dec. 1853, *GW* xiv. 334.

32. Engelberg, i. 396.

33. 'Prokesch von Osten, Anton Franz Count (1795–1876)', *Neue deutsche Biographie*, vol. xx (Berlin, 2001), 739–40.

34. Bismarck to Manteuffel, 12 Feb. 1853, cited in Engleberg, i. 384.

35. Ibid. 384.

36. Gerlach, *Briefe*, 28 Jan. 1853, pp. 33–4.

37. Leopold von Gerlach Diary, 27 July 1853, Engelberg, i. 403–4.

38. Willms, 100.

39. Pflanze, i. 90.

40. Engelberg, i. 424.

41. Willms, 100.

42. Bismarck to Leopold von Gerlach, Frankfurt, Maundy Thursday 13 Apr. 1854, *GW* xiv. 352.

43. Bismarck to Brother, 10 May 1854, *Bismarck Briefe*, No. 144, pp. 174–5.

44. 10 July 1854, ibid., No. 147, p. 177.

45. Ibid. 179, n. 1.

46. Bismarck to Leopold von Gerlach, Frankfurt, 15 Dec. 1854, *GW* xiv. 374–5.

47. Bismarck to Leopold von Gerlach, Frankfurt, 21 Dec. 1854, *GW* xiv. 375.

48. Engelberg, i. 424.

49. *Bismarck Briefe*, 181, n. 1.

50. Bismarck to Brother, Frankfurt, 26 Mar. 1855, ibid. No. 154, p. 181.

51. Bismarck to Leopold von Gerlach, 2 Feb. 1855, *GW* xiv. 381.

52. Engelberg, i. 428.

53. Ibid.

54. Tiedemann, 281.

55. Urbach, 61.

56. Bismarck to Leopold von Gerlach, Frankfurt, 10 Feb. 1855, *GW* xiv. 384.

57. <http://www.famousquotesandauthors.com/topics/revolution_and_reform_quotes.html>.

58. *Letters of the Empress Frederick*, 6.

59. Ibid. 7.

60. Bismarck to General Leopold von Gerlach, Frankfurt, 8 Apr. 1856, *GW* xiv. 439.

61. Pflanze, i. 81.

62. Bismarck to Leopold von Gerlach, Berlin, 2/4 May 1860, *GW* xiv. 549.

63. Bismarck to Leopold von Gerlach, Frankfurt, 15 Sept. 1857, *GW* xiv. 415.

64. Bismarck to Leopold von Gerlach, Frankfurt, 2 May 1857, *GW* xiv. 464–8.

65. Gerlach to Bismarck, *Briefe*, 6 May 1857, No. 103, pp. 208–13.

66. Bismarck to Leopold von Gerlach, Frankfurt, 30 May 1857, *GW* xiv. 470.

67. Leopold von Gerlach to Bismarck, *Briefe*, 22 Dec. 1857, No. 107, p. 223.

68. Ibid., *Briefe*, 23 Feb. 1858, No. 109, p. 229.
69. Leopold von Gerlach, *Briefe*, No. 110, 1 May 1860, pp. 229–32.
70. Bismarck to Leopold von Gerlach, Berlin, 2/4 May 1860, *GW* xiv. 549.
71. *Bismarck, Man & Statesman*, i. 52–3.
72. David Barclay in his biography of Frederick William IV gives a vivid account of the increasing incapacity of the King, who from 1853 on lost memory and capacity to use words. 8 October 1858, after another stroke, when he regained consciousness 'he remained unable to attach proper words to people or objects. Although his condition began to stabilize, everyone realized that it would be a long time before he could resume the activities of his office' (Barclay, 279).
73. Leopold von Gerlach, *Briefe*, 1 May 1860, No 110, pp. 231–2.
74. Pflanze, i. 140.
75. Ibid. 82.
76. Klaus-Jürgen Bremm, *Von der Chaussee zur Schiene: Militär und Eisenbahnen in Preußen 1833 bis 1866*, Militärgeschichtliche Studien (Munich: Oldenbourg, 2005).
77. 'Moltke', *Neue deutsche Biographie*, ed. Historischen Kommission bei der Bayerischen Akademie der Wissenschaften (Berlin: Duncker & Humblot, 1953), xviii. 13.
78. Bucholz, 33–4.
79. Ibid. 33.
80. Molte, *Neue deutsche Biographie*, 14.
81. Bucholz, 40–1.
82. Moltke, *NDB* 14–15.
83. Bucholz, 49.
84. Walter, 500–15.
85. 8 July 1870, Holstein, *Memoirs*, 41.
86. 9 Jan. 1871, Versailles, Verdy du Vernois, *Im grossen Hauptquartier*, 239.
87. 3 Sept. 1870, Waldersee, 95.
88. Bismarck to Stadtrat Gaertner, Frankfurt, 3 Feb. 1858, *GW* xiv. 484.
89. Letters of the Empress Frederick, 11.
90. Kurt Börries, 'Friedrich Wilhelm IV', *Allgemeine deutsche Biographie & Neue deutsche Biographie* (Digitale Register), vol. v (Berlin, 1961), 565.
91. Otto Pflanze, *Bismarck and the Development of Germany: The Period of Unification, 1815–1871* (Princeton: Princeton University Press, 1971), 121–2.
92. Ibid. 134.
93. Wagner, 293ff.
94. Bismarck to Leopold von Gerlach, Frankfurt, 20 Feb. 1859, *GW* xiv. 484.
95. Bismarck to Brother, Frankfurt, 29 Apr. 1858, *GW* xiv. 488.
96. Roon, i. 342.
97. Walter, 210, n. 81.
98. Roon, i. 213.
99. Princess Augusta to Roon, 22 Oct. 1848, ibid. 219.
100. Roon to Princess Augusta, 6 Nov. 1848, ibid. 225.

101. Ibid. 226.

102. Princess Augusta to Major Roon, 10 Dec. 1848, ibid. 231.

103. Prince William to Roon, 9 Jan. 1849, ibid. 231.

104. Ibid. 233–4.

105. Ibid. 257.

106. Anna to Roon, 31 Dec. 1850, ibid. 261.

107. Ibid. 266–7.

108. Roon to Bismarck, Coblenz, 14 July 1852, ibid. 267–8.

109. Roon to Perthes, 9 Nov. 1857, ibid. 334–5.

110. Ibid. 343–4.

111. Ibid. 348.

112. Ibid. 350–2.

113. The United States Constitution Online: <http://www.usconstitution.net/
     const.html#Am2>.

114. Pflanze, i. 105.

115. Clark, *Iron Kingdom*, 407.

116. Richard L. Gawthrop, 'Literacy Drives in Pre-Industrial Germany', in Robert
     F. Arnove and Harvey J. Graff (eds.), *National Literacy Campaigns: Historical and
     Comparative Perspectives* (New York: Springer, 1987), 29.

117. Pflanze, i. 105.

118. Karl Demeter, *Das Deutsche Heer und seine Offiziere* (Berlin, 1930), 13–29 and
     69–95.

CHAPTER 6

1. Wolfgang Wippermann, 'Otto von Manteuffel', *Allgemeine deutsche Biographie*,
   vol. xx (Leipzig, 1884), 270–1. <http://mdz10.bib-bvb.de/~db/bsb00008378/
   images/index.html>.

2. *Bismarck, Man & Statesman,* i. 232.

3. Bismarck to Johanna, Berlin, 15 Jan. 1859, *GW* xiv. 496.

4. Otto Count Stolberg-Wernigerode, 'Bismarck', *Neue deutsche Biographie*, vol. ii
   (Berlin, 1955), 270. <http://mdz10.bib-bvb.de/~db/0001/bsb00016318/
   images/index.html?id=00016318&fip=81.129.122.54&no=19&seite=297>.

5. Roon to Anna, 9 Jan. 1859, Roon, i. 360.

6. Roon to Anna, 10 Jan. 1859, ibid. 361–2.

7. Roon to Anna, 11 Jan. 1859, ibid. 362.

8. Roon, ibid. 363–4.

9. Stern, 14–15.

10. Ibid. 17.

11. Bismarck to Freiherr Georg von Werther, Frankfurt, 25 Feb. 1859, *GW* xiv.
    501.

12. Bismarck to Brother, Frankfurt, 3 Mar. 1859, *GW* xiv. 502.

13. Bismarck to Johanna, 17 Mar. 1859, *GW* xiv. 504.

14. Bismarck to Johanna, Berlin, 22 Mar. 1859, *GW* xiv. 506.

15. Bismarck to Sister, Petersburg, 19/31 Mar. 1859, *Bismarck Briefe*, No. 210, pp. 253–4.

16. Bismarck to Brother, Petersburg, 8 May 1859, *GW* xiv. 519.

17. Bismarck to Johanna, Petersburg, 28 Apr. 1859, *GW* xiv. 515.

18. Bismarck to Johanna, St Petersburg, 4 Apr. 1859, *GW* xiv. 511.

19. Bismarck to Frau Peterhof, 28 June 1859, *GW* xiv. 529.

20. Bismarck to Johanna, Petersburg, 2 July 1859, *GW* xiv. 533.

21. Bismarck to Otto von Wentzel, Petersburg, 1 July 1859, *GW* xiv. 531–2.

22. Roon, i. 372.

23. Kenney, *Ideology and Foreign Policy*, 36.

24. Beller, 69.

25. Odo Russell to Lady William, 23 Mar. 1852, Urbach, 28.

26. 'Villafranca, Conference of', *Encyclopædia Britannica* Online (2008). <http://proxy.library.upenn.edu:3225/eb/article-9075366>.

27. Bismarck to Brother, Petersburg, 8 May 1859, *GW* xiv. 519.

28. Bismarck to Schleinitz, Petersburg, 12 May 1859, *GW* iii. 35 ff.

29. Bucholz, 66–7.

30. Roon to Perthes, 15 June 1859, Roon, i. 375.

31. *Bismarck, Man & Statesman*, i. 251.

32. Engelberg, i. 477.

33. Bismarck to Brother, Berlin, 3 Aug. 1859, *GW* xiv. 536.

34. Planze, ii. 58.

35. Bismarck to Brother, St Petersburg, 15 July 1860, *GW* xiv. 556.

36. Bismarck to Sister, Berlin, 24 Sept. 1859, *GW* xiv. 538.

37. Bismarck to Johanna, Lazienki Palace, 19 Oct. 1859, *GW* xiv. 541.

38. Roon to Anna, 24 Oct. 1859, Roon, i. 388.

39. Roon to Anna, 28 Oct. 1859, ibid. 389–90.

40. Heinz Kraft, 'Adold Heinrich von Brandt', *Neue deutsche Biographie*, vol. ii (Berlin, 1955), 531.

41. General Heinrich von Brandt to Major Albrecht von Stosch, Berlin, 19 Oct. 1859, Stosch, 48.

42. Roon to Anna, 4 Nov. 1859. Roon, i. 391.

43. Ibid. 402–5.

44. Pflanze, ii. 10.

45. 'Clemens Theodor Perthes', *Neue deutsche Biographie*, vol. xx (Berlin, 2001), 202.

46. Perthes to Roon, 4 Dec. 1859, Roon, i. 409.

47. Walter, 32, 'Once more, let me repeat: there is no research on the Roon reforms.'

48. Ibid. 25–6.

49. Ibid. 33.

50. Karl Georg Albrecht Ernst von Hake (1768–1835), *Allgemeine deutsche Biographie*, vol. x (Leipzig, 1879), 394–6. Hake belonged to the 'Napoleonic' generation and served twice as Minister of War. The *ADB* says of him: 'not a statesman of the highest rank or a field commander, nor an organizational genius but a solid person and a restless worker, who served his Fatherland with true and useful service' (ibid. 396).

51. Walter, 341.

52. Duncker, 183.

53. 'August Reichensperger, (1808–1895)', *Allgemeine deutsche Biographie & Neue deutsche Biographie* (Digitale Register), vol. xxi (Berlin, 2003), 309–10.

54. Bismarck to Moritz, 12 Feb. 1860, Pflanze, i. 143, n. 39.

55. Bismarck to Johanna, Berlin, 7 May, *GW* xiv. 551.

56. Roon, ii. 19–20.

57. Bernhard von Poten, 'Edwin Freihher von Manteuffel', *Allgemeine deutsche Biographie & Neue deutsche Biographie* (Digitale Register), vol. lii, Nachträge bis 1899 (Leipzig, 1906), 178.

58. Craig, 'Portrait of a Political General', 2.

59. Ibid. 2, n. 4.

60. Ibid. 32.

61. Schweinitz, 214–16.

62. *PC* 21/11, 14 Mar. 1883, p. 4. <http://amtspresse.staatsbibliothek-berlin.de/vollanzeige.php?file=9838247%2F1883%2F1883–03–14.xml&s=4>.

63. Craig, 'Portrait of a Political General', 32, n. 108.

64. Ibid. 11–12.

65. Ibid. 12.

66. Stefan Hartmann, 'Manteuffel', *Neue deutsche Biographie*, vol. xvi (Berlin, 1990), 88.

67. Bismarck to Leopold von Gerlach, Frankfurt, 19 Dec. 1857, *GW* xiv. 481.

68. Bismarck to Brother, Berlin, 12 May 1860, *GW* xiv. 553.

69. Ibid.

70. Schlözer to Brother, 2 June 1860, Schlözer, 149.

71. Bismarck to Geh. Legationsrath Wentzel, Petersburg, 16 June 1860, *GW* xiv. 554–5.

72. Engelberg, i. 529.

73. Bismarck to Sister, Zarskoe-Selo, 4 Oct. 1860, *GW* xiv. 562–3.

74. Holstein, *Memoirs*, 4–6.

75. Pflanze, i. 173.

76. Craig, 'Portrait of a Political General', 13.

77. Hermann von Petersdorff, 'Twesten' (1820–70), *Allgemeine deutsche Biographie*, vol. xxxix (Leipzig, 1895), 35.

78. Ibid. 35 and Pflanze, i. 171.

79. Von Petersdorff, 'Twesten', 35–6.

80. Roon, ii. 21.

81. <http://www.dhm.de/lemo/html/kaiserreich/innenpolitik/fortschrittspartei/index.html>.
82. Roon, ii. 50.
83. Bismarck to Roon, 1–3 July 1861, Roon, ii. 29–32.
84. Ibid. 30.
85. Bismarck to Alexander Ewald von Below-Hohendorf (1800–81), Stolpmünde, 18 Sept. 1861, *GW* xiv. 578.
86. Bismarck to Sister Malwine, Petersburg, 8 Nov. 1861, *Bismarck Briefe*, No. 258, p. 322.
87. 'Sitzverteilung in der Zweiten Kammer des Landtags 1848–1870', *Wahlen in Deutschland bis 1918: Landtage Königreich Preußen.* <http://www.wahlen-in-deutschland.de/klPreussen.htm>.
88. Craig, 'Portrait of a Political General', 19.
89. Craig, *The Politics*, 137.
90. 'Sitzverteilung in der Zweiten Kammer des Landtags 1848–1870', *Wahlen in Deutschland bis 1918: Landtage Königreich Preußen.* <http://www.wahlen-in-deutschland.de/klPreussen.htm>.
91. 'Urwählerstatistik 1849–1913, Preussen', *Wahlen in Deutschland bis 1918 Landtage Königreich Preußen.* <http://www.wahlen-in-deutschland.de/klPreussen.htm>.
92. Bismarck to Roon, 12 Apr. 1862, Roon, ii. 79–80.
93. Bismarck to von Wentzel, 19 Apr. 1862, *Bismarck Briefe*, No. 264, pp. 330–1.
94. Bismarck to Johanna, 17 May 1862, *Bismarck Briefe*, No. 265, 332.
95. Roon, ii. 86.
96. Unpublished memo, 21 May 1862, cited in Schoeps, 235.
97. Bismarck to Johanna, 23 May 1862, *Bismarck Briefe*, No. 266, 332.
98. Bismarck to Johanna, Berlin, 25 May 1862, *Bismarck Briefe*, No. 268 p. 334; Bismarck to Brother, 25 May 1862, No. 267, ibid. 333.
99. Roon, ii. 92.
100. Roon to Bismarck, 4 June 1862, ibid. 93.
101. Ibid. 94.
102. Bismarck to Roon, Paris, 8 June 1862, ibid. 97.
103. Roon to Bismarck, Berlin, 26 June 1862, ibid. 99.
104. Moneypenny and Buckle, ii. 765.
105. Bismarck to Roon, Paris, 5 July 1862, Roon, ii. 101.
106. Bismarck to Johanna, 14 July 1862, *Bismarck Briefe*, No. 279, 345–6.
107. Roon to Perthes, 6 July 1862, Roon, ii. 106–7.
108. Orloff, 38.
109. Ibid. 56–7.
110. Ibid. 57.
111. Ibid. 88.
112. Bismarck to Katharina Orloff, Letter No. 5, Biarritz, 21 Oct. 1865, ibid. 113.
113. Roon to Bismarck, Zimmerhausen, 29 Aug. 1862, Roon, ii. 109.

114. Bismarck to Roon, Toulouse, 12 Sept. 1862, *Bismarck Briefe*, No. 290, 361.
115. Roon, ii. 115.
116. *Bismarck, Man & Statesman*, i. 293.
117. Roon, ii. 120–1; and also Pflanze, i. 180.
118. *Bismarck, Man & Statesman*, i. 294.
119. Ibid.
120. *Bismarck, Man & Statesman*, i. 295.
121. Crown Prince's diary, Schoeps, 31.
122. Engelberg, i. 518.
123. Stern, 28.
124. Petersdorff, 338.
125. Kleist-Retzow to Ludwig von Gerlach, 22 Sept. 1862, ibid. 340.
126. Bismarck to von Wentzel, 28 Sept. 1862, *Bismarck Briefe*, No. 281, p. 363.
127. Stosch to von Holtzendorff, Magdeburg, 28 Sept. 1862, Stosch, 52.
128. Bismarck's speech before Landtag Budget Committee, 'Blut und Eisen', 30 Sept. 1862, Pflanze, i. 183–4.
129. Gall, *The White Revolutionary*, i. 206.
130. *Bismarck, Man & Statesman*, i. 313–14.
131. Schoeps, 105.
132. Kurd von Schlözer, 3 Oct. 1862, Pflanze, i. 179.
133. Schoeps, 105.

CHAPTER 7

1. Perthes to Roon, 28 Apr. 1864, Roon, ii. 238.
2. Ibid. 260–1.
3. Kurd von Schlözer, 3 Oct. 1862, Pflanze, i. 179.
4. Ibid. 169.
5. Ibid. 182.
6. Adolf Graf von Kleist (1793–1866) to Hans von Kleist, 9 Nov. 1862, Petersdorff, 342.
7. Manteuffel to Roon, 5 Dec. 1862, Craig, 'Portrait of a Political General', 26.
8. Clark, *Iron Kingdom*, 522.
9. Bismarck to Prince Henry VII of Reuss, 23 Nov. 1862, *GW* xiv. 629.
10. Engelberg, i. 532.
11. Brunck, 36.
12. Huber, vol. ii, section II.1.
13. Brunck, 64 n. 1.
14. Bismarck to Johanna, 7 Oct. 1862, *Bismarck Briefe*, No. 292, p. 363.
15. Pflanze, ii. 35.
16. Holstein, *Memoirs*, 6.
17. Pflanze, ii. 45–6.
18. Ibid. 48, n. 45.

19. Stosch to von Normann, Prödlitz (Bohemia), 17 July 1866, Stosch, 102.
20. *Bismarck, Man & Statesman*, ii. 331.
21. Stern, 30.
22. *Bismarck, Man & Statesman*, ii. 329, 330, 333, 334.
23. Ibid. 370.
24. Roon, ii. 127; Brunck, 101.
25. Pflanze, i. 193.
26. *Bismarck, Man & Statesman*, ii. 342–3.
27. Ibid. 346.
28. Pflanze, i. 195.
29. Lucius, 2.
30. Bismarck Speech, 31 Mar. 1863, *GW* x. 179.
31. Ludwig von Gerlach to Hans von Kleist, 23 Apr. 1863, Petersdorff, 347.
32. Bismarck to Motley, Berlin, 17 Apr. 1863, *Bismarck Briefe*, No. 297, pp. 366–7.
33. Motley, *Family*, 174–8.
34. Pflanze, i. 210.
35. *Bismarck, Man & Statesman*, ii. 350.
36. Princess Victoria to Queen Victoria, 8 June 1863, *Letters of the Empress Frederick*, 41–2.
37. Bismarck to Roon, Carlsbad, 6 July 1863, *Bismarck Briefe*, No. 299, pp. 369–70.
38. Bismarck to Johanna, Nuremberg, 19 July 1863, ibid., No. 303, p. 372.
39. Pflanze, i. 197.
40. *Bismarck, Man & Statesman*, ii. 375–6.
41. Bismarck to Johanna, Baden, 29 Aug. 1863, *Bismarck Briefe*, No. 312, p. 377.
42. Huber, 32–3.
43. Oncken, 59.
44. Footman, 175.
45. Lassalle to Dammer, 12 May 1863, Oncken, 360.
46. George Meredith, *The Tragic Comedians* (Westminster: Archibald Constable & Co. 1902).
47. Roberts, 174.
48. Meredith, 57.
49. Hans Wolfram von Hentig, 'Sophie Gräfin von Hatzfeldt', *Neue deutsche Biographie*, vol. viii (Berlin, 1969), 67.
50. Georg Brandes, *Ferdinand Lassalle* (1881) English edn. (London: William Heineman, New York: The Macmillan Company, 1911), 22–3.
51. Ibid. 24.
52. Ibid. 30–1.
53. Oncken, 254–5.
54. Ferdinand Lassalle, 2 Feb. 1839, *Tagebuch*, 85–6.
55. Iring Fetscher, 'Lassalle', *Neue deutsche Biographie*, vol. xiii (Berlin, 1982), 662.
56. Ibid.
57. Brandes, *Lassalle*, 24.

58. Oncken, 228–9.

59. Ibid. 230; Studt, 236–7.

60. Oncken, 243–4.

61. Ibid. 236–7.

62. Ibid. 256.

63. Footman, 156.

64. Ibid. 153–4.

65. Lassalle to Countess Hatzfeldt, 3 Mar. 1862, Footman, 162–3.

66. Haenisch, 119.

67. Ibid. 119.

68. Oncken, 379.

69. Ibid. 467.

70. Marx to Engels, ibid. 473.

71. Karl Marx, *Das Kapital: Kritik der politischen Ökonomie* (Stuttgart: Albert Kroner Verlag, 1969), 5. Foreword to the first German edition, London 25 July 1867 (translated by JS).

72. Oncken, 373–4.

73. Ibid. 374.

74. Studt, 245–8.

75. Ibid. 251–2.

76. Willy Andreas, 'Arthur von Brauer', *Neue deutsche Biographie*, vol. ii (Berlin, 1955), 543–4.

77. Studt, 251.

78. Ibid. 251–2.

79. Holstein, *Memoirs*, 52 f.

80. *Bismarck, Man & Statesman*, ii. 357.

81. Roon, ii. 167.

82. *PC* 1/15, 7 Oct. 1863. <http://amtspresse.staatsbibliothek-berlin.de/vollanzeige.php?file=9838247/1863/1863–10–07.xml&s=1>.

83. Ibid.

84. 'Sitzverteilung in der Zweiten Kammer des Landtags 1848–1870', *Wahlen in Deutschland bis 1918: Landtage Königreich Preußen*. <http://www.wahlen-in-deutschland.de/klPreussen.htm>.

85. Hans von Kleist to Bismarck, 6 Nov. 1863, Petersdorff, 356.

86. Roon, ii. 170.

87. *PC* 1/22, 25 Nov. 1863, p. 2. <http://amtspresse.staatsbibliothek-berlin.de/verzeichnis.php>.

88. Ibid. 1.

89. Bismarck to unknown recipient, Berlin, 22 Dec. 1862, *Bismarck Briefe*, No. 295, p. 365.

90. Pflanze, i. 236.

91. Clark, *Iron Kingdom*, 524.

92. Pflanze, i. 237.

93. Grenville, 253.
94. *Bismarck, Man & Statesman*, ii. 10.
95. Ibid. 12 and 13.
96. Ibid. i. 359.
97. Schoeps, 55.
98. Ibid. 56.
99. Pflanze, i. 242.
100. Roon, ii. 189.
101. Stern, 39.
102. Roon to Perthes, 17 Jan. 1864, Roon, ii. 180.
103. John Prest, 'Russell, John [formerly Lord John Russell], first Earl Russell (1792–1878)', *Oxford Dictionary of National Biography* (Oxford: Oxford University Press, Sept. 2004). Online edn., Jan. 2008: <http://www.oxforddnb.com/view/article/24325>.
104. Ibid.
105. Pflanze, i. 248.
106. Embree, 29.
107. Ibid. 29–30.
108. Bismarck to Roon, 21 Jan. 1864, Roon, ii. 171–2.
109. *Bismarck, Man & Statesman*, ii. 379–80.
110. Holstein, *Memoirs*, 25.
111. Bismarck to Roon, end Mar. 1864, Roon, ii. 226.
112. Embree, 45.
113. Roon to King, 16 Mar. 1864, Roon, ii. 214 and 215.
114. Pflanze, i. 249.
115. Craig, *Fontane*, 84.
116. Bismarck to Graf Arnim-Boitzenburg, 16 May 1864, *Bismarck Briefe*, No. 331, p. 388.
117. Bismarck to Motley, Berlin, 23 May 1864, *Bismarck Briefe*, No. 332, p. 389.
118. Motley to Bismarck, Vienna, 28 May 1864; Motley, *Family*, 201–2.
119. Bismarck to Theodor von Bismarck-Bohlen, Berlin, 23 May 1864, *Bismarck Briefe*, No. 333, p. 391.
120. Roon to Moritz von Blanckenburg, 24 May 1864, Roon, ii. 243.
121. Pflanze, i. 252.
122. *Bismarck, Man & Statesman*, ii. 36.
123. Roon, ii. 245.
124. Ibid. 247.
125. Ibid. 248.
126. *Bismarck, Man & Statesman*, ii. 30–1.
127. Pflanze, ii. 253.
128. Ibid. 253.
129. Eyck, *Bismarck*, i. 624.
130. *Bismarck, Man & Statesman*, ii. 32.
131. Moneypenny and Buckle, ii. 80.

132. Brunck, 150.
133. Roon to Moritz von Blanckenburg, 26 Mar. 1866, Roon, ii. 259.
134. Stern, 44–5.
135. Brunck, 143.
136. Pflanze, i. 249.
137. Bismarck to Sister, Carlsbad, 27 June 1864, *Bismarck Briefe*, No. 336, p. 392.
138. Roon, ii. 254.
139. Bismarck to Johanna, Carlsbad, 20 July 1864, *GW* xiv. 672.
140. Bismarck to Brother, Vienna, 22 July 1864, *Bismarck Briefe*, No. 340, p. 394.
141. Mary Motley to daughter, 1 Aug. 1864, Motley, *Family*, 209–14.
142. Moneypenny and Buckle, ii. 82.
143. Pflanze, i. 255.
144. Stern, 51.
145. Bismarck to Roon, Reinfeld, 22 Sept. 1864, Roon, ii. 284.
146. *PC* 2/45, Nov. 1864, p. 1. <http://amtspresse.staatsbibliothek-berlin.de/vollanzeige.php?file=9838247/1864/1864-11-02.xml&s=1>.
147. Franz Freiherr von Samaruga, 'Mensdorff', *Allgemeine deutsche Biographie*, vol. xxi (Leipzig, 1885), 366.
148. Pflanze, i. 259.
149. *Bismarck Briefe*, No. 362, p. 408, n. 4.
150. Pflanze, i. 260.
151. Ibid.
152. Stern, 8.
153. William I to Roon, 25 Apr. 1865, Roon, ii. 329.
154. Manteuffel to the King, 2 May 1865, Craig, 'Portrait of a Political General', 25.
155. Röhl, 'Kriegsgefahr', 97.
156. Pflanze, i. 261.
157. Manteuffel to Roon, 4 June 1865, Roon, ii. 321.
158. Stern, 60.
159. Röhl, 'Kriegsgefahr', 97.
160. Brunck, 144.
161. Wolfgang Köllmann, 'August von der Heydt', *Neue deutsche Biographie*, vol. ix (Berlin, 1972), 75.
162. August von der Heydt to Bismarck, 22 June 1865, Brunck, 146.
163. Radtke, 356.
164. Ibid. 17.
165. Bismarck to Roon, 3 July 1865, *Bismarck Briefe*, No. 365, p. 410.
166. Röhl, 'Kriegsgefahr', 94 and n. 34
167. Ibid. 97 and Bismarck to Eulenburg, 4 July, ibid. 98.
168. Bismarck to Eulenburg, 11 July 1865, ibid. 98–9.
169. Karl Wippermann, 'Otto von Camphausen', *Allgemeine deutsche Biographie*, vol. xlvii, Nachträge bis 1899 (Leipzig, 1903), 429.
170. Stern, 64.

171. Bismarck to Eulenburg, 11 July 1865, Röhl, 'Kriegsgefahr', 99.
172. 'Oppenheim Familie', *Allgemeine deutsche Biographie & Neue deutsche Biographie* (Digitale Register) vol. xix (Berlin, 1999), 559.
173. Brophy, *Capitalism, Politics, and Railroads in Prussia*, 156–7.
174. Nikolaus von Preradowich, 'Blome', *Neue deutsche Biographie*, vol. ii (Berlin, 1955), 315.
175. Bismarck to Eulenburg, 30 July 1865, Röhl, 'Kriegsgefahr', 101.
176. Tiedemann, 281.
177. Bismarck to Eulenburg, 1 Aug. 1875, Röhl, 'Kriegsgefahr', 99.
178. Roon to Moritz von Blanckenburg, 1 Aug. 1865, Roon, ii. 354.
179. Stern, 64–5.
180. Chotek to Mensdorff, 12 Aug. 1865, Stern, 64.
181. Pflanze, i. 263.
182. Bismarck to Eulenburg, 18 Aug. 1865, Röhl, 'Kriegsgefahr', 102.
183. Lawrence D. Steefel, 'The Rothschilds and the Austrian Loan of 1865', *Journal of Modern History*, 8/1 (Mar. 1936), 36.
184. *Budissiner Nachrichten*, 11 June 1865, in Green, 267.
185. Stosch to von Holtzendorff, Magdeburg, 31 Aug. 1865, Stosch, 63.
186. Busch, i. 490.
187. Wawro, *Austro-Prussian War*, 17.
188. Walter, 580–1.
189. Stosch to von Holtzendorff, Magdeburg, 2 Oct. 1865, Stosch, 63.
190. Eyck, *Bismarck and the German Empire*, 108; Pflanze, i. 265; Wawro, 42–3.
191. 3 Jan. 1866, Ludwig von Gerlach, *Nachlass*, i. 474.
192. A. W. Ward, 'Loftus, Lord Augustus William Frederick Spencer (1817–1904)', rev. H. C. G. Matthew, *Oxford Dictionary of National Biography* (Oxford: Oxford University Press, 2004). Online edn., Jan. 2008: <http://www.oxforddnb.com/view/article/34586>.
193. Loftus, 38.
194. *PC* 4/10, 7 Mar. 1866, p. 2. <http://amtspresse.staatsbibliothek-berlin.de/vollanzeige.php?file=9838247/1866/1866-03-07.xml&s=2>.
195. Ibid. 1.
196. Eyck, *Bismarck and the German Empire*, 111, Stern, 70.
197. Bucholz, 114.
198. Lord Clarendon to Loftus, 7 Mar. 1866, Loftus, 43.
199. Gräfin Hatzfeldt to Mensdorff, 17 Mar. 1866, Schoeps, 177.
200. Roon to Moritz von Blanckenburg, 26 Mar. 1866, Roon, ii. 259.
201. Stosch to von Holtzendorff, Magdeburg, 14 May 1865, Stosch, 62.
202. *Im Ring der Gegner Bismarcks: Denkschriften und politischer Briefwechsel Franz v. Roggenbachs mit Kaiserin Augusta und Albrecht v. Stosch, 1865–1896*, 2nd edn., ed. Julius Heyderhoff (Leipzig: Koehler & Amelang, 1943).
203. Börner, *William I*, 269.
204. Roon, ii. 260.

205. Roon, ii. 260.
206. Moltke to Roon, 5 Apr. 1866, Roon, ii. 262.
207. Bucholz, 116–17.
208. Crown Prince to Schweinitz, 1 Apr. 1866, Schweinitz, 23.
209. Engelberg, i. 574.
210. Eyck, *Bismarck and the German Empire*, 115.
211. Ibid., 11 Apr. 1866, p. 1. <http://amtspresse.staatsbibliothek-berlin.de/vollan-zeige.php?file=9838247/1866/1866–04–11.xml&s=1>.
212. Anderson, 97.
213. Engelberg, i. 575.
214. Count Adolph von Kleist to Gerlach, 10 Apr. 1866, Gerlach, *Nachlass*, ii. 1265–6.
215. Prince Albrecht von Preussen to Ludwig von Gerlach, Berlin, 4 May 1866, ibid. 1272–4.
216. Hans von Kleist-Retzow to Ludwig von Gerlach, Kieckow, 16 Apr. 1866, ibid. 1268–9.
217. Geheimrat J. Bindewald to Ludwig von Gerlach, Berlin, 2 May 1866, ibid. 1271.
218. Prince Albrecht von Preussen to Ludwig von Gerlach, Berlin, 4 May 1866, ibid. 1272–4.
219. Ludwig von Gerlach, 5 May 1866, published in the *Kreuzzeitung*, No. 105, 8 May 1886, Gerlach, *Tagebuch*, 478.
220. Lucius, 28.
221. Pflanze, i. 303.
222. *PC* 4/19, 9 May 1866, p. 3. <http://amtspresse.staatsbibliothek-berlin.de/vol-lanzeige.php?file=9838247/1866/1866–05–09.xml&s=3>.
223. Stosch to his wife, Berlin, 26 May 1866, Stosch, 74.
224. Bismarck to von der Goltz, 30 May 1866, *GW* v. 429.
225. Stosch to his wife, Berlin, 30 May 1866, Stosch, 76.
226. Walter, 221.
227. Bucholz, 120.
228. Roon, ii. 275.
229. *PC* 4/23, 6 June 1866, p. 1. <http://amtspresse.staatsbibliothek-berlin.de/vol-lanzeige.php?file=9838247/1866/1866–06–06.xml&s=1>.
230. Bismarck to Duke Ernst von Saxe-Coburg-Gotha, 9 June 1866, *Bismarck Briefe*, No. 382, p. 424.
231. Bismarck, Memorandum to Federal Princes, 10 June 1866, *GW* v. 534.
232. Bismarck to Heinrich von Treitschke, 11 June 1866, *Bismarck Briefe*, No. 383, pp. 425–6.
233. Hermann von Petersdorff, 'Treitschke', *Allgemeine deutsche Biographie*, vol. lv, Nachträge bis 1899 (Leipzig, 1910), 282.
234. Stern, 85.
235. Eyck, *Bismarck and the German Empire*, 118.
236. Arsène Lagrelle, *A travers la Saxe, Souvenirs et études* (Paris, 1866) in Green, 28.
237. Zimmer, 74–5.

238. *The Death of Wallenstein* by Friedrich Schiller, trans. Samuel Taylor Coleridge. Project Gutenberg. <http://www.gutenberg.org/dirs/6/7/8/6787/6787.txt>.

239. Eyck, *Bismarck and the German Empire*, 123–4.

240. Ibid. 127.

241. Sterne, 205.

242. Loftus, 60.

243. Wawro, *Austro-Prussian War*, 53.

244. Zimmer, 95–101.

245. Ibid. 62.

246. Craig, *Fontane*, 87.

247. Ibid. 63.

248. Bismarck to Roon, 17 June 1866, Roon, ii. 277.

249. Zimmer, 89.

250. Wawro, *Austro-Prussian War*, 55.

251. Stosch to Holtzendorff, 20 Aug. 1866, Stosch, 113.

252. Ibid. 55.

253. Ibid. 199–201.

254. Wawro, *Austro-Prussian War*, 227.

255. Zimmer, 120–1.

256. Walter, 64.

257. Ibid. 74.

258. Craig, *Battle of Königgrätz*, 26.

259. Stosch to wife, Neise (Silesia), 20 June 1866 (Stosch, 84) 'Promotion has arrived, Madame General! My first bit of General's equipment—a few "ellen" of red cloth which we sewed on'.

260. 3 July 1866, Stosch, 94.

261. *PC* 4/27, 4 July 1866, p. 4. <http://amtspresse.staatsbibliothek-berlin.de/vollanzeige.php?file=9838247/1866/1866-07-04.xml&s=1}>.

262. Rudolf Bamberger to Ludwig, 6 July 1866, Koehler, 91.

263. Bismarck to Johanna, Hohenmauth, Monday 9 July 1866, *Bismarck Briefe*, No. 387, p. 429.

264. Stosch to von Normann, Prödlitz (Bohemia), 17 July 1866, Stosch, 102.

265. Moltke to Wife, 23 July 1866, Moltke, *Gesammelte Schriften*, vi. 496.

266. Engelberg, i. 613.

267. Lucius, 118–19.

268. Engelberg, i. 614.

269. *PC* 4/31, 1 Aug. 1866, p. 1. <http://amtspresse.staatsbibliothek-berlin.de/vollanzeige.php?file=9838247/1866/1866-08-01.xml&s=1>.

270. Pflanze, i. 315.

271. Sterne, 210.

272. Ibid. 212–13, n. 50.

273. Ibid. 213.

274. Pflanze, i. 316.

CHAPTER 8

1. *PC* 4/30, 25 July 1866, p. 2. <http://amtspresse.staatsbibliothek-berlin.de/vol-lanzeige.php?file=9838247/1866/1866–07–25.xml&s=2>.
2. Bismarck to Johanna, Brünn, 18 July 1866, *Bismarck Briefe*, No. 389, p. 431.
3. Engelberg, i. 619.
4. L. Mitteis, *Allgemeine deutsche Biographie*, vol. i, Nachträge bis 1899 (Leipzig, 1905), 652 ff. <http://mdz10.bib-bvb.de/~db/bsb00008408/images/index. html?id=00008408&fip=81.129.122.54&no=17&seite=652>.
5. Pflanze, i. 331.
6. Clark, *Iron Kingdom*, 544.
7. Cited in Walter, 65.
8. Petersdorff, 381.
9. Bismarck to Johanna, Prague, 3 Aug. 1866, *Bismarck Briefe*, No. 390, p. 432; and also in Petersdorff, 383.
10. Engelberg, i. 627.
11. *PC* 4/30, 8 Aug. 1866, p. 1. <http://amtspresse.staatsbibliothek-berlin.de/ vollanzeige.php?file=9838247/1866/1866–08–08.xml&s=1>.
12. Petersdorff, 383–4.
13. Brunck, 167.
14. Emil Breslaur, *Allgemeine Zeitung des Judenthums*, 25 Sept. 1866, pp. 622–3.
15. Brunck, 169.
16. Schoeps, 113–14.
17. Klara von Eyall, 'Mevissen', *Neue deutsche Biographie*, vol. xvii (Berlin, 1994), 277–81.
18. Pflanze, i. 331.
19. Koehler, 92–3.
20. 'Photographs from the Reichstag', *Die Gartenlaube*, 15/18 (Apr.), 285–6.
21. Bismarck to Bernhard, Varzin, 7 July 1867, *Bismarck Briefe*, No. 394, p. 435.
22. Bismarck to Motley, Varzin, 7 Aug. 1869, Motley, *Correspondence*, 221–2.
23. Motley to Mary Motley, Hôtel du Nord, Berlin, 1 Aug. 1872, Motley, *Correspondence*, iii. 274 ff.).
24. Roggenbach, 57–8, n. 2.
25. Queen Augusta to Freiherr von Roggenbach, Berlin, 9 Jan. 1867, Roggenbach, 68–9.
26. Pflanze, ii. 409.
27. Schweinitz, 37.
28. Verfassung des Norddeutschen Bundes: <http://de.wikisource.org/wiki/ Verfassung_des_Norddeutschen_Bundes#Artikel_1>.
29. Pflanze, i. 353.
30. Wahl des konstituierenden Reichstages: <http://de.wikipedia.org/wiki/ Reichstag_(Norddeutscher_Bund)#Wahl_des_konstituierenden_ Reichstages>
31. Schuder, 67.

32. Pflanze, i. 357.
33. <http://www.hgisg-ekompendium.ieg-mainz.de/Dokumentation_ Datensaetze/Multimedia/Staatenwelten/Norddeutscher_Bund.pdf>.
34. Stosch to wife, Versailles, 25 Jan. 1870, Stosch, 227.
35. *GW* vi. b. 15.
36. Ibid. 15–16.
37. Brunck, 206.
38. Ibid.
39. Ibid.
40. Hans Heffter, 'Delbrück', *Neue deutsche Biographie*, vol. iii (Berlin, 1957), 577–9. <http://mdz10.bib-bvb.de/~db/0001/bsb00016319/images/index. html?seite=595>.
41. Holstein, *Memoirs*, 51.
42. Hollyday, 144.
43. 27 Mar. 1875, Lucius, 47–8.
44. Stosch to Gustav Freytag, Berlin, 18 Aug. 1867, Stosch, 132–3.
45. Anderson, 3.
46. Ulrich von Hehl, 'Peter Reichensperger', *Neue deutsche Biographie*, vol. xxi (Berlin, 2003), 310–11.
47. Anderson, 243.
48. Ibid. 63.
49. Ibid. 100.
50. Riotte, 85.
51. *Wahlen in Deutschland bis 1918 Reichstagswahlen Preußische Provinz Hannover.* <http://www.wahlen-in-deutschland.de/kuPrHannover.htm>.
52. F. Nachpfahl, 'Windthorst', *Allgemeine deutsche Biographie*, vol. lv, Nachträge bis 1899 (Leipzig, 1910), 99.
53. Anderson, 140.
54. Ibid. 99–100.
55. Ibid. 107.
56. Ulrich von Hehl, 'August Reichensperger', *Neue deutsche Biographie*, vol. xxi (Berlin, 2003), 309–10.
57. Anderson, 108.
58. Stosch to Freytag, 15 Mar. 1868, Stosch, 137.
59. Bismarck to State Minister von Mühler, 27 Feb. 1868, *GW* vib. 283.
60. Decrees of the First Vatican Council, *Historical Discovery Presents the Councils of the Church.* <http://www.geocities.com/Heartland/Valley/8920/churchcoun-cils/Ecum20.htm#papalinfallibilitydefined>.
61. Spitzemberg, 80, n. 30.
62. Roggenbach to Queen Augusta, Berlin, 22 June 1869, Roggenbach, No. 22, p. 105.
63. Bismarck to Eulenburg, 19 Jan. 1869, in Brunck, 222.
64. *Bismarck, Man & Statesman*, ii. 225.

65. King William to Bismarck, 22 Feb. 1869, *Correspondence of William I. & Bismarck*, i. 107–8.
66. Bismarck to Roon, Berlin, 22 Feb. 1869, *Bismarck Briefe*, No. 404, p. 442.
67. King William to Bismarck, op. cit. n. 65 above.
68. Ibid. 227.
69. Stosch to Freytag, 9 Mar. 1869, Stosch, 152.
70. Clark, *Conversion*, 163, n. 170.
71. Bismarck to Roon, Varzin, 29 Aug. 1869, *Bismarck Briefe*, No. 410, 449.
72. Roon to Moritz von Blanckenburg, 16 Jan. 1870, Roon, ii. 419.
73. Moritz von Bismarck to Roon, 21 Jan. 1870, ibid. ii. 420.
74. Bartlett, 278.
75. Willms, 219–20.
76. Clark, 'Marshal Prim', 318.
77. Pflanze, i. 253; Willms, 220.
78. Willms, 220.
79. Halperin, 85.
80. Gerwarth, 72.
81. Halperin, 85.
82. Waldersee, 49.
83. Bartlett, 280.
84. Halperin, 87.
85. Pflanze, i. 454.
86. Crown Princess to Queen Victoria, 12 Mar. 1870, *Letters of the Empress Frederick*, 71.
87. Pflanze, i. 455–6.
88. Ibid. 456.
89. *Bismarck, Man & Statesman*, ii. 89. <http://www.archive.org/stream/bismarck-manstate02bismuoft/bismarckmanstate02bismuoft_djvu.txt>.
90. Willms, 223.
91. Bartlett, 276.
92. Ibid. 282.
93. Willms, 224.
94. Waldersee, 71–2.
95. Crown Princess to Queen Victoria, 6 June 1870, *Letters of the Empress Frederick*, 72.
96. 7 July 1870, Diary Entry, Waldersee, 72.
97. 8 July 1870, Waldersee, 73–4.
98. 9 July 1870, Waldersee, 76.
99. Willms gives an excellent account of this stage of the crisis, 225–6.
100. Pflanze, ii. 81.
101. Pflanze, i. 466.
102. *Kriegstagebuch Herbert Bismarcks* quoted in Stern, 130.
103. Engelberg, i. 721.

104. 12 July, diary entry, Waldersee, 79–80.

105. Willms, 228.

106. Ibid.

107. Lucius, 17 Jan. 1877, p. 98.

108. Crown Princess to Queen Victoria, 16 July 1870, *Letters of the Empress Frederick*, 75.

109. Bucholz, 162–3.

110. Lucius, 3–4.

111. 21 July 1870, Waldersee, 83.

112. Moltke, *Franco-German War*, Appendix, pp. 423–47.

113. Bernhard von Poten, 'Steinmetz', *Allgemeine deutsche Biographie*, vol. xxxvi (Leipzig, 1893), 18.

114. Waldersee, 84.

115. Willms, 232.

116. Ibid. 233.

117. 2 Aug. 1879, Mainz, Waldersee, 86.

118. Moltke, *Franco-Prussian War*, 18.

119. 5 Aug. 1870, *War Diary of Emperor Frederick*, 31, 41–2.

120. Moltke, *Franco-Prussian War*, 63.

121. Moltke, *Franco-Prussian War*, 114.

122. Ibid. 115.

123. 3 Aug. 1870, Waldersee, 86.

124. 24 Aug., ibid.

125. 9 Sept. 1870, Waldersee, 95.

126. Ibid. 97.

127. Bronsart, 89.

128. Stern, 138.

129. Ibid. 148.

130. Waldersee, 98.

131. Moltke, *Franco-Prussian War*, 128.

132. Ibid. 127.

133. Waldersee, 98–9.

134. Bronsart, 107–8.

135. Ferrières, 4 Oct. 1870, Waldersee, 100.

136. 7 Oct., ibid. 101.

137. Keudell, 469.

138. 23 Oct. 1870, Waldersee, 102–4.

139. Urbach, 54.

140. Ibid.

141. Richard Davenport-Hines, 'Russell, Odo William Leopold, first Baron Ampthill (1829–1884)', *Oxford Dictionary of National Biography* (Oxford University Press, Sept. 2004). Online edn., Jan. 2008: <http://www.oxforddnb.com/view/article/24332>.

142. Lady William Russell to Sir Austen Henry Layard, 18 Oct. 1870, in Urbach, 47.

143. Davenport-Hines, 'Russell', *ODNB*.

144. Urbach, 69.

145. Bronsart, 212.

146. Crown Prince, 14 Dec. 1870, in *Letters of the Empress Frederick*, 107.

147. Bronsart, 227.

148. Ibid. 233–7.

149. Bronsart, 233–7.

150. Stosch to Wife, Versailles, 22 Dec. 1870, Stosch, 17.

151. Bronsart, 249.

152. Diary, Versailles 26 Dec. 1870, Waldersee, 116–18.

153. Versailles, 31 Dec. 1870, *Emperor Frederick's Diary*, 241.

154. 4 Jan. 1871, ibid. 246.

155. Ibid. 247.

156. Stosch to wife, Versailles, 6 Jan. 1871, Stosch, 221.

157. 8 Jan. 1871, *Emperor Frederick's Diary*, 253.

158. 9 Jan. 1871, ibid. 254.

159. HQ Versailles, 13 Jan. 1871, *Emperor Frederick's Diary*, 257–8.

160. Jörg, a leader in the Patriot Party in Bavaria, became one of the most important figures in Catholic social action after unification. Bernhard Zittel, 'Jörg', *Neue deutsche Biographie*, vol. x (Berlin, 1974), 461.

161. Anderson, 29, n. 25.

162. Keudell, 463.

163. Pflanze, i. 500.

164. Ibid. 464.

165. Karl Erich Born, 'Friedenthal', *Neue deutsche Biographie*, vol. v (Berlin, 1961), 447.

166. Schuder, 109–10.

167. *PC* 8/49, 7 Dec. 1870, p. 1. <http://amtspresse.staatsbibliothek-berlin.de/vollanzeige.php?file=9838247/1870/1870–12–07.xml&s=1>.

168. Bismarck to Johanna, HQ Versailles, 12 Dec. 1870, *GW* xiv. 803.

169. *PC* 8/49, 14 Dec. 1870, p. 1.

170. Kleist to von Blanckenburg, Petersdorff, 406.

171. Keudell, 465.

172. Pflanze, i. 504.

173. Clark, *Iron Kingdom*, 67.

174. HQ Versailles, 16 Jan. 1871, *Emperor Frederick's Diary*, 263–4.

175. 17 Jan. 1871, ibid. 265–6.

176. 18 Jan. 1871, Bronsart, 298.

177. *War Diary of Emperor Frederick*, 272.

178. 8 June 1873, Lucius, 33–4.

179. Stern, 146.

180. Holstein, *Memoirs*, 79. The 'Prince of Arcadia's full title was Georg Albert, Prince von Schwarzburg- Rudolstadt, who reigned in that tiny state from 1869 to 1890.
181. Crown Princess to Queen Victoria, 20 Jan. 1871, *Letters of the Empress Frederick*, 116.
182. Ibid. 229.
183. *War Diary of the Emperor Frederick*, 292 and 294.
184. Bronsart, 310.
185. Erich Angermann, 'Otto Camphausen', *Neue deutsche Biographie*, vol. iii (Berlin, 1957), 115.
186. Stern, 151.
187. Ibid. 154.
188. Ibid. 154.
189. HQ Versailles, 6 Mar. 1871, *Emperor Frederick's Diary*, 328.
190. Spitzemberg, 122.
191. Ibid. 124.
192. Source: <http://www.bismarckhering.com/index-eng.php3>.

CHAPTER 9

1. Moneypenny and Buckle, ii. 473–4.
2. Crown Princess to Queen Victoria, 11 Dec. 1870, *Letters of the Empress Frederick*, 110.
3. Bismarck, NFA p. vii.
4. *Wahlen in Deutschland bis 1918, Reichstagswahlen. Ergebnisse reichsweit.* <http://www.wahlen-in-deutschland.de/krtw.htm>.
5. Keudell, 476.
6. 22 Sept. 1870, *Emperor Frederick's Diary*, 130.
7. Pflanze, ii. 186.
8. Ibid. 187.
9. Bismarck to von Werthern, 17 Apr. 1871, NFA 56–7.
10. Anderson, 144–5.
11. Bismarck to Brassier, 1 May 1871, NFA, No. 85, p. 94.
12. Pflanze, ii. 194.
13. Ibid. 195.
14. Heinz Starkulla, 'Karl Jentsch', *Neue deutsche Biographie*, vol. v (Berlin, 1974), 412–13.
15. Anderson, 151.
16. Bismarck to Tauffkirchen, 30 June 1871, NFA, No. 149, p. 161.
17. Engelberg, ii. 106–7.
18. Pflanze, ii. 201.
19. Hermann Granier, 'Maximilian Graf von Schwerin', *Allgemeine deutsche Biographie*, vol. xxxiii (Leipzig, 1891), 433.

20. Schoeps, 116–17.
21. Stephan Skalweit, 'Falk', *Neue deutsche Biographie*, vol. v (Berlin, 1961), 6.
22. Ibid.
23. Engelberg, ii. 107.
24. Ibid., ii. 110.
25. Anderson, 433, n. 61.
26. Ibid. 154–5.
27. Ibid. 156.
28. Schoeps, 229.
29. Anderson, 157.
30. Ibid. 160.
31. Schoeps, 230.
32. Pflanze, ii. 208.
33. Urbach, 157.
34. Petersdorff, 423.
35. Ibid. 424–5.
36. Kurt Gassen, 'Andrae', *Neue deutsche Biographie*, vol. i (Berlin, 1953), 274.
37. Andrae-Roman to Gerlach, 15 Feb. 1872, Gerlach, *Nachlass*, i. 68.
38. Petersdorff, 413.
39. Lucius, 8.
40. Karl Erich Born, 'Robert Freiherr Lucius von Ballhausen', *Neue deutsche Biographie*, vol. xv (Berlin, 1987), 278–9.
41. Ibid. 9–10.
42. 27 Apr. 1871, Waldersee, 131.
43. Kent, 56.
44. Pflanze, ii. 197.
45. 15 May 1871, Waldersee, 134–5.
46. Bismarck to Mühler, Varzin, 25 July 1871, NFA, No. 154, pp. 166–7.
47. Bismarck to Johanna, Gastein, 22 August 1871, ibid., No. 163, p. 176.
48. Promemoria über die Verfassungswirren in Österreich, ibid., No. 161, pp. 174–5.
49. Runderlass, Bad Gastein, 24 Aug. 1871, NFA, No. 165, pp. 178–9.
50. Runderlass an die Missionen in St Petersburg, Wien, London, Rom, München, Lissabon, Haag, Berlin, 14 May 1872, ibid., No. 307, pp. 346–7.
51. Urbach, 120–1.
52. *Measuring Wealth*: <http://www.measuringworth.com/index.html>.
53. Willy Andreas, 'Arthur von Brauer', *Neue deutsche Biographie*, vol. ii (Berlin, 1955), 543.
54. Arthur von Brauer, *Im Dienst Bismarcks* (Berlin, 1936), cited in Pflanze, ii. 282.
55. Stern, 172 and 565, n. 45.
56. Bismarck to William I, Berlin, 15 May 1873, NFA, No. 437, pp. 521–2.
57. Bismarck to William I, 16 May 1873, ibid., No. 438, p. 525.
58. Henckel to Tiedemann, 20 Jan. 1879, Tiedemann, 327–8.

59. Michael Turner, 'Output and Price in UK Agriculture, 1867–1914 and the Great Agricultural Depression Reconsidered', *Agricultural History Review*, 40/1 (1992), Table 3, pp. 47–8.

60. Sartorius von Waltershausen, 261–2.

61. See Jeffrey Fear, *Organizing Control: August Thyssen and the Construction of German Corporate Management* (Cambridge, Mass.: Harvard University Press, 2005) for a brilliant analysis of the role of accountancy in the construction of the concept of the enterprise. The numbers 'made' the company a reality.

62. Stern, 189.

63. Kent, 87.

64. Bismarck to Delbrück, Varzin, 3 June 1872, NFA, No. 316, pp. 356–7.

65. Bismarck to Falk, Varzin, 11 June 1872, ibid., No. 319, p. 358.

66. Bundesverfassung der Schweizerischen Eidgenossenschaft vom 29. Mai 1874. <http://www.verfassungen.de/ch/verf74-i.htm>.

67. Swiss Minister to Germany to the President of the Swiss Confederation, 23 Feb. 1873, *Documents diplomatiques suisses*, iii, No. 2, pp. 7–8.

68. This neat summary can be found in Pflanze, ii. 203.

69. Anderson, 173.

70. Engelberg, ii. 119.

71. Russell to Granville, 18 Oct. 1872, Kent, 38, n. 1.

72. Ernst Deuerlein, 'Georg Graf von Herling', *Neue deutsche Biographie*, vol. viii (Berlin, 1969).

73. Ibid. 146.

74. Ibid. 178.

75. Odo to Hastings, 23 Nov. 1874, Urbach, 170.

76. Urbach, 69.

77. Ibid. 162.

78. 12 Nov. 1874, Hohenlohe memoirs, quoted in Pflanze, ii. 278.

79. Roggenbach to Stosch, 30 Aug. 1874, Roggenbach, 162–4.

80. Wagner, 303–13.

81. Itzenplitz to Bismarck, 18 Sept. 1869, Brunck, 225, n. 144.

82. Pflanze, ii. 210–11.

83. Spenkuch, 93.

84. Blanckenburg to Kleist, 15 Aug. 1872, ibid. 96, n. 36.

85. Ibid. 360.

86. Wagner, 314.

87. Paret, 131.

88. Eulenburg to Bismarck, 25 Oct. 1872, Brunck, 227–8.

89. Bismarck to Eulenburg, Varzin, 27 Oct. 1872, NFA, No. 343, pp. 386–7.

90. Ernst von Sennft-Pillsach to Bismarck, 3 July 1872, Schoeps, 340.

91. Pflanze, ii. 210–11.

92. Stern, 260.

93. Promemoria, Varzin, 2 Nov. 1872, NFA, No. 345, pp. 388–90.

94. Brunck, 230–1.

95. Wagner, 314.

96. Spitzemberg, pp. 136–7, n. 12.

97. Bismarck to Roon,Varzin, 12 Nov. 1872, NFA, No. 349, p. 394.

98. Bismarck to Wilhelm I,Varzin, 13 Nov. 1872, ibid., No. 350, pp. 394–5.

99. Bismarck to Roon,Varzin, 13 Dec. 1872, ibid., No 360, p. 408.

100. Bismarck to Roon,Varzin, 13 Dec. 1872, ibid. No. 361, pp. 409–10.

101. The horrible Arnim case has no equal in Bismarck's treatment of subordinates. George Kent has written an excellent monograph on this dreadful affair: *Arnim and Bismarck* (Oxford: Clarendon Press, 1968).

102. Helma Brunck has an extremely useful appendix in her *Bismarck und das preussische Staatsministerium*, 343–8, in which all the ministries and the incumbents with excellent short biographies are set out. This excellent monograph should be better known than it is. Nobody had taken it out from the University Library in Cambridge since it appeared in 2005 until I did.

103. Pflanze, ii. 337.

104. Ibid. 337–340; Schoeps, 161.

105. Petersdorff, 428.

106. 18 July 1879, Spitzemberg, 179–80.

107. Tiedemann, entry for 18 Jan. 1875, p. 2.

108. Ibid. 2–4.

109. Ibid. 222.

110. Ibid. 208.

111. Ibid. 33.

112. Ibid., 25 Jan. 1876, p. 39 and 20 Feb. 1876, p. 42.

113. Tiedemann to Count Herbert Bismarck, Berlin, 30 Sept. 1881, ibid. 460.

114. The episode in Tiedemann's words can be found in Chapter 1 above, p. 10.

115. <http://www.ewtn.com/library/ENCYC/P9QUODNU.HTMhttp://www.ewtn.com/library/ENCYC/P9QUODNU.HTM>.

116. Engelberg, ii. 121.

117. Spitzemberg, 153.

118. Pflanze, ii. 242.

119. Tiedemann, 11 July 1876, p. 51.

120. Ibid., 29 Sept. 1876, p. 91.

121. Ibid., 3 Dec. 1876, p. 103.

122. Ibid. 101.

123. Ibid., 11 June 1876, p. 51.

124. Ibid. 95.

125. Ibid., 4 Jan. 1877, p. 107.

126. Ibid., 28 Jan. 1877, p. 111.

127. Pflanze, ii. 266.

128. Eyck, *Bismarck and the German Empire*, 216.

129. Tiedemann, 24.

130. Urbach, 138–9.

131. Hillgruber, *Bismarcks Aussenpolitik*, 141.

132. Eyck, *Bismarck and the German Empire*, 219.

133. Bismarck to William I, 4 May 1875, *Correspondence of William I. and Bismarck*, i. 162.

134. Engelberg, ii. 171.

135. Hildebrand, *Das vergangene Reich*, 32.

136. James Stone offers a different reading of the 'war scare'. He argues that Bismarck throughout the 1870s used the threat of war to undermine the monarchist forces in France and that he continued after 1875 to pursue the same tactics for the same ends but more cautiously. He needed a 'republican France' because he thought it less likely to be acceptable to the conservative powers as an ally. James Stone and Winfried Baumgart, *The War Scare of 1875: Bismarck and Europe in the Mid-1870s* (Wiesbaden: Franz Steiner Verlag, 2010).

137. See Notiz, Varzin, 5 Aug. 1875, NFA, No. 278, ii. 409, nn. 1 and 2 and other dispatches, Herbert Bismarck to von Bülow, Nos. 286–9.

138. Sir Edwin Pears, *Forty Years in Constantinople, 1873–1915* (New York: D. Appleton and Co., 1916), 16–19. Internet Modern History Source Book: <http://www.fordham.edu/halsall/mod/1876massacre-bulgaria>.

139. Hermann von Petersdorff, 'Stosch', *Allgemeine deutsche Biographie*, vol. liv, Nachträge bis 1899 (Leipzig, 1908), 610.

140. Pflanze, ii. 423.

141. Bismarck to von Bülow, Varzin, 1 Oct. 1876, NFA, vol. ii, 1874–1876, No. 407, pp. 592–3.

142. Bismarck 'Diktat', Varzin, 9 Nov. 1876, NFA, No. 438, pp. 644–5.

143. Pflanze, ii. 428.

144. Engelberg, ii. 200–1.

145. <http://www.deutsche-schutzgebiete.de/kissinger_diktat.htm>.

146. Sir William White to Sir Robert Morier, 16 Jan. 1877, Ramm, 65.

147. Tiedemann, 126.

148. Spitzemberg, 165.

149. Tiedemann, 127.

150. Eugen Richter to Paul Richter, 5 Apr. 1877, Pflanze, ii. 370.

151. Russell to Lord Derby, 7 Apr. 1877, *Letters of the Empress Frederick*, 149.

152. Tiedemann, 132 and 133.

153. Spitzemberg, 165–6.

154. 28 Apr. 1877, Lucius, 110.

155. October (no date) Bismarck as recorded by Busch, ii. 158.

156. Tiedemann, 176.

157. Ibid. 176–7.

158. Tiedemann to wife, 30 Nov. and 7 Dec. 1877, Tiedemann, 216–17.

159. Ibid. 212, 216–17, Lucius, 118.

160. Lucius, 122–3.

161. William I and Bismarck, 30 Dec. 1877, *Correspondence of William I. & Bismarck*, No. 229, pp. 184–5.
162. Pflanze, ii. 378.
163. Normann to Roggenbach, Wiesbaden, 22 Nov. 1877, Roggenbach, 187–8.
164. Stosch to Roggenbach, Berlin, 27 Dec. 1877, ibid. 190–1.

CHAPTER 10

1. Tiedemann, 220.
2. Ibid. 225.
3. Pflanze, ii. 379.
4. Green, 305, discusses the inconsistency of national and state politics even within the same party.
5. Pflanze, ii. 379–80.
6. Eyck, Bismarck and the German Empire, 232.
7. Ibid.
8. Ibid.
9. 26 Jan. 1873, Diary Entry, Bamberger, 298.
10. Günter Richter, 'Wilhelm von Kardorff', *Neue deutsche Biographie*, vol. xi (Berlin, 1977), 150.
11. Pflanze, ii. 454–5.
12. Brunck, 266.
13. Tiedemann, 265–6.
14. There is a full account of the two assassination attempts and of Hödel and Nobiling in Pflanze, ii. 392ff.
15. Tiedemann, 263.
16. Spitzemberg, 171.
17. Tiedemann, 271.
18. *Wahlen in Deutschland bis 1918, Reichstagswahlen. Ergebnisse reichsweit*: <http://www.wahlen-in-deutschland.de/krtw.htm>.
19 Moneypenny and Buckle, ii. 1183–4.
20. Francis Charles Hastings Russell, ninth duke of Bedford (1819–91), was Liberal MP for Bedfordshire from 1847 to 1872, when (26 May) he succeeded to the dukedom on the death of his first cousin, William, eighth duke. (E. M. Lloyd, and Thomas Seccombe, 'Russell, Lord George William (1790–1846)', rev. James Falkner, *Oxford Dictionary of National Biography* (Oxford University Press, 2004). Online edn., Jan. 2008: <http://www.oxforddnb.com/view/article/24310>).
21. Odo to Hastings Russell, 12 June 1878, Urbach, 193.
22. Lytton Strachey, 346.
23. Disraeli to Queen Victoria, 12 June 1878, Moneypenny and Buckle, ii. 1189.
24. Ibid. 1186–7.
25. Disraeli to Queen Victoria, 13 June 1878, ibid. 1189–90.
26. Urbach, 193.

27. Moneypenny and Buckle, ii. 1191.
28. Ibid. 1194.
29. Schweinitz to Anna Schweinitz, 25 June 1878, Schweinitz, 137.
30. Disraeli Diary, 21 June 1878, Moneypenny and Buckle, ii. 1196.
31. Ibid.
32. Ibid. 1201.
33. Ibid. 1203.
34. Urbach, 194.
35. Disraeli Diary Entry, 5 July 1878, Moneypenny and Buckle, ii. 1203–4.
36. Pflanze, ii. 412.
37. Tiedemann, 299.
38. Petersdorff, 472–3.
39. Tiedemann, 300 and 302.
40. Anderson, 216.
41. Lasker in *PC* 16/43, 23 Oct. 1878. <http://amtspresse.staatsbibliothek-berlin.de/vollanzeige.php?file=9838247/1878/1878–10–23.xml&s=2>.
42. Tiedemann, 305–7.
43. *PC* loc. cit. n. 41 above.
44. Lucius, 143.
45. Pflanze, ii. 467.
46. Tiedemann, 315.
47. Bismarck to William I, 9 Nov. 1878, *Correspondence of William I. and Bismarck*, vol. i, No. 232, p. 188.
48. Pflanze, ii. 409.
49. *PC* 16/45, 6 Nov. 1878, *Amtspresse Preussens*. <http://amtspresse.staatsbibliothek-berlin.de/vollanzeige.php?file=9838247%2F1878%2F1878–11–06.xml&s=1>.
50. *PC* 16/52, 27 Dec. 1878, p. 2. <http://amtspresse.staatsbibliothek-berlin.de/vollanzeige.php?file=9838247/1878/1878–12–27.xml&s=1>.
51. Ibid. 3.
52. Tiedemann, 326.
53. *PC* 17/5, 29 Jan. 1879, p. 1.
54. Erich Angermann, 'Forckenbeck', *Neue deutsche Biographie*, vol. v (Berlin, 1961), 297.
55. Pflanze, ii. 475.
56. Bamberger, 330–1.
57. Lucius, 154.
58. Bismarck, 21 Dec. 1892, cited in Schoeps, 131.
59. *PC* 17/8, 19 Feb. 1879, p. 2. <http://amtspresse.staatsbibliothek-berlin.de/vollanzeige.php?file=9838247/1879/1879–02–19.xml&s=2>.
60. Pflanze, ii. 480.
61. Anderson, 219.
62. Stern, 205–6.
63. Anderson, 221.

64. Anderson, 228.
65. Manfred Weitlauff, 'Moufang', *Neue deutsche Biographie*, vol. xviii (Berlin, 1997), 233.
66. Anderson, 229.
67. Engelberg, ii. 259.
68. Lucius, 158–9.
69. Pflanze, ii. 489.
70. Niall Ferguson, 'Public Finance and National Security: The Domestic Origins of the First World War Revisited', *Past and Present*, 142 (Feb. 1994), 141–68.
71. Pflanze, ii. 511.
72. Anderson, 233.
73. Wolfgang Neugebauer, 'Puttkamer', *Neue deutsche Biographie*, vol. xxi (Berlin, 2003), 21.
74. Schoeps, 110–11.
75. Engelberg, ii. 263.
76. Karl Erich Born, 'Friedenthal', *Neue deutsche Biographie*, vol. v (Berlin, 1961), 447.
77. Schoeps, 112.
78. Lucius, 168.
79. Ibid. 168–9.
80. Both of his parents died in Auschwitz and he himself escaped at the very last minute to Sweden. The entry in the theological reference work calls it 'his decidedly Prussian spirit' which came out in work after his return to Germany in 1947. See entry 'Hans-Joachim Schoeps, 1909–1980', Horst Robert Balz, Gerhard Krause, Gerhard Müller (eds.), *Theologische Realenzyklopädie*. TRE online: <http://www.digento.de/titel/106392.html>.
81. Bismarck to King Ludwig of Bavaria, 4 Aug. 1879, Schuder, 84.
82. *PC* 17/36, 3 Sept. 1879, p. 2. <http://amtspresse.staatsbibliothek-berlin.de/vollanzeige.php?file=9838247/1879/1879–09–03.xml&s=2>.
83. Hermann Dechent 'Andrassy', *Neue deutsche Biographie*, vol. i (Berlin, 1953), 274.
84. Engelberg, ii. 281.
85. Pflanze, ii. 514.
86. Ibid.
87. Hildebrand, *Das vergangene Reich*, 66–7.
88. Pflanze, ii. 505.
89. *PC* 17/39, 24 Sept. 1879, p. 4.
90. Pflanze, ii. 507.
91. Lucius, 176.
92. Ibid. 178.
93. *PC* 17/41, 9 Oct. 1879, p. 2.
94. Richard Wagner, *Judaism in Music* (1850), trans. William Ashton Ellis. <http://users.belgacom.net/wagnerlibrary/prose/wagjuda.htm>.

95. Ibid.
96. Freytag, 102.
97. *Evangelische Kirchenzeitung* no. 80 (1865) in Clark, *Conversion*, 162.
98. Stern, 499.
99. Pulzer, table 2.2, p. 52.
100. Mosse, 115–16.
101. Ibid. 202.
102. Moneypenny and Buckle, ii. 1202.
103. Sartorius, 286 and 317.
104. Rosenberg, 55.
105. Ibid. 93 and 95.
106. Otto Glagau, 'Der Börsen- und Gründungsschwindel in Berlin', *Die Gartenlaube*, No. 499 (1874), 788.
107. Ibid. 790.
108. Uwe Puschner, 'Marr', *Neue deutsche Biographie*, vol. xvi (Berlin, 1990), 248.
109. Hermann von Petersdorff, 'Treitschke', *Allgemeine deutsche Biographie*, vol. lv, Nachträge bis 1899 (Leipzig, 1910), 306.
110. Treitschke, 10.
111. Pulzer, *Jews and the German State*, 96.
112. Treitschke, 10.
113. Fritz Martini, 'Auerbach', *Neue deutsche Biographie*, vol. i (Berlin, 1953), 434.
114. Schuder, 185.
115. Anderson, 251.
116. Stern, 513–14.
117. Hans-Joachim Schoeps, 'Fechenbach', *Neue deutsche Biographie*, vol. v (Berlin, 1961), 36.
118. Anderson, 252 and 449, n. 24.
119. Ibid. 253.
120 Pastor, ii. 191.
121. Schuder, 196.
122. Stern, 519.
123. Koehler, 231–2.
124. Anderson, 300.
125. Koehler, 231.
126. Pulzer, *Jews and the German State*, 97.
127. Schuder, 197.
128. Pulzer, *Jews and the German State*, 97.
129. Fontane to Philipp zu Eulenburg, 12 Mar. 1881, in Craig, *Fontane*, 114–15.
130. Karl Wippermann, 'Lasker', *Allgemeine deutsche Biographie*, vol. xix (Leipzig, 1884), 748–9.
131. Schuder, 205–6.
132. Lucius, 6 Jan. 1884, p. 278.
133. Pflanze, iii. 111.

134. Ibid.

135. Bamberger, 285.

136. Ibid. 285–6.

137. Lucius, 284.

138. Wipperman, 'Lasker', *Allgemeine deutsche Biographie*, 750.

139. Lucius, 216.

140. Ibid. 217.

141. 31 Mar. 1880, Tiedemann, 376–7.

142. Tiedemann had been appointed by Bismarck to represent him at Bundesrat meetings and had attended that day. Tiedemann, 378.

143. 6 Apr. 1880, ibid. 380–1.

144. Spitzemberg, 183.

145. 13 May 1880, ibid. 391.

146. 12 Oct. 1880, ibid. 400.

147. 18 Oct. 1880, 13 May 1880, ibid. 400, 391.

148. Stolberg to Tiedemann, 29 Jan. 1881, ibid. 416.

149. 'Weshalb ich meine Stellung beim Fürsten Bismarck abgab', ibid. 419.

150. Ibid. 20.

151. Lucius, 183–4; Pflanze, ii. 527.

152. Lucius, 186.

153. 25 Dec. 1880, Lucius, 192.

154. Lucius describes this fine clothing, ibid. 204.

155. Eberhard von Vietsch, 'Herbert von Bismarck', *Neue deutsche Biographie*, vol. ii (Berlin, 1955), 268.

156. Philipp zu Eulenburg, 'Herbert Bismarcks Tragödie', in *Aus Fünfzig Jahren*, 106.

157. Brandes, 419.

158. Reinhard Stumpf, 'Loe', *Neue deutsche Biographie*, vol. xv (Berlin, 1987), 14.

159. Snyder, 159.

160. Ibid. 159.

161. Stern, 257.

162. Eulenburg, *Aus 50 Jahren*, 93.

163. Eberhard von Vietsch, 'Herbert von Bismarck', *Neue deutsche Biographie*, vol. ii (Berlin, 1955), 268.

164. 1 Jan. 1888, Spitzemberg, 238.

165. Snyder, 161.

166. Eulenburg, *Aus 50 Jahren*, 105.

167. 11 Dec. 1886, Waldersee, 307.

168. Stern, 258.

169. Lucius, 210.

170. Ibid., 17 July 1881, p. 213.

171. *Wahlen in Deutschland bis* 1918 *Reichstagswahlen*, op. cit.

172. Pflanze, iii. 71.

173. Ibid. 73.

174. *PC* 20/3, 18 Jan. 1882, p. 1.

175. Anderson, 303.

176. 18 Feb. 1882, Holstein, *Diaries*, 7.

177. Anderson, 304.

178. Lucius, 225.

179. Anderson, 304.

180. *New Advent, Catholic Encyclopedia*: <http://www.newadvent.org/cathen/08703b.htm>.

181. Anderson, 292.

182. Lucius, 242.

183. Koch and Laqueur, 757.

184. Pflanze, iii. 100.

185. Koch and Laqueur, 760.

186. Ibid. 762.

187. Ibid. 776.

188. Pflanze, ii. 54–5.

189. Ibid.

190. Ibid. 53, n. 67.

191. Koch and Laqueur, 759.

192. Pflanze, iii. 100–1.

193. Koch and Laqueur, 759.

194. *PC* 20/2, 11 Jan. 1882, pp. 2–3. <http://amtspresse.staatsbibliothek-berlin.de/vollanzeige.php?file=9838247/1882/1882–01–11.xml&s=2>.

195. Peter Koch, 'Theodor Lohmann', *Neue deutsche Biographie*, vol. xv (Berlin, 1987), 130.

196. *Neueste Mittheilungen*, 2/65, ed. H. Klee (Berlin), Friday 15 June 1883, p. 1. <http://amtspresse.staatsbibliothek-berlin.de/vollanzeige.php?file=11614109/1883/1883–06–15.xml&s=1>.

197. Pflanze, iii. 139–40.

198. Lucius, 312.

199. Spitzemberg, 218.

200. Eulenburg, *Aus 50 Jahren*, 117.

201. Craig, Fontane, 109.

202. Eulenburg, *Aus 50 Jahren*, 128.

203. Ibid.

204. *Neueste Mittheilungen*, 6/4, 11 Jan. 1887, pp. 5–6. <http://amtspresse.staatsbibliothek-berlin.de/vollanzeige.php?file=11614109/1887/1887–01–11.xml&s=5>.

205. Spitzemberg, 227–8.

206. Anderson, 342 and 467, n. 64.

207. Ibid. 345.

208. Ibid. 350–2.

209. *Wahlen in Deutschland bis 1918 Reichstagswahlen*, op. cit.

210. Anderson, 59.
211. Pflanze, iii. 234.
212. 11 Mar. 1887, Waldersee, 319.
213. Ibid.
214. Pflanze has a fine section on the Reinsurance Treaty, iii. 248–53.
215. Holstein, *Memoirs*, 127.

CHAPTER 11

1. Eulenberg, *Korrespondenz*, i. 17.
2. Hull provides the best account of these events in ch. 5, 'Philipp Eulenburg: Decline and Fall', pp. 109ff.
3. Eulenburg, *Korrespondenz*, i. 45.
4. Martin Sabrow, 'Walter Rathenau', *Neue deutsche Biographie*, vol. xxi (Berlin, 2003), 176.
5. Hull, 17.
6. Ibid. 15.
7. 2 Apr. 1886, Waldersee, 286–7.
8. 31 May 1886, ibid. 327.
9. Holstein to Eulenburg, 16 June 1886, Eulenburg, *Korrespondenz*, vol. i, No. 76, pp. 179–80.
10. *Letters of the Empress Frederick*, 224–5.
11. Crown Prince to Stosch, Hollyday, 132.
12. Ibid. 235.
13 *Letters of the Empress Frederick*, 225.
14. Crown Princess to Queen Victoria, 27 Oct. 1887, ibid. 250.
15. Ibid. 232.
16. Crown Princess to Queen Victoria, 23 Apr. 1887, ibid. 214.
17. *Letters of the Empress Frederick*, 192.
18. 20 Jan. 1888, Waldersee, 354.
19. 3 Feb. 1888, ibid. 357.
20. *Neueste Mittheilungen*, 7/14, Tuesday 7 Feb. 1888, p. 1. <http://amtspresse.staats-bibliothek-berlin.de/vollanzeige.php?file=11614109/1888/1888–02–07.xml&s=1>.
21. Pflanze, iii. 279.
22. Emperor Frederick to Bismarck, 12 Mar. 1888, *Letters of the Empress Frederick*, 289–91.
23. Pflanze, iii. 281; Lucius, 433.
24. 13 Mar. 1888, Waldersee, 373.
25. Fontane to Martha Fontane, 14 Mar. 1888, Craig, *Fontane*, 115.
26. Crown Princess to Queen Victoria, 16 Mar. 1888, *Letters of the Empress Frederick*, 292–3.
27. 18 Mar. 1888, Waldersee, 375.

28. Pflanze, iii. 281–2.
29. 24 Mar. 1888, Waldersee, 379–80.
30. 27 Mar. 1888, ibid. 379–80.
31. 4 Apr. 1888, ibid. 382.
32. Philipp Konrad Count zu Eulenburg to his son Philipp, Berlin, 17 June 1888, Eulenburg, *Korrespondenz*, No. 183, p. 299.
33. Clark, *Kaiser Wilhelm II*, 1.
34. Crown Princess to Queen Victoria, 28 May 1870, Pflanze, iii. 288.
35. Ibid. 289–90.
36. Clark, *Kaiser Wilhelm II*, 6.
37. 28 June 1887, Holstein, *Correspondence*, 346–7.
38. 15 Nov. 1887, Crown Princess to Queen Victoria, *Letters of the Empress Frederick*, 256–7.
39. Crown Prince William to Eulenburg, Berlin, 12 Apr. 1888, Eulenburg, *Korrespondenz*, No. 169, p. 284.
40. 10 July 1888, Waldersee, 412.
41. Homberger to Bamberger, 17 Nov. 1888, in Bamberger, 430.
42. Röhl, *William II*, ii. 134.
43. Ibid. 135.
44. *Neueste Mittheilungen*, 8/4, Monday 14 Jan. 1889, p. 1.
45. Engelberg, ii. 444.
46. Friedrich-Christian Stahl, 'Albedyll', *Neue deutsche Biographie*, vol. i (Berlin, 1953), 122.
47. Engelberg, ii. 445.
48. Pflanze, iii. 331.
49. Engelberg, ii. 447.
50. Pflanze, iii. 345–6.
51. Schoeps, 42.
52. Walter Bussmann, 'Berlepsch', *Neue deutsche Biographie*, vol. ii (Berlin, 1955), 683.
53. Michael Epkenhahn, 'Rottenburg', *Neue deutsche Biographie*, vol. xxii (Berlin, 2005), 141.
54. Heinrich Otto Meissner, 'Bötticher', *Neue deutsche Biographie*, vol. ii (Berlin, 1955), 413.
55. Pflanze, iii. 348–9.
56. Rohl, *Wilhelm II*, ii. 263.
57. Holstein, *Memoirs*, 157.
58. Holstein to Eulenburg, Berlin, 27 Jan. 1890, Eulenburg, *Korrespondenz*, No. 293, pp. 421–3.
59. Lucius, 509.
60. Waldersee, 103–4.
61. Empress Frederick to Queen Victoria, 20 Feb. 1890, *Letters of the Empress Frederick*, 407.

62. 28 Feb. 1890, Bamberger, 441–3.
63. *Wahlen in Deutschland bis 1918 Reichstagswahlen Ergebnisse reichsweit.*
64. Röhl, *Wilhelm II*, ii. 288.
65. Pflanze, iii. 364.
66. Holstein to Eulenburg, 7 Mar. 1890, Eulenburg, *Korrespondenz*, No. 338, p. 482.
67. Röhl, *Wilhelm II*, ii. 296.
68. Ibid. ii. 289.
69. Anderson, 386–7.
70. Bismarck, *Gedanken und Erinnerungen*, 640–1; Bamberger diary entry 28 Mar. 1890, *Bismarcks Grosses Spiel*, 446. There are differences between the Bismarckian version of the conversation and others that circulated. That the meeting was stormy is not in doubt.
71. Eulenburg, *Aus 50 Jahren*, 235.
72. Röhl, *Wilhelm II*, ii. 299.
73. August Graf zu Eulenburg to Philipp Eulenburg, Berlin, 17 Mar. 1890, Eulenburg, *Korrespondenz*, No. 359, p. 503.
74. Eulenburg, *Aus 50 Jahren*, 237.
75. 17 Mar. 1890, Lucius, 523–4.
76. Hans Körner, 'Hermann von Lucanus', *Neue deutsche Biographie* (Digitale Register) vol. xv (Berlin, 1987), 270.
77. Bismarck, *Gedanken und Erinnerungen*, 650.
78. Ibid. 653–4.
79. William II to Franz Joseph, 3–5 Apr. 1890, in Röhl, *Wilhelm II*, ii. 309–16.
80. Spitzemberg, 271–1.
81. Ekkhard Verchau, 'Marschall von Bieberstein', *Neue deutsche Biographie*, vol. xvi (Berlin, 1990), 256.
82. Holstein, *Memoirs*, 131.
83. 23 Mar. 1890, Lucius, 525.
84. Chlodwig Hohenlohe-Schillingsfürst, *Memoirs*, ii. 423.
85. Spitzemberg, 273.
86. 29 Mar. 1890, ibid. 275–6.
87. 29 Mar. 1890, Lucius, 525.
88. 29 Mar. 1890, Bamberger, 426.
89. Engelberg, ii. 478.
90. Martin Glaubrecht, 'Emil Hartmeyer', *Neue deutsche Biographie* (Digitale Register), vol. viii (Berlin, 1969), 6.
91. Philipp Eulenburg to Karl Heinrich von Boetticher, Stuttgart, 21 Mar. 1891, Eulenburg, *Korrespondenz*, No 491, p. 658.
92. Bismarck, *Gedanken und Erinnerungen*, 607–14.
93. Alden, 31.
94. Heinrich Otto Meissner, 'Caprivi', *Neue deutsche Biographie*, vol. iii (Berlin, 1957), 136.
95. Ibid. 137.

96. *Neueste Mittheilungen*, 9/50, ed. O. Hammann (Berlin), Friday, 27 June 1890, p. 1. <http://amtspresse.staatsbibliothek-berlin.de/vollanzeige.php?file=11614109/1890/1890-06-27.xml&s=1>.

97. Anderson, 389.

98. Spitzemberg, 288–9.

99. Bernhard von Poten, 'Maximilian von Versen' (1833–1893), *Allgemeine deutsche Biographie* (Digitale Register), vol. liv, Nachträge bis 1899 (Leipzig, 1908), 741–2. Commanding General in Berlin from 24 Mar. 1890, a cavalry officer with diplomatic and international experience.

100. Petersdorff, 520.

101. Pflanze, iii. 396.

102. 'COUNT BISMARCK WEDDED; A BRILLIANT GATHERING', *New York Times*, 22 June 1892. NY Times Archive: <http://query.nytimes.com/gst/abstract.html?res=9502E2D91538E233A25751C2A9609C94639ED7CF>.

103. Robert Gerwarth, *The Bismarck Myth: Weimar Germany and the Legacy of the Iron Chancellor* (Oxford: University Press, 2005).

104. Spitzemberg, 307.

105. Ibid. 320.

106. Pflanze, iii. 404; Hohenlohe-Schillingsfürst, *Memoirs*, 464.

107. Pflanze, iii. 405.

108. Spitzemberg, 322.

109. Hohenlohe-Schillingsfürst, *Memoirs*, 466.

110. Karl Erich Born, 'Botho Eulenburg', *Neue deutsche Biographie*, vol. iv (Berlin, 1959), 680–1.

111. Nichols, 40–1.

112. Günter Richter, 'Chlodwig Hohenlohe-Schillingsfürst', *Neue deutsche Biographie*, vol. ix (Berlin, 1972), 487–9.

113. Roggenbach to Stosch, 28 Jan. 1895, Stosch, No. 130, p. 407.

114. Spitzemberg, 330–1.

115. Ibid. 335–6.

116. Alexander von Hohenlohe, *Aus meinem Leben*, 264 ff.

117. Pflanze, iii. 410.

118. Bismarck to William Bismarck, 30 July 1895, *GW* xiv. 1020.

119. Manfred, 597–8.

120. Sidney B. Fay, *Origins of the First World War*, 'Breakdown of the wire to Russia in 1890'. <http://yamaguchy.netfirms.com/7897401/fay/origin_102.html#N_56_>.

121. Aufzeichnung Eulenburgs 27 Oct. 1896, No. 1269, Eulenburg, *Korrespondenz*, iii. 1745.

122. Eulenburg to Wilhelm II, Liebenberg, 3 Nov. 1896, ibid. No. 1270, pp. 1746–7.

123. Hank, 599–600.

124. Ibid. 597, n. 3.

125. Ibid. 599 ff.
126. 29 Nov. 1898, Eulenburg, *Aus 50 Jahren*, 270–1.
127. Herbert von Bismarck to Ludwig von Plessen, 31 July 1898, in Engelberg, ii. 523.
128. Eulenburg, *Aus 50 Jahren*, 276.
129. Pflanze, iii. 428.
130. Ibid. iii. 427–8.
131. 3 Aug. 1898, Spitzemberg, 373.
132. Eulenburg, *Aus 50 Jahren*, 279.

CONCLUSION

1. Odo Russell to Morier, 15 May 1875, Urbach, 141.
2. Spitzemberg, 238.
3. Disraeli Diary Entry, 5 July 1878, Moneypenny and Buckle, ii. 1203–4.
4. 26 Jan. 1873, Diary Entry, Bamberger, 298.
5. Pflanze, i. 179.
6. Ibid. ii. 163–5.
7. Perthes to Roon, 28 Apr. 1864, Roon, ii. 238.
8. Queen Victoria to Sir Henry Ponsonby, 9 Apr. 1888, *Letters of the Empress Frederick*, 296.
9. Von Blanckenburg to von Kleist, 17 Jan. 1873, Petersdorff, 415.
10. Röhl, *Wilhelm II*, ii. 296.
11. Disraeli Diary, 21 June 1878, Moneypenny and Buckle, ii. 1201.
12. May 1886, Schweinitz, 214–16.
13. 24 Sept. 1859, Bismarck to Brother, *GW* xiv. 538.
14. Pflanze, ii. 58.
15. Disraeli to Victoria, Congress of Berlin, 17 June 1878, Moneypenny and Buckle, ii. 1194.
16. Hermann Granier, 'Maximilian Graf von Schwerin', *Allgemeine deutsche Biographie*, vol. xxxiii (Leipzig, 1891), 433.
17. Immanuel Kant, paras. 116-17, *The Metaphysic of Right*. <http://www.allacademic.com/meta/p_mla_apa_research_citation/0/8/8/8/0/pages88808/p88808-28.php>.
18. Engelberg, i. 456.
19. Aufzeichnung des Oberleutnant Bauers über die Rückwirkungen der innenpolitischen Situation auf das Feldherr, Deist, *Militär und Innenpolitik im Weltkrieg 1914–1918*, No. 464, ii. 1243.
20. Eulenburg to Kaiser Wilhelm II, 26 Mar. 1890, in Röhl, *Wilhelm II*, ii. 326.
21. Pflanze, ii. 241.
22. W. H. Auden, *A Selection by the Author* (Harmondsworth: Penguin Books, 1958), 66.

23. Werner Conze, 'Paul von Hindenburg', *Neue deutsche Biographie*, vol. ix (Berlin, 1972), 178.

24. Max Weber, *Parlament und Regierung im neugeordneten Deutschland: Zur politischen Kritik des Beamtentums und Parteiwesens* (Max Weber, *Gesammelte politische Schriften*, ed. Johannes Winckelmann, 5th edn. (Tübingen, 1988), 310–20. <http://www. zeno.org/Soziologie/M/Weber,+Max/Schriften+zur+Politik/Parlament+und +Regierung+im+neugeordneten+Deutschland/I.+Die+Erbschaft+ Bismarcks>.

Bibliography

PRINTED PRIMARY SOURCES

Allgemeine deutsche Biographie, electronic version, ed. Historischen Kommission bei der Bayerischen Akademie der Wissenschaften and Bayerischen Staatsbibliothek, Feb. 2007.

Bamberger, Ludwig, *Bismarcks grosses Spiel: Die geheimen Tagebücher Ludwig Bambergers*, ed. Dr Ernst Feder (Frankfurt am Main: Societäts-Verlag, 1932).

Bismarck, Otto von, *Die politischen Reden des Fürsten Bismarcks: Historisch-kritische Gesamtausgabe*, ed. Horst Kohl (Stuttgart: Cotta, 1892).

—— *Bismarck Briefe, 1836–1873*, 8th printing, ed. Horst Kohl (Bielefeld/Leipzig: Verlag Delhagen & Klasing, 1900).

—— *Gedanken und Erinnerungen* (Stuttgart/Berlin: J.S. Cotta, 1928).

—— *Bismarck: Die Gesammelten Werke*, ed. Wolfgang Windelband and Werner Frauendienst. 1st edn., 15 vols. (Berlin: Deutscheveralgsanstalt, 1933) (abbreviated *GW*).

—— *Gesammelte Werke*, ed. Konrad Canis, Lothar Gall, Klaus Hildebrand, and Eberhard Kolb, Neue Friedrichsruher Ausgabe (Paderborn: F. Schöningh, 2004–) (abbreviated NFA).

—— *Bismarck, the Man & the Statesman: Being the Reflections and Reminiscences of Otto, Prince Von Bismarck*, 2 vols. (London: Harper & Brothers, 1899). Questia Online Library: <http://www.questia.com/PM.qst?a=o&d=77734130>.

Brandes, Georg, *Berlin als deutsche Reichshauptstadt: Erinnerungen aus den Jahren 1877–1883*, trans. from the Danish by Peter Urban-Halle, ed. Erik M. Christensen and Hans-Dietrich Loock (Berlin: Colloquium Verlag, 1989).

Bronsart von Schellendorf, Paul, *Geheimes Kriegstagebuch 1870–1871*, ed. Peter Rassow (Bonn: Athenäum-Verlag, 1954).

Burke, Edmund, *Reflections on the Revolution in France And on the Proceeding in Certain Societies in London Relative to That Event in a Letter Intended to Have Been Sent to a Gentleman in Paris. 1790.* Ed. L. G. Mitchell (Oxford: Oxford University Press, 1993) p. 142. Also available online, Harvard Classics, Vol. 24: <http://www.bar-Heby.com/24/3>.

Busch, Moritz, *Bismarck. Some Secret Pages of His History: Being a Diary Kept by Dr. Moritz Busch during Twenty-Five Years' Official and Private Intercourse with the Great Chancellor* (London: Macmillan, 1898).

Documents diplomatiques suisses, 1848–1945. vol. ii (1.1 1866–24.12.1872) (Bern: Benteli Verlag, 1985); vol. iii (1.1873–31.12. 1889) (Bern: Benteli Verlag, 1986); vol. iv (1.1.1890–31.12 1904) (Bern: Benteli Verlag, 1994).

Duncker, Max, *Politischer Briefwechsel aus seinem Nachlass*, ed. Johannes Schulze (Osnabrück: Biblio Verlag, 1967).

Eulenburg-Hertefeld, Philipp Fürst zu, *Aus 50 Jahren: Erinnerungen des Fürsten Philipp zu Eulenburg-Hertefeld* (Berlin: Verlag von der Gebrüder Paetel, 1923).

—— *Philipp Eulenburgs politische Korrespondenz*, ed. John C. G. Röhl (Boppard am Rhein: H. Boldt, 1976–83).

Fontane, Theodor, *Irrungen Wirrungen* (1888), in Theodor Fontane, ed. *Gesammelte Werke: Jubiläumsausgabe. Erste Reihe in fünf Bänden* (Berlin: S. Fischer Verlag, 1919).

Frederick III, Emperor, *The War Diary of the Emperor Frederick III 1870–1871*, trans. and ed. A. R. Allinson (London: Stanley Paul & Co., 1927).

Frederick, Empress, *The Letters of the Empress Frederick*, ed. Sir Frederick Ponsonby (London: Macmillan & Co. Ltd, 1929).

Freytag, Gustav, *Soll und Haben* (Waltrop/Leipzig: Manuscriptum Verlagsbuchandlung, 2002).

Gentz, Friedrich von, *Briefe von und an Friedrich von Gentz*, ed. Friedrich Carl Wiitichen (Munich/Berlin: R. Oldenbourg, 1909).

Gerlach, Ernst Ludwig, *Aus dem Nachlass: Erster Teil Tagebuch 1848–1866, Zweiter Teil. Briefe, Denkschrifte, Aufzeichnungen*, ed. Hellmutt Diwald (Göttingen: Vandenhoek & Ruprecht, 1970).

—— *Die Civilehe und der Reichskanzler* (Berlin, 1874). Digitale bibliothek published by the Max Planck Institut für Rechtsgeschichte: <http://dlib-pr.mpier.mpg.de>.

Gerlach, General Leopold von, *Briefe an Otto von Bismarck*, ed. Horst Kohl (Stuttgart/Berlin: J. G. Cotta'sche Bunchandlung Nachfolger, 1912).

Glagau, Otto, 'Der Börsen- und Gründungsschwindel in Berlin', *Die Gartenlaube*, 49 (1874), 788–90.

Hohenlohe-Schillingsfürst, Alexander von, *Aus meinem Leben* (Frankfurt am Main; Frankfurter-Societäts-Drückerei GmbH, 1925).

Hohenlohe-Schillingsfürst, Chlodwig, *Memoirs of Prince Chlodwig of Hohenlohe-Schillingsfürst*, English edn., ed. George W. Chrystal (New York: The Macmillan Company; London: William Heineman, 1906).

Holstein, Friedrich von, *The Holstein Papers: The Memoirs, Diaries and Correspondence of Friedrich von Holstein 1837–1909*, ed. Norman Rich and M. H. Fisher (Cambridge: Cambridge University Press, 1955, 1957, 1962), vol. i *Memoirs and Political Observations*; vol. ii *Diaries*; vol. iii *Correspondence 1861–1896*.

Judenthum: Allgemeine Zeitung des Judenthums, 26 Sept. 1866, Leipzig Internet Archiv Jüdischer Periodika: <http://www.compactmemory.de/index_p.aspx?ID_0=3>.

Keudell, Robert von, *Fürst und Fürstin Bismarck: Erinnerungen aus den Jahren 1846 bis 1872*, 3rd edn. (Berlin & Stuttgart, 1902).

Lassalle, Ferdinand, *Tagebuch*, ed. Paul Lindau (Breslau: Schlesische Buchdruckerei, 1891).

Loftus, Lord Augustus, *The Diplomatic Reminiscences of*, 2 vols. (London: Cassell & Company Ltd. 1894).

Lucius von Ballhausen, Robert Sigmund Maria Joseph, *Bismarck-Erinnerungen des Staatsministers Freiherrn Lucius von Ballhausen*, 4th edn. (Stuttgart/Berlin: Cotta, 1921).

Macaulay, Thomas Babbington, Lord Macaulay, *Critical and Historical Essays contributed to 'The Edinburgh Review'* (London: Longmans, Green & Co., 1883).

Marwitz, Friedrich August Ludwig von der, *Preussens Verfall und Aufstieg*, ed. Friedrich Schinkel (Breslau: Wilhelm Gottl. Korn Verlag, 1932).

—— *Ein Preussischer Patriot: Selbstzeignisse aus Tagebüchern und Denkschriften Ludwigs von der Marwitz*, ed. Walter Kayser (Munich: Albert Langer/Georg Müller, 1939).

—— *Ein märkischer Edelmann im Zeitalter der Befreiungskriege*, ed. F. Meusel, No. 1 (Berlin: Ernst Siegfried Mittler & Sohn, 1908).

Meredith, George, *The Tragic Comedians: A Study in a Well Known Story* (Westminster: Archibald Constable & Co. 1902).

Moltke, Helmuth von, *His Life and Character: Journals, Letters, Memoirs*, trans. Mary Herms (New York: Harper & Brothers, 1892).

—— *Letters to his Mother and Brothers*, trans. Clara Bell and Henry W. Fischer (New York: Harper & Brothers, 1892).

—— *The Franco-German War of 1870–71*, introd. Michael Howard (London: Greenhill Books; Novato, Calif.: Presidio Press, 1992).

—— *Gesammelte Schriften und Denkwürdigkeiten des Generalfeldmarschalls Grafen Helmuth von Moltke*, 8 vols. (Berlin: Ernst Siegfried Mittler & Sohn, 1892–3).

Motley, J. L., *Morton's Hope; or the Memoirs of a Provincial*, 2 vols. (New York: Harper & Brothers, 1839).

—— *John Lothrop Motley and his Family: Further Letters and Records*, ed. Susan St John Mildmay and Herbert St John Mildmay (London: The Bodley Head; New York: John Lane Company, 1910).

—— *The Correspondence of John Lothrop Motley*, ed. George William Curtis, 3 vols. (New York/London: Harper & Brothers, 1900).

Orloff, Nicholas W., *Bismarck und Katharina Orloff: Ein Idyll in der hohen Politik* (Munich: C. H. Beck'sche Verlagsbuchhandlung, 1944).

Petersdorff, Hermann von, *Kleist Retzow: Ein Lebensbild* (Stuttgart/Berlin: J. G. Cotta'sche Buchhandlung Nachfolger, 1907).

Provinzial-Correspondenz (PC) (1863–84), *Neueste Mittheilungen* (1882–94). <http://amtspresse.staatsbibliothek-berlin.de/index.html>.

Roggenbach, Franz von, *Im Ring der Gegner Bismarcks: Denkschriften und politischer Briefwechsel Franz v. Roggenbachs mit Kaiserin August a und Albrecht von Stosch 1865–1896* (Leipzig: Koehler and Ameling, 1943).

Roon, Waldemar, Graf von, *Denkwürdigkeiten aus dem Leben des Generalfeldmarschalls, Kriegsministers Grafen von Roon: Sammlung von Briefen, Schriftstücken und Erinnerungen*, 3rd edn., 2 vols. (Breslau: E. Trewendt, 1892).

Rühs, Friedrich, *Die Rechte des Christenthums und des deutschen Volks: vertheidigt gegen die Ansprüche der Juden und ihrer Verfechter* (Berlin: Realschulbuchhandlung, 1816).

Schlözer, Kurd von, *Petersburger Briefe 1857–1862* (Berlin/Leipzig: Deutsche Verlags-Anstalt, 1923).

Schweinitz, Lothar von, *Briefwechsel des Botschafters von Schweinitz* (Berlin: Verlag vom Reimer Hobbing, 1928).

Spitzemberg, Hildegard Freifrau Hugo von, *Das Tagebuch der Baronin Spitzemberg: Aufzeichnungen aus der Hofgesellschaft*, ed. Rudolf Vierhaus (Göttingen: Vandenhoek & Ruprecht, 1961).

Stosch, Albrecht von, *Denkwürdigkeiten des Generals und Admirals Albrecht von Stosch, Briefe und Tagebücher*, ed. Ulrich von Stosch (Stuttgart/Leipzig: Deutsche Verlags-Anstalt, 1904).

Tiedemann, Christoph von, *Sechs Jahre Chef der Reichskanzlei unter dem Fürsten Bismarck* (Leipzig: Verlag von S. Hirzel, 1909).

Treitschke, Heinrich von, 'Unsere Ansichten', *Preussische Jahrbücher*, 44 (Nov. 1879).

Trollope, Anthony, *Barchester Towers* (1857) (London: Penguin, 1994).

Verdy du Vernois, Julius Adrian Friedrich Wilhelm von, *Im grossen Hauptquartier, 1870–71: Persönliche Erinnerungen*, 3rd edn. (Berlin: E. S. Mittler, 1896)

—— *With the Royal Headquarters in 1870–71* (London, 1897), repr. in AMS edition (New York: AMS Press, Inc, 1971).

Waldersee, Alfred, *Denkwürdigkeiten des General-Feldmarschall Alfred Grafen von Waldersee*, ed. Heinrich Otto Meisener, vol. i: *1832–1888* (Osnabrück, 1967).

William I, *The Correspondence of William I. and Bismarck, with other letters from and to Prince Bismarck*, trans. J. A. Ford, with portrait and facsimile letters (New York: F. A. Stokes, 1903).

ONLINE REFERENCE SOURCES

Allgemeine deutsche Biographie:
    <http://de.wikipedia.org/wiki/Allgemeine_Deutsche_Biographie>.

Biographisches Lexikon des Kaiserthums Österreich: <http://alo.uibk.ac.at/webinterface/library/COLLECTION_V01?objid=11104>.

Büchmann, Georg, *Geflügelte Worte: Der Citatenschatz des deutschen Volkes* (Berlin: Haude & Spener'sche Buchhandlung (F. Weidling), 1898). <http://susning.nu/buchmann/>.

Neue deutsche Biographie: <http://www.ndb.badw-muenchen.de/index_e.htm>.

Wahlen in Deutschland bis 1918 Reichstagswahlen: <http://www.wahlen-in-deutschland.de/akurtwalg.htm>.

SECONDARY SOURCES

Anderson, Margaret Lavinia, *Windthorst: A Political Biography* (Oxford: The Clarendon Press, 1987).

Barclay, David E., *Frederick William IV and the Prussian Monarchy, 1840–1861* (Oxford: The Clarendon Press, 1995).

Beller, Steven, *Francis Joseph* (London: Longman, 1996).

Berdahl, Robert M., *The Politics of the Prussian Nobility: The Development of a Conservative Ideology, 1770–1848* (Princeton: Princeton University Press, 1988).

Börner, Karl Heinz, *Wilhelm I. deutscher Kaiser und König von Preussen: Eine Biographie* (Berlin: Akademie-Verlag, 1984).

Brandes, Georg, *Ferdinand Lassalle* (London: William Heineman; New York: The Macmillan Company, 1911).

Brophy, James M., *Capitalism, Politics, and Railroads in Prussia, 1830–1870* (Columbus, Oh.: Ohio State University Press, 1998).

—— *Popular Culture and the Public Sphere in the Rhineland, 1800–1850* (Cambridge: Cambridge University Press, 2007).

Brunck, Helma, *Bismarck und das preussische Staatsministerium 1862–1890* (Berlin: Duncker & Humblot, 2004).

Bucholz, Arden, *Moltke and the German Wars* (Basingstoke: Palgrave Publishers Ltd, 2001).

Clark, Christopher, *The Politics of Conversion: Missionary Protestantism and the Jews in Prussia 1728–1941* (Oxford: Clarendon Press, 1995).

—— *Iron Kingdom: The Rise and Downfall of Prussia 1600–1947* (London: Allen, 2006).

—— *Kaiser Wilhelm II* (Harlow/New York: Longman, 2000).

Craig, Gordon A., *The Politics of the Prussian Army, 1640–1945* (Oxford/New York: Oxford University Press, 1955).

—— *Theodor Fontane: Literature and History in the Bismarck Reich* (Oxford: Oxford University Press, 1999).

—— *The Battle of Königgrätz: Prussia's Victory over Austria, 1866* (Philadelphia: University of Pennsylvania Press, 2003).

Deist, Wilhelm, *Militär und Innenpolitik im Weltkrieg 1914–1918* (Düsseldorf: Droste Verlag, 1970).

Embree, Michael, *Bismarck's First War: The Campaign of Schleswig and Jutland 1864* (Solihull: Helion & Company Ltd., 2006).

Engelberg, Ernst, *Bismarck*, vol. i: *Urpreusse und Reichsgründer* (Berlin: Akademie-Verlag, 1985); vol. ii: *Das Reich in der Mitte Europas* (Berlin: Akademie-Verlag, 1990).

Epstein, Klaus, *The Genesis of German Conservatism* (Princeton, NJ: Princeton University Press, 1966).

Eyck, Erich, *Bismarck*, 3 vols. (Erlenbach-Zürich: Eugen Rentsch Verlag, 1941, 1943, 1944).

—— *Bismarck and the German Empire*, 2nd edn. (London: Allen & Unwin, 1963).

Fear, Jeffrey, *Organizing Control: August Thyssen and the Construction of German Corporate Management* (Cambridge, Mass.: Harvard University Press, 2005).

Fischer, Horst, *Judentum, Staat und Heer in Preussen im frühen 19. Jahrhundert: Zur Geschichte der staatlichen Judenpolitik* (Tübingen: Mohr, 1968).

Foerster, Roland G., *Generalfeldmarschall von Moltke: Bedeutung und Wirkung.* (Munich: R. Oldenbourg Verlag, 1991).

Footman, David, *Ferdinand Lassalle: Romantic Revolutionary* (New Haven: Yale University Press, 1947).

Frie, Ewald, *Friedrich August Ludwig von der Marwitz 1777–1837: Biographie eines Preussen* (Paderborn: Schöningh, 2001).

Gall, Lothar, *Bismarck: The White Revolutionary*, trans. J. A. Underwood, 2 vols. (London: Unwin Hyman, 1986).

—— *Bismarck: Der weisse Revolutionär* (Frankfurt am Main: Verlag Ulstein GmbH, Propyläen Verlag, 1980).

—— (ed.), *Otto von Bismarck und die Parteien* (Paderborn: Ferdinand Schöningh, 2001).

Gerwarth, Robert, *The Bismarck Myth: Weimar and the Legacy of the Iron Chancellor*, Oxford Historical Monographs (Oxford: Oxford University Press, 2005; pbk. 2007).

Green, Abigail, *Fatherlands: State-Building and Nationhood in Nineteenth-Century Germany* (Cambridge: Cambridge University Press, 2001).

Grenville, J. A. S., *Europe Reshaped, 1848–1878* (Hassocks: Harvester Press, 1976).

Guglia, Eugen, *Friedrich Gentz: Eine Biographische Studie* (Vienna: Wiener Verlag, 1900).

Haenisch, Konrad, *Lassalle Mensch und Politiker* (Berlin: Franz Schneider Verlag, 1923).

Hank, Manfred, *Kanzler ohne Amt: Fürst Bismarck nach seiner Entlassung 1890–1898* (Munich: Tuduv-Verlagsgesellschaft, 1977).

Hildebrand, Klaus, *Deutsche Aussenpolitik 1871–1918* (Munich: Oldenbourg, 1989).

—— *Das vergangene Reich: deutsche Aussenpolitik von Bismarck bis Hitler 1871–1945* (Stuttgart: Deutsche Verlags-Anstalt, 1995).

Hillgruber, Andreas, *Bismarcks Aussenpolitik* (Freiburg: Rombach, 1972).

—— 'Die Krieg-in-Sicht-Krise 1875: Wegscheide der Politik der europäischen Großmächte in der späten Bismarckzeit', in Ernst Schulin (ed.), *Studien zur europäischen Geschichte: Gedenkschrift für Martin Göhring* (Wiesbaden: Franz Steiner, 1968), 239–53.

Holborn, Hajo, *A History of Modern Germany* (London: Eyre & Spottiswoode, 1965).

Hollyday, Frederick B. M., *Bismarck's Rival: A Political Biography of General and Admiral Albrecht von Stosch* (Durham, NC: Duke University Press, 1960).

Huber, E. R., *Deutsche Verfassungsgeschichte seit 1789* (Stuttgart: W. Kohlhammer, 1957–90).

Hull, Isabel V., *The Entourage of Kaiser Wilhelm II, 1888–1918* (Cambridge: Cambridge University Press, 1982).

Imlah, Albert Henry, *Economic Elements in the Pax Britannica: Studies in British Foreign Trade in the Nineteenth Century* (Cambridge, Mass.: Harvard University Press, 1958).

Keinemann, Friedrich, *Westfalen im Zeitalter der Restauration und der Julirevolution, 1815–1833: Quellen zur Entwicklung der Wirtschaft, zur materiellen Lage der Bevölkerung und zum Erscheinungsbild der Volksstimmung* (Münster in Westfalen: Aschendorff, 1987).

Kenney, John, 'Ideology and Foreign Policy in the Nineteenth Century: France, Austria and the Unification of Italy. (PhD. University of Pennsylvania, 2010).

Kent, George O., *Arnim and Bismarck* (Oxford: Clarendon Press, 1968).

Koehler, Benedikt, *Ludwig Bamberger: Revolutionär und Bankier* (Stuttgart: Deutsche-Verlagsanstalt GmbH, 1999).

Kuhn, Ulrich, *Der Grundgedanke der Politik Bismarcks* (Dettelbach: J. H. Roll, 2001).

Lerman, Katherine Anne, *Bismarck*, Profiles in Power (Harlow/New York: Pearson Longman, 2004).

Lytton Strachey, Giles, *Queen Victoria* (New York, Harcourt Brace, 1921).

Mann, Golo, *Friedrich von Gentz: Gegenspieler Napoleons Vordenker Europas* (Frankfurt am Main: S. Fischer Verlag, 1995).

Marcks, Erich, *Bismarcks Jugend 1815–1848* (Stuttgart: Cotta, 1915).

—— *Bismarck: Eine Biographie*, vol. i (Stuttgart/Berlin: J. G. Cotta'sche Buchhandlung Nachfoler, 1915).

Mazura, Uwe, *Zentrumspartei und Judenfrage 1870/71–1933: Verfassungsstaat und Minderheitenschütz* (Mainz: Matthias-Grünewald-Verlag, 1994).

Mosse, W. E., *Jews in the German Economy: The German-Jewish Economic Elite, 1820–1935* (Oxford: Clarendon Press, 1987).

Moneypenny, W. F., and Buckle, G. E., *The Life of Benjamin Disraeli*, 2 vols. (London: John Murray, 1929).

Nichols, J. Alden, *Germany after Bismarck: The Caprivi Era, 1890–1894* (Cambridge, Mass.: Harvard University Press, 1958).

Oncken, Hermann, *Lassalle: Eine Politische Biographie*, 3rd edn. (Stuttgart/Berlin: Deutsche Verlags-Anstalt, 1920).

Paret, Peter, *Yorck and the Era of Prussian Reform 1807–1815* (Princeton: Princeton University Press, 1966).

Pastor, Ludwig, *August Reichensperger 1808–1895*, 2 vols. (Freiburg, 1899).

Pflanze, Otto, *Bismarck and the Development of Germany*, 2nd edn., 3 vols. (Princeton: Princeton University Press, 1990).

Pulzer, Peter G. J., *Jews and the German State: The Political History of a Minority, 1848–1933* (Oxford: Blackwell, 1992).

Radtke, Wolfgang, *Die preussische Seehandlung zwischen Staat und Wirtschaft in der Frühphase der Industrialisierung*, introd. Otto Büsch (Berlin: Colloquium Verlag, 1981).

Ramm, Agatha, *Sir Robert Morier: Envoy and Ambassador in the Age of Imperialism* (Oxford: The Clarendon Press, 1973).

Rich, Norman, *Friedrich von Holstein: Politics and Diplomacy in the Era of Bismarck and Wilhelm II*, 2 vols. (Cambridge: Cambridge University Press, 1965).

Roberts, Neil, *Meredith and the Novel* (Basingstoke: Macmillan Press Ltd., 1997).

Röhl, J. C. G., *Germany without Bismarck: The Crisis of Government in the Second Reich 1890–1900* (London: B. T. Batsford, 1967).

—— *Young Wilhelm: The Kaiser's Early Life 1859–1888*, trans. Jeremy Gaines and Rebecca Wallach (Cambridge: Cambridge University Press, 1998).

—— *Wilhelm II: The Kaiser's Personal Monarchy, 1888–1900*, trans. Sheila de Bellaigue (Cambridge: Cambridge University Press, 2004).

Romeo, Rosario, *Dal Piemonte sabaudo all'Italia liberale* (Torino: Einaudi, 1963).

Rosenberg, Hans, *Grosse Depression und Bismarckzeit: Wirtschaftsablauf, Gesellschaft und Politik in Mitteleuropa* (Berlin: W. de Gruyter, 1967).

Sartorius von Waltershausen, August, *Deutsche Wirtschaftsgeschichte, 1815–1914*, 2nd edn. (Jena: G. Fischer, 1923).

Schoeps, Hans Joachim, *Bismarck über Zeitgenossen, Zeitgenossen über Bismarck* (Frankfurt am Main: Verlag Ullstein/Propyläen, 1972).

Schroeder, Paul W. *The Transformation of European Politics, 1763–1848* (Oxford: Clarendon Press, 1994).

Schuder, Rosemarie, *Der 'Fremdling aus dem Osten': Eduard Lasker—Jude, Liberaler, Gegenspieler Bismarcks* (Berlin: Verlag für Berlin-Brandenburg, 2008).

Solomou, Solomos, *Phases of Economic Growth, 1850–1973: Kondratieff Waves and Kuznets Swings* (Cambridge: Cambridge University Press, 1987).

Spenkuch, Hartwin, *Das preussische Herrenhaus: Adel und Bürgertum in der Ersten Kammer des Landtages, 1854–1918* (Düsseldorf: Droste, c.1998).

Steinberg, Jonathan, *Yesterday's Deterrent: Tirpitz and the Birth of the German Battle Fleet* (Aldershot: Gregg Revivals, 1992).

Stern, Fritz, *Gold and Iron: Bismarck, Bleichröder and the Building of the German Empire* (London: George Allen and Unwin Ltd, 1977).

Stone, James, and Baumgart, Winfried, *The War Scare of 1875: Bismarck and Europe in the Mid-1870s* (Wiesbaden: Franz Steiner Verlag, 2010).

Studt, Christoph, *Lothar Bucher (1817–1892): Ein politisches Leben zwischen Revolution und Staatsdienst* (Göttingen: Vandenhoeck & Ruprecht, 1992).

Sweet, Paul R., *Friedrich von Gentz, Defender of the Old Order* (Madison: The University of Wisconsin Press, 1941).

Tal, Uriel, *Christians and Jews in Germany: Religion, Politics, and Ideology in the Second Reich, 1870–1914*, trans. Noah Jonathan Jacobs (Ithaca, NY: Cornell University Press, 1975).

Tudesq, André-Jean, *L'Élection présidentielle de Louis-Napoléon Bonaparte, 10 décembre 1848* (Paris: Arman Colin, 1965).

Urbach, Karina, *Bismarck's Favourite Englishman: Lord Odo Russell's Mission to Berlin* (London/New York: I. B. Tauris, 1999).

Wagner, Patrick, *Bauern, Junker und Beamte: lokale Herrschaft und Partizipation im Ostelbien des 19. Jahrhunderts* (Göttingen: Wallstein, 2005).

Walter, Dierk, *Pressische Heeresreformen 1807–1870: Militärische Innovation und der Mythos der 'Roonschen Reform'* (Paderborn: Ferdinand Schöningh, 2003).

Wawro, Geoffrey, *The Austro-Prussian War: Austria's War with Prussia and Italy in 1866* (Cambridge/New York: Cambridge University Press, 1996).

—— *The Franco-Prussian War: The German Conquest of France in 1870–1871* (Cambridge/New York: Cambridge University Press, 2003).

Wienfort, Monika, *Patrimonialgerichte in Preussen: ländliche Gesellschaft und bürgerliches Recht 1770–1848/49* (Göttingen:Vandenhoeck & Ruprecht, 2001).

Willms, Johanes, *Bismarck: Dämon der Deutschen. Anmerkungen zu einer Legende* (Munich: Kindler Verlag, 1997).

Zimmer, Frank, *Bismarcks Kampf gegen Kaiser Franz Joseph: Königgrätz und seine Folgen* (Graz:Verlag Styria, 1996).

ARTICLES

Bartlett, C. J., 'Clarendon, the Foreign Office and the Hohenzollern Candidature, 1868–1870', *The English Historical Review*, 75/295 (Apr. 1960), 276–84.

Clark, Chester W., 'Marshal Prim and the Question of the Cession of Gibraltar to Spain in 1870', *The Hispanic American Historical Review*, 19/3 (Aug. 1939), 318–23.

Clark, Christopher, 'Confessional Policy and the Limits of State Action: Frederick William III and the Prussian Church Union 1817–40', *The Historical Journal*, 39/4 (Dec. 1996), 985–1004.

Craig, Gordon A., 'Portrait of a Political General: Edwin von Manteuffel and the Constitutional Conflict in Prussia', *Political Science Quarterly*, 66/1 (Mar. 1951), 1–36.

Ferguson, Niall, 'Public Finance and National Security: The Domestic Origins of the First World War Revisited', *Past and Present*, 142 (Feb. 1994), 141–68.

Halperin, S. William, 'The Origins of the Franco-Prussian War Revisited: Bismarck and the Hohenzollern Candidature', *The Journal of Modern History*, 45/1 (Mar. 1973), 83–91.

Herwig, Holger H., Review Article: 'Andreas Hillgruber: Historian of "Grossmachtpolitik" 1871–1945', *Central European History*, 15/2 (June 1982), 186–98.

Koch, Richard, and Laqueur, Naomi B., 'Schweninger's Seminar', *Journal of Contemporary History*, 20/4, Medicine, History and Society (Oct. 1985), 757–79.

Riotte, Torsten, 'The House of Hanover: Queen Victoria and the Guelph Dynasty', in Karina Urbach (ed.), *Royal Kinship: Anglo-German Family Networks 1815–1918* (Munich: K. G. Saur, 2008).

Röhl, John C. G., 'Kriegsgefahr und Gasteiner Konvention: Bismarck, Eulenburg und die Vertagung des preussisch-österreichischen Krieges in Sommer 1865', in

Imanuel Geiss and Bernd Jürgen Wendt (eds.), *Deutschland in der Weltpolitik des 19. und 20. Jahrhunderts. Fritz Fischer zum 65, Geburtstag* (Düsseldorf: Bertelsmann Verlag, 1973).

Snyder, Louis L., 'Political Implications of Herbert von Bismarck's Marital Affairs, 1881, 1892', *The Journal of Modern History,* 36/2 (June 1964), 155–69.

Steefel, Lawrence D., 'The Rothschilds and the Austrian Loan of 1865', *The Journal of Modern History,* 8/1 (Mar. 1936), 27–39.

Steinberg, Jonathan, 'Carlo Cattaneo and the Swiss Idea of Liberty', in C. A. Bayly and Eugenio Biagini (eds.), *Giuseppe Mazzini and the Globalisation of Democratic Nationalism,* Proceedings of the British Academy, 152 (Oxford/New York: Oxford University Press, 2008).

Sterne, Margaret, 'The End of the Free City of Frankfort', *The Journal of Modern History,* 30/3 (Sept. 1958), 203–14.

Turner, Michael, 'Output and Price in UK Agriculture, 1867–1914 and the Great Agricultural Depression Reconsidered', *Agricultural History Review* (1992).

Photographic Acknowledgements

© akg-images: frontispiece, plates 3, 4, 6a, 6b, 7, 9, 14, 16; © akg-images/Bismarck Museum, Friedrichsruh: plate 2; © akg-images/Lower Saxony State Museum, Hanover: plate 22; © akg-images/Old National Gallery, Berlin: plates 10, 19, 20; © akg-images/ullstein bild: plate 24; © The Art Institute of Chicago (Franz von Lenbach, German, 1836–1904, Prince Otto von Bismarck, 1896, oil on canvas, 125.6 x 94.3 cm, Gift of Mr. and Mrs. Otto K. Eitel, 1956.1205): plate 1; Federal Archives, Koblenz: plates 11 (146-2004-0099), 17 (183-R29818), 23 (183-R68588), 25 (146-1990-023-06A); Federal Office for Central Services and Unresolved Property Issues, Berlin: plate 18; private collection: plate 15; © 2010 Scala, Florence/BPK, Berlin: plates 8, 21, 26; © 2010 Scala, Florence/BPK, Berlin/Bavarian State Library, Munich: plate 13; © 2010 Scala, Florence/Jörg P. Anders/BPK/Old National Gallery, Berlin: plate 5; © 2010 Scala, Florence/BPK, Berlin/Prussian Palaces and Gardens, Potsdam: plate 12; from *Prince von Bismarck in Friedrichsruh*, 1892, by Christian Wilhelm Allers: plate 27

Index